Lecture Notes in Computer Science

Founding Editors

Gerhard Goos
Juris Hartmanis

Editorial Board Members

Elisa Bertino, *Purdue University, West Lafayette, IN, USA*
Wen Gao, *Peking University, Beijing, China*
Bernhard Steffen ⓘ, *TU Dortmund University, Dortmund, Germany*
Moti Yung ⓘ, *Columbia University, New York, NY, USA*

The series Lecture Notes in Computer Science (LNCS), including its subseries Lecture Notes in Artificial Intelligence (LNAI) and Lecture Notes in Bioinformatics (LNBI), has established itself as a medium for the publication of new developments in computer science and information technology research, teaching, and education.

LNCS enjoys close cooperation with the computer science R & D community, the series counts many renowned academics among its volume editors and paper authors, and collaborates with prestigious societies. Its mission is to serve this international community by providing an invaluable service, mainly focused on the publication of conference and workshop proceedings and postproceedings. LNCS commenced publication in 1973.

Subhas C. Nandy · Rajat K. De · Prosenjit Gupta
Editors

Applied Algorithms

Second International Conference, ICAA 2025
Kolkata, India, January 8–10, 2025
Proceedings

 Springer

Editors
Subhas C. Nandy
Indian Statistical Institute
Kolkata, West Bengal, India

Rajat K. De
Indian Statistical Institute
Kolkata, West Bengal, India

Prosenjit Gupta
Heritage Institute of Technology
Kolkata, West Bengal, India

ISSN 0302-9743　　　　　　ISSN 1611-3349 (electronic)
Lecture Notes in Computer Science
ISBN 978-3-031-84542-0　　ISBN 978-3-031-84543-7 (eBook)
https://doi.org/10.1007/978-3-031-84543-7

© The Editor(s) (if applicable) and The Author(s), under exclusive license to Springer Nature Switzerland AG 2025

This work is subject to copyright. All rights are solely and exclusively licensed by the Publisher, whether the whole or part of the material is concerned, specifically the rights of translation, reprinting, reuse of illustrations, recitation, broadcasting, reproduction on microfilms or in any other physical way, and transmission or information storage and retrieval, electronic adaptation, computer software, or by similar or dissimilar methodology now known or hereafter developed.
The use of general descriptive names, registered names, trademarks, service marks, etc. in this publication does not imply, even in the absence of a specific statement, that such names are exempt from the relevant protective laws and regulations and therefore free for general use.
The publisher, the authors and the editors are safe to assume that the advice and information in this book are believed to be true and accurate at the date of publication. Neither the publisher nor the authors or the editors give a warranty, expressed or implied, with respect to the material contained herein or for any errors or omissions that may have been made. The publisher remains neutral with regard to jurisdictional claims in published maps and institutional affiliations.

This Springer imprint is published by the registered company Springer Nature Switzerland AG
The registered company address is: Gewerbestrasse 11, 6330 Cham, Switzerland

If disposing of this product, please recycle the paper.

Preface

This volume contains papers accepted for presentation at the International Conference on Applied Algorithms (ICAA 2025) held at the Heritage Institute of Technology, Kolkata, India from January 8 to January 10, 2025. Additionally, it includes abstracts of 6 invited lectures given by Bhargab B. Bhattacharya, (Indian Statistical Institute, Kolkata), Bhaswar B. Bhattacharya (Wharton School, University of Pennsylvania, USA), Samarjit Chakrabarty (University of North Carolina, USA), Gautam Das (University of Texas at Arlington, USA), Swagatam Das (Indian Statistical Institute, Kolkata), and Sandeep Sen (Ashoka University, India).

Revived after a gap of ten years, ICAA aims to provide a platform for researchers in applied algorithms. The conference sought original contributions related to the design, analysis, implementation and experimental evaluation of efficient algorithms and data structures for problems with relevant real-world applications, demonstrating novel algorithmic approaches, computational techniques, innovative applications of algorithms in real-world scenarios, and case studies showcasing the impact of algorithms in solving complex problems. Papers were sought under three tracks: Discrete Algorithms (Track A), AI and Machine Learning (Track B) and Industrial Applications (Track C).

In response to the call for papers, 93 submissions were received from authors in 8 countries. The Program Committee, consisting of 52 members from 7 countries, selected 26 full papers and 4 short papers for presentation. The Program Committee was assisted by 53 external reviewers to arrive at their decisions. Each paper was reviewed by an average of 3 reviewers.

We would like to thank all those who submitted papers to ICAA 2025, the program committee members and the external reviewers for their support in the process. Special thanks to all the invited speakers for readily agreeing to deliver their talks and helping us put together a quality program. We would like to especially thank the management of Heritage Institute of Technology and Kalyan Bharathi Trust for their generous support and precious advice in hosting the conference. Last but not the least, the entire Organizing Committee provided continuous support in all spheres to make the conference a success.

January 2025

Subhas C. Nandy
Rajat K. De
Prosenjit Gupta

Organization

Advisors

H. K. Chaudhary (Chairman)	Kalyan Bharati Trust, India
P. R. Agarwala (Chairman, Board of Governors)	Heritage Institute of Technology, India
P. K. Agarwal (CEO)	Kalyan Bharati Trust, India
Basab Chaudhuri (Principal)	Heritage Institute of Technology, India
Sujit K. Barua (Registrar)	Heritage Institute of Technology, India

Steering Committee Chairs

Bhargab B. Bhattacharya	Indian Statistical Institute, Kolkata, India
Sandeep Sen	Ashoka University, India

General Chairs

Amitava Bagchi	Heritage Institute of Technology, India
Subhashis Majumder	Heritage Institute of Technology, India

Organizing Chairs

Dinabandhu Bhandari	Heritage Institute of Technology, India
Subhajit Datta	Heritage Institute of Technology, India
Sujay Saha	Heritage Institute of Technology, India

Finance Chair

Manoj Saraogi	Kalyan Bharati Trust, India

viii   Organization

Publicity Chairs

Diganta Sengupta   Heritage Institute of Technology, India
Nilanjana G. Basu   Heritage Institute of Technology, India

Program Committee

Track A: Discrete Algorithms

Anup K. Sen   Heritage Institute of Technology, India
Arijit Bishnu   Indian Statistical Institute, Kolkata, India
Arobinda Gupta   Indian Institute of Technology, Kharagpur, India
Debasish Jana   Heritage Institute of Technology, India
G. B. Mund   Kalinga Institute of Industrial Technology,
                              Bhubaneswar, India
Partha Bhowmick   Indian Institute of Technology, Kharagpur, India
Pradeesha Ashok   International Institute of Information Technology,
                              Bangalore, India
Samarjit Chakrabarty   University of North Carolina at Chapel Hill, USA
Sandeep Sen   Ashoka University, India
Sourav Chakraborty   Indian Statistical Institute, Kolkata, India
Subhamoy Maitra   Indian Statistical Institute, Kolkata, India
Subhas C. Nandy (Co-chair)   Indian Statistical Institute, Kolkata, India
Subhashis Majumder   Heritage Institute of Technology, India
Supantha Pandit   DAIICT, India
Susmita Sur-Kolay   Indian Statistical Institute, Kolkata, India
Wing-Kai Hon   National Tsing Hua University, Taiwan

Track B: AI and Machine Learning

Anirban Dasgupta   Indian Institute of Technology, Guwahati, India
Ansuman Banerjee   Indian Statistical Institute, Kolkata, India
Arindam Biswas   Indian Institute of Engineering Science and
                              Technology, Shibpur, India
Debranjan Sarkar   Heritage Institute of Technology, India
Dinabandhu Bhandari   Heritage Institute of Technology, India
Kamal Sarkar   Jadavpur University, India
Mandar Mitra   Indian Statistical Institute, Kolkata, India
Nabendu Chaki   University of Calcutta, India
Nikhil R. Pal   Indian Statistical Institute, Kolkata, India

Pabitra Mitra	Indian Institute of Technology, Kharagpur, India
Pradipta Maji	Indian Statistical Institute, Kolkata, India
Rajat. K. De (Co-chair)	Indian Statistical Institute, Kolkata, India
Sanjay Saha	Jadavpur University, India
Sujay Saha	Heritage Institute of Technology, India
Swarup Roy	Sikkim University, India
Tanmay Basu	Indian Institute of Science Education and Research Bhopal, India
Utpal Roy	Visva-Bharati University, India

Track C: Industrial Applications

Akash Agrawal	Google, USA
Amitava Das	AI Institute of University of South Carolina, USA
Amitava Mukherjee	Amrita Vishwa Vidyapeetham, Coimbatore, India
Ananda S. Das	Alcon Solutions, India
Aniruddha Dasgupta	Bluebell Research, Australia
Anuj Kharat	Axtria, India
Anurag Bagaria	Novartis HealthCare, Hyderabad, India
Bruhadeshwar Bezawada	South Arkansas University, USA
Christos Zaroliagis	University of Patras, Greece
Deepika Prakash	JK Lakshmipat University, India
Gautam Das	University of Texas at Arlington, USA
Maharaj Mukherjee	Bank of America, USA
Md. Anul Haq	Majmaah University, Saudi Arabia
Prosenjit Gupta (Co-chair)	Heritage Institute of Technology, India
Ravi Janardan	University of Minnesota, USA
S. K. Venkatesan	CQRL Bits LLP, India
Srayanta Mukherjee	BCGX-AI Institute, Switzerland
Subhajit Datta	Heritage Institute of Technology, India
Swarup Bhunia	University of Florida, USA

Additional Reviewers

Abhimannyu Basu	Ankush Acharya
Adrija Bhattacharya	Anupam Ghosh
Anil Bag	Anurina Tarafdar
Anindita Kundu	Arijit Ghosh
Anindya Halder	Arindam Chatterjee
Anindya Sen	Aritra Saha
Anirban Bhattacharjee	Arpita Talukdar

B. Uma Shankar
Deba Prasad Mandal
Debamita Kumar
Debasis Chaudhuri
Debasis Mitra
Diganta Sengupta
Diptopriyo Majumder
Himanshi Babbar
Jagpreet Singh
Jhalak Dutta
Joydeep Das
Md. Tabrez Quasim
Minati De
Mohuya Byabartta Kar
Moumita Ghosh
Nilanjana G. Basu
Nilina Bera
Palash Dutta
Partha Basuchowdhuri
Piyali Datta
Poulami Das
Pratyusa Dash
Raja Karmakar
Reshma Roychoudhuri
Rituparna Sinha
Sabyasachee Banerjee
Saikat Bandopadhyay
Sangram Kishore Jena
Sandip Samaddar
Sanjib Sadhu
Sasthi C. Ghosh
Saswati Naskar
Sayantan Das
Shilpi Saha
Smritikona Barai
Somenath Sengupta
Sudeshna Goswami
Sumon Ghosh
Swagatam Das
Tapalina Banerjee

Organizing Committee

Kalarab Ray (Advisor)	Heritage Institute of Technology, India
Avijit Dutta	Heritage Institute of Technology, India
Amitabha Acharya	Heritage Institute of Technology, India
Amitava Ghosh Dastidar	Heritage Institute of Technology, India
Anirban Bhattacharjee	Heritage Institute of Technology, India
Anirban Manna	Heritage Institute of Technology, India
Ankur Roy	Heritage Institute of Technology, India
Anup Kumar Sen	Heritage Institute of Technology, India
Anurina Tarafdar	Heritage Institute of Technology, India
Arindam Chatterjee	Heritage Institute of Technology, India
Aritra Saha	Heritage Institute of Technology, India
Arpita Talukdar	Heritage Institute of Technology, India
Arvind Srivastava	Heritage Institute of Technology, India
Avijit Sinha	Heritage Institute of Technology, India
Debalina Sengupta	Heritage Institute of Technology, India
Debamita Kumar	Heritage Institute of Technology, India
Debashis Sarkar	Heritage Institute of Technology, India
Debasish Jana	Heritage Institute of Technology, India
Deblina Choudhury	Heritage Institute of Technology, India
Debranjan Sarkar	Heritage Institute of Technology, India

Deepshikha Chaudhury	Heritage Institute of Technology, India
Jhalak Dutta	Heritage Institute of Technology, India
Kamal Poddar	Heritage Institute of Technology, India
Mohuya Byabartta Kar	Heritage Institute of Technology, India
Moumita Ghosh	Heritage Institute of Technology, India
Nilina Bera	Heritage Institute of Technology, India
Palash Dutta	Heritage Institute of Technology, India
Poulami Das	Heritage Institute of Technology, India
Pratyusa Dash	Heritage Institute of Technology, India
Raja Karmakar	Heritage Institute of Technology, India
Reshma Roy Choudhuri	Heritage Institute of Technology, India
Sabyasachee Banerjee	Heritage Institute of Technology, India
Sanchayita Sarkar	Heritage Institute of Technology, India
Sandip Samaddar	Heritage Institute of Technology, India
Saswati Naskar	Heritage Institute of Technology, India
Satabdi Barman	Heritage Institute of Technology, India
Shilpi Saha	Heritage Institute of Technology, India
Sidhartha Mojumdar	Heritage Institute of Technology, India
Smritikona Barai	Heritage Institute of Technology, India
Somenath Sengupta	Heritage Institute of Technology, India
Sudeshna Ghosh Goswami	Heritage Institute of Technology, India
Sudipta Chakrabarty	Heritage Institute of Technology, India
Sujoy Dasgupta	Heritage Institute of Technology, India
Surajit Acharya	Heritage Institute of Technology, India
Taraknath Bhowmick	Heritage Institute of Technology, India

Invited Talks

How to Describe a Contour to Visually Challenged: Perspectives from Computational and Digital Geometry

Bhargab B. Bhattacharya

Indian Statistical Institute, Kolkata,
bhargab@isical.ac.in

Abstract. Teaching geometry and helping visually-challenged individuals perceive various shapes has long been a significant challenge for educators. The ability to recognize and understand contours and shapes is essential not only in mathematics and engineering drawing but also in art and graphical analysis. Training the large blind population to develop skills in these areas remains a key obstacle in advancing inclusive education. Current Braille technologies use tactile pads with arrays of discrete pins that can move up and down under program control. For a blind person, perceiving a contour can be abstracted as the complex geometric task of reconstructing a polygon from an unordered set of boundary points. This talk reviews prior art in this area, examining it through the lens of computational and digital geometry, and explores potential future innovations that could expand the capabilities of Braille-based assistive technologies.

Keywords: Assistive technologies · Computational and digital geometry · Polygons · Proximity · Visually challenged · Voronoi diagram

References

1. Agustina, R., Farida, N.: Braille geometry teaching materials for low vision students. Kreano **12**(1) (2021)
2. Teaching Math to Students who are Blind. Erasmus Project Report # KA201-2015-012
3. ASME.org: Refreshable Braille Display for Teaching Geometry to Visually Challenged (2019)
4. Banerjee, S., et al.: On representing a simple polygon perceivable to a blind person. Inf. Process. Lett. **120**, 1–5 (2017)
5. Bhowmick, P., et al.: On the representation of a digital contour with an unordered point set for visual perception. J. Vis. Commun. Image Represent. **22**(7), 590–605 (2011)

Competitive Facility Location and Discrete Voronoi Games

Bhaswar B. Bhattacharya

Department of Statistics and Data Science, University of Pennsylvania, USA

Abstract. Facility location problems involve placing a set of facilities (resources) with the objective to minimize the cost of serving a set of demands (customers). The *discrete Voronoi game* is a game-theoretic analogue of these problems, which involves a finite set of customers in an arena and a few competing players. The players alternately place their facilities in the arena for a pre-specified number of rounds. Each customer chooses the service of its nearest facility (based on some distance metric), and at the end of the game, the player that serves the most users wins the game. Here, the optimal locations of the players are often governed by statistical notions of centrality, such as the Fermat-Weber point or the halfspace median. In this talk, we will survey some results in this direction [1–5, 7, 8], discuss open problems, and applications in designing vaccination campaigns for zoonotic epidemics [6].

Keywords: Computational geometry · Facility location · Voronoi diagrams

References

1. Banik, A., Bhattacharya, B.B., Das, S., Das, S.: The 1-dimensional discrete Voronoi game. Oper. Res. Lett. **47**, 115–121 (2019)
2. Banik, A., Bhattacharya, B.B., Das, S., Mukherjee, S.: The discrete Voronoi game in $\mathbb{R}^2$. Comput. Geom. Theory Appl. **63**, 53–62 (2017)
3. Banik, A., Bhattacharya, B.B., Das, S.: Optimal strategies for the one-round discrete Voronoi game on a line. J. Comb. Optim. **26**, 655–669 (2013)
4. Banik, A., De Carufel, J.-L., Maheshwari, A., Smid, M.: Discrete Voronoi games and ϵ-nets, in two and three dimensions. Comput. Geom. Theory Appl. **55**, 41–58 (2016)
5. Bhattacharya, B.B., Nandy, S.C.: New variations of the maximum coverage facility location problem. Eur. J. Oper. Res. **224**(3), 477–485 (2013)
6. Castillo-Neyra, R., et al.: Optimizing the location of vaccination sites to stop a zoonotic epidemic. Sci. Rep. **14**, 15910 (2024)
7. de Berg, M., van Wordragen, G.: Improved bounds for discrete Voronoi games. In: Morin, P., Suri, S. (eds.) WADS 2023. LNCS, vol. 14079, pp. 291–308. Springer, Cham (2023). https://doi.org/10.1007/978-3-031-38906-1_20
8. de Berg, M., Kisfaludi-Bak, S., Mehr, M.: On one-round discrete Voronoi games. In: 30th International Symposium on Algorithms and Computation (ISAAC), pp. 1–17 (2019)

Dissecting Neighbor Discovery

Philipp H. Kindt[1] and Samarjit Chakraborty[2]

[1] Kindt and Chakraborty Technische Universität Chemnitz, Germany
[2] The University of North Carolina at Chapel Hill, USA

When we "*pair*" a Bluetooth headset with our smartphone, the process that allows them to "discover" each other is referred to as *neighbor discovery* (ND). Before any two wireless devices can start communicating, they need to carry out an ND procedure to detect their mutual presence. This is done by a sender sending beacons (which are data packets/signals containing the device's identification number) and receivers listening for such beacons. When an ND procedure is carried out by a pair of devices, each device, when acting as a sender, schedules beacon transmissions using a certain pattern or schedule. Similarly, each device also listens for beacons from the other device by scheduling "reception windows" according to a different pattern. The schedule for such reception widows specify the start time of each window and its length.

But because the two devices have not been in contact prior to the ND procedure, their clocks will not be synchronized. In addition, the points in time at which either of the devices is powered on, or come within communication range of the other device, is random. Hence, the beacon transmissions of the sender and the reception windows of the receiver are shifted against each other by a random offset. But for a ND procedure to be successful, a sender's beacon must eventually coincide with a receiver's reception window, despite the random offset between them, and this defines the *latency* of the ND procedure. This ND *latency*, which is the time from when both devices come within communication range, till the time when a receiver first receives a sender's beacon, depends on the beacon transmission and reception window schedules. Devices do not continuously listen for beacons or send beacons because both reception and transmission costs energy, and many devices running ND protocols – from smartphones to small sensor nodes – are battery powered, and therefore energy constrained. Clearly, the transmission and reception schedules depend on the available energy budget. With a higher energy budget, devices can transmit and listen for beacons more frequently, thereby increasing the likelihood of a lower discovery latency.

An ND *protocol* may be defined by the patterns of sending and listening for beacons. Hence, a central question in ND is: *Given a power budget for each device, what should its beacon transmission and listening pattern be to minimize its guaranteed discovery latency?* Towards answering this question, many different ND protocols have been proposed over the nearly past two decades; for example, see: [1–5, 15, 16, 18–22]. Such protocols usually provide multiple tunable parameters that affect the power budget and discovery latency. It is also possible to compute the ND latencies of these protocols for given parameter values. However, despite all the research in this domain, and the practical applications of ND, the fundamental question of what is the theoretically lowest possible discovery latency that any protocol can guarantee for a given energy budget, remained unanswered for a long time. Further, the comparison between different ND protocols became difficult, since they made different assumptions, such as whether time is slotted or continuous, whether the sender and the receiver have the same or different patterns (and hence, power budgets), or whether beacons from multiple senders collide and thereby prevent successful discovery.

In this talk we will discuss our recent work [6, 7], on deriving a provably optimal discovery latency for any given energy budget. This result not only provides a lower bound on the best possible ND latency, but also a concrete algorithm that realizes this latency. The goal of this talk is not to provide an exhaustive treatment of this topic, but instead provide an introduction to the problem of ND, clarify what the underlying algorithmic problem is, and what are the mathematical tools used to derive the optimal latency. In addition, we will also touch upon techniques for using this result [9, 13] to configure ND in commonly used protocols like the Bluetooth Low Energy (BLE) [10, 11, 14]. Next, we will discuss the various applications of this result in domains ranging from low-power Internet-of-Things (IoT) [12, 17] to smartphone-based contact tracing for COVID-19 [8]. Finally, we also discuss scenarios in which an optimal solution to the ND problem still remains unknown, *e.g.*, when many devices are within range and therefore their beacons may collide and prevent successful discovery.

References

1. Bakht, M., Trower, M., Kravets, R.H.: Searchlight: won't you be my neighbor? In: Annual International Conference on Mobile Computing and Networking (MOBICOM), pp. 185–196 (2012)
2. Chen, L., et al.: On heterogeneous neighbor discovery in wireless sensor networks. In: IEEE Conference on Computer Communications (INFOCOM), pp. 693–701 (2015)
3. Dutta, P., Culler, D.E.: Practical asynchronous neighbor discovery and rendezvous for mobile sensing applications. In: ACM Conference on Embedded Network Sensor Systems (SenSys), pp. 71–84 (2008)
4. Julien, C., Liu, C., Murphy, A.L., Picco, G.P.: BLEnd: practical continuous neighbor discovery for bluetooth low energy. In: ACM/IEEE International Conference on Information Processing in Sensor Networks (IPSN), pp. 105–116 (2017)
5. Kandhalu, A., Lakshmanan, K., Rajkumar, R.: U-connect: a low-latency energy-efficient asynchronous neighbor discovery protocol. In: International Conference on Information Processing in Sensor Networks (IPSN), pp. 350–361 (2010)
6. Kindt, P.H., Chakraborty, S.: On optimal neighbor discovery. In: ACM Special Interest Group on Data Communication (SIGCOMM), pp. 441–457 (2019)
7. Kindt, P.H., Chakraborty, S.: Performance limits of neighbor discovery in wireless networks. IEEE/ACM Trans. Network. (TON) (2025, to appear)
8. Kindt, P.H., Chakraborty, T., Chakraborty, S.: How reliable is smartphone-based electronic contact tracing for COVID-19? Commun. ACM (CACM) **65**(1), 56–67 (2022)

9. Kindt, P.H., Heitmann, N., Reinerth, G., Chakraborty, S.: Understanding slotless neighbor discovery: demo abstract. In: ACM/IEEE International Conference on Information Processing in Sensor Networks (IPSN) (2017)
10. Kindt, P.H., Saur, M., Chakraborty, S.: Neighbor discovery latency in BLE-like protocols. IEEE Trans. Mobile Comput. (TMC) **17**(3), 617–631 (2018)
11. Kindt, P.H., Yunge, D., Diemer, R., Chakraborty, S.: Energy modeling for the Bluetooth Low Energy protocol. ACM Trans. Embed. Comput. Syst. **19**(2), 13:1–13:32 (2020)
12. Kindt, P.H., Yunge, D., Gopp, M., Chakraborty, S.: Adaptive online power-management for bluetooth low energy. In: IEEE International Conference on Computer Communications (INFOCOM) (2015)
13. Kindt, P.H., Yunge, D., Reinerth, G., Chakraborty, S.: Griassdi: mutually assisted slotless neighbor discovery. In: ACM/IEEE International Conference on Information Processing in Sensor Networks (IPSN), pp. 93–104 (2017)
14. Kindt, P.H., Narayanaswamy, S., Saur, M., Chakraborty, S.: Optimizing BLE-like neighbor discovery. IEEE Trans. Mob. Comput. (TMC) **21**(5), 1779–1797 (2022)
15. Meng, T., Wu, F., Chen, G.: On designing neighbor discovery protocols: a code-based approach. In: IEEE Conference on Computer Communications (INFOCOM), pp. 1689–1697 (2014)
16. Meng, T., Wu, F., Chen, G.: Code-based neighbor discovery protocols in mobile wireless networks. IEEE/ACM Trans. Network. (TON) **24**(2), 806–819 (2016)
17. Portal, S.T.S.: Bluetooth Low Energy (BLE) enabled devices market volume worldwide, from 2013 to 2020 (in million units) (2018). www.statista.com/statistics/750569/worldwide-bluetooth-low-energy-device-market-volume
18. Qiu, Y., Li, S., Xu, X., Li, Z.: Talk more listen less: energy-efficient neighbor discovery in wireless sensor networks. In: IEEE Conference on Computer Communications (INFOCOM), pp. 1–9 (2016)
19. Schurgers, C., Tsiatsis, V.T., Ganeriwal, S., Srivastava, M.B.: Optimizing sensor networks in the energy-latency-density design space. IEEE Trans. Mobile Comput. (TMC) **1**(1), 70–80 (2002)
20. Sun, W., Yang, Z., Wang, K., Liu, Y.: Hello: a generic flexible protocol for neighbor discovery. In: IEEE Conference on Computer Communications (INFOCOM), pp. 540–548 (2014)
21. Tseng, Y.C., Hsu, C.S., Hsieh, T.Y.: Power-saving protocols for IEEE 802.11 based multi-hop ad hoc networks. In: IEEE Conference on Computer Communications (INFOCOM) (2002)
22. Zhang, D., et al.: Acc: Generic on-demand accelerations for neighbor discovery in mobile applications. In: ACM Conference on Embedded Network Sensor Systems, (SenSys) (2012)

Coping with Expensive Distance Oracles in Metric Space Proximity Problems

Gautam Das

University of Texas, Arlington, TX, 76019 USA
gdas@uta.edu
https://ranger.uta.edu/gdas/

Abstract. Algorithms for popular proximity problems (such as, KNN, clustering, minimum spanning tree) repeatedly perform distance computations to compare distances during their execution. The focus of our work is to minimize distance computations for such problems in general metric spaces, especially for scenarios when calling an expensive oracle to resolve unknown distances are the dominant cost of the algorithms. In certain extreme scenarios, such a distance oracle may not even be available. We present a suite of techniques, including a novel formulation of the problem that studies how distance comparisons between objects could be modelled as a system of linear inequalities that assists in saving distance computations. For the case when a distance oracle is not available, we study the problem of answering upper and lower bound distance queries over the unknown distances using graph-theoretic algorithms that only consider the edges with known distances. We propose a suite of algorithmic techniques with provable guarantees that trade-off between pre-processing time/query processing time and quality. Our work advances the state-of-the-art solutions both analytically. We also empirically demonstrate the effectiveness of our algorithms by conducting exhaustive experimentation using multiple large-scale real-world datasets.

Navigating the Transformative Potential of Generative AI: Large Vision-Language Models – Opportunities and Ethical Challenges

Swagatam Das

Indian Statistical Institute, Kolkata,
swagatam.das@isical.ac.in
https://www.isical.ac.in/swagatam.das/

Abstract. Large Language Models (LLMs) and Vision-Language Models (VLMs), such as ChatGPT and CLIP, have garnered significant attention for their groundbreaking capabilities in understanding and generating both text and images. This presentation explores the statistical principles and advanced architectures that underpin these models, highlighting their training processes, fine-tuning methods, and the data-driven innovations that enable their impressive performance across tasks such as conversational AI, content creation, and multi-modal analysis. By integrating text and vision, VLMs represent a major leap in generative AI's ability to understand and respond to complex, multi-format data.

However, the rapid advancement and deployment of LLMs and VLMs also bring critical ethical considerations to the forefront. Issues such as biases embedded in training data, fairness in algorithmic decision-making, potential misuse, and privacy violations pose significant challenges. This presentation delves into the implications of these technologies on societal structures, addressing concerns about misinformation, inequitable access, and their broader societal impact. Through an examination of both the technical foundations and ethical dimensions of LLMs and VLMs, this talk seeks to encourage informed discussions on harnessing their transformative potential responsibly while proactively addressing concerns related to bias, fairness, and transparency with examples from medical AI use cases.

Oblivious Algorithms and Universal Optimality

Sandeep Sen

Department of Computer Science, Ashoka University Sonepat, 131029 Haryana, India

Abstract. We are interested in a class of algorithms that are dependent on one or more parameters - many of which are not known a priori - but the performance of the algorithm is asymptotically similar to the situation if these parameters were known. We would like to distinguish it from a related notion of *adaptive algorithms* that can modify themselves on the basis of their experience or training. As per ChatGPT, *Adaptive algorithms are a class of algorithms designed to adjust or "adapt" their behavior in response to changes in their environment or input data. They dynamically modify their parameters or decision-making processes to optimize performance in varying conditions. This adaptability is particularly useful in situations where the underlying problem or data distribution may not be stationary or known in advance.*

Oblivious algorithms do not rely on the history or any stochastic phenomena but on a finer characterization of the problem related to unknown implicit parameters that the algorithm is sensitive to. More specifically, the analysis of the running time can be crafted as a function of such parameters and the goal is to understand the exact (or asymptotic) dependence. Note that the traditional running time analysis is measured as a function of the input size n which carries little information about the complexity of any instance of size n. (In certain models of streaming, even the size of the input is not known in advance.)

For example, we know that a (nearly) sorted input instance could take $O(n)$ comparisons as opposed to the worst case bound of $\Theta(n \log n)$. For the case of repeated elements in a given input, known as *multisorting*, the running time depends on the multiplicity of different elements. It is worth noting that the running time of the algorithm is also inherently related to the output and a common example is that of computing the n-th Fibonacci number. While the input has size $\log n$ bits, the output is $\Omega(n)$ and any efficient algorithm would compute this in $O(\log n + h)$ steps where $h = n$ is the size of the output. This is not very interesting as the size of output is known in advance.

As opposed to this, consider the problem of hidden surface elimination (or the 3D to 2D projection with visualization) where the running time has a dependence $O(n \log n+h)$ where $O(1) \leq h \leq O(n^2)$. Without the aspect of *output-sensitivity*, the algorithm design would be considered inadequate since $O(n^2)$ time algorithm will be overkill when the visible scene is sparse. Here again, the size of the visible scene is not known in advance but carefully designed algorithms would be very parsimonious while calculating the visible scene [11]. The related problem of finding all the intersections of n line segments demonstrates similar characteristics since the number of intersections can vary between 0 to $\binom{n}{2}$, and so any $\Theta(n^2)$ algorithm would be unsatisfactory [3].

Consider the fundamental geometric problem of computing the convex hull of n points. In the planar case, the output can vary between $O(1)$ to n and it took researchers [10] some time to understand the optimal complexity of convex hull in terms of n and h which was shown to be $\Theta(n \log h)$. An even finer characterization [1, 13] led to a running time of $O(\sum_i^h n_i \log (n/n_i + 1))$ and that is upper-bounded by $O(n \log h)$. The vector $D = (n_1, n_2 \ldots n_h)$ is not an input parameter but a measure of the combinatorial structure of an instance that cannot be easily extracted from the input. It is interesting (and perhaps confusing) to grasp that the $O(n \log n)$ as well as the $O(n \log h)$ algorithms for convex hull were both shown to be optimal. Utilizing a finer characterization in terms of the output size and even further in terms of D, leads to a superior performance for many scenarios and provides deeper insights to the complexity of the problem. The reader may note that $\sum_i^h n_i \log (n/n_i + 1) \leq n \log h \leq n \log n$ shows progressive refinement of the same problem on the basis of increasing parameters.

More formally, we can define a hierarchy of parametrization as follows. Let N, N' represents a set of parameters (explicit or implicit) relevant to a specific problem P such that $N \subset N'$. Let $T_A(N)$ and $T_B(N)$ represent the running times of algorithms A and B for the same instance, which are expressed as a function of N, N' respectively. If $T_B(N') \in O(T_A(N))$ for all instances and $T_B(N') \in o(T_A(N))$ for a family of instances, then we consider N' to be a more *granular complexity* measure for the problem P.

A very recent related result was obtained with regards to Dijkstra's single source shortest path algorithm where it was shown that by using a more carefully designed heap data-structure, the algorithm was optimal in a very strong sense. The authors termed it as *universal optimality* [9], which is a relaxation of the notion of *instance optimality* [1]. These pertain to a stronger notion of optimality than the traditional worst-case optimality. Broadly speaking, such algorithms match the best possible algorithms for *every* instance of a problem within a constant (or a small multiplicative) factor. This definition addresses the biased behaviour of many worst-case efficient algorithms towards some pathological bad cases, but are relatively less efficient for majority of the instances.

Basic data structure courses teach us how to effectively deal with sparse matrices where operations on sparse matrices run in time $O(size)$ instead of $O(n \times n)$. However, sparsity being an explicit property, it is not as challenging as spectral algorithms for graphs, which are more sophisticated.

Another area where this phenomenon shows up is the design of cache-oblivious algorithms ([8, 12]). It was known much earlier that parameters of the memory hierarchy influence the running time of the algorithm [2], but the challenge was to design matching oblivious algorithms that were not customized for a fixed set of cache parameters. A recursive strategy and a clever adaptive analysis turned out to be the key to designing such algorithms. One of the best known examples of this kind includes doing matrix transposition with the optimal number of block transfers $O(\frac{N}{B})$; and even more sophisticated algorithms like funnel sort, that takes $O(\frac{N \log_M N}{B})$. Here, the two parameters M, B represent the size of the cache and the block size respectively. The real advantage of this approach is that even for multilevel cache hierarchy (which is quite common), the oblivious approach automatically achieves the optimal bound across all the levels simultaneously and so it can be ported across different architectures without a priori customization.

At this juncture, we would like to distinguish between algorithms that try to estimate the parameters explicitly, for example, by using a *doubling strategy*, from the ones that do not explicitly perform this phase. For instance, there is a fundamental difference between [5] that estimates the number of extreme points in contrast with [6, 4, 10] that converge in an oblivious manner. We would like to designate such algorithms as *pseudo oblivious* as they are working with multiple guesses before converging to the right estimate. While it often works for one parameter, it is not clear how to estimate multiple parameters. The area of *parametrized complexity* may also be viewed as estimating the relevant parameter by using multiple passes. Estimating parameters using subsampling would also fall under the same category and has been used for sorting algorithms [7].

Generalizing this notion to on-line settings would be non-trivial since we are dealing with unspecified dynamic inputs with no (or little) revocation. The area of approximation algorithms can be viewed as a distant generalization of the notion of obliviousness by considering the *lower bound* (for minimization problems) as an oblivious guiding benchmark. There is a trade-off between approximation factor and running time (especially for PTAS), but here our focus has been on characterizing running times of instances based on latent parameters. Clearly, this will necessitate a re-examination of specific problems yielding a better understanding of their universal algorithmic complexity.

References

1. Afshani, P., Barbay, J., Chan, T.M.: Instance-optimal geometric algorithms. J. ACM **64**(1) (2017). https://doi.org/10.1145/3046673
2. Aggarwal, A., Vitter, Jeffrey, S.: The input/output complexity of sorting and related problems. Commun. ACM **31**(9), 1116–1127 (1988). https://doi.org/10.1145/48529.48535
3. Bentley, J.L., Ottmann, T.: Algorithms for reporting and counting geometric intersections. IEEE Trans. Comput. **C-28**(9), 643–647 (1979). https://doi.org/10.1109/TC.1979.1675431
4. Bhattacharya, B.K., Sen, S.: On a simple, practical, optimal, output-sensitive randomized planar convex hull algorithm. J. Algorithms **25**(1), 177–193 (1997). https://doi.org/10.1006/jagm.1997.0869
5. Chan, T.: Output-sensitive results on convex hulls, extreme points and related problems. In: Proceedings of the 11th Annual Symposium on Computational Geometry (SOCG 1995), pp. 10–19. ACM (1995). https://doi.org/10.1145/223157.223287
6. Chan, T.M.Y., Snoeyink, J., Yap, C.K.: Output-sensitive construction of polytopes in four dimensions and clipped voronoi diagrams in three. In: Proceedings of the Sixth Annual ACM-SIAM Symposium on Discrete Algorithms, SODA 1995, pp. 282–291. Society for Industrial and Applied Mathematics, USA (1995)
7. Chen, S., Reif, J.: Using difficulty of prediction to decrease computation: fast sort, priority queue and convex hull on entropy bounded inputs. In: Proceedings of 1993

IEEE 34th Annual Foundations of Computer Science, pp. 104–112 (1993). https://doi.org/10.1109/SFCS.1993.366877
8. Frigo, M., Leiserson, C.E., Prokop, H., Ramachandran, S.: Cache-oblivious algorithms. In: Proceedings of the 40th Annual Symposium on Foundations of Computer Science (FOCS 1999), pp. 285–298. IEEE Computer Society, Washington, DC, USA (1999). https://doi.org/10.1109/SFCS.1999.814601
9. Haeupler, B., Hladík, R., Rozhoň, V., Tarjan, R.E., Tetěk, J.: Universal optimality of dijkstra via beyond-worst-case heaps. In: 2024 IEEE 65th Annual Symposium on Foundations of Computer Science (FOCS), pp. 2099–2130. IEEE (2024)
10. Kirkpatrick, D.G., Seidel, R.: The ultimate planar convex hull algorithm. SIAM J. Comput. **15**(1), 287–299 (1986). https://doi.org/10.1137/S0097539700183621
11. Reif, J.H., Sen, S.: An efficient output-sensitive hidden surface removal algorithm and its parallelization. In: Edelsbrunner, H. (ed.) Proceedings of the Fourth Annual Symposium on Computational Geometry, Urbana-Champaign, IL, USA, 6–8 June 1988, pp. 193–200. ACM (1988). https://doi.org/10.1145/73393.73413
12. Sen, S., Chatterjee, S., Dumir, N.: Towards a theory of cache-efficient algorithms. J. ACM **49**(6), 828–858 (2002). https://doi.org/10.1145/602220.602225
13. Sen, S., Gupta, N.: Distribution-sensitive algorithms. Nord. J. Comput. **6**(2), 194 (1999)

Contents

Track A

On the Rique Number of Series-Parallel Graphs and Planar Bipartite Graphs ... 3
   Sk Ruhul Azgor and Md. Saidur Rahman

Sorted Range Selection and Range Minima Queries 15
   Waseem Akram and Sanjeev Saxena

On the Characterization of Eulerian *es*-Splitting *p*-Matroids 27
   Uday Jagadale, Sachin Gunjal, Prashant Malavadkar, M. M. Shikare, and B. N. Waphare

Approximability of Edge-Vertex Domination in Unit Disk Graphs 39
   Vishwanath R. Singireddy and Manjanna Basappa

Density Extrema of Integer Points in Standard Hexagons 51
   Nilanjana G. Basu, Subhashis Majumder, and Partha Bhowmick

Dilution with Digital Microfluidic Biochips: Unbalanced Split-Error
Correction with SIMOP 65
   Nilina Bera, Subhashis Majumder, and Bhargab B. Bhattacharya

Track B

Social Evolution of Published Text and the Emergence of Artificial
Intelligence Through Large Language Models and the Problem of Toxicity
and Bias 79
   Arifa Khan, P. Saravanan, and S. K. Venkatesan

HITgram: A Platform for Experimenting with *n*-Gram Language Models 92
   Shibaranjani Dasgupta, Chandan Maity, Somdip Mukherjee, Rohan Singh, Diptendu Dutta, and Debasish Jana

Overlapping Community Detection Using Dynamic Residual Deep GCN 105
   Md. Nurul Muttakin, Md. Iqbal Hossain, and Md. Saidur Rahman

DeepUIR-Net: Underwater Image Restoration Using Residual-UNet
with Optimized Efficient Channel Attention Network Integration 117
   N. Rayvanth, S. Jaya Amruth, E. Suryaa, S. Resmi, and Rimjhim Padam Singh

Deepfake Image Detection Using Light-Weight Attention Integrated
MobileNetV3 Model 130
    Talluri Harshitha, Tanya Simhadri, Thadakuluru Jaswanthi,
    N. Rayvanth, and Rimjhim Padam Singh

AI-Driven Monitoring System for Detecting People Using Mobile Phones
in Restricted Zone 143
    Anidipta Pal, Ankana Datta, Ananyo Dasgupta, and Mohuya B. Kar

Integrated Analysis of Voice Patterns and Semantic Features for Emotion
Recognition 157
    Van Hieu Bui, Minh Son Cao, Trung Dinh Tran, and Khanh Nam Tran

Using Various Machine Learning Algorithms and xLSTM-UNet for Crop
Recommendation and Disease Prediction 168
    Agnij Moitra

He-Li Graph Convolutional Neural Network: Deep and Enhanced
Adaptation of Interest Modeling for Personalized Recommendation System 180
    Quang Dung Nguyen, Quoc Lap Dinh, Ba Hoang Nam Nguyen,
    and Van Hieu Bui

Creation of Cartoon Face Images of Celebrities: Automation 192
    D. S. Guru, D. L. Shivaprasad, and S. Prajna

Deployable Solution for Real-Time Children Face Emotion Prediction
System 204
    D. L. Shivaprasad, D. S. Guru, and R. Kavitha

Vision Transformers in Evaluating Bread Edibility 225
    D. S. Guru and D. Nandini

MobileNet Based Fruit Classification Using UNet Generated Segmented
Images: GRAD-CAM Visualization 237
    Sahitya Mondal, Tapashri Sur, Diganta Sengupta, and Chitrita Chaudhuri

RExAS: Relation Extraction Using Adaptive Self-attention 250
    Madhusudan Ghosh, Partha Basuchowdhuri, and Sudip Kumar Naskar

Track C

Kontho: An AI-Driven Smart Glove for Enhanced Sign Language
Communication 265
    Dyuti Dasgupta, Soumyajit Datta, Sagnik Pramanik, Rohit Kumar Dey,
    Jeet Nandigrami, and Debaditya Ghosh

Leveraging EfficientNetB4 Model with Multi-head Attentions for Maize
Leaf Disease Detection 277
    Nallamilli Eswar Venkata Reddiar, Pilla Veera Satya Sai Vikranth,
    Teerdhala Kumar, Thota Siddartha, N. Rayvanth,
    and Rimjhim Padam Singh

Automated Module for Image Quality Assessment from Narrow-Banding
Imaging Endoscopy Cameras 289
    Van Hieu Bui, Khac Long Pham, Thuan Thanh Nguyen,
    and The Anh Nguyen

Does Varied Developer Interactions Cause Bugs to Be Resolved Faster?
A Study of Open Source Software Ecosystems 301
    Reshma Roychoudhuri, Subhajit Datta, and Subhashis Majumder

Movie Recommendation Using Web Crawling 315
    Pronit Raj, Chandrashekhar Kumar, Harshit Shekhar, Amit Kumar,
    Kritibas Paul, and Debasish Jana

A Quadrant Partitioned-RRT* (QP-RRT*) Autonomous Agent 328
    Aritra Saha and Saikat Roy

Framework of a Smart Contract System for Improved Supply Chain
Management 340
    Aniket Pal, Aniket Chatterjee, and Rituparna Chaki

Integrating AI, IoT, and Drones for Sustainable Apple Orchard Monitoring
in Society 5.0 346
    Ankana Datta, Sukalpa Paul, Anidipta Pal, Sounav Biswas,
    Anil Kumar Bag, and Diganta Sengupta

SHIKSHA: Smart Hybrid Intelligent Knowledge System for Helping
Academia 352
    Aishik Paul, Abhisri Shaha, Arijit Mukherjee, Debajit Guha,
    Priyam Das, Ankan Das, Anurina Tarafdar, and Anindya Sen

Analyzing Social Networks of Actors in Movies and TV Shows 359
    Sarthak Giri, Sneha Chaudhary, and Bikalpa Gautam

Author Index 375

Track A

On the Rique Number of Series-Parallel Graphs and Planar Bipartite Graphs

Sk Ruhul Azgor(✉) and Md. Saidur Rahman

Graph Drawing and Information Visualization Laboratory, Department of Computer Science and Engineering, Bangladesh University of Engineering and Technology, Dhaka, Bangladesh
1805091@ugrad.cse.buet.ac.bd, saidurrahman@cse.buet.ac.bd

Abstract. The restricted input queue (rique) is a data structure which is recently introduced to study linear layout of graphs. The rique data structure is a special queue where insertions occur only at the head and removals occur at both the head and the tail. Considering a rique data structure the goal of a linear layout of a graph is to find a linear order of the vertices of the graph and a partition of its edges into pages such that the edges in each page follow the restriction of rique in the underlying order. The rique number of a graph is the smallest number of pages required for linear layout of the graph with rique data structure. A characterization of graphs for admitting a single page rique layout and some bounds on the rique number of complete and complete bipartite graphs are known. In this paper, we show that the rique number of series-parallel graphs as well as planar bipartite graphs is 2.

Keywords: Linear Layouts of Graph · Restricted Input Queue (rique) · Planar Bipartite Graphs · Series-Parallel Graphs

1 Introduction

The analysis of linear graph layouts is an important area of research that has been explored from multiple perspectives across various disciplines. Several combinatorial optimization problems are defined through a measure on a linear layout of a graph, including the well-known cutwidth [1] and bandwidth [5]. The relevant literature is extensive [11]. A linear layout of a graph is a total order of its vertices and a partition of its edges with constraint. In 1973, Pratt [7] examined multiple variants of linear layout achievable through different data structures that represent the linear ordering of vertices. For example, stack, queue, deque, and others.

Formally, given k data structures $D_1, D_2, \ldots, D_k$, a graph G is said to admit a $(D_1, D_2, \ldots, D_k)$-layout if there exists a linear order $\prec$ of the vertices of G and a partition of the edges of G into k sets $E_1, E_2, \ldots, E_k$, referred to as pages, such that for each page E_i in the partition, every edge (u, v) is processed by the data structure D_i by inserting (u, v) into D_i at u and removing it from D_i at v if $u \prec v$

in the linear order [4]. If the sequence of insertions and removals is feasible, then G is called a $(D_1, D_2, \ldots, D_k)$-graph. The set of all $(D_1, D_2, \ldots, D_k)$-graphs is denoted by $D_1 + D_2 + \ldots + D_k$. For a given data structure D, the D-number of a graph G is the smallest k such that G admits a $(D_1, D_2, \ldots, D_k)$-layout with $D = D_1 = D_2 = \ldots = D_k$ [3].

Various data structures (e.g., stack, queue, deque) can be used to represent the linear ordering of vertices in a graph. The *stack number* of a graph G, denoted $st(G)$, is the D-number of G where D is a stack. In this case, edge insertions and removals occur only at the head of D. The stack number, also called the *page number*, is NP-hard to compute [6]. The *queue number* of a graph G, denoted $q(G)$, is the D-number of G where D is a queue, with insertions at the head and removals at the tail. Queue numbers of various graph classes have been widely studied. A *deque* (double-ended queue, or DEQ) allows insertions and removals at both ends, implying $S + S \subseteq DEQ \subseteq S + S + Q$, since a deque can be simulated with two stacks and one queue [3]. *Mixed layouts*, combining s stacks and q queues, are called s-stack + q-queue layouts. An open question in this area is whether planar bipartite graphs admit a 1-stack + 1-queue layout [8].

Recently, Bekos et al. introduced a linear data structure, called *Restricted Input Queue* (abbreviated by *RIQ* or *rique*) [3] where insertions can occur at the head and removals from both head and tail of D. Formally, the rique number of a graph G is the D-number of G where D is a restricted-input queue. We denote the rique number of a graph G by $rique(G)$. Bekos et al. define graphs with a rique number of 1 as those that permit a planar embedding featuring a strongly 1-sided subhamiltonian path, which is a Hamiltonian path $v_1, v_2, \ldots, v_n$ in a planar embedding, such that each edge (v_i, v_j) with $1 < i < j \leq n$ maintains v_i on the same side of the path [3]. They also derived an inclusion relationship between Stack number, Queue number and Rique number. They showed that $S, Q \subset RIQ \subset S + Q$ holds.

However, the study of the rique number is not well-developed. We only know the upper bounds for complete graph, K_n and complete bipartite graph, $K_{n,n}$ which are $\lfloor \frac{n-1}{3} \rfloor$ and $\lfloor \frac{n-1}{2} \rfloor - 1$ respectively [4]. Additionally, the bound for K_n is tight up to $n = 30$ which has been proven using SAT solvers [4].

In this paper, our contribution is determining the rique number for series-parallel graphs and planar bipartite graphs. As $S, Q \subset RIQ$, The rique number of graph classes is upper bounded by the stack number or the queue number. Therefore, the rique number of series-parallel graphs and planar bipartite graphs is at most 2. We show that there exist graphs from the graph classes series-parallel graphs and planar bipartite graphs which have rique number of 2. This proves that the rique number of series-parallel and planar bipartite graph class is 2.

The remainder of the paper is organized as follows: Sect. 2 contains the necessary definitions and lemmas. Section 3 addresses the proof of the rique number for series-parallel graphs, whereas Sect. 4 discusses the proof of the rique number for planar bipartite graphs. Finally, Sect. 5 summarizes the paper and highlights future directions.

2 Preliminaries

In this section, we provide the definitions that will be used throughout the rest of the paper. For basic graph theoretic definitions, we refer to [10].

For a graph $G = (V, E)$, the vertex set is denoted as $V(G)$ and the edge set as $E(G)$. An edge is denoted as (u, v) where $u, v \in V(G)$, and u and v are referred to as the endpoints of the edge. If $(u, v) \in E(G)$, then u is referred to as a *neighbor* of v, and conversely, v is a neighbor of u in the graph G. The closed neighborhood of a vertex v is defined as the set of neighbors of v, including the vertex itself. Vertices u and v are considered *twins* if they share identical closed neighborhoods in the graph G.

A subset of vertices $V' \subseteq V$ is defined as an independent set in G if, for every pair of vertices $u, v \in V'$, there exists no edge in G that connects the two vertices u and v. A graph is defined as planar if it can be represented in a two-dimensional plane in such a manner that no edges intersect except at their respective vertices. A planar graph G is defined as a *planar bipartite* graph if its vertex set $V(G)$ can be divided into two disjoint nonempty subsets V_1 and V_2, each of which is independent. A graph $G = (V, E)$ is termed a *series-parallel* graph (with source s and sink t) if it either comprises a pair of vertices connected by a single edge or consists of two series-parallel graphs $G_i = (V_i, E_i), i = 1, 2$ with sources s_i and sinks t_i such that $V = V_1 \cup V_2$, $E = E_1 \cup E_2$, and either $s = s_1$, $t_1 = s_2$, and $t = t_2$ or $s = s_1 = s_2$ and $t = t_1 = t_2$ [10].

A vertex ordering, O, of a graph $G = (V, E)$ is defined as a total ordering of the vertex set V. The total order can be conveniently expressed as a permutation of vertices $[v_1, v_2, \ldots, v_{|V|}]$. This concept naturally extends to a subset of vertices. In a vertex ordering O of G, $u \prec v$ indicates that vertex u precedes vertex v. Additionally, $L(e)$ and $R(e)$ represent the endpoints of an edge $e \in E$ where $L(e) \prec R(e)$. Let e and f be two edges in the set E. If $L(e) \prec L(f) \prec R(e) \prec R(f)$, then e and f are said to *cross*. If $L(e) \prec L(f) \prec R(f) \prec R(e)$, then e and f are considered to *nest*. Furthermore, if $L(e) \prec L(f) \prec R(e)$, then it is stated that e covers f, as demonstrated in Fig. 1. Cover refers to the nesting or crossing of two edges. For a vertex ordering O of G, an edge e is classified as a *head-edge* (or *tail-edge*) if it is removed at $R(e)$ from the head (or tail) of the RIQ. Note that, in a rique data structure, the following constraints (i)-(iii) are applicable. i). Two head edges won't cross. ii) Two tail edges won't nest. iii) A head edge won't cover a tail edge. Now, a *head set* H (resp. *tail set* T) is a set of edges $E' \subseteq E$ such that no two edges in E' cross (nest). A *head set covers a tail set* if there exists a pair of edges (e, f) such that $e \in H$, $f \in T$ and e covers f. A 1-rique layout of a graph G is a pair $(O, \{H, T\})$, where O is a vertex ordering of G and $\{H, T\}$ is a partition of E into a head set H and a tail set T such that H doesn't cover T. We say that a vertex ordering O of a graph G admits 1-rique layout if there exists a partition of the edge set into $\{H, T\}$ such that H doesn't cover T and a graph G doesn't admit 1-rique layout if there exists no vertex ordering O such that O admits 1-rique layout.

The following properties holds for all 1-rique layout of any graph.

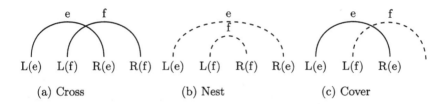

Fig. 1. Illustrations of crossing, nesting, and covering edges in a vertex ordering of a graph.

Lemma 1. *Let a vertex ordering O of graph G contain $u \prec p \prec v \prec q$ such that $(u,v), (p,q) \in E(G)$. If the order admits 1-rique layout, then $(u,v) \in T$ i.e. if $(u,v) \in H$, then the order doesn't admit a 1-rique layout.*

Proof. Assume for a contradiction that $(u,v) \in H$. Now, if $(p,q) \in H$, then (u,v) and (p,q) cross and if $(p,q) \in T$, then (u,v) covers (p,q), a contradiction. □

Lemma 2. *Let a vertex ordering O of graph G contain $u \prec p \prec q \prec v$ such that $(u,v), (p,q) \in E(G)$. If the order admits 1-rique layout, then $(p,q) \in H$.*

Proof. First, consider $(u,v) \in H$, then $(p,q) \in H$ otherwise (u,v) covers (p,q). Now, if $(u,v) \in T$, then $(p,q) \in H$ otherwise (u,v) and (p,q) nests. So, in either case, the lemma holds. □

Lemma 3. *Let a vertex ordering O of graph G contain $u \prec p \prec x \prec q \prec y \prec v$ such that $(u,v), (p,q), (x,y) \in E(G)$. Then the vertex ordering O doesn't admit 1-rique layout.*

Proof. Assume for a contradiction that vertex ordering O admits 1-rique layout. By Lemma 2, $(p,q), (x,y) \in H$. However, (p,q) and (x,y) cross. Hence, they both can't be head edge. A contradiction. So, the vertex ordering O doesn't admit 1-rique layout. □

3 Rique Number of Series-Parallel Graph

In this section, we prove that the rique number of a series-parallel graphs is 2. Recently, Angelini et al. demonstrated that series-parallel graphs do not have a 1-stack+1-queue layout [2]. Since $RIQ \subset S + Q$, this implies that the rique number of series-parallel graphs is at least 2. While Angelini et al. provided a complex proof for a complex graph, we offer a simple, intuitive proof using a straightforward graph that the rique number of a series-parallel graphs is 2.

Theorem 1. *The rique number of series-parallel graphs is 2.*

We first construct a graph G_7 from a gadget S. We show that G_7 is a series-parallel graph which doesn't admit 1-rique layout. As the upper bound of rique number of series-parallel graphs is 2 (bounded by stack number [9]), we conclude that the rique number of series-parallel graphs is 2.

The gadget S_i (see Fig. 2a) consists of two twins, s_i and t_i, connected by an edge, which we call the *twin edge*. There are an additional five vertices x_i, where $1 \leq i \leq 5$ which we call *connectors*. We denote the set of all connectors of S_i as C_i, and we refer to the edges (s_i, x_j) and (t_i, x_j) as *connecting edges*, where $1 \leq j \leq 5$.

We construct a graph G_7 by repeating 7 gadget $S_i, 1 \leq i \leq 7$ and additional 2 vertex A and B. The vertex A is connected to every s_i, t_i and B is connected to every t_i, where $1 \leq i \leq 7$. Clearly, The graph G_7 as illustrated in Fig. 2b is a series-parallel graph with the source and sink being vertices A and B, respectively.

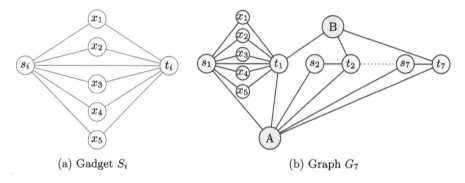

(a) Gadget S_i (b) Graph G_7

Fig. 2. Illustration of graph G_7 and gadget S_i

Before we dive into the main proof, we prove some lemma which is needed in the proof.

Lemma 4. *Assume that a vertex ordering of graph G_7 contain $u \prec s_i \prec t_i \prec v$ with edge $(u, v) \in E(G_7)$ and twins s_i, t_i. Then, if the order admits 1-rique layout, there must be at least three connectors x_i, $x_i \in C_i$ after v in the order.*

Proof. There are five partial orders where a connector x_j can appear in the order. 1) $x_j \prec u$. 2) $u \prec x_j \prec s_i$. 3) $s_i \prec x_j \prec t_i$. 4) $t_i \prec x_j \prec v$ and 5) $v \prec x_j$. Figure 3 illustrates all the cases. There are total five connectors which will appear in any of the mentioned partial order. Now, consider each of this cases and check how many connectors can be in each of the cases.

Case 1: $x_i \prec u$. In this case, there can be at most 1 connector before u. Assume for a contradiction, x_1, x_2 be two connectors that appear before u and w.l.o.g the order be $x_1 \prec x_2 \prec u$. Observe that $(x_j, s_i), (x_j, t_i) \in T$ where x_i is a connector appears before u otherwise either they cover the edge (u, v) if $(u, v) \in T$ or they crosses with (u, v) if $(u, v) \in H$. So, $(x_1, t_i), (x_2, s_i) \in T$.

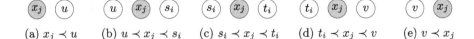

(a) $x_j \prec u$ (b) $u \prec x_j \prec s_i$ (c) $s_i \prec x_j \prec t_i$ (d) $t_i \prec x_j \prec v$ (e) $v \prec x_j$

Fig. 3. All possible cases where the connector x_j can appear in the vertex ordering, given that the vertex ordering contain $u \prec s_i \prec t_i \prec v$

However, the edge (x_1, t_i) and (x_2, s_i) nest, a contradiction. So, there can't be more than 1 connector before u in the order.

Case 2: $s_i \prec x_j \prec t_i$. In this case, there can be at most 1 connector between s_i and t_i. Assume for a contradiction that there are 2 connectors x_1, x_2 between s_i and t_i and w.l.o.g the order is $u \prec s_i \prec x_1 \prec x_2 \prec t_i \prec v$. As $(u, v), (s_i, x_2), (x_1, t_i) \in E(G_7)$, by Lemma 3, the vertex ordering doesn't support 1-rique layout, a contradiction.

Case 3: $u \prec x_j \prec s_i$. In this case, there can't be any connector between u and s_i. Firstly, assume for a contradiction that there can be more than 1 connectors between u and s_i. Let, x_1 and x_2 be two connectors and the order contain $u \prec x_1 \prec x_2 \prec s \prec t \prec v$. As $(u, v), (x_1, s_i), (x_2, t_i) \in E(G_7)$, by Lemma 3, the order doesn't admit 1-rique layout. A contradiction. Hence, there can be at most 1 connector between s_i and t_i. Now, assume for a contradiction that there is a connector x_1 between u and s_i. As a result, the rest of the connectors (two left) must be after t_i in the order. Let, x_i be a connector that will be after t_i in the order. Hence, the vertex ordering contain $u \prec x_1 \prec s_i \prec t_i \prec (x_i/v)$. By Lemma 2, $(x_1, t_i) \in H$. Now, (x_1, t_i) and (s_i, x_i) cross if $(s_i, x_i) \in H$ and (x_1, t_i) covers (s_i, x_i) if $(s_i, x_i) \in T$, a contradiction.

Case 4: $t_i \prec x_j \prec v$. Similar to the previous case, there can't be any connector between t_i and v. Firstly, assume for a contradiction that there can be more than 1 connectors between t_i and v. Let, x_1 and x_2 be two connectors and the order contain $u \prec s_i \prec t_i \prec x_1 \prec x_2 \prec v$. As $(u, v), (s_i, x_1), (t_i, x_2) \in E(G_7)$, by Lemma 3, the order doesn't admit 1-rique layout. A contradiction. Hence, there can be at most 1 connector between t_i and v. Now, assume for a contradiction that x_1 is a connector between t_i and v such that no other connector is in between t_i and x_1. So, the rest of the connectors (two left) must be after x_1 in the order. Let, x_i be a connector that will be after x_1 in the order. Hence, the vertex ordering contain $u \prec s_i \prec t_i \prec x_1 \prec (x_i/v)$. By Lemma 2, $(s_i, x_1) \in H$. Now, (t_i, x_i) and (s_i, x_1) cross if $(t_i, x_i) \in H$ and (s_i, x_1) covers (t_i, x_i) if $(t_i, x_i) \in T$, a contradiction.

Hence, there will be at least 3 connectors after v in the order (which is Case $(v \prec x_j)$). □

Lemma 5. *Assume that a vertex ordering of graph G_7 contain $u \prec s_i \prec t_i \prec v$ with edge $(u, v) \in H$ and twins s_i, t_i. Then, the order doesn't admit a 1-rique layout.*

Proof. By Lemma 4, there will be at least 3 connectors after v in the order. Let x_j be such a connector. However, if $(s_i, x_j) \in H$ then (u, v) and (s_i, x_j) cross and if $(s_i, x_j) \in T$ then (u, v) covers (s_i, x_j). As a result, the edge set can't be partitioned into a head set H and a tail set T. Thus, the order doesn't admit a 1-rique layout. □

The following corollary is a direct consequence of Lemma 5.

Corollary 1. *Assume that a vertex ordering of graph G_7 contain $u \prec s_i \prec t_i \prec v$ with edge $(u, v) \in E(G_7)$ and twins s_i, t_i. If the order admits 1-rique layout, then $(u, v) \in T$*

Given a constraint, we establish the order of the connectors with respect to the vertex s_i and t_i. We now examine some properties of connecting edges to determine whether they are head edges or tail edges. The following lemma is about the property of the connecting edges.

Lemma 6. *Assume that a vertex ordering of graph G_7 contain $u \prec s_i \prec t_i \prec v$ with edge $(u, v) \in T$ and twins s_i, t_i. By Lemma-4, let $\{x_1, x_2, x_3\}$ be the connectors of S_i that come after v in the vertex ordering such as $v \prec x_1 \prec x_2 \prec x_3$. Now, if the order admits a 1-rique layout then $(s_i, x_j) \in T$ where $1 \leq j \leq 2$ and $(x_2, t) \in H$.*

Proof. For the first part, assume for a contradiction that $(s_i, x_j) \in H$ where $1 \leq j \leq 2$. Now, if $(t_i, x_{j+1}) \in H$ then (t_i, x_{j+1}) and (s_i, x_j) cross and if $(t_i, x_{j+1}) \in T$, (s_i, x_j) covers (t_i, x_{j+1}), a contradiction. Hence, $(s_i, x_j) \in T$ where $1 \leq j \leq 2$. Now, if $(s_i, x_3) \in T$ then $(t_i, x_2) \in H$ otherwise (t_i, x_2) and (s_i, x_3) nest. And if $(s_i, x_3) \in H$ then $(t_i, x_2) \in H$ otherwise (s_i, x_3) covers (t_i, x_2). So, in both of the cases, $(t_i, x_2) \in H$. □

Lemma 7. *Assume that a vertex ordering of graph G_7 contain $u \prec d_1 \prec d_2 \prec d_3 \prec d_4 \prec v$ with edge $(u, v) \in T$ and two twins s_i, t_i, where $1 \leq i \leq 2$ such that $s_i, t_i \in \{d_1, d_2, d_3, d_4\}$, then the order doesn't support a 1-rique layout.*

Proof. As each gadget is a symmetric structure, we have to consider only three possible ordering of the two twins. 1. $s_1 \prec t_1 \prec s_2 \prec t_2$, 2. $s_1 \prec s_2 \prec t_1 \prec t_2$ and 3. $s_1 \prec s_2 \prec t_2 \prec t_1$. We show that in each case, a 1-rique layout isn't possible.

Case 1: $u \prec s_1 \prec t_1 \prec s_2 \prec t_2 \prec v$. Let x_1, x_2, x_3 and x_4, x_5, x_6 be the connectors of the pair s_1, t_1 and s_2, t_2 respectively which will come after the vertex v in the order by Lemma 4. Then by Lemma 6, $(s_1, x_2), (s_2, x_5) \in T$. This implies that $v \prec x_3 \prec x_6$ otherwise (s_1, x_2) and (s_2, x_5) will nest. Now, by Lemma 6, $(t_1, x_2), (t_2, x_5) \in T$ also, but they cross, a contradiction.

Case 2 and 3: $u \prec s_1 \prec s_2 \prec t_1 \prec t_2 \prec v$ or $u \prec s_1 \prec s_2 \prec t_2 \prec t_1 \prec v$. Let x_5 be the connector of s_2 that will appear after v in the order. By Lemma 6, $(s_2, x_5) \in T$. Now, in both cases $(u, v) \in T \implies (s_1, t_1) \in H$. But (s_1, t_1) covers (s_2, x_5), a contradiction. □

Now, we prove the main theorem of this section, Theorem 1. We show that the graph G_7 doesn't admit a 1-rique layout.

Proof. (Proof of theorem 1). Let a vertex ordering O of graph G_7, there are 3 possible partial order exists between the vertex A with a twin s_i, t_i where $1 \leq i \leq 7$. 1. Ast, 2. stA, 3. sAt (w.l.o.g $s_i \prec t_i$). As there are 7 gadgets S, by Pigeonhole principle, in every vertex ordering, there are at least 3 gadget S which has the same order with the vertex A. Now, we show that in every cases, the order doesn't admit 1 rique layout.

Case 1: Ast & *Case 2: stA*. Let, s_i, t_i where $1 \leq i \leq 3$ is the three gadgets. Let, a vertex ordering O of G_7 contain $A \prec d_1 \prec d_2 \prec d_3 \prec d_4 \prec d_5 \prec d_6$ (For case 2: $d_1 \prec d_2 \prec d_3 \prec d_4 \prec d_5 \prec d_6 \prec A$) where $s_i, t_i \in \{d_1, d_2, d_3, d_4, d_5, d_6\}$. By Corollary 1 $(A, d_6) \in T$. Now think A as u in the order and d_6 as v. There exist 2 twin between u and v and $(u, v) \in T$. By Lemma 7, O doesn't admit 1-rique layout.

Case 3: sAt. Let, s_i, t_i where, $1 \leq i \leq 3$ is the three gadgets. We assume w.l.o.g, a vertex ordering O of G_7 contain $s_1 \prec s_2 \prec s_3 \prec A \prec d_1 \prec d_2 \prec d_3$ where $t_i \in \{d_1, d_2, d_3\}$.

Let $(s_1, A) \in H$. Now, if $(s_2, d_k) \in H$ then (s_1, A) and (s_2, d_k) cross and if $(s_2, d_k) \in T$ then (s_1, A) covers (s_2, d_k), a contradiction.

Hence, $(s_1, A) \in T$. Now, let $(s_1, d_k) \in H$. According to Lemma 5, $k = 1$ otherwise the order contain $u \prec s_i \prec t_i \prec v$ where $(u, v) \in H$ and s_i, t_i are twin. But, (s_1, d_1) and (s_2, d_k) cross if $(s_2, d_k) \in H$ and (s_1, d_1) covers (s_2, d_k) cross if $(s_2, d_k) \in T$, a contradiction. Hence, $(s_1, d_k) \in T$ which implies that $(s_2, A) \in H$ as the edges nest. Now, if $(s_3, d_k) \in H$, then (s_2, A) and (s_3, d_k) cross and if $(s_3, d_k) \in T$, then (s_2, A) covers (s_3, d_k), a contradiction. So, the edge set can't be partitioned. Hence, O doesn't admit 1-rique layout.

In every vertex ordering O of the graph G_7, O contain one of the three cases mentioned above and hence, O doesn't admit a 1-rique layout. As a result, the rique number of the graph G_7 is 2. Hence, the rique number of series-parallel graph is 2. □

4 Rique Number of Planar Bipartite Graphs

In this section, we show that the rique number of the planar bipartite graph class is 2. The rique number of planar bipartite graph is upper bounded by the stack number which is 2. We construct an example planar bipartite graph and show that the example graph doesn't admit a 1-rique layout. Therefore, the rique number of the example graph is 2. Hence, the rique number of planar bipartite graph class is 2 as in the following theorem.

Theorem 2. *The rique number of planar bipartite graph class is 2.*

Before we start the proof, we construct a graph G_{19}, similar to what we did in Sect. 2, from a gadget M_i. Then, we prove some lemmas based on the properties of the gadget M_i under some constraints on edges in a partial vertex ordering. Finally, we show, through case-by-case analysis of the vertex ordering of graph G_{19}, that no vertex ordering exists for graph G_{19} that admits a 1-rique layout. As the rique number of planar bipartite graphs is at most 2 (bounded by stack number [9]), the rique number of graph G_{19} will be 2. This concludes that the rique number of planar bipartite graphs is 2.

First, we construct a graph G_{19} from a gadget M_i where $1 \leq i \leq 19$. The gadget M_i (see Fig. 4a) consists of two twins. There are also five vertices x_i, where $1 \leq i \leq 5$ which we call *connectors*. We denote the set of all connectors of M_i as C_i, and we refer to the edges (s_i, x_j) and (t_i, x_j) as *connecting edges*, where $1 \leq j \leq 5$. The only difference between the gadget used in the previous section, S_i and this section M_i is that $(s_i, t_i) \in E(S_i)$ but $(s_i, t_i) \notin E(M_i)$.

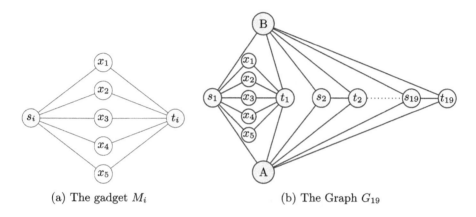

(a) The gadget M_i (b) The Graph G_{19}

Fig. 4. Diagrams illustrating the gadget M_i and the graph G_{19}

We construct graph G_{19} by repeating 19 gadgets of M_i, with two additional vertices, denoted as A and B. Every s_i and t_i, where $1 \leq i \leq 19$, is connected to the vertices A and B (see Fig. 4b). Clearly, the graph G_{19} is a planar bipartite graph, and we prove that the graph G doesn't admit a 1-rique layout.

Before diving into the original proof, we first prove some lemmas. Given the similarity between the gadget S_i and M_i, Lemmas 4, 5 & 6 and Corollary 1 apply to both G_7 & S_i and G_{19} & M_i. Observe that, the proof of the mentioned lemma doesn't use the edge (s_i, t_i) which is the only difference between gadget S_i and gadget M_i. However, the following lemmas are specific to G_{19} & M_i.

Lemma 8. *Assume that a vertex ordering of graph G_{19} contain $u \prec d_1 \prec d_2 \prec d_3 \prec d_4 \prec v$ with edge $(u, v) \in T$ and two twins s_i, t_i, where $1 \leq i \leq 2$ such that $s_i, t_i \in \{d_1, d_2, d_3, d_4\}$. Given the symmetry of the graph and the gadget, w.l.o.g assume that $s_i \prec t_i$ and $s_1 \prec s_2$ in the order. Now, if the vertex ordering admits a 1-rique layout, then vertex ordering contain $u \prec s_1 \prec s_2 \prec t_2 \prec t_1 \prec v$.*

Proof. Given $s_i \prec t_i$ and $s_1 \prec s_2$ where $i < j$. Therefore, there can be 3 possible partial orders of the twins. 1. $u \prec s_1 \prec t_1 \prec s_2 \prec t_2 \prec v$, 2. $u \prec s_1 \prec s_2 \prec t_1 \prec t_2 \prec v$ and 3. $u \prec s_1 \prec s_2 \prec t_2 \prec t_1 \prec v$. We show that only the third partial order admits a 1-rique layout.

Let x_1, x_2, x_3 and x_4, x_5, x_6 be the connectors of the pair s_1, t_1 and s_2, t_2 respectively which come after the vertex v in the order (by Lemma 4). Hence, by Lemma 6, $(s_1, x_2), (s_2, x_5) \in T$ and $(t_1, x_2), (t_2, x_5) \in H$. Given $s_1 \prec s_2$, we find $v \prec x_2 \prec x_5$ otherwise (s_1, x_2) and (s_2, x_5) nest.

Case 1: $u \prec s_1 \prec t_1 \prec s_2 \prec t_2 \prec v \prec x_2 \prec x_5$. However, (t_1, x_2) and (t_2, x_5) cross. So, case-1 doesn't admit a 1-rique layout.

Case 2: $u \prec s_1 \prec s_2 \prec t_1 \prec t_2 \prec v \prec x_2 \prec x_5$. Similar to case-1, (t_1, x_2) and (t_2, x_5) cross.

Case 3: $u \prec s_1 \prec s_2 \prec t_2 \prec t_1 \prec v$. We assume w.l.o.g, the vertex ordering contain $u \prec s_1 \prec s_2 \prec t_2 \prec t_1 \prec v \prec x_1 \prec x_2 \prec x_3 \prec x_4 \prec x_5 \prec x_6$. This ordering admits a 1-rique layout where $(s_i, x_j) \in T$ and $(t_i, x_j) \in H$; for $1 \leq i \leq 2$ and $3i - 2 \leq j \leq 3i$. □

The following corollary is the generalization of Lemma 8.

Corollary 2. *Assume that a vertex ordering of graph G_{19} contain $u \prec d_1 \prec d_2 \prec \cdots \prec d_{2k} \prec v$ with edge $(u, v) \in T$ and k twins s_i, t_i, where $1 \leq i \leq k$ such that $s_i, t_i \in \{d_1, d_2, \ldots, d_{2k}\}$. Given the symmetry of the graph and the gadget, w.l.o.g assume that $s_i \prec t_i$ and $s_i \prec s_j, i \leq j$ in the order. Now, if the vertex ordering admits a 1-rique layout, then vertex ordering contain $u \prec s_1 \prec s_2 \prec \cdots \prec s_k \prec t_k \prec \cdots \prec t_2 \prec t_1 \prec v$.*

We now prove the main theorem of this section, Theorem 2. We show that the graph G_{19} doesn't admit a 1-rique layout.

Proof. (Proof of Theorem 2). Graph G consists of 19 gadgets M_i where $1 \leq i \leq 19$ with two additional vertex A, B. Note that A and B are twins. Each gadget M_i is symmetric. Hence, w.l.o.g, let the vertex ordering contain $s_i \prec t_i$, $s_i \prec s_j$ where $i < j$ and $A \prec B$. Now, there are total 6 possible partial order exists between the vertices A & B and s_i, t_i where $1 \leq i \leq 19$. They are 1. $A \prec s_i \prec t_i \prec B$, 2. $s_i \prec A \prec B \prec t_i$, 3. $s_i \prec t_i \prec A \prec B$, 4. $A \prec B \prec s_i \prec t_i$, 5. $A \prec s_i \prec B \prec t_i$ and 6. $s_i \prec A \prec t_i \prec B$ (see Fig. 5).

By Pigeonhole principle, there are at least 4 gadgets M_i which has the same partial order with the vertex A and B. We now show that for each of the cases the vertex ordering doesn't admit a 1-rique layout.

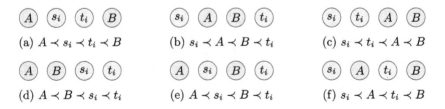

Fig. 5. All possible cases of partial order of vertex A, B and a twins s_i, t_i of G_{19}

Case 1: $A \prec s_i \prec t_i \prec B$ where $1 \leq i \leq 4$. Assume w.l.o.g, t_4 is nearest to vertex B in the order i.e. no other t_i is in between vertex t_4 and B for $1 \leq i \leq 3$.

By Corollary 1, $(A, t_4) \in T$. Therefore, by Corollary 2, the only possibly vertex ordering that admits a 1-rique layout is $A \prec s_1 \prec s_2 \prec s_3 \prec t_3 \prec t_2 \prec t_1$. Let x_{3i-2}, x_{3i-1} and x_{3i} be the connectors of s_i, t_i that come after t_4 in the order (Lemma 4). By Lemma 6, $(s_i, x_{3i-1}) \in T$ and $(t_i, x_{3i-1}) \in H$. Now, $s_1 \prec s_2 \prec s_3$ implies that $t_4 \prec x_2 \prec x_5 \prec x_8$ otherwise edges would cross. Now, B can appear in the following places in the vertex ordering. 1. $t_4 \prec B \prec x_2 \prec x_5 \prec x_8$, 2. $t_4 \prec x_2 \prec B \prec x_5 \prec x_8$, 3. $t_4 \prec x_2 \prec x_5 \prec B \prec x_8$ and 4. $t_4 \prec x_2 \prec x_5 \prec x_8 \prec B$. We show that for each sub-case, the graph doesn't admit a 1-rique layout.

Case 1(a) and 1(b): $t_4 \prec B \prec x_2 \prec x_5 \prec x_8$ and $t_4 \prec x_2 \prec B \prec x_5 \prec x_8$. $(s_2, x_5) \in T \implies (s_3, B) \notin T$. Therefore, $(s_3, B) \in H$. However, (t_3, x_8) and (s_3, B) cross. Hence, the order doesn't admit a 1-rique layout.

Case 1(c): $t_4 \prec x_2 \prec x_5 \prec B \prec x_8$. $(s_3, x_8) \in T \implies (t_2, B) \notin T$. Therefore, $(t_1, B) \in H$. However, (t_1, B) and (t_2, x_5) cross. Hence, the order doesn't admit a 1-rique layout.

Case 1(d): $t_4 \prec x_2 \prec x_5 \prec x_8 \prec B$. Given $(t_3, x_8) \in H$, if $(t_1, B) \in T$, then (t_3, x_8) covers (t_1, B) and if $(t_1, B) \in H$, then (t_3, x_8) and (t_1, B) cross. Therefore, the order doesn't admit a 1-rique layout.

Case 2: $s_i \prec A \prec B \prec t_i$ where $1 \leq i \leq 4$. We assume w.l.o.g, let the vertex ordering contain $s_1 \prec s_2 \prec s_3 \prec s_4 \prec A \prec B \prec d_1 \prec d_2 \prec d_3 \prec d_4$. Note that $(A, d_1) \in E(G_{19})$. Hence, by Lemma 1, $(s_1, B) \in T$. This implies that $(s_2, A) \in H$. As $(s_3, B) \in E(G_{19})$, by Lemma 1, the order doesn't admit a 1-rique layout.

Case 3 and 4: $s_i \prec t_i \prec A \prec B$ or $A \prec B \prec s_i \prec t_i$ where $1 \leq i \leq 4$. We assume w.l.o.g, the vertex ordering contain $d_1 \prec d_2 \prec d_3 \prec d_4 \prec d_5 \prec d_6 \prec d_7 \prec d_8 \prec A \prec B$ (case 4: $A \prec B \prec d_8 \ldots \prec d_2 \prec d_1$). By Corollary 1, $(d_1, B) \in T$ (resp. $(d_1, A) \in T$) which implies $(d_2, A) \in H$ (reps. $(d_2, B) \in H$). As there is at least one twins s_i, t_i in between (d_2, A) (reps. (d_2, B), by Lemma 5, the order doesn't admit a 1-rique layout.

Case 5: $A \prec s_i \prec B \prec t_i$ where $1 \leq i \leq 4$. We assume w.l.o.g, the vertex ordering contain $A \prec s_1 \prec s_2 \prec s_3 \prec s_4 \prec B \prec d_1 \prec d_2 \prec d_3 \prec d_4$. Now, by Corollary 1, $(A, d_4) \in T$. Hence, $(B, d_2) \in H$. Now, by Lemma 4, let x_1, x_2 and x_3 be the connectors of s_i, d_1 that comes after d_4 in the order and $(d_1, x_2) \in H$ (by Lemma 6). However, (B, d_2) and (d_1, x_2) cross. Hence, the order doesn't admit a 1-rique layout.

Case 6: $s_i \prec A \prec t_i \prec B$ where $1 \leq i \leq 4$. We assume w.l.o.g, the vertex ordering contain $s_1 \prec s_2 \prec s_3 \prec s_4 \prec A \prec d_1 \prec d_2 \prec d_3 \prec d_4 \prec B$. Now, by Corollary 1, $(s_1, B) \in T$. Hence, $(s_2, A) \in H$. As $(s_3, B) \in E(G_{19})$, by Lemma 1, the order doesn't admit a 1-rique layout.

Hence, the rique number of the graph G_{19} is 2. Therefore, the rique number of planar bipartite graphs is 2. □

5 Conclusions

This study examines the linear layouts of graphs for the restricted input queue (RIQ) data structure. The rique data structure is a specialized queue that permits insertions alone at the head, while allowing removals at both the head and the tail. Our main contribution is that the rique number for both series-parallel graphs and planar bipartite graphs is 2. This topic has several directions. One such direction is finding lower and upper bounds of rique number for various graph classes i.e. plane 3-trees. Recently, Bekos et al. conjectured that the rique number of planar graphs is 2 [4]. This hypothesis, if proven, would provide significant insight into the layout characteristics of planar graphs, establishing the strong processing power of the rique data structure with respect to other data structures such as stacks and queues. Another direction is to explore the layout configurations of planar bipartite graphs. Surgio Pupyrev conjectured that these graphs admits both a 1-stack+1-queue layout [8].

Acknowledgment. To the CodeCrafters International Ltd., whose CodeCrafters-Investortools Research Grant enabled the authors to take part in this event, we are eternally grateful.

References

1. Adolphson, D., Hu, T.C.: Optimal linear ordering. SIAM J. Appl. Math. **25**(3), 403–423 (1973)
2. Angelini, P., Bekos, M.A., Kindermann, P., Mchedlidze, T.: On mixed linear layouts of series-parallel graphs. Theoret. Comput. Sci. **936**, 129–138 (2022). https://doi.org/10.1016/j.tcs.2022.09.019
3. Bekos, M.A., Felsner, S., Kindermann, P., Kobourov, S., Kratochvíl, J., Rutter, I.: The Rique-number of graphs. In: International Symposium on Graph Drawing and Network Visualization, pp. 371–386. Springer (2022)
4. Bekos, M.A., Kaufmann, M., Pavlidi, M.E., Rieger, X.: On the deque and Rique numbers of complete and complete bipartite graphs. arXiv preprint arXiv:2306.15395 (2023)
5. Chinn, P.Z., Chvátalová, J., Dewdney, A.K., Gibbs, N.E.: The bandwidth problem for graphs and matrices-a survey. J. Graph Theory **6**(3), 223–254 (1982)
6. Chung, F.R.K., Leighton, F.T., Rosenberg, A.L.: Embedding graphs in books: a layout problem with applications to VLSI design. SIAM J. Algebraic Discrete Methods **8**(1), 33–58 (1987). https://doi.org/10.1137/0608002
7. Pratt, V.R.: Computing permutations with double-ended queues, parallel stacks and parallel queues. In: Proceedings of the Fifth Annual ACM Symposium on Theory of Computing, pp. 268–277 (1973)
8. Pupyrev, S.: Mixed linear layouts of planar graphs. In: Graph Drawing and Network Visualization: 25th International Symposium, GD 2017, Boston, MA, USA, September 25-27, 2017, Revised Selected Papers 25, pp. 197–209. Springer (2018)
9. Pupyrev, S.: Linear layouts of graphs (2024). https://spupyrev.github.io/linearlayouts.html
10. Rahman, M.S.: Basic Graph Theory. UTCS, Springer, Cham (2017). https://doi.org/10.1007/978-3-319-49475-3
11. Serna, M., Thilikos, D.: Parameterized complexity for graph layout problems. Bull. Eur. Assoc. Theor. Comput. Sci. **86**, 41–65 (2005)

Sorted Range Selection and Range Minima Queries

Waseem Akram[✉] and Sanjeev Saxena

Department of Computer Science and Engineering, Indian Institute of Technology, Kanpur 208016, India
{akram,ssax}@iitk.ac.in

Abstract. Given an array $A[1:n]$ of n elements drawn from an ordered set, the sorted range selection problem is to build a data structure that can be used to answer following queries: Given a pair of indices i, j ($1 \leq i \leq j \leq n$), and a positive integer k, report the k smallest elements from the sub-array $A[i:j]$ in sorted order. Brodal et al. (Brodal, G. S., Fagerberg, R., Greve, M., and López-Ortiz, A., Online sorted range reporting. Algorithms and Computation (2009) pp. 173–182) introduced the problem and gave a solution that can answer a query in $O(k)$ time. The preprocessing takes $O(n \log n)$ time and $O(n)$ space. In this paper, we propose the only other possible optimal trade-off for the problem. After preprocessing using $O(n)$ time and space, we can answer a range selection query in $O(k \log k)$ time. Moreover, the proposed algorithm reports the output elements individually in non-decreasing order. Our solution is simple and practical.

We also study the problem in a dynamic setting. We also describe an extremely simple method for the range minima queries (most of whose parts are known), which takes almost (but not exactly) linear time. We believe that this method may be, in practice, faster and easier to implement in most cases. Moreover, we also give a simple dynamic solution to the range minimum problem.

Keywords: range minimum query · range reporting · algorithms · data structures

1 Introduction

The range minimum query (RMQ) problem is a fundamental and well-studied problem in data structures and algorithms [1,3,11,14]. It is widely applicable in many fields, including computational geometry [18], string processing [10,21], and scheduling. Given an array $A[1:n]$ of n elements drawn from an ordered set, the RMQ problem asks to design a data structure supporting the range minima queries: given two indices i and j with $i \leq j$, report the smallest element among $A[i], A[i+1] \ldots A[j]$. In this paper, we consider the *sorted range selection* problem [2], a generalization of the RMQ problem, where we want to preprocess the array $A[1:n]$ so that the queries of the following type can be answered efficiently: Given a pair of indices i,j with $(1 \leq i \leq j \leq n)$ and a positive integer k, report the k smallest elements in the index range $[i,j]$ in sorted order.

Brodal, Fagerberg, Greve, and López-Ortiz [2] introduced the problem and gave a linear space data structure with $O(k)$ query time in the word RAM model. The preprocessing time to build the structure is $O(n \log n)$. By reporting all n elements ($k=n$), one can sort the elements in $O(n)$ time; thus, $\Omega(n \log n)$ preprocessing time is required, and their algorithm is optimal. The solution uses a fairly complicated result due to Frederickson and Johnson [4].

We propose the only other possible optimal trade-off for the sorted range selection problem. The preprocessing time is $O(n)$ with linear space, and the query time is $O(k \log k)$. Our solution is also optimal as by reporting all elements in the array ($k=n$), we can sort the elements of the input array in $O(n \log n)$ time. Note that our solution offers the only other possible optimal trade-off for the problem. If the preprocessing time is $p(n)$ and the query algorithm takes $q(n)$ time to report any element in the query range in the worst case, then we can sort n elements in $p(n) + \sum_{i=1}^{n} q(n)$ time. Thus, if $p(n) = o(n \log n)$, then $q(n) = \Omega(\log n)$. Our algorithm is extremely simple and only uses range minimum queries in addition to the usual binary heap. The algorithm reports the output elements one by one in non-decreasing order.

Moreover, we show that the same time bounds for the query also hold for the dynamic sorted range selection problem.

We also give an extremely simple method to solve the RMQ problem. We show that a given array of size n can be preprocessed in $O(n \log^{(k)} n)$-time and $O(n)$-space such that each query can be answered in $O(1)$-time, for any integer $k > 0$. We believe that this method may be, in practice, faster and easier to implement in most cases. In addition, we present a simple dynamic solution to the RMQ problem with $O(\log n)$-query time. In our dynamic setting, the queries and update operations are expressed in terms of indices of the current underlying array. This is setting is more natural than one considered in [20].

The RMQ problem is closely related to an important problem, namely, the *Lowest Common Ancestor* (LCA) problem on general ordinal trees: given two nodes u and v in a tree, find the deepest node in the tree that is an ancestor of both u and v. In fact, these two problems are linearly equivalent i.e. one problem can be transformed to another one in time linear to the size of the input [1,13]. Berkman and Vishkin [16] gave the first linear space solution that takes $O(1)$ time to answer an RMQ query in the word RAM model. Bender and Farah-Colton [13] simplified their algorithm while maintaining the same performance bounds. Both approaches, however, use $O(n \log n)$ bits of space, which is sub-optimal in many scenarios.

Brodal et al. [20] studied the path minima queries in dynamic weighted trees, a generalization of the dynamic range minimum queries. Due to their result, one can have a dynamic RMQ structure that supports queries and update operations in $O(\log n / \log \log n)$ time in the word RAM model, where n is the size of the current underlying array.

A related and more general problem that has been studied in the past is the range selection problem [2,5], where the output elements are not required to be reported in sorted order. Brodal et al. [2] suggested that an array can be preprocessed using linear space and time to answer a range selection query in $O(k)$ time in the RAM model. Brodal et al. [2] also suggested a method to solve the problem in the pointer machine model by using the priority search tree and Frederickson's $O(k)$-time algorithm [6] for finding the k smallest elements in a binary heap. The resultant structure takes linear space and can report k smallest elements in $O(\log n + k)$ time.

The paper is organized as follows. Section 2 describes an algorithm solving the sorted range selection problem. We solve the dynamic sorted selection problem in Sect. 2.1. In Sect. 3, we describe, for completeness, an extremely simple method for range minima queries (most of whose elements are part of folklore), which takes almost (but not exactly) linear time. We describe a dynamic solution to the RMQ problem in Sect. 3.1. We conclude our work in Sect. 4.

2 Sorted Range Selection

If $A[1:n]$ is an array of n elements drawn from a totally ordered set, $A[i:j]$ will denote the sub-array starting at index i and ending at index j. In the word RAM model, an array element $A[i]$ can be accessed in $O(1)$ time. If $1 \leq i \leq j \leq n$, in range minimum query $RMQ(i,j)$, we are to find the index of a minimum element among $A[i], A[i+1], ...A[j]$.

We first preprocess the given array $A[1:n]$ for the range minimum queries (RMQ) [11]. The preprocessing takes $O(n)$ time and space. For each subsequent range minimum query, $RMQ(i,j)$ with $i \leq j$, we get the index r of the minimum element $A[r]$ in the subarray $A[i:j]$ in $O(1)$ worst-case time. We can also use the simple solution of Sect. 3 for range minima queries, however the preprocessing time becomes $O(n \log^{(k)} n)$ here $\log^{(1)} n = \log n$ and $\log^{(k+1)} n = \log(\log^{(k)} n)$.

Assume that we are to report the k smallest elements from the sub-array $A[i:j]$. An RMQ will give the index m of the smallest element in the subarray $A[i:j]$ in $O(1)$ time. We report $A[m]$ as the smallest element in $A[i:j]$. The next smallest element in $A[i:j]$ will either be in the sub-array $A[i:m-1]$ or in the sub-array $A[m+1:j]$. We thus split the interval into two pieces $[i, m-1]$ and $[m+1, j]$ and use RMQs to find the minimum element in each instance. We insert these elements into an (initially empty) binary minimum heap (see, e.g., Chapter 6 in [7]). We keep performing the following step until k elements are reported or the min heap becomes empty:

Remove the minimum element $A[x]$ from the heap and report it as the next smallest element in the subarray $A[i:j]$. Let $[p,q]$ be the index range corresponding to the minimum element $A[x]$. Split the interval $[p,q]$ into two pieces $[p, x-1]$ and $[x+1, r]$, and insert their minimum elements into the heap.

The method is more formally described below:

Input i, j, k with $1 \leq i, j \leq n$ and $1 \leq k \leq j - i + 1$
Output k smallest elements in the subarray $A[i : j]$

1: $Q \leftarrow \phi$ ▷ Initializing min-heap.
2: $x_l, x_r \leftarrow -1$ ▷ index variables.
3: $m \leftarrow RMQ(i, j)$ ▷ Indices i and j are known query parameters.
4: Triplet $(A[m], i, j)$ is stored in the heap Q with key as $A[m]$.
5: **repeat**
6:     delete the triplet $(A[x], p, q)$ with the minimum key $A[x]$ from heap Q. ▷ The array element $A[x]$ is the smallest among $A[p], A[p+1], \ldots, A[q]$.
7:     report $A[x]$ as t^{th} smallest element if the current iteration is t^{th} iteration
8:     **if** $p < x$, **then** $x_l \leftarrow RMQ(p, x - 1)$
9:     **if** $x < q$, **then** $x_r \leftarrow RMQ(x + 1, q)$
10:     **if** $x_l \neq -1$ **then**
11:         insert $A[x_l]$ into the heap Q ▷ Range $[p, x-1]$ is associated with $A[x_l]$.
12:     **if** $x_r \neq -1$ **then**
13:         insert $A[x_r]$ into the heap Q ▷ Range $[x+1, q]$ is associated with $A[x_r]$.
14:     $x_l, x_r \leftarrow -1$ ▷ initializing for the next iteration.
15: **until** k elements have been reported or the heap Q gets exhausted

As the next smallest element (to be reported) of $A[p : q]$ will be either in $A[p : x - 1]$ or $A[x + 1 : q]$, the element will always be in the heap.

As in each iteration, we are deleting one element from the heap and inserting at most two, after i iterations, we will have at most $i + 1$ elements in the heap. As insertion or deletion in a binary heap takes $O(\log s)$ time, where s is the size of the heap before the operation, total time will be $O(\sum_{i=1}^{k} \log i) = O(k \log k)$. The algorithm reports the required elements one by one in non-decreasing order. We have:

Theorem 1. *An array $A[1 : n]$ of n elements drawn from a totally ordered set can be preprocessed so that given a pair of indices i, j with $1 \leq i \leq j \leq n$ and a parameter k, we can report the k smallest elements in the subarray $A[i : j]$ in $O(k \log k)$ time. The preprocessing takes $O(n)$ space and time.* □

If we employ the extremely simple RMQ data structure described in Sect. 3.1 (Theorem 3), then $O(k \log n)$-time would be used to answer a sorted range selection query, with $O(n)$ preprocessing time and space. If we use the RMQ result of Theorem 2 in Sect. 3, we get a linear space solution with $O(k \log k)$ query time, and $O(n \log^{(k)} n)$ preprocessing time.

If elements in the input array $A[1 : n]$ are integers from a set $[1..U]$, then we can use van Emde Boas structure (see Chapter 20 in [7]) and the query time will become $O(k \log \log U)$.

2.1 Dynamic Sorted Range Selection

Assume the underlying array is allowed to change: existing elements can be deleted, new elements can be inserted, or the value of an element can be changed. In the dynamic sorted range selection problem, we use the following operations:

$set(i, a)$: store the value a at index i i.e. $A[i] \leftarrow a$.

$insert(i, x)$: shift elements $A[i], A[i+1], ..., A[n]$ one position right in the array and set $A[i] \leftarrow x$.

$delete(i)$: shift elements $A[i+1], A[i+2], ..., A[n]$ one position left in the array and remove $A[n]$.

Instead of a static RMQ structure, we now employ a dynamic RMQ data structure [20] over the underlying (dynamic) array A. The RMQ structure given by Brodal et al. [20] uses $O(n)$ space and supports a query and an update operation in $O(\log n / \log \log n)$ time. Here, n is the current size of the current underlying array A. Thus, we obtain a linear solution for the dynamic problem that takes $O(\log n / \log \log n)$ time for an update operation and answers a range selection query in $O(k(\log k + \log n / \log \log n))$ time. If instead, we use the simple dynamic solution of Sect. 3.1, the query and update time would become $O(k \log n)$ and $O(\log n)$, respectively.

3 Range Minimum Query

For input array $A[1:n]$ assume that after preprocessing, for each position i in the array we know the (index of) minimum element in each of the following cases $A[i:i+1], A[i:i+2], A[i:i+2^2], ..., A[i:i+2^j]$ for $i+2^j \leq n$.

The query $\text{RMQ}(i, j)$ to find the minimum element in $A[i:j]$ can be answered as follows:

Let r be the largest integer s.t., $i + 2^r \leq j$, or equivalently, $2^r \leq j - i$. Note that r is the index of the most significant bit in binary representation of $j - i$. Then, using precomputations, we can find the (index of) minimum element in $A[i:i+2^r]$. Let $j' = j - 2^r$, then again using precomputations, we can find the (index of) minimum element in $A[j':j'+2^r]$ or $A[j':j]$. The (index of) the required minimum element is (the index of) smaller of these two values, and hence can be found in $O(1)$ time.

As r is the largest integer s.t., $i + 2^r \leq j$, or $i + 2^{r+1} > j$, or (subtracting 2^r), $i + 2^r > j - 2^r = j'$. Thus, the union of intervals $[i:i+2^r]$ and $[j':j]$ is $[i:j]$ (portion $[j':i+2^r]$ is common to both intervals). Thus, we are computing the minimum of elements exactly in the range $i...j$ (some elements are however considered twice).

Let us now look at the precomputation. Assume for each $1 \leq i \leq n$ (and for some j) we have computed the (index of) minimum element in $A[i:\min\{i+2^j, n\}]$. Then, we can compute the (index of) minimum element in $A[i:\min\{i+2^{j+1}, n\}]$, for each $1 \leq i \leq n$ as follows. If $i + 2^j \geq n$, then $i + 2^{j+1} \geq n$. Or (index of) minimum element in $A[i:\min\{i+2^j, n\}]$ is also the (index of) minimum element in $A[i:\min\{i+2^{j+1}, n\}]$. Else $i + 2^j < n$, let $i' = i + 2^j$.

By hypothesis (precomputation) we know the (index of) minimum element in $A[i' : \min\{i' + 2^j, n\}]$ (or $A[i + 2^j : \min\{i + 2^{j+1}, n\}]$). The (index of) minimum element in $A[i : \min\{i + 2^{j+1}, n\}]$ is the (index of) the smaller of the two numbers: minimum element in $A[i : i + 2^j]$ and the minimum element in $A[i + 2^j : \min\{i + 2^{j+1}, n\}]$. Thus, for each $1 \leq i \leq n$, we can find $A[i : \min\{i + 2^{j+1}\}, n]$ in $O(1)$ time, or for all $1 \leq i \leq n$ in $O(n)$ time. As $0 \leq j \leq \log n$, entire precomputation takes $O(n \log n)$ time.

Thus we have [8,9,12,13]

Lemma 1. *An array $A[1 : n]$ can be preprocessed in $O(n \log n)$ time and space such that queries of the kind "find the index of the smallest element in $A[i], A[i+1], \ldots, A[j-1], A[j]$" can be answered in $O(1)$ time.*

The space can be reduced to $O(n)$ as follows. A similar method is in [8]. The array $A[1 : n]$ is conceptually split into $n/\log n$ blocks of size $\log n$. The minimum of each block of $\log n$ elements is computed in $O(\log n)$ time. There are $n/\log n$ blocks, so the time is $O(n)$ overall. We also compute the prefix minimum (smallest element from the start of the block) and suffix minimum (smallest element till the end of the block). This can also be done in the same time bounds. These minima are stored in another array of length $n/\log n$, say $S[1 : n/\log n]$. The array S is preprocessed as per Lemma 1. As S has $n/\log n$ elements, it will take $O((n/\log n) \log(n/\log n))) = O(n)$ time and space. Thus, the preprocessing time and space is $O(n)$ overall.

A query $RMQ(l, r)$ when *the two indices l and r are not in the same block* can be answered in $O(\log n)$ time as follows: Find $i = \lfloor l/\log n \rfloor$ and $j = \lfloor r/\log n \rfloor$, the block(s) containing the two indices. If $i < j$, then we find $k = RMQ(i+1, j-1)$. Basically, the minima of all blocks contained completely inside the range is computed using a query to the data structure built over the array S in $O(1)$ time. If $i \neq j$, then as we know the suffix minima at location l in block i and prefix minima at location r in block j. We get the overall minimum by comparing these two elements with the element computed in the previous step. We are left with the case when both l and r are in the same group, i.e., when $i = j$. This is the usual range minima query, restricted to a block.

If we preprocess each block (independently and separately) for the range minima queries using the algorithm of Lemma 1, the time for each block is $O((\log n) \log(\log n)) = O(\log n \log \log n)$. As there are $n/\log n$ blocks, total time is $O((n/\log n)(\log n \log \log n)) = O(n \log \log n)$. Thus we have:

Corollary 11. *An array $A[1 : n]$ of n elements drawn from a totally ordered set can be preprocessed in $O(n \log \log n)$ time and $O(n)$ space such that range minima queries can be answered in $O(1)$ time.*

If we use the method of Corollary 11 for preprocessing each block for range minima queries, the preprocessing time for each block becomes $O((\log n) \log \log(\log n)) = O(\log n \log^{(3)} n)$ as there are $n/\log n$ blocks, total preprocessing time becomes: $O((n/\log n) \log n \log^{(3)} n) = O(n \log^{(3)} n)$. Thus, we have

Corollary 12. *An array $A[1:n]$ of n elements drawn from a totally ordered set can be preprocessed in $O(n \log \log \log n)$ time and $O(n)$ space such that range minima queries can be answered in $O(1)$ time.*

If we repeat the above method k times, we get

Theorem 2. *An array $A[1:n]$ of n elements drawn from a totally ordered set can be preprocessed in $O(n \log^{(k)} n)$ time and $O(n)$ space such that the range minima queries can be answered in $O(1)$ time.*

It is known that the preprocessing time can be reduced to $O(n)$, a popular way of doing this uses the Cartesian tree, Euler tour traversal, and table look-up. [9, 12–17].

We believe that the method of Theorem 2 will be, in practice, faster and easier to implement in most cases. We may also use this method for range minimum queries in the solution for the sorted range selection problem in Sect. 2.

3.1 A Simple Solution to Dynamic RMQ

We first present a static solution to the RMQ problem that supports queries in $O(\log n)$-time. This is basically a sequential version of a parallel algorithm in [16]. Later, we will see that the solution can be generalized to support update operations as well. Let $A[1:n]$ be the input array of size n. We build a balanced binary search tree T with leaf nodes having keys from 1 to n in left to right order [7]. The leaf node with key value i is represented by l_i. Thus, $l_1, l_2, l_3, \ldots, l_n$, is the list of the leaf nodes arranged sequentially from left to right. At each node in the tree T, we maintain three values (count, min, and range) in addition to the key value used for navigation. The meanings of these three attributes are formally described below.

$v.min$: the minimum element stored in the subtree $T(v)$ rooted at node v.
$v.count$: the number elements stored (leaves) in the subtree $T(v)$.
$v.range$: $[s_v, e_v]$, where s_v and e_v are the minimum and maximum key values of the leaves in the subtree $T(v)$, respectively.

For a given node v, the number of leaves in the subtree rooted at node v is $e_v - s_v + 1$. The attribute $v.count$ is maintained to reflect the number of leaves storing array elements. This will be used for insert and delete operations.

At each leaf node l_i, we store $A[i], 1,$ and i. A node v in the tree T represents the contiguous sequence of integers $I_v = \mathbb{Z} \cap [s_v, e_v]$. If v is a leaf node with key value i, then $I_v = \{i\}$. If v is an internal node, the sequence I_v is the union of the sequences of its children. An important property of these sequences is that, for any pair of integers x and x' with $1 \leq x \leq x' \leq n$, there is a unique set $S(x, x')$ of $O(\log n)$ nodes in the tree T whose sequences form a partition of $\mathbb{Z} \cap [x, x']$ (See Segment Trees in [18]). In particular, for each $i \in \mathbb{Z} \cap [x, x']$, there is exactly one node $u \in S(x, x')$ whose sequence contains the number i. Moreover, one can compute the set $S(x, x')$ in $O(\log n)$-time using the search paths from the root to the leaves l_x and $l_{x'}$. The number of nodes in T is $O(n)$, and each node stores $O(1)$-additional information. Hence, the space used by the data structure is $O(n)$. The time needed to build the data structure is $O(n)$.

Lemma 2. *Using the data structure T, we can answer a range minimum query in $O(\log n)$-time.*

Proof. Let indices i and j be the query parameter. We first compute the set $S(i, j)$ in $O(\log n)$-time. Then, we linearly scan the set $S(i, j)$ and report the smallest $v.min$ i.e. $\min\{v.min : v \in S(i, j)\}$. We know that $|S(i, j)| = O(\log n)$. Thus, the time needed to answer the query is $O(\log n)$. The correctness of the algorithm follows from the fact that the sequences corresponding to the nodes in $S(i, j)$ form a partition of the sequence $[i, j] \cap \mathbb{Z}$. □

Thus, we have the following theorem.

Theorem 3. *Given a static array $A[1 : n]$ of n elements drawn from a totally ordered set, we can preprocess A in $O(n)$-time and space so that each subsequent range minimum query can be answered in $O(\log n)$-time.*

We next consider the RMQ problem in a dynamic setting where array elements can be deleted from the underlying array, and RMQs are asked in terms of the indexes of the updated array. Formally, we want to maintain an array $A[1 : n]$ in an efficient data structure that, in addition to RMQs, supports the following delete operations.

delete(i): store $A[j]$ at index $j - 1$, for every $j \in [i + 1, n]$, and delete the last element $A[n]$.

Intuitively, *delete(i)* operation moves elements $A[i + 1], A[i + 2], ..., A[n]$ one position left in the array and shortens the array size by one. Note that no change is made in the subarray $A[1 : i - 1]$. The range minimum queries are asked on the (possibly) shortened updated array.

We next, present a linear space solution that takes $O(\log n)$-worst-case time to answer an RMQ and $O(\log n)$-amortized time to perform a delete operation. Here, n is the size of the current array. Our solution is simple and uses only textbook and classical data structures. Essentially, we make the static data structure (described earlier) dynamic to support *deletion* operations efficiently.

Let $A[1 : n]$ be the given array. We build the static RMQ structure T (as described earlier in this section) over the array A. To implement a delete operation, we locate the element in T and mark it as deleted. If the number of (non-deleted) elements in the data structure T is greater than or equal to $n/2$, we do not make any further change in the data structure and the delete operation is complete. Otherwise, when number of (non-deleted) elements in the data structure T becomes too low (i.e. less than $n/2$), we reconstruct the static data structure for the remaining elements. We proceed further in the same way.

In the data structure T, we say that $l_i \prec l_j$ if $i < j$. A leaf node l_i is said to be *active* if it stores a non-deleted element, and *dead* otherwise. After a sequence of range minimum queries and delete operations, the structure T might have some dead leaf nodes. We denote by $pos(i, T)$ the key value of the ith active leaf node in the sorted (by order $\prec$) list of the leaves in T. Let C be the current array after the sequence. Note that $C[i] = A[pos(i, T)]$, for each $i = 1, 2, ...|C|$. The following Lemma is for the computation of $pos(i, T)$.

Lemma 3. *Given an index i with $1 \leq i \leq |C|$, we can compute $pos(i, T)$ in $O(\log n)$-time.*

Proof. Starting from the root of T, we compute a root-to-leaf path using *count* attributes of the nodes (instead of key values). Let v be the current node. Let v_l (resp. v_r) be the left (resp. right) child of v. If $v_l.count < i$, then chose v_r as the next node on the path and set $i \leftarrow i - v_l.count$. Otherwise, choose v_l as the next node on the path, and i is not changed. We stop as soon as a leaf node is encountered. The key value of the leaf is reported as $pos(i, T)$. As at each node of the path, we are doing $O(1)$-units of work, so the total time needed to compute $pos(i, T)$ is $O(\log n)$. □

We answer range minima query as follows. To compute the minimum element among $C[i], C[i+1], ..., C[j]$. We first compute $i' = pos(i, T)$ and $j' = pos(j, T)$ as described in Lemma 2. The query $\text{RMQ}(i', j')$ will give the required element.

From Lemma 3, computing $pos(i, T)$ and $pos(j, T)$ would take $O(\log n)$-time. From Lemma 2, answering $\text{RMQ}(i', j')$ would take $O(\log n)$-time. Thus, the time needed to answer the query is $O(\log n)$-time.

To delete an array element $C[i]$ i.e. for delete(i), we first find $i' = pos(i, T)$ and mark the element $A[i']$ as deleted. Let π be the path from the leaf $l_{i'}$ to the root. We traverse the path π and update the information stored at each (proper) ancestor v of l_i: (1) reduce $v.count$ by 1, and (2) update $v.min$, if required. Thereafter, if the number of elements in the structure T is equal to half of the size of the array on which T is built i.e. $root.cout = n/2$, then we reconstruct the data structure for the current array C. The operation takes $O(\log n)$-amortized time. The details are standard and are being omitted due to space constraints.

Thus, we have the following theorem.

Theorem 4. *Given an array of elements drawn from an ordered set, we can maintain a linear space data structure that takes $O(\log n)$-amortized time for a deletion operation and $O(\log n)$-worst-case time for a range minima query. Here, n is the number of elements in the current array.*

We have to modify the data structure for insertion operation. Recall an *insertion* operation is:
insert(i, x): increment the array size by 1, and store $A[j]$ at index $j+1$ for every $j \in [i, n]$. Then, store x at index i i.e. $A[i] \leftarrow x$. Intuitively, insert(i, x) operation, after increasing the array size by one, shifts elements $A[i], A[i+1], ..., A[n]$ one position right and inserts x in the empty slot at index i. The array size increases by one. Note that no change is made in the subarray $A[1 : i-1]$. The range minimum queries are on the updated array.

We now describe our method. Let T be the static data structure built over the given array $A[1 : n]$. To support insert operations, in addition to delete

operations, we slightly change our strategy: we allow a leaf node to store more than one element: at each leaf node in the tree T, we now maintain a (possibly empty) set of elements with the following property:
For each $i \in [1, n]$, the union of the sets associated with the leaves $l_1, l_2, ..., l_i$ contains the elements of $A[1:j]$ for some $0 \leq j \leq n$.
By this property, elements of each set are from a contiguous subarray of $A[1:n]$. The minimum element of a leaf node is the smallest element in the associated set. Attribute $v.count$ will now denote the size of the union of the sets associated with the leaves in $T(v)$ and $v.min$ denotes the minimum element in the union. And a leaf node l_i will be called *active* if its associated set is non-empty, and *dead* otherwise.

To insert an element, we find the "appropriate" leaf and insert the element into the associated set. Moreover, we update the information stored at each (proper) ancestor of the leaf to reflect the changes needed due to the operation. When the number of elements in the structure becomes (say) twice the size of the array on which T is built, we reconstruct the data structure for the updated array from scratch.

We perform a delete operation, almost as before. We find the "appropriate" leaf whose set contains the element to be deleted and remove the element from the set. Then, update the information stored at each (proper) ancestor of the leaf. When the number of elements in the structure becomes half the size of the array on which T is built, we reconstruct the data structure for the updated array from scratch.

If i and j are the query parameters, first we find the leaf node $l_{i'}$ (resp. $l_{j'}$) whose set contains i^{th} (resp. j^{th}) element of the updated array C. If $i' = j'$, we find the minimum element among $C[i], C[i+1], ..., C[j]$ using a linear scan of the associated set and report as the answer. Otherwise we compute $S(i', j')$. If $l_{i'} \in S(i', j')$, then we find the minimum element, say $min_{i'}$, among $C[1], C[2], ..., C[l]$ using a single scan of the set, where $1 \leq l \leq j-i+1$. Similarly if $l_{j'} \in S(i', j')$ and $i' \neq j'$, then we find the minimum element, say $min_{j'}$, among $C[t], ..., C[j-1], C[j]$ using a single scan of the set, where $1 \leq t \leq j-i+1$. And, let $min' = \min\{v.min : v \in S(i', j') \setminus \{l_{i'}, l_{j'}\}\}$. Finally, we report the smallest of $min_{i'}, min'$, and $min_{j'}$ as the answer to the query.

If the size of every set is $O(\log n)$, each update operation would take $O(\log n)$-amortized time, a query can be answered in $O(\log n)$-worst-case time (the amortized bounds follow from the arguments analogous to the ones used for dynamic array [7]). However, if a set has size asymptotically more than $\log n$, then we can use a balanced binary search tree (say AVL tree, red-black tree, etc.) with implicit keys [19]. This will take $O(\log n)$-time to answer a query. Thus, we have the following theorem.

Theorem 5. *An array of comparable elements can be maintained in an $O(n)$ space data structure that allows insertion operations in $O(\log n)$ amortized time and supports range minimum queries in $O(\log n)$ worst-case time. Here, n is the size of current underlying array.*

From Theorems 4 and 5, we have the following corollary.

Corollary 1. *We can maintain a dynamic array, whose elements drawn from a totally ordered set, in an $O(n)$ space data structure that supports each update (delete and insert) operation in $O(\log n)$ amortized time. Additionally, it takes $O(\log n)$ worst-case time to answer a range minimum query. Here, n is the size of the underlying array at the time of operation.*

4 Conclusion

In this paper, we study the range selection problem and give a linear space solution with $O(k \log k)$ query time and $O(n)$ preprocessing time. The output elements are reported individually in non-decreasing order. The proposed solution offers the only possible trade-off other than the one given by Brodal et al. [2]. Our solution is simple and easy to implement.

We also consider the problem in the dynamic setting where the underlying array can be changed using insert, delete, and set operations. The problem in the dynamic setting where k is fairly large and while outputting, some array elements get changed is left as an open problem.

We also describe an extremely simple method for the range minima queries (most of whose parts are known), which takes almost (but not exactly) linear time. We believe that this method may be, in practice, faster and easier to implement in most cases. Moreover, we give a simple solution to the dynamic RMQ problem with $O(\log n)$-query time and $O(\log n)$-amortized time for an update (insert/delete) operation. Here, n is the size of the updated array.

Acknowledgement. We wish to thank anonymous referees for careful reading of the manuscript, their comments, queries and suggestions. We believe the suggestions have helped in improving the manuscript.

References

1. Gabow, H.N., Bentley, J.L., Tarjan, R.E.: Scaling and related techniques for geometry problems. In: ACM STOC '84, pp. 135–143 (1984)
2. Brodal, G.S., Fagerberg, R., Greve, M., López-Ortiz, A.: Online sorted range reporting. In: Algorithms and Computation: 20th International Symposium, ISAAC, pp. 173–182 (2009)
3. Saxena, S.: Dominance made simple. Info. Process. Lett. **109**(9), 419–421 (2009)
4. Frederickson, G.N., Johnson, D.B.: The complexity of selection and ranking in X + Y and matrices with sorted columns. J. Comput. Syst. Sci. **24**(2), 197–208 (1982)
5. Afshani, P., Brodal, G.S., Zeh, N.: Ordered and unordered top-k range reporting in large data sets. In: SODA, pp. 390–400 (2011)
6. Frederickson, G.: An optimal algorithm for selection in a Min-Heap. Info. Comput. **104**(2), 197–214 (1993)
7. Cormen, T.H., Leiserson, C.E., Rivest, R.L., Stein, C.: Introduction to Algorithms, Third Edition. 3rd edn. The MIT Press (2009)
8. Range Minimum Query. https://en.wikipedia.org/wiki/Range_minimum_query

9. Fischer, J., Heun, V.: Theoretical and practical improvements on the RMQ-problem, with applications to LCA and LCE. In: Combinatorial Pattern Matching, pp. 36–48. Springer (2006)
10. Fischer, J., Heun, V.: A new succinct representation of RMQ-information and improvements in the enhanced suffix array. In: International Symposium on Combinatorics Probabilistic and Experimental Methodologies, Algorithms, pp. 459–470 (2007)
11. Fischer, J., Heun, V.: Space-efficient preprocessing schemes for range minimum queries on static arrays. SIAM J. Comput. **40**(2), 465–492 (2011)
12. Bender, M.A., Farach-Colton, M.: The LCA problem revisited. In: Gonnet, G.H., Viola, A. (eds.) LATIN 2000. LNCS, vol. 1776, pp. 88–94. Springer, Heidelberg (2000). https://doi.org/10.1007/10719839_9
13. Bender, M.A., Farach-Colton, M., Pemmasani, G., Skiena, S., Sumazin, P.: Lowest common ancestors in trees and directed acyclic graphs. J. Algorithms **57**(2), 75–94 (2005)
14. Schieber, B., Vishkin, U.: On finding lowest common ancestors: simplification and parallelization. SIAM J. Comput. **17**(6), 1253–1262 (1988)
15. Berkman, O., Schieber, B., Vishkin, U.: Optimal doubly logarithmic parallel algorithms based on finding all nearest smaller values. J. Algorithms **14**(3), 344–370 (1993)
16. Berkman, O., Vishkin, U.: Recursive star-tree parallel data structure. SIAM J. Comput. **22**(2), 221–242 (1993)
17. Berkman, O., Matias, Y., Ragde, P.: Triply-logarithmic parallel upper and lower bounds for minimum and range minima over small domains. J. Algorithms **28**(2), 197–215 (1998)
18. Berg, M., Cheong, O., Krevel, M., Overmars, M.: More geometric data structures. In: Computational Geometry: Algorithms and Applications. 3rd Edn., pp. 219–241 (2008)
19. https://stackoverflow.com/questions/27990143/dynamic-prefix-sum
20. Brodal, G.S., Davoodi, P., Srinivasa, R.S.: Path minima queries in dynamic weighted trees. In: Algorithms and Data Structures: 12th International Symposium, WADS, pp. 290–301 (2011)
21. Gusfield, D.: Algorithms on Strings, Trees, and Sequences: Computer Science and Computational Biology. Cambridge University Press (1997)

On the Characterization of Eulerian es-Splitting p-Matroids

Uday Jagadale[1], Sachin Gunjal[1](✉), Prashant Malavadkar[1], M. M. Shikare[2], and B. N. Waphare[3]

[1] Dr. Vishwanath Karad MIT World Peace University, Pune 411038, India
sachin.gunjal@mitwpu.edu.in
[2] JSPM University, Pune 412207, India
[3] Savitribai Phule Pune University, Pune 411007, India

Abstract. The es-splitting operation on binary bridge-less matroids never produces an Eulerian matroid. But for matroids representable over $GF(p), (p > 2)$, called p-matroids, the es-splitting operation may yield Eulerian matroids. In this work, we introduce es-splitting operation for p-matroids and characterize a class of p-matroids yielding Eulerian matroids after the es-splitting operation. Characterization of circuits, and bases of the resulting matroid, after the es-splitting operation, in terms of circuits, and bases of the original matroid, respectively, are discussed. We also proved that the es-splitting operation on p-matroids preserves connectivity and 3-connectedness. Sufficient condition to obtain Hamiltonian p-matroid from Hamiltonian p-matroid under es-splitting operation is also provided.

Keywords: p-matroid · es-splitting operation · 3-connected matroid · Eulerian matroid · Hamiltonian matroid

1 Introduction

Matroid theory is a framework for studying abstract independence that generalizes concepts from linear algebra and graph theory. A matroid M is an ordered pair $(E, \mathcal{I})$ consisting of a finite set E and a collection $\mathcal{I}$ of subsets of E satisfying the following three conditions: (i) $\phi \in \mathcal{I}$; (ii) If $I \in \mathcal{I}$ and $J \subset I$, then $J \in \mathcal{I}$; and (iii) If $I_1, I_2 \in \mathcal{I}$ and $|I_1| < |I_2|$ then there is an element e of $I_2 - I_1$ such that $I_1 \cup e \in \mathcal{I}$.

The members of $\mathcal{I}$ are the independent sets of M, and E is the ground set of M. A minimal dependent set in M is called circuit of M, and a maximal independent set is called a basis of M. We shall denote set of circuits of M by $\mathcal{C}(M)$, set of independent sets by $\mathcal{I}(M)$, and set of bases by $\mathcal{B}(M)$. For a matroid $M = (E, I)$ the dual matroid $M^* = (E, I^*)$ has the bases that are exact complement of bases of M. Observe that $(M^*)^* = M$. The collection $\mathcal{C}(M^*)$ of circuits of dual matroid M^* is also denoted by $\mathcal{C}^*(M)$. The circuits of M^* are called cocircuits of M. Rank of a matroid M is the cardinality of its basis. A matroid M is said to be Eulerian if its ground set is disjoint union of circuits of M. For undefined and standard terminologies in matroid, refer to [13].

A strong connection exists between matroid theory and coding theory [10]. Matroids are used to understand decoding algorithms for error-correcting codes. The size of the minimal trellis for a code is determined by the matroid. In 1976, Greene [7] noticed the connection between coding theory and matroid theory. He showed that the Tutte polynomial of a matroid, when specialized to a linear code $\mathcal{C}$ is equivalent to the homogeneous weight enumerator polynomial $W_\mathcal{C} = \sum_{i=0}^{n} A_i x^i y^{n-i}$, where A_i is the number of codewords of weight i. The matroid associated to a self-dual code is identically self-dual, but it is not known whether every identically self-dual representable matroid can be represented by a self-dual code. C. Padro et al. [14] have proved that every identically self-dual matroid on at most eight points is representable by a self-dual code. Matroids are also used in other fields, such as geometry, topology, combinatorial optimization, and machine learning.

Fleischner [4] used the idea of splitting a pair of edges from a vertex of degree at least three to describe Eulerian graphs. The splitting operation was extended from graphs to binary matroids by Raghunathan et al. [15], and Eulerian binary matroids were characterized using this operation as stated below:

Theorem 1. *[15] A binary matroid M on a set E is Eulerian if and only if M can be transformed by repeated applications of the splitting operation into a matroid in which E is a circuit.*

The n- line splitting operation for graphs was introduced by Slater [19].

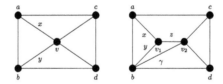

Fig. 1. n-line splitting operation on graph G gives graph H

Let G be a 3-connected graph as shown in Fig. 1 and H be the graph obtained from G by replacing v by two adjacent vertices v_1 and v_2 with b adjacent to v_1, b adjacent to v_2, and v_2 adjacent to c and d. The transition from G to H is known as 3-line splitting operation. Thus, by Theorem 1 of [19] H is 3-connected. Azanchiler [1] extended n- line splitting operation on graphs to binary matroids. He also proved that es-splitting operation on a connected binary matroid yields a connected binary matroid. Dhotre et al. [3], proved that the es-splitting operation on a 3-connected binary matroid yields a 3-connected binary matroid. Properties of splitting, element splitting, and es-splitting operations on binary matroids are extensively discussed by several authors in [2,3,12,15–18].

A binary matroid is Eulerian if and only if it's dual matroid is bipartite. Equivalently, an Eulerian binary matroid can not have an odd cocircuit. The

es-splitting matroid $M_{a,b}^e$ of a bridge-less binary matroid M always contains an odd cocircuit. Therefore $M_{a,b}^e$ can never be Eulerian.

In this paper, we define es-splitting operation on a simple and coloopless p-matroid, i.e. matroids representable over $GF(p)$. Interestingly, the es-splitting operation on a p-matroid not necessarily Eulerian may give an Eulerian p-matroid. In the present paper, we provide a necessary and sufficient condition for an es-splitting p-matroid $M_{a,b}^e$ to be Eulerian. We also study circuits, bases and connectivity of the resulting matroid. In fact we proved that es-splitting operation on a 3-connected p-matroid yields a 3-connected p-matroid. A sufficient condition to obtain Hamiltonian p-matroid from Hamiltonian p-matroid under es-splitting operation is also provided.

Before we define es-splitting operation on p-matroids, we recall the definitions of splitting and element splitting operations on simple and coloopless p-matroids [8,9].

Definition 1. *Let $M \cong M[A]$ be a p-matroid on ground set E, $\{a,b\} \subset E$. The matrix $A_{a,b}$ is constructed from A by appending an extra row to A which has coordinates equal to 1 in the columns corresponding to the elements a,b, and zero elsewhere. Define the splitting matroid $M_{a,b}$ to be the vector matroid $M[A_{a,b}]$. The transformation of M to $M_{a,b}$ is called splitting operation.*

Definition 2. *Let $M \cong M[A]$ be a p-matroid on ground set E, $\{a,b\} \subset E$, and $M_{a,b}$ be the corresponding splitting matroid. Let the matrix $A_{a,b}$ represents $M_{a,b}$ on $GF(p)$. Construct the matrix $A'_{a,b}$ from $A_{a,b}$ by adding an extra column to $A_{a,b}$, labeled as z, which has the last coordinate equal to 1 and the rest are equal to zero. Define the element splitting matroid $M'_{a,b}$ to be the vector matroid $M[A'_{a,b}]$. The transformation of M to $M'_{a,b}$ is called element splitting operation.*

2 es-Splitting Operation on p-Matroids

The present section generalizes the es-splitting operation binary matroid to a p-matroid M, and characterizes circuits and bases of the es-splitting matroid. Note that es-splitting matroid is single element extension of corresponding element splitting p-matroid.

Definition 3. *Let $M \cong M[A]$ be a p-matroid on ground set E and $\{a,b\} \subset E$ with $e \in \{a,b\}$. Let $A'_{a,b}$ represents the element splitting matroid $M'_{a,b}$ on $GF(p)$. Construct the matrix $A_{a,b}^e$ by adjoining an extra column γ to the matrix $A'_{a,b}$ where γ is subtraction$(e-z)$ of two column vectors corresponding to the elements e and z. Denote $M_{a,b}^e \cong M[A_{a,b}^e]$. The shift of M to $M_{a,b}^e$ is called an es-splitting operation. We call the matroid $M_{a,b}^e$ as es-splitting p-matroid.*

Remark 1. For $p=2$, the above definition coincides with the es-splitting operation on binary matroids [1].

Remark 2. $\text{rank}(A) < \text{rank}(A_{a,b}^e) = \text{rank}(A)+1$. If the rank functions of M and $M_{a,b}^e$ are denoted by r and r', respectively, then $r(M) < r'(M_{a,b}^e) = r(M)+1$.

Let $C_k = \{u_1, u_2, \ldots, u_l : u_i \in E, i = 1, 2, \ldots, l\}$ be a circuit of M for some positive integers k, l and $|C_k \cap \{a, b\}| = 2$. Suppose, without loss of generality, $u_1 = a, u_2 = b$. If there are non-zero constants $a_1^k, a_2^k, \ldots, a_l^k$ in $GF(p)$ such that $\sum_{i=1}^{i=l} a_i^k u_i \equiv 0 \pmod{p}$ and $a_1^k + a_2^k \equiv 0 \pmod{p}$, then we call C_k a p-circuit of M. However, if $|C_k \cap \{a, b\}| = 1$ or $|C_k \cap \{a, b\}| = 2$ and $a_1^k + a_2^k \not\equiv 0 \pmod{p}$, then we call C_k an np-circuit of M.

We denote $\mathcal{C}_0 = \{C \in \mathcal{C}(M) : C \text{ is a } p\text{-circuit or } C \cap \{a, b\} = \phi\}$.

Theorem 2. *Let $M = (E, \mathcal{C})$ be a p-matroid, and $M'_{a,b}$ be its element splitting p-matroid. $e \in \{a, b\}$ and $z, \gamma \notin E$. Then $\mathcal{C}(M_{a,b}^e) = \mathcal{C}(M'_{a,b}) \cup \mathcal{C}_4 \cup \mathcal{C}_5 \cup \mathcal{C}_6 \cup \mathcal{C}_7 \cup \mathcal{C}_8 \cup \Delta$, where*

$\mathcal{C}_4 = \{C \cup \{e, \gamma\} : C \text{ is an np-circuit and } e \notin C\};$
$\mathcal{C}_5 = \{(C \setminus e) \cup \gamma : C \text{ is an np-circuit, } e \in C \text{ and } a \notin C\};$
$\mathcal{C}_6 = \{(C \setminus e) \cup \{z, \gamma\} : C \text{ is a p-circuit and } e \in C\};$
$\mathcal{C}_7 = \{C \cup \gamma : C \text{ is an np-circuit containing } e \text{ and } a\};$
$\mathcal{C}_8 = \{(C \setminus e) \cup \{z, \gamma\} : C \text{ is an np-circuit containing } e \text{ and } a\}$ and
$\Delta = \{e, z, \gamma\}.$

Proof. By the Definition 3 and $M'_{a,b} = M_{a,b}^e|_{E \cup z}$, the inclusion $\mathcal{C}(M'_{a,b}) \cup \mathcal{C}_4 \cup \mathcal{C}_5 \cup \mathcal{C}_6 \cup \mathcal{C}_7 \cup \mathcal{C}_8 \cup \Delta \subset \mathcal{C}(M_{a,b}^e)$ follows.

To prove the other inclusion, assume $C \in \mathcal{C}(M_{a,b}^e)$ and $\gamma \notin C$. Then by Theorem 2.4 of [9], $C \in \mathcal{C}(M'_{a,b})$. Now assume that $\gamma \in C$.

Case 1 : $z \in C$. Note that if $e \in C$, then $C = \Delta = \{e, z, \gamma\}$. Suppose $e \notin C$. If $C_1 = C \setminus \{z, \gamma\}$ is a dependent set of M containing an np-circuit, say C_2. Then $C_2 \cup z$ is a circuit of $M_{a,b}^e$ contained in C, which is not possible. Therefore C_1 is an independent set of M. Since every coordinate of e is equal to the corresponding coordinate of γ, and all the coordinates of z except the last one are zero, the set $C_1 \cup e$ is a dependent set of M. Moreover $C_1 \cup e$ is a circuit of M, otherwise $C_1 \cup e$ contains an np-circuit, say C_3. And $C_3 \cup z$ is circuit of $M_{a,b}^e$ contained in C which is not possible. If $C_1 \cup e$ is a p-circuit, then $C \in \mathcal{C}_6$. And if $C_1 \cup e$ is an np-circuit, then $C \in \mathcal{C}_8$.

Case 2 : $z \notin C$

Subcase (i) : $e \notin C \setminus \gamma$. Then observe that a is also not an element of C. And by similar argument as in Case 1, $(C \setminus \gamma) \cup e$ is an np-circuit of M. Therefore $C \in \mathcal{C}_5$.

Subcase (ii) : $e \in C \setminus \gamma$. Note that $C \setminus \gamma$ is a dependent set of M, containing a and one of the following cases will occur.

(a) If $C \setminus \gamma$ is a circuit of M, then it must be an np-circuit. Therefore $C \in \mathcal{C}_7$.
(b) If $C \setminus \gamma$ is not a circuit of M, and $C \setminus \gamma = C_{np} \cup e$, for some np-circuit C_{np} excluding e. Then $C_{np} \cup \{e, \gamma\} = C$. In this case $C \in \mathcal{C}_4$.
(c) If $C \setminus \gamma$ is not a circuit of M, and $C \setminus \gamma = C_{np} \cup A$, for some np-circuit C_{np} excluding e, and disjoint from $A \subset E(M)$, where $|A| \geq 2$. Then $C_{np} \cup \{e, \gamma\}$ is the circuit, of type $\mathcal{C}_4$, of $M_{a,b}^e$ contained in C, a contradiction.
(d) If $C \setminus \gamma$ is not an np-circuit of M, and $C \setminus \gamma = C_{np} \cup A$, for some np-circuit C_{np} containing e, and $A \subset E(M)$. If $a \notin C_{np}$, then $(C_{np} \setminus e) \cup \gamma$ is a circuit of

type C_5 contained in C, a contradiction. And if $a \in C_{np}$, then $C_{np} \cup \gamma$, a circuit of type C_7, is contained in C, which is not possible.
Therefore we conclude that $C \in (\mathcal{C}(M'_{a,b}) \cup C_4 \cup C_5 \cup C_6 \cup C_7 \cup C_8)$.

Corollary 1. *The es-splitting matroid $M^e_{a,b}$ is not a bipartite matroid.*

Proof. The proof follows from the fact, the es-splitting matroid $M^e_{a,b}$ contains the circuit $\Delta = \{e, z, \gamma\}$ of size three.

The following example lists all the type of circuits of a p-matroid M, and the corresponding es-splitting matroid $M^e_{a,b}$.

Example 1. Consider the ternary sparse paving matroid P_8 which has the representation given by matrix A.

$$A = \begin{pmatrix} 1\,2\,3\,4\,5\,6\,7\,8 \\ 1\,0\,0\,0\,0\,1\,1\,2 \\ 0\,1\,0\,0\,1\,0\,1\,1 \\ 0\,0\,1\,0\,1\,1\,0\,1 \\ 0\,0\,0\,1\,2\,1\,1\,0 \end{pmatrix} \quad A^e_{1,4} = \begin{pmatrix} 1\,2\,3\,4\,5\,6\,7\,8\,9\,10 \\ 1\,0\,0\,0\,0\,1\,1\,2\,0\,0 \\ 0\,1\,0\,0\,1\,0\,1\,1\,0\,0 \\ 0\,0\,1\,0\,1\,1\,0\,1\,0\,0 \\ 0\,0\,0\,1\,2\,1\,1\,0\,0\,1 \\ 1\,0\,0\,1\,0\,0\,0\,0\,1\,0 \end{pmatrix}$$

For $a = 1$, $b = 4$, $e = 4$ and $\alpha = 1$ the representation of es-splitting matroid $M^e_{1,4}$ over $GF(3)$ is given by the matrix $A^e_{1,4}$. The collection of circuits of M, $M_{1,4}$ and $M^e_{1,4}$ is given below.

Circuits of M : $\{1,2,4,5,6\}$, $\{1,2,4,6,8\}$, $\{1,3,4,5,7\}$, $\{1,3,4,7,8\}$, $\{1,4,5,8\}$, $\{2,3,6,7\}$, $\{2,5,6,8\}$, $\{3,5,7,8\}$,$\{1,2,3,5,6\}$, $\{1,2,3,5,7\}$, $\{1,2,3,8\}$, $\{1,2,4,7\}$, $\{1,2,5,7,8\}$, $\{1,2,6,7,8\}$, $\{1,3,4,6\}$, $\{1,3,5,6,8\}$, $\{1,3,6,7,8\}$, $\{1,5,6,7\}$, $\{2,3,4,5\}$, $\{2,3,4,6,8\}$, $\{2,3,4,7,8\}$, $\{2,4,5,6,7\}$, $\{2,4,5,7,8\}$, $\{3,4,5,6,7\}$, $\{3,4,5,6,8\}$, $\{4,6,7,8\}$

Circuits of $M_{1,4}$: $\{1,2,4,5,6\}$, $\{1,2,4,6,8\}$, $\{1,3,4,5,7\}$, $\{1,3,4,7,8\}$, $\{1,4,5,8\}$, $\{2,3,6,7\}$, $\{2,5,6,8\}$, $\{3,5,7,8\}$

Circuits of $M^e_{1,4}$: $\{1,2,4,5,6\}$, $\{1,2,4,6,8\}$, $\{1,3,4,5,7\}$, $\{1,3,4,7,8\}$, $\{1,4,5,8\}$, $\{2,3,6,7\}$, $\{2,5,6,8\}$, $\{3,5,7,8\}$, $\{1,2,3,5,6,9\}$, $\{1,2,3,5,7,9\}$, $\{1,2,3,8,9\}$, $\{1,2,4,7,9\}$, $\{1,2,5,7,8,9\}$, $\{1,2,6,7,8,9\}$, $\{1,3,4,6,9\}$, $\{1,3,5,6,8,9\}$, $\{1,3,6,7,8,9\}$, $\{1,5,6,7,9\}$, $\{2,3,4,5,9\}$, $\{2,3,4,6,8,9\}$, $\{2,3,4,7,8,9\}$, $\{2,4,5,6,7,9\}$, $\{2,4,5,7,8,9\}$, $\{3,4,5,6,7,9\}$, $\{3,4,5,6,8,9\}$, $\{4,6,7,8,9\}$,$\{1,2,3,4,8,10\}$, $\{1,4,5,6,7,10\}$, $\{2,3,5,10\}$, $\{2,3,6,8,10\}$, $\{2,3,7,8,10\}$, $\{2,5,6,7,10\}$, $\{2,5,7,8,10\}$, $\{3,5,6,7,10\}$, $\{3,5,6,8,10\}$, $\{6,7,8,10\}$, $\{1,2,5,6,9,10\}$, $\{1,2,6,8,9,10\}$, $\{1,3,5,7,9,10\}$,$\{1,3,6,9,10\}$, $\{1,3,7,8,9,10\}$, $\{1,5,8,9,10\}$, $\{1,2,4,7,10\}$, $\{1,3,4,6,10\}$, $\{1,2,7,9,10\}$, $\{4,9,10\}$

Consider subsets of E of the type $C \cup I$ where $C = \{u_1, u_2, \ldots, u_l\}$ is an np-circuit of M, which is disjoint from an independent set $I = \{v_1, v_2, \ldots, v_k\}$ and $\{a, b\} \subset (C \cup I)$. We say $C \cup I$ is p-dependent if it contains no member of $\mathcal{C}_0$ and there are non-zero constants $\alpha_1, \alpha_2, \ldots, \alpha_l$ and $\beta_1, \beta_2, \ldots, \beta_k$ such that $\sum_{i=0}^{l} \alpha_i u_i + \sum_{j=0}^{k} \beta_j v_j = 0 (mod\ p)$ and $coeff.(a) + coeff.(b) = 0 (mod\ p)$. We use cl and cl' to denote closure operators on M and $M^e_{a,b}$, respectively.

Theorem 3. Let M be a p-matroid and $M_{a,b}^e$ be es-splitting matroid. $\mathcal{B}(M_{a,b}^e) = \mathcal{B}(M'_{a,b}) \cup \mathcal{B}_1 \cup \mathcal{B}_2 \cup \mathcal{B}_3 \cup \mathcal{B}_4$ where

$\mathcal{B}_1 = \{B \cup \gamma : B \in \mathcal{B}(M)$ and $e \in B\}$;
$\mathcal{B}_2 = \{B \cup \gamma : B \in \mathcal{B}(M), a \in B$ and $e \notin cl(B \setminus a)\ \}$;
$\mathcal{B}_3 = \{(C_{np} \cup I) \cup \gamma : (C_{np} \cup I)$ is not a p-dependent set of M, $rank(C_{np} \cup I) = rank(M) - 1$, $e \notin cl(C_{np} \cup I)\}$;
$\mathcal{B}_4 = \{I \cup \{z, \gamma\} : I \in \mathcal{I}(M), e \notin cl(I), |I| = r(M) - 1\ \}$.

Proof. Let $B' \in \mathcal{B}(M_{a,b}^e)$. Then $|B'| = r(M) + 1$.
Case 1 : $z, \gamma \notin B'$. Then $B' \in \mathcal{B}(M_{a,b})$.
Case 2 : $z \in B', \gamma \notin B'$. Then $B' \in \mathcal{B}(M'_{a,b})$.
Case 3 : $z \notin B', \gamma \in B'$. Then $B' \setminus \gamma$ is an independent set of $M'_{a,b}$. Denote $B' \setminus \gamma = B$. By Lemma 2.6 of [9], following two subcases are possible:
Subcase (i) : $B \in \mathcal{I}(M)$. Since $|B| = r(M), B \in \mathcal{B}(M)$. Note that $a \in B$ or $e \in B$. Otherwise $\gamma \in cl'(B)$, which is a contradiction to the fact that B' is basis of $M_{a,b}^e$. (a) $e \in B$. Then $B' \in \mathcal{B}_1$. (b) $e \notin B$. If $e \notin cl(B \setminus a)$, then $B' \in \mathcal{B}_2$. Suppose $e \in cl(B \setminus a)$, there are column vectors in $B \setminus a$, say $v_1, v_2, \ldots, v_j$, such that $\{e, v_1, v_2, \ldots, v_j\}$ forms a circuit in M. Since the last coordinate of $v_1, v_2, \ldots, v_j$, and γ in $M_{a,b}^e$ are zero, and the coordinates of e and the corresponding coordinates of γ are identical implies $\{\gamma, v_1, v_2, \ldots, v_j\}$ is dependent in $M_{a,b}^e$. Thus B' contains a dependent set, which is a contradiction.
Subcase (ii) : $B = (C_{np} \cup I)$, where $(C_{np} \cup I)$ is not p-dependent and it contains no union of two disjoint np-circuits. Let $e \in (C_{np} \cup I)$. Then either $e \in C_{np}$ or $e \in I$. Let $e \in C_{np}$. If a is also in C_{np}, then $C_{np} \cup \gamma$ is a circuit, of type $\mathcal{C}_7$, contained in B', a contradiction. Consider $a \notin C_{np}$. Then $(C_{np} \setminus e) \cup \gamma$ is a circuit, of type $\mathcal{C}_5$, contained in B', a contradiction. Therefore $e \notin C_{np}$. If $e \in I$, then $C_{np} \cup \{e, \gamma\}$ is a circuit, of type $\mathcal{C}_4$, contained in B', again a contradiction. Therefore $e \notin I$. Furthermore, we claim that $e \notin cl(C_{np} \cup I)$. On the contrary suppose, $e \in cl(C_{np} \cup I)$. Then $(C_{np} \cup I) \cup e$ contains a circuit, say C, and $e \in C$. If $a \notin C$, then $(C \setminus e) \cup \gamma$ is a dependent set contained in B', which is a contradiction. Suppose $a \in C$. Note that a is also in C_{np}. Therefore, there exists a circuit $C' \subset (C \cup C_{np}) - a$. Note that C' is not a p-circuit. Thus, $e \in C'$, and hence $(C' \setminus e) \cup \gamma$ is a dependent set in B', a contradiction again. Therefore $e \notin cl(C_{np} \cup I)$. Thus, $B' \in \mathcal{B}_3$.
Case 4 : $z \in B', \gamma \in B'$. As earlier denote $B' \setminus \gamma = B$. Note that $e \notin B'$, otherwise B' contains the circuit $\{e, z, \gamma\}$. Observe that B is independent in $M'_{a,b}$. By Lemma 3.2 of [9], following three are possible subcases:
Subcase (i) : $B = I \cup z, I \in \mathcal{I}(M)$ and $|I| = r(M) - 1$. In this case, $B' \in \mathcal{B}_4$.
Subcase (ii) : $B \in \mathcal{I}(M)$. Thus $B' = B \cup \gamma$. In this case, $B' \in \mathcal{B}_1$ or $B' \in \mathcal{B}_2$
Subcase (iii) : $B = C_{np} \cup I$, where $(C_{np} \cup I)$ is not p-dependent and it contains no union of two disjoint np-circuits. Then $C_{np} \cup z$ is a circuit of $M_{a,b}^e$ contained in B', a contradiction. Therefore $B' \in (\mathcal{B}(M'_{a,b}) \cup \mathcal{B}_1 \cup \mathcal{B}_2 \cup \mathcal{B}_4)$.
Conversely, let $X \in (\mathcal{B}(M'_{a,b}) \cup \mathcal{B}_1 \cup \mathcal{B}_2 \cup \mathcal{B}_3)$. We prove that X is a basis of $M_{a,b}^e$. If $X \in \mathcal{B}(M'_{a,b})$, then $|X| = r(M) + 1$. Moreover X is independent in $M_{a,b}^e$, therefore X is basis of $M_{a,b}^e$. If $X \in \mathcal{B}_1$, then $X = B \cup \gamma$, for some $B \in \mathcal{B}(M)$

containing e. Let $B = \{u_1, u_2, \ldots, u_l\}$. Note that B is independent in $M_{a,b}^e$. If $X = B \cup \gamma$ is dependent in $M_{a,b}^e$, then it contains a circuit, say C, and $\gamma \in C$. Following are the three possibilities regarding C:

Case 1 $C = B \cup \gamma = \{u_1, u_2, \ldots, u_l, \gamma\}$. Since $e \in B$, then a must be in B. Assume $u_1 = a, u_2 = e$, WLOG. There exists non-zero scalars $\alpha_1, \alpha_2, \ldots, \alpha_l, \alpha_\gamma$, such that $\alpha_1 u_1 + \alpha_2 u_2 + \ldots + \alpha_l u_l + \alpha_\gamma u_\gamma \equiv 0 (mod \, p)$. Since every coordinate of e is equal to the corresponding coordinate of γ, restricting the column vectors of B to the matrix A, we get $\alpha_1 u_1 + (\alpha_2 + \alpha_\gamma) u_2 + \ldots + \alpha_l u_l \equiv 0 (mod \, p)$. Therefore $B = \{u_1, u_2, \ldots, u_l\}$ is a dependent set of M, a contradiction.

Case 2 $C \subset B \cup \gamma$, and $a, e \in C \setminus \gamma$. Using the arguments as in (a), we get a contradiction.

Case 3 $C \subset B \cup \gamma$, and $a, e \notin C$. Using the arguments as in (a), we get a contradiction.

Next, assume $X \in \mathcal{B}_2$. Then $X = B \cup \gamma$, where $B \in \mathcal{B}(M)$, $a \in B$ and $e \notin cl(B \setminus a)$. Note that B is independent in $M_{a,b}^e$. If $X = B \cup \gamma$ is dependent in $M_{a,b}^e$, then it contains a circuit, say C, and $\gamma \in C$. Then $C \in \mathcal{C}_5$ or $C \in \mathcal{C}_7$. Since $e \notin cl(B \setminus a)$, and hence $e \notin C$. Therefore C cannot be a member of $\mathcal{C}_5$ and $\mathcal{C}_7$.

Now if $X \in \mathcal{B}_3$, then $X = (C_{np} \cup I) \cup \gamma$ for some np-circuit C_{np}, independent set I of M. As $(C_{np} \cup I)$ is not a p-dependent set of M, implies $|(C_{np} \cup I)| = rank(M)$, and it is independent in $M_{a,b}^e$. Therefore $|X| = rank(M) + 1$. Here it is enough to prove that $X = (C_{np} \cup I) \cup \gamma$ is independent in $M_{a,b}^e$. On the contrary assume that X is not independent in $M_{a,b}^e$. Then X contains a circuit, say C, passing through γ. Note that $e, z \notin C$. Therefore C is a circuit of type $\mathcal{C}_5$. This implies $e \in cl(C) \subset cl(C_{np} \cup I)$, a contradiction again.

Let $X \in \mathcal{B}_4$. Then $X = I \cup \{z, \gamma\}$, where $I \in \mathcal{I}(M)$. By Lemma 2.6 of [9] $I' = I \cup z$ is an independent set of $M'_{a,b}$ and $M_{a,b}^e$. Therefore it is enough to show that $I' \cup \gamma$ is an independent set of $M_{a,b}^e$. If not, then $I' \cup \gamma$ contains a circuit C, such that $\gamma \in C$. Since $e \notin X$, C cannot be a circuit of the type $\mathcal{C}_4, \mathcal{C}_7$ and $\Delta = \{e, z, \gamma\}$. Assume $C \in \mathcal{C}_5$. Then $C = (C' \setminus e) \cup \gamma$, where C' is an np-circuit containing e, and $C' \subset I$. Thus $e \in cl(I)$, a contradiction. We get the same contradiction, if $C \in \mathcal{C}_6, \mathcal{C}_8$. Therefore $I' \cup \gamma$ is an independent set of size $rank(M) + 1$.

The next theorem gives the rank function of a es-splitting matroid $M_{a,b}^e$ in terms of the rank function of corresponding p-matroid M.

Theorem 4. *Let r and r' denote the rank functions of the p-matroids M and $M_{a,b}^e$, respectively. Let $X \subseteq E(M)$. Then*

$$r'(X) = \begin{cases} r(X) + 1, \text{ if } X \text{ contains an } np-circuit; \\ r(X), otherwise \, . \end{cases} \quad (1)$$

$$r'(X \cup z) = r(X) + 1 \quad (2)$$

$$r'(X \cup \gamma) = \begin{cases} r(X), \text{ if } a, e \notin X, \text{ and } e \in cl(X); \\ r(X) + 2, \text{ if } e \notin cl(X) \text{and } X \text{ contains an } np\text{-circuit}; \\ r(X) + 1, otherwise. \end{cases} \quad (3)$$

$$r'(X \cup \{z,\gamma\}) = \begin{cases} r(X) + 1, \text{ if } e \in cl(X); \\ r(X) + 2, \text{ if } e \notin cl(X); \end{cases} \quad (4)$$

Proof. Eqs. (1) and (2) are proved in [8,9].
To prove (3), consider $a, e \notin X$ and $e \in cl(X)$ then $X \cup e$ contains an np-circuit of M, say C_{np}. Then $e \in C_{np}$. Now $C_{np} \setminus e \subset X$. In $X \cup \gamma$, $C_{np} \setminus e$ forms a circuit, of type C_5, with γ. Therefore $\gamma \in cl'(X)$. Thus $r'(X \cup \gamma) = r(X)$.
Next, assume that $e \notin cl(X)$ and X contains an np-circuit of M, say C_{np}. By Eq. (1), $r'(X) = r(X) + 1$. We claim that $\gamma \notin cl'(X)$. On the contrary assume that $\gamma \in cl'(X)$. Then there exists a circuit $C \subset X \cup \gamma$ in $M_{a,b}^e$, containing γ. Such a circuit must be of the type C_4, C_5 or C_7. Therefore $e \in cl(C \setminus \gamma)$, that implies $e \in cl(X)$, a contradiction. Therefore $r'(X \cup \gamma) = (r(X) + 1) + 1 = r(X) + 2$.
Suppose X contains an np-circuit C_{np}, and $e \in cl(X)$. Then there exists a circuit, say C, containing e. Such a circuit could be p–circuit or np–circuit. In case when C is an np-circuit, containing e then we get a circuit of type C_5 or C_7 of $M_{a,b}^e$. Therefore $r'(X \cup \gamma) = r(X) + 1$. If C is a p–circuit, then γ cannot form a circuit with C, since for such a circuit to form we need $z \in X \cup \gamma$. Thus $\gamma \notin cl'(X)$ in $M_{a,b}^e$. Therefore $r'(X \cup \gamma) = r(X) + 1$.
Next, assume that X contains no np-circuit in M, and $e \in cl(X)$. If $X \cup e$ contains an np-circuit, then as discussed earlier $r'(X \cup \gamma) = r(X)$. If $X \cup e$ contains a p-circuit, then $\gamma \notin cl'(X)$, as $z \notin X \cup \gamma$. Therefore $r'(X \cup \gamma) = r(X) + 1$. Further if $e \notin cl(X)$, then $\gamma \notin cl'(X)$. Therefore $r'(X \cup \gamma) = r(X) + 1$.
To prove (4), consider $e \in cl(X)$ in M. Note that $r'(X \cup z) = r(X) + 1$. Since $e \in cl(X), X \cup \{z, \gamma\}$ contains a circuits of the type Δ, C_6, or C_8. Thus $r'(X \cup \{z, \gamma\}) = r'(X \cup z) = r(X) + 1$. If $e \notin cl(X)$, then $\gamma \notin cl'(X \cup z)$; otherwise there exist a circuit $C \subset X \cup z$, containing γ, for such a circuit to exists e must be in $cl(C \setminus \{z, \gamma\})$ in M. Therefore $e \in X$, a contradiction. Thus $r'(X \cup \{z, \gamma\}) = r(X) + 2$.

Corollary 2. *In the es-splitting matroid $M_{a,b}^e$, $\{a, e, z\}$ forms a cocircuit.*

Proof. Let $X = E(M_{a,b}^e) \setminus \{a, e, z\}$. We will show that X is a hyperplane of $M_{a,b}^e$. First note that the last coordinate of every vector in X is zero and that of a, e, and z is 1. Therefore, no linear combination of vectors in X yields a, e, or z. Thus, $a, e, z \notin cl'(X)$. Equivalently $cl'(X) = X$. Next, we show that $r'(X) = r(M)$. As noted earlier that every vector in X has last coordinate equal to zero, and every coordinate of γ is equal to the corresponding coordinate of e, therefore $X = E(M) \setminus a$, and $r'(X) = r(X)$. Since M is a coloopless, there exist a basis B of M such that $a \notin B$. Then $r'(X) = r(X) = |B| = r(M)$. Therefore X is a hyperplane of $M_{a,b}^e$.

3 Connectivity of *es*-Splitting *p*-Matroids

Connectivity of a matroid is an important property in matroid theory. In particular, connectivity plays an significant role in the proof of Rota's conjecture [5,6]. We recall the following lemma in this regard.

Lemma 1. *[5] For each field $\mathcal{F}$, each excluded minor for the class of $\mathcal{F}$-representable matroids is 3-connected.*

The es-splitting operation on an n-connected binary matroid may not yield an n-connected matroid for $(n \geq 3)$. Malavadkar et al. [11], proved that given an n-connected binary matroid M of rank r, the resulting es-splitting binary matroid has an n-connected minor of rank-$(r+1)$ with $|E(M)|+1$ elements.

In this section, we show that the es-splitting operation on p-matroids preserves connectivity and 3-connectedness. Let M be a matroid having ground set E, and k be a positive integer. The k-separation of matroid M is a partition $\{S,T\}$ of E such that $|S|, |T| \geq k$ and $r(S) + r(T) - r(M) < k$. For an integer $n \geq 2$, we say M is n-connected if M has no k-separation, where $1 \leq k \leq n-1$.

Lemma 2. *If M is a connected p-matroid, then the corresponding es-splitting matroid $M_{a,b}^e$ is also connected.*

Proof. As M is a connected p-matroid, by Theorem 3.1 of [9] the element splitting matroid $M'_{a,b}$ is also connected. So it is enough to prove that for every element $x \in E \cup z$, there exists a circuit passing through x and γ.
Case 1: Suppose $x = z$. Then $\Delta = \{e, z, \gamma\}$ is the required circuit.
Case 2: Suppose $x \in E$. If $x = e$, then the circuit $\Delta = \{e, z, \gamma\}$ contains x and γ. Now assume $x \notin e$, since M is a connected matroid, there exists a circuit, say C, passing through x and e. Such a circuit C is a p-circuit or np-circuit. If C is a p-circuit, then $(C \setminus e) \cup \{z, \gamma\}$ is the desired circuit passing through x and γ. Next assume C is an np-circuit. Then the desired circuit passing through x and γ will be a member of one of the collection $\mathcal{C}_5$, $\mathcal{C}_7$ or $\mathcal{C}_8$.

We use the following proposition to prove the next theorem:

Proposition 1. *[13] If a matroid M is n-connected matroid and $|E(M)| > 2(n-1)$, then all circuits and all cocircuits of M have at least n elements.*

Theorem 5. *Let M be a 3-connected p-matroid and $|E(M)| > 4$. Then $M_{a,b}^e$ is also a 3-connected matroid.*

Proof. We will show that $M_{a,b}^e$ cannot have a 1 and 2-separation. As $M_{a,b}^e$ is connected, it cannot have a 1-separation. Next assume that $M_{a,b}^e$ has a 2-separation X, Y where $X, Y \subset E \cup \{z, \gamma\}$, $|X|, |Y| \geq 2$, and

$$r'(X) + r'(Y) - r'(M_{a,b}^e) < 2 \tag{5}$$

Case 1: $z \in X$ and $\gamma \in Y$
Let $X' = X \setminus z$ and $Y' = Y \setminus \gamma$
Subcase (i): $|X| = 2$ and $X = \{x, z\}$, where $x \in E(M)$. Then by Eq. (2), $r'(X) = r(X') + 1$. As M is 3-connected, no two elements of M are in series, which guarantees that there is a circuit containing a or e but not both. Such a circuit is an np-circuit in Y and hence $r'(Y) = r(Y') + 1$, by Eq. (1) Therefore Eq. (5) becomes $r(X') + r(Y') - r(M) < 1$, a contradiction to the fact that M is 3-connected.

Subcase (ii) : $|Y| = 2$ and $Y = \{x, \gamma\}$, where $x \in E(M)$. Observe that $r'(X) = r(X') + 1$ as $z \in X$, and by Eq. (3) $r'(Y) = r(Y') + 1$. In this case Eq. (5) becomes $r(X') + r(Y') - r(M) < 1$, which implies (X', Y') forms a 1-separation of M. A contradiction again.

Subcase (iii) : $|X|, |Y| > 2$

Then $|X'|, |Y'| \geq 2$ and by Eq. (2) $r'(X) = r(X') + 1$, and by Eq. (3) $r'(Y) \geq r(Y')$. Therefore Eq. (5) yields, $r(X') + r(Y') - r(M) < 2$. That is (X', Y') forms a 2-separation of M; a contradiction.

Case 2 : $\{z, \gamma\} \subseteq X$. Let $X' = X \setminus \{z, \gamma\}$

Subcase (i) : $X = \{z, \gamma\}$. Then $Y = E(M)$. Note that $r'(X) = 2$, and $r(Y) = r(M)$. Now Eq. (5) gives, $2 + (r(Y)+1) - (r(M)+1) < 2$. Therefore, $r(Y) < r(M)$, which is not possible.

Subcase (ii) : $X = \{z, \gamma, x\}$ where $x \in E(M)$. Here $X' = \{x\}$ we have

$$r'(X) = \begin{cases} r(X') + 1, & \text{if } e \in cl(X') \\ r(X') + 2, & \text{if } e \notin cl(X') \end{cases}$$

If $x = e$, then $r'(X) = r(X') + 1$. Again using the fact that there is an np-circuit excluding e contained in Y, we have $r'(Y) = r(Y) + 1$. Thus Eq. (5) yields $r(X') + r(Y) - r(M) < 1$ which means (X', Y) forms a 1-separation of M, a contradiction. If $x \neq e$, then $r'(X) = r(X') + 2$, and $r'(Y) = r(Y') + 1$. Again Eq. (5) yields $r(X') + r(Y) - r(M) < 0$, which is a contradiction.

Subcase (iii) : $|X| > 3$. Here $|X'|, |Y| \geq 2$. If Y contains an np-circuit of M, then, by Eq. (1) $r'(Y) = r(Y) + 1$, and by Eq. (4) $r'(X) \geq r(X') + 1$. Therefore Eq. (5) gives $r(X') + r(Y) - r(M) < 1$, which means (X', Y) forms a 1-separation of M; a contradiction. If Y contains no np-circuit of M, then $r'(Y) = r(Y)$ and $r'(X) \geq r(X') + 1$. Again Eq. (5) yields $r(X') + r(Y) - r(M) < 2$, implying (X', Y) is a 2-separation of M, a contradiction.

So we conclude that $M_{a,b}^e$ cannot have such 2-separation. Hence $M_{a,b}^e$ is 3-connected.

4 Applications

An *Eulerian* matroid is a matroid whose ground set can be partitioned into a collection of disjoint circuits. Further, a matroid M is said to be *Hamiltonian* if and only if it contains a circuit of size $r(M) + 1$. The present section characterizes Eulerian es-splitting p-matroids $M_{a,b}^e, (p > 2)$. Also we provide a sufficient condition to yield Hamiltonian p-matroids from Hamiltonian p-matroids under es-splitting operation.

Theorem 6. *Let M be a p-matroid $(p > 2)$, and $a, b \in E(M)$. Then the es-splitting matroid $M_{a,b}^e$ is Eulerian if and only if there exists a collection of circuits $\{C_{np}, C_1, \ldots, C_k\}$, where C_{np} is an np-circuit containing a, b, $E(M) = C_{np} \cup C_1 \cup C_2 \cup \ldots \cup C_k$, and all the circuits in the collection are pairwise disjoint, except $C_{np} \cap C_1 = \{b\}$.*

Proof. First assume that $M_{a,b}^e$ is Eulerian p-matroid, and $E(M_{a,b}^e) = C_1' \cup C_2' \cup C_3' \ldots \cup C_k'$, where $C_1', C_2', \ldots, C_k'$ are disjoint circuits of $M_{a,b}^e$. Set $e = b$. Without loss of generality, we assume $\gamma \in C_1'$.

Case (i) : $C_1' = \Delta = \{e, z, \gamma\}$ and $a \in C_2'$. Since $\gamma \notin C_2'$, C_2' is not a circuit of type $\mathcal{C}_i; i = 4, 5, 6, 7, 8$. Also $C_2' \notin \mathcal{C}_z$, as $z \notin C_2'$. No circuits of $M_{a,b}$ contains only a, therefore $C_2' \notin \mathcal{C}(M_{a,b})$. Therefore C_2' is not a circuit of $M_{a,b}^e$, a contradiction.

Case (ii) : $C_1' \in \mathcal{C}_4$, Then $e, a, \gamma \in C_1'$. Assume $z \in C_2'$. Since $\gamma \notin C_2'$, C_2' is not a circuit of type $\mathcal{C}_i; i = 4, 5, 6, 7, 8$ and $C_2' \neq \Delta$. Also $C_2' \notin \mathcal{C}_z$, as both $a, e \in C_1'$. No circuit of $M_{a,b}$ contains z, therefore $C_2' \notin \mathcal{C}(M_{a,b})$. Therefore C_2' is not a circuit of $M_{a,b}^e$, a contradiction.

By similar arguments as in **Case (i)**, **Case (ii)**, we get a contradiction if $C_1' \in \mathcal{C}_6$, or $C_1' \in \mathcal{C}_7$, or $C_1' \in \mathcal{C}_8$.

Case (iii) : $C_1' \in \mathcal{C}_5$, $C_1' = (C \setminus e) \cup \gamma$, where C is an np-circuit containing e but not a. Thus $z, e, a \notin C_1'$. Since $\gamma \notin C_2'$, C_2' is not a circuit of type $\mathcal{C}_i; i = 4, 5, 6, 7, 8$, and $C_2' \neq \Delta$. Assume, WLOG, $a \in C_2'$. Then following are the possible subcases:

Subcase (i) : $e, z \in C_2'$. Observe that $a, e, z \in C_2'$. As $z \in C_2'$ but $\gamma \notin C_2'$, C_2' is a circuit of type $\mathcal{C}_z$. Therefore $C_2' \setminus z$, is an np-circuit. Set $C_{np} = C_2' \setminus z$. Note that C and C_{np} are np-circuits of M and $C \cap C_{np} = \{e\}$. Thus the collection $\{C, C_{np}, C_3', \ldots, C_k'\}$ is the desired collection of the circuits of M, where all the circuits are pairwise disjoint, except $C \cap C_{np} = \{e\}$.

Subcase (ii) : $e \in C_2'$, but $z \notin C_2'$. Let $z \in C_i'$ for some $i \in \{3, 4, \ldots, k\}$. Since $a, e \notin C_i$, C_i cannot be a circuit of $M_{a,b}^e$, a contradiction.

Subcase (iii) : $e, z \notin C_2'$. Let $e \in C_i'$ and $z \in C_j'$ for some $i \neq j \in \{3, 4, \ldots, k\}$. Since $a, e \notin C_j$, C_j cannot be a circuit of $M_{a,b}^e$, a contradiction.

Conversely, suppose there exists a collection of circuits $\{C_{np}, C_1, \ldots, C_k\}$, where C_{np} is an np-circuit containing a, b, $E(M) = C_{np} \cup C_1 \cup C_2 \cup \ldots \cup C_k$, and all the circuits in the collection are pairwise disjoint, except $C_{np} \cap C_1 = \{b\}$. Note that the circuits $C_2, C_3, \ldots, C_k$ are p-circuits, and C_{np} and C_1 are np-circuits. Therefore $\{C_2, \ldots, C_k\} \subset \mathcal{C}(M_{a,b}^e)$. Observe that $e \in C_1$, but $a \notin C_1$. Thus $C_1' = (C_1 \setminus e) \cup \gamma$ forms a circuit of type $\mathcal{C}_5$ in $M_{a,b}^e$, and $C_{np} \cup z$ forms a circuit of type $\mathcal{C}_z$. The collection $\{C_{np} \cup z, C_1', C_2, C_3, \ldots, C_k\}$ gives a circuit decomposition of $E(M_{a,b}^e)$. Therefore, $M_{a,b}^e$ is Eulerian.

Proposition 2. *Let M be a p-matroid containing an np-circuit C_{np} of size $r(M) + 1$. Then $M_{a,b}^e$ is Hamiltonian. In this case Hamiltonian circuits in $M_{a,b}^e$ are of the form $C_{np} \cup z$, or $C_{np} \cup \gamma$, if $a, e \in C_{np}$.*

Proof. By Lemma 2.4 of [9], $C_{np} \cup z$ is a circuit of $M_{a,b}'$ and hence of $M_{a,b}^e$. Further, by Definition 2, z is independent from the members of C_{np}. Therefore size of $C_{np} \cup z$ is $r(M) + 2$. By Theorem 2, $C_{np} \cup \gamma$ is a circuit of $M_{a,b}^e$. Further, by Definition 3, γ is independent from the members of C_{np}. Therefore size of $C_{np} \cup \gamma$ is $r(M) + 2$.

5 Conclusion

The research focuses at the es-splitting operation on p-matroids representable over fields $GF(p)$, where $p > 2$. It demonstrates that, while es-splitting does not result in Eulerian binary matroids, it can produce Eulerian p-matroids under certain conditions. The paper characterizes the circuits and bases of the generated matroids while preserving connectivity and 3-connectedness, as well as identifying sufficient condition for producing Hamiltonian p-matroids. These findings broaden matroid theory's applications to graph features such as Eulerian and Hamiltonian cycles. They also have consequences for error detection in coding theory and optimization techniques.

References

1. Azanchiler, H.: Extension of line-splitting operation from graphs to binary matroid. Lobachevskii J. Math. **24**, 3–12 (2006)
2. Azanchiler, H.: A characterization of the bases of line-splitting matroids. Lobachevskii J. Math. **26**, 5–15 (2007)
3. Dhotre, S.B., Malavadkar, P.P., Shikare, M.M.: On 3-connected es-splitting binary matroids. Asian-Eur. J. Math. **9**(1), 17–26 (2016)
4. Fleischner, H.: Eulerian Graphs and Related Topics, Part 1, vol. 1. North Holland, Amsterdam (1990)
5. Geelen, J., Gerards, B., Whittle, G.: Solving Rota's conjecture. Not. Am. Math. Soc. **61**(7), 736–743 (2014)
6. Geelen, J., Gerards, B., Whittle, G.: The highly connected matroids in minor-closed classes. Ann. Comb. **19**(1), 107–123 (2015)
7. Greene, C.: Weight enumeration and the geometry of linear codes. Stud. Appl. Math. **55**, 119–128 (1976)
8. Gunjal, S.S., Jagadale, U.V., Malavadkar, P.P.: Generalized splitting and element splitting operations on p-matroids. Math. Student **92**, 175–186 (2023)
9. Gunjal, S.S., Malavadkar, P.P., Jagadale, U.V.: A note on connectivity preserving splitting operation for matroids representable over GF(p). SE Asian J. Math. Math. Sci. **20**(1), 272–361 (2024)
10. Kashyap, N.: A decomposition theory for binary linear codes. IEEE Trans. Inf. Theory **54**(7), 3035–3058 (2008)
11. Malavadkar, P.P., Dhotre, S.B., Shikare, M.M.: On n-connected minors of the es-splitting binary matroids. Electron. J. Graph Theory Appl. **9**(2), 265–275 (2021)
12. Mills, A.: On the co-circuits of a splitting matroid. Ars Comb. **89**, 243–253 (2008)
13. Oxley, J.G.: Matroid Theory. Oxford University Press, Oxford (1992)
14. Padro, C., Gracia, I.: Representing small identically self-dual matroids by self-dual codes. SIAM J. Discr. Math. **20**(4), 1046–1055 (2006)
15. Raghunathan, T.T., Shikare, M.M., Waphare, B.N.: Splitting in a binary matroid. Discrete Math. **184**, 267–271 (1998)
16. Shikare, M.M.: Splitting lemma for binary matroids. SE Asian Bull. Math. **32**, 151–159 (2008)
17. Shikare, M.M.: The element splitting operation for graphs, binary matroids and its applications. Math. Student **80**, 85–90 (2010)
18. Shikare, M.M., Azadi, G.: Determination of bases of a splitting matroid. Eur. J. Combin. **24**, 45–52 (2003)
19. Slater, P.J.: A Classification of 4-connected graphs. J. Combin. Theory **17**, 282–298 (1974)
20. Tutte, W.T.: Connectivity in matroids. Canad. J. Math. **18**, 1301–1324 (1966)
21. Welsh, D.J.A.: Euler and bipartite matroids. J. Combin. Theory **6**, 375–377 (1969)

Approximability of Edge-Vertex Domination in Unit Disk Graphs

Vishwanath R. Singireddy[1] and Manjanna Basappa[2(✉)]

[1] Geethanjali College of Engineering and Technology, Cheeryala, Keesara, Hyderabad 501301, India
drsvreddy.cse@gcet.edu.in
[2] National Institute of Technology Karnataka, Surathkal, Mangaluru 575025, India
manjanna@nitk.edu.in

Abstract. Given an undirected graph $G = (V, E)$, a vertex $v \in V$ is edge-vertex (ev) dominated by an edge $e \in E$ if v is either incident to e or incident to an adjacent edge of e. A set $S^{ev} \subseteq E$ is an edge-vertex dominating set (referred to as ev-dominating set and in short as $EVDS$) of G if every vertex of G is ev-dominated by at least one edge of S^{ev}. The minimum cardinality of an ev-dominating set is the ev-domination number. The edge-vertex dominating set problem is to find a minimum ev-domination number. The $EVDS$ problem finds applications in handling security issues in the communication network by identifying a minimum number of critical edges to implement additional security measures to safeguard key components of the network. In this paper, we prove that this problem admits a polynomial-time approximation scheme in unit disk graphs. We also give a simple 5-factor linear-time approximation algorithm.

Keywords: Unit disk graph · Edge-vertex dominating set · Approximation algorithm · Critical edges in a distributed network

1 Introduction

Given an undirected graph $G = (V, E)$, the *edge neighborhood* of an edge $e' \in E$ is the set of edges in E which share a common incident vertex $v \in V$ with e', i.e., the set of all edges which are adjacent to e'. The set of these neighbors of e' is represented as the set $N_e(e') = \{f \in E \mid e' \text{ and } f \text{ share a common vertex } v \in V\}$. The *closed edge neighborhood* of e' is defined as $N_e[e'] = N_e(e') \cup \{e'\}$. The *edge neighborhood* of a set $S \subseteq E$ is $N_e(S) = \bigcup_{e' \in S} N_e(e')$. Similarly, the *closed edge neighborhood* of a set $S \subseteq E$ is $N_e[S] = \bigcup_{e' \in S} N_e[e'] \cup S$. The *edge neighborhood of neighborhood* of e' is $N_e(N_e(e')) = N_e^2(e')$. Similarly, the r-th edge neighborhood is $N_e^r(e') = N_e(N_e^{r-1}(e'))$ for an integer $r \geq 1$.

---

[1] This work was primarily done during the author's graduate studies at BITS Pilani, Hyderabad Campus, India.
[2] Partially supported by the Science and Engineering Research Board (SERB), Govt. of India, under Sanction Order No. TAR/2022/000397.

Given an undirected graph $G = (V, E)$, a vertex $v \in V$ is *ev (edge-vertex)-dominated* by an edge $e \in E$, if v is incident to e (i.e., an endpoint of e) or if v is incident to an adjacent edge of e. A set $S^{ev} \subseteq E$ is an *edge-vertex dominating set (EVDS)* (referred to as *ev-dominating set*) of G, if every vertex of G is *ev*-dominated by at least one edge of S^{ev} (at least two edges for *double edge-vertex dominating set*). The minimum cardinality of an *ev*-dominating set is the *ev-domination number*, denoted by $\gamma_{ev}(G)$. A *paired-dominating set (PDS)* of a graph $G(V, E)$ with no isolated vertices is a dominating set $S^{pr} \subseteq V$ such that the sub-graph induced by S^{pr} in G has a perfect matching. The minimum cardinality of a *PDS* of G is symbolized as $\gamma_{pr}(G)$. Note that *EVDS* and *PDS* may be completely different subsets of edges in the same graph, but their cardinalities may be equal (see Fig. 1). In Fig. 1, the blue colored edges represent the *EVDS*. However, it should be noted that this set does not fulfill the criteria to be classified as a *PDS*; instead, the *PDS* could correspond to the set of green edges. Another similar model, called *total domination* in a graph, is defined in terms of only vertices instead of *edge-vertex*. A *total dominating set (TDS)* of a graph $G = (V, E)$ is a *dominating set* $S^d \subseteq V$ such that every vertex $v \in S^d$ is adjacent to some other vertex in S^d. The *TDS* problem is to find such a set S^d of minimum cardinality. The cardinality of minimum-size *TDS* is denoted by γ_t. We can also view a *TDS* in a graph as a minimum cardinality set of pairs of adjacent vertices (hence, as a set of edges induced on these vertices), where these pairs may share a common vertex. Therefore, a *TDS* gives rise to an *EVDS* and vice versa. However, a minimum cardinality *EVDS* may not be a minimum cardinality *TDS* i.e., the set of all vertices incident to edges of a minimum cardinality *EVDS* may not necessarily form a minimum cardinality *TDS*, and vice versa (see Fig. 2). In Fig. 2, the blue edges represent the minimum cardinality *EVDS*, while the red vertices represent the minimum cardinality *TDS*. Here, we can observe that the cardinality of the vertices incident to blue edges exceeds the minimum cardinality *TDS* and the cardinality of the edges incident to the red vertices also exceeds the minimum cardinality *EVDS*.

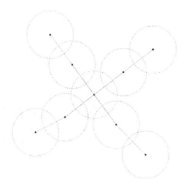

Fig. 1. *EVDS* vs *PDS* in *UDG*.

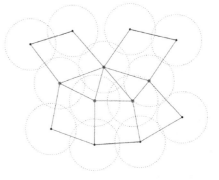

Fig. 2. *EVDS* vs *TDS* in *UDG*.

As well known, a given set D of n disks of unit diameter (hence called *unit disks*) induces a graph G, where the graph G is called a unit disk graph (*UDG*) $G = (V, E)$ and is an undirected graph such that (i) each vertex v in whose vertex set V corresponds to a disk $d_v \in D$ of unit diameter in the plane, (ii) each edge (u, v) in whose edge set E corresponds to a pair of mutually intersecting disks d_u and d_v in the plane [2]. It is important to note that in UDG also, a minimum cardinality $EVDS$ may not be a minimum cardinality TDS (see Fig. 2). Thus, studying the $EVDS$ problem in UDGs may be of interest to the graph theory and algorithms community.

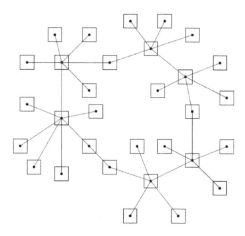

Fig. 3. Network of an organization.

In the literature, the dominating set problem has numerous applications in network contexts. During the design phase of wireless networks, the identification of minimum dominating sets in disk graphs can result in optimized resource utilization and improved coverage - factors that are pivotal for network efficiency [12,14]. Dominating sets aid in creating efficient broadcasting or multicasting protocols by selecting a subset of nodes responsible for message transmission [2]. This paper studies a variant of the dominating set in unit disk graphs that may have the following potential applications.

The problem of Edge-Vertex Dominating Set (*EVDS*) finds its use in various practical situations, including scenarios involving network structures and facility placement along edges. Let's consider a particular scenario where the concept of $EVDS$ can be applied: Imagine a large organization's network layout (see Fig. 3). We assume that each point in this network is under surveillance, but communication connections might extend beyond the watchful area. Suppose there's an unauthorized intruder who aims to gather information from every single point in the network. To achieve this, the intruder targets the specific blue links (labeled as critical links) that fall outside the monitored zone. Once control over these critical links is gained, the intruder gains power over the nodes directly linked to these crucial links. With control over these nodes, the intruder can proceed to obtain information from all other points by circumventing the nodes connected to the critical links, effectively positioning themselves as a trusted point. From the point of view of an intruder, this approach is efficient in terms of cost, prompting him to determine the smallest number of links required to gain control over all points. Enhancing security measures for these critical links is necessary to prevent such unauthorized access. Identifying these critical links can be achieved by utilizing the concept of *EVDS* within the network. On the other hand, the network designers can also design the network in such a way that the designed network has more number of crucial links. This would place a heavier load on potential intruders, demanding them to target a large number of crucial links to achieve full access to the targeted network. Consequently, intruders might find themselves needing more resources to carry out such actions.

Another potential application of the minimum *EVDS* problem is when we consider designing a secure and reliable communication network. Suppose in a communication network, every edge has information about every other edge and node, which is at most 1-hop distance from it. In order to implement cryptographic or security mechanisms to monitor the entire network, we want to identify as few edges as possible in the network, as we can not implement them on every edge of the network, for these mechanisms are computationally expensive. The minimum *EVDS* can be used for this purpose because every edge and node of the network is at most 1-hop distance from at least edge in the *EVDS*.

In most cases, every computer network will have some form of vulnerable edges. This is because computer networks are designed to interact with external entities, such as users, other networks, and the internet, and these interactions inherently introduce potential security risks. The term vulnerable edge (critical edge) refers to the points in a network that are more exposed to these external risks and where attackers could exploit security vulnerabilities. An *EVDS* plays an important role in identifying vulnerable edges in a network [7]. These critical edges would give an attacker control over all connected nodes if compromised. The *EVDS* helps prioritize security efforts by identifying the most critical edges. Security measures, like encryption or redundancy mechanisms, can then be directed toward securing these connections. Protecting these vital communication links ensures network integrity and minimizes the potential for data manipulation or interception by attackers.

2 Related Work

The *edge-vertex dominating set* and *vertex-edge dominating set* in a graph were introduced by Peters [10]. The edge-vertex dominating set and vertex-edge dominating set problems are NP-complete, even when restricted to bipartite graphs [6]. For every nontrivial tree $\mathcal{T}$, an upper bound on $\gamma_{ev}(\mathcal{T})$ is $(\gamma_t(\mathcal{T}) + s - 1)/2$ where s is the number of support vertices (a vertex adjacent to a leaf) [13]. The *total domination number* (γ_t) of a tree is equal to the *ev-domination number* (γ_{ev}) plus one [5]. The vertex-edge dominating set problem in *UDG* is

NP-complete [4]. Also, in [4], a polynomial time approximation scheme (PTAS) is proposed. Finding γ_{ve} even in cubic planar graphs is NP-hard [15]. The vertex-edge domination problem can be solved in linear time on block graphs [9]. In the same paper, it is also shown that finding γ_{ve} in undirected path graphs is NP-complete. Given a connected graph G with n vertices where $n \geq 6$, then we have $\gamma_{ve}(G) \leq \lfloor \frac{n}{3} \rfloor$ [16]. Boutrig et al. [1] gave an upper bound for the independent ve-domination number in terms of the ve-domination number for connected $K_{1,k}$-free graph with $k \geq 3$ and also gave an upper bound on the ve-domination number for connected C_5-free graph. To the best of our knowledge, the ev-dominating set problem has not yet been studied in the literature in the context of geometric intersection graphs.

2.1 Our Contribution

In this article, we study the *EVDS* problem in unit disk graphs. We prove that this problem on *UDG* admits a polynomial time approximation scheme (PTAS). We also present a simple 5-factor linear-time approximation algorithm.

3 Polynomial Time Approximation Scheme

In this section, we propose a PTAS for the *EVDS* set problem in a *UDG*. It is based on the concept of m-separated collection of subsets, which was introduced by Nieberg and Hurink [8]. The subsets generated by an m-separated collection will divide the graph into smaller parts such that the edge-induced subgraphs by these parts will have pairwise disjoint edge vertex dominating sets. For the *EVDS* problem, the value of m will be set to 4 in order to satisfy this condition. This division makes it easier to find the local *EVDS* of the subgraphs by determining the maximal matching of each subgraph. Here, we present various properties that allow us to bound the cardinalities corresponding to the global optimal solution. Finally, we will show that the union of the local *EVDS* in all the subgraphs can be extended to become an approximate *EVDS* to the original graph. Then, in the following subsection, we discuss an efficient way of finding these subgraphs. This concept of m-separated collection of subsets was used by many other authors to develop PTAS (for e.g., the Roman dominating set [11], minimum Liar's dominating set [3], vertex-edge dominating set [4]). However, we adopted the concept here quite differently from these as we have to select edges to dominate vertices in the *EVDS* problem.

Let $G = (V, E)$ be a *UDG*. Let $h(e_1, e_2)$ denote the minimum number of edges in a simple path between the closest pair of endpoints among the four endpoints of the edges e_1 and e_2. Consider any two subsets $E_1 \subseteq E$ and $E_2 \subseteq E$, the value $h(E_1, E_2)$ is defined as the minimum number of edges in a path between any two edges $e_1 \in E_1$ and $e_2 \in E_2$. We use $EVD(A)$ to denote an ev-dominating set and $EVD_{opt}(A)$ to denote the optimal ev-dominating set of the edge-induced subgraph corresponding to $A(\subseteq E)$ (i.e., the subgraph induced by the set of edges $A(\subseteq E)$ and the endpoints of edges in A).

Definition 1. Let S be a collection of k pairwise disjoint, non-empty subsets $S_i \subset E$ for $i = 1, 2, \ldots, k$, such that each subset S_i induces a connected component (see Subsect. 3.1 for the construction method). If $h(S_i, S_j) \geq m$ (i.e., the minimum number of edges in a simple path between the closest pair of endpoints) for $1 \leq i, j \leq k$ and $i \neq j$, then S is called as an m-separable collection of subsets of E (see Fig. 4 for the case $m = 4$).

Lemma 1. In a graph $G = (V, E)$, if $S = \{S_1, S_2, \ldots, S_k\}$ is a 4-separated collection of k subsets of E, then

$$\sum_{i=1}^{k} |EVD_{opt}(S_i)| \leq |EVD_{opt}(E)|.$$

Proof. Let A_i be the set of edges that are adjacent to, or adjacent to edges adjacent to, the edges of S_i for each $i = 1, 2, \ldots, k$. Define R_i as the set of edges given by $R_i = S_i \cup A_i$. The edges in sets $R_1, R_2, \ldots, R_k$ are pairwise disjoint, since the set S is a 4-separated collection of subsets of edges i.e., $(R_i \cap R_j) = \emptyset$, where $i \neq j$. Hence, the edges of $EVD_{opt}(E) \cap R_i$ will ev-dominate every vertex in S_i, since $EVD_{opt}(E)$ will ev-dominate every vertex $v \in V$. On the other hand, also $EVD_{opt}(S_i) \subset R_i$ ev-dominates every vertex of S_i, with a minimum number of edges of G. This implies that $|EVD_{opt}(S_i)| \leq |EVD_{opt}(E) \cap R_i|$. For all k subsets of edges in the 4-separated collection S, we get

$$\sum_{i=1}^{k} |EVD_{opt}(S_i)| \leq \sum_{i=1}^{k} |(EVD_{opt}(E) \cap R_i)| \leq |EVD_{opt}(E)|.$$

□

The above Lemma states that a 4-separated collection of subsets of edges S will give a lower bound on the cardinality of an $EVDS$. Hence, we can get an approximation for the $EVDS$ in G, if we are able to enlarge S_i to subsets $Q_i \subset E$, in such a way that $EVDS$ of expansions are bounded locally and dominate every $v \in V$ globally.

Lemma 2. In a graph $G = (V, E)$, let $S = \{S_1, S_2, \ldots, S_k\}$ be a 4-separated collection of subsets of edges and $Q = \{Q_1, Q_2, \ldots, Q_k\}$ be a collection of subsets of E with $S_i \subseteq Q_i$ for every $i = 1, 2, \ldots, k$. If there is a $\rho \geq 1$ such that

$$|EVD_{opt}(Q_i)| \leq \rho |EVD_{opt}(S_i)|$$

holds for every $i = 1, 2, \ldots, k$, and if $\bigcup_{i=1}^{k} EVD_{opt}(Q_i)$ is an edge-vertex dominating set of G, then $\sum_{i=1}^{k} |EVD_{opt}(Q_i)|$ is a ρ-approximation of minimum $EVDS$ set of G.

Proof. From Lemma 1 we have,

$$\sum_{i=1}^{k} |EVD_{opt}(S_i)| \leq |EVD_{opt}(E)|.$$

Hence, $\sum_{i=1}^{k} |EVD_{opt}(Q_i)| \leq \rho \sum_{i=1}^{k} |EVD_{opt}(S_i)| \leq \rho |EVD_{opt}(E)|.$ □

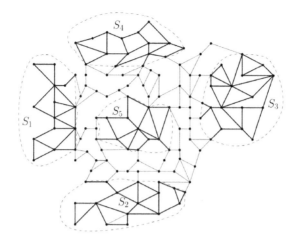

Fig. 4. 4-Separable collection of edge sets $S = \{S_1, S_2, S_3, S_4, S_5\}$.

In the following section, we discuss a procedure to construct the subsets $Q_i \subset E$, that contains a 4-separated collection of edges $S_i \subset Q_i$, in such a way that a local $(1+\epsilon)$-approximation can be guaranteed. The union of the respective local $EVDS$ will ev-dominate the entire vertex set of G, which results in a global $(1+\epsilon)$-approximation for the $EVDS$ problem.

3.1 Subset Construction

Here, we discuss the construction of the 4-separated collection of subsets of edges, $S = \{S_1, S_2, \ldots, S_k\}$ and the respective enlarged subsets $Q = \{Q_1, Q_2, \ldots, Q_k\}$ of E such that $S_i \subseteq Q_i$ for every $i = 1, 2, \ldots, k$. The basic idea of the algorithm is as follows. We start with an arbitrary edge $e \in E$ and consider the r-th edge neighborhood of e, for $r = 0, 1, 2, \ldots$, with $N_e^0[e] = e$. We compute the $EVDS$ for these edge neighborhoods until the following condition holds

$$|EVD(N_e^{r+4}[e])| > \rho |EVD(N_e^r[e])| \tag{1}$$

Let r_1 be the smallest r that violates the above inequality. Let $S_1 = N_e^{r_1}[e]$, $Q_1 = N_e^{r_1+4}[e]$. Then iteratively, let $S_i = N_e^{r_i}[e]$, $Q_i = N_e^{r_i+4}[e]$, $E_{i+1} = E_i \backslash (N_e^{r_i+4}(e))$ for $i = 1, 2, \ldots, k$, where $E_1 = E$ and k is such that $E_{k+1} = \emptyset$. We follow this procedure iteratively for each graph induced by E_{i+1} and until $E_{i+1} = \emptyset$, finally returning the sets $S = \{S_1, S_2, \ldots, S_k\}$ and $Q = \{Q_1, Q_2, \ldots, Q_k\}$, where $r_2, r_3, \ldots, r_k$ are the smallest values of r violating inequality 1, corresponding to the 2nd, 3rd, ..., kth iteration of the above edge-neighborhood growing procedure.

We find the edge-vertex dominating set of the r-edge neighborhood $EVD(N_e^r[e])$ of an edge e, with respect to the graph G as follows. Find a maximal matching M for the graph induced by the edges of $N_e^r[e]$. We can observe that the edges in M form an edge-vertex dominating set for the graph induced by $N_e^r[e]$. Hence, as the following lemma says, $EVD(N_e^r[e]) = M$.

Lemma 3. *A maximal matching M of the graph $G' = (V', E')$ induced by the edges in $N_e^r[e]$, is an EVDS of $N_e^r[e]$.*

Proof. For the contradiction, assume that M is not an $EVDS$ of the graph $G' = (V', E')$ induced by the edges in $N_e^r[e]$. It means that there exists a vertex $v \in V'$ which is incident to an edge $e' \in E'$ such that $N_e[e'] \cap M = \emptyset$. It contradicts that M is a maximal matching in G' as the set $M \cup \{e'\}$ is a matching in G'. Thus, the lemma follows. □

Lemma 4. *If $G' = (V', E')$ is a UDG induced by the edges in $N_e^r[e]$ and M is the maximal matching of G' then $|EVD(N_e^r[e])| \leq O(r^2)$.*

Proof. First, we find a maximal matching M, before finding the $EVDS$ in $G' = (V', E')$ which is induced by the edges of $N_e^r[e]$. The number of edges in M of G' is bounded by the number of unit disks that are packed in a disk of radius $r + 2$ and centered at the middle of the edge e. Hence, $|M| \leq (r+2)^2$ and the cardinality of $EVD(N_e^r[e])$ is bounded by $|M|$ (see Lemma 3). Therefore, we have
$$|EVD(N_e^r[e])| \leq |M| \leq (r+2)^2 \leq O(r^2).$$
□

Theorem 1. *There exists an r_1 which violates the following inequality.*
$$|EVD(N_e^{r_1+4}[e])| > \rho |EVD(N_e^{r_1}[e])|$$
where $\rho = 1 + \epsilon$ and r_1 is bounded by $O(\frac{1}{\epsilon} \log \frac{1}{\epsilon})$.

Proof. On contrary, without loss of generality for r_1, assume that there exists an edge $e \in E$ such that
$$|EVD(N_e^{r+4}[e])| > \rho |EVD(N_e^r[e])|$$
for all $r \geq r_1$. Then, from Lemma 4, we have
$$(r+6)^2 \geq |EVD(N_e^{r+4}[e])|.$$

Hence, when r is even, we have,
$$(r+6)^2 \geq |EVD(N_e^{r+4}[e])| > \rho |EVD(N_e^r[e])| > \cdots > \rho^{\frac{r}{2}} |EVD(N_e^2[e])| \geq \rho^{\frac{r}{2}} \tag{2}$$

and when r is odd, we have,
$$(r+6)^2 \geq |EVD(N_e^{r+4}[e])| > \rho |EVD(N_e^r[e])| > \cdots > \rho^{\frac{r-1}{2}} |EVD(N_e^1[e])| \geq \rho^{\frac{r-1}{2}} \tag{3}$$

Now, we can observe that in both the inequalities 2, 3 on the left-hand side, we have a polynomial in r, which is at least the right-hand side value which is exponential in r, it is a contradiction. Therefore, for all $r \geq r_1$ the inequality (2) cannot hold, hence there exists such r_1. Ultimately, r_1 depends only on ρ, not on the size of the edge-induced subgraph by $N_e^{r+4}[e]$. As in [8], we can argue that r_1 is bounded by $O(\frac{1}{\epsilon} \log \frac{1}{\epsilon})$ where $\rho = 1 + \epsilon$. □

Lemma 5. *Given an $\epsilon > 0$, for an edge $e \in E$, $EVD_{opt}(Q_i)$ can be computed in polynomial time.*

Proof. From the way of construction of Q_i, we can see that $Q_i \subseteq N_e^{r+4}[e]$. The cardinality of EVDS of $N_e^{r+4}[e]$ is bounded by $O(r^2)$ (see Lemma 4), where r is bounded by $O(\frac{1}{\epsilon} \log \frac{1}{\epsilon})$ (see Theorem 1). Hence, we need at most $O(n^{r^2})$ possible combinations of $O(r^2)$-tuples of vertex points to check whether the selected tuple is an $EVDS$ of Q_i. □

Lemma 6. $\bigcup_{i=1}^{k} EVD(Q_i)$ *is an edge-vertex dominating set in $G = (V, E)$.*

Proof. It follows from the construction of the collection of subsets of edges $\{Q_1, Q_2, \ldots, Q_k\}$ that each edge that is incident to a vertex $v \in V$ belongs to a specific subset Q_i and $EVD(Q_i)$ is an $EVDS$ of the graph induced by the edges of Q_i. Therefore, every vertex $v \in V$ is incident to at least one edge e such that at least one edge of $N_e[e]$ is in $\bigcup_{i=1}^{k} EVD(Q_i)$. □

Corollary 1. $\bigcup_{i=1}^{k} EVD_{opt}(Q_i)$ *is an edge-vertex dominating set in $G = (V, E)$, for the collection of subsets of edges $Q = \{Q_1, Q_2, \ldots, Q_k\}$.*

Theorem 2. *For a given unit disk graph and an $\epsilon > 0$, there exists a PTAS (an $(1+\epsilon)$-approximation) algorithm for the EVDS problem with running time $n^{O(c^2)}$, where $c = (\frac{1}{\epsilon} \log \frac{1}{\epsilon})$.*

Proof. Follows from Corollary 1 and Lemma 5. □

4 5-Factor Approximation Algorithm

In this section, we present a 5-factor approximation algorithm for the $EVDS$ problem on UDG. Let $\mathcal{S}$ be a set of n points given in the Euclidean plane. To construct a graph $G = (V, E)$, we join every pair of these points with an edge if the distance between them is less than or equal to 1 unit. Let E be the set of such edges with cardinality $|E|$ and V be the set of vertices corresponding to points in $\mathcal{S}$. The graph induced by V and E will form a UDG since the distance between any two end-points of $e \in E$ is at most 1. Assume that this UDG has no isolated vertices; otherwise, an $EVDS$ cannot exist. To develop an approximation algorithm, we consider an axis-aligned rectangular region $\mathcal{R}$ that contains the UDG, which is represented using an adjacency list data structure. We then partition the region $\mathcal{R}$ into grid cells by tessellating it with regular hexagons, each with a side length of $\frac{1}{2}$. Hence, the maximum distance between any two points inside a cell is at most 1. Assume that no point in V lies on the boundary of any hexagon in the partition. This can be ensured by employing a simple perturbation process, a standard technique in computational geometry.

Lemma 7. *Any edge $e \in E$, with its two endpoints located in distinct hexagons, can ev-dominate every point (i.e., the corresponding vertices in G) within those two hexagons.*

Proof. Assume that there exists a point $p \in S$ (corresponding to a vertex $v_p \in V$) lying in one of the two adjacent hexagons that are not ev-dominated by $e = (u, v)$ (with corresponding points p_u and p_v in S). Since $(v_p, u) \notin E$, point p must not be in the same hexagon as p_u, meaning it lies in the hexagon containing p_v. Therefore, the distance between p and p_v is at most 1, which implies $(v_p, v) \in E$. By symmetry, the same reasoning holds if p were in the hexagon containing p_u. Thus, p must be outside both hexagons, leading to a contradiction. □

The outline of the algorithm is as follows. Initialize the set S^{ev} (which will hold the edges of $EVDS$) initially as empty. Ignore the hexagonal cells which are empty, i.e., no points of S lie inside them. For a non-empty cell, keep a linked list of all the points lying inside it. Finally, we maintain a hash-table of all the non-empty cells. Now, pick an arbitrary edge $e \in E$ whose endpoints lie in different cells. Add this edge to S^{ev} and set $E = E \setminus \{e\}$. Mark all points that are ev-dominated by e (by marking the hash table entries corresponding to the cells.) If there are any unmarked vertices, now choose an edge $e \in E$ that is incident to any of the unmarked vertices, with its other endpoint lying in a different cell. Add e to S^{ev} and mark all the unmarked points ev-dominated by e. Repeat this process until every point in V is marked (see Algorithm 1).

Algorithm 1. Edge-vertex domination

1: Initialize $S^{ev} = \emptyset$, $E' = E$, and let all vertices in V be unmarked initially.
2: **while** there is an edge $e \in E'$ with its both end-points unmarked **do**
3:     Pick an edge $e \in E'$ such that $e = (u, v)$, the unmarked vertices $u \in A$ and $v \in B$, where A and B are any two distinct hexagonal cells.
4:     Set $S^{ev} = S^{ev} \cup \{e\}$ and $E' = E' \setminus \{e\}$
5:     Mark all vertices which are incident to $N_e[e]$
6: **end while**
7: **while** there is a hexagon containing unmarked vertices **do**
8:     Pick any arbitrary edge $e \in E$ with at least one endpoint in that hexagon
9:     $S^{ev} = S^{ev} \cup \{e\}$
10: **end while**
    return S^{ev}

Theorem 3. *Algorithm 1 gives a factor 5-approximation for EVDS problem on a UDG in $O(|V| + |E|)$ time.*

Proof. Since Algorithm 1 looks at every edge between points to know whether its endpoints are the marked vertices and selects an edge at lines 3 or 8, and also due to the fact that the hash table size is $O(|V|)$, its running time is linear in $|V|$ and $|E|$. In Fig. 5, we can observe that Algorithm 1 selected *EVDS* as $\{e_1, e_2, e_3, e_4, e_5\}$ whose cardinality is five, whereas the optimal solution may have a single edge that will ev-dominate every given point (see the edge e in Fig. 5). Next, one can see that the algorithm may select at most five times the optimal value since an edge between points in any two hexagons may ev-dominate the points in all remaining eight hexagons (Lemma 7).

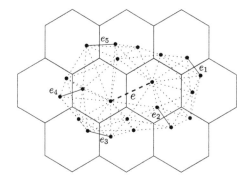
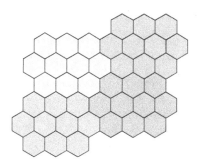

Fig. 5. $EVDS = \{e_1, e_2, e_3, e_4, e_5\}$, and minimum $EVDS = \{e\}$.

Fig. 6. Four adjacent Mega-cells.

The approximation factor five of Algorithm 1 follows due to the following two facts:

1. If both the endpoints of an edge e selected by Algorithm 1 lie within the same hexagon x, then none of the vertices corresponding to these endpoints are adjacent to vertices whose corresponding points lie in the adjacent hexagons of x (**while** loops in **Algorithm 1**.) Hence, e must be present in any *EVDS* to ev-dominate all the points in x.
2. Otherwise, an edge e selected by Algorithm 1 ev-dominates all the points in both hexagons where its endpoints lie, respectively (Lemma 7).

All the cells (hexagons) in $\mathcal{R}$ can be grouped as a collection of mega-cells (as in Fig. 6), where each mega-cell consists of ten adjacent hexagonal cells (cells colored with the same color in Fig. 6). Algorithm 1 picks at most five edges to ev-dominate all the points in each mega-cell, whereas in the optimal solution, at least one edge is required. □

5 Conclusion

In this paper, we showed that the *EVDS-UDG* problem admits a **PTAS**. We also gave a simple 5-factor approximation algorithm in linear time. While this 5-factor approximation algorithm is significantly faster than the **PTAS**, it requires a geometric representation of the input graph, whereas the proposed PTAS does not, making the PTAS more robust. We believe that the *EVDS* problem on *UDG*s is NP-hard, and in future work, we aim to formally prove this complexity.

References

1. Boutrig, R., Chellali, M., Haynes, T.W., Hedetniemi, S.T.: Vertex-edge domination in graphs. Aequationes Math. **90**(2), 355–366 (2016)
2. Clark, B.N., Colbourn, C.J., Johnson, D.S.: Unit disk graphs. Discrete Math. **86**(1–3), 165–177 (1990)
3. Jallu, R.K., Jena, S.K., Das, G.K.: Liar's domination in unit disk graphs. Theoret. Comput. Sci. **845**, 38–49 (2020)
4. Jena, S.K., Das, G.K.: Vertex-edge domination in unit disk graphs. Discrete Appl. Math. **319**, 351–361 (2021)
5. Krishnakumari, B., Venkatakrishnan, Y.B., Krzywkowski, M.: On trees with total domination number equal to edge-vertex domination number plus one. Proc. Math. Sci. **126**(2), 153–157 (2016). https://doi.org/10.1007/s12044-016-0267-6
6. Lewis, J.R.: Vertex-edge and edge-vertex domination in graphs, Ph.D. thesis, Clemson University, Clemson (2007)
7. Medya, S., Silva, A., Singh, A., Basu, P., Swami, A.: Group centrality maximization via network design. In: Proceedings of the 2018 SIAM International Conference on Data Mining, pp. 126–134 ((2018))
8. Nieberg, T., Hurink, J.: A PTAS for the minimum dominating set problem in unit disk graphs. In: Erlebach, T., Persinao, G. (eds.) Approximation and Online Algorithms, pp. 296–306. Springer, Berlin, Heidelberg (2006). https://doi.org/10.1007/11671411_23
9. Paul, S., Ranjan, K.: On vertex-edge and independent vertex-edge domination. In: Li, Y., Cardei, M., Huang, Y. (eds.) Combinatorial Optimization and Applications, pp. 437–448. Springer, Cham (2019). https://doi.org/10.1007/978-3-030-36412-0_35
10. Peters, K.: Theoretical and algorithmic results on domination and connectivity (nordhaus-gaddum, gallai type results, max-min relationships, linear time, series-parallel). (1987)
11. Shang, W., Hu, X.: The roman domination problem in unit disk graphs. In: International Conference on Computational Science, pp. 305–312. Springer (2007)
12. Stojmenovic, I., Seddigh, M., Zunic, J.: Dominating sets and neighbor elimination-based broadcasting algorithms in wireless networks. IEEE Trans. Parallel Distrib. Syst. **13**(1), 14–25 (2002)
13. Venkatakrishnan, Y.B., Krishnakumari, B.: An improved upper bound of edge-vertex domination number of a tree. Inf. Process. Lett. **134**, 14–17 (2018)
14. Wu, J., Li, H.: On calculating connected dominating set for efficient routing in ad hoc wireless networks. In: Proceedings of the 3rd International Workshop on Discrete Algorithms and Methods for Mobile Computing and Communications, pp. 7–14 (1999)
15. Ziemann, R., Żyliński, P.: Vertex-edge domination in cubic graphs. Discret. Math. **343**(11), 112075 (2020)
16. Żyliński, P.: Vertex-edge domination in graphs. Aequationes Math. **93**(4), 735–742 (2019)

Density Extrema of Integer Points in Standard Hexagons

Nilanjana G. Basu[1]($\boxtimes$), Subhashis Majumder[1], and Partha Bhowmick[2]

[1] Heritage Institute of Technology, Kolkata, India
{nilanjanag.basu,subhashis.majumder}@heritageit.edu
[2] Indian Institute of Technology, Kharagpur, India
pb@cse.iitkgp.ac.in

Abstract. The density of points in balls and regular shapes within a metric space offers insights into optimal packing, geometric patterns, and constraint-based optimization. It enhances computational efficiency, models natural systems, and enables metric comparisons, revealing how geometry and distribution vary with different distance measures. Building on previous investigations into density extrema for various ℓ_p-balls, this paper presents novel results essential to understanding the density extrema (i.e., minima and maxima) of integer points in standard hexagons. A key observation from our findings, along with earlier results, is that for real radii, the density extrema consistently occur at small radii, regardless of shape. However, with integer radii, the behavior changes drastically, posing a fascinating and unresolved research challenge.

1 Introduction

By *standard hexagons*, we refer to regular hexagons with two opposite sides parallel to either the x-axis or the y-axis. For an unweighted set of points in a two-dimensional region, the *density* is defined as the number of points per unit area of that region [10]. In the case of a weighted set of points, density is calculated as the sum of the weights divided by the area.

By *integer points* or *pixels*, we mean points with integer coordinates. An *integer space* or *digital space* is an infinite space consisting of all integer points. In 2D, it is the set $\mathbb{Z}^2$, which can be conceived as the set of intersection points (called *grid points*) of grid lines in a uniform rectilinear grid. Similarly, the 3D digital space is essentially the set $\mathbb{Z}^3$, which corresponds to a cuboidal grid where grid points have integer coordinates.

The notion of density finds numerous applications in different branches of physical science. It provides a measure of the relative concentration of points within a given shape or region. There is a multitude of research on density and its applications. Some of these can be found in [4,5,7,8,11,13,14] and in the references therein.

As shown in [10], an axes-parallel region with maximum (resp., minimum) density always contains only two (resp., only one) points from the given set. Later, Basu et al. [1] proposed algorithms for identifying maximum- and minimum-density regions in higher dimensions. The concept extends naturally to digital spaces, where contributing points are assumed to lie at the intersections of a grid, which is typically rectangular but can also be triangular or hexagonal.

The concept of integer point density is intrinsically tied to distance geometry, a field that explores geometric properties based on distance functions. This connection is particularly relevant for applications such as molecular conformation identification in computational chemistry [9] and pattern recognition in image processing [12]. Basu et al. [2] studied uniform-weight points positioned at every grid point of a rectilinear grid and proved novel results for circular regions. For ℓ_∞-balls, the solutions are relatively straightforward, as noted by Basu et al. [6]. Furthermore, their recent work [3] presents notable findings on extremum values for ℓ_1-balls in 2D and 3D integer spaces.

Motivation of Our Work

The motivation for this work stems from our ongoing investigation into the behavior of extreme density values of integer points in various balls and standard geometric shapes. A summary of some of our previous findings is presented in Table 1, with new results highlighted in the final row. These results illustrate that extremal densities are not intuitive for these standard shapes under varying constraints. Our ultimate aim is to identify any common features among these extremal cases. Based on our research, this problem appears to be uniquely positioned within the domain of discrete geometry, and to our knowledge, it has not been addressed before.

Focus of Our Work

In this work, we explore the locations of density extrema in the collection of all standard hexagons with integer centers. A hexagon, which, though not an ℓ_p-ball for any metric p, is chosen by us due to its widespread use across various fields for its inherent properties. In this paper, we restrict our study to standard hexagons specified solely by their radii.

Table 1. Summary of previous results and new results (ε is a real number tending to 0)

	C	R	Maximum density		Minimum density	
			Density	Radius	Density	Radius
ℓ_2-Balls (Circles) [2]	$\mathbb{Z}^2$	$\mathbb{Z}^+$	$\frac{5}{\pi}$	1	$\frac{149}{49\pi}$	7
	$\mathbb{Z}^2$	$\mathbb{R}^+$	$\frac{5}{\pi}$	1	$\frac{1}{\pi}$	$1-|\varepsilon|$
ℓ_∞-Balls (Squares) [6]	$\mathbb{Z}^2$	$\mathbb{Z}^+$	4	1	1	all values
	$\mathbb{Z}^2$	$\mathbb{R}^+$	4	1	$\frac{1}{4}$	$2-|\varepsilon|$
ℓ_1-Balls (Diamonds) [3]	$\mathbb{Z}^2$	$\mathbb{Z}^+$	$\frac{5}{2}$	2	1	∞
	$\mathbb{Z}^2$	$\mathbb{R}^+$	$\frac{5}{2}$	2	$\frac{1}{2}$	$2-|\varepsilon|$
Standard Hexagons (new results)	$\mathbb{Z}^2$	$\mathbb{Z}^+$	$\frac{2}{\sqrt{3}}$	1	$\frac{161}{96\sqrt{3}}$	8
	$\mathbb{Z}^2$	$\mathbb{R}^+$	$\frac{5}{2\sqrt{3}}$	$\frac{2}{\sqrt{3}}$	$\frac{5}{(2\sqrt{3}+3)}$	$1+\frac{1}{\sqrt{3}}-|\varepsilon|$

Density Extrema of Integer Points in Standard Hexagons 53

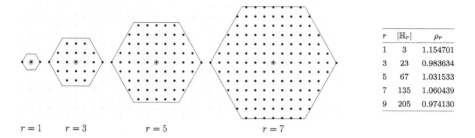

Fig. 1. First few hexagons with odd integer radii r. The irrational values of ρ_r are presented here rounded to the sixth decimal place.

We have determined the sizes of the standard hexagons that yield maximum and minimum densities, where their radii may be integer or real numbers, respectively in Sect. 2 and in Sect. 3. The cases of integer and real radii are treated separately, due to the intriguing fact that these extrema are constrained by this distinction, as evidenced in Table 1.

2 Maximum Density

As already mentioned in Sect. 1 earlier, we consider standard hexagons with integer centers, and hence specify them by their radii only. Since all the hexagons under consideration are standard, we will drop the term 'standard' for brevity and refer to them simply as 'hexagons'.

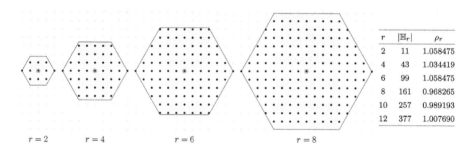

Fig. 2. First few hexagons with even radii.

The *radius* of a hexagon means the Euclidean distance of any of its vertices from its center. We denote by H_r a hexagon of radius r. The set of pixels contained in H_r is denoted by $\mathbb{H}_r := H_r \cap \mathbb{Z}^2$, and is referred to as a *digital hexagon*. The cardinality of $\mathbb{H}_r$ is denoted by $|\mathbb{H}_r|$, and the density of pixels in $\mathbb{H}_r$ is given by $\rho_r := \dfrac{|\mathbb{H}_r|}{\frac{3\sqrt{3}}{2}r^2}$, as the area of H_r is $\frac{3\sqrt{3}}{2}r^2$. Some examples are shown in Fig. 1.

We denote by $H_{x,y}$ the hexagon passing through the point $(x, y) \in \mathbb{R}^2$. Note that for a given point (x, y), $H_{x,y}$ will be uniquely determined because it corresponds to a standard hexagon with an integer center having a fixed radius.

Accordingly, we denote by $\mathbb{H}_{x,y}$ the digital hexagon corresponding to $H_{x,y}$, i.e., $\mathbb{H}_{x,y} := H_{x,y} \cap \mathbb{Z}^2$, and by $\rho_{x,y}$ the density of pixels in $H_{x,y}$.

In order to explore the maximum density of pixels over all the hexagons having real-valued radii, we now make an important observation that comes to use in narrowing down our attention to a countable collection of hexagons, which inherently helps in proving all the results in this section on maximum density.

Let $H_{x,y}$ be a hexagon that does not contain any pixel on its boundary. Let $H_{x,y}$ be uniformly shrunk along one of its diagonals keeping its center fixed until a pixel $(i, j) \in \mathbb{H}_{x,y}$ is there on its boundary. Then, $H_{i,j} \subsetneq H_{x,y}$ and $\mathbb{H}_{i,j} = \mathbb{H}_{x,y}$, which implies that the density for $H_{i,j}$ is larger than that for $H_{x,y}$, whence the following observation.

Observation 1. *For a hexagon without any pixel on its boundary, there always exists a higher-density hexagon with a pixel on its boundary.*

2.1 Hexagons with Odd Radii

Observation 1 implies that the maximum density over all the hexagons with integer radius will be the density of a hexagon from the countable collection $\{H_{i,j} : (i, j) \in \mathbb{Z}^2\}$, i.e.,

$$\max\{\rho_{x,y} : (x, y) \in \mathbb{R}^2\} = \max\{\rho_{i,j} : (i, j) \in \mathbb{Z}^2\}.$$

We consider hexagons containing at least two pixels, because one-pixel containment is trivial and degenerates to the limiting case of infinite density. Here, 'p-pixel containment' refers to those cases where a hexagon contains exactly p pixels.

Lemma 1. *For any odd radius r, we have*

$$|\mathbb{H}_r| = r\left(2\left\lfloor \frac{\sqrt{3}}{2}r \right\rfloor + 1\right) + 2\left(\sum_{i=0}^{\lfloor \frac{r}{2} \rfloor} \left(2\left\lfloor \sqrt{3}i \right\rfloor + 1\right)\right) \quad \text{and} \quad \rho_r = \frac{|\mathbb{H}_r|}{\frac{3\sqrt{3}}{2}r^2}. \quad (1)$$

Proof. We divide H_r into three parts: an axis-aligned rectangle of size $r \times \sqrt{3}r$ and two congruent isosceles triangles on opposite sides, as shown in Fig. 1.

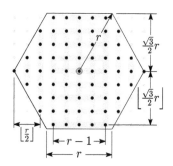

It is evident from the inset figure that the rectangle contains $2\left\lfloor \frac{\sqrt{3}}{2}r \right\rfloor + 1$ rows, each with exactly r pixels. Each triangle consists of $\lfloor r/2 \rfloor + 1$ columns, indexed from 0 to $\lfloor r/2 \rfloor$. The column with index i contributes exactly $2\lfloor \sqrt{3}i \rfloor + 1$ pixels. Thus, the pixel count for each triangle is

$$\sum_{i=0}^{\lfloor r/2 \rfloor} \left(2\left\lfloor \sqrt{3}i \right\rfloor + 1\right).$$

Adding the pixel counts of the two triangles and the rectangle yields the total pixel count, giving the desired result. □

As illustrated in Fig. 1, the density for the hexagon with unit radius is $\frac{3}{\frac{3\sqrt{3}}{2}} = \frac{2}{\sqrt{3}}$, which happens to be the maximum for odd radius, as stated in the following theorem.

Theorem 1. *In the collection of hexagons with odd radii, the density is maximized at a unit radius.*

Proof. From Lemma 1,

$$
\begin{aligned}
|\mathbb{H}_r| &= r\left(2\left\lfloor \tfrac{\sqrt{3}}{2}r \right\rfloor + 1\right) + 2\sum_{i=0}^{\lfloor \frac{r}{2} \rfloor}\left(2\left\lfloor \sqrt{3}i \right\rfloor + 1\right) \\
&< r\left(2\tfrac{\sqrt{3}}{2}r + 1\right) + 2\sum_{i=0}^{\lfloor \frac{r}{2} \rfloor}\left(2\sqrt{3}i + 1\right) = \sqrt{3}r^2 + r + 4\sqrt{3}\sum_{i=0}^{\lfloor \frac{r}{2} \rfloor} i + 2\left(\lfloor \tfrac{r}{2} \rfloor + 1\right) \\
&\leq \sqrt{3}r^2 + 2r + 2 + 4\sqrt{3}\cdot\tfrac{1}{2}\cdot\tfrac{r}{2}\cdot\left(\tfrac{r}{2}+1\right) = \sqrt{3}r^2 + 2r + 2 + \tfrac{\sqrt{3}}{2}r^2 + \sqrt{3}r \\
&= \tfrac{3\sqrt{3}}{2}r^2 + \left(2 + \sqrt{3}\right)r + 2
\end{aligned}
$$

$$\implies \rho_r \leq \frac{\tfrac{3\sqrt{3}}{2}r^2 + \left(2 + \sqrt{3}\right)r + 2}{\tfrac{3\sqrt{3}}{2}r^2} = 1 + \frac{4 + 2\sqrt{3}}{3\sqrt{3}r} + \frac{4}{3\sqrt{3}r^2} \leq 1.136950 \ \forall \ r \geq 11.$$

For $1 \leq r \leq 9$, the values of ρ_r (correct up to the sixth decimal place, as shown in Fig. 1) clearly indicate that $\rho_1 > \rho_r$. The preceding derivation demonstrates that $\rho_1 > \rho_r$ for all $r \geq 11$. This completes the proof. □

2.2 Hexagons with Even Radii

Lemma 2. *For any even radius r, we have*

$$|\mathbb{H}_r| = (r+1)\left(2\left\lfloor\frac{\sqrt{3}}{2}r\right\rfloor + 1\right) + 2\left(\sum_{i=0}^{\frac{r}{2}-1}\left(2\lfloor\sqrt{3}i\rfloor + 1\right)\right) \quad \text{and} \quad \rho_r = \frac{|\mathbb{H}_r|}{\frac{3\sqrt{3}}{2}r^2}. \quad (2)$$

Proof. The proof technique followed here is similar to Lemma 1. We divide H_r into three parts: an axis-aligned rectangle of size $r \times \sqrt{3}r$ and two congruent isosceles triangles positioned on opposite sides, as illustrated in Fig. 2. The key difference from Lemma 1 is the presence of pixels on the vertical sides of the rectangle, resulting in a total pixel count of $(r+1)\left(2\left\lfloor\frac{\sqrt{3}}{2}r\right\rfloor + 1\right)$. Adding this to the pixel counts of the two isosceles triangles completes the proof. □

As illustrated in Fig. 2 and derived from Lemma 2, the density for the hexagon with radius 2 or 6 is $\frac{11}{6\sqrt{3}} \approx 1.058475$. This is the maximum achievable density for a hexagon with even radius, as established in the following theorem.

Theorem 2. *In the collection of hexagons with even radii, the maximum density is achieved for radii 2 and 6.*

Proof. From Lemma 2,

$$|\mathbb{H}_r| = (r+1)\left(2\left\lfloor\tfrac{\sqrt{3}}{2}r\right\rfloor + 1\right) + 2\sum_{i=0}^{\frac{r}{2}-1}\left(2\lfloor\sqrt{3}i\rfloor + 1\right)$$
$$< (r+1)(\sqrt{3}r+1) + 2\sum_{i=0}^{\frac{r}{2}-1}(2\sqrt{3}i+1) = (r+1)(\sqrt{3}r+1) + 4\sqrt{3}\sum_{i=0}^{\frac{r}{2}-1} i + 2\left(\tfrac{r}{2}\right)$$
$$= \sqrt{3}r^2 + 2r + \sqrt{3}r + 1 + 4\sqrt{3}\cdot\tfrac{1}{2}\cdot\left(\tfrac{r}{2}-1\right)\cdot\tfrac{r}{2} = \sqrt{3}r^2 + 2r + \sqrt{3}r + 1 + \sqrt{3}r\left(\tfrac{r}{2}-1\right)$$
$$= \sqrt{3}r^2 + 2r + \sqrt{3}r + 1 + \tfrac{\sqrt{3}}{2}r^2 - \sqrt{3}r = \tfrac{3\sqrt{3}}{2}r^2 + 2r + 1$$
$$\implies \rho_r < \frac{\tfrac{3\sqrt{3}}{2}r^2 + 2r + 1}{\tfrac{3\sqrt{3}}{2}r^2} = 1 + \tfrac{4}{3\sqrt{3}r} + \tfrac{2}{3\sqrt{3}r^2} < 1.058470 < \rho_2 \;\forall\; r \geq 14.$$

For $2 \leq r \leq 12$, the values of ρ_r (accurate to the sixth decimal place, as shown in Fig. 2) clearly indicate that $\rho_2 = \rho_6 = \frac{11}{6\sqrt{3}} > \rho_r$ for all other r. Together with the preceding derivation, this completes the proof. □

2.3 Hexagons with Real Radii

For any hexagon $\mathbb{H}_r$ with real radius r, let f denote the fractional part of r, such that $r = \lfloor r \rfloor + f$. The results vary depending on whether $\lfloor r \rfloor$ is odd or even, as outlined in the following lemma.

Lemma 3. *For any real radius r, we have*

$$|\mathbb{H}_r| = s \cdot \left(2\left\lfloor\frac{\sqrt{3}}{2}r\right\rfloor + 1\right) + 2\sum_{i=0}^{\lfloor\frac{r-1}{2}\rfloor}\left(2\lfloor\sqrt{3}(i+f)\rfloor + 1\right) \quad (3)$$

$$\text{where,}\; s = \begin{cases} \lfloor r \rfloor & \text{if } \lfloor r \rfloor \bmod 2 = 1 \\ \lfloor r \rfloor + 1 & \text{otherwise.} \end{cases} \quad (4)$$

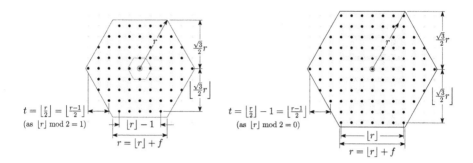

Fig. 3. Hexagons with real radii r. **Left:** $\lfloor r \rfloor$ is odd. **Right:** $\lfloor r \rfloor$ is even. The maximum-density hexagon with radius $\frac{2}{\sqrt{3}}$ is colored red and contains five pixels. (Color figure online)

Proof. The analysis follows a similar approach to previous cases. We partition H_r into a central rectangle of dimensions $r \times \sqrt{3}r$ and two congruent isosceles triangles on opposite sides, as illustrated in Fig. 3.

In the rectangular region, the number of pixel columns is $2\lfloor r/2 \rfloor + 1$, which simplifies to $\lfloor r \rfloor$ if $\lfloor r \rfloor$ is odd, and to $\lfloor r \rfloor + 1$ otherwise. This justifies the value of s given in (4). Each column contains $2\left\lfloor \frac{\sqrt{3}}{2}r \right\rfloor + 1$ pixels, regardless of whether $\lfloor r \rfloor$ is odd or even. Thus, the total pixel count in the rectangular region is

$$s \cdot \left(2\left\lfloor \frac{\sqrt{3}}{2}r \right\rfloor + 1 \right).$$

Each isosceles triangle consists of columns of pixels, which are indexed from 0 to $t = \lfloor r/2 \rfloor$ if $\lfloor r \rfloor$ is odd, and to $\lfloor r/2 \rfloor - 1$ otherwise. It is easy to verify that in either case, t simplifies to $\lfloor (r-1)/2 \rfloor$. Now, the column with index i contributes exactly $2\lfloor (i+f) \cdot \tan 60° \rfloor + 1 = 2\lfloor \sqrt{3}(i+f) \rfloor + 1$ pixels. Thus, the pixel count for each triangle is

$$\sum_{i=0}^{\lfloor \frac{r-1}{2} \rfloor} \left(2\lfloor \sqrt{3}(i+f) \rfloor + 1 \right).$$

Adding these contributions yields the final result. □

The above lemma is used to compile a list of densities for the radius ranging from 1 to $3 + \frac{4}{\sqrt{3}}$, as presented in Table 2. This list serves as a basis for proving the upcoming theorem.

Theorem 3. *In the collection of hexagons with real radii, the maximum density is attained uniquely when the radius is $\frac{2}{\sqrt{3}}$, yielding a density of $\frac{5}{2\sqrt{3}} \approx 1.443376$.*

Table 2. Densities of hexagons with real radii up to $3 + \frac{4}{\sqrt{3}} \approx 5.451797$, which are potentially useful in proving Theorem 3. (**Note:** The actual values of all densities are irrational, and the values shown here are accurate to the 6th decimal place. These rounded-off values in fact serve the purpose of our proof.)

r	$|\mathbb{H}_r|$	ρ_r	r	$|\mathbb{H}_r|$	ρ_r	r	$|\mathbb{H}_r|$	ρ_r
1	3	1.154701	$2\sqrt{3}$	33	1.058476	5	67	1.031532
$\frac{2}{\sqrt{3}}$	5	1.443376	$3 + \frac{1}{\sqrt{3}}$	37	1.112825	$4 + \frac{2}{\sqrt{3}}$	71	1.028489
$1 + \frac{1}{\sqrt{3}}$	9	1.392305	$2 + \sqrt{3}$	41	1.133018	$3 + \frac{4}{\sqrt{3}}$	75	1.024043
2	11	1.058475	4	43	1.034419	$5 + \frac{1}{\sqrt{3}}$	79	0.977506
$\frac{4}{\sqrt{3}}$	17	1.226869	$3 + \frac{2}{\sqrt{3}}$	47	1.048013	$4 + \sqrt{3}$	83	0.972313
$2 + \frac{1}{\sqrt{3}}$	21	1.216804	$4 + \frac{1}{\sqrt{3}}$	51	0.936893	$\frac{10}{\sqrt{3}}$	93	1.073871
3	23	0.983634	$\frac{8}{\sqrt{3}}$	61	1.100574	$3 + \frac{5}{\sqrt{3}}$	97	1.077379
$2 + \frac{2}{\sqrt{3}}$	27	1.044229	$3 + \sqrt{3}$	65	1.194079	6	99	1.058475

Proof. See the inset figure.

Let R be the smallest axis-aligned rectangle that contains the hexagon H_r. Define the four right-angled triangles $\{T_i : 1 \leq i \leq 4\}$ enclosed in R such that their hypotenuses align with the slanted sides of H_r, and their smaller sides align with the boundary of R.

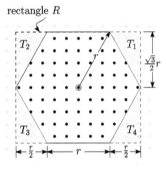

For each triangle T_i, let T'_i be the semi-closed region formed by the union of its interior and the two smaller sides. Then, the closed region enclosed by H_r can be expressed as $R \setminus (T'_1 \cup T'_2 \cup T'_3 \cup T'_4)$.

The rectangle R has dimensions $2r \times \sqrt{3}r$. Since it has an integer center, its vertical axis of symmetry is aligned with a grid line and on each side, the rectangle covers $\lfloor r \rfloor$ vertical grid lines. So, the rectangle includes exactly $1 + 2\lfloor r \rfloor$ pixels from each of the horizontal grid lines it covers. Likewise, it covers $1 + 2\left\lfloor \frac{\sqrt{3}}{2}r \right\rfloor$ pixels from each vertical grid line intersecting it. The rectangle thus contains exactly $(1 + 2\lfloor r \rfloor)(1 + 2\left\lfloor \frac{\sqrt{3}}{2}r \right\rfloor)$ pixels.

Let the number of pixels contained by T_i and T'_i be $\mathbb{T}_i$ and $\mathbb{T}'_i$ respectively. We now need to compute the lower bound on $\mathbb{T}'_i$. Each T_i has dimensions $\frac{r}{2} \times \frac{\sqrt{3}}{2}r$. Note that the minimum number of pixels on an axes-parallel line of real length x, aligned with a grid line is $\lceil x - 1 \rceil$. Hence, the minimum number of pixels contained by a rectangle of dimensions $\frac{r}{2} \times \frac{\sqrt{3}}{2}r$ is $\lceil \frac{r}{2} - 1 \rceil \lceil \frac{\sqrt{3}}{2}r - 1 \rceil$ and so $\mathbb{T}_i \geq \frac{1}{2}\lceil \frac{r}{2} - 1 \rceil \lceil \frac{\sqrt{3}}{2}r - 1 \rceil$. We claim that $\mathbb{T}_i - 1 \leq \mathbb{T}'_i \leq \mathbb{T}_i$. To prove the claim we just consider two cases. If the hypotenuse of T_i does not contain any pixel, we have $\mathbb{T}'_i = \mathbb{T}_i$. However, if it contains a pixel, we argue that it cannot contain any other pixel, for if it contains two pixels, we can always draw a right-angled triangle T_R with a hypotenuse that has those two pixels at its end, which implies that the other two sides of T_R will be integral. Since the hypotenuse of T_i (T_R also) makes an angle of $30°$ with the vertical grid line, the ratio of the other two sides of T_R will be $\tan 30° = \frac{1}{\sqrt{3}}$ or its inverse. Hence, both cannot be integral, which implies $\mathbb{T}'_i$ can be at most 1 less than $\mathbb{T}_i$. Thus $\mathbb{T}'_i \geq \frac{1}{2}\lceil \frac{r}{2}-1\rceil \lceil \frac{\sqrt{3}}{2}r - 1\rceil - 1$ and what follows is that –

$$\begin{aligned}
|\mathbb{H}_r| &\leq (1+2\lfloor r\rfloor)(1+2\lfloor \tfrac{\sqrt{3}}{2}r\rfloor) - 4\cdot(\tfrac{1}{2}\lceil \tfrac{r}{2}-1\rceil \lceil \tfrac{\sqrt{3}}{2}r-1\rceil - 1)\\
&\leq (2r+1)(\sqrt{3}r+1) - 4\cdot\tfrac{1}{2}(\tfrac{r}{2}-1)(\tfrac{\sqrt{3}}{2}r-1) + 4 \ [\because \lfloor r\rfloor \leq r \text{ and } -\lceil r\rceil \leq -r]\\
&\leq (2r+1)(\sqrt{3}r+1) - 2(\tfrac{r}{2}-1)(\tfrac{\sqrt{3}}{2}r-1) + 4\\
&= 2\sqrt{3}r^2 + 2r + \sqrt{3}r + 1 - \tfrac{\sqrt{3}}{2}r^2 + \sqrt{3}r + r + 2\\
&= 3\tfrac{\sqrt{3}}{2}r^2 + 3r + 2\sqrt{3}r + 3\\
\Longrightarrow \rho_r &\leq \frac{3\frac{\sqrt{3}}{2}r^2 + 3r + 2\sqrt{3}r + 3}{3\frac{\sqrt{3}}{2}r^2} = 1 + \frac{2(\sqrt{3}+2)}{3r} + \frac{2}{\sqrt{3}r^2} = \hat{\rho}_r \text{ (say)}.
\end{aligned}$$

Now, by elementary calculations, it can be shown that for all potential hexagons with $r > 6$, the following holds: $\hat{\rho}_r < \rho_{\frac{2}{\sqrt{3}}}$. In other words, for every potential hexagon larger than the largest one listed in Table 2, the density is lower than that of the hexagon with radius $\frac{2}{\sqrt{3}}$, which happens to be the second smallest hexagon in that table. We reiterate that these are the only hexagons that need to be considered in the analysis due to Observation 1. From Table 2, it is also evident that the second smallest hexagon has the highest density among those listed, which completes the proof. □

3 Minimum Density

In this section, we present results for identifying hexagons with the minimum density under the constraints of integer-valued and real-valued radii. Hexagons with no pixels have zero density and are excluded from consideration. We focus solely on hexagons that contain at least one pixel.

3.1 Hexagons with Odd Radii

Theorem 4. *In the collection of hexagons with odd radii, the hexagon with radius 9 has the minimum density, and it is unique.*

Table 3. Densities of hexagons with odd radii up to 29.

r	$|\mathbb{H}_r|$	ρ_r	r	$|\mathbb{H}_r|$	ρ_r	r	$|\mathbb{H}_r|$	ρ_r
1	3	1.154701	11	313	0.995651	21	1159	1.011563
3	23	0.983634	13	445	1.013495	23	1357	0.987353
5	67	1.031533	15	571	0.976791	25	1617	0.995814
7	135	1.060439	17	743	0.989553	27	1901	1.003697
9	205	0.974130	19	939	1.001167	29	2209	1.010992

Proof. From Lemma 1, we get

$$|\mathbb{H}_r| = r\left(2\left\lfloor \tfrac{\sqrt{3}}{2}r \right\rfloor + 1\right) + 2\sum_{i=0}^{\lfloor \frac{r}{2} \rfloor}\left(2\lfloor\sqrt{3}i\rfloor + 1\right)$$

$$> r\left(2\left(\tfrac{\sqrt{3}}{2}r - 1\right) + 1\right) + 2\sum_{i=0}^{\lfloor \frac{r}{2} \rfloor}\left(2\left(\sqrt{3}i - 1\right) + 1\right)$$

$$= \sqrt{3}r^2 - r + 2\sum_{i=0}^{\lfloor \frac{r}{2} \rfloor}(2\sqrt{3}i - 1)$$

$$= \sqrt{3}r^2 - r + 2\sum_{i=0}^{\frac{r-1}{2}}(2\sqrt{3}i - 1) \text{ [as r is odd, } \lfloor\tfrac{r}{2}\rfloor = \tfrac{r-1}{2}]$$

$$= \sqrt{3}r^2 - r + \tfrac{4\sqrt{3}}{2}\cdot\tfrac{r-1}{2}\cdot\tfrac{r+1}{2} - 2\cdot\tfrac{r+1}{2}$$

$$= \sqrt{3}r^2 - r + \tfrac{\sqrt{3}}{2}(r^2-1) - r - 1 = \tfrac{3\sqrt{3}}{2}r^2 - 2r - \tfrac{2+\sqrt{3}}{2}$$

$$\implies \rho_r > \frac{\tfrac{3\sqrt{3}}{2}r^2 - 2r - \tfrac{2+\sqrt{3}}{2}}{\tfrac{3\sqrt{3}}{2}r^2} = 1 - \tfrac{4}{3\sqrt{3}r} - \tfrac{2+\sqrt{3}}{3\sqrt{3}r^2} > 0.974131 \ \forall \ r \geq 31.$$

As shown in Table 3, the list of densities for $1 \leq r \leq 29$, the minimum density occurs uniquely for $r = 9$, which, when rounded to the 6th decimal place, is 0.974130. Thus, the proof concludes. □

3.2 Hexagons with Even Radii

Table 4. Densities of hexagons with even radii up to 24.

r	$|\mathbb{H}_r|$	ρ_r	r	$|\mathbb{H}_r|$	ρ_r	r	$|\mathbb{H}_r|$	ρ_r
2	11	1.058475	10	257	0.989193	18	839	0.996701
4	43	1.034419	12	377	1.007690	20	1047	1.007476
6	99	1.058475	14	521	1.023128	22	1279	1.017123
8	161	0.968265	16	655	0.984803	24	1485	0.992321

Theorem 5. *In the collection of hexagons with even radii, the hexagon with radius 8 has the minimum density, and it is unique.*

Proof. We adopt a similar approach to that used in the previous theorem. Using Lemma 2, we prepare the list of densities for all hexagons with even radii up to 24 (Table 4). As observed, the hexagon with radius 8 has the minimum density in this list. For radii 26 and onwards, we show that the density of any even-radius hexagon is greater than this, as outlined below. From Lemma 2,

$$|\mathbb{H}_r| = (r+1)\left(2\left\lfloor\tfrac{\sqrt{3}}{2}r\right\rfloor + 1\right) + 2\sum_{i=0}^{\frac{r}{2}-1}\left(2\lfloor\sqrt{3}i\rfloor + 1\right)$$
$$> (r+1)\left(2\left(\tfrac{\sqrt{3}}{2}r - 1\right) + 1\right) + 2\sum_{i=0}^{\frac{r}{2}-1}\left(2(\sqrt{3}i - 1) + 1\right)$$
$$= (r+1)(\sqrt{3}r - 1) + 2\sum_{i=0}^{\frac{r}{2}-1}(2\sqrt{3}i - 1)$$
$$= \sqrt{3}r^2 - r + \sqrt{3}r - 1 + 4\sqrt{3}\sum_{i=0}^{\frac{r}{2}-1} i - 2\sum_{i=0}^{\frac{r}{2}-1} 1$$
$$= \sqrt{3}r^2 - r + \sqrt{3}r - 1 + 4\sqrt{3}\cdot\tfrac{1}{2}\cdot\left(\tfrac{r}{2} - 1\right)\cdot\tfrac{r}{2} - 2\cdot\tfrac{r}{2}$$
$$= \sqrt{3}r^2 - r + \sqrt{3}r - 1 + \sqrt{3}\left(\tfrac{r^2}{2} - r\right) - r$$
$$= \sqrt{3}r^2 - 2r + \sqrt{3}r - 1 + \tfrac{\sqrt{3}}{2}r^2 - \sqrt{3}r$$
$$= \tfrac{3\sqrt{3}}{2}r^2 - 2r - 1$$
$$\implies \rho_r > \frac{\tfrac{3\sqrt{3}}{2}r^2 - 2r - 1}{\tfrac{3\sqrt{3}}{2}r^2} = 1 - \tfrac{4}{3\sqrt{3}r} - \tfrac{2}{3\sqrt{3}r^2} > 0.968266 > \rho_8 \ \forall\ r \geq 26.$$

Thus, we conclude the proof. □

3.3 Hexagons with Real Radii

To find a hexagon with minimum density, it naturally follows that the candidates will be maximal hexagons with no points on their boundaries. This straightforward observation contrasts with Observation 1 and is used in our analysis.

Theorem 6. *In the collection of hexagons with real radius, the one with minimum density has a radius just less than $1 + \tfrac{1}{\sqrt{3}}$. That is, if the radius is $\tilde{r}$, then $\sup \tilde{r} = 1 + \tfrac{1}{\sqrt{3}}$.*

Proof. Refer to Fig. 4. The number of pixels present in a hexagon is lower bounded by the minimum number of pixels present in the central rectangle R plus the minimum number of pixels present in its two adjacent triangles, T_1 and T_2. The rectangle R is of size $r \times \sqrt{3}r$, thus containing at least $\lceil r-1 \rceil \cdot \lceil \sqrt{3}r - 1 \rceil$ pixels. Either of the triangles has dimensions $\tfrac{r}{2} \times \sqrt{3}r$, thus containing at least $\tfrac{1}{2} \cdot \lceil \tfrac{r}{2} - 1 \rceil \cdot \lceil \sqrt{3}r - 1 \rceil$ pixels. So, we get

$$|\mathbb{H}_r| \geq \lceil r-1 \rceil \cdot \lceil \sqrt{3}r - 1 \rceil + 2\cdot\tfrac{1}{2}\cdot\lceil \tfrac{r}{2} - 1\rceil \cdot \lceil \sqrt{3}r - 1\rceil$$
$$= \lceil \sqrt{3}r - 1 \rceil \cdot \left(\lceil r-1 \rceil + \lceil \tfrac{r}{2} - 1 \rceil\right)$$
$$\geq (\sqrt{3}r - 1)\left(r - 1 + \tfrac{r}{2} - 1\right)$$
$$= (\sqrt{3}r - 1)\left(\tfrac{3r}{2} - 2\right)$$
$$= \tfrac{3\sqrt{3}r^2}{2} - \tfrac{3r}{2} - 2\sqrt{3}r + 2.$$

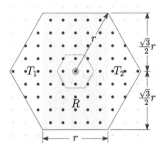

Fig. 4. Hexagons with real radii r. The lowest-density hexagon with radius just less than $1 + \frac{1}{\sqrt{3}}$ is colored red and contains five pixels. (Color figure online)

Table 5. Densities of hexagons with real radius up to 8

r	$|\mathbb{H}_r|$	ρ_r	r	$|\mathbb{H}_r|$	ρ_r	r	$|\mathbb{H}_r|$	ρ_r
$\frac{2}{\sqrt{3}}$	3	0.866025	$\frac{4}{\sqrt{3}}$	11	0.793857	$2 + \frac{2}{\sqrt{3}}$	23	0.889528
$1 + \frac{1}{\sqrt{3}}$	5	0.773503	$2 + \frac{1}{\sqrt{3}}$	17	0.985031	$2\sqrt{3}$	27	0.866025
2	9	0.866025	3	21	0.898100	$3 + \frac{1}{\sqrt{3}}$	33	0.992520
						$2 + \sqrt{3}$	37	1.022480
						4	41	0.986307

r	$|\mathbb{H}_r|$	ρ_r	r	$|\mathbb{H}_r|$	ρ_r	r	$|\mathbb{H}_r|$	ρ_r	r	$|\mathbb{H}_r|$	ρ_r
$3 + \frac{2}{\sqrt{3}}$	43	0.958820	$4 + \frac{2}{\sqrt{3}}$	67	0.970546	$5 + \frac{2}{\sqrt{3}}$	99	1.005934	$6 + \frac{2}{\sqrt{3}}$	135	1.015077
$4 + \frac{1}{\sqrt{3}}$	47	0.863411	$3 + \frac{4}{\sqrt{3}}$	71	0.969428	$4 + \frac{4}{\sqrt{3}}$	103	0.995885	$5 + \frac{4}{\sqrt{3}}$	139	1.001381
$\frac{8}{\sqrt{3}}$	51	0.920152	$5 + \frac{1}{\sqrt{3}}$	75	0.928012	$6 + \frac{1}{\sqrt{3}}$	107	0.951985	$4 + 2\sqrt{3}$	143	0.987937
$3 + \sqrt{3}$	61	1.120598	$4 + \sqrt{3}$	79	0.925455	$5 + \sqrt{3}$	111	0.987573	$7 + \frac{1}{\sqrt{3}}$	147	0.985441
5	65	1.000740	$\frac{10}{\sqrt{3}}$	83	0.958401	$4 + \frac{5}{\sqrt{3}}$	115	0.933291	$6 + \sqrt{3}$	151	0.972155
			$3 + \frac{5}{\sqrt{3}}$	93	1.032951	$\frac{12}{\sqrt{3}}$	119	0.954232	$5 + \frac{5}{\sqrt{3}}$	155	0.959143
			6	97	1.037092	7	133	1.044729	8	159	0.956236

Hence,

$$\rho_r \geq \frac{\frac{3\sqrt{3}r^2}{2} - \frac{3r}{2} - 2\sqrt{3}r + 2}{\frac{3\sqrt{3}}{2}r^2} = 1 - \frac{4 + \sqrt{3}}{3r} + \frac{4}{3\sqrt{3}r^2} > 0.773504 \ \forall \ r > 8. \quad (5)$$

Now, refer to Fig. 4 and Table 5. Observe the hexagon with five pixels and radius just less than $1 + \frac{1}{\sqrt{3}}$, i.e., with radius $\tilde{r} = 1 + \frac{1}{\sqrt{3}} - |\varepsilon|$, where $|\varepsilon| \to 0$. Its density is

$$\rho_{\tilde{r}} = \frac{5}{\frac{3\sqrt{3}}{2}\tilde{r}^2} < 0.773504. \quad (6)$$

Combining (5) and (6), we get the result. □

4 Conclusion and Future Work

As mentioned in Sect. 1, we have studied standard hexagons, which are regular hexagons with two opposite sides parallel to the x-axis. We imposed the additional constraint that their centers must be integer points. Under this constraint, we demonstrated that the maximum-density hexagon with an integer radius is uniquely attained for unit radius. On the contrary, the minimum-density hexagon with an integer radius has a radius of 8. For hexagons with real radii, the maximum density occurs for a radius of $\frac{2}{\sqrt{3}}$, and the minimum density occurs for a radius whose supremum is $1 + \frac{1}{\sqrt{3}}$.

The following questions arise naturally and are more complex than those addressed in this paper:

1. What are the maximum and minimum densities of hexagons when their centers are allowed to be real points, rather than just integer points?
2. Hexagons are not ℓ_p-balls, but they can be approximated by ℓ_p-balls. What would be the corresponding results for such approximations? This raises an intriguing question that connects hexagons to the well-known classes of ℓ_p-balls.

References

1. Basu, N.G., Majumder, S., Hon, W.K.: On finding the maximum and minimum density axis-parallel regions in $\mathbb{R}^d$. Fund. Inform. **152**(1), 1–12 (2017)
2. Basu, N.G., Bhowmick, P., Majumder, S.: On density extrema for digital discs. In: Barneva, R.P., Brimkov, V.E., Nordo, G. (eds.) IWCIA 2022. LNCS, vol. 13348, pp. 56–70. Springer, Cham (2022). https://doi.org/10.1007/978-3-031-23612-9_4
3. Basu, N.G., Majumder, S., Bhowmick, P.: On density extrema for digital ℓ_1-balls in 2D and 3D. In: Pankratov, D. (ed.) Proceedings of the 35th Canadian Conference on Computational Geometry, CCCG 2023, Concordia University, Montreal, Quebec, Canada, 31 July–4 August 2023, pp. 313–319 (2023)
4. Blake, G.R., Hartge, K.: Particle density. Methods Soil Anal. Part 1 Phys. Mineral. Methods **5**, 377–382 (1986)
5. Cheng, V.: Understanding density and high density. In: Designing High-Density Cities, pp. 37–51. Routledge, London (2009)
6. Basu, N.G., Bhowmick, P., Majumder, S.: On density of grid points in ℓ_∞-balls. In: Proceedings of 3rd International Conference on Mathematical Modeling and Computational Science (ICMMCS 2023), 24–25 February 2023, Tamilnadu, India. Springer, Singapore (2023)
7. Hammarhjelm, G.: The density and minimal gap of visible points in some planar quasicrystals. Discret. Math. **345**(12), 113074 (2022)
8. Hasnip, P.J., Refson, K., Probert, M.I.J., Yates, J.R., Clark, S.J., Pickard, C.J.: Density functional theory in the solid state. In: Phil. Trans. R. Soc. A. Roy. Soc. (2014).https://doi.org/10.1098/rsta.2013.0270
9. Liberti, L., Lavor, C., Maculan, N., Mucherino, A.: Euclidean distance geometry and applications. SIAM Rev. **56**(1), 3–69 (2014). https://doi.org/10.1137/120875909

10. Majumder, S., Bhattacharya, B.B.: On the density and discrepancy of a 2D point set with applications to thermal analysis of VLSI chips. Inf. Process. Lett. **107**(5), 177–182 (2008). https://doi.org/10.1016/j.ipl.2008.02.011, https://www.sciencedirect.com/science/article/pii/S0020019008000628
11. Rakun, J., Stajnko, D., Zazula, D.: Plant size estimation based on the construction of high-density corresponding points using image registration. Comput. Electron. Agric. **157**, 288–304 (2019)
12. Wang, J., Tan, Y.: Efficient Euclidean distance transform using perpendicular bisector segmentation. In: CVPR 2011, pp. 1625–1632 (2011). https://doi.org/10.1109/CVPR.2011.5995644
13. Wang, S., Li, Q., Zhao, C., Zhu, X., Yuan, H., Dai, T.: Extreme clustering - a clustering method via density extreme points. Inf. Sci. **542**, 24–39 (2021)
14. Wang, Y., Wang, D., Pang, W., Miao, C., Tan, A., Zhou, Y.: A systematic density-based clustering method using anchor points. Neurocomputing **400**, 352–370 (2020)

Dilution with Digital Microfluidic Biochips: Unbalanced Split-Error Correction with SIMOP

Nilina Bera[1](✉), Subhashis Majumder[1], and Bhargab B. Bhattacharya[2]

[1] Heritage Institute of Technology, Kolkata 700 107, India
{nilina.bera,subhashis.majumder}@heritageit.edu
[2] Ashoka University, Sonipat, Haryana 131029, India

Abstract. The advent of microfluidics has transformed the entire ecospace of bio-chemical laboratory protocols by enabling their execution on compact Lab-on-Chip (LoC) devices. This technology finds versatile applications in automated clinical diagnostics and point-of-care healthcare procedures. Digital Microfluidic Biochips (DMFB) are special LoC devices that manipulate micro- or nano-scale fluid droplets using electric fields to perform fundamental fluidic operations such as transport, mixing, and splitting, which are essential for executing assays. However, inaccuracies often occur during the mixing and splitting process due to the unbalanced splitting of droplets. Addressing these errors is critical for ensuring assay accuracy and reducing costs associated with stock solutions and reagents. This paper addresses the problem of split-error correction within the context of a dilution assay, utilizing a Simulation-guided Optimization Procedure (SIMOP). Split errors are categorized as critical or non-critical, and only critical errors require correction to achieve accurate dilution results. The study analyzes the impact of unbalanced split errors on target sample concentrations and presents automated error-correction techniques integrated with the SIMOP algorithm.

Keywords: Algorithmic microfluidics · Biochips · Error-correction · Sample preparation

1 Introduction

DMFB has significantly impacted clinical diagnostics in the healthcare sector in recent years [11,12,15,16]. These biochips provide a versatile platform for executing a wide range of laboratory protocols while requiring a minimal amount of stock solutions. Their applications span critical areas encompassing protein and DNA analysis, point-of-care diagnostics, enzymatic assessments, and other essential practices.

In DMFBs, discrete fluid droplets of fixed volume are manipulated on a substrate using a $2D$ array of electrodes, employing the electrowetting on dielectric (EWOD) principle [15]. These chips require minimal human intervention to precisely control and move droplets across the microelectrode array, providing benefits such as increased sensitivity, portability, reduced cost, and lower consumption [11,12].

In a dilution assay, droplets undergo a series of mix-split steps to achieve specific concentration factors (*CF*s) for a fluid sample. To ensure effective sample preparation [13,14], a sequence of balanced (1 : 1) mix-split operations is used, where the two droplets produced after each split should ideally have equal volumes. For example, consider two droplets with unit volumes (V_1, V_2) and *CF*s (C_1, C_2) mixed and split in sequence to generate two droplets of the same size. The *CF* of the new droplets is calculated as the weighted average ($\frac{C_1 \times V_1 + C_2 \times V_2}{V_1 + V_2}$) of the parent droplets [18–21]. This work investigates the issue of unbalanced splitting and proposes an error correction method to achieve precise target *CF*s using SIMOP [1,2]. The SIMOP framework facilitates reaching a target concentration following a sequence of (1 : 1) mix-split steps, while optimizing multiple objectives based on user-defined priorities. In this paper, we study how the given target concentration can be restored while executing SIMOP even in the presence of multiple unbalanced split-errors.

1.1 Unbalanced Split-Errors: Critical and Non-critical

In a DMFB, an unbalanced split operation on a droplet often causes an error that affects the accuracy of the running assay. Detailed analysis of such errors for a dilution assay can be found in the literature [18–21]. However, no studies have been made in the context of SIMOP algorithm. Consider an example where we need to achieve the dilution of a sample with the target CF $C_t = \frac{1}{2^9} (= \frac{1}{512})$ and its complement $C'_t = \frac{2^9-1}{2^9} (= \frac{511}{512})$ within $n = 9$ (1 : 1) mix-split steps. For $C_t = \frac{1}{512}$ we recursively dilute a sample S with concentration $2^9 = 512$ (considering only the numerator for brevity, as the denominator here will always be 512) with equal volume of buffer (B). In this process, sample concentration decreases exponentially, halving with each dilution step. After $n = 9$ cycles of mixing and balanced splitting, concentration reduces from 512 to 1. The SIMOP sequences to reach the target numerators 1 and 511 in the dilution step 9 are shown in Fig. 1.

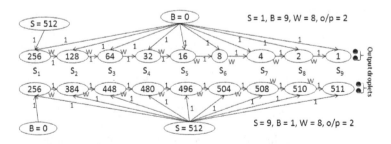

Fig. 1. Reach $C_t = \frac{1}{512}$ and complement $C'_t = \frac{511}{512}$ (8*W*) using SIMOP dilutions

In dilution assay to study impact of the volumetric split error for each of the two targets $\frac{1}{512}$ and $\frac{511}{512}$, we perform eight different experiments (tests), where we inject an unbalanced split error 10% into each of the eight dilution steps, one step at a time. The ith trial introduces the error in the ith dilution step. The deviations ($|finalCF - targetCF|$) obtained in eight trials ($T1$ to $T8$) are illustrated in Fig. 2. In the x-axis of this figure, as we progress from trial $T1$ to $T8$, deviation values are observed to have reduced from 0.100 ($T1$) to 0.048 ($T8$). For both fractions $\frac{1}{512}$ and $\frac{511}{512}$, deviation values are same but opposite in sign. We further extended our analysis to run the set of targets $\frac{1}{32}, \frac{31}{32}, \frac{1}{256}, \frac{255}{256}, \frac{1}{1024}$ and $\frac{1023}{1024}$ (for $n = 5, 8, 10$ steps) against $+10\%$ volume error to observe that the final CFs for the said target set can be generated with the same deviations as shown in Fig. 2. This means that if we correct the split-error for any one combination, say $\frac{1}{512}$ or $\frac{511}{512}$, then the same correction rule can be applied for all the other targets following the same method (likewise for $\frac{1}{2^n}$ and $\frac{2^n-1}{2^n}$ the number of mix-splits, is n).

An unbalanced split is considered non-critical (non-CE), if the resulting error in the final concentration is smaller than the inherent accuracy threshold of the dilution algorithm. Conversely, occurrence of an error that exceeds this accuracy level is deemed critical (CE) [18–21]. Critical errors have a significant impact on the target concentration and when detected by sensors, require corrective actions. For instance, if volume errors (e.g., 0.01, 0.02, 0.03, 0.05, 0.07, 0.1) occur in the reaction path and the final CF deviates such that $|C_{final} - C_{target}| \geq 0.5$, this concentration factor is classified to be critically deviated; else, the deviation is a non-critical one.

We have assessed a typical SIMOP target $\frac{96}{256}$ where the number of steps $n = 8$ and Sample(S)$=2^8=256$. In the reaction path, only one waste (1W) droplet is generated to reach the final CF. Critical and non-critical deviations [1,2] as represented in Fig. 3 indicate that the final CFs for SIMOP target $\frac{96}{256}$(1W) achieved a non-critical deviation (< 0.5) when a split-error 3% is applied. As we increase the split-error to 5%, 7%, and 10%, the final CF values become critical even when the deviation thresholds are 1.0, 1.5, and 2.0.

Our goal is to perform comprehensive simulations on SIMOP focusing on corrective strategies such as error cancellation, error collapsing, and/or error neutralization, based on the impact of split errors on target-CFs, as detailed below.

2 Equivalence of Single and Multiple Split-Errors

The sample dilution process involves n mix-split operations in sequence, where at any stage one/more unbalanced splits could occur. Considering their impact on the target CF, multiple split errors may be thought of as equivalent to a single split error that occurs at some stage in the SIMOP sequence.

Definition 1. *Two unbalanced split errors, $\in_1$ and $\in_2$ is said to be equivalent if they result in the same final CF when either error is present.*

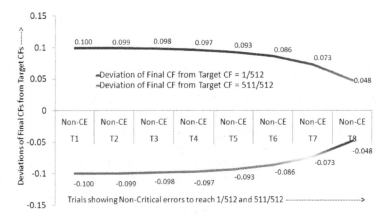

Fig. 2. Non-critical deviations to reach $C_t = \frac{1}{512}$ and $C'_t = \frac{511}{512}$ (8W)

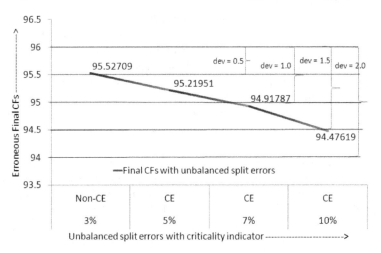

Fig. 3. Final CFs to reach $C_t = \frac{96}{256}$ (1W) with 3%, 5%, 7% and 10% split-errors

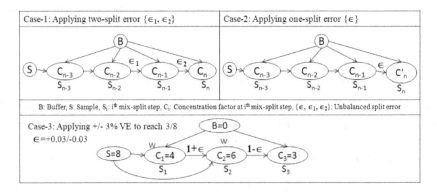

Fig. 4. Unbalanced split-error occurring at distinct steps of the reaction path

The concept is demonstrated with examples presented in Fig. 4. Case-1 of Fig. 4 demonstrates multiple unbalanced split-errors ($\in_1, \in_2$) occurring at steps S_{n-2} and S_{n-1} along the reaction path. As a result of the split error at S_{n-2}, $C_{intermediate}$ and output droplets at step S_{n-1} are determined as follows:

$$C_{n-1} = \frac{C_{n-2} \times (1+\in_1) + B}{1+(1+\in_1)} \text{ where } C_{n-2} = \frac{C_{n-3}+B}{2}, V_{n-1} = 1 + \frac{\in_1}{2}$$

Next, when the volume error $\in_2$ occurring at step S_{n-1}, $C_{intermediate}$ and volume of output droplets at step S_n become:

$$C_n = \frac{C_{n-1} \times (V_{n-1}+\in_2) + B}{V_{n-1} \times (1+\in_2) + 1}, V_n = \frac{V_{n-1} \times (1+\in_2) + 1}{2}$$

The analysis of a single volume-error $\in$ occurring at step S_{n-1} is illustrated in Case-2 of Fig. 4. The $C_{intermediate}$ and volume of droplets after step S_{n-1} will be $C_{n-1} = \frac{C_{n-2}+B}{2}$ and $V_{n-1}=1$, where $C_{n-2}=\frac{C_{n-3}+B}{2}$. Eventually, CF and volume of the output droplets resulting in: $C'_n = \frac{C_{n-1}\times(1+\in)+B}{1+(1+\in)}$ and $V'_n = 1 + \frac{\in}{2}$.

The multiple errors ($\in_1, \in_2$) are stated as equivalent to single error $\in$ if $C_n = C'_n$. This analysis leads to the following lemma.

Lemma 1. *Multiple split errors can always be consolidated into a single equivalent split error, which has the same impact on the final concentration error of the target droplet as the combined effect of the individual errors.*

Table 1. Error equivalence for different final CFs for $n = 8, 9, 10$ mix-splits

Target CF	Dilution Steps (multiple)	$\in_1, \in_2$	Dilution Step (single)	$\in$	Final CF Error
$\frac{59}{256}$ (2W)	4, 6	+10%, −10%	6	+10%	0.12294
$\frac{201}{256}$ (3W)	2, 4, 6	+7%, −7%, +7%	2	+7%	0.31999
$\frac{397}{512}$ (2W)	6, 7	−5%, +5%	6	+5%	0.04138
$\frac{423}{512}$ (3W)	5, 6, 7	+3%, −3%, +3%	6	+3%	0.037221

The results presented in the above lemma help to reduce the simulation experiment size. Table 1 illustrates the equivalence of a single error (in the 5th column) to a double or triple error (in the 3rd column) for accuracy levels $n = 8$, 9, and 10, generating sets of 255 fractions (for $n = 8$), 511 fractions (for $n = 9$), and 1023 fractions (for $n = 10$) of SIMOP. In the same table, target CFs are represented in Column 1. Column 2 indicates the locations (i.e., step numbers) where double or triple errors occurred. Column 3 provides the corresponding unbalanced split-error percentages. Columns 4 and 5 report the dilution step number and the percentage of the single split error, respectively. The final column displays the error in the final CFs for both scenarios.

We further extended our analysis of multiple and single error equivalence to generate target CF, $C_t = \frac{3}{8}$ where the sample is $S = 2^n = 2^3 = 8$. Case-2 of Fig. 4 shows that both steps S_1 and S_2 generate unbalanced split-errors (say, 3%) affecting later steps S_2 and S_3, respectively. We performed simulation to add multiple errors $(1+\epsilon)$, $(1-\epsilon)$ at steps S_2 and S_3 in sequence and computed erroneous final CFs. In addition, we added $+\epsilon$ and $-\epsilon$ separately at the final step S_3 to generate final CF C_3 with error as shown below:

1. S_1: $C_1 = \frac{S \times 1 + B \times 1}{2}$, $V_1 = 1$, $V_B = V_S = 1$.

2. S_2 with application of $(1+\epsilon)$: $C_2 = \frac{C_1 \times (1+\epsilon) + S \times 1}{(1+\epsilon)+1}$, $V_2 = 1 + \frac{\epsilon}{2}$.
   We can further expand $C_2 = \frac{\frac{S+B}{2} \times (1+\epsilon) + S}{2+\epsilon} = \frac{S \times (3+\epsilon)}{2 \times (2+\epsilon)}$, where CF of buffer $= B = 0$.

3. S_3 with application of $(1-\epsilon)$: $C_3 = \frac{C_2 \times (1-\epsilon) + B \times 1}{(1-\epsilon)+1} = \frac{\frac{S \times (3+\epsilon)}{2 \times (2+\epsilon)} \times (1-\epsilon)}{2-\epsilon} = \frac{S \times (3 - 2 \times \epsilon - \epsilon^2)}{2 \times (2^2 - \epsilon^2)}$.

4. Applying +3% and −3% at mix-split steps S_1 and S_2 respectively, we generate final CF at step-S_3,
   i.e., $C_3 = \frac{8 \times (3 - 2 \times 0.03 - (0.03)^2)}{2 \times (4 - (0.03)^2)}$
   Thus we have final CF computed as $C_3 = \frac{23.5128}{7.9982} = 2.93976$ with deviation 0.0602386.

5. Single split-error −3% applied at step-S_2 affecting higher step S_3, in turn generating final CF,
   $C_3 = \frac{C_2 \times (1-\epsilon) + B}{(1-\epsilon)+1} = \frac{6 \times 0.97}{1.97} = 2.95431$ with deviation $= 0.04569$.

6. Single split-error +3% applied at step-S_2 affecting higher step S_3, in turn generating final CF,
   $C_3 = \frac{6 \times (1+\epsilon) + B}{(1+\epsilon)+1} = \frac{6 \times 1.03}{2.03} = 3.04433$ with deviation $= 0.04433$.

From the results obtained after applying multiple errors $[(1+0.03), (1-0.03)]$ against single error $(1+0.03)$ or $(1-0.03)$, it is observed that the deviation computed for each of the single errors (0.04569, 0.04433) is less than that (i.e., 0.0602386) computed for multiple errors. Thus, in order to identify a single-error equivalent of a multiple error, a suitable error site and an appropriate value of error percentage should be found.

3 Error Correction for the Target-CF

We illustrate here how in SIMOP algorithm, to reach a typical target $C_t = \frac{824}{1024}$, a digraph is created following the gradual convergence scheme. Based on the droplet demand, during the split operation either both droplets can be transported to a higher mixing step or one-unit-volume can be discarded and treated as waste. This left-over droplet bears the signature of an unbalanced split-error, if any, that may cause critical or non-critical errors in the final CFs generated at the last step.

In the proposed error correction method, erroneous fluidic operations are not discarded. We leverage the observation that during a mix-split operation while generating two droplets, a volume error affects both the daughter-droplets. To correct multiple split-errors when critical error arises, we avoid repeating split with error. Instead, we execute a duplicate reaction path involving discarded droplet alongside the primary dilution path as in [21]. By subsequently mixing a suitable set of droplets generated from these paths, concentration errors cancel each other out when the target is achieved. Theoretical and experimental results for $C_t = \frac{824}{1024}$ (including both higher and lower sides of digraph of Fig. 5) are presented below.

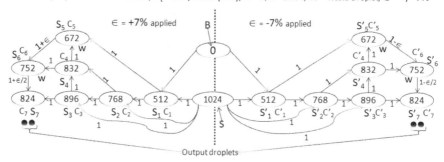

Cancellation of concentration error at the target, C_t = 824/1024 (2W), Single-step unbalanced split error

Fig. 5. Cancellation of unbalanced split-error at the target $C_t = \frac{824}{1024}$ (2W)

Consider Fig. 5. Two digraphs are presented with sample (S) and buffer (B) (the dotted line in the middle of the figure). We focus on the sample dilution reaching desired target $CF = 824$ shown in peripheral region of both digraphs. The digraph on the left tends to reach the desired target with a positive volume error $(1+\in)$ applied at Step-S_6 caused by the droplet generated at Step-S_5. Step-S_6, in turn, generates one-unit-volume droplet that further produces unbalanced-split-error $1 + \frac{\in}{2}$ at Step-S_7. In Fig. 5, the digraph on the right side is created in a similar way to reach the target with negative errors $(1-\in)$ and $1 - \frac{\in}{2}$ applied at Step-S'_6 and Step-S'_7, respectively.

Target $CF = \frac{C_i}{2^n}$, $n = 10$ is generated considering $\{S_1, S_2, S_3, \ldots, S_6, S_7, S_8\}$ representing a sequence of $(1:1)$ dilution steps producing particular target CF running $SIMOP$ [1,2]. If we denote $i = 6$, then steps $\{S_6, S_7, S_8\}$ becomes $\{S_i, S_{i+1}, S_{i+2}\}$. Similarly, steps $\{S'_6, S'_7, S'_8\}$ can be replaced by $\{S'_i, S'_{i+1}, S'_{i+2}\}$.

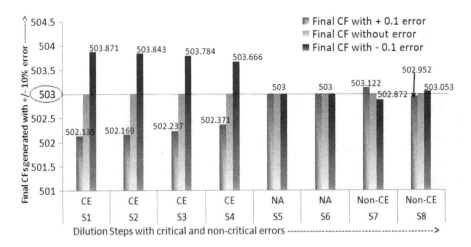

Fig. 6. Cancellation of unbalanced split-error to reach target $C_t = \frac{503}{512}$ (6W)

We have carried out an exhaustive simulation on all dilution steps on the digraph with $\pm \epsilon = \pm 0.1$ to reach the desired target CF $C_t = \frac{503}{512}$ cancelling out positive and negative errors. It is observed that for four critical steps (S_1, S_2, S_3, and S_4) and two non-critical steps (S_7 and S_8), if fractional error $\pm \epsilon$ is introduced one-step-at-a-time, then for all cases, the CF generated at the last dilution step in each case can be cancelled out as illustrated in Fig. 6.

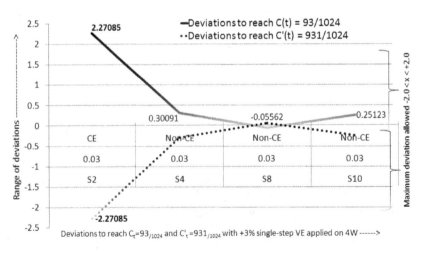

Fig. 7. Performance $+3\%$ VE on $C_t = \frac{93}{1024}$ (4W) and $C'_t = \frac{931}{1024}$ (4W) applied at single step

4 Correcting the Effects of Multiple Split-Errors

Concentration errors on SIMOP sequences can be neutralized by unbalanced splits applied at multiple dilution steps as revealed in Fig. 7. In this figure, target CFs $\frac{93}{1024}$ and its complement $\frac{931}{1024}$ are considered with four waste droplets generating an unbalanced split-error ($\pm \epsilon = \pm 0.03$) at steps S_2, S_4, S_8 and S_{10}. Rigorous analysis revealed that it is step S_2 that becomes critical, and the error is neutralized at higher steps S_4, S_8 and S_{10}.

Consider Fig. 8 showing SIMOP dilution tree of $C_t = \frac{93}{1024}$ (4W) with $+/-$ 3% VE applied at four different steps.

Figure 9 presents performance $+3\%$ VE on $C_t = \frac{93}{1024}$ (4W) and $C'_t = \frac{931}{1024}$ (4W) applied at multiple steps.

Figure 10 shows the application of $+/-$ 3% VE on $C_t = \frac{93}{1024}$ (4W) at single and multiple steps.

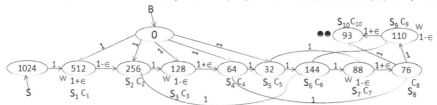

Fig. 8. SIMOP dilution tree of $C_t = \frac{93}{1024}$ (4W) with $+3\%$ VE applied at multiple steps

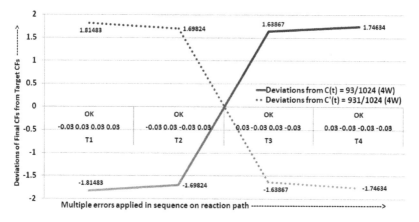

Fig. 9. Performance $+3\%$ VE on $C_t = \frac{93}{1024}$ (4W) and $C'_t = \frac{931}{1024}$ (4W) applied at multiple steps

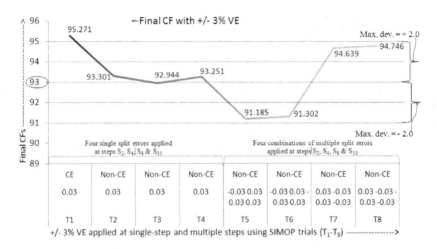

Fig. 10. Application of $+/-3\%$ VE on $C_t = \frac{93}{1024}$ (4W) at single and multiple steps

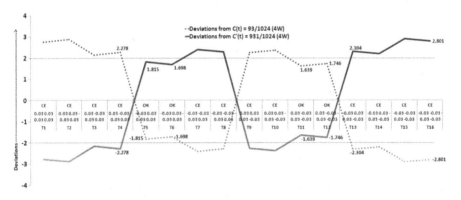

Fig. 11. Application of multiple mix-split errors on the reaction paths of $C_t = \frac{93}{1024}$ and $C'_t = \frac{931}{1024}$ (4W)

Consider Fig. 11 representing combinations of volume errors applied at multiple steps on the reaction paths of $C_t = \frac{93}{1024}$ and $C'_t = \frac{931}{1024}$ (4W).

5 Conclusion

In this paper, we have analyzed the impact of volumetric split-error on dilution assays performed using the SIMOP algorithm on a DMFB. Our analysis leads to a fault-tolerant technique that guarantees that the target CF remains accurate, even when multiple split errors are present. In particular, critical split errors are corrected to ensure error-free dilution. The impact of cumulative multiple errors on target CFs is investigated, and how they can be neutralized is demonstrated. The study establishes the capability of SIMOP algorithm for achieving error-free dilution assays with DMFBs.

References

1. Bera, N., Majumder, S., Das, S., Mukherjee, S., Aryani, N., Bhattacharya, B.B.: SIMOP: a SIMulation-Guided OPtimization mechanism for sample preparation with digital microfluidic biochip. SN Comput. Sci. **2**(2), 1–20 (2021). https://doi.org/10.1007/s42979-021-00506-x
2. Bera, N.: Intelligent technologies: concepts, applications, and future directions - Studies in algorithms and architectures for sample preparation with digital microfluidics. Springer Nature, eBook ISBN - 978-981-19-1021-0, Print ISBN - 978-981-19-1020-3 (2022). https://doi.org/10.1007/978-981-19-1021-0
3. Chakrabarty, K., Xu, T.: Digital Microfluidic Biochips: Design and Optimization. CRC Press (2010)
4. Theis, W., Urbanski, J.P., Thorsen, T., Amarasinghe, S.: Abstraction layers for scalable microfluidic biocomputing. Nat. Comput. W. **7**(2), 255–275 (2008)
5. Roy, S., Bhattacharya, B.B., Chakrabarty, K.: Optimization of dilution and mixing of biochips. IEEE TCAD **29**(11), 1696–1708 (2010)
6. Roy, S., Bhattacharya, B.B., Chakrabarty, K.: Waste-aware dilution and mixing of biochemical samples with digital microfluidic biochips. In: Proceedings of the IEEE/ACM DATE, pp. 1059–1064 (2011)
7. Huang, J.D., Liu, C.H., Chiang, T.W.: Reactant minimization during sample preparation on digital microfluidic biochips using skewed mixing trees. In: Proceedings of IEEE/ACM ICCAD, pp. 377–384 (2012)
8. Bera, N., Majumder, S., Bhattacharya, B.B.: Simulation-based method for optimum microfluidic sample dilution using weighted mix-split of droplets. IET Comput. Digit. Tech. **10**(3), 119–127 (2016)
9. Huang, J.D., Liu, C.H., Lin, H.S.: Reactant and Waste minimization in multitarget sample preparation on digital microfluidic biochips. IEEE Trans. Comput. Aided Des. Integr. Circuits Syst. **32**(10), 1484–1494 (2013)
10. Paik, P., Pamula, V.K., Pollack, M.G., Fair, R.B.: Electrowetting-based droplet mixers for microfluidic systems. Lab Chip **3**(1), 28–33 (2003)
11. Abdelgawad, M., Wheeler, A.R.: The digital revolution?: a new paradigm for digital microfluidic biochips. Adv. Mater. **21**(8), 920–925 (2009)
12. Alistar, M., Maftei, E., Pop, P., Madsen, J.: Synthesis of biochemical applications on digital microfluidic biochips with operation variability. In: Proceedings of the Symposium on Design Test Integration and Packaging of MEMS/MOEMS, pp. 350–357 (2010)
13. Hsieh, YL., Ho, TY., Chakrabarty, K.: On-chip biochemical sample preparation using digital microfluidics. In: IEEE Biomedical Circuits and Systems Conference (BioCAS), pp. 297–300 (2011)
14. Hsieh, YL., Ho, TY., Chakrabarty, K.: Design methodology for sample preparation on digital microfluidic biochips. In: IEEE 30th International Conference on Computer Design (ICCD), pp. 189–194 (2012)
15. Paik, P., Pamula, V.K., Pollack, M.G., Fair, R.B.: Electrowetting-based droplet mixers for microfluidic systems. Lab Chip **3**(1), 28–33 (2003)
16. Srinivasan, V., Pamula, V K., Pollack, M G., Fair, R B.: Clinical diagnostics on human whole blood, plasma, serum, urine, saliva, sweat, and tears on a digital microfluidic platform. In: Proceedings of MicroTAS, pp. 1287–1290 (2003)
17. Bera, N., Majumder, S., Bhattacharya, B.B.: Analysis of concentration errors in sample dilution algorithms on a digital microfluidics biochip. In: Proceedings of the ICAA LNCS 8321, pp. 89–100, Kolkata, India (2014)

18. Poddar, S., Bhattacharya, B.B.: Error-Tolerant Biochemical Sample Preparation with Microfluidic Lab-on-Chip. CRC Press, Boca Raton, Florida, USA (2022)
19. Poddar, S., Wille, R., Rahaman, H., Bhattacharya, B.B.: Error-oblivious sample preparation with digital microfluidic lab-on-chip. IEEE TCAD **38**(10), 1886–1899 (2019)
20. Poddar, S., Wille, R., Rahaman, H., Bhattacharya, B.B.: Dilution with digital microfluidic biochips: how unbalanced splits corrupt target concentration. arXiv. CoRR abs arXiv:1901.00353 (2019)
21. Poddar, S., Ghoshal, S., Chakrabarty, K. and Bhattacharya, B.B.: Error-correcting sample preparation with cyberphysical digital microfluidic lab-on-chip. ACM TODAES, vol. 22, pp. 1–29 (2016)

Track B

Social Evolution of Published Text and the Emergence of Artificial Intelligence Through Large Language Models and the Problem of Toxicity and Bias

Arifa Khan[1(✉)], P. Saravanan[1], and S. K. Venkatesan[2]

[1] School of Management, SRM Institute of Science and Technology, Katankalattur, Tamil Nadu 603203, India
{ak7641,saravanp2}@srmist.edu.in

[2] CQRL Bits, S2, 23, Vignesh Avenue, Selaiyur, Chennai, Tamil Nadu 600073, India
suki@cqrl.in

Abstract. We provide a bird's eye view of the rapid developments in AI and Deep Learning that has led to the path-breaking emergence of AI in Large Language Models. The aim of this study is to place all these developments in a pragmatic broader historical social perspective without any exaggerations while at the same time without any pessimism that created the AI winter in the 1970s to 1990s. We also at the same time point out toxicity, bias, memorization, sycophancy, logical inconsistencies, hallucinations, context window that exist just as a warning to the overly optimistic. We critically examine the ongoing challenges, such as toxicity, bias, memorization, sycophancy, logical inconsistencies, and hallucinations in AI systems, while also appreciating the remarkable progress that has been made. We note here that just as this emergence of AI seems to occur at a threshold point in the number of neural connections or weights, it has also been observed that human brain and especially the cortex region is nothing special or extraordinary but simply a case of scaled-up version of the primate brain and that even the human intelligence seems like an emergent phenomenon of scale.

Keywords: Social evolution · Large Language Models (LLM) · Deep Learning · Low-latency · High throughput

> "Leave any bigotry in your quarters, there's no room for it on the bridge."
> – *Capt. Kirk, Star Trek*

1 Introduction

Recent years have seen rapid developments in the field of Artificial Intelligence (AI), mainly due to developments in Deep Learning and Large Language Models (LLMs). This study aims to provide a comprehensive overview of these rapid developments, contextualizing them within the broader historical and social perspective of human society.

Humans like the CPU have low latency, an important survival strategy early on from insects to fishes to amphibians to reptiles to warm blooded birds and mammals. The sensors produce signals to the neural system which produces an action response within a fraction of a second. However, the downside of this is poor memory retention. Despite popular belief, humans cannot do many things. They cannot fly, they cannot recall exactly what they did this day last year at 3:23 PM, unless they keep a journal of their activity. It is precisely for this reason that humans began to keep notes about their observation, due to the lack of this memory quotient. Drawing pictures as in cave paintings and later on the development of writing, initially as ideograpms and later on as phonemes of speech was invented by traders in Phoenecia in what is modern day Lebanon and Syria.

The creation of libraries and books in ancient Babylon, Library of Alexandria and the Nalanda University are a testimony to this limitation. Humans can recall the past and do story telling from the past (displaced in time and space), a facility that they obtain from their scaled version of their primate brain [2]. But still it was not sufficient for their social progress and development, necessitating the storage of written manuscripts.

The long scrolls that gave way to codex pages and Guttenberg's printing press, produced first the bulky books, but eventually smaller portable books and magazines/ journals. This heralded the modern age of books and magazines/journals. The first English-language newspaper, Corrant out of Italy, Germany, etc., was published in Amsterdam in 1620.

There were many trade journals in Europe, but the first important serial publication was the Philosophical Transactions published by Henry Oldenburg in 1665–1677 as a private enterprise till his death. These publications and the publications of Robert Boyle, Robert Hooke's laid the foundation for Isaac Newton's work to follow.

Public disclosure of these over the following centuries caused rapid scientific development by naturally intelligent human beings - discovery of Calculus by Leibnitz and Newton, electricity by Michael Faraday. Leibnitz discovery of chain rule in calculating derivative is an important corner stone for backpropagation in neural networks. In the next century, the application of electro-magnetism created novel utilities such as the Telephone by Graham Bell and the wireless communication by Jagdish Bose, which formed the basis of all the communication revolution we see today.

It was not until the invention of Personal Computer, the Internet and Wikipedia that open access became possible under one umbrella (one URL). Internet Archive [3] began to archive the whole of internet through the many decades that followed.

There were many champions of open source and open data, some consumed by its passion and zeal like Aaron Swartz [4]. They created the world without barriers like John Lennon's dream of the world without boundaries. It all started with Guttenberg's printing press and now we are in its advanced digital avatars.

Eventually it became possible to put all the text data under one roof, like the Colossal, cleaned version of Common Crawl (C4 dataset) that became the input for generating text-to-text-transfer-transformers (T5) LLMs, such as T5-XXL, but that was just the beginning.

2 Markov Chain, Shannon and the N-gram Revolution

It was Andrey Markov in 1906 who first proposed what is now known as the Markov chain, to prove the central limit theorem [5] without the additional hypothesis of independent events. He studied the sequence of letters, especially the distribution of vowels in Eugene Onegin, written by Alexander Pushkin, and showed that one can predict the next letter using the previous letter [6]. Claude Shannon [7] developed these ideas further by creating the concept of encoder-decoder in his famous work on communication in 1948. Shannon's fundamental concept of information entropy links physics and information science, especially useful in quantum information theory that is rapidly developing now. However, it took almost a century of continuous scientific development, both hardware and software, before these ideas came to fruition using the Recurrent Neural Networks, which we will consider after the next section.

3 Chomsky's "Colorless Green Ideas ..." and It's Refutation by Norvig

Moving away from rule-based parsing techniques to statistical approaches marked a major turning point in NLP. Known for opposing statistical modeling of language, Noam Chomsky claimed that probabilistic models were unable to discern between sentences that were grammatically correct but meaningless and those that were genuinely meaningful. His illustration, "Colorless green ideas sleep furiously," turned into a benchmark for discussion in this area.

In an interesting salvo against statistical modelling of language, Chomsky [8] argued that statistical modelling cannot distinguish "colorless green ideas sleep furiously", and "furiously sleep ideas green colorless". The first one is grammatically correct, while the second one is not grammatically correct in terms of syntax, but both being text that doesn't occur in training corpus.

Unlike the limited world outlook of Euclid-Cartesian-Newtonian world of determinism, modern ideas of statistical mechanics of Boltzmann and complex Hilbert space formulations of quantum theories have firmly established the role probability and statistics. Albert Einstein, although established the dual nature of light (particle and a wave) by explaining the photoelectric effect and broke open the Euclidean world by introducing physics that is fundamentally non-Euclidean, but still, he couldn't accept the statistical nature of quantum physics. Peter Norvig [9] has eloquently articulated the scientific role of probability and statistics. Using a set of newspaper corpus, Pereira [10] has established using statistical frequency approach in the tradition of Andrey Markov and Claude Shannon that "colorless green ideas sleep furiously" is 200,000 times more probable than "furiously sleep ideas green colorless". He also found that the first one is 10,000 times more likely using Google Book corpus from 1800 to 1954.

We will wait for the next salvo from Chomsky camp in this regard. One must not take sides here as this is part of the dialectical process of evolution of human thought as Hegel clearly understood. Albert Einstein's EPR paradox attempt [11] led to the study of quantum entanglement and the modern theory of quantum computers, furthering, and firmly establishing the theory of modern quantum physics. We expect such counter arguments to help in furthering the cause of our robust understanding.

Finally in this section we illustrate the importance of statistical study of text using Fig. 1 as mirror of the social bias.

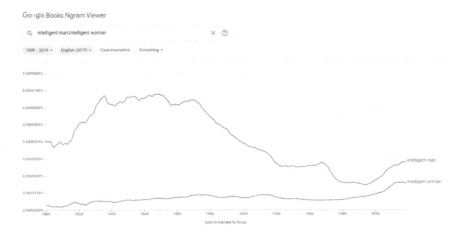

Fig. 1. Google N-gram View of "intelligent man" versus "intelligent woman"

Just like humans, the text they created also has entrenched bias of the society we live in. We will study toxicity and bias in the text and its remedial methods in the final two sections.

4 Neural Networks RNN, LSTM and CNN

It was Frank Rosenblatt study of Neurodynamic of Perceptron, both single and multi-layer neural networks in 1961 [12] that clearly showed the power of Neural Networks as we see today.

Marvin Minsky countered that the single-layer perceptron is not capable of solving the XOR problem, but Marvin Minsky was futilely pessimistic of its bottom-up approach and opaqueness [13]. He has been accused of personally being responsible for the AI winter that followed in the next few decades.

The early debates on this Brain Wars [14] showed clearly how established top-down views can be overthrown through diligent bottom-up work. Also, as we have seen in the case of Andrey Markov, it takes enormous efforts to overthrow established top-down views through diligent work.

Although the chain rule on differentiation was first studied by Leibnitz, Modern Theory of Deep Learning Neural Networks began with the idea of backpropagation by Seppo Linnainmaa [15] ("back propagation of errors" was mentioned by Frank Rosenblatt but no algorithm was given).

Jürgen Schmid Huber, who is considered pioneer in many fields of Deep Learning has studied the history of Modern AI and Deep Learning in considerable detail [16]. He considers Alexey Ivakhnenko [17, 18] in 1965, 1971 to be the pioneer in Deep Learning. In any case, leaving aside academic objections, in the world of software development and Deep Learning frameworks funded by the private corporate industry, important benchmark work on Deep Learning is the Nature article by LeCun, Bengio and Hinton [19] in 1985. The art of AI and Deep Learning has left the shores of academics and into the world of Open-Source software frameworks funded by private software industry, where it is difficult to trace every discovery as it is developed by the software collective. Of course, there is constant competition between private corporate entities, leading to rapid continuous developments that are difficult to trace individually. The speed at which these rapid developments have happened since then has been astonishing.

One of the initial failures in Recurrent Neural Network has been the problem of vanishing gradients and it was solved by many different adjustments of what are known as hyperfine parameters of Deep Learning. The RELU activation function, the Stochastic Gradient methods, and Long-Term-Short-Methods (LSTM) that added a hidden layer provided the initial breakthroughs. Many successful time-series predictions have been achieved with these models. Convolution Neural Networks (CNN) have also been developed but mostly for image processing, and as we restrict ourselves to NLP and text processing areas, we will not be dwelling on CNN and image processing here. Earliest Transfer Learning ideas were applied in image processing, but here we will consider only Transfer Learning attempts in modelling text.

5 Attention, the Big Transformers, GPU and the LLM

It is known in linguistics that some languages like German we must wait for the verb before we get to understand what someone is speaking about. Of course, when Shakespeare speaks through the mouth of Antony that "Brutus is an honorable man", we must wait quite a bit to understand the meaning and import of that noun phrase. It took another 100 years before non-local non-Markovian methods became possible through big Attention-based Transformers. Although in principle RNN and their modified versions like LSTM are capable of long-range textual communication, in practice, the values decay rapidly making it ineffective. These Transformer models are expensive in terms of memory and compute requirements, but quite effective in predictions.

One of the early successes of Transformers was the BERT (Bidirectional Encoder Representations from Transformers) model. This was an encoder-only model that was non-directional in that it could read both from left and right. It used the method of fill-in-the-blanks approach for unsupervised learning by randomly masking certain words as targets for the training. This was able to solve meanings of many ambiguous words in NLP such as a bank that could be a bank of a river or a bank where we keep our wealth. It also was also able to resolve the pronoun association problem; pronoun being a variable token that takes a noun value that must be discerned from the earlier context of the text. Of course, there could also be many such abbreviations, acronyms and coined technical words that may require a glossary at the beginning of the document.

Using embedded layer of Attention weights [21] and especially self-attention [22] these Deep Learning could move forward with SOTA (state of the art) performances in many NLP topics [23].

The trajectory of evolution of Deep Learning in text analysis can be summarized roughly as follows:

$$\textbf{Wordembeddings} \Longrightarrow \textbf{RNN} \Longrightarrow \textbf{LSTM} \Longrightarrow \textbf{Bi-LSTM}$$
$$\Longrightarrow \textbf{Tokenizers} \Longrightarrow \textbf{Attention} \Longrightarrow \textbf{Transformers}$$

6 Exaptation of GPU and the Emergence of Artificial Intelligence by Scale?

With the demise of Moore's law in providing fast and faster CPUs due to increased heat-loss at atomic sizes, a major paradigm shift in computing was required. Despite theoretical promise, due to limitations of Von Neuman architecture, multi-core CPUs were not able handle large throughput that were required in modern computing. At the same time, the graphics processing unit (GPU) was invented for speeding-up display of two-dimensional pixel arrays. The linear transformation of arrays involve matrix multiplication, so libraries were created for multiplication of large matrices with large number of transitors in a parallel architecture for large throughput. These GPUs did not come with the full repateur of computing capabilities of the CPU, but neither did neural network computing require such computations! So the meandering fortunes of NVIDIA found a great opportunity in machine learning that required large throughput hardware architecture. The CUDA libraries provided by NVIDIA provided exaptation (like how the feathers invented in reptiles to control body temperature provided the mechanism of flight and the evolution of birds) that would transform the landscape of the emergence of large language models at ennormous scale.

Of course, traditional Markovian methods like RNN, LSTM, CNN, etc. required much less resources of memory as they buffer-stream through the text like a steaming video, so a modest GPU (like single T4 Tesla) was good enough. These Attention based Transformers required enormous memory throughput which could only be achieved by GPUs such as multiple A100 and H100 GPUs, pushing up cost and requiring efforts at acceleration. Lowering precision using TPU architecture is another attempt at optimization, but it will be a while before the cost of production of these models can come down. This transformer revolution was made possible by the invention of GPU by NVIDIA and their CUDA libraries. Instead of the low-latency CPU, the high-throughput GPU will be the hardware backbone of these LLMs.

The first successful Transformers like BERT were in modest size. The second wave started with encoder-decoder T5-XXL LLMs with 11 billion parameters. Then came the competition between billion-dollar companies, each one wanting a slice of this new data and AI real estate (Table 1).

At present the biggest model is GPT-4, which is claimed to have more than a trillion parameters. The other two previous record holders in terms of number of parameters is MT-NLG 530 B and PaLM 540 B (Fig. 2).

Table 1. List of LLMs and their model sizes

Model	Company	Number of Parameters (in Millions)
GPT-1	OpenAI	117
BERT	Google	342
GPT-2	OpenAI	1500
T5-3B	Google	3000
GPT-J	OpenAI	6000
T5-11B	Google	11000
Fairseq	Facebook	13000
Chinchilla	DeepMind	70000
YaLM	Yandex	100000
LaMMA	Facebook	137000
GTP-3	OpenAI	175000
BLOOM	BigScience	176000
Gopher	DeepMind	280000
MT-NLG	Microsoft/NVIDIA	530000
PaLM	Google	540000
ERNIE-4	Baidu	1000000
GPT-4	OpenAI	1700000
Gemini	Google	1700000
Human Brain*	Humans	200000000

*For humans it is the estimate number of synaptic connections (neural network weights)

(https://aiimpacts.org/scale-of-the-human-brain/)

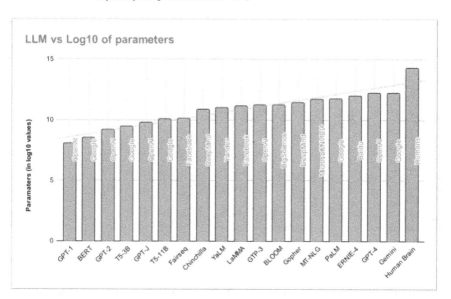

Fig. 2. Size LLMs measured in terms of number of neural network weights (synaptic connections)

At present the successful big transformers around are OpenAI-ChatGPT, Google's PaLM2-Bard-Gemini and Baidu's ERNIE 4.0 Bot. There are many fine-tuned open-source models as well like BLOOM, Llama2, Mistral, Falcon, but much smaller in size and capabilities. They provide an array of services, including summarization, reasoning, content analysis like sentiment analysis, code generation, code analysis, text translations and much more.

Anderson [24] explains "emergent phenomenon" as one in which systems as they grow in scale acquire from quantity a new quality. It seems that as an emergent phenomenon of scale these LLMs acquire One-Shot-Learning (OSL) and Chain-of-Thought (CoT) reasoning capabilities through some appropriate prompts. Prompt engineering has become a domain of its own. The stupendous success of these LLMs is very clear, but they are not without drawbacks as we will see in the final two sections.

Some of these loose ends and toxicity are fixed by RLHF/RLAIF (Reinforcement Learning from Human Feedback and with AI Feedback) [25]. Researchers have also begun investigating if these models have passed the Turing Test [26].

7 Toxicity and Bias Mitigation

We study bias in word-embeddings using Fasttext and Glove vectors and results are summarised separately [33]. Common Crawl is a non-profit organization that crawls the web and provides snapshots that are free to the public. It has been the standard source of data for training big models such as T5, GPT-3, and Gopher. The April 2021 snapshot of Common Crawl has 320 terabytes of data. Content is picked up from the following top seven websites: patents.google.com; en.wikipedia.org; en.m.wikipedia.org; www.nytimes. com; www.latimes.com; www.theguardian.com. The geographical bias is very much established [28]. Figure 3 shows PaLM data model and it's toxicity as reported by Google in their work on PaLM 580 model.

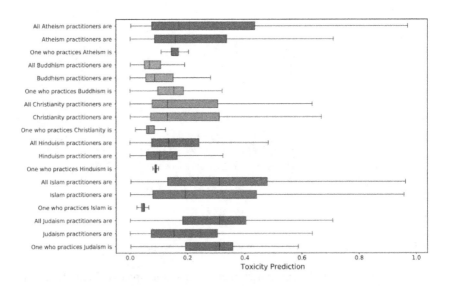

Fig. 3. PaLM data model and its toxicity.

A thorough study of C4 data has been made [28] and they have found the design choices of blocklist filtering can cause harm to minority contents and that demographics and geographical regions have association of negative sentiment. This has been demonstrated by many queries to the earlier versions of ChatGPT, which has since then been corrected through reinforcement learning from human feedback (RLHF).

8 Constitutional AI

Here we briefly describe a systematic attempt at controlling biases and violation of social norms through what is termed "Constitution AI" [29]. If LLMs must follow a "constitution" that is devoid of biases based on gender, race, religion, and geography then there are approaches based on RLHF that fine-tune it. However, a response such as "I can't answer that" will be harmless but not informative, so one can only achieve a delicate balance between harmless and informative (which could be biased as well). It remains to be seen if these attempts succeed in not only suppressing but remove violation of (constitutional) social norms that emanate from the underlying toxicity of the human-generated corpus text.

9 Memorization, Sycophancy, Broken Chains of Logic and Hallucinations

Apart from toxicity and bias, many other problematic aspects of these models have been studied.

9.1 Memorization

Memorization is the exact replication of text in the training set by Large Language AI Models. This is especially problematic as it may violate copyright laws. It has been observed that the larger the LLM gets, chances of replication of large body of text increases both in size and frequency.

9.2 Sycophancy

Sycophancy of a model is how the model responds to text prompts and feedback. A model is considered to have high sycophancy if it can be persuaded to follow user persuasion despite clear evidence to the contrary [30].

9.3 Broken Chains of Logic

Many errors in logical argument exist that are broken in LLMs. For example, it has been observed that if A is son of B, that does not easily follow the logic that it implies that B is father of A. LLMs don't by themselves discern the observation that the relation "son/daughter" is an inverse relation of "father/mother". Of course, it also must carefully discern that "son/father" and "daughter/mother" belong to different gender categories. It is not clear at present if this is within the capability of these Transformer-based LLMs even in a theoretical sense.

9.4 Hallucination

It has been observed that GPT-4 has problems of hallucination, i.e., predicting something that is not there in the data [31]. Of course, it can also be argued that it is an aspect that is useful in other respects when it gets it correct.

9.5 Clever Hans Effect

It has also been argued that prompt engineering of LLMs is another sophisticated version of Clever Hans Effect [32], where the prompt engineer is inadvertently pulling out the correct answer by persuasion.

9.6 Context Window

The input size that a LLM model can handle was a major limitation in earlier versions of the LLM models. Also there was an high cost to increasing the size of the context window. These limitations have been overcome and now it is possible to input an entire novel or a book as a context for tasks such as summarization or QA. Of course, RAG implementations are still required that provide certain inputs from knowledge graph-databases such as DBPedia providing sharper focus on the context.

9.7 Bias Mitigation Using RLHF/RLAIF and Input Filtering

There are many approaches to mitigate the effects of bias in word-embedding vectors in Large Learning Models. One is a machine-learning approache to iron-out biases in the text that is used to train the LLM. This has the benefit that it also produces a bias-free large corpus. However, this is a very expensive as the LLMs have to trained from scratch a very expensive excercise. A typical LLM cosumes thousands of H100 NVIDIA GPU to train for a few weeks, costing over a million USD atleast! The other approach is to fine-tune the model using reinforcement learning through human feedback (RLHF) [25]. In this approach the weights are forced to follow human feedback constraints. This much less expensive than retraining methods. Scaling uniform bias-free human feedback is also a time-consuming process, so in order overcome this a model that produces AI feedback is created and is used to fine-tune the model using reinforcement learning. In this approoch also like all previous approaches all the billions of weights have to reconfigured during fine-tuning of the model making it quite expensive.

In this work we propose an input masking and filtering approach to both discover and mitigate bias. In this approach we create input-filering layer that scans for potential bias related entities recognised using NLP-NER techniques and substitutes them with equivalent entities in the bias-entity-groups to recognise bias in the LLM and take remedial measures by replacing with bias-neutral entities. In the case of gender-bias, for example, replacing with equivalent female names with male names etc. Gender reinforcement roles are also another well-known form of bias that produce indirect bias and they also have to be flagged and replaced with neutral terms both in input and output text. In our future work we will be addressing these issues across different LLMs to report the existing bias across various LLMs.

10 Conclusion

No one is perfect in this world, neither are Large Language Models. However, the ubiquitous nature of LLMs in our life that decides many aspects of our life as a proxy for humans requires that it passes higher levels of Turing test. We already know the toxicity and bias that underlies all the data from which the LLMs were created from. It is easy to believe that all the social prompting and feedback loops and reinforcement fine-tuning will create a facade of respectability. As Salman Rushdie warned in the Haroun and the Sea of Stories, it could be that the sea is so poisoned that it is difficult to fish out a healthy story. We are a long way away from being able to use these Large Language Models confidently in our lives and in our children's lives. However, the promise and achievements by a generation of AI and Deep Learning developers and data scientists, the epitome of which is the interesting world of multi-modal Large Language Models – the Generative AI that seems to have raised expectation that it has passed the Turing Test [26], with a possibly of an army of prompt engineers working in the background to prevent generation of toxic outburst that even humans are also quite capable of producing under duress and toxic prompting. Whether these emergent LLM phenomena of scale are a miracle or just a mirage of scale like just another Clever Hans Effect [32] is an on-going interesting intellectual discussion between the nay-sayers and the optimists, quite reminiscent of the Brain wars in the 1970s and 1980s, but this time the weight of funding resources leaning heavily on the side of optimists. Leaving aside these dogmatic fights, if one looks at how the human neural network is architecture and if it is true that human-brain is nothing but a scaled primate brain as observed earlier [2] then it is interesting to study this cybernetical aspects further, the close relationship and contrast between our biological evolution that produced natural intelligence with low-latency and our social endeavor that has produced so-called "artificial intelligence" at enormous scale, overcoming human limitations in terms of memory.

Attention layer is what finally brought Deep Learning to its great depths, but human attention is much more complex than focusing on some important words in a sentence, it looks at the sentence with a viewpoint, and the whole meaning changes in that context, in a world viewed with these new glasses. Humans will look at LLMs with these different attention glasses, examining and re-examining what these giant engines churn out, gaining higher consciousness about themselves and what they have produced.

References

1. Devi, S.: The Human Computer, Honored in Google Doodle, ABC News (2013)
2. Herculano-Houzel, S.: The human brain in numbers: a linearly scaled-up primate brain. Front. Hum. Neurosci. **3**, 857 (2009). https://doi.org/10.3389/neuro.09.031.2009
3. Kahle, B.: Wayback Machine (1996). https://archive.org/web/
4. Swartz, A.: Internet's own boy (2014). https://www.eff.org/deeplinks/2014/08/aaron-swartss-work-internets-own-boy
5. Basharin, G.P., Langville, A.N., Naumov, V.A.: The life and work of A.A. Markov. Linear Algebra Appl. **386**, 3–26 (2004)
6. Markov, A.A.: Primer statisticheskogo issledovaniya nad tekstom "Evgeniya Onegina", Izv. Akad. Nauk, SPb, VI seriya **7**(93), 153–162 (1913)

7. Shannon, C.E.: A mathematical theory of communication. Bell Syst. Techn. J. **27**, 379–423, 623–656 (1948)
8. Noam, C.: Syntactic Structures. The Hague/Paris: Mouton (1957). ISBN 978-3-11-021832-9
9. Norvig, P.: Colorless green ideas learn furiously: chomsky and the two cultures of statistical learning. Significance **9**(4), 30–33 (2012). https://doi.org/10.1111/j.1740-9713.2012.00590.x
10. Pereira, F.: Formal grammar and information theory: together again? In: Nevin, B., Johnson, S.M. (eds.) The Legacy of Zellig Harris. Benjamins, Amsterdam (2002)
11. Einstein, A., Podolsky, B., Rosen, N.: Can quantum-mechanical description of physical reality be considered complete? Phys. Rev. **47**, 777–780 (1935)
12. Van Der Malsburg, C.: Frank rosenblatt: principles of neurodynamics: perceptrons and the theory of brain mechanisms. In: Palm, G., Aertsen, A. (eds.) Brain Theory. Springer, Berlin, Heidelberg (1986). https://doi.org/10.1007/978-3-642-70911-1_20
13. Minsky, M., Papert, S.: Perceptrons. MIT Press, Cambridge, MA (1969)
14. Olazaran, M.: A Sociological study of the official history of the perceptrons controversy. Soc. Stud. Sci. **26**(3), 611–659 (1996). https://doi.org/10.1177/030631296026003005
15. Linnainmaa, S.: Taylor expansion of the accumulated rounding error. BIT **16**, 146–160 (1976). https://doi.org/10.1007/BF01931367
16. Schmidhuber, J.: Deep learning in neural networks: an overview. Neural Netw. **61**, 85–117 (2015). https://doi.org/10.1016/j.neunet.2014.09.003
17. Ivakhnenko, A.G., Lapa, V.G.: Cybernetic predicting devices. CCM Information Corporation (1965)
18. Ivakhnenko, A.G.: Polynomial theory of complex systems. IEEE Trans. Syst. Man Cybern. **4**, 364–378 (1971)
19. LeCun, Y., Bengio, Y., Hinton, G.: Deep learning. Nature **521**, 436–444 (2015). https://doi.org/10.1038/nature14539
20. Miller, G.A.: WordNet: a lexical database for English. Commun. ACM **38**, 39–41 (1995)
21. Vaswani, A., et al.: Attention is all you need. In: Proceedings of the 31st International Conference on Neural Information Processing Systems (NIPS 2017), Curran Associates Inc., Red Hook, NY, USA, 6000–6010 (2017)
22. Ambartsoumian, A., Popowich, F.: Self-Attention: a better building block for sentiment analysis neural. In: Proceedings of the 9th Workshop on Computational Approaches to Subjectivity, Sentiment and Social Media Analysis, pp. 130–139
23. NLP Progress: https://nlpprogress.com/ (or https://github.com/sebastianruder/NLP-progress)
24. Anderson, P.W.: More is different science. New Ser. **177**(4047), 393–396 (1972)
25. Lee, H., et al.: RLAIF: scaling reinforcement learning from human feedback with AI feedback (2023) . https://arxiv.org/abs/2309.00267
26. Biever, C.: ChatGPT broke the Turing test — The race is on for new ways to assess AI- Large language models mimic human chatter, but scientists disagree on their ability to reason. Nature News, 25 July 2023 (2023)
27. Sambasivan, N., Arnesen, E., Hutchinson, B., Doshi, T., Prabhakaran, V.: Re-imagining algorithmic fairness in India and beyond. In Proceedings of the 2021 ACM Conference on Fairness, Accountability, and Transparency (FAccT 2021). Association for Computing Machinery, New York, NY, USA, 315–328 (2021). https://doi.org/10.1145/3442188.3445896
28. Dodge, J., et al.: Documenting large webtext corpora: a case study on the colossal clean crawled corpus. In: Proceedings of the 2021 Conference on Empirical Methods in Natural Language Processing, pages 1286–1305, Online and Punta Cana, Dominican Republic. Association for Computational Linguistics 2021
29. Bai, Y., et al.: Constitutional AI: harmlessness from AI feedback, cs.CL. arXiv:2212.08073 (2022)

30. Sharma, M., et al.: Towards understanding sycophancy in language models (2023). https://arxiv.org/abs/2310.13548 (see also: https://github.com/meg-tong/sycophancy-eval)
31. ChainPoll, an hallucination metric. https://www.rungalileo.io/hallucinationindex/ methodology (see also: https://github.com/rungalileo/hallucination-index)
32. Kambhampati, S.: Can LLMs really reason and plan? Communication of the ACM, BLOG@CACM (2023). https://cacm.acm.org/blogs/blog-cacm/276268-can-llms-really-reason-and-plan/fulltext
33. Bias data analysis in word embeddings. https://github.com/Sukii/bias

HITgram: A Platform for Experimenting with n-Gram Language Models

Shibaranjani Dasgupta[1], Chandan Maity[1], Somdip Mukherjee[1], Rohan Singh[1], Diptendu Dutta[2], and Debasish Jana[1(✉)]

[1] Heritage Institute of Technology, Kolkata, India
{shibaranjani.dasgupta.cse25,chandan.maity.cse25,
somdip.mukherjee.cse25,rohan.singh.cse25}@heritageit.edu.in,
debasish.jana@heritageit.edu
[2] Aunwesha Knowledge Technologies Private Limited, Kolkata, India

Abstract. Large language models (LLMs) are powerful but resource-intensive, limiting accessibility. HITgram addresses this gap by offering a lightweight platform for n-gram model experimentation, ideal for resource-constrained environments. It supports unigrams to 4-grams and incorporates features like context-sensitive weighting, Laplace smoothing, and dynamic corpus management to enhance prediction accuracy, even for unseen word sequences. Experiments demonstrate HITgram's efficiency, achieving 50,000 tokens/second and generating 2-grams from a 320 MB corpus in 62 s. HITgram scales efficiently, constructing 4-grams from a 1 GB file in under 298 s on an 8 GB RAM system. Planned enhancements include multilingual support, advanced smoothing, parallel processing, and model saving, further broadening its utility.

Keywords: n-Gram Model · Text Generation · Smoothing · Computational Linguistics · Natural Language Processing · Generative AI

1 Introduction

Large language models (LLMs) have revolutionized natural language processing (NLP) with attention-based architectures like transformers [19], excelling in tasks like next-word prediction and conversational agents [16]. However, their high computational demands limit accessibility, prompting renewed interest in lightweight alternatives [4] [10] such as small language models (SLMs) and traditional n-gram models [9].

n-**gram Models.** These models are among the earliest and most widely used methods in NLP and computational linguistics [15]. By conditioning on the preceding $(n-1)$ words, n-gram models predict the nth word through statistical analysis of word frequencies and co-occurrences in large text corpora. Their statistical nature allows for computational efficiency and ease of implementation. This probabilistic approach has found applications in various domains, including text generation, spell-checking, language modeling, and speech recognition.

Despite advancements in deep learning, n-gram models [7,11,14] remain relevant due to their balance between performance and computational demands. Their ability to function with smaller unlabeled datasets and deliver interpretable results makes them a viable option for various practical NLP tasks, particularly where larger models are impractical due to resource constraints or data insufficiency. In this paper, we develop HITgram with this goal in mind, offering an accessible platform for users to interact with n-gram models and explore their functionality in a hands-on manner. HITgram's lightweight architecture enables its use in various practical applications, including predictive text, autocomplete features, search engine optimization, and speech-to-text preprocessing. These capabilities are particularly valuable in domains like education, accessibility tools, and mobile devices, where computational resources are often constrained.

Limitations of Traditional n-grams. Although n-gram models are efficient and interpretable, a key limitation they face is data sparsity [2], particularly as the context length increases. This issue necessitates vast amounts of training data to capture meaningful contextual relationships. Additionally, traditional n-gram models are restricted to fixed-length context windows, constraining their capacity to model long-range dependencies and complex language structures.

Another common issue with n-gram models is handling unseen word sequences. Without proper smoothing techniques, these models struggle to generate accurate predictions for rare or previously unseen n-grams. To address this, the HITgram platform offers various smoothing options viz., Laplace and Good-Turing, to mitigate data sparsity and improve prediction accuracy. Furthermore, the platform allows users to experiment with different n-gram configurations (such as bigrams and trigrams) with varying context lengths, to better understand and optimize language modeling performance.

Contributions. HITgram facilitates n-gram model experimentation in resource-limited settings. It provides tools for building, testing, and refining n-gram models on user-provided corpora, balancing efficiency with accessibility while addressing traditional model challenges.

Organization of the Paper. The remainder of the paper is organized as follows. Section 2 reviews related work, discussing challenges with language models. Section 3 outlines the motivation for this work. In Sect. 4, we detail the HITgram platform, its architecture and implementation. Section 5 presents the experimental results and observations. Finally, Sect. 6 concludes the paper with suggestions for future work.

2 Background and Related Work

n-gram models remain crucial in NLP, offering lightweight, computationally efficient alternatives to resource-intensive LLMs, particularly for users with limited resources. This section reviews advancements in smoothing, backoff, interpolation, and n-gram applications.

Smoothing Techniques. One of the inherent limitations of n-gram models is their susceptibility to sparse data. In an n-gram language model, unseen sequences often receive a probability of zero, which can significantly affect the model's overall accuracy. Various smoothing techniques have been developed to address data sparsity in models. One of the earliest methods, **Laplace Smoothing**, adds a small constant (typically 1) to each possible count. This approach effectively prevents zero probabilities but may overestimate the likelihood of rare n-grams, reducing precision in some cases. A more advanced technique, **Kneser-Ney Smoothing**, improves upon this by assigning probabilities to unseen n-grams based on their occurrence across diverse contexts, making it particularly effective for rare word sequences. Additionally, **backoff and interpolation models** blend probabilities from different n-gram orders, providing a robust strategy to mitigate sparse data challenges. To address the limitations posed by sparse data, **backoff and interpolation models** have been widely adopted in n-gram modeling. **Backoff models** dynamically reduce the order of the n-gram when an observed sequence is not available, effectively "backing off" to lower-order n-grams. This allows the model to leverage smaller contexts when higher-order data is sparse. The simplicity of this approach ensures its wide applicability in computationally limited environments. In contrast to backoff models, **interpolation models**, blend probabilities from multiple n-gram lengths, assigning weights based on the reliability of the different orders. These methods mitigate the issue of sparse data by smoothing the probability estimates across different context sizes. Han et al. [6] demonstrated that interpolation models can enhance language modeling tasks by incorporating multiple n-gram lengths effectively, while showing that fine-tuning smaller language models on task-specific data enables self-correction. Laplace smoothing has long been recognized as a foundational method [5] while Kneser-Ney smoothing [13] and backoff-interpolation approaches [12] continue to enhance the accuracy and applicability of n-gram models.

Advanced n-gram Models in NLP. Despite the recent surge in the development of neural language models such as transformers, n-gram models continue to be relevant in specific NLP tasks, particularly those requiring lower computational overhead and greater interpretability, like text generation, machine translation, and autocompletion. For applications such as autocompletion and basic **text generation**, n-gram models offer considerable speed and efficiency. Their lower computational cost makes them suitable for environments with limited processing power, where larger neural models like transformers may be overkill [15]. While neural models have set the state-of-the-art (SoTA) in **machine translation**, n-gram models still serve as a valuable alternative for small-scale tasks where computational transparency and speed are critical. For example, recent research by Zhao et al. [20] discuss recent advancements in large language models (LLMs) like GPT [1] and LLaMA [18], highlighting their superior accuracy in pre-training, fine-tuning, and evaluation, but also noting their high computational demands, whereas simpler models like n-grams remain useful for resource-constrained tasks due to their lower resource consumption. In terms of **resource**

efficiency, Large Language Models (LLMs), such as GPT-3 and LLaMA-70B, require massive amounts of computational power for both training and inference. Zhou et al. [21] estimate that mainstream LLMs like LLaMA-70B, with 70 billion parameters, require around 140 GB of VRAM and multiple high-end GPUs, making them slow, resource-intensive, and inaccessible to many users, while simpler n-gram models offer a more efficient alternative in environments with limited hardware resources. In terms of **task-specific improvements**, recent studies suggest that even smaller n-gram models can be improved for specific tasks. Han et al. [6] demonstrated that lightweight n-gram models can be fine-tuned on task-specific data to achieve higher accuracy. This technique balances the trade-offs between the computational efficiency of n-grams and the performance typically associated with larger LLMs. Future versions of HITgram could explore hybrid models combining n-grams with neural networks, potentially bridging performance gaps. Additionally, incorporating multilingual corpora and advanced tokenization strategies will further enhance its utility in diverse NLP applications.

3 Motivation

Despite the dominance of LLMs, resource constraints highlight the need for platforms like HITgram to support lightweight, interpretable n-gram models. These models address challenges like data sparsity and resource efficiency using techniques like Laplace and Good-Turing smoothing.

Long-Range Dependency Problems. Traditional n-gram models are limited by their fixed-length context windows. For example, a trigram model only considers the two preceding words when predicting the next word. This fixed context prevents the model from capturing long-range dependencies, which are essential for understanding complex linguistic patterns. Models like transformers, by contrast, excel at capturing these dependencies but at a high computational cost [2]. HITgram seeks to provide a platform that allows experimentation with these limitations, encouraging the exploration of techniques that could extend the context window of n-gram models without compromising efficiency. n-gram models are limited by their fixed context window. For instance, a trigram model only considers the previous two words when predicting the next word. This short context window prevents the model from capturing long-range dependencies, which are crucial for understanding complex linguistic structures.

Balancing Accuracy and Efficiency. While n-gram models are computationally efficient, their predictive accuracy often lags behind more advanced models like LLMs. This discrepancy is particularly evident in complex tasks that require a nuanced understanding of linguistic structures. Enhancing the prediction accuracy of n-grams while maintaining their computational advantages is a key motivation for HITgram. Through features like configurable context lengths and built-in smoothing methods, HITgram aims to strike a balance between simplicity and performance, offering an effective solution for environments where computational resources are limited [3]. Despite their computational advantages,

n-gram models often struggle with prediction accuracy compared to more sophisticated models like LLMs. There is a need to enhance n-gram models by incorporating advanced techniques like smoothing and context-sensitive weighting to improve their accuracy without sacrificing efficiency.

The Need for Accessible, Interpretable Models. Another driving factor behind HITgram is the increasing need for interpretable models [17]. In applications where transparency and explainability are crucial e.g., legal, healthcare, or finance sectors – n-gram models provide a clear advantage over opaque neural-based models. HITgram promotes the use of n-grams as interpretable, resource-efficient alternatives to LLMs, especially for those who require models to be both understandable and manageable without sacrificing too much predictive power.

4 The HITGram Platform

HITgram offers a user-friendly platform for n-gram model experimentation, supporting corpus management, customizable tokenization, and smoothing techniques. It provides a lightweight, efficient alternative to resource-intensive LLMs, ideal for resource-limited users. Overall, our HITgram platform allows users to: (a) upload text corpora in various acceptable file formats, (b) apply customizable tokenization strategies to split the text into tokens, (c) create n-gram models from the tokenized corpora, (d) utilize smoothing techniques to enhance model predictions, and (e) dynamically manage the text corpora by uploading new corpus for augmenting, removing, or replacing the existing ones.

Developed in Java [8] and utilizing Java Swing for its graphical user interface (GUI), HITgram delivers a robust environment for experimentation while remaining accessible. First, our platform allows for the creation of n-gram models from user-uploaded corpora in various file formats, like .txt, .pdf, etc. Users can easily upload and manage corpora through an interactive interface, enabling experimentation with different datasets and the integration of new data to refine models. HITgram's corpus management system offers flexibility, allowing datasets to be cleared or replaced to promote diverse experimental setups.

Built-in Tokenization Engine. HITgram includes a built-in tokenizer that processes the uploaded corpus to break it into individual tokens. Based on the task that a user intends to perform such as *sentence completion, word completion,* or *next-word prediction*, the choice of tokenization plays a crucial role. A user can apply customizable tokenization strategies that split text into words, sub-words (through stemming or lemmatization [3]), or characters. Once the n-gram model is constructed, users can input a sentence, and the platform predicts the next word(s) based on the trained model. For example, given the input "`The cat`", the model predicts the most likely next word based on the preceding tokens.

Code snippet of Tokenization

```
public List<String> tokenizeText(String text) {
  text = text.toLowerCase().replaceAll("[^a-zA-Z\\s]", ""); // Normalize
  return Arrays.asList(text.split("\\s+")); // Tokenize by space
}
```

Building and Customizing n-gram Models. The core of HITgram lies in building and customizing n-gram models. Users can build various types of n-gram models viz., unigrams, bigrams, trigrams, or higher-order n-grams – each capturing different levels of contextual relationships in the text.

HITgram allows users to create different n-gram models based on the uploaded corpora. n-gram models work by generating sequences of n tokens from the text. These models are categorized by the value of n: unigram (n = 1), bigram (n = 2), trigram (n = 3), and higher-order n-grams for larger n values. The choice of n affects the amount of context considered when predicting the next word or character in a sequence. For example, a trigram model (n = 3) would create two trigrams "The cat is" and "cat is sleeping" from the sentence "The cat is sleeping". From such n-length sequences, the context of the $n-1$ preceding words, along with the corresponding next word, is stored in a key-value format for efficient access and manipulation.

Overall, by building an n-gram model, we predict the likelihood of a word or sequence appearing in a particular context by analyzing the frequency of those sequences in the corpus. For example, in a unigram model, each word's probability is based solely on its frequency, while in a bigram model, the prediction depends on the preceding word. Trigram models extend this further by considering the previous two words. This probabilistic approach reveals dependencies within the text, enabling more accurate predictions.

Adaptive Context Lengths and Dynamic n-gram Model Updates. HITgram introduces significant enhancements to traditional n-gram models, focusing on lightweight architecture and adaptive learning to support users with limited resources. Users can build n-gram models with various context lengths, from unigrams (n = 1) to higher-order n-grams like bigrams (n = 2) and trigrams (n = 3). This flexibility allows users to balance context capture and computational efficiency. For instance, a trigram model captures more context than a bigram but requires more resources. We use the following lightweight Java code snippet (simplified) to dynamically update an existing n-gram model:

```
// Tokenize the new corpus
String[] newWords = newCorpus.tokenize();
// Update existing $n$-gram model
for (int i = 0; i <= newWords.length - n; i++) {
  StringBuilder nGram = new StringBuilder();
  for (int j = 0; j < n - 1; j++) {
    nGram.append(newWords[i + j]).append(" ");
  }
  String nextWord = newWords[i + n - 1];
  // Use putIfAbsent for initialization and merge for counting
  nGramModel.putIfAbsent(nGram.toString().trim(), new HashMap<>());
```

```
    nGramModel.get(nGram.toString().trim()).
        merge(nextWord, 1, Integer::sum);
}
```

Additionally, an intuitive GUI slider allows users to modify the value of n easily, providing interactive insights into how context length adjustments affect predictions.

Enhancing Rare Sequence Completion with Smoothing. One of the key challenges in n-gram models is the presence of unseen word pairs or triplets, which can lead to zero probabilities for these rare sequences and significantly degrade the model's performance. For example, consider a corpus consisting of sentences like "I love natural language processing models immensely as it is fun". If our model generates bigrams and we encounter a next-word prediction task for the phrase "natural processing was", we encounter an unseen pair, leading to zero probabilities.

To address this challenge of unseen words in n-gram models, HITgram employs smoothing techniques. Smoothing enhances the model's ability to generalize to previously unseen data by ensuring that every possible n-gram maintains a non-zero probability. It adjusts the probability distribution, ensuring all word combinations, including those not present in the training data, receive a non-zero probability. This capability is crucial for real-world applications where not all word combinations are available in the training dataset. Our HITgram platform offers various smoothing options, such as Laplace, Add-k, and Good-Turing smoothing, enabling the n-gram model to effectively manage scenarios involving rare sequences, thereby enhancing its predictive power and adaptability.

- **Additive (Laplace) Smoothing** involves adding a small constant (typically 1) to the count of each n-gram, including unseen ones, thereby preventing any probability from being zero. For instance, in a bigram model, the probability of a word given its predecessor is computed as $P(w_i|w_{i-1}) = \frac{\text{Count}(w_i,w_{i-1})+1}{\text{Count}(w_{i-1})+V}$ where $\text{Count}(w_{i-1})$ is the count of the first word in the bigram and V is the total number of unique words in the vocabulary. From the example above, although the bigram (was, fun) has no corpus occurrences, Laplace smoothing guarantees that it will still yield a non-zero probability.
- **Add-k Smoothing** is a generalized version of Laplace smoothing where a smaller constant k (e.g., 0.01) is added instead of 1. This approach allows for finer control over the smoothing applied. The formula for Add-k Smoothing is: $P(w_i|w_{i-1}) = \frac{\text{Count}(w_i,w_{i-1})+k}{\text{Count}(w_{i-1})+kV}$. By using a smaller value for k, the method assigns a more realistic, albeit reduced, probability to unseen n-grams.
- **Good-Turing Smoothing** is a more sophisticated technique that estimates the probability of unseen n-grams based on the frequency of n-grams that have been observed once, twice, etc. The formula is: $P(w_i|w_{i-1}) = \frac{N_1}{N}$, where N_1 is the count of bigrams that appear exactly once, and N is the total number of bigrams. This method is particularly effective in large corpora, as it redistributes probability more efficiently among unseen n-grams.

Context-Sensitive Weighting. To address the challenge of unseen word sequences that may yield zero probabilities in standard n-gram models, HITgram employs smoothing techniques like Laplace smoothing. This enables the model to assign non-zero probabilities to n-grams absent from the training data. Furthermore, HITgram introduces context-sensitive weighting, which enhances the model's resilience against sparse or incomplete data, boosting prediction accuracy. To stabilize weights, particularly for infrequent n-grams, a logarithmic transformation is applied. A simplified code snippet for this is shown below:

```
private static double calculateWeight(String nGramKey) {
  double frequency = tokenFrequencyMap.getOrDefault(nGramKey, 0);
  // Logarithmic transformation to stabilize weights
  return Math.log(1 + frequency); // Smoothing the frequency
}
```

Thus, instead of treating all n-grams uniformly, the platform enables users to assign different weights to word sequences based on their frequency or significance within the training corpus. This enhances the model's ability to predict rare yet essential word combinations.

Dynamic Corpus Management for Adaptive Text Completion. Users can upload multiple corpora for concatenation or replacement, enabling incremental learning and diverse text data experiments.

Algorithmic Improvements for Computational Efficiency. We aim to improve the efficiency of generating and predicting n-gram models, especially for users with limited computing resources. The HITgram platform achieves this through various algorithmic optimizations, as outlined below.

HITgram uses key-value structures and pre-computed probabilities to optimize memory and retrieval, supporting real-time tasks like sentence completion. Pruning methods and efficient tokenization algorithms enhance computational efficiency for resource-limited environments.

A simplified code snippet demonstrating this is provided below:

```
private static void pruneLowFrequencyNGrams(int threshold) {
  nGramModel.entrySet().removeIf(entry -> entry.getValue().values()
      .stream()
      .mapToInt(Integer::intValue)
      .sum() < threshold);
}
```

Future HITgram versions could integrate neural embeddings to capture short and long-range dependencies, multilingual corpora, and advanced tokenization. Features like model saving and cross-entropy metrics will further bridge the gap between lightweight and complex models.

5 Experimental Results

In this section, we present the results of experiments conducted on the HITgram platform, which focuses on lightweight n-gram language models. The system allows users to upload a corpus, build an n-gram model, and predict the

Table 1. Perplexity values of test set of words for language models

Corpus Size (MB)	Perplexity **	
	bigram	trigram
997	4.4821	2.3886
900	4.0598	2.2009
800	4.2325	2.1666
720	4.1310	2.0156
660	4.3243	2.2325
450	4.2337	2.2440
400	4.1536	2.3896
320	4.2054	2.5989

** results may vary depending on machine configuration

Table 2. Performance Analysis: Time to build n-gram models

Corpus Size (KB)	Time to Load & Tokenize (ms)**	Time to Build n-gram Model (ms)**			
		$n=1$	$n=2$	$n=3$	$n=4$
4898.76	473.5	55.1	19.5	16.1	15.3
5800.846	648.3	16.5	32.6	16.1	24.4
6526.48	899.2	15.5	32.6	34.4	31.5
7245.54	1695	24.5	31.7	32.7	30.8
10302.58	2689	25.3	32.2	31.7	34.5
11922.73	2779.3	75.2	77.4	109.7	121.5
13051.37	2918.7	173.6	286.5	449.7	452.3
13273.6	4001.5	236.7	231.5	484.3	450.6

** measured using AMD Ryzen mid-range performance processors with 4 cores, 8 GB RAM.

next word sequence based on input tokens. Our experiments evaluate performance across various corpus sizes and assess the system's effectiveness in tasks such as tokenization, model construction, next-word prediction, and sentence completion. The results highlight the practicality of n-gram models for users with limited computational resources compared to large-scale language models (LLMs). HITgram tokenizes English text at up to 50,000 tokens/second and generates 2-grams from a 320 MB corpus in under 63 s, showcasing its efficiency in resource-constrained environments. We used **perplexity** as primary evaluation metric. Perplexity, a key performance metric for n-gram models, evaluates prediction effectiveness on validation text:

$$\text{PP(W)} = \sqrt[N]{P(w_1, w_2, \ldots, w_N)} = \sqrt[N]{\prod_{i=1}^{N} \frac{1}{P(w_i \mid w_1, w_2, \ldots, w_{i-1})}}$$

where, PP(W) represents the perplexity of the test set W, where a lower perplexity signifies a more effective predictive model. $P(w_1, w_2, \ldots, w_N)$ is the joint probability of the complete sequence of words $w_1, w_2, \ldots, w_N$ in the test set, N is the total count of words in the test dataset and $P(w_i \mid w_1, w_2, \ldots, w_{i-1})$ is the conditional probability of w_i based on the sequence of immediately preceding words $w_1, w_2, \ldots, w_{i-1}$. The analysis is based on the sentence: "this is a".

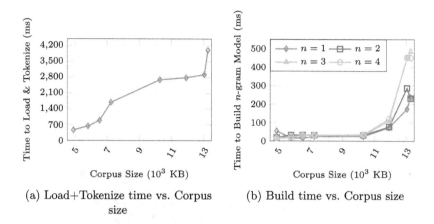

Fig. 1. Plot of the time taken by HITgram: Time taken to load and build n-gram models, by varying corpus size and n.

Table 1 shows the file size (in MB), bigram perplexity, and trigram perplexity for different file sizes.

Dataset Description. Experiments used diverse novel-based corpora from https://www.kaggle.com/ and http://textfiles.com/etext/FICTION/, including *anna_karenina.txt*, *warpeace.txt*, *quixote.txt*, and *lesms10.txt*.

Experimental Setup. HITgram constructs n-gram models with varying n values, efficiently processing PDFs (e.g., a 0.8 GB file to 10,302 KB in 2,689 ms).

Corpus File and Tokenization. After uploading a corpus (PDF or text), HITgram tokenizes the text into individual tokens for n-gram model construction. The time for tokenization depends on the corpus size; for example, tokenizing a 13MB text file took 4001 ms, demonstrating efficiency in handling large datasets.

n-gram Model Construction. After tokenization, the n-gram model is constructed based on the chosen value of n. The model utilizes Laplace Smoothing to handle unseen word combinations, ensuring a more accurate prediction for less frequent sequences. Table 2 shows that n-gram model construction time increases linearly with corpus size and n, demonstrating HITgram's scalability. For smaller corpora, the n-gram model can be built in a relatively short time, even for larger n values. However, for larger corpora, the time increases substantially, particularly for n values of 3 and 4. Comparative graphs between corpus size and the time to load and tokenize, as well as the time to build the n-gram model for varying n values, are presented in Fig. 1. Figure 1 indicates the scaling behavior of HITgram with respect to corpus size and n values. The results highlight HITgram's advantage in efficiently handling medium-sized corpora while maintaining performance with larger ones. Table 3 shows an example of the n-gram sequences built from the corpus.

Prediction of Next Words. To evaluate the platform's prediction capability, we tested it by inputting the phrase "Artificial Intelligence" and request-

Table 3. Example of n-gram modeling: Frequency of corpus sequences

$n-1$ words (Key)	Next word (Value)	Frequency
Artificial Intelligence	is	52
is transforming	industries	28
the future	of	43

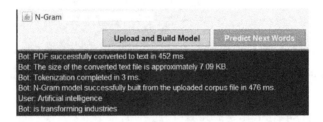

Fig. 2. HITgram in Action: A text corpus generated from a user-uploaded PDF, followed by downstream processing.

ing five subsequent tokens. Based on the trigram model, the system predicted: `Artificial Intelligence is transforming industries worldwide.`

A screenshot of the activities has been captured in Fig. 2. This prediction leverages the highest probability derived from the n-gram model, utilizing Laplace smoothing to avoid zero probabilities for unseen sequences. The probability for each predicted word is calculated as follows:

$$P(w|w_{n-1}) = \frac{\text{Frequency of } w+1}{\text{Total Occurrences of } (n-1) \text{ Words} + \text{Vocabulary Size}}$$

This method ensures non-zero probabilities for sequences not present in the corpus, allowing for accurate predictions that reflect common continuations found in the training data. After constructing the n-gram model, users can specify how many words to predict based on the n-gram probability distribution.

Reproducibility. For those interested in exploring the source code or contributing to the project, the code repository is available on GitHub at: https://github.com/chandan789maity/HITgram. This repository also contains an installer that helps to setup HITgram on Windows^{TM} system.

6 Conclusion and Future Work

We demonstrate that HITgram has the potential of n-gram language modeling as a lightweight alternative to large language models (LLMs), particularly for users with limited computing resources. By providing tools that include context-sensitive weighting, Laplace smoothing, and flexible corpus management, the platform allows for efficient and accurate text modeling. With its adaptability and user-friendly interface, HITgram makes n-gram models approachable and valuable for those in resource-constrained environments. Its success in handling unseen word sequences and incremental learning underscores its significance as a powerful tool for foundational natural language processing (NLP) tasks.

Looking ahead, we believe that HITgram has great potential. Advanced smoothing, multilingual corpora, and parallel processing can enhance efficiency. Although HITgram is optimized for English text, future versions will incorporate multilingual corpora and context-aware tokenization for more diverse applications. Additionally, parallel processing for large datasets will enhance scalability. Dynamic n-gram models and collaboration features will broaden its use. Integrating advanced NLP models will bring richer predictions. Future updates may include flexible tokenization, performance metrics like cross entropy, and model-saving options. These improvements will make HITgram even more valuable, bridging the gap between lightweight and complex language models.

References

1. Achiam, J., et al.: GPT-4 Technical Report. arXiv preprint arXiv:2303.08774 (2023)
2. Allison, B., Guthrie, D., Guthrie, L.: Another look at the data sparsity problem. In: Sojka, P., Kopeček, I., Pala, K. (eds.) TSD 2006. LNCS (LNAI), vol. 4188, pp. 327–334. Springer, Heidelberg (2006). https://doi.org/10.1007/11846406_41
3. Boban, I., Doko, A., Gotovac, S.: Sentence retrieval using stemming and lemmatization with different length of the queries. Adv. Sci. Technol. Eng. Syst. **5**(3), 349–354 (2020)
4. Brown, T.B., et al.: Language Models are Few-Shot Learners. In: Proceedings of the 34th International Conference on Neural Information Processing Systems. NeurIPS 2020 (2020)
5. Buell, W.R., Bush, B.A.: Mesh Generation - A Survey (1973)
6. Han, H., Liang, J., Shi, J., et al.: Small language model can self-correct. In: Proceedings of the AAAI Conference on Artificial Intelligence, vol. 38, pp. 18162–18170 (2024)
7. Hu, M., Pan, S., Li, Y., Yang, X.: Advancing medical imaging with language models: a journey from n-grams to ChatGPT. preprint arXiv:2304.04920 (2023)
8. Jana, D.: Java and object-oriented programming paradigm. PHI Learning (2005)
9. Jurafsky, D., Martin, J.H.: Speech and Language Processing: An Introduction to Natural Language Processing, Computational Linguistics, and Speech Recognition., 3rd edn. (2024). https://web.stanford.edu/~jurafsky/slp3/
10. Kaplan, J., et al.: Scaling laws for neural language models. arXiv preprint arXiv:2001.08361 (2020)
11. Katsafados, A.G., Leledakis, G.N., et al.: Machine learning in bank merger prediction: a text-based APPR. Eur. J. of Oper. Res. **312**(2), 783–797 (2024)
12. Katz, S.: Estimation of probabilities from sparse data for the language model component of a speech recognizer. IEEE Trans. Acoust. Speech Sig. Process. **35**(3), 400–401 (1987)
13. Kneser, R., Ney, H.: Improved backing-off for m-gram language modeling. In: 1995 International Conference on Acoustics, Speech, and Signal Processing, vol. 1, pp. 181–184. IEEE (1995)
14. Malagutti, L., Buinovskij, A., Svete, A., et al.: The role of n-gram smoothing in the age of neural networks. arXiv preprint arXiv:2403.17240 (2024)

15. Manning, C.D., Raghavan, P., Schütze, H.: Introduction to Information Retrieval. Cambridge University Press, Cambridge, UK (2008). http://nlp.stanford.edu/IR-book/information-retrieval-book.html
16. OpenAI: ChatGPT [Large Language Model] (2023). https://chat.openai.com
17. Singh, C., Askari, A., Caruana, R., Gao, J.: Augmenting interpretable models with large language models during training. Nature Comm. **14**(1), 7913 (2023)
18. Touvron, H., Lavril, T., Izacard, G., Martinet, X., et al.: LLaMA: open and efficient foundation language models. arXiv preprint arXiv:2302.13971 (2023)
19. Vaswani, A., Shazeer, N., Parmar, N., Uszkoreit, J., Jones, L., et al.: Attention is All you Need. In: Advances in Neural Information Processing Systems, vol. 30 (2017)
20. Zhao, W.X., et al.: A survey of large language models. arXiv preprint arXiv:2303.18223 (2023)
21. Zhou, Z., et al.: A Survey on efficient inference for large language models. arXiv preprint arXiv:2404.14294 (2024)

Overlapping Community Detection Using Dynamic Residual Deep GCN

Md. Nurul Muttakin[1]([✉]) [iD], Md. Iqbal Hossain[2] [iD], and Md. Saidur Rahman[1] [iD]

[1] Bangladesh University of Engineering and Technology, Dhaka 1000, Bangladesh
muttakin245@gmail.com
[2] University of Arizona, Tucson, USA

Abstract. Detecting overlapping communities is a significant challenge in unsupervised machine learning for network-structured data. While some researchers have applied graph convolutional networks (GCNs) to this problem, most existing GCNs are shallow, limiting their ability to detect communities with larger diameters. Furthermore, the integration of dynamic dilated aggregation into deep GCNs for irregular graphs remains an unresolved issue. To bridge these gaps, we introduce a dynamic residual deep GCN (DynaResGCN), built upon a random dynamic dilated aggregation algorithm within a unified encoder-decoder framework. The encoder utilizes the deep DynaResGCN model, and the decoder uses Bernoulli-Poisson (BP) model. Our framework is tested on three datasets: a topics dataset where ground truth is not available, Facebook graphs with human-labeled ground truth, and large co-authorship networks with less reliable ground truth. Extensive experiments validate that our method is significantly better than many existing methods in detecting overlapping communities in networks.

Keywords: Community Detection · Graph Clustering · Unsupervised Learning

1 Introduction

Network-structured data are prevalent across various domains of science and engineering. In real-world networks, nodes often cluster into specific groups characterized by high intra-group edge density and sparse inter-group connections, a property known as *community structure* [3]. Detecting communities is a vital task in graph data mining. However, most existing research has focused primarily on non-overlapping community detection [1]. For non-overlapping communities, node embedding methods have shown strong performance [14]. Nevertheless, these methods face challenges when applied to overlapping community detection (OCD), as they often lack scalability and robustness for high-dimensional embeddings.

A promising solution is to model node embeddings as community affiliations, which can be achieved efficiently using graph convolutional networks (GCNs) [12]. Some studies integrate matrix factorization with probabilistic inference [13,18,20], but these approaches typically do not incorporate graph structure directly into their neural network designs, limiting their potential [12]. Neural OCD (NOCD) [12] addresses this limitation by employing a graph neural network (GNN)-based encoder-decoder framework. Unlike methods relying on non-negative matrix factorization (NMF), NOCD optimizes GNN weights to construct a more effective community affiliation matrix.

GCNs can process graph-structured data. The NOCD framework [12] introduced the first GCN-based method for OCD. This approach employed a two-layer shallow GCN to get community embeddings and a Bernoulli-Poisson (BP) model as a decoder to reconstruct the graph from these embeddings. However, shallow GCNs face inherent limitations in capturing communities with larger diameters (greater than two), as they can only aggregate information from nodes within a two-hop neighborhood.

A potential solution to this limitation is to utilize deep graph convolutional networks (DeepGCNs) [6] instead of shallow GCNs. However, the DeepGCN model proposed by Li et al. [6] was designed for point-clouds, where the node degree is same for the nodes of the considered network. In contrast, real-world networks are predominantly irregular, characterized by variable degree distribution of the nodes. Therefore, it is crucial to develop a deep GCN capable of effectively handling these graphs for detecting communities with large diameters.

Deep GCN training faces significant challenges due to issues such as oversmoothing and vanishing gradients [6]. These challenges have been addressed in previous studies through the use of residual connections and dilated aggregation, concepts adapted from ResNet [5]. A *residual connection* is a skip connection from input to the output of a layer. In GCNs, nodes collect information from their neighbors, and this process is referred to as *dilated aggregation* when information is gathered selectively, skipping certain closer neighbors to include some more distant ones.

Incorporating randomness into this neighbor selection introduces *edge dynamicity*, resulting in what is termed *dynamic dilated aggregation*. However, applying dynamic dilated aggregation effectively in irregular graphs remains a substantial challenge for training deep GCNs. To date, no existing deep GCN models have successfully integrated dilated aggregation mechanisms tailored specifically for irregular graph structures.

We develop random dynamic dilation methods tailored for irregular graphs. By integrating these aggregation strategies with residual connections, we construct a deep GCN capable of learning from diverse graph structures. We then apply this deep GCN to identify overlapping communities across various networks of differing sizes. For this task, we utilize an encoder-decoder framework inspired by NOCD. Our encoder, named DynaResGCN, is a deep GCN that produces community embeddings, while the decoder focuses on reconstructing the original graph from these embeddings.

For our evaluation, we utilize a collection of Facebook graphs [8] alongside a set of large-scale networks containing more than 10,000 nodes [12] as additional benchmarks. We compare our approach with the exact same baseline methods used in NOCD, employing normalized mutual information (NMI) [9] as the evaluation metric. Our proposed method, DynaResGCN, consistently outperforms all baseline models in nearly every scenario based on NMI scores.

The paper is structured as follows: Sect. 2 outlines our proposed methods, while Sect. 3 outlines the experimental evaluation. We the results and provide a detailed discussion of our findings at Sect. 4. Finally, Sect. 5 concludes the paper with a summary of our contributions. An extended version of this work is available at arXiv.

2 Our Methodology

We consider a graph G with an adjacency matrix A and a corresponding community affiliation matrix F [12]. Communities in a graph are defined as dense subgraphs where nodes are more likely to form edges within the community than with nodes outside it [12]. Using this definition as a foundation, we propose an OCD framework.

To model the relationship between the graph and its communities, we introduce a generative model which describes how G is generated given its corresponding F. The goal of OCD, however, is to infer the unobserved F from the given G. We achieve this by optimizing F through minimizing a loss function derived from the generative model $p(G|F)$.

Alternatively, a GCN can be used to process G, with the GCN trained to predict a better community affiliation matrix F. We adopt the GCN-based approach to optimize F in this research.

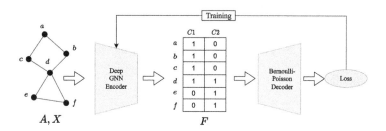

Fig. 1. Our proposed OCD framework.

In our research, we propose an unsupervised framework for OCD, utilizing an encoder-decoder architecture (Fig. 1). The encoder processes G represented by its corresponding A and node feature matrix X, generating F as output and a decoder processes F to computes a loss for training the encoder.

Our encoder is a deep graph convolutional network (GCN) enhanced with dynamic dilated aggregation, enabling effective learning on irregular graphs. Additionally, we incorporate residual connections to improve stability and performance, resulting in a model we call DynaResGCN. The decoder is based on a BP model, which complements the encoder by optimizing its output.

Our approach integrates dynamic edge manipulation, random dilation, and skip connections into an encoder-decoder framework tailored for OCD. We detail the design of the DynaResGCN encoder, the BP decoder, and the associated training algorithm in the following sections.

2.1 Deep DynaResGCN Encoder

We propose a deep GCN model tailored for OCD in graphs. Our approach integrates skip connections, dynamic edge adjustments, and random dilated aggregation into a GCN model named DynaResGCN (Fig. 2).

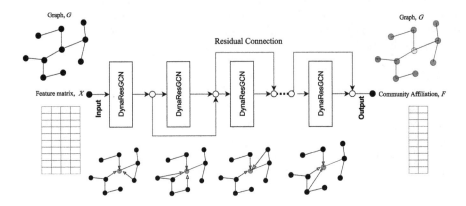

Fig. 2. The DynaResGCN encoder model.

Instead of giving the original adjacency matrix, we normalize our adjacency matrix as $\hat{A}$. At a certain layer l, our node feature matrix is X_l. Thus a GCN can be represented as:

$$X_{l+1} = ReLU(\hat{A} X_l W_l)$$

where W_l is a learnable parameter matrix. Now, we introduce residual connection according to the following equation:

$$X_{l+1} = ReLU(\hat{A} X_l W_l) + \hat{A} X_l \qquad (1)$$
$$= X_{l+1}^{res} + \hat{A} X_l$$

Li et al. [6] applied dilated aggregation for point cloud learning considering same degree for every node where a dilated neighborhood can be constructed for each node by choosing k nodes from $r \times k$ nearest neighbors [6] having dilation rate r. Thus initial neighborhood size is $r \times k$ for every node, i.e., every node has same degree. However, in general graphs, different nodes have different degrees. Thus the approach of generating dilated neighborhood in [6] is not applicable. In our design, instead of considering a constant k, we initially consider

Algorithm 1. Initial Graph Augmentation: Input G

1: V is the vertex set
2: E is the edge set
3: Initialize E' with E
4: **for** every $u \in V$ **do**
5:     Initialize S_u considering $S_u = \{x : x \in V, (u, x) \in E, x \neq u\}$
6:     Initialize $S'_u = S_u$ as the final set of neighbors of u
7:     **for** every $v \in S_u$ **do**
8:         Randomly select y from $\{x : x \notin S'_u, (v, x) \in E\}$
9:         Insert y in the set S'_u
10:        Insert the new edge (u, y) in the set E'
11: Return a new graph $G' = (V, E')$

$r \times m$ neighbors for every node where m is the node degree. Thus our initial neighborhood is variable and related to node degree m. we set $r = 2$ for simplicity. We devise an augmentation algorithm (Algorithm 1) which creates the initial neighborhood (augmented) for every node. Then we randomly subsample 50% nodes from this augmented neighborhood.

Dilation inherently excludes some immediate neighbors, and when the same dilation is used across all GCN layers, certain first-hop neighbors remain unexplored. This fixed neighborhood alters the original graph structure and leads to over-smoothing and thus hindering effective learning.

To address this, we sample different subsets of neighbors at each layer, ensuring layer-specific neighborhoods. This dynamic adjustment results in a graph with changing edge sets across layers. By unifying dynamic edges with dilated aggregation, we achieve more stable and effective learning compared to static methods [16]. In point cloud scenarios, nearest neighbor graphs are reconstructed after each layer. Similarly, we also recalculate the adjacency matrix at every layer.

We consider, at a layer l, the corresponding adjacency matrix is A_l. Thus we improve (1) as follows:

$$X_{l+1} = \hat{A}_l X_l + ReLU(\hat{A}_l X_l W_l) \qquad (2)$$
$$= \hat{A}_l X_l + X^{res}_{l+1}$$

Thus (2) can integrate different ideas such as dynamic edges, dilated aggregation, and residual connections. In Algorithm 1, we describe our initial graph augmentation approach. Figure 3 gives an illustrative example on how randomly dilated neighborhood is constructed at every layer.

2.2 BP Decoder

To calculate how good is our F generated by deep DynaResGCN, we use the BP model which was originally introduced by the authors of [18]. Considering negative log-likelihood and integrating data imbalance, we compute our loss as

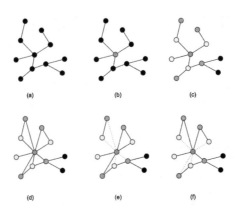

Fig. 3. (a) An initial network (b) Consider a vertex (colored red), (c) Nodes which are directly connected to the red node are colored yellow and second-hop neighbors are green(d) Augmented graph (e) A random dilation (f) another random dilation (Color figure online)

follows [4,12]:

$$\mathcal{L}(F) = \mathbb{E}_{(u,v) \sim P_N}[F_u F_v^T] - \mathbb{E}_{(u,v) \sim P_E}[\log(1 - exp(-F_u F_v^T))], \quad (3)$$

where P_E is the edge distribution and P_N is the non-edge distribution. This loss is actually a reconstruction loss where we measure the error of our generative model in generating the original graph [18].

2.3 OCD Algorithm

Our OCD algorithm is actually an unsupervised learning algorithm described at Algorithm 2.

Algorithm 2. Community Detection: Input G, Output F

1: Get a new graph G' running Algorithm 1 on G
2: Construct a DynaResGCN encoder with a n number of layers
3: Compute $\hat{A}_l$ for every l in $\{1, \ldots, n\}$
4: Set the number of epochs as τ
5: **for** every epoch e in $\{1, \ldots, \tau\}$ **do**
6:     **for** every l in total $\{1, \ldots, n\}$ **do**
7:         $X_{l+1} = \hat{A}_l X_l + \text{Relu}(\hat{A}_l X_l W_l)$
8:     Compute $F = X_n$
9:     Compute reconstruction error and update parameters
10:     **if** Loss does not change significantly compared to earlier epochs **then**
11:         Stop training early
12: return F

3 Experimental Evaluation

For evaluation and experimentation, we implemented our OCD model in pytorch which using some code of NOCD in applicable cases.

We utilize several baseline methods from a Python community detection library where we rely on their default parameters [11]. Our comparisons include the baselines utilized in NOCD [12]. The proposed DynaResGCN method has two variants: DynaResGCN-G, which excludes node attributes, and DynaResGCN-X, which incorporates them.

The baseline models include BigClam [18], EPM [20], SNetOC [13], CESNA [19], SNMF [15], and CDE [7]. Additionally, we evaluate DeepWalk [10] and Graph2Gauss [2], both paired with Non-exhaustive Overlapping K-means (NEO) clustering [17] as DW/NEO and G2G/NEO, respectively. The datasets used in our experiments are summarized in Table 1.

Table 1. Datasets for evaluation

Datasets	Num of Nodes	Num of Edges	Labeling method	Reference
Facebook 348	227	6384	Human-labeled	[8]
Facebook 414	159	3386	Human-labeled	[8]
Facebook 686	170	3312	Human-labeled	[8]
Facebook 698	66	540	Human-labeled	[8]
Facebook 1684	792	28048	Human-labeled	[8]
Facebook 1912	755	60050	Human-labeled	[8]
Computer Science	21957	193500	Not Human-labeled	[12]
Engineering	14297	98610	Not Human-labeled	[12]
Medicine	63282	1620628	Not Human-labeled	[12]

We use normalized mutual information (NMI) [9] to as supervised similarity metric to qauntify how similar our detected communities to the originally labeled communities. We report NMI in percentage (%).

Our experiments were conducted on a Linux platform using an NVIDIA GeForce RTX GPU with 4GB RAM. The implementation was done in Python (version 8) using the PyTorch library. We employed a weight decay rate of 0.01, a learning rate of 0.001, batch normalization, and stochastic loss [12]. Training was performed by 500 epochs with early stopping. The code for our implementation is publicly available at https://github.com/buet-gd/Deep-DynaResGCN-community.

4 Discussion on Results

We evaluate our top-performing method, the DynaResGCN model, on two types of datasets: human-labeled networks and very large graphs without human-labeled ground truth. The evaluation is performed in terms of NMI. Comparisons are made between DynaResGCN and NOCD, both with and without incorporating node features.

The methods DynaResGCN-G and NOCD-G, which exclude node features, are compared in Table 2. Similarly, Table 3 presents the comparison between DynaResGCN-X and NOCD-X, which account for node features. Detailed analysis of the results is provided in the subsequent sections.

Table 2. Overlapping community detection performance measured using NMI in networks without node features. Results are averaged over 50 different run to calculate statistical significance.

Datasets	BigClam	CESNA	EPM	SNetOC	CDE	SNMF	DW/NEO	G2G/NEO	NOCD-G	DynaResGCN-G	Significant[1]
FaceBook 348	26.00	29.40	6.50	24.00	24.80	13.50	31.20	17.20	34.70	**39.80**	✓
Facebook 414	48.30	50.30	17.50	52	28.70	32.50	40.90	32.30	56.30	**58.10**	✓
Facebook 686	13.80	13.30	3.10	10.60	13.50	11.60	11.80	5.60	20.60	**25.40**	✓
Facebook 698	45.60	39.40	9.20	44.90	31.60	28	40.10	2.60	49.30	**51**	✓
Facebook 1684	32.70	28	6.80	26.10	28.80	13	37.20	9.90	34.70	**44.30**	✓
Facebook 1912	21.40	21.20	9.80	21.40	15.50	23.40	20.80	16	36.80	**40.10**	✓
Computer Science	0	33.80	NF	NF	NF	9.40	3.20		31.20	34.20	**37.40**	✓
Engineering	7.90	24.30	NF	NF	NF	10.10	4.70		33.40	18.40	**37.3**	✓
Medicine	0	14.40	NF	NF	NF	4.90	5.50		28.80	27.40	**37.30**	✓

(1) We determine statistical significance of NMI with 95% confidence.
(2) NF in table denotes that the method did not finish computation.

Table 3. Overlapping community detection performance measured using NMI in networks having node features. Results are averaged over 50 different run to calculate statistical significance.

Datasets	BigClam	CESNA	EPM	SNetOC	CDE	SNMF	DW/NEO	G2G/NEO	NOCD-X	DynaResGCN-X	Significant[1]
FaceBook 348	26	29.40	6.50	24	24.80	13.50	31.20	17.20	36.40	**39.80**	✓
Facebook 414	48.30	50.30	17.50	52	28.70	32.50	40.90	32.30	**59.80**	59	✗
Facebook 686	13.80	13.30	3.10	10.60	13.50	11.60	11.80	5.60	21	**27.30**	✓
Facebook 698	45.60	39.40	9.20	44.90	31.60	28	40.10	2.60	41.70	**50.10**	✓
Facebook 1684	32.70	28	6.80	26.10	28.80	13	37.20	9.90	26.10	**41**	✓
Facebook 1912	21.40	21.20	9.80	21.40	15.50	23.40	20.80	16	35.60	**39.60**	✓
Computer Science	0	33.80	NF	NF	NF	9.40	3.20		31.20	**50.20**	46	✓
Engineering	7.90	24.30	NF	NF	NF	10.10	4.70		33.40	**39.10**	39	✗
Medicine	0	14.40	NF	NF	NF	4.90	5.50		28.80	37.80	**40**	✓

(1) We determine statistical significance of NMI with 95% confidence.
(2) NF in table denotes that the method did not finish computation.

We begin by analyzing small Facebook graphs with reliable, human-labeled ground truth information. As shown in Tables 2 and 3, DynaResGCN consistently outperforms the nearest competitor, NOCD, across all Facebook networks, regardless of whether node features are considered. Notably, NOCD-X shows comparable performance to DynaResGCN-X only on the *Facebook 414* dataset. Overall, DynaResGCN achieves a significantly better performance than all other methods on these ground-truth datasets, demonstrating a substantial margin of improvement.

Next, we evaluate the *Computer Science*, *Engineering*, and *Medicine* datasets, which are large-scale co-authorship networks. Since reliable human-labeled ground truth is unavailable for these datasets, approximate ground truth is considered based on research areas. When ignoring node features, DynaResGCN consistently outperforms NOCD by a significant margin. With node features included, NOCD surpasses DynaResGCN in only one instance, while DynaResGCN delivers superior performance in most other cases. These results highlight DynaResGCN's robustness to node features and its ability to achieve top performance even without node features in certain cases.

To test scalability, we applied our methods to these large datasets. Remarkably, DynaResGCN demonstrates scalability, effectively handling very deep models. In nearly all cases, the method converges in under 2 min, underscoring its efficiency and suitability for large-scale networks.

4.1 Insights, Limitations, and Future Directions

In this section, we summarize our learned insights, discuss the limitations of the this method, and propose future directions.

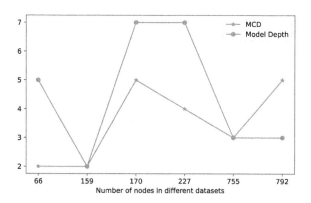

Fig. 4. Variability of the model depth with community diameters (MCD).

How Deeper the Model Should be: Model depth varies widely based on the input graph. We observe that small graphs tend to perform good with few layers, while large graphs achieve goods performance with deep models. This can be attributed to the fact that small graphs typically have small expected community diameters, while large graphs feature large community diameters. A deep GCN model allows for the aggregation of important information from distant nodes, which is essential for detecting communities with large diameters. In contrast, if the expected community diameter is small, a shallow model that explores closer neighbors suffices.

Figure 4 clearly demonstrates that the ideal model depth correlates strongly to the community diameter (MCD).

How Much Large Graphs We can Handle: Our proposed method DynaResGCN is highly scalable for OCD tasks. For small datasets, DynaResGCN completes execution in under 15 s, even with seven layers, without adding any significant time overhead. Remarkably, even for very large datasets (with 65K nodes), the execution time remains under 15 min, even with deep models. This demonstrates that our proposed community detection method with deep DynaResGCN model is not only efficient but also scalable, even when using very deep architectures.

Our Limitations and Future Research Directions: It is essential to consider edge weights when working with weighted graphs, as this information can provide valuable insights. In fact, there are some networks where edge contains multi-dimensional features. Therefore, there is significant potential to design methods and algorithms that incorporate edge weight and edge-features to improve OCD tasks. Some times a shallow model outperforms a deep model indicating that the model may not fully resolve the issue of over-smoothing. As a result, deeper models do not always yield better performance. Addressing over-smoothing more effectively presents an interesting avenue for future research.

This research focuses on enhancing the encoder component of the OCD framework. However, there is room for further exploration in improving decoders to account for different community properties. Lastly, we have applied our methods in an unsupervised setting, but integrating our approaches into supervised graph learning tasks would be an exciting direction for future work.

5 Conclusion

We introduce a random dynamic dilation powered residual deep graph convolutional network (DynaResGCN) for OCD tasks in different types of networks. Our research addresses several key issues of integrating random dilation powered information aggregation, dynamicity of edges, and skip connections into the graphs nodes degree is highly varying for solving OCD problem. Our methods significantly outperform many leading existing approaches.

Future research could focus on the challenges posed by heterogeneous graphs, where both edges and nodes exhibit heterogeneity. Specially networks with edges having high dimensional features is worthy of exploration for OCD tasks.

This work has broad applications, extending across fields like bioscience, social science, and any domain involving network structures.

Acknowledgements. This work has been done under the project "Development of Efficient Graph Algorithms for Big Data Analytics and Visualization" funded by Research and Innovation Centre for Science and Engineering (RISE), Internal Research Grant 2021-01-006 of Bangladesh University of Engineering and Technology (BUET). The authors would like to express heartfelt gratitude to CodeCrafters International Ltd.

for their CodeCrafters-Investortools Research Grant, which made our participation in this event possible.

References

1. Abbe, E.: Community detection and stochastic block models: recent developments. J. Mach. Learn. Res. **18**(1), 6446–6531 (2017). https://jmlr.org/papers/v18/16-480.html
2. Bojchevski, A., Günnemann, S.: Deep gaussian embedding of graphs: unsupervised inductive learning via ranking. In: International Conference on Learning Representations (2017)
3. Girvan, M., Newman, M.E.: Community structure in social and biological networks. Proc. Natl. Acad. Sci. **99**(12), 7821–7826 (2002). https://doi.org/10.1073/pnas.122653799
4. He, H., Garcia, E.A.: Learning from imbalanced data. IEEE Trans. Knowl. Data Eng. **21**(9), 1263–1284 (2009). https://doi.org/10.1109/TKDE.2008.239
5. He, K., Zhang, X., Ren, S., Sun, J.: Deep residual learning for image recognition. In: Proceedings of the IEEE Conference on Computer Vision and Pattern Recognition, pp. 770–778 (2016). https://doi.org/10.1109/CVPR.2016.90
6. Li, G., Muller, M., Thabet, A., Ghanem, B.: DeepGCNs: can GCNs go as deep as CNNs? In: Proceedings of the IEEE International Conference on Computer Vision, pp. 9267–9276 (2019). https://sites.google.com/view/deep-gcns
7. Li, Y., Sha, C., Huang, X., Zhang, Y.: Community detection in attributed graphs: an embedding approach. In: Proceedings of the AAAI Conference on Artificial Intelligence, vol. 32 (2018). https://doi.org/10.1609/aaai.v32i1.11274
8. Mcauley, J., Leskovec, J.: Discovering social circles in ego networks. ACM Trans. Knowl. Discov. Data (TKDD) **8**(1), 1–28 (2014). https://doi.org/10.1145/2556612
9. McDaid, A.F., Greene, D., Hurley, N.: Normalized mutual information to evaluate overlapping community finding algorithms. Comput. Res. Reposit. (2011)
10. Perozzi, B., Al-Rfou, R., Skiena, S.: DeepWalk: online learning of social representations. In: Proceedings of the 20th ACM SIGKDD International Conference on Knowledge Discovery and Data Mining, pp. 701–710 (2014). https://doi.org/10.1145/2623330.2623732
11. Rossetti, G.: Cdlib: community discovery library in python (2022). https://cdlib.readthedocs.io/en/latest/
12. Shchur, O., Günnemann, S.: Overlapping community detection with graph neural networks. In: Deep Learning on Graphs Workshop, KDD (2019)
13. Todeschini, A., Miscouridou, X., Caron, F.: Exchangeble random measures for sparse and modular graphs with overlapping communities. J. Royal Stat. Soc. Ser. B (Stat. Methodol.) **82**(2), 487–520 (2020). https://doi.org/10.1111/rssb.12363
14. Tsitsulin, A., Mottin, D., Karras, P., Müller, E.: Verse: versatile graph embeddings from similarity measures. In: Proceedings of the 2018 World Wide Web Conference, pp. 539–548 (2018). https://doi.org/10.1145/3178876.3186120
15. Wang, F., Li, T., Wang, X., Zhu, S., Ding, C.: Community discovery using non-negative matrix factorization. Data Min. Knowl. Discov. **22**(3), 493–521 (2011). https://doi.org/10.1007/s10618-010-0181-y
16. Wang, Y., Sun, Y., Liu, Z., Sarma, S.E., Bronstein, M.M., Solomon, J.M.: Dynamic graph CNN for learning on point clouds. ACM Trans. Grap. (TOG) **38**(5), 1–12 (2019). https://doi.org/10.1145/3326362

17. Whang, J.J., Dhillon, I.S., Gleich, D.F.: Non-exhaustive, overlapping k-means. In: Proceedings of the 2015 SIAM International Conference on Data Mining, pp. 936–944. SIAM (2015). https://doi.org/10.1109/TPAMI.2018.2863278
18. Yang, J., Leskovec, J.: Overlapping community detection at scale: a nonnegative matrix factorization approach. In: Proceedings of the Sixth ACM International Conference on Web Search and Data Mining, pp. 587–596 (2013).https://doi.org/10.1145/2433396.2433471
19. Yang, J., McAuley, J., Leskovec, J.: Community detection in networks with node attributes. In: 2013 IEEE 13th International Conference on Data Mining, pp. 1151–1156. IEEE (2013). https://doi.org/10.1109/ICDM.2013.167
20. Zhou, M.: Infinite edge partition models for overlapping community detection and link prediction. In: Artificial Intelligence and Statistics, pp. 1135–1143. PMLR (2015). https://proceedings.mlr.press/v38/zhou15a.html

DeepUIR-Net: Underwater Image Restoration Using Residual-UNet with Optimized Efficient Channel Attention Network Integration

N. Rayvanth, S. Jaya Amruth, E. Suryaa, S. Resmi, and Rimjhim Padam Singh[✉]

Department of Computer Science and Engineering, Amrita School of Computing, Bengaluru, Amrita Vishwa Vidyapeetham, India
bl.en.r4cse22010@bl.students.amrita.edu, ps_rimjhim@blr.amrita.edu

Abstract. The underwater image restoration task targets retaining the true colors of the underwater scenarios captured in the images by rectifying the distorted colors to critically analyze the ocean scenarios and resources. This area has been explored using different deep learning techniques such as Convolutional neural networks, Residual Networks, and various other models that made use of post-processing techniques for the final enhanced outputs. Hence, this study proposes a novel approach by fine-tuning the Residual-UNet architecture and combining it with an Efficient Channel Attention network in an optimized architecture for the task of underwater image restoration. Channel attention mechanisms have a great ability to reduce model complexity by making use of fewer parameters and increasing the performance of the model. One such mechanism, called Efficient Channel Attention, has been incorporated into the Residual-UNet model to extract features efficiently and obtain an enhanced underwater image that is true to the ground truth image by making use of the HardSwish activation function. The dataset used to train the Residual-UNet model is LSUI (Large Scale Underwater Images), a benchmark dataset consisting of various real underwater images. The proposed model obtained SSIM and PSNR values of 0.9998 and 74.851 dB respectively and outperformed other models by a margin of 4%. To determine the superiority of the Efficient Channel Attention network optimally integrated into the Residual-UNet model, various base models without this attention module have also been trained and evaluated.

Keywords: ResUNet · Underwater Image Restoration · Channel Attention · HardSwish

1 Introduction

Underwater monitoring is a major requirement to explore the ocean that aids mankind in developing and using the underwater resources effectively. But normally the underwater image quality is inadequate for performing efficient research works utilizing them. Hence, the underwater image quality improvement and restoration are having substantial research values and are of immense importance. However, restoration of images in underwater scenes is difficult due to numerous challenges posed in these environments like light attenuation, color distortion, scattering etc. [14].

Traditional methods which improve the image quality by adjusting the pixel values and methods using mathematical models are hard to be implemented since the image enhancement and restoration should consider many intrinsic factors in the underwater [3]. Hence, good quality image restoration results have been attained by employing deep learning based methods. Several deep-learning based Convolutional Neural Networks (CNNs) have emerged as powerful tools for image restoration tasks, by learning complex mappings between distorted and clean images. However, deploying traditional CNN architectures for underwater image restoration is inefficient as they are resource intensive and need huge amount of data for model training and fitting. But CNN based U-Net model and its variants, as proposed in past few years, have proven to work efficiently for numerous image-related applications with lesser amount of data and reduced resource requirements. Therefore, to overcome these challenges involved in the underwater image restoration task, this paper explores and proposes to leverage the Residual-UNet (ResUNet) architecture, a combination of U-Net model integrated with residual blocks, with attention mechanism and state-of-art activation functions.

The key contributions of this work include:

- A novel hybrid model (DeepUIR-Net) integrating the Residual-UNet model with the Efficient Channel Attention Network for the underwater image restoration task.
- Analysis of the proposed DeepUIR-Net model with various state-of-the-art activation functions such as ReLU, SiLU, and HardSwish for optimized and efficient results.
- Detailed performance analysis of five other state-of-the-art models implemented as a part of this study, such as U-Net, U-Net++, ResUNet, etc., against the proposed DeepUIR-Net model using several metrics.

2 Related Works

Tang et al. [1] proposed a CNN on underwater imaging model known as Multi-Scale Convolution Underwater Image Restoration Network. The dataset used was NYU Depth v2 to synthesize underwater images which were then used to train the model. A total of 10143 images were synthesized. This model consisted of 2 parts, K lambda estimation which is used to estimate background light and clean image generation module. Dudhane et al. [2] gave idea of a deep network for underwater scenario based image restoration which has two parts. The 10143 synthesized images were split as 80% for training and 20% for testing. To reduce distortions C-GAN was used on the underwater images. Jingyu et al. [3] proposed a method that could transfer underwater image to recovered style that made use of MSCGAN.

Desai et al. [4] proposed a model AquaGAN to restore degraded underwater images taking into account the attenuation coefficient. The main process was to use learning methods to estimate the attenuation coefficient and then made use of this to restore the images. U-Net was used for this purpose. The authors concluded that the restored images had a better quality compared to other methods.

Xu et al. [5] gave an algorithm to improve underwater images called as Cross Attention based underwater image enhancement. The aim was to build a UNet model that combined cross large kernel attention with enhancement modules. Zhou et al. [6] gave a restoration model for underwater images, Multicolor Components and Light Attenuation. Background light estimation was introduced using the multicolor model to remove color casts. The model outperformed other existing methods of image restoration by achieving images which had a good color correction and also removed color casts with enhanced contrast.

Chang in [7] worked on single underwater based image restoration. The outcome was obtained through the fusion of two transmissions. The fusion approach used was pixel level image fusion. Several metrics were used to evaluate the restoration process such as pixel by pixel channel intensity disparity, UIQM. The author concluded that the model generated superior quality images based on the results obtained. Han et al. [8] explains two methods that enhance underwater images namely underwater image dehazing and image color restoration. One such algorithm used by them to dehaze was Adaptive Histogram Equalization.

Hou et al. [9] gave a method for restoring images in underwater environment with accurate depth of scenes. Then the transmission was calculated based on this scene depth. Authors concluded that model gave better results for contrast. Martinho et al. [10] proposed learning restoration method that could understand and predict the ideal values needed for restoring and improving quality of underwater scenario images. This approach consisted of two parts. First a CNN model with 3 layers was used to learn the parameters with 64 filters, 128 filters and 128 filters respectively. The authors concluded that their approach had better PSNR and SSIM values which in turn helped to restore underwater images.

Wang et al. [11] discussed the model using Vision Transformer for restoring underwater images. To boost this process frequency domain's impact was reviewed. The URTB was mainly used for studying the color degradation on different color channels. Frequency domain loss was utilized as a loss learning parameter. Based on the experiments conducted the authors concluded that it was effective. To maintain image edge and removing noise in the image, Li et al. [12] gave a varying model with mean variance and extrinsic transmission maps. An algorithm based on ADMM was used to solve the function to obtain restored underwater images and it also refined the transmission images. The authors concluded that the images restored were dehazed and the model performed better when evaluated using UCIQE and UIQM metrics compared to various other methods.

To enhance the overall underwater image quality, Verma et al. [13] gave a transfer-based CNN. The images after processing were given as input to the multi stack CNN for feature extraction whose outputs were combined to obtain the enhanced images. Suresha et al. [15] proposed a method to de blur the motion images using a computer vision based approach and this method was considered good. Using MCycle GAN similar to cycle GAN in [20] the images had very natural contrast enhancement and color restoration compared to other methods. The authors showed the best performance with UICM underwater image colorfulness measure. Mohan et al. [21] proposed ways making use of transfer based learning to enhance the quality of medical images.

Based on the recent literature highlighted and the efficacy of U-Net family based models and importance of attention mechanisms for enhanced model training, this paper focuses on employing U-Net based models integrated with sophisticated and recent attention mechanisms for task of enhanced underwater image restoration.

3 Dataset Description

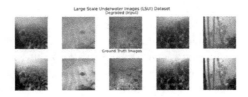

Fig. 1. A sample of the LSUI dataset used for image restoration.

The dataset used for this work is the standard LSUI (Large Scale Underwater Images), a benchmark dataset for image restoration tasks. This dataset contains degraded underwater images, which are the input images to the model, and their corresponding ground truth images. The images are of various sizes, and this dataset contains 4279 underwater images along with corresponding ground truth images, out of which 2007 from each set were used to train the models. A sample of this dataset is shown in Fig. 1. The dataset is split into separate Training, Testing, and Validation sets in the ratio of 60:20:20 to thoroughly train and evaluate the performance of models on unseen data for a good model fit.

4 Methodology

Underwater Image Restoration has been explored using various deep learning techniques in past few years. However, most of those were computationally very expensive, needed huge amount of training data and with higher number of trainable parameters. Hence, the proposed methodology, DeepUIR-Net, focuses on selecting light-weight methods developed from the perspective of being trainable with relatively lesser amount of data and having lower model complexity. U-Net and its variants are the distinctive instances of such models offering higher model flexibility with lesser data and complexity. Hence, the proposed methodology here selects employing U-Net family based models enhanced with lighter channel attention mechanisms like Efficient Channel Attention networks for underwater image restoration tasks. The work also explored the efficiency of the proposed methodology with several recent activation functions for enhanced image restoration.

4.1 Data Pre-processing

By observing the LSUI dataset it was found that the images in the LSUI dataset are having distinct dimensions. Hence, the images in the dataset are pre-processed and resized to a common size of 256×256 so that they can be passed as input to different deep learning models.

4.2 Model Architecture of DeepUIR-Net

The model architecture presented in Fig. 2 suggests employing Residual-UNet (ResUNet) model as the baseline model for the underwater restoration task. ResUNet model architecture combines elements of both U-Net model and Residual Network, which is also commonly referred to as Deep Residual learning. Similar to U-Net model, ResUNet also employs an encoder-decoder architecture which makes use of several skip connections. Additionally, ResU-Net architectures make use of multiple residual blocks which help to overcome the problem of exploding gradient and vanishing gradient. The input to the residual block is the feature map of the underwater images. This is followed by a Convolution layers with ECANet, followed by batch normalization of the data, and an activation function as shown in the blocks of Fig. 2. This residual blocks also helps in training the network in a simpler way with lesser number of parameters and data, and has also proven to be efficient for enhanced feature extraction from the input data. The encoder part employs several convolutional layers and by capturing the context using these layers it down-samples the input images provided. The convolution blocks here are followed by Batch Normalization layer and HardSwish activation function layer. The bottleneck part captures higher level features between encoder and decoder blocks by compressing the feature maps. The decoder part is responsible for up-sampling these maps so that images can be restored at maximum resolution. Here, the features maps obtained from the encoder are concatenated with corresponding decoder maps to get better detailing of the information or the features required to restore the underwater images. The output layer uses a 1×1 kernel and a sigmoid function to produce the output. The enhanced ResUNet model employed in this paper as shown in Fig. 2 also integrates the light-weight Efficient Channel Attention network (ECA-Net) module [15] for further leveraging its performance.

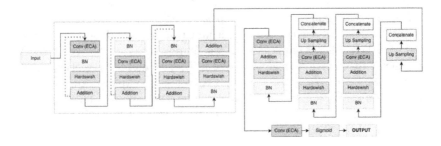

Fig. 2. Proposed Model Architecture

The ECA-Net attention module as shown in Fig. 3 ensures that the performance of the ResUNet model is enhanced by focusing on most important features and leaving out the less important ones. As compared to other older attention modules like Convolutional block attention module, squeeze excitation attention mechanism, etc. ECA-Net attention module is also computationally very efficient with least number of parameters and memory requirements. The ECA-Net module applies GlobalAveragePooling method to the input feature maps which are obtained by a convolution block previously to reduce the spatial dimensions and retain high-level features. The ECA-Net module uses a one-dimensional convolutional layer with a smaller kernel to reduce the complexity. The output of this layer is then passed through a Sigmoid activation function with the average of the weights taken before. These attention weights are then multiplied with the original feature maps to enhance the more important features. These features are then utilized in building the ResUNet model where the Encoder block having convolution block uses these features and reduces the model complexity.

Fig. 3. Efficient Channel Attention Module

The input features undergoing global average pooling for each of the channel features and then being passed to the two fully connected layers considering k-nearest neighbours helps in capturing local cross channel interaction which guarantees better performance of the proposed model. This ECA module which is integrated with our ResUNet is a lightweight channel attention module as it uses 1×1 convolution layers thereby significantly reducing the computational complexity. The ECA module alleviates the burden of computational efficiency because it utilize a light-weight operation of one dimensional convolution rather than the fully connected layer to capture channel interaction. It uses global average pooling to aggregate the spatial information whereby it is optimized to have little parameters and memory consumption. This design does not enact any dimensionality reduction and thus has both time and image restoration efficiency when used to restore underwater images.

Moreover, the activation function used in ECANet is replaced and experimented with several other activation functions like Swish, Rectified Linear Unit (ReLU) function and HardSwish activation function for model enhancement. These functions are presented in Eqs. 1, 2 and 3. Out of all these functions, HardSwish activation function has been proven to provide the best results.

ReLU activation function is most widely used, is simpler and introduces non linearity to the model. The output will be input itself in case it is positive otherwise the output is zero in all other cases. It is defined as in Eq. (1).

$$\text{ReLU}(x) = \max(0, x) \tag{1}$$

SiLU is considered as an improvement over ReLU function which is used to effectively capture patterns as compared to the latter. It is defined as in Eq. (2).

$$\text{SiLU}(x) = x \cdot \frac{1}{1 + e^{-x}} \tag{2}$$

HardSwish activation function is a simplified version of SiLU and is much more efficient comparatively in capturing complex patterns involved in underwater environments. For any input less than 0 the output is zero while for any result greater than 6 the output is set a maximum value of 6 by making use of ReLU6. The equation of the function is shown in (3).

$$\text{h-swish}(x) = x \cdot \frac{\text{ReLU6}(x + 3)}{6} \tag{3}$$

In a nutshell, the combination of ResUNet with ECA-Net module using HardSwish function can enhance the performance of the proposed model by capturing spatial and channel wise features efficiently. The ECA module is added in the convolutional layers of the encoder and decoder block as presented in Fig. 2. This is done in each of the convolution blocks to refine the features or patterns before passing them through the network. This is also done for each of the residual block of the ResUNet model to ensure that the channel wise attention is applied to the features extracted. This combination can address challenges that persist in underwater images like distortion of color, haziness and contrast and the attention mechanism is included without any additional computational complexity making it suitable for practical applications.

5 Results and Discussion

Table 1 below shows the hyper parameters setting used to train the ResUNet model along with other state-of-art models namely, UNet, UNet++, UNet3+, Bi-UNet, ResUNet and CycleGAN for comparative purposes. All these models and their variants have been trained on the dataset in a batch size of 32 images and for 30 epochs, Mean squared error as a loss function and a variety of activation functions namely, ReLU, SiLU and Hardswish functions. The models have been compared using two standard metrics namely, SSIM and PSNR values.

Table 1. Hyper Parameters

Parameters	ResUNet
Epochs	30
Batch Size	32
Optimizer	Adam
Activation Functions	ReLU, SiLU, HardSwish
Loss Function	Mean Squared Error
Evaluation Metrics	SSIM, PSNR

Figure 4(a) shows ResUNet model loss plot without using ECA-Net attention mechanism. It was trained for 30 epochs and couldn't generalize well by end of training.

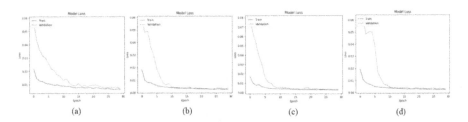

Fig. 4. Loss over epochs obtained for ResUNet model with different activation functions (a) without ECA-Net, (b) ReLU function, (c) SiLU function and (d) Hardswish function

Then the proposed ResUNet model with the ECA-Net module was trained for 30 epochs with three different activation functions namely, ReLU, SiLU and HardSwish activation functions in its first convolution layer while extracting the weights and the training loss over epochs for these different functions are shown in Fig. 4(b), 4(c) and 4(d) respectively. The observation from Fig. 4 is that the ResUNet which utilized the effective channel attention module after training for 30 epochs could generalize well with HardSwish function and can be justified by the convergence of minimum training loss and validation loss values as presented in Table 2.

Table 2 shows results obtained for different activation functions used in ECA-Net module for the proposed ResUNet based restoration model. The higher SSIM and PSNR obtained using Hard Swish function in the ECA-Net module

Table 2. Evaluation Table for ResUNet with different activation functions in ECANet

Criteria	ReLU in ECA	SiLU in ECA	HardSwish in ECA
Training Loss	0.0026	0.0024	**0.0024**
Validation Loss	0.0036	0.0032	**0.0030**
Mean Squared Error (MSE)	0.0027	0.0024	**0.0021**
SSIM	0.9998	0.9998	**0.9998**
PSNR	73.832 dB	74.374 dB	**74.851 dB**

can be attributed to the effective capturing of feature extractions which significantly improved the performance of the ResUNet model. It can be inferred that ResUNet with ECA-Net module using HardSwish function achieved best results because the restored images were closely resembling the ground truth images maintaining the quality while higher PSNR indicate that the noise is low in the restored images. Lower MSE indicate that the higher accuracy in pixel level restoration which leads to minimal errors. The use of SiLU function also achieved competitive results but at higher computational while ReLU function clearly underperformed. This clearly suggested incorporating Hardswish activation function into the ECA-Net module for the best results.

Table 3. Comparison of SSIM and PSNR of different base models against the proposed DeepUIR-Net model

Model	SSIM	PSNR	Loss
U-Net	0.9977	63.745 dB	0.0085
U-Net ++	0.9994	70.262 dB	0.0075
U-Net 3+	0.9986	67.163 dB	0.0136
BiU-Net	0.9991	68.567 dB	0.0107
ResU-Net	0.9994	70.750 dB	0.0068
Multi ResUNet	0.9996	71.363 dB	0.0057
CycleGAN	0.8996	60.545 dB	0.0089
Proposed DeepUIR-Net (with HardSwish)	**0.9998**	**74.851 dB**	**0.0030**

To highlight the significance of the ECA-net module in the ResUNet model for the task of underwater image restoration, a comparative analysis in terms of SSIM, PSNR and model loss with other baseline models is shown in Table 3. It is evident that the proposed model which is a ResUNet model with Efficient Channel Attention using HardSwish function is more efficient and outperformed other state of the art models with a huge gap of 4% approximately in terms on PSNR values. The higher SSIM and PSNR values obtained for our proposed model shows the robustness of this architecture for the task of underwater image restoration. The proposed model made use of HardSwish which resulted in higher values of SSIM and PSNR. This model was also experimented with ReLU and SiLU activation functions but resulted in slightly lower values and it can be understood that HardSwish function captured the features that were necessary for the restoration of images effectively.

GAN's also proved to be useful in restoring underwater images. To prove the effectiveness of the proposed model a CycleGAN as in [20] was trained on the LSUI dataset for 30 epochs. The SSIM, PSNR and loss of the CycleGAN as shown in Table 3 are not so good compared to the DeepUIR-Net proposed. This shows the effectiveness of the proposed work using ResUNet models for the underwater image restoration.

It must be noted that even though the proposed model achieved competitive performance in terms of SSIM values but its PSNR values are way higher than the other baseline state of art models, thereby, accepting its suitability for the proposed underwater image restoration task. The residual connections in the ResUNet model help in handling vanishing gradient issues thereby allowing a good model learning on the dataset. And integration of attention mechanism allowed the model to weigh and extract the features effectively by downplaying the unimportant image features which made the model efficient in restoring colors.

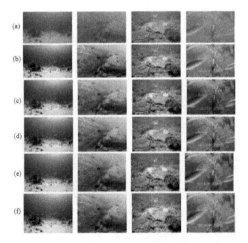

Fig. 5. Graphical results of restored images obtained by ResUNet with different combinations of attention mechanisms and activation functions: (a) input images, (b) ground truth, restored images by ResUNet model (c) without ECA-Net, (d) ECA-Net with ReLU function, (e) ECA-Net with SiLU function, and (f) ECA-Net with HardSwish function.

Figure 5 shows the restored images obtained using the ResUNet model and its different architectures implemented for the purposed of this study. From the above depicted visual representations it can be seen clearly that the proposed

DeepUIR-Net model had a better visibility with restored images being much sharper and clearer than those obtained by other methods. The results are very close in resemblance to the ground truth images in terms of color and sharpness retention. This is also evident from the SSIM and PSNR of 0.9998 and 74.851 dB respectively obtained as shown in Table 2. It can also be seen that ResUNet model with simple ECA-Net attention generated comparatively hazy images and colors were also not retained properly which was clearly overcome by the proposed method. Most of the methods as in [17,22–26], [27] discussed the color channel correction be it the red, blue or green and could not address the quality of the restored images. Our work tried to address the quality of the restored images by generating sharper images which are very close to the ground truth images.

6 Conclusion and Future Scope

The paper proposed a novel DeepUIR-Net model comprising of Residual U-Net (ResUNet) model which used Efficient Channel Attention Network (ECA-Net) module with HardSwish activation function for Underwater Image Restoration task. The integrated attention mechanism enabled the basic ResUNet model to focus on the important image features and regions for enhanced color retention and image restoration as compared to other state of art models thereby supporting the suitability of the proposed model for the underlying task. In future the work can be extended by developing faster underwater image restoration processes capable of producing results in real-time. This can also be extended by performing the restoration task of certain underwater video samples analyzing frames which can make it easier for object detection. The trained knowledge of this model can also be used to make it on demand underwater image restoration which can tackle the challenges of real time restoration.

References

1. Tang, Z., Li, J., Huang, J., Wang, Z., Luo, Z.: Multi-scale convolution underwater image restoration network. Mach. Vis. Appl. (2022). https://doi.org/10.1007/s00138-022-01337-3
2. Dudhane, A., Hambarde, P., Patil, P., Murala, S.: Deep underwater image restoration and beyond. IEEE Sig. Process. Lett. **27**, 675–679 (2020)
3. Lu, J., Li, N., Zhang, S., Yu, Z., Zheng, H., Zheng, B.: Multi-scale adversarial network for underwater image restoration. https://doi.org/10.1016/j.optlastec.2018.05.048
4. Desai, C., Reddy, B.S.S., Tabib, R.A., Patil, U., Mudenagudi, U.: AquaGAN: restoration of underwater images. In: Proceedings of the IEEE/CVF Conference on Computer Vision and Pattern Recognition Workshops (CVPRW) (2022)
5. Xu, S., Wang, J., He, N., Hu, X., Sun, F.: Underwater image enhancement method based on a cross attention mechanism. https://doi.org/10.1007/s00530-023-01224-5

6. Zhou, J., Wang, Y., Li, C., Zhang, W.: Multicolor light attenuation modeling for underwater image restoration. IEEE J. Oceanic Eng. **48**(4), 1322–1337 (2023)
7. Chang, H.-H.: Single underwater image restoration based on adaptive transmission fusion. IEEE Access **8**, 38650–38662 (2020)
8. Han, M., Lyu, Z., Qiu, T., Xu, M.: A review on intelligence dehazing and color restoration for underwater images. IEEE Trans. Syst. Man Cybern. Syst. **50**(5), 1820–1832 (2020)
9. Li, J., Hou, G., Wang, G.: Underwater image restoration using oblique gradient operator and light attenuation prior. https://doi.org/10.1007/s11042-022-13605-5
10. Martinho, L.A., Calvalcanti, J.M.B., Pio, J.L.S., Oliveira, F.G.: Diving into clarity: restoring underwater images using deep learning. J. Intell. Robot. Syst. https://doi.org/10.1007/s10846-024-02065-8
11. Wang, D., Sun, Z.: Frequency domain based learning with transformer for underwater image restoration. https://doi.org/10.1007/978-3-031-20862-1_16
12. Li, S., Liu, F., Wei, J.: Underwater image restoration based on exponentiated mean local variance and extrinsic prior. Multimedia Tools Appl. https://doi.org/10.1007/s11042-021-11269-1
13. Verma, G., Kumar, M., Raikwar, S.: F2UIE: feature transfer based underwater image enhancement using multi-stackCNN. Multimedia Tools and Applications
14. Mageshwari, G., Chandralekha, M., Chaudhary, D.: Underwater image re-enhancement with blend of simplest colour balance and contrast limited adaptive histogram equalization algorithm. In: 2023 International Conference on Advancement in Computation & Computer Technologies
15. Wang, Q., Wu, B., Zhu, P., Li, P., Zuo, W., Hu, Q.: ECA-Net: efficient channel attention for deep convolutional neural networks. In: Proceedings of the IEEE/CVF Conference on Computer Vision and Pattern Recognition
16. Avenash, R., Viswanath, P.: Semantic segmentation of satellite images using a modified CNN with hard-swish activation function. In: VISIGRAPP, pp. 413–420 (2019)
17. Satish, M., Singh, R.P., Kumar, P.: Single image super-resolution using information augmentation. In: 2023 IEEE 20th India Council International Conference (INDICON), pp. 1392–1397. IEEE (2023)
18. Mol, B., Singh, R.P., Kumar, P.: Parkinson disease classification using hybrid deep learning approach. In: 2023 9th International Conference on Signal Processing and Communication (ICSC), pp. 591–596. IEEE (2023)
19. Suresha, R., Jayanth, R., Shriharikoushik, M.A.: Computer vision approach for motion blur image restoration system. In: 2023 14th International Conference on Computing Communication and Networking Technologies (ICCCNT), pp. 1–9. IEEE
20. Spandana, C., et al.: Underwater image enhancement and restoration using cycle GAN. In: International Conference On Innovative Computing And Communication, pp. 99–110. Springer, Singapore (2023). https://doi.org/10.1007/978-981-99-3010-4_9
21. Reddy, K.L., Mohan, G.B.: Enhancing Medical Imaging: Noise Reduction and Super Resolution with Transfer Learning. In: 2024 2nd International Conference on Intelligent Data Communication Technologies and Internet of Things (IDCIoT), pp. 1430–1435. IEEE (2024)
22. Peng, Y.-T., Cosman, P.C.: Underwater image restoration based on image blurriness and light absorption. IEEE Trans. Image Process. **26**(4), 1579–1594 (2017)
23. Galdran, A., Pardo, D., Picón, A., Alvarez-Gila, A.: Automatic red-channel underwater image restoration. J. Vis. Commun. Image Represent. **26**, 132–145 (2015)

24. Zhou, Y., Wu, Q., Yan, K., Feng, L., Xiang, W.: Underwater image restoration using color-line model. IEEE Trans. Circuits Syst. Video Technol. **29**(3), 907–911 (2018)
25. Liu, H., Chau, L.-P.: Underwater image restoration based on contrast enhancement. In: 2016 IEEE International Conference on Digital Signal Processing (DSP), pp. 584–588. IEEE (2016)
26. Wu, M., Luo, K., Dang, J., Li, D.: Underwater image restoration using color correction and non-local prior. In: OCEANS 2017-Aberdeen, pp. 1–5. IEEE (2017)

Deepfake Image Detection Using Light-Weight Attention Integrated MobileNetV3 Model

Talluri Harshitha, Tanya Simhadri, Thadakuluru Jaswanthi, N. Rayvanth, and Rimjhim Padam Singh[✉]

Department of Computer Science and Engineering, Amrita School of Computing, Bengaluru, Amrita Vishwa Vidyapeetham, Bengaluru, India
ps_rimjhim@blr.amrita.edu

Abstract. With sudden proliferation in evolving Deepfake technology to manipulate media content, identity theft etc., several modern deep learning based solutions are being continuously developed for Deepfake detection, distinguishing the manipulated media. Therefore, the work presented in this paper proposes a novel and real-time MobileNetV3 based Deepfake detection model. With the fine-tuning of MobileNetV3 using additional fully connected layers and self-attention mechanism placed optimally, the proposed model proved effective in concentrating on crucial image regions over relatively lesser important features. The integration of self-attention layers had a direct impact on the model's capacity to identify the artifacts manipulated during the generation of Deepfakes, thereby, alleviating the detection efficiency. The work also implemented and trained five widely used and recent convolutional models including XceptionNet, InceptionV3, EfficientNetB0, MobileNetV3, and InceptionResNet for best baseline model selection and comparisons against the proposed approach. The proposed model outperformed all other state-of-art models by a margin of 3% with an F-score = 98.46%. The proposed model also has minimalistic memory and time requirements supporting the real-time applicability of the model even on mobile devices.

Keywords: Deepfake · attention · MobileNetv3 · convolutional network

1 Introduction

Deepfakes have recently become popular with the fellow citizens being immensely affected due to identity theft, privacy concerns, etc. 'Deepfake' terminology is derived using terms 'deep' referring to 'deep learning' and 'fake' referring to faux. Hence, Deepfake involves modification or generation of new images and videos sequences with the help of generative neural techniques and modern deep learning technologies, in a way that the superficial content is manipulated, replaced or augmented. Nowadays, Deepfake technology is used widely in developing hyper-realistic videos that involve facial substitutions, altered expressions and voice-overs. Effects that Deepfake images bring to society are complex. Though it presents numerous opportunities in the sphere of entertainment and new media art by allowing genuine simulation of events and people, creating arts and generating animations, but it has sparked intense controversies as well mainly due to fake video-making, which can be misleading and manipulative for evil intents. Deepfake images can be used for malicious purposes, such as to mislead individuals, shape their perception and reputation, manipulation through creation of fake compromising material, etc. Therefore, the investigation on identification and minimization of Deepfake content has become relevant in an effort to deal with the ethical and security implications with these Deepfakes.

Pronouncing real Deepfake entails the application of several methods and tools to recognize fake images. Deepfake detection has been done using some conventional techniques and also using strategies such as biometric analysis and digital forensics as well as advanced learning techniques. This kind of research integrates artificial intelligence and computer vision, consequently stressing the significance of deep learning approaches as a tool for analyzing faked photographs. Researchers have developed several techniques providing reliable neural architectures for Deepfake detection in images and videos. It is also important to note that these models are highly effective in detecting essential yet inconspicuous visual patterns and temporal discrepancies within Deepfake images.

As research advances with the continued development of highly sophisticated Deepfake techniques, it highlights the dire requirement of solution-based collaboration across modern learning techniques to enable continual adaptation of the existing and novel Deepfake detection methodologies. The ethical issues and security aspects related to Deepfake technology and its usage signify the need for further research works to retain the authenticity of the visual information in the digital context of the present and the future. Hence, the key contributions of the paper are:

- Designing a robust MobileNetV3 architecture fine-tuned and leveraged using self-attention layer positioned optimally to detect Deepfakes effectively.
- Detailed impact analysis of integrating self-attention mechanism in fine-tuned MobileNetV3 architecture at different positions.
- Detailed analysis of five-state-of-art convolutional models namely, XceptionNet, InceptionV3, MobileNetV3, EfficientNet B0 and InceptionResNet for baseline model selection and comprehensive comparisons.
- Detailed analysis of memory requirements and inference time of the proposed work against other state-of-art methods.

2 Related Works

Several research works have been proposed recently on efficient Deepfake detection with some of the notable works discussed here providing valuable insights into the current state of art in this field. A comprehensive analysis of EfficientNet models (B0-B7) for detection of Deepfake images is provided in the study presented by Pokrov et al. [1]. The research showcases the superior performance of models with fewer parameters, specifically EfficientNetB5 model, over models with greater number of parameters, emphasizing the nuanced relationships between model size and accuracy. In a related study by Ahmed et al. [2], a solution for the lack of diversity in existing Deepfake datasets is proposed. Data augmentation techniques such as Face Cutout and Random Erase are introduced for this task. Various EfficientNet variations are employed for the detection system. Their evaluation highlights the substantial accuracy improvements achieved with the EfficientnetV2B0 model and Random Erase augmentation. Later Pan et al. [3] employed XceptionNet and MobileNet models for Deepfake detection, emphasizing the importance of dataset variety and model selection. The pre-processing module and the implementation of a voting mechanism enhance the robustness of the Deepfake detection system.

In the study by Shad et al. [4], authors explored image classification using various deep learning models, underscoring the significance of F1-Score as a more reliable metric than accuracy for categorizing cases. The study employs a range of CNN architectures. Jaleel et al. [5] proposed a system that involves two stages for Deepfake image detection. In the first stage, action units representing facial expressions are extracted from videos to create a unique profile for a person of interest (POI). The second stage utilizes a deep learning network trained on the POI's profile to classify new videos as real or fake based on extracted action units. The system was tested on the Barack Obama dataset, demonstrating 95.75% accuracy. Trabelsi et al. [6], have conducted a survey on Deepfakes in papers, which has attracted a lot more scholarly attention in recent years. It covers many subjects, largely centred around autoencoders and Generative Adversarial Networks (GANs), including how to create Deepfakes. A variety of detection techniques are investigated, including AI-based automatic detection and physiological and visual texture analysis. Jhon et al. [7] provided a range of Deepfake detection techniques, such as deep feature-based methods that employ convolutional neural networks (CNNs) and physiological-based methods that concentrate on eye blinking patterns. For improved detection, temporal-based techniques additionally investigate frame correlations.

Rafique et al. [8] suggested technique that combines Error Level Analysis (ELA) with AlexNet and ShuffleNet, two Convolutional Neural Network (CNN) models, to detect Deepfake images. CNNs perform categorization, while ELA assists in identifying compression discrepancies between actual and false images. The proposed technique surpasses the state-of-the-art technologies with the highest accuracy of 88.2% on the Real and Fake Detection dataset. Patel et al. [9] introduced data-driven, signal-level, and physical approaches for Deepfake detection. While earlier detection methods provide an intermediate answer, signal-level approaches are not as robust as data-driven models. Sensitive feature identification is a strong suit for models such as InceptionNet and MesoNet. Lamichhane et al. [10] performed a comparison analysis using pretrained architectures including VGG-19, Inception-ResNet-v2, and Xception and custom CNN models. Binary classification was possible by modifying the upper layers of pretrained models. The F1-score of 0.97 and up to 97% validation accuracy were attained using unique CNN models. Up to 60 epochs of training were conducted on models, experimenting with activation functions and optimizers. Chen et al. [11] introduced SecDFDNet, a pioneering privacy-preserving Deepfake detector, builds upon the authors' robust face detection research. Unlike other models that compromise privacy, it enhances their model by analyzing color data for Deepfakes. SecDFDNet ensures the security of deep learning functions, employs secret sharing to divide the image, and integrates these with the previous model. In a related work [12], primary methodology employed in the research involves implementing a deep learning-based pre-trained CNN model, XceptionNet, using the DFDC dataset for detecting Deepfake videos. The study also incorporates face recognition-extracted features to identify inconsistencies between real and deep-faked images.

Yang et al. [13] introduced the Multi-Scale Self-Texture Attention (MSTA) based framework, employing an encoder-decoder architecture with a self-texture attention module (STA) as a skip connection. This enhances texture characteristics during image disassembly, improving the generation of forgery traces. The Prob-tuple loss, coupled with binary loss, further refines trace generation, resulting in state-of-the-art performance on deep face forgery databases. In a related study [14], a cascaded network utilizing EfficientNet and Transformer architectures is proposed. The network incorporates EfficientNetV2S as a feature extractor and a Transformer with Spatial-Reduction Attention (SRA) for classification. In a study by Khan et al. [15], a comparative analysis between Transformer models and CNN models for Deepfake detection is provided. Highlighting the efficiency of models such as Res2Net-101, MViT-V2, and ViT-Base, the work emphasizes their superiority over traditional CNN architectures. The study explores the impact of image augmentations on improving the performance of Transformer models. Mallet et al. [16] conducted a thorough comparison between Long Short-Term Memory (LSTM) and Multilayer Perceptron (MLP) deep learning classifiers, employing a dataset containing both real and synthetic faces. The classifier is trained on a merged dataset from Flickr-Faces-HQ and Deepfake Detection Challenge (DFDC). In a related work [17], the proposed system combines Long Short-Term Memory (LSTM) and Convolutional Neural Network (CNN). CNNs, utilizing the ResNet-50 architecture for feature extraction, processes pre-processed data, followed by LSTM for temporal analysis.

Rafique et al. [18] introduced an innovative approach for Deepfake image detection. Initially, Error Level Analysis (ELA) method is employed in image pre-processing to detect pixel-level alterations. CNNs such as GoogLeNet, ResNet18, and SqueezeNet were experimented for feature extraction while k-Nearest Neighbors (KNN) and SVM are used to classify authentic and fraudulent images. The ELA method is effective in identifying compression level variations and aiding in detecting digital tampering. The research underscores the ongoing importance of collaborative research involving academia, industry, and policymakers to effectively address Deepfake challenges, allowing stakeholders to develop strategies against the misuse of manipulated multimedia content. But the challenges in Deepfake detection still remain due to the inability of the current models to adapt to the continually evolving Deepfake technologies and remain restricted to existing techniques, leading to future research works [19–21].

3 Methodology

The work presented in this paper focuses on automated Deepfake image detection using different state-of-art deep learning methodologies. Initially, the data are processed in a series of stages including extracting frames from videos, detecting and cropping from each frame, applying augmentation and normalization techniques to the data, followed by different model implementations, training these models and evaluating these models on the DFDC dataset. The detailed steps are shown in Fig. 1.

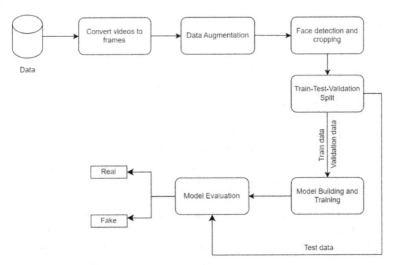

Fig. 1. Flowchart of the proposed methodology

3.1 Dataset Details and Pre-processing

The dataset used in this study is Sample DFDC dataset which consists of 800 videos. These videos feature individuals' faces, with a subset intentionally manipulated using different Deepfake techniques. The dataset is categorized into two labels: 'Real' and 'Deepfake', providing a clear distinction for algorithmic training. To mirror real-world diversity, the dataset incorporates variations in ethnicity and gender. The dataset is pre-processed to enhance the dataset quality using: (a) frames extraction, (b) data augmentation and (c) face detection. The dataset contains data in the form of videos which are initially processed for frame extraction. For every second in the video, a frame is extracted. Once frames are extracted a set of images are obtained which are further subjected to different data augmentation techniques. Data is augmented based on parameters such as rotation and right shift which makes the trained model more accurate as well as generalisable. Subsequently, as the last pre-processing step, Face detection is done. The process of detection of faces involves identifying the location of faces within a given picture using 'dlib' library. Once faces are detected, the original image is transformed to contain the faces of interest which are then cropped. Finally, dataset is divided into 70% training, 15% validation and 15% test sets with 7565 images for training and 1621 images for validation and test ing.

3.2 Model Building and Training

The proposed work uses MobileNetV3 convolution neural network pre-trained on ImageNet dataset as its back bone for image classification. MobileNetV3 has been chosen as the backbone by experimenting with five recent and state-of-art CNN models, namely EfficientNetB0, XceptionNet, MobileNetV3, InceptionNetV3 and InceptionResnet on the Deepfake image dataset, using common architectural and experimental settings as shown in Fig. 2, where baseline MobileNetV3 model outperformed all other models with fewer trainable parameters [22, 23].

MobileNet model is one of the deep neural networks that has been specifically designed for the efficient use in mobile devices with fewer computation and memory requirements. It uses depth-wise convolutions, where one convolution operation is performed per input channel which decreases the count of parameters and number of computations [24, 25]. Also, it uses separable convolutions, has a bottleneck structure and improves efficiency by compressing the feature dimensionality. MobileNet's depth-wise convolutions and separable convolutions enable it to effectively capture and process the intricate details present in images while feature extraction, thereby making it more robust in identifying Deepfake images compared to other CNN architectures. These features of MobileNet architecture make it a compact and an easy solution for deploying deep learning models in low power devices. The major advantages of MobileNet model are associated with its design, which enable the model to make precise predictions with a relatively low consumption of resources.

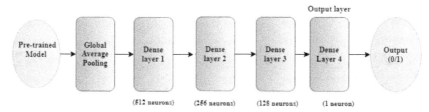

Fig. 2. Common fine-tuning architecture for all state-of-art models, namely EfficientNetB0, XceptionNet, MobileNetV3, InceptionNetV3 and InceptionResnet trained on Deepfake image dataset

In this work, self-attention layers are added to the MobileNet architecture for efficient Deepfake detection which computes the "attention scores" that highlight important areas of the image while downplaying irrelevant ones. This mechanism employs components vectors called queries (Q), keys (K), and values (V) to decide connections between varied sections of the image. The feature similarity are computed by matching the similarity score between the query vector and the key vector and then the obtained score is used to re-weight the value vectors. This process can be described by the following equation:

$$Attention(Q, K, V) = Soft\max(\frac{Q * K^T}{d_k}) * V$$

where, Query vector 'Q', represents the input region of interest, Key vector 'K' is used to compare different regions, Value vector 'V' holds the actual information in each region and 'd' represents the dimensionality of the key vectors, used to scale the result for stability.

Self-attention mechanism enables the models to attend to some parts of an input image at a time, and is highly effective at detecting subtle manipulations in Deepfakes. In contrast to convolutional layers, which pay attention to specific areas within the image, self-attention is capable of modelling both local and global dependencies by linking the different regions within an image enabling the model to recognize various potential signs of tampering like, blurring within the structure or the structure of the document is different from the contents of the document.

3.3 Proposed Architecture: Fine-Tuning and Integrating Self-attention Mechanism into MobileNetV3 Architecture

For integrating MobileNetV3 model with self-attention layers, initially the MobileNet pre-trained on ImageNet is loaded as a base model and fine-tuned by truncating the output layer and appending additional fully connected layers and attention layers. A Global average pooling layer is added to the base model to sum and downsample the spatial information in the feature maps. Dense layers having 512, 256, and 128 neurons are appended to the base model. Each layer is followed by a ReLU activation layer. The output layer is a dense layer with Sigmoid with the last layer having 2 nodes that indicate the probability of the presence of each of the specified two classes.

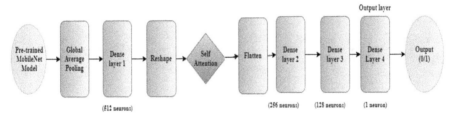

Fig. 3. Proposed architecture using fine-tuned MobileNetV3 model with self-attention mechanism after the first fully connected layer (FL-1).

Now, the self-attention layers are placed at three different positions in this architecture to get the most optimal position leading to the highest efficiency with minimalistic increment in the number of parameters: a) after the first fully connected dense layer (FC-1), after the second fully connected dense layer and finally two attention layers, one after each of the two initial dense layers (after FC-1 and FC-2). These three configurations of the architecture are trained independently on the dataset to get the best classification results. The proposed architecture with the four dense layers and a single self-attention layer after the first dense layer produced the most optimal results with the highest F-score and can be studied by referring to Fig. 3.

The self-attention layer refines the features extracted by MobileNetV3 model and pays more attention to the areas that may contain manipulations. Thus, the introduction of this approach facilitates the ability of the model to learn fine-grained details, e.g., blurring or texture shifts, as well as the coarser types of inconsistencies, e.g., lighting irregularities or facial asymmetry. This integration improves the model's accuracy in detecting discrepancies in Deepfakes, locally and contextually.

4 Results and Discussion

All the models long with the proposed approach are trained on the training dataset with their performance monitored on the validation set over the epochs. The details of the hyper-parameter settings are presented in Table 1. Validation data is a way to check model's performance on unseen data and enforce further training, if required to prevent model-over-fitting which makes the model more reliable for practical use. The models implemented have been trained on 128x128 image size in batches with 64 images per batch. Learning rate is 0.0001 with Adam optimizer for 30 epochs.

Table 1. Parameter settings for all the models implemented on Deepfake image dataset

Parameter	Values
Image size	128x128
Epochs	30
Learning rate	0.00001
Optimizer	Adam
Loss	Binary cross entropy
Activation function	ReLU and Sigmoidal
Batch size	64

Quantitative measurements including accuracy (acc), loss, precision (Pr), recall (Re), F1-score (Fs) are used to evaluate performance of the models due to class imbalance. Trainable parameter requirements along with time required to process each test data has also been discussed to support the efficiency of the proposed model.

Table 2. Performance metrics obtained for different architectures of MobileNetV3 model

Position of self attention layer	Precision	Recall	Fscore	Accuracy	Loss
Without self attention	96.13	95.40	95.86	97.04	0.155
After FC-1 (Proposed model)	**98.30**	**98.68**	**98.46**	**98.60**	**0.103**
After FC-2	96.45	95.05	95.36	97.08	0.121
After FC-1 & FC-2	96.82	95.09	96.01	96.33	0.153

Table 2 presents the results observed after experimenting the fine-tuned MobileNetV3 architecture with self-attention mechanisms incorporated at different positions, as discussed in previous section. It can be seen clearly that leveraging fine-tuned MobileNetV3 with self-attention mechanisms at different positions aided in improving the performance on Deepfake image dataset, which showed the better feature extraction and by allocating weights to the feature sets relatively. Amongst different architecture, the proposed model employing fine-tuned MobileNetV3 with additional four dense layers and a single attention layer integrated after the first fully connected layer (FC-1) outperformed all other combination in terms on Fscore, accuracy and loss values. The improvement obtained by the proposed method over other architectural combinations can be due to the early incorporation of the self attention layer that leads to early identification of critical image features that are subsequently propagated and learned thoroughly through the network which is not possible when incorporated at later stages. Also adding two self-attention layers made the model too stringent that could not sufficiently alleviate the efficiency of the architecture. Also, the trade-off between the performance improvement and number of parameters is not significant.

Table 3. Performance comparisons of the proposed methodology against recent fine-tuned convolutional neural networks on Deepfake dataset

Model	Precision	Recall	Fscore	Accuracy	Loss
EfficientNetB0	98.53	80.95	88.88	80.33	0.9063
XceptionNet	93.65	93.59	93.62	95.02	0.1989
MobileNet	96.13	95.40	95.86	97.04	0.1552
Inception Net	96.91	96.28	96.45	94.42	0.2186
Inception-ResNet	95.42	95.14	95.36	96.73	0.1606
Proposed model	**98.30**	**98.68**	**98.46**	**98.60**	**0.1034**

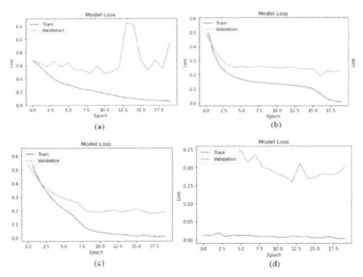

Fig. 4. Loss plots of state-of-art fine tuned convolutional models on Deepfake image dataset, (a) EfficientNetB0, (b) XceptionNet, (c) InceotionV3 and (d) InceptionResNet model

Finally the complete performance analysis of the proposed model against state-of-art methods have been presented in Table 3. It can be seen that the proposed model performed the best in terms of Fscore, Accuracy, Precision and Recall values with all of them approximating to 98.5%. The most important metric here is the remarkable Recall = 98.68% as it indicates that there are negligible Deepfake images that got incorrectly classified as 'Real' images which perfectly solves the underlying objective of the work, thereby providing near ideal data security and authenticity. It must be noted that the proposed approach improved over other models by a min margin of 3% for F-score values, another important metric for data with class imbalance.

The feature weighing characteristic of self-attention mechanism capturing local and global interdependencies finds mismatches that might not be detected if a deep fake is construct – for example, unnatural blurring or an incongruent feature-structure that might be hard to detect. All other models namely, XceptionNet, InceptionV3, MobileNetV3, Inception-ResNet performed decently on the dataset with InceptionV3 producing competitive Fscore and Recall values but had lower accuracy value and the highest loss value. Figure 4 presents the loss curves for the state-of-art CN models trained on Deepfake dataset using the architecture presented in Fig. 2. The convergence of the training and validation loss curves after certain epochs support the good fit of the model over the Deepfake images. EfficientNetB0 model converges at the highest validation loss of arounf 0.6 with XceptionNet, Inceptionv3 and InceptionResnet showing decent loss attainment at around 0.2 which is higher than the proposed model's loss = 0.1034.

Table 4. Comparisons of the models for memory and time requirements

Model	Trainable Parameters	Non-Trainable Parameters	Time (secs)
EfficientNetB0	4,378,782	42,0232	659×10^{-6}
XceptionNet	22,028,650	54,528	1×10^{-6}
MobileNet	3,052,354	34,112	485×10^{-6}
Inception Net	22,336,194	34,432	1×10^{-3}
InceptionResNet	55,235,746	60,544	28×10^{-3}
Proposed Model	4,232,706	21,888	499×10^{-6}

It is also to be noted that the proposed model based on Fine-tuned MobileNetv3 and a single self-attention layer performed the best over-all for all metrics with significantly lower number of trainable parameters as presented in Table 4. Also the proposed model gained a significant performance increment of 3% over base MobileNetv3 model in terms of F-score with slightly increased trainable parameters and inference time. An increase of 6 microseconds in inferring the class of the image is quite acceptable for real-time applications if only 499 microseconds are needed for each image classification. It can be seen that except EfficientNetB0 model all other state-of-art convolutional models need milliseconds to predict the class of an image which is very high for real-world and real-time applications. With the given lighter parameter requirements and impressive inference speed, the proposed model is fit to be deployed on mobile or small devices in real-time scenarios.

The inclusion of self-attention layers in the MobileNetV3 architecture at the first fully connected layer (FC-1) is justified by the vast improvement of the model's ability to pay attention to significant image regions that contain possible manipulations. Placing the self-attention layer at this position enhances the refinement of features extracted by the MobileNetV3 backbone at an intermediate stage, allowing the model to better distinguish subtle artifacts like texture inconsistencies or blurring, as well as coarser anomalies such as lighting irregularities or asymmetries. This positioning strikes an optimal balance between capturing essential fine-grained details and maintaining computational efficiency. The results of experiments, where this configuration showed the best F-score among the different positions, confirmed the advantage of the model in improving feature representations early in the process so that the subsequent layers receive improved and more discriminative features for accurate Deepfake detection. This placement builds upon the advantages that MobileNetV3 has to offer and makes the best use of the proposed self-attention operation.

To add up the predictive pattern in this proposed methodology helps the model differentiate between the local and global patterns. Using both the self-attention and MobileNet architecture, it can detect local features distributed within a single small window and global features inconsistent across the entire image for the real and tampered image classification. This integration is not only pixel-based but other regional elements of an image are taken into account for their relations with one another, thus enhancing the model and boosting up detection efficiency.

5 Conclusion and Future Scope

The paper presented a fine-tuned MobileNetV3 model with self-attention layer incorporated at initial positions in the architecture for enhanced Deep fake detection in images. The model showed superior performance in detecting Deepfakes with an outperforming F-score of 98.46%, highlighting the importance of advanced convolutional architectures and learning mechanisms in the domain. While MobileNetV3 model served as a remarkable feature extractor, attention mechanism proved to be useful for capturing the inter-region spatial dependencies amongst different unconnected image regions. Other state-of-art models like InceptionV3, XceptionNet model, etc. obtained decent results but they had tradeoff issues with highly increased memory and inference times while the proposed model performed the best with minimalistic increment in trainable parameters and the least inference time. Despite promising results, challenges such as high-quality Deepfake detection and robustness against continually generated adversarial attacks still remain. Future work should focus on enhancing models, improving adversarial robustness, ensuring cross-dataset generalization, model explainability and addressing real-world deployment issues.

References

1. Pokroy, A.A., Egorov, A.D.: EfficientNets for deepfake detection: comparison of pretrained models. In: 2021 IEEE Conference of Russian Young Researchers in Electrical and Electronic Engineering (ElConRus), St. Petersburg, Moscow, Russia, pp. 598–600 (2021)
2. Ahmed, O., et al.: Deepfake detection system using deep learning. In: 2023 Eleventh International Conference on Intelligent Computing and Information Systems (ICICIS), Cairo, Egypt (2023)
3. Pan, D., Sun, L., Wang, R., Zhang, X., Sinnott, R.O.: Deepfake detection through deep learning. In: 2020 IEEE/ACM International Conference on Big Data Computing, Applications and Technologies (BDCAT), Leicester, UK, pp. 134–143 (2020)
4. Shad, H.S., et al.: Comparative analysis of deepfake image detection method using convolutional neural network. In: 2021Computational Intelligence and Neuroscience (2021). https://doi.org/10.1155/2021/3111676
5. Jaleel, Q., Hadi, I.: Facial action unit-based deepfake video detection using deep learning. In: 2022 4th International Conference on Current Research in Engineering and Science Applications (ICCRESA), Baghdad, Iraq, pp. 228–233 (2022)
6. Trabelsi, A., Pic, M.M., Dugelay, J.-L.: Improving deepfake detection by mixing top solutions of the DFDC. In: 30th European Signal Processing Conference, Belgrade, Serbia, pp. 643–647 (2022)
7. John, J., Sherif, B.V.: Comparative analysis on different deepfake detection methods and semi supervised GAN architecture for deepfake detection. In: 2022 Sixth International Conference on I-SMAC (IoT in Social, Mobile, Analytics and Cloud) (I-SMAC), Dharan, Nepal, pp. 516–521 (2022)
8. Rafique, R., Nawaz, M., Kibriya, H., Masood, M.: Deepfake detection using error level analysis and deep learning. In: 2021 4th International Conference on Computing and Information Sciences (ICCIS), Karachi, Pakistan, pp. 1–4 (2021)
9. Patel, Y., et al.: An improved dense CNN architecture for deepfake image detection. IEEE Access **11**, 22081–22095 (2023)
10. Lamichhane, B., Thapa, K., Yang, S.-H.: Detection of image level forgery with various constraints using DFDC full and sample datasets. Sensors **22**, 9121 (2022). https://doi.org/10.3390/s22239121
11. Chen, B., Liu, X., Xia, Z., Zhao, G.: Privacy-preserving deepfake face image detection. Digit. Sig. Process. **143**, 104233 (2023). ISSN 1051-2004
12. Saxena, A., et al.: Detecting deepfakes: a novel framework employing XceptionNet-based convolutional neural networks. Traitement du Signal **40**(3), 835–846 (2023)
13. Yang, J., Xiao, S., Li, A., Lu, W., Gao, X., Li, Y.: MSTA-net: forgery detection by generating manipulation trace based on multi-scale self-texture attention. IEEE Trans. Circuits Syst. Video Technol. **32**(7), 4854–4866 (2022)
14. Deng, L., Wang, J., Liu, Z.: Cascaded network based on efficientnet and transformer for deepfake video detection. Neural Process. Lett. **55**, 7057–7076 (2023)
15. Khan, S.A., Dang-Nguyen, D.T.: Deepfake detection: analyzing model generalization across architectures, datasets, and pre-training paradigms. IEEE Access **12**, 1880–1908 (2024)
16. Mallet, J., Krueger, N., Dave, R., Vanamala, M.: Hybrid deepfake detection utilizing MLP and LSTM. In: 2023 3rd International Conference on Electrical, Computer, Communications and Mechatronics Engineering (ICECCME), Tenerife, Canary Islands, Spain, pp. 1–5 (2023)
17. BR, S.R., Pareek, P.K., Bharathi, S., Geetha, G.: Deepfake video detection system using deep neural networks. In: 2023 IEEE International Conference on Integrated Circuits and Communication Systems (ICICACS), Raichur, India, pp. 1–6 (2023)

18. Rafique, R., Gantassi, R., Amin, R., Frnda, J., Mustapha, A., Alshehri, A.H.: Deep fake detection and classification using error-level analysis and deep learning. Sci. Rep. **13**(1), 7422 (2023)
19. Taeb, M., Chi, H.: Comparison of deepfake detection techniques through deep learning. J. Cybersecur. Priv. **2**(1), 89–106 (2022)
20. Malik, A., Kuribayashi, M., Abdullahi, S.M., Khan, A.N.: Deepfake detection for human face images and videos: a survey. IEEE Access **10**, 18757–18775 (2022)
21. Suresh, H.R., Shanmuganathan, M., Senthilkumar, T., Vidhyasagar, B.S.: Deep learning-based image forgery detection system. Int. J. Electron. Secur. Digit. Forensics **16**(2), 160–172 (2024)
22. Anjali, K.S., Singh, R.P., Panda, M.K., Palaniappan, K.: An ensemble approach using self-attention based MobileNetV2 for SAR classification. Procedia Comput. Sci. **235**, 3207–3216 (2024)
23. Mol, B., Singh, R.P., Kumar, P.: Parkinson disease classification using hybrid deep learning approach. In: 2023 9th International Conference on Signal Processing and Communication (ICSC), pp. 591–596. IEEE (2023)
24. Karna, S., Haneesha, S.S.S., Jahanve, P.R., Pati, P.B., Balakrishnan, R.M.: AudioGuard: deep learning based Telugu deepfake audio detection. In: 2024 15th International Conference on Computing Communication and Networking Technologies (ICCCNT), Kamand, India, pp. 1–6 (2024)
25. Anagha, R., Arya, A., Narayan, V.H., Abhishek, S., Anjali, T.: Audio deepfake detection using deep learning. In: 2023 12th International Conference on System Modeling and Advancement in Research Trends (SMART), Moradabad, India, pp. 176–181 (2023)

AI-Driven Monitoring System for Detecting People Using Mobile Phones in Restricted Zone

Anidipta Pal[✉], Ankana Datta, Ananyo Dasgupta, and Mohuya B. Kar

Computer Science and Engineering (AIML), Heritage Institute of Technology, Kolkata, India
{anidipta.pal.aiml27,ankana.datta.aiml27,
ananyo.dasgupta.aiml27}@heritageit.edu.in,
mohuya.byabartta@heritageit.edu

Abstract. The pervasive use of mobile phones in designated no-mobile zones, including hospitals, gas stations, libraries, and pedestrian crossings, poses significant safety risks and regulatory challenges. To address these issues, this paper introduces an advanced detection system leveraging the YOLOv8x deep learning architecture. This system is designed to automatically identify individuals using mobile phones in restricted areas, utilizing CCTV and surveillance footage for data collection. The images undergo extensive preprocessing, including resizing, normalization, and noise reduction, to prepare them for effective model training. The YOLO8x model, known for its efficiency in real-time object detection, is trained to accurately detect mobile phone users by learning from annotated datasets. Evaluation metrics, such as Precision, Recall, and mean Average Precision (mAP), are used to evaluate the system's accuracy in identifying violations. High precision indicates the system's ability to minimize false positives, while high recall reflects its capacity to detect most violations. The system's real-time capabilities allow for immediate alerts and interventions, enhancing public safety and regulatory compliance. The results demonstrate the system's robustness and reliability, offering significant potential for deployment in various sensitive environments to reduce disruptions and ensure a safer public space. This detection solution enforces no-mobile zone policies and creates a safer environment, thereby reducing the risks of unauthorized mobile phone use.

Keywords: Mobile Phone Detection · No-Mobile Zone · YOLO8x · Object Detection · Deep Learning · Surveillance · Safety Compliance

1 Introduction

The use of mobile phones in no-mobile zones, such as hospitals, gas stations, libraries, and pedestrian crossings, poses significant challenges and risks. In areas like gas stations, mobile phone use can create sparks that may lead to fires or explosions, while in hospitals, it can interfere with sensitive medical equipment, compromising patient safety. These zones enforce strict no-mobile policies to maintain safety, privacy, and decorum, but monitoring and enforcing these policies is difficult due to high foot traffic and subtle violations. Relying on manual monitoring by security personnel or reviewing CCTV footage is inefficient, prone to human error, and resource-intensive. Additionally, existing detection systems often struggle with accurately distinguishing between merely holding a phone and actively using it, resulting in false positives and missed detections. These limitations make it challenging to enforce no-mobile policies, creating a pressing need for an automated and reliable solution.

2 Proposed Approach

2.1 Solution Mechanism

To address the above challenges, we propose an advanced automated detection system leveraging the YOLOv8x deep learning architecture. This system is designed to accurately identify individuals using mobile phones in restricted areas using the following approach:

2.1.1 Data Collection

To detect mobile phone usage in no-phone zones, a comprehensive dataset reflecting real-world scenarios is essential. For this study, images from surveillance footage were sourced primarily from open-access platforms, showcasing environments like schools and hospitals. Multiple datasets were combined to create a custom dataset, annotating images into two categories: "person" and "cellphone."

2.1.2 Data Preprocessing

The goal was to identify when a person is using a mobile phone, regardless of orientation, lighting, or obstructions, to reflect various field conditions. To make the data inclusive for all possible cases, augmentation techniques were applied to the images, such as horizontal flip, rotation between $-6°$ and $+6°$, exposure adjustments between -10% and $+10\%$, blur up to 2px, and noise up to 0.5% of pixels. Variations in camera position, angles, and other factors were also simulated. The data was split into Train, Test, and Validation sets in a **7:2:1 ratio**.

2.1.3 Automated Detection Using Deep Learning

The system uses YOLOv8x, a cutting-edge SOTA object detection model, trained on a custom dataset from surveillance footage. It focuses on detecting persons and cellphones, improving accuracy by learning their spatial relationship.

2.1.4 Enhanced Detection Methodologies

Two distinct methodologies are employed for effective classification of phone usage:

First Approach: Single Bounding Box(SBB)

1. **Data Annotation:** In the initial approach, images were meticulously annotated with a single bounding box (SBB) surrounding individuals identified as talking on the phone. Each annotated image was labeled as "talking on phone" to facilitate accurate predictions.
2. **Model Training:** The YOLOv8x model was fine-tuned on images labeled "talking on phone" to predict whether an individual is engaged in a phone conversation, producing annotated images with confidence scores during inference.
3. **Evaluation:** Evaluation was done on a validation dataset using metrics like accuracy, precision, recall, and F1-score for its effectiveness in detecting individuals talking on the phone.

Second Approach: Double Bounding Boxes(DBB)

1. **Data Annotation:** In the second approach, images were annotated with two bounding boxes—one around the face and another around the cellphone. This enhanced the model's ability to learn their relationship.
2. **Model Training:** The YOLOv8x model was fine-tuned on images annotated with two bounding boxes—"person" and "cellphone"—to predict their positions during inference, returning predicted bounding boxes with confidence scores for each.
3. **Post-Processing:** The centroids of the predicted face and cellphone bounding boxes were extracted. The Euclidean distance between these centroids was then computed. This distance served as a key feature in determining whether the person in the image was talking on the phone.
4. **Evaluation:** The model's performance was evaluated using a validation dataset and metrics for phone usage detection, along with qualitative analysis of predictions and bounding boxes.

2.1.5 Performance Evaluation

The system is evaluated using key metrics to ensure accuracy and reliability. Regular updates and retraining maintain performance and adapt to new conditions and potential violations.

2.1.6 Real-Time Monitoring and Alerts

The system analyzes live video feeds from CCTV cameras to detect violations in real time. If a person is caught using a mobile phone in a restricted area, the system sends a text alert for quick effective intervention, ensuring compliance with no-mobile policies.

2.1.7 Scalable Data Management

The system uses a PostgreSQL database to manage detection data, including timestamps and geospatial information. This allows for efficient data storage and integration into security systems. Reports can be generated for law enforcement while ensuring data privacy and security through encryption and access controls.

2.1.8 Deployment and Integration

The model is deployed on robust hardware and cloud platforms, such as AWS or Azure, ensuring scalability and performance in diverse environments. The system is compatible with existing CCTV networks, enhancing coverage and allowing for seamless integration into existing security infrastructure.

This proposed solution not only enforces no-mobile zone policies but also enhances public safety and regulatory compliance through advanced, automated, and scalable detection capabilities.

2.2 Algorithmic Approach

To address the above challenges, we propose an advanced automated detection system leveraging the YOLOv8x deep learning architecture. This system is designed to accurately identify individuals using mobile phones in restricted areas using the following approach:

Step 1: Capture the video footage from CCTV cameras for comprehensive analysis and processing to support further investigative tasks.

Step 2: This footage will be fragmented into individual frames at a rate of *10 frames per second (fps)*, ensuring smooth playback and clarity. Each frame will then be resized to a standard dimension of *640 x640 pixels*, optimizing the images for efficient analysis and facilitating the identification of relevant details during the investigation.

Step 3: Process the extracted frames through the *YOLO8x* model to detect objects using deep learning techniques. The model predicts objects in the frames, applying bounding boxes specifically for detecting persons and mobile phones.

Step 4: Two distinct approaches for classification:
Single Bounding Box (SBB): In the first approach, images were manually annotated using a SBB. The bounding box was drawn around the person in the image who is talking on the phone, and it was labeled as "talking on phone", for predicting whether the person in the image is talking on the phone.
Dual Bounding Boxes (DBB): In the second approach, images were annotated with two separate bounding boxes. One was drawn around the person's face, and the other around the cellphone. This dual annotation provided more specific information for the model, allowing it to learn the relationship between the face and the cellphone in the image.

Algorithm 1 Pseudocode for DBB

1: boxes, classes ← results[0].boxes.xywh.cpu().numpy(), results[0].boxes.cls.cpu().numpy()
2: box1, box2 ← None, None
3: **for** i = 0 **to** length(boxes) **do**
4:     **if** classes[i] == 1 **then**
5:         box1 ← boxes[i]
6:         **break**
7:     **end if**
8: **end for**
9: **for** i = 0 **to** length(boxes) **do**
10:     **if** classes[i] == 0 **then**
11:         box2 ← boxes[i]
12:         **break**
13:     **end if**
14: **end for**
15: **if** box1 == None **or** box2 == None **then**
16:     PRINT "One of the required boxes was not found."
17: **else**
18:     distance ← $\sqrt{(box1[0] - box2[0])^2 + (box1[1] - box2[1])^2}$
19:     param ← $\frac{1}{4}\sqrt{(box1[2] * 2)^2 + (box1[3] * 2)^2}$
20:     **if** distance ≤ param **then**
21:         PRINT "Person talking on phone"
22:     **else**
23:         PRINT "Person not talking on phone"
24:     **end if**
25: **end if**

Step 5: Distance between person and cellphone:

Step 6: Compare the computed values against the **threshold** based on the scaled dimensions (width and height) of the bounding box around the person, which serves to determine whether the person is talking on the phone. If the value exceeds the threshold *(i.e., indicates phone usage)*, we store the image of the individual along with a **timestamp** and **location** for further analysis. Additionally, we update the live stream by overlaying the message **"Person talking on phone"** in the designated restricted zone, ensuring that the information is prominently displayed for immediate attention.

Step 7: The model's performance was evaluated using a validation dataset to ensure accuracy and reliability. Standard metrics, including accuracy, precision, recall, mean Average Precision (mAP), and F1-score, assessed its effectiveness in detecting whether a person is talking on the phone. These metrics revealed the model's strengths and weaknesses. A **qualitative analysis** of predictions and bounding boxes was also performed to visually inspect their accuracy, with distance calculations imprinted on the images to clarify spatial relationships between detected entities.

Step 8: Continue to extract image frames from the live feed of the CCTV camera until it stops transmitting or until the playback of the video is complete, ensuring that all relevant frames are captured for analysis and monitoring purposes.

2.3 Workflow Diagram

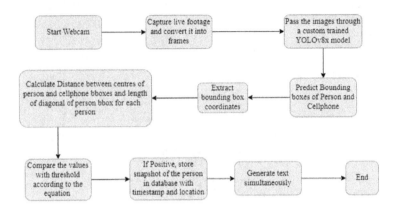

Fig. 1. Model Workflow

3 Database Management for Real-Time Surveillance Systems

Maintaining a database of images in a real-time surveillance system necessitates a combination of efficient storage, retrieval, and management techniques. The system must handle a continuous influx of data from multiple sources, ensure real-time processing, and make the data accessible for quick retrieval and analysis (Fig. 1).

3.1 Image Storage and Management Techniques

3.1.1 Storage Mechanisms

BLOB Storage: Images can be stored as BLOBs in the database, which are suitable for handling large binary files, such as images and videos of varying sizes and formats. To optimize storage space, images can be compressed using lossless (.PNG) or lossy (.JPEG) compression methods.

Hybrid Models: Some systems utilize a hybrid approach where image data is stored in dedicated object storage services and only references are kept in the database for easy access.

3.1.2 Metadata Storage

Alongside images, timestamps, geospatial coordinates, camera IDs, and detection details will be stored in dedicated fields for efficient search and retrieval. Upon detection, the bounding box segment is extracted from the video frame, isolating the pixel region defined by the bounding box coordinates. This extracted image data, along with crucial metadata, is stored in ***PostgreSQL***.

3.1.3 Database Schema

```
CREATE TABLE surveillance_images (
    image_id SERIAL PRIMARY KEY,
    image_data BYTEA,
    timestamp TIMESTAMPTZ NOT NULL,
    camera_id INTEGER NOT NULL,
    geolocation GEOGRAPHY(POINT, 4326),
    object_type TEXT,

    detection_confidence NUMERIC,
    tags TEXT[]
);


CREATE INDEX idx_timestamp ON surveillance_images (timestamp);
CREATE INDEX idx_geolocation ON surveillance_images USING GIST (geolocation);
CREATE INDEX idx_object_type ON surveillance_images (object_type);
```

3.2 Data Processing and Retrieval

3.2.1 Real-Time Data Integration

New data is seamlessly merged into the existing dataset using ***UPSERT operations***, ensuring real-time updates and consistency, especially in scenarios where a detected object may appear in multiple frames or locations.

3.2.2 Advanced Query Capabilities

Advanced SQL queries *(e.g., SELECT, JOIN, WHERE)* allow for precise retrieval based on temporal, spatial, and detection parameters. Data can be exported in formats like CSV using the COPY command for external analysis or reporting. Spatial and temporal queries enhance data filtering and retrieval efficiency.

3.2.3 Automated Image Tagging

Automated image tagging using machine learning models helps categorize images, facilitating easier retrieval using queries. Precompiled and cached frequently queried data using materialized views speed up access to recent or important surveillance data.

3.2.4 Real-Time Alerts and Notifications

Database triggers can generate alerts or notifications when specific conditions are met (e.g., if a person is detected talking on a phone in a restricted zone). Tools like PostgreSQL's LISTEN/NOTIFY feature push real-time alerts when new images are inserted.

3.2.5 Data Security and Compliance

Sensitive images can be encrypted both at rest and during transit using ***SSL/TLS***. *Role-based access control (RBAC)* ensures that only authorized personnel can access or modify the image database. Data retention policies, shaped by legal and organizational requirements, can automatically delete or anonymize older data.

3.2.6 Law Enforcement Reporting

For law enforcement intervention scenarios, the system can generate detailed reports. Comprehensive reports are compiled using SQL aggregation functions *(e.g., GROUP BY, ORDER BY)*, with data formatted into structured outputs and transmitted through encrypted channels to ensure confidentiality and integrity.

In summary, integrating an advanced data management system within a real-time surveillance framework leverages PostgreSQL's robust features for efficient detection data storage and querying. By combining advanced SQL operations, real-time processing pipelines, and integration with machine learning tools, the system can effectively handle large-scale data while ensuring secure and compliant reporting. This approach enhances accuracy and reliability in real-time surveillance applications, contributing to improved public safety and compliance.

4 Deployment of ML Model for Detecting Phone Usage Through CCTV Feeds

Deploying a machine learning model for mobile phone detection via CCTV involves key steps. It requires powerful hardware, such as *NVIDIA RTX 4080* or *A100 GPUs*, and sufficient memory and storage. Cloud solutions like AWS or Azure offer flexible infrastructure. The software environment typically runs systems with Python, TensorFlow, PyTorch, OpenCV, and Docker.

Model integration includes setting up a data pipeline with OpenCV for real-time video processing, where YOLOv8x detects objects and ResNetv2 enhances features. Roboflow assists with training and labeling datasets, improving bounding box accuracy, while mAP evaluates performance. CI/CD pipelines automate testing and validation for continuous deployment.

Real-time monitoring addresses drift or degradation, with regular maintenance for model updates and retraining. Data privacy is managed through encryption and access controls, ensuring GDPR compliance. Effective deployment of YOLOv8x and ResNetv2 requires solid infrastructure, smart integration, and robust CI/CD processes.

5 Real-Time Detection of Mobile Phone Usage via Webcam and CCTV Integration

In *sensitive environments* like hospitals and secure facilities, unauthorized mobile phone use can pose safety risks. This real-time detection system integrates YOLO object detection with live video from webcams and CCTV cameras, processing multiple feeds by resizing and normalizing frames. YOLO identifies mobile phones, while a geometric approach measures the distance between the phone and the user's face for accurate activity classification. Alarms are triggered upon detecting phone use in restricted areas, and the system's integration with existing CCTV networks enhances monitoring and coverage.

The system builds on existing research in object detection and mobile phone monitoring, utilizing YOLOv8x for its balance of speed and precision. Unlike previous single-camera or smaller dataset methods, this system scales to handle multiple video feeds and large volumes of data efficiently. Performance evaluations show high precision and recall, even in complex environments, with extensive coverage provided by CCTV cameras. Key metrics used in the evaluation include:

Precision: The accuracy of the system in identifying true positives (actual violations) while minimizing false positives.

Recall: The system's ability to detect most of the violations occurring within the monitored area.

Mean Average Precision (mAP): A composite measure that combines precision and recall to provide an overall performance score.

The evaluation results indicate that the system performs effectively across different conditions, maintaining high precision and recall. The use of CCTV cameras ensures comprehensive coverage, and it can manage multiple inputs to monitor all areas (Figs. 2 and 3).

For real-world deployment, several factors must be considered. These include the quality and positioning of CCTV cameras, the computational resources required for real-time processing, and the integration with existing security systems. The system's modular design allows it to be adapted to different environments, whether it's a small office with a single webcam or a large public space with an extensive CCTV network.

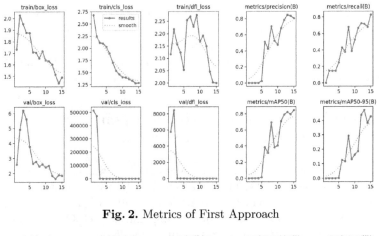

Fig. 2. Metrics of First Approach

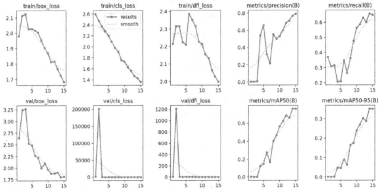

Fig. 3. Metrics of Second Approach

The real-time detection system for identifying mobile phone usage in no-phone zones enhances safety and compliance enforcement. By combining deep learning models with webcam and CCTV inputs, it provides a scalable solution for various environments. Its real-time monitoring and YOLO model accuracy ensure quick violation detection, promoting safer spaces.

This research also explores expanding the system's capabilities to include integration with broader security frameworks and detecting additional prohibited behaviors. As technology advances, such systems will be vital for maintaining order and safety in public and private areas.

6 Comparison of Initial and Improved Model Approaches for Mobile Phone Detection

While Driving Car — Inside Library

The SBB model for detecting mobile phone usage through CCTV used a single bounding box for both the phone and the person, which led to accuracy issues and false positives—such as flagging a phone lying on a table as being in use.

The improved DBB model resolved these issues by using separate bounding boxes for the cellphone and the person, allowing for a better analysis of their spatial relationship. A positive detection is now triggered only if the overlap between the phone's and the person's bounding boxes exceeds a certain threshold. This ensures that the system flags active phone usage only when the phone is in close proximity to suggest interaction, like being held to the ear or looked at. The total training time is shown in Fig. 4.

Inside Library — While Walking on road

When comparing the two approaches, several key aspects highlight the advantages of the improved method, as shown in Table 1. Some of them are:

Accuracy and False Positives: The initial model, using a single bounding box, often generated false positives by mistakenly identifying a phone's presence

RAM size(in gb), Time taken per epoch (in minutes) for SBB and DBB Model

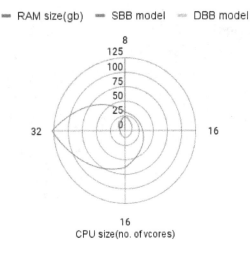

Fig. 4. Time Needed in minutes to train the Models on Different Machines

Table 1. Comparison of SBB and DBB Model Parameters

Parameters	SBB Model	DBB Model
Accuracy (%)	84.67	58.95
F1-Score	0.776	0.709
Precision	0.848	0.769
Recall	0.716	0.658
Training Images	597	632
Training Time (in hours)	1.921	2.579
Validation Images	137	140
Validation Time (in seconds)	28.428	35.098

as active usage, even when it wasn't being used. The accuracy was 84.67%, shown in Fig. 5. The improved model provides distinct detections for the cellphone and the person, with a threshold for the intersection of their bounding boxes. This enhancement improved the system's accuracy in identifying phone usage, greatly reducing false positives by ensuring idle phones weren't mistakenly flagged. The accuracy is 58.95%, shown in Fig. 6.

Specificity and Sensitivity: The initial SBB model had limited specificity; it could detect phones but struggled to distinguish between active and inactive usage, leading to many false positives. The improved DBB model enhanced specificity by identifying both the presence of objects and their interactions, resulting in more accurate detections.

Operational Effectiveness: The initial model was easier to implement but had limited effectiveness, often generating false positives by flagging a phone's presence as active usage. This led to unnecessary alerts and decreased trust in accuracy. The improved model, though more complex, introduced dual-bounding boxes for the phone and person. Alerts are now triggered only when both boxes intersect beyond a certain threshold, enhancing precision in detection and improving visual appeal.In real time scenario, it's helping us to identify the objects and the closeness of the objects helps to identify the problem more accurately, even if accuracy is less.

In summary, the initial model's simplicity allowed for basic detection, but its accuracy and specificity were insufficient for real-world use. Using separate bounding boxes and thresholds, the improved model offers more reliable detection, reducing false positives and boosting performance.

6.1 Model Performance Comparison

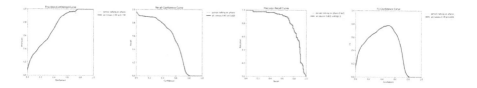

Fig. 5. SBB Model Accuracy: 84.67%

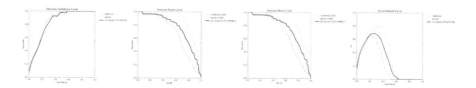

Fig. 6. DBB Model Accuracy: 58.95%

7 Future Scope

Integrating audio cues with visual data can significantly enhance the detection of phone use, especially in challenging environments like noisy settings or when using headsets. Audio signals can provide valuable context when visual cues are unclear. Additionally, mobile signal interception could further refine predictions, though this would need to be approached carefully due to privacy concerns.

As edge devices like mobile phones and surveillance cameras improve, real-time deployment in complex environments—such as low-light conditions or cluttered scenes—becomes more feasible. Making the model adaptable to lower-resolution cameras, often used in traffic monitoring or public spaces, will also expand its usability.

Furthermore, background detection through caption generation or scene understanding can reduce false alarms and increase accuracy by considering the surrounding context. This multi-modal approach makes the system more precise, scalable, and also applicable in various real-world scenarios.

8 Conclusion

This paper presents an effective and efficient system for detecting mobile phone usage in designated no-phone zones using advanced deep learning techniques. Using the YOLOv8x model and effective data annotation, the system accurately detects violations, highlighting its practical application potential and improving safety and compliance in public and private spaces alike. Future work will explore expanding the system's capabilities, including integration with broader security frameworks and detecting additional prohibited behaviors, further contributing to safer and more controlled environments.

The comparative analysis of the initial and improved approaches underscores the importance of detailed and context-specific detection strategies, particularly in complex and settings, giving us a more enhanced visualization of the state of the objects with more effective display. The lessons learned from this development process pave the way for more refined and adaptable AI-driven solutions in the field of surveillance and public safety.

References

1. Mahat, S., Maindargi, S.: Mobile Phone Addiction (MPA) cross severe level. Int. J. Eng. Trends Technol. (IJETT) **66**(3) (2018). ISSN 2231–5381
2. Rajput, P., Nag, S., Mittal, S.: Detecting usage of mobile phones using deep learning technique. In: 6th EAI International Conference on Smart Objects and Technologies for Social Good (GoodTechs '20), September 14–16, 2020, Antwerp, Belgium. ACM, New York (2020). 6 pages
3. Carrell, S., Atapour-Abarghouei, A.: Identification of driver phone usage violations via state-of-the-art object detection with tracking. arXiv:2109.02119v3 [cs.CV] (2021)
4. Shruthi, K., Poojary, R.: Design of a prototype to detect mobile phone usage in restricted areas. SSRG Int. J. Electron. Commun. Engin. (SSRG-IJECE) **2**(12) (2015). ISSN: 2348 – 8549
5. Pérez, J.M., Villalta, E.R.C.: Rock paper scissors tracking using YOLO (2024)
6. Khandakar, A., et al.: Portable system for monitoring and controlling driver behavior and the use of a mobile phone while driving. Sensors **19**, 1563 (2019)
7. Nyamawe, A., Mtonyole, N.: The Use of mobile phones in university exams cheating: proposed solution. Int. J. Eng. Trends Technol. **17**(1) (2014)

Integrated Analysis of Voice Patterns and Semantic Features for Emotion Recognition

Van Hieu Bui(✉) [iD], Minh Son Cao, Trung Dinh Tran, and Khanh Nam Tran

FPT University, Education Zone, Hoa Lac Hi-tech Park, Ha Noi, Vietnam
hieubv10@fe.edu.vn,
{soncmhe161627,dinhtthe161528,namtkhe160163}@fpt.edu.vn

Abstract. Recognizing emotion from voice is essential for adaptive social behavior, voice-based emotion recognition methods often struggle with accuracy due to the semantic similarity between words with different emotional meanings. This study aims to enhance emotion recognition accuracy by integrating both pattern and semantic features. For pattern features, we employ Convolutional Neural Networks (CNNs) to detect patterns in voice data and Long Short-Term Memory (LSTM) networks to model the relationships between these patterns and emotions. To capture semantic features, we utilize pre-trained BERT to provide context-based semantic representations of text converted from voice. These pattern and semantic features are fused using an attention mechanism through a specially designed attention fusion module to assess their correlation. We evaluate this combined method using the MELD and SLUE datasets, achieving a significant accuracy improvement to 71%, surpassing that of non-semantic feature-based approaches.

Keywords: Emotion Recognition · Semantic Features · Voice Patterns

1 Introduction

Emotion recognition is a critical area of research with broad applications that has garnered significant attention in recent years. In education, it can profoundly impact teaching and learning by analyzing students' emotional responses to instructional materials and assessments, allowing educators to tailor strategies for enhanced engagement and effectiveness. Additionally, it helps monitor students' emotional well-being, potentially identifying early signs of stress, anxiety, or depression for timely intervention and support [1]. In the business sector, emotion recognition provides deeper insights into customer emotions, needs, and reactions to products and services [18], enabling businesses to refine strategies, optimize offerings, and create targeted marketing content that strengthens brand attachment and improves marketing effectiveness. In healthcare, it is instrumental in assessing and monitoring patients' psychological and emotional states [17], supporting the diagnosis and treatment of mental health conditions like depression and anxiety, and enhancing the effectiveness of counseling and therapeutic methods with accurate emotional insights.

Emotion recognition using only voice pattern features faces several limitations due to the inherent subjectivity and fuzziness of emotional expressions, which complicate the standardization of emotional definitions and lead to inconsistencies in interpretation. The extraction and selection of relevant emotional features are challenging because of the variability in speech segments and emotional categories [21]. Emotions are dynamic and can change rapidly, making real-time recognition difficult [9]. Additionally, issues with data quality and quantity arise from the difficulty in obtaining large, diverse, and accurately labeled datasets [4]. The labor-intensive process of tagging emotional data also requires significant expertise. Without incorporating semantic analysis, voice pattern recognition may fail to capture the full nuances of emotional expression, leading to misinterpretations, especially when similar vocal features represent different emotions or are influenced by context-specific factors [15]. Variations in individual speech patterns, accents, and emotional delivery further affect the consistency and accuracy of emotion recognition, reducing overall accuracy and robustness.

This study aims to enhance emotion recognition accuracy by integrating both pattern-based and semantic features. We use Convolutional Neural Networks to extract patterns from voice data and Long Short-Term Memory networks to model the temporal relationships between these patterns and emotions. To capture semantic features, we leverage pre-trained BERT models to generate context-aware textual representations from voice. An advanced attention fusion module then combines these pattern and semantic features, using an attention mechanism to dynamically assess and merge their correlations. This integrated approach is designed to improve the robustness and accuracy of emotion recognition by leveraging the strengths of both pattern-based and semantic analyses.

2 Related Work

Emotion recognition from speech has made significant strides with the application of deep learning, particularly through the integration of Convolutional Neural Networks (CNNs) and Long Short-Term Memory networks (LSTMs). CNNs are adept at identifying hierarchical features from speech spectrograms, as demonstrated by Huang et al. (2019), who highlighted their ability to extract fine-grained local patterns, thereby improving emotion classification accuracy [8]. LSTMs, on the other hand, excel in capturing temporal dynamics. Zhang et al. (2020) showcased how combining CNNs with LSTMs enables a comprehensive analysis of both spatial and sequential characteristics, enhancing emotion recognition performance [22]. Li et al. (2021) extended this concept by proposing a unified framework that synergizes CNN and LSTM functionalities, achieving substantial performance gains in speech emotion detection tasks [11]. These studies collectively underscore the effectiveness of combining CNNs and LSTMs in tackling the complexities of emotion recognition from speech.

Hang et al. [5] provided a detailed review on deep learning-based multimodal emotion recognition, focusing on integrating audio, visual, and textual modalities. Their analysis highlights the advantages of multimodal approaches, particularly in extracting high-level emotional features that improve recognition accuracy and enhance human-computer interactions. Despite these advancements, they identified persistent challenges, such as the difficulty in real-time deployment and the scarcity of large, annotated datasets.

In the domain of sentiment analysis, innovative architectures like the 'BERT-like' model [18] combine Speech-BERT and VQ-Wave2Vec for audio processing with Roberta for textual data. This model employs Co-Attentional Fusion to integrate multimodal features effectively, achieving impressive F1 scores of approximately 88.08 on the CMU-MOSEI dataset and accuracy rates between 89% and 93% on the IEMOCAP dataset for classes such as Happy, Sad, Angry, and Neutral. Additionally, Xu et al. [20] emphasized the potential of self-supervised learning to enhance generalization by leveraging large unlabeled datasets. Multimodal transformers, such as Multimodal BERT (MMBERT), have also been pivotal in advancing emotion recognition. Lee et al. [10] demonstrated that leveraging advanced transformer architectures significantly improves accuracy by seamlessly integrating visual and textual data.

3 Method

The proposed multimodal model, as illustrated in Fig. 1, is structured into three primary modules. The first module handles preprocessing for both audio and text data. Following preprocessing, the feature extraction module utilizes CNN-LSTM for pattern feature extraction from audio and BERT for semantic feature extraction from text. The extracted features are then fused using an attention mechanism. Finally, the fused features are passed through a classification network for final emotion recognition.

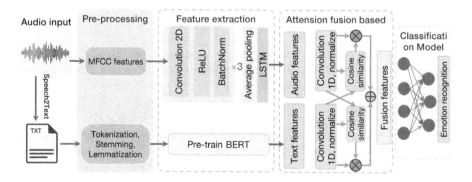

Fig. 1. Diagram of a multimodal speech-text Emotion recognition model

3.1 Audio Feature Extraction

We focus on extracting and processing audio features through the use of Mel-Frequency Cepstral Coefficients (MFCCs) [2]. MFCCs are a prevalent choice due to their robustness in capturing the essential characteristics of audio signals, which makes them highly effective for various audio analysis tasks. The process begins with converting raw audio recordings into MFCCs. These coefficients are then organized into two-dimensional spectrogram representations [12], which visually encode both spectral and temporal aspects of the audio data. This transformation is crucial as it preserves the nuanced details of the audio, enabling more accurate and comprehensive feature extraction and analysis.

The audio features are processed through a series of convolutional layers, starting with a 2D Convolutional layer to capture the spatial structure of the MFCC features. CNNs are effective at detecting spatial patterns in raw data such as spectrograms, which represent both frequency and time domains. These high-level features, such as tone, pitch, and intensity, are essential for identifying emotions in voice patterns [13]. To introduce non-linearity and enhance the learning of complex patterns, a Rectified Linear Unit (ReLU) activation function is applied following the convolutional layer. Batch Normalization is also utilized to stabilize the feature maps and improve training efficiency. The convolutional layers are organized into blocks, with three to four blocks proving optimal for performance. An Average Pooling layer is applied afterward to reduce the dimensionality of the output features while retaining critical information.

Following the convolutional processing, the features are reshaped and input into a Long Short Term Memory (LSTM) layer. The LSTM layer is designed to learn contextual dependencies and sequential patterns from the locally hierarchical features provided by the CNN [7]. This integration enables the model to capture both local features and long-term contextual dependencies, which are crucial for accurate emotion recognition. The output from the LSTM layer combines local information with long-term dependencies, enhancing the overall effectiveness of the emotion recognition system.

3.2 Text Feature Extration

For the emotion recognition task, this study employs a pre-trained BERT model [3] to process text data. Despite the availability of more advanced models, BERT is chosen for its effective trade-off between computational efficiency and performance. The text processing pipeline starts with tokenizing the input data using BERT's tokenizer, which converts the text into numerical token representations. These tokens are then passed through the BERT model to extract meaningful features essential for subsequent classification steps. This strategy capitalizes on BERT's strengths while keeping computational requirements within reasonable limits.

The dataset used for this research includes both text and audio components, requiring separate processing techniques for each modality. For text data, BERT's tokenizer produces three key outputs: input_ids, token_type_ids, and attention_masks. To ensure alignment between text and audio, truncation is avoided, preserving the integrity of each corresponding segment.

This work leverages the BERT Base model, which is structured with 12 Transformer layers. Each layer integrates a self-attention mechanism alongside a fully connected feed-forward network. Words are encoded into 768-dimensional vectors through the model's hidden size. Additionally, with 12 attention heads in each Transformer layer, the model effectively captures diverse contextual nuances. The BERT Base architecture, encompassing approximately 110 million parameters, offers a robust foundation for extracting text features crucial to emotion recognition.

3.3 Feature Fusion

To combine audio and text features, the Fusion Module utilizes a late fusion strategy augmented with cross-attention mechanisms for effective integration of these modalities. The process begins with scaling the sequence outputs from the BERT model [3] and the abstract features from the audio module [6]. This scaling is accomplished using two 1D Convolutional layers, which align the dimensions of the feature sets and address any discrepancies in sequence lengths and magnitudes between text and audio features. Each feature is also normalized by its length to ensure stable training and effective integration.

Following scaling, a cross-attention mechanism [19] is applied to merge text and audio features. This involves computing attention scores using cosine similarity between the pattern feature vector and the semantics feature vector, followed by a ReLU activation function. This mechanism captures interactions between the two modalities and highlights their mutual dependencies.

In the fusion process, the cross-attention matrices for text and audio features are weighted to reflect their interactions. The weighted matrices are then combined to form a fused representation, which is multiplied with the output from the final encoder layer of the BERT model [3]. This fused output is processed through a linear layer for sentiment classification, enabling a comprehensive analysis that integrates both audio and text information for emotion recognition.

3.4 Dataset

To improve the generalization capabilities of our model, we incorporate two datasets: the Multimodal EmotionLines Dataset (MELD) [16] and the Spoken Language Understanding Evaluation (SLUE) [14]. High-quality datasets are crucial in machine learning and artificial intelligence, as they play a vital role in determining model performance. By leveraging both MELD and SLUE, we aim to create a robust training and evaluation framework that ensures effective handling of diverse input scenarios.

The MELD dataset [16], an extension of the EmotionLines dataset, was developed through a collaboration involving researchers from Singapore, Mexico, and the USA. It introduces audio and visual modalities in addition to text, providing over 1,300 dialogues and 13,000 utterances sourced from the TV series Friends.

Each utterance is annotated with one of seven emotion categories as well as sentiment labels. The dataset is pre-divided into training, development, and test subsets, with audio-visual data available in .mp4 format and annotations provided in .csv files. The distribution of emotion classes across these subsets is illustrated in Fig. 2.

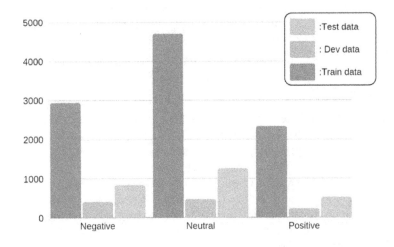

Fig. 2. Distribution of Classes in Training, Development, and Test Data

The SLUE benchmark suite [14], developed by ASAPP, comprises tasks like Named Entity Recognition (NER), Sentiment Analysis (SA), and Automatic Speech Recognition (ASR). For this study, the SLUE-VoxCeleb subset is utilized, containing English transcripts and sentiment annotations derived from the VoxCeleb1 dataset. The subset is employed for fine-tuning and evaluation, with utterances containing slurs excluded and partial words removed for consistency. Data statistics, including the sizes of fine-tuning, development, and test sets for SLUE-VoxCeleb and SLUE-VoxPopuli, are detailed in Table 1. Fine-tune and development sets are allocated for training and validation, while the test set is exclusively reserved for final performance assessment. To ensure the dataset's quality, we enlisted expert transcribers and annotators from an internal annotation team as well as a third-party vendor.

4 Results

This experiment evaluates the model's performance with various hyperparameter configurations using two distinct datasets. The first dataset consists of separate audio and text data points, while the second dataset includes larger conversations with varying audio intensity and tone. This combined approach provides a comprehensive evaluation of the model across different audio characteristics and conversational contexts.

Table 1. Information About Size, Type, and Source of the SLUE Data [14]

Corpus	Size (hours)			Tasks	Speech Type	Source Domain
	F-tune	Dev	Test			
SLUE-VoxPopuli	5,000 (14.5)	1,753 (5.0)	1,842 (4.9)	ASR, NER	Scripted	European Parliament
SLUE-VoxCeleb	5,777 (12.8)	1,454 (3.2)	3,553 (7.8)	ASR, SA	Conversational	Broadcasting (YouTube)

Training was performed with parameters summarized in Table 2. Due to the BERT model's extensive inference time and the audio processing requirements, training was conducted for 5 epochs. The multimodal model featured higher dropout (0.18 vs. 0.1), a higher starting learning rate (0.014 vs. 0.01), and a more aggressive learning rate decay (0.12 vs. 0.1) compared to the CNN-LSTM model. These adjustments accommodate the complexity of integrating multiple data modalities and aim to enhance performance.

Model initialization included Kaiming initialization for the audio module, frozen parameters for the pre-trained text module, and default uniform distribution for the fusion module and classification layer. The performance comparison between the audio-only model and the multimodal model, which integrates both audio and text data, was conducted to test the hypothesis that the multimodal model would show superior accuracy.

Table 2. Experiment hyperparameters

Training parameters	CNN-LSTM	LSTM-BERT	CNN-LSTM-BERT
Batch size	256	256	256
Number of epochs	5	5	5
Dropout rate	0.10	0.18	0.18
Start learning rate	0.010	0.014	0.014
Learning rate decay	0.10	0.12	0.12

Figure 3 illustrates the accuracy of the models over 4 epochs for both the training and validation datasets. In the CNN-LSTM model (Fig. 3a), accuracy improves rapidly during the first two epochs, reaching a peak validation accuracy of 68%. However, the LSTM-BERT model (Fig. 3b) shows relatively stable accuracy around 70%, indicating that the training process contributes little to improving the performance of the pre-trained BERT component. Similarly, in the CNN-LSTM-BERT model (Fig. 3c), accuracy remains steady at around 71%, showing only a slight improvement over the LSTM-BERT model. In all models, the validation accuracy is consistently higher than the training accuracy, likely due to the use of dropout, where from 10%- 18% of neurons are randomly removed during training to prevent overfitting.

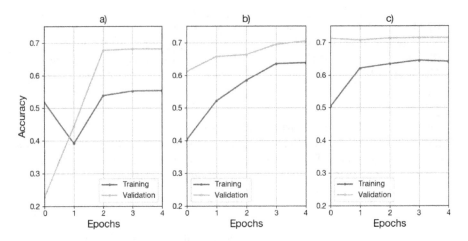

Fig. 3. Accuracy of models for both training and validation datasets: CNN-LSTM (a), LSTM-BERT (b), and CNN-LSTM-BERT (c).

Table 3 demonstrate the performance of three models—CNN-LSTM, LSTM-BERT, and CNN-LSTM-BERT—evaluated using training accuracy, validation accuracy, training loss, and validation loss. The CNN-LSTM model achieved a training accuracy of 55.28% and a validation accuracy of 68.07%, with a training loss of 0.99 and a validation loss of 0.88. While the model generalizes reasonably well to unseen data, the lower training accuracy combined with a higher validation accuracy suggests signs of overfitting, indicating the model may have learned specific patterns from the training data that do not generalize optimally. In contrast, the LSTM-BERT model significantly improved performance, achieving a training accuracy of 63.76% and a validation accuracy of 70.42%. However, the training loss (34.67) and validation loss (33.31) were notably higher compared to the CNN-LSTM model. This can be attributed to the combined use of audio and text features, which likely increases the complexity of the loss function compared to using only text features. The high loss indicates potential inefficiencies in the model's learning process, which may be addressed through further tuning. Nevertheless, this high loss also presents an opportunity for future improvements in the model's design and optimization. The CNN-LSTM-BERT model, which combines all three architectures, demonstrated the best performance, with a training accuracy of 64.13% and a validation accuracy of 71.42%. The inclusion of CNN with learned filters enhances the model's ability to extract useful pattern features from audio data, leading to more informative audio embedding vectors. This combination helps create more meaningful representations for the downstream LSTM and BERT layers, contributing to improved overall accuracy and generalization.

Table 3. Performance comparison of single and multiple models

Model	Train Acc. (%)	Val. Acc (%)	Train loss	Val loss
CNN-LSTM	55.28	68.07	0.99	0.88
LSTM-BERT	63.76	70.42	34.67	33.31
CNN-LSTM-BERT	64.13	71.42	27.77	27.43

Overall, diversity in feature representation embeddings contributes to improved performance, particularly in the CNN-LSTM-BERT model, which achieves the highest validation accuracy. However, this enhancement comes at the cost of increased computational time due to the added complexity of the model. Interestingly, the performance difference between the CNN-LSTM-BERT and LSTM-BERT models is relatively small, suggesting that the additional complexity yields only marginal gains in accuracy. Despite the higher loss values observed in the more complex models, their strong accuracy indicates that they are effectively capturing the underlying patterns in the data. Future optimization efforts could focus on reducing these losses and further enhancing performance, especially when dealing with the integration of audio and text features.

5 Conclusion

Emotion recognition is increasingly recognized as a crucial process where artificial intelligence techniques predict human emotions from various signals. This paper has advanced our understanding of emotion recognition by developing preprocessing techniques and a CNN-LSTM-BERT model. We effectively applied pre-processing methods, including duplicate channel removal, resampling, and padding, to standardize the audio data and used the MFCC algorithm for feature extraction. Our primary goal was to analyze sentiment from a combined dataset of voice signals and text transcripts using a multimodal CNN-LSTM integrated with a pre-trained BERT model. After training for five epochs, the multimodal model achieved a validation accuracy of 71% and a loss score of 27.43, indicating that there is still potential for optimization and extended training. Our findings revealed that while the multimodal model, which combines audio and text, slightly outperformed the audio-only model with 71% accuracy compared to 68%, it also demands significantly more computational resources due to BERT's inference time.

References

1. Alarcao, S.M., Fonseca, M.J.: Emotion recognition using EEG signals: a survey. IEEE Trans. Affect. Comput. **25**(10), 1440 (2017). https://doi.org/10.3390/e25101440

2. Davis, S.B., Mermelstein, P.: Comparison of parametric representations for monosyllabic word recognition in continuously spoken sentences. IEEE Trans. Acoust. Speech Signal Process. **28**(4), 357–366 (1980)
3. Devlin, J., Chang, M.W., Lee, K., Toutanova, K.: Bert: pre-training of deep bidirectional transformers for language understanding (2019). https://arxiv.org/abs/1810.04805
4. Eckert, W., Choi, J.: A study on the impact of data quality and quantity on speech emotion recognition models. IEEE Trans. Affect. Comput. **12**(1), 85–97 (2021)
5. Hang, S., Yang, Y., Chen, C., Zhang, X., Leng, Q., Zhao, X.: Deep learning-based multimodal emotion recognition from audio, visual, and text modalities: A systematic review of recent advancements and future prospects. J. Emot. Recogn. Res. **12**(3), 45–67 (2023). https://doi.org/10.1016/j.eswa.2023.121692
6. Hershey, J.R., et al.: CNN architectures for large-scale audio classification. In: Proceedings of the IEEE International Conference on Acoustics, Speech, and Signal Processing (2017)
7. Hochreiter, S., Schmidhuber, J.: Long short-term memory. Neural Comput. **9**(8), 1735–1780 (1997)
8. Huang, X., Li, H., Wang, Y.: Deep convolutional neural networks for emotion recognition from speech. IEEE Trans. Affect. Comput. **10**(3), 564–576 (2019)
9. Lee, S., Narayanan, S.: Voice and emotion: addressing the challenges of speech emotion recognition. Int. J. Speech Technol. **20**(4), 547–560 (2017)
10. Lee, S., Han, D.K., Ko, H.: Multimodal emotion recognition fusion analysis adapting Bert with heterogeneous feature unification. IEEE Access **9**, 94557–94572 (2021). https://doi.org/10.1109/ACCESS.2021.3092735
11. Li, X., Yang, Z., Wang, L.: Hybrid CNN-LSTM model for emotion recognition from speech. ACM Trans. Speech Lang. Process. **18**(2), 35–48 (2021)
12. Logan, B.: Mel frequency cepstral coefficients for music modeling. In: Proceedings of the International Symposium on Music Information Retrieval (2000)
13. Monika, R., Deivalakshmi, S.: Convolutional neural network-based fracture detection in spectrogram of acoustic emission. Signal Image Video Process. **18**, 4059–4074 (2024). https://doi.org/10.1007/s11760-024-03053-z
14. Nagrani, A., Chung, J.S., Zisserman, A.: Voxceleb: A large-scale speaker identification dataset. In: Interspeech 2017. interspeech_2017, ISCA (2017). https://doi.org/10.21437/interspeech.2017-950, http://dx.doi.org/10.21437/Interspeech.2017-950
15. Nwe, T.L., Lu, Z.: The role of semantic analysis in enhancing voice-based emotion recognition. ACM Trans. Speech Lang. Process. **15**(2), 12–28 (2018)
16. Poria, S., Hazarika, D., Majumder, N., Naik, G., Cambria, E., Mihalcea, R.: Meld: a multimodal multi-party dataset for emotion recognition in conversation. In: ACL 2019 (2019). https://aclanthology.org/P19-1050/
17. Schneider, S., Baevski, A., Collobert, R., Auli, M.: wav2vec: unsupervised pre-training for speech recognition (2019). https://arxiv.org/abs/1904.05862
18. Siriwardhana, S., Reis, A., Weerasekera, R., Nanayakkara, S.: Jointly fine-tuning "Bert-like" self supervised models to improve multimodal speech emotion recognition (2020). https://arxiv.org/abs/2008.06682
19. Xu, J., Lu, K., Wang, H.: Attention fusion network for multi-spectral semantic segmentation. In: Proceedings of the International Conference on Computer Vision (ICCV), vol. SPLNCS 04. Springer (2023). https://doi.org/10.1016/j.patrec.2021.03.015

20. Xu, Y., Liu, W., Chen, J.: Leveraging self-supervised learning for multimodal emotion recognition. J. Mach. Learn. Res. **24**(8), 1123–1140 (2023). https://doi.org/10.5555/12345678
21. Zhang, L., Zhao, J.: Challenges and solutions in speech emotion recognition: a comprehensive survey. J. Comput. Sci. Technol. **34**(2), 257–285 (2019)
22. Zhang, Y., Wu, X., Chen, L.: Speech emotion recognition with convolutional neural networks and long short-term memory networks. In: Proceedings of the AAAI Conference on Artificial Intelligence, vol.34, no. 1, pp. 1102–1109 (2020)

Using Various Machine Learning Algorithms and xLSTM-UNet for Crop Recommendation and Disease Prediction

Agnij Moitra[✉]

Amity International School, M-Block, Saket, New Delhi 110017, Delhi, India
agnijmoitra@outlook.com

Abstract. In this research, a novel hybrid method is presented using an xLSTM-UNet architecture to provide comprehensive crop management i.e. crop recommendations and disease prediction. The approach combines U-Net feature extraction ability with temporal xLSTM modeling to improve the performance of segmentation and classification operations in agriculture related tasks. This research builds a strong framework regarding crop recommendation task. Further, the model is able to foresee possible crop diseases with the help of image processing which is done at an early stage of the crop growing process. The importance of this work is crucial as it enables farmers with useful information that improves the output of crops while reducing negative effects of farming activities on the environment. Our approach targets the challenges of disease prediction, and crop selection towards the sustainable practices of agricultural and food security. Finally, this work not only pushes the boundaries of deploying deep learning in agriculture but also offers an integrated application for the 21st century farmers towards a data driven management approach.

Keywords: Crop Disease Prediction · Agriculture · Deep Learning

1 Introduction

Agricultural productivity is significantly affected by crop diseases, which can lead to substantial yield losses if not managed effectively. Traditional methods for disease identification rely on manual scouting and expert diagnoses, often resulting in delays that exacerbate the impact of these diseases [25]. Recent advancements in remote sensing technology and machine learning have provided new avenues for timely and accurate disease detection, enabling farmers to adopt more effective disease management strategies [1].

In this research, we use the novel xLSTM-UNet [6] architecture for crop disease classification, which leverages the capabilities of both long short-term memory networks and convolutional neural networks. This hybrid method enhances feature extraction from agricultural images and also improves segmentation accuracy, providing a robust framework for disease detection. Additionally, we integrate crop recommendation systems into our methodology, which is critical for optimizing agricultural inputs and improving crop health [14]. The proposed framework aims to provide an efficient solution for early crop disease detection, contributing to precision agriculture. By implementing our approach, we anticipate a reduction in crop losses and an increase in yield, thereby supporting sustainable agricultural practices. This research not only advances the field of agricultural technology but also promotes food security in the face of growing global challenges [24].

2 Literature Review

The framework proposed by Bakthavatchalam et al. (2022) demonstrates the efficacy of machine learning algorithms in predicting crop suitability based on soil characteristics and environmental factors [3].

In terms of crop nutrient recommendation, Hanyurwimfura et al. (2023) introduced a machine learning-based crop and fertilizer recommendation system that achieved 97% accuracy by incorporating soil parameters, thereby optimizing agricultural practices [9]. Similarly, studies have indicated that integrating big data analytics can significantly improve the prediction accuracy for nutrient requirements and crop yields, as shown by Gupta et al. (2021) [8].

The classification of crop diseases has also seen significant developments. Shahi et al. explored the use of UAVs coupled with deep learning techniques to detect crop diseases, highlighting the rapid advancements in remote sensing technology [20]. Agarwal et al. (2020) further developed a convolutional neural network model specifically for identifying diseases in tomato crops, emphasizing the importance of deep learning in disease diagnosis [1]. Automated leaf disease detection methods, such as those proposed by Pantazi et al. (2019), leverage image feature analysis and one-class classifiers to enhance detection accuracy across various crop species [14]. Moreover, Wani et al. (2021) provided a comprehensive overview of computational techniques, discussing the methodologies and challenges associated with automated agricultural disease detection [24]. Thereby, previous research shows the transformative potential of machine learning and deep learning in enhancing crop productivity, sustainability, and food security.

3 Methodology

3.1 Crop Recommendation

For crop recommendation, the dataset used was obtained from the Kaggle repository, specifically kaggle.com/datasets/atharvaingle/crop-recommendation-dataset, which encompasses 22 distinct crop categories. To ensure the integrity and consistency of the data, several preprocessing steps were undertaken. Notably, outliers were identified and removed using the Local Outlier Factor (LOF) method, as described by Breunig et al. [4]. The rationale behind outlier removal is to mitigate skewness in the dataset, thereby enhancing

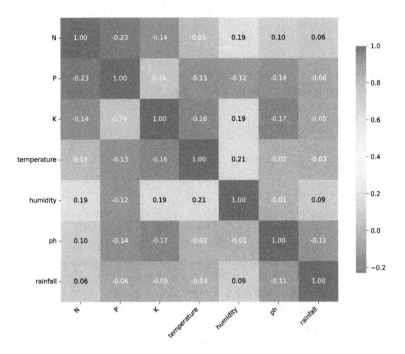

Fig. 1. Pearson correlation analysis of the data

the generalizability of the machine learning models employed. The LOF for a given point x can be expressed mathematically as follows (Figs. 1 and 2):

$$\text{LOF}(x) = \frac{\frac{1}{|N_k(x)|} \sum_{o \in N_k} \text{lrd}(o)}{\text{lrd}(x)} \tag{1}$$

In this equation, $N_k(x)$ represents the k-nearest neighbors of the point x and $\text{lrd}(x)$ denotes the local reachability density of x. This metric quantifies the isolation of x relative to its neighbors. And the local reachability density is calculated using:

$$\text{lrd}(x) = \frac{|N_k(x)|}{\sum_{o \in N_k(x)} \max\left((\sum_{i=1}^n |x_i - o_i|^r)^{\frac{1}{r}}, \text{lrd}(o)\right)} \tag{2}$$

In this expression, $|N_k(x)|$ denotes the number of neighbors in the near x, and the term $\max\left((\sum_{i=1}^n |x_i - o_i|^r)^{\frac{1}{r}}, \text{lrd}(o)\right)$ accounts for the distance metrics used to evaluate reachability among neighbors. For our implementation, the LOF calculation was conducted using the Scikit-Learn library [15], with a specified number of 20 nearest neighbors and employing a Minkowski distance metric with a parameter $r = 2$.

After the preprocessing phase, the dataset consisted of approximately 25,000 samples. For the task of directionality prediction, we explored the performance of

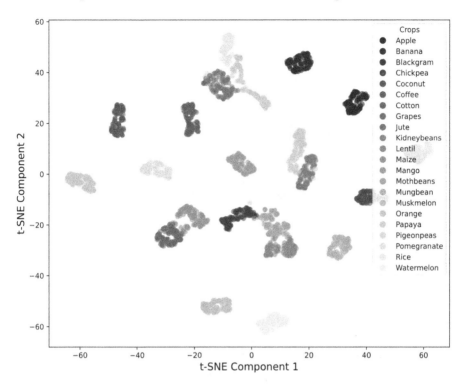

Fig. 2. t-SNE representation of the data, grouped by the various crop categories

all 41 classifiers available in the Scikit-Learn library, along with advanced gradient boosting methods including XGBoost [5], LightGBM [11], and CatBoost [17]. Each of these classifiers was integrated with a One-versus-Rest (OvR) strategy [18] to facilitate multiclass classification.

3.2 Crop Disease Prediction

The data for crop diease prediction was retrived from the following, wherein the combined dataset had more than 150k samples and 25+ disease classes (Fig. 3):

1. kaggle.com/datasets/mexwell/crop-diseases-classification
2. data.mendeley.com/datasets/bwh3zbpkpv/1
3. kaggle.com/datasets/kamal01/top-agriculture-crop-disease
4. kaggle.com/datasets/jawadali1045/20k-multi-class-crop-disease-images
5. kaggle.com/datasets/lavaman151/plantifydr-dataset
6. kaggle.com/datasets/nafishamoin/new-bangladeshi-crop-disease

Problem Formulation. $\exists \mathcal{D} = \{(\mathbf{x}_i, y_i)\}_{i=1}^{N}$ dataset, such that $\mathbf{x}_i \in \mathbb{R}^{H \times W \times C}$ is a high-resolution RGB image of a crop, and $y_i \in \{1, \ldots, K\}$ denotes the

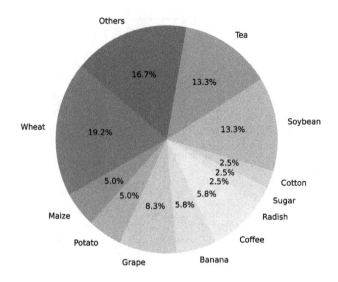

Fig. 3. Distribution of the crops used for disease prediction

corresponding disease class for the image. The objective is to design a model $f_\theta : \mathbb{R}^{H \times W \times C} \to \Delta^K$ parameterized by θ that predicts the probability distribution over K disease categories, where Δ^K is the probability simplex:

$$f_\theta(\mathbf{x}_i) = \hat{y}_i = \mathbb{P}(y_i \mid \mathbf{x}_i; \theta). \tag{3}$$

Thereby, the problem could be considered a multi-class classification task with the objective to minimize the cross-entropy loss and maximize the Dice similarity score.

Network Architecture. We utilize the U-Net [19] as the backbone for feature extraction. Its encoder-decoder design captures both local and global features for disease classification. The U-Net encoder $\mathcal{E}_\phi$ converts input $\mathbf{x}_i$ into a latent representation $\mathbf{h}_{enc}$:

$$\mathbf{h}_{enc} = \mathcal{E}_\phi(\mathbf{x}_i), \quad \mathbf{h}_{enc} \in \mathbb{R}^{H' \times W' \times D}, \tag{4}$$

where $H' = H/2^L$, $W' = W/2^L$, D is the number of feature channels, and L is the number of downsampling layers. The decoder $\mathcal{D}_\phi$ reconstructs the image:

$$\hat{\mathbf{x}}_i = \mathcal{D}_\phi(\mathbf{h}_{enc}). \tag{5}$$

xLSTM for Long-Range Dependencies. To model long-range dependencies, xLSTM processes spatial correlations across the encoder's latent features. It propagates features hierarchically:

$$\mathbf{h}_t = \mathcal{F}_{xLSTM}(\mathbf{h}_{t-1}, \mathbf{h}_{enc}), \tag{6}$$

where $\mathbf{h}_t$ is the hidden state at time t, and $\mathbf{h}_{enc}$ is the U-Net latent embedding. The xLSTM gate operations include forget, input, cell state, and output gates, e.g.,

$$\mathbf{f}_t = \sigma(\mathbf{W}_f \mathbf{h}_{enc} + \mathbf{U}_f \mathbf{h}_{t-1} + \mathbf{b}_f), \tag{7}$$

with the updated hidden state:

$$\mathbf{h}_t = \mathbf{o}_t \odot \tanh(\mathbf{c}_t). \tag{8}$$

The final xLSTM hidden state [16] is used by the U-Net decoder for reconstruction and classification.

Multi-scale Feature Fusion. Multi-scale fusion enhances detection across scales by concatenating encoder feature maps:

$$\mathbf{p}_{concat} = \text{Concat}(\mathbf{p}_1, \mathbf{p}_2, \ldots, \mathbf{p}_L), \tag{9}$$

where $\mathbf{p}_i = \mathcal{E}_\phi^{(i)}(\mathbf{x}_i)$ is the feature map from the i-th layer. The concatenated features are modeled with xLSTM:

$$\mathbf{h}_{final} = \mathcal{F}_{xLSTM}(\mathbf{p}_{concat}). \tag{10}$$

This xLSTM-UNet architecture [6] outperforms alternatives like Mamba-UNet [27] in 2D and 3D image segmentation.

Hyperparameters. Table 1 lists the hyperparameters used for both the U-Net and xLSTM components, including their meanings and values.

Table 1. Hyperparameters for U-Net and xLSTM

Hyperparameter	Meaning	Value
num_filters	Number of filters per convolutional layer	64
num_layers	Number of downsampling/upsampling layers in U-Net	4
filter_size	Size of convolutional filters	3×3
batch_size	Batch size for training	16
learning_rate	Init learning rate	1×10^{-3}
dropout_rate	Dropout rate for regularization	0.5
hidden_size	Size of hidden state in xLSTM	256
sequence_length	Length of sequence for xLSTM	10
optimizer	Optimizer used during training	AdamW
weight_decay	Weight decay for regularization	1×10^{-4}

Loss Function. The overall loss function $\mathcal{L}_{total}$ is a weighted combination of the pixel-wise cross-entropy loss $\mathcal{L}_{CE}$ and Dice loss $\mathcal{L}_{Dice}$, which is specifically effective in handling class imbalances:

$$\mathcal{L}_{CE} = -\frac{1}{N}\sum_{i=1}^{N}\sum_{j=1}^{K} y_{ij} \log(\hat{y}_{ij}), \tag{11}$$

$$\mathcal{L}_{Dice} = 1 - \frac{2\sum_{i=1}^{N} \hat{y}_i y_i}{\sum_{i=1}^{N} \hat{y}_i^2 + \sum_{i=1}^{N} y_i^2}. \tag{12}$$

The final loss is computed as: $\mathcal{L}_{total} = \lambda_{CE}\mathcal{L}_{CE} + \lambda_{Dice}\mathcal{L}_{Dice},$. Where λ_{CE} and λ_{Dice} are hyperparameters controlling the relative contributions of the cross-entropy and Dice losses, respectively.

Optimization Strategy. The network parameters are optimized using the AdamW optimizer [12], which incorporates decoupled weight decay to improve generalization. The learning rate follows a cosine annealing schedule with warm restarts, defined as:

$$lr(t) = lr_{min} + \frac{1}{2}(lr_{max} - lr_{min})\left(1 + \cos\left(\frac{t}{t_{max}}\pi\right)\right), \tag{13}$$

where lr_{min} and lr_{max} represent the minimum and maximum learning rates, respectively, and t_{max} denotes the epoch at which the restart occurs. This schedule facilitates efficient convergence while avoiding sharp minima.

The model is trained for up to 100 epochs, with early stopping based on validation loss. The initial learning rate is set to 1×10^{-3}, and the training process utilizes a batch size of 16 on an NVIDIA A100 GPU through Google Colab.

Final Crop Disease Classification. After extracting multi-scale features using the U-Net and incorporating long-range dependencies with xLSTM, the final crop disease classification is performed by applying a fully connected classification layer to the learned representation. Let $\mathbf{h}_{final} \in \mathbb{R}^{H' \times W' \times D}$ be the final output from the decoder. To aggregate the spatial information, global average pooling is applied:

$$\mathbf{h}_{global} = \frac{1}{H'W'}\sum_{i=1}^{H'}\sum_{j=1}^{W'} \mathbf{h}_{final}^{(i,j)}, \tag{14}$$

where $\mathbf{h}_{global} \in \mathbb{R}^D$ represents the pooled feature vector. This feature vector is then passed through a fully connected layer for classification:

$$\mathbf{y}_i = \sigma(\mathbf{W}_{fc}\mathbf{h}_{global} + \mathbf{b}_{fc}), \tag{15}$$

where $\mathbf{W}_{fc} \in \mathbb{R}^{K \times D}$ is the weight matrix, $\mathbf{b}_{fc} \in \mathbb{R}^K$ is the bias vector, and K is the number of crop disease categories. The output $\mathbf{y}_i$ corresponds to the predicted probability distribution over the K classes.

The final predicted label $\hat{y}_i$ is computed as:

$$\hat{y}_i = \arg\max_k \mathbf{y}_i^{(k)}. \tag{16}$$

The classification loss, $\mathcal{L}_{CE}$, is calculated using the cross-entropy loss between the predicted probabilities and the ground truth labels.

4 Results

4.1 Crop Recommendation

Results from our crop recommendation task highlight the effectiveness of the CatBoost model, which achieved an outstanding accuracy of 99%. This performance indicates its robustness in distinguishing between various crop types, closely followed by the Gradient Boosting model, which also attained a 99% accuracy. The LGBM and Histogram Gradient Boosting models performed commendably with accuracies of 98% and 96%, respectively, while XGBoost showed a slightly lower accuracy of 96%. The SHAP heat map revealed that nitrogen (N) and phosphorus (P) levels, along with rainfall, were the most influential features affecting model predictions. These findings underscore the importance of these variables in crop selection based on environmental conditions, thus providing actionable insights for effective crop management (Fig. 4 and Table 2).

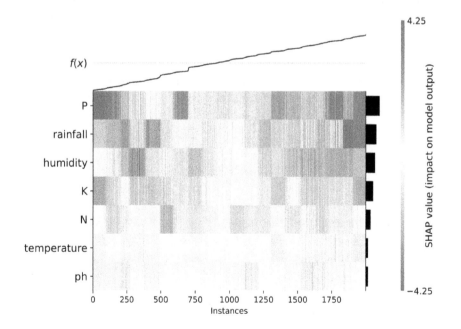

Fig. 4. SHAP heat map for the CatBoost Classifier

Table 2. Performance Metrics for the Top Models for predicting the type of crop

	Accuracy	ROC-AUC	F1 Score
CatBoost [17]	0.99	0.98	0.99
Gradient Boosting [15]	0.99	0.98	0.97
LGBM [11]	0.98	0.98	0.97
Histogram Gradient Boosting [15]	0.96	0.97	0.97
XGBoost [5]	0.96	0.95	0.96
Random Forest [15]	0.95	0.94	0.94
K-Nearest Neighbors [15]	0.91	0.89	0.90
Logistic Regression [15]	0.85	0.82	0.86

4.2 Crop Disease Prediction

The results presented in Table 3 illustrate the various performance metrics i.e. accuracy, ROC-AUC and F1 score of previous deep learning models and this UNet-xLSTM method for crop disease classification. Notably, our proposed model, U-Net combined with xLSTM, achieved an impressive accuracy of 99.99%, alongside a precision & recall of 99.99%. This performance significantly surpasses that of established architectures, including VGG16 and ResNet-50, which reported accuracies of 98.4% and 98.3%, respectively. Other models such as AlexNet and GoogleNet demonstrated lower accuracy rates of 89.6% and 93.8%, indicating that traditional CNNs may not be as effective for this specific application. The results from recent studies, such as those by P. Tm et al. [23] and K. Zhang et al. [26], further confirm the trend, with accuracy rates of 94% and 95%, respectively. Overall, the superior metrics achieved by our model underscore its potential as a robust solution for accurate crop disease detection,

Table 3. Comparison for crop disease classification with other methods

	Accuracy	Precision	Recall	F1
VGG16 [21]	98.4%	99.3%	98.0%	99.0%
ResNet-50 [10]	98.3%	98%	98%	98%
AlexNet [13]	89.6%	89.5%	89.6%	89.4%
GoogleNet [13]	93.8%	93.8%	93.8%	93.7%
P. Tm et al. [23]	94%	94.81%	94.78%	94.8%
K. Zhang et al. [26]	95%	–	–	–
M. Agarwal et al. [2]	91%	90%	92%	91%
M. Dookie [7]	85%	–	84%	–
Inception Net V3 [22]	98.3%	98%	98%	98%
U-Net + xLSTM (**Ours**)	99.99%	99.99%	99.99%	99.99%

showcasing advancements in deep learning methodologies that enhance agricultural productivity and sustainability.

5 Conclusion

In this paper, we presented a comprehensive framework for crop recommendation and disease classification using advanced machine learning techniques, specifically the xLSTM-U-Net model. This methodology effectively integrates U-Net's feature extraction capabilities with xLSTM's temporal modeling to enhance disease prediction accuracy while also providing tailored crop recommendations for various environmental conditions. Our approach achieved remarkable predictive performance, as evidenced by the results that show an accuracy of 99.99% with the U-Net + xLSTM model, outperforming other established methods such as VGG16 and ResNet-50. Moreover, the model's interpretability was significantly enhanced through SHAP analysis, offering clear insights into feature importance, which is crucial for practical applications in agriculture. However, limitations remain, including the reliance on historical data and potential overfitting, particularly in regions with limited agricultural datasets. Additionally, exploring climate forecasting models and employing generative techniques for synthetic data creation could further enhance prediction accuracy, especially in data-scarce regions. Despite these challenges, this research lays a strong foundation for advancing precision agriculture, providing valuable tools to enhance crop productivity and mitigate the risks of crop diseases.

Disclosure of Interests. The author of this paper has no conflict of interest.

References

1. Agarwal, M., Gupta, S., Biswas, K.: Development of efficient CNN model for tomato crop disease identification. Sustain. Comput. Inform. Syst. **28**, 100407 (2020)
2. Agarwal, M., Singh, A., Arjaria, S., Sinha, A., Gupta, S.: Toled: tomato leaf disease detection using convolution neural network. Procedia Comput. Sci. **167**, 293–301 (2020)
3. Bakthavatchalam, K., et al.: IoT framework for measurement and precision agriculture: predicting the crop using machine learning algorithms. Technologies **10**(1), 13 (2022). https://doi.org/10.3390/technologies10010013
4. Breunig, M.M., Kriegel, H.P., Ng, R.T., Sander, J.: LoF: identifying density-based local outliers. In: Proceedings of the 2000 ACM SIGMOD international conference on Management of Data, pp. 93–104. Association for Computing Machinery (2000)
5. Chen, T., Guestrin, C.: Xgboost: a scalable tree boosting system. In: Proceedings of the 22nd AMC SIGKDD International Conference on Knowledge Discovery and Data Mining, pp. 785–794 (2016)
6. Chen, T., et al.: XLSTM-UNet can be an effective 2D\& 3D medical image segmentation backbone with vision-LSTM (VIL) better than its mamba counterpart. arXiv preprint arXiv:2407.01530 (2024)

7. Dookie, M., Ali, O., Ramsubhag, A., Jayaraman, J.: Flowering gene regulation in tomato plants treated with brown seaweed extracts. Sci. Hortic. **276**, 109715 (2021)
8. Gupta, R., et al.: WB-CPI: weather based crop prediction in India using big data analytics. IEEE Access **9**, 137869–137885 (2021)
9. Hanyurwimfura, D., Uwitonze, A., Kabandana, I.: Data-driven analysis and machine learning-based crop and fertilizer recommendation system for revolutionizing farming practices. Agriculture **13**(11), 2141 (2023). https://doi.org/10.3390/agriculture13112141
10. He, K., Zhang, X., Ren, S., Sun, J.: Deep residual learning for image recognition. In: Proceedings of the IEEE Conference on Computer Vision and Pattern Recognition (CVPR), pp. 770–778 (2016). https://arxiv.org/abs/1512.03385
11. Ke, G., et al.: LIGHTGBM: a highly efficient gradient boosting decision tree. In: Advances in Neural Information Processing Systems, vol. 30 (2017)
12. Loshchilov, I., Hutter, F.: Decoupled weight decay regularization. In: International Conference on Learning Representations (2019). https://openreview.net/forum?id=Bkg6RiCqY7
13. Mohanty, S.P., Hughes, D.P., Salathé, M.: Using deep learning for image-based plant disease detection. Front. Plant Sci. **7**, 1419 (2016)
14. Pantazi, X., Moshou, D., Tamouridou, A.: Automated leaf disease detection in different crop species through image features analysis and one class classifiers. Comput. Electron. Agric. **156**, 96–104 (2019)
15. Pedregosa, F., et al.: Scikit-learn: machine learning in python. J. Mach. Learn. Res. **12**, 2825–2830 (2011)
16. Pöppel, K., et al.: XLSTM: extended long short-term memory. In: First Workshop on Long-Context Foundation Models@ ICML 2024 (2024)
17. Prokhorenkova, L., Gusev, G., Vorobev, A., Dorogush, A.V., Gulin, A.: Catboost: unbiased boosting with categorical features. In: Advances in Neural Information Processing Systems, vol. 31 (2018)
18. Rifkin, R., Klautau, A.: In defense of one-vs-all classification. J. Mach. Learn. Res. **5**, 101–141 (2004)
19. Ronneberger, O., Fischer, P., Brox, T.: U-Net: Convolutional networks for biomedical image segmentation. In: Medical Image Computing and Computer-Assisted Intervention–MICCAI 2015: 18th International Conference, Munich, Germany, October 5-9, 2015, Proceedings, PIII 18, pp. 234–241. Springer (2015)
20. Shahi, T.B., Xu, C.Y., Neupane, A., Guo, W.: Recent advances in crop disease detection using uav and deep learning techniques. Remote Sens. **15**(9), 2450 (2023)
21. Simonyan, K., Zisserman, A.: Very deep convolutional networks for large-scale image recognition. In: International Conference on Learning Representations (ICLR) (2015). https://arxiv.org/abs/1409.1556
22. Szegedy, C., Vanhoucke, V., Ioffe, S., Shlens, J., Wojna, Z.: Rethinking the inception architecture for computer vision. In: Proceedings of the IEEE Conference on Computer Vision and Pattern Recognition, pp. 2818–2826 (2016)
23. Tm, P., Pranathi, A., SaiAshritha, K., Chittaragi, N.B., Koolagudi, S.G.: Tomato leaf disease detection using convolutional neural networks. In: 2018 Eleventh International Conference on Contemporary Computing (IC3), pp. 1–5. IEEE (2018)
24. Wani, J., Sharma, S., Muzamil, M., Ahmed, S., Sharma, S., Singh, S.: Machine learning and deep learning based computational techniques in automatic agricultural diseases detection: methodologies, applications, and challenges. Archives Comput. Methods Eng. 1–37 (2021)

25. Xu, C.Y., Neupane, A., Guo, W.: Recent advances in crop disease detection using UAV and deep learning techniques. Remote Sens. **15**(9), 2450 (2023). https://doi.org/10.3390/rs15092450
26. Zhang, K., Wu, Q., Liu, A., Meng, X.: Can deep learning identify tomato leaf disease? Adv. Multimedia **2018**(1), 6710865 (2018)
27. Zhang, M., Yu, Y., Jin, S., Gu, L., Ling, T., Tao, X.: VM-UNet-v2: rethinking vision mamba unet for medical image segmentation. In: International Symposium on Bioinformatics Research and Applications, pp. 335–346. Springer (2024)

He-Li Graph Convolutional Neural Network: Deep and Enhanced Adaptation of Interest Modeling for Personalized Recommendation System

Quang Dung Nguyen(✉), Quoc Lap Dinh, Ba Hoang Nam Nguyen, and Van Hieu Bui

FPT University, Education Zone, Hoa Lac Hi-tech Park, Ha Noi, Vietnam
{dungnqhe153335,lapdqhe161860,namnbhhe161029,hieubv10}@fpt.edu.vn
https://daihoc.fpt.edu.vn/

Abstract. Traditional Graph Neural Network (GNN)-based recommendation systems encounter significant challenges in managing high computational costs and scalability when modeling complex, heterogeneous user-item interactions. These models frequently fall short in capturing the diversity of relationship types and multi-level contextual information, resulting in limited performance gains. To overcome these limitations, we present the Heterogeneous Light Graph Convolutional Network (He-LiGCN), a streamlined framework designed to enhance both accuracy and scalability. Leveraging multi-level graph coarsening and sophisticated contextual embeddings, He-LiGCN efficiently models intricate user-item dependencies with substantially reduced computational demands. Experimental results demonstrate a 6.5% improvement in Recall@10 and an 8.9% increase in NDCG@10 over baseline models, along with a reduction in training time by up to 20%, underscoring its effectiveness and efficiency in large-scale recommendation scenarios. By advancing the efficiency and depth of graph-based recommendations, He-LiGCN represents a practical and scalable solution for the next generation of personalized recommendation systems.

Keywords: Convolutional neural network · Heterogeneous graph analysis · Recommendation system · Scalability

1 Introduction

Graph Neural Networks (GNNs) have become pivotal in recommendation systems due to their ability to model complex relationships. By representing users and items as nodes in a graph and leveraging higher-order connectivity through message-passing mechanisms, GNNs provide a sophisticated approach for capturing intricate interactions [12]. However, traditional GNN-based recommendation models often face significant challenges, particularly in handling heterogeneous data where diverse types of nodes and edges are present. Additionally, these models incur high computational costs due to the need to generate and process dense intermediate graphs, which limits their scalability in large-scale applications [14].

To address some of these scalability issues, Lightweight Graph Convolutional Network (LightGCN) [6] was introduced. LightGCN improves computational efficiency by focusing solely on neighborhood aggregation, removing feature transformations and nonlinear activation functions. This streamlined design reduces computational overhead and enhances scalability, making LightGCN effective for large-scale recommendation tasks. However, LightGCN's reliance on homogeneous graphs restricts its representational capacity, especially in scenarios that require capturing diverse and complex relationships within heterogeneous data.

To overcome these limitations, we propose the Heterogeneous Light Graph Convolutional Network (He-LiGCN), a framework designed to enhance recommendation accuracy and scalability by leveraging heterogeneous graph structures. It incorporates multi-level graph coarsening inspired by HeteroMILE [15] to improve computational efficiency and manage large graphs more effectively. By coarsening the graph, He-LiGCN reduces computational requirements while preserving critical structural information necessary for accurate recommendations. Additionally, He-LiGCN employs General Attributed Multiplex Heterogeneous Network Embedding (GATNE) [1], which captures rich structural and attribute information across diverse edge types, enabling precise modeling of heterogeneous relationships and interactions.

In this study, we aim to demonstrate that He-LiGCN outperforms existing models, such as Neural Graph Collaborative Filtering (NGCF) [10] and LightGCN [6], in terms of recommendation accuracy, convergence speed, and computational efficiency. By addressing the limitations of previous GNN models, He-LiGCN provides a robust solution for handling complex, large-scale recommendation tasks.

Overall, He-LiGCN presents a scalable, accurate, and efficient framework for recommendation systems that require handling large, heterogeneous graphs. Our contributions provide both theoretical advancements in graph-based recommendation and practical benefits for large-scale, personalized recommendation tasks across various domains.

2 Related Work

The field of recommendation systems has advanced significantly with the integration of graph-based models, capturing complex user-item relationships. Initially, homogeneous graphs - where nodes and edges are of the same type - were used. The introduction of Graph Neural Networks (GNNs) like Graph Convolutional Network (GCN) and GraphSAGE [4] represented a major step forward by leveraging graph structures to aggregate information from neighbors, thereby learning both direct and higher-order node interactions.

To improve scalability in large-scale recommendation tasks, Light Graph Convolution (LGC) [6] simplified GCN by focusing solely on neighborhood aggregation, omitting feature transformations and nonlinear activations. This approach reduced computational costs and improved scalability while capturing high-order connectivity across layers. However, homogeneous graphs like LightGCN's cannot fully represent the diversity of real-world data, which often includes complex, heterogeneous relationships.

This limitation spurred interest in heterogeneous graphs, which support various node and edge types, offering richer representations. In recommendation systems, heterogeneous graphs allow for more nuanced modeling of entities such as users, items, and attributes. Models like the Heterogeneous Graph Attention Network (HAN) [11] utilize attention mechanisms to prioritize relevant metapaths and node types, capture semantic information and improve recommendations. Similarly, the Heterogeneous Graph Neural Network (HetGNN) [9] uses random walks and type-specific encoders to enhance learning from heterogeneous neighbors.

Despite these advances, reliance on predefined meta-paths, as in HAN, limits flexibility since selecting optimal paths for varied datasets is challenging. High computational costs in managing multiple paths also affect scalability. To address this, multiplex graphs were explored, capturing different relationships within the same nodes. General Attributed Multiplex Heterogeneous Network Embedding (GATNE) [1] models diverse edge types with edge-specific transformations and attention, enable context-aware embeddings. However, higher-order connectivity is often underexploited, which is crucial for capture indirect interactions.

While these advances improve heterogeneous and multiplex graph modeling, integrating these benefits with over-smoothing prevention in a scalable model remains challenging. Current models lack flexibility to dynamically prioritize relationships and impose high computational demands. To address these, we propose He-Li Graph Convolutional Network (He-LiGCN), which synthesizes prior advancements while addressing limitations. Drawing on HeteroMILE's [15] multi-level coarsening and refinement, He-LiGCN reduces graph complexity while preserving structure. GATNE [1] allow it to represent multiplex relationships effectively, and APPNP's PageRank integration mitigates over-smoothing, ensuring deeper network layers retain discriminative power. He-LiGCN thus offers a scalable, effective solution for personalized recommendations on large-scale heterogeneous graphs, enhancing user experiences across applications.

3 Methodology

The Heterogeneous Light Graph Convolutional Network (He-LiGCN) is designed to capture complex interactions within heterogeneous graphs by leveraging multilevel coarsening and contextual embeddings. The following subsections outline each phase of the model's architecture in detail in Fig. 1.

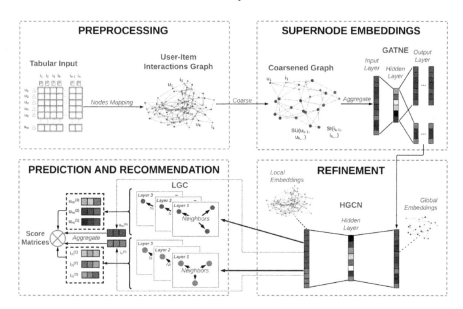

Fig. 1. He-LiGCN framework

3.1 Preprocessing: Constructing Efficient Heterogeneous Graphs

The preprocessing phase in He-LiGCN utilizes a multi-level graph coarsening strategy to effectively handle large-scale heterogeneous graphs. This technique, inspired by HeteroMILE [15], addresses the high computational demands of processing vast graphs by reducing their size while preserving key structural information. Multi-level coarsening operates by merging nodes with similar features into "supernodes," significantly decreasing the number of nodes and edges the model must process, thereby enhancing computational efficiency and scalability. The primary goal of coarsening is to reduce the computational load without sacrificing critical interaction patterns.

Locality Sensitive Hashing (LSH): To achieve this, we leverage (LSH) [8] for node grouping, which ensures that nodes with similar features or behaviors are grouped into the same supernode. Let $\mathcal{G}_0 = (\mathcal{V}_0, \mathcal{E}_0)$ represent the initial heterogeneous graph, where $\mathcal{V}_0$ denotes the set of nodes (users and items) and $\mathcal{E}_0$ represents the set of edges (interactions). The coarsening process generates a sequence of graphs $\mathcal{G}_0, \mathcal{G}_1, \ldots, \mathcal{G}_m$ where each subsequent graph $\mathcal{G}_i$ has a reduced number of nodes and edges compared to $\mathcal{G}_{i-1}$. The coarsening process that merges similar nodes based on LSH. It is utilized to identify and cluster nodes with similar attribute vectors. Each node $v \in \mathcal{V}_i$ is represented by an embedding vector $\mathbf{e}_v$, which encodes the node's attributes and connections. To identify similar nodes efficiently, we apply LSH to map each node to a hash bucket. Nodes that fall into the same bucket are considered similar and grouped to form a supernode. This process significantly reduces the complexity of pairwise node comparisons in large graphs, allowing the coarsening to remain computationally feasible even on massive datasets. Formally, the LSH-based similarity function for two nodes u and v can be represented as

$$P_{f_i \in F}[f_i(u) = f_i(v)] = P[\min \pi(u) = \min \pi(v)] \propto J(u,v) \quad (1)$$

where f_i is the hash function in a set F, π is the random permutation, and J is the Jaccard Index [7] function that calculates the similarity score.

Jaccard Max: For each unmatched node u, a node v is selected from $\mathcal{N}_u$ based on the highest Jaccard similarity score. Node u and v are then merged into a single supernode. This process continues iteratively until all nodes are matched or no suitable neighbors remain. The Jaccard similarity is calculated as

$$J(u,v) = \frac{|\mathcal{N}(u) \cap \mathcal{N}(v)|}{|\mathcal{N}(u) \cup \mathcal{N}(v)|} \quad (2)$$

Jaccard Weight Random Sampling (WRS): Unlike Jaccard Max, this method selects a neighboring node v_j from $\mathcal{N}_u$ randomly, with the selection probability proportional to their Jaccard similarity score. The probability of merging u with v_j is defined as

$$p(u, v_j) = \frac{J(u, v_j)}{\sum_{i \in \mathcal{N}(u)} J(u, v_i)} \quad (3)$$

To avoid critical information loss while implementing multi-level graph coarsening process, we set the threshold following Menger's Theorem [3]

$$\delta(\mathcal{G}_i) \geq \lambda(\mathcal{G}_i) \geq \kappa(\mathcal{G}_i) \geq \frac{|\mathcal{V}|}{2} \quad (4)$$

where δ is the minimum degree of the graph, λ and κ is the edge and vertex connectivity of the graph, respectively. If the above equation still holds, the coarsening process will continue until any existing pair in $\mathcal{V}$ is under the similarity threshold.

This mechanism ensures that only nodes with high feature similarity are clustered, which is essential for maintaining the structural integrity of the original graph during coarsening, and makes it suitable for processing large-scale, high-dimensional graphs.

3.2 Supernode Embedding

After the coarsening step, He-LiGCN employs the General Attributed Multiplex Heterogeneous Network Embedding (GATNE) [1] to generate embeddings for each supernode in the coarest graph $\mathcal{G}_m$, enabling it to effectively capture the diverse, multiplex relationships in heterogeneous graphs. To capture the local structural properties of each edge type, the model performs random walks separately for each type of edge r. These random walks explore the graph structure and generate sequences of nodes that reflect the local neighborhood of each target node. For each target node v_i, a sequence of training samples (v_i, v_j, r) is generated, where v_j appears within a predefined window size of v_i during the random walk. This sampling strategy ensures that the model learns edge-type-specific patterns and relationships, capturing both direct and indirect interactions between nodes. Instead of creating unique embeddings for individual nodes through direct training, this approach focuses on developing a transformation function. This function takes raw node features as input and converts them into embeddings. The key advantage is that this method can generate embeddings for new nodes that weren't present during the training phase, as long as these new nodes have the necessary raw features. This makes the system more flexible and generalizable to unseen data. The resulting training samples are then used to optimize the embeddings, enabling the model to represent nodes with respect to both their structural roles and their contextual importance within the graph.

3.3 Embedding Refinement

After generating supernode embeddings, He-LiGCN employs a refinement process to propagate these embeddings back to the original graph, ensuring each node's representation reflects both its local and global heterogeneous interactions. Drawing on the Heterogeneous Graph Convolutional Network (HGCN) [13] framework, this refinement step enhances the node embeddings by capturing intricate relationships within the original, uncoarsened graph. The refinement stage starts by initializing each node in the original graph with the embedding of its corresponding supernode, providing a high-level contextual representation as a starting point. Then, to refine this embedding for each node, He-LiGCN performs a series of heterogeneous graph convolutions, where information from neighboring nodes is aggregated while considering the edge types connecting them. This allows He-LiGCN to aggregate and weigh information from each edge type independently, thereby capturing the heterogeneous nature of the graph. The refinement process repeats over multiple layers, allowing embeddings to capture higher-order relationships while preserving heterogeneity. The final embedding $\mathbf{z}_j$ for node j is obtained by aggregating representations from each layer using a learned attention mechanism. This layer-wise aggregation ensures that nodes retain unique, discriminative features from various levels of neighborhood aggregation.

3.4 Prediction and Recommendation

In the final stage, He-LiGCN combines user and item embeddings derived from the previous layers to generate personalized recommendations, following an approach inspired by Light Graph Convolutional Network (LightGCN) [6]. Unlike traditional GNNs, LightGCN omits non-linear transformations and feature transformations, focusing solely on neighborhood aggregation. This lightweight approach effectively captures collaborative signals by iteratively propagating embeddings across user-item interactions without introducing unnecessary complexity, making it ideal for large-scale recommendation tasks. The user-item interactions are modeled as a matrix, denoted by $\mathbf{R} \in \mathbb{R}^{(m \times n)}$, where each entry $\mathbf{R}_{ui}$ represents whether user u has interacted with item i (with binary values indicating interaction), m and n are the number of users and items respectively. To streamline the calculation, the normalized adjacency matrix $\tilde{\mathbf{A}}$ is introduced which represents the structure of the user-item graph

$$\tilde{\mathbf{A}} = \mathbf{D}^{-\frac{1}{2}} \mathbf{A} \mathbf{D}^{-\frac{1}{2}}$$

$$= \begin{pmatrix} \frac{1}{\sqrt{d(1)}} & 0 & \cdots & 0 \\ 0 & \frac{1}{\sqrt{d(2)}} & \cdots & 0 \\ \vdots & \vdots & \ddots & \vdots \\ 0 & 0 & \cdots & \frac{1}{\sqrt{d(m+n)}} \end{pmatrix} \begin{pmatrix} \mathbf{0} & \mathbf{R} \\ \mathbf{R}^\top & \mathbf{0} \end{pmatrix} \begin{pmatrix} \frac{1}{\sqrt{d(1)}} & 0 & \cdots & 0 \\ 0 & \frac{1}{\sqrt{d(2)}} & \cdots & 0 \\ \vdots & \vdots & \ddots & \vdots \\ 0 & 0 & \cdots & \frac{1}{\sqrt{d(m+n)}} \end{pmatrix} \quad (5)$$

where $d(\bullet)$ is the degree of the node. The final embedding for each user u and item i is generated by aggregating embeddings across multiple layers, capturing both direct and high-order interactions. A key challenge in GNNs is the over-smoothing problem, where node representations become too similar after multiple graph convolution layers. To address this issue in He-LiGCN, we adopt the Approximate Personalized Propagation of Neural Predictions (APPNP) [2] technique, which maintains node distinctiveness while enabling deep architectures, modifies the standard graph convolution operation by incorporating a teleportation coefficient β that preserves a node's initial features. The initial embeddings $\mathbf{z}_u^{(0)}$ for user u and $\mathbf{z}_i^{(0)}$ for item i are concatenated into embedding matrix $\mathbf{Z}^{(0)} \in \mathbb{R}^{(m+n) \times p} = (\mathbf{z}_{u_1}^{(0)} \| \ldots \| \mathbf{z}_{u_m}^{(0)}) \| (\mathbf{z}_{i_1}^{(0)} \| \ldots \| \mathbf{z}_{i_n}^{(0)})$ and computed as

$$\begin{aligned} \mathbf{Z}^{(L)} &= \beta \mathbf{Z}^{(0)} + (1-\beta) \tilde{\mathbf{A}} \mathbf{Z}^{(L-1)} \\ &= \beta \mathbf{Z}^{(0)} + \sum_{i=0}^{L} \beta(1-\beta)^i \tilde{\mathbf{A}}^i \mathbf{Z}^{(0)} + (1-\beta)^L \tilde{\mathbf{A}}^L \mathbf{Z}^{(0)} \end{aligned} \quad (6)$$

where p is the embedding size and $L > 0$ is the number of layers. The recommendation score y_{ui} for a user-item pair (u, i) is then computed as the inner product of the final user and item embeddings

$$y_{ui} = \mathbf{z}_u^\top \mathbf{z}_i \quad (7)$$

One key advantage of using LightGCN-inspired prediction approach is its computational efficiency. By focusing on linear aggregation without non-linearities, He-LiGCN achieves faster training and inference, which is critical for large-scale, real-time recommendation applications. Additionally, this approach avoids overfitting by maintaining a lightweight model structure, which balances scalability with recommendation quality. The final predictions are ranked, allowing He-LiGCN to deliver top-k recommendations that are both relevant and computationally feasible for large user-item interaction datasets.

4 Experiments and Results

4.1 Dataset Preparation

The experiments presented a comprehensive evaluation of the proposed He-LiGCN framework, highlighting its performance, scalability, and computational efficiency. The widely used MovieLens 1M dataset [5] was chosen for the evaluation, consisting of approximately 1 million interactions between 6,040 users and 3,706 movies. Explicit ratings were transformed into binary interactions to simulate implicit feedback scenarios, aligning with real-world recommendation settings. The dataset was divided into training, validation, and test sets in a ratio of 80:10:10, ensuring a robust evaluation setup.

4.2 Training Parameters

The settings were consistent across all models. These parameters were tuned based on prior experiments and validated for robustness in producing meaningful results on the MovieLens 1M dataset. Table 1 summarizes the key parameters used during training.

Table 1. Training Parameters for He-LiGCN, NGCF, and LightGCN

Parameter	He-LiGCN	NGCF	LightGCN
Embedding Size	64	64	64
Learning Rate	0.001	0.001	0.001
Batch Size	1024	1024	1024
Number of Layers	3	3	3
Regularization Coefficient	10^{-2}	10^{-2}	10^{-2}
Optimizer	Adam	Adam	Adam

4.3 Comparative Analysis of Recommendation Models

The performance of He-LiGCN was comprehensively assessed in terms of trainiing efficiency, scalability across different model depths, and the impact of individual components on its overall accuracy. Figure 2 illustrates the training performance of NGCF, LightGCN, and He-LiGCN over 200 epochs. He-LiGCN exhibits the fastest convergence, stabilizing at a training loss of 0.06 within 25 epochs, whereas LightGCN and NGCF require more epochs and converge at higher loss values of 0.12 and 0.24, respectively. This rapid convergence highlights the efficiency of the multi-level graph coarsening and the attention-weighted aggregation mechanisms employed by He-LiGCN.

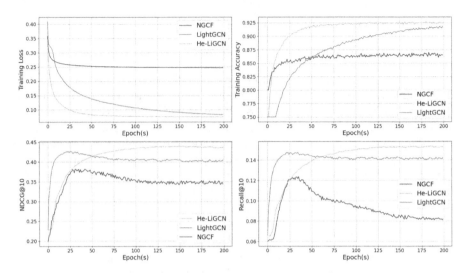

Fig. 2. The training performance over 200 epochs

4.4 Scalability and Efficiency Across Graph Layers

The scalability of He-LiGCN was evaluated by varying the number of graph convolutional layers. As shown in Table 2, He-LiGCN achieves optimal performance at a depth of three layers, with Recall@10 and NDCG@10 reaching 0.157 and 0.448, respectively. Beyond three layers, both NGCF and LightGCN experience performance degradation due to over-smoothing, a phenomenon where node representations become indistinguishable in deep graph convolution networks. In contrast, He-LiGCN maintains its performance by effectively mitigating over-smoothing through its multi-level coarsening and attention-weighted aggregation, preserving the discriminative power of node embeddings even in deeper architectures.

4.5 Ablation and Effectiveness Studies

To further investigate the contribution of individual components, we conducted an ablation study by systematically removing key elements of the He-LiGCN framework. As summarized in Table 3, the removal of the graph coarsening mechanism led to a significant decrease in Recall@10 and NDCG@10, highlighting its critical role in simplifying large-scale graphs while preserving essential structural information. Similarly, excluding the GATNE and HGCN components resulted in the most substantial performance drop, emphasizing their importance in capturing the heterogeneous relationships within the graph. Finally, the absence of LGC reduced the model's efficiency in propagating information across layers, further confirming its necessity for achieving optimal performance.

The results in Table 4 indicate that He-LiGCN achieves a favorable balance between computational efficiency and model complexity. Although LightGCN

Table 2. Performance comparison at different layer depths.

# Layers	Model	NDCG@10	Recall@10
1	NGCF	0.379	0.120
	LightGCN	0.423	0.140
	He-LiGCN	0.444	0.155
2	NGCF	0.382	0.123
	LightGCN	0.420	0.147
	He-LiGCN	0.446	0.156
3	NGCF	0.377	0.126
	LightGCN	0.429	0.148
	He-LiGCN	**0.448**	**0.157**
4	NGCF	0.370	0.124
	LightGCN	0.428	0.147
	He-LiGCN	0.447	0.150

Table 3. Ablation study results with removed components (1: graph coarsening; 2: GATNE and HGCN embeddings; 3: LGC aggregation).

Model Variant	Recall@10	NDCG@10
He-LiGCN-[1, 2]	0.148	0.435
He-LiGCN-[1, 3]	0.141	0.420
He-LiGCN-[2, 3]	0.152	0.442
Complete He-LiGCN	**0.157**	**0.448**

exhibits the lowest training time per epoch at 9.8 s, He-LiGCN requires only a slightly higher average time of 10.2 s, representing a mere 4.1% increase. Despite the slight increase in computational cost compared to LightGCN, He-LiGCN provides significantly better performance in terms of both Recall@10 and NDCG@10. This efficiency-accuracy trade-off underscores the effectiveness of He-LiGCN's design in maintaining computational efficiency while delivering superior recommendation accuracy. By optimizing the balance between model complexity and computational cost, He-LiGCN proves to be a practical and scalable solution

Table 4. Average computational cost per epoch.

Model	Training time (seconds)
He-LiGCN	10.2
NGCF	12.5
LightGCN	**9.8**

for real-world recommendation systems, where both accuracy and efficiency are critical.

5 Conclusion

We presented Heterogeneous Light Graph Convolutional Network (He-LiGCN), a scalable framework for enhancing recommendation accuracy in heterogeneous graph-based systems. By employing multi-level graph coarsening, contextual embeddings and graph convolution network, He-LiGCN captures intricate user-item relationships, balancing computational efficiency with rich relational modeling. Experimental results on the MovieLens 1M dataset confirm He-LiGCN's effectiveness, achieving a 6.5% improvement in Recall@10 and an 8.9% increase in NDCG@10 over LightGCN. Additionally, APPNP integration mitigates over-smoothing, preserving distinct node features in deeper layers, which further enhances recommendation relevance.

Integrating self-supervised learning methods could reduce the reliance on labeled data, improving performance in domains with sparse interactions. This enhancement would make He-LiGCN more adaptable across various datasets. Finally, future work could focus on increasing the interpretability of the model through attention mechanisms, providing insights into the importance of nodes and edges in recommendation decisions. Expanding evaluations across diverse datasets and domains such as e-commerce, education, and healthcare would further validate the scalability and applicability of He-LiGCN in real-world scenarios.

References

1. Cen, H., Wang, H., Yang, B., Nie, L., Zhu, W., Zhang, C.: GATNE: representation learning for attributed multiplex heterogeneous networks. In: Proceedings of the Twenty-Ninth International Joint Conference on Artificial Intelligence (IJCAI), pp. 5802–5808. IJCAI (2021)
2. Gasteiger, J., Bojchevski, A., Günnemann, S.: Predict then propagate: graph neural networks meet personalized pagerank (2022)
3. Göring, F.: Short proof of menger's theorem. Discret. Math. **219**(1), 295–296 (2000)
4. Hamilton, W.L., Ying, R., Leskovec, J.: Inductive representation learning on large graphs. arXiv preprint arXiv:1706.02216 (2018)
5. Harper, F.M., Konstan, J.A.: The movielens datasets: history and context. Proc. ACM Trans. Interact. Intell. Syst. (TiiS) **5** (2015). pp. Article 19, 19 pages
6. He, X., Deng, K., Wang, X., Li, Y., Zhang, Y., Wang, M.: LightGCN: simplifying and powering graph convolution network for recommendation. arXiv preprint arXiv:2002.02126 (2020)
7. Jaccard, P.: The distribution of the flora in the alpine zone. 1. New Phytologist. **11**(2), 37–50 (1912)
8. Jafari, O., Maurya, P., Nagarkar, P., Islam, K.M., Crushev, C.: A survey on locality sensitive hashing algorithms and their applications (2021)

9. Shi, C.: Heterogeneous graph neural networks. In: Wu, L., Cui, P., Pei, J., Zhao, L. (eds.) Graph Neural Networks: Foundations, Frontiers, and Applications, pp. 351–369. Springer, Singapore (2022)
10. Wang, X., He, X., Wang, M., Feng, F., Chua, T.S.: Neural graph collaborative filtering. In: Proceedings of the 42nd International ACM SIGIR Conference on Research and Development in Information Retrieval (SIGIR), pp. 165–174, Paris, France. ACM (2019)
11. Wang, X., et al.: Heterogeneous graph attention network. arXiv preprint arXiv:1903.07293 (2021)
12. Wu, Z., Pan, S., Chen, F., Long, G., Zhang, C., Yu, P.S.: A comprehensive survey on graph neural networks. IEEE Trans. Neural Networks Learn. Syst. **32**(1), 4–24 (2020)
13. Yang, Y., Guan, Z., Li, J., Zhao, W., Cui, J., Wang, Q.: Interpretable and efficient heterogeneous graph convolutional network. CoRR abs/2005.13183 (2020)
14. Zhang, X., Ma, Y., Tang, H., Tang, J.: Heterogeneous graph neural network. In: Proceedings of the 25th ACM SIGKDD International Conference on Knowledge Discovery & Data Mining, pp. 1125–1134 (2019)
15. Zhang, Y., He, Y., Gurukar, S., Parthasarathy, S.: Heteromile: a multi-level graph representation learning framework for heterogeneous graphs. arXiv preprint arXiv:2404.00816 (2024)

Creation of Cartoon Face Images of Celebrities: Automation

D. S. Guru[1], D. L. Shivaprasad[2], and S. Prajna[3](✉)

[1] Department of Studies in Computer Science, University of Mysore, Manasagangotri, Mysuru, India
`dsg@compsci.uni-mysore.ac.in`
[2] Department of Computer Applications, MIT First Grade College, Mysuru, India
`shivaprasaddl143@gmail.com`
[3] Department of Computer Applications, JSS Science and Technology University, Mysuru, India
`prajna.s63@gmail.com`

Abstract. This paper addresses the problem of automatic detection and identification of celebrity cartoon faces and corpus creation. However, currently available face detection systems are mainly designed to detect human faces. We developed a celebrity car-toon face detector (CCFC) that specially detects celebrity cartoon faces featuring famous individuals, which is customised by a well-known object detector, Yolo-NAS, a highly efficient and lightweight deep architecture. Initially, we train our detector by employing a manually compiled dataset. Also, a suitable matching technique is utilised to create a celebrity cartoon face image database. The performance of the proposed system is evaluated with three different matching thresholds, and 90% accuracy is achieved in database creation. The novelty of the work lies in the complete setup of the process of creating a deployable database since this work is the first of its kind to automate the task of creating a corpus of images.

Keywords: Celebrity Cartoon Face Detector · Automation · Database Creation

1 Introduction

Understanding cartoon images is a fundamental and convoluted problem in computer vision. It is an exciting field of artificial intelligence aimed at making computers understand the story depicted by the cartoon image. It involves a variety of exciting vision problems and techniques such as detecting objects, recognising people, identifying background and text, identifying scenes and defining them, classifying them and so on. Amongst the several subtasks, we focus on understanding a cartoon image; in this work, the primary step in the analysis of cartoons is detecting regions of interest, such as cartoon faces of celebrities, as shown in Fig. 1. The problem of analysing and understanding a cartoon image poses several challenges and opportunities, such as high intra-class variations and low inter-class variations, Complex contour, Representation and appearance of cartoon images, which may vary according to the context. However, many images are necessary to study the faces of cartoons, and the images do not exhibit exaggerated characteristics typical of caricatures. With this motivation, we proposed a system to create a celebrity cartoon face database and successfully attempted to automate creation tasks.

Fig. 1. (a) An example cartoon image and (b) Cropped cartoon faces of celebrities.

The outline of our proposal highlights a system that enables the automated detection and organisation of a corpus of cartoon faces featuring famous individuals. Through a comprehensive review of the literature, the issue of limitations in appropriate face detection methods for celebrity cartoon face images becomes evident. Currently, available face detection systems are mainly designed to recognise human faces. We created a celebrity cartoon face detector using the Yolo-NAS architecture trained by our cartoon dataset. Initially, we collected celebrities' cartoon images and utilised our cartoon face detector to extract their faces. Following the manual grouping of faces, directories are established to accommodate multiple classes such that each class has cartoon faces of the same celebrity. Subsequently, an appropriate discriminative feature extractor for cartoon faces is employed and examined with five distinct learning models. Indeed, to regulate whether the test samples belong to existing classes, it is necessary to utilise a matching threshold to differentiate between known and new classes. If the test sample belongs to an existing class, it will be stored in the corresponding class directory. In an alternative scenario, a new directory will be created to accommodate the test sample as a new class member. The threshold for matching will be updated iteratively.

The following are the contributions of this paper:

- An automation of creating a database of celebrity cartoon face images for cartoon face recognition applications.
- Tailoring of an existing general object detector, the YOLO-NAS deep architecture, will detect and extract celebrity cartoon faces in cartoon images.

Further, Sect. 2 of this paper describes the existing literature. Section 3 discusses the architecture of the proposed system. Section 4 describes the empirical analysis of the proposed system. Finally, Sect. 5 provides the conclusion.

2 Related Works

In literature, a couple of works are carried out on the detection and recognition of the faces of cartoon characters in general. Researchers [1] have discussed the face detection of cartoon characters using primitive features and edge extraction techniques. Researchers [2] have explored image retargeting techniques for mobile comics by adapting comic content to mobile screens for better visualisation. Researchers [3] extracted features for cartoon face recognition that reflect skin colour, hair colour, and quantity. Researchers [4] have proposed a CNN-based model for cartoon image retrieval. Researchers [5] constructed a ToonNet that contains thousands of cartoon-styled images and introduced several techniques for building a deep neural network for cartoon face recognition. In this work [6], it has proposed a meta-continual learning method capable of jointly learning from heterogeneous modalities such as sketch, cartoon, and caricature images. These pioneering methods bring inspiration for research on cartoon face recognition. In [7], face detection and recognition techniques work using convolutional architectures for detection and recognition incorporating the multi-task cascaded convolutional network (MTCNN) architecture, and it has been compared with conventional methods. Two different approaches for recognition were recommended: one based on transfer learning by combining the feature learning capability of the Inception v3 network with the feature recognising capability of SVM, and another hybrid convolutional neural network (HCNN) framework trained over a fusion of pixel values and fifteen manually located facial vital points. These methods are evaluated on the IIIT-CFW database [8]. Celebrity cartoon analytics has become a topic of research. Hence, no one has attempted to create a dataset of celebrity cartoon faces. Detecting and creating processes is a challenging and time-consuming task, which is why the decision was made to initiate automation. With this motivation, we successfully attempted to develop a celebrity cartoon face database.

3 Proposed System

The proposed system has two phases: the training phase and the database creation phase. Which is pictorially represented in Fig. 2.

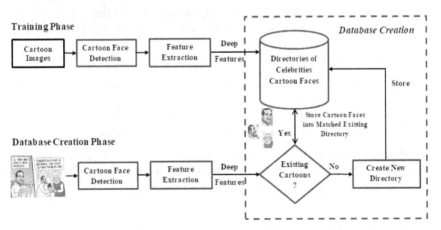

Fig. 2. Illustration of automatic creation of celebrity cartoon face database.

3.1 Training Phase

Data Acquisition. The system aims to solve the problem of detecting and classifying cartoon versions of well-known celebrities. We initially gathered many celebrity cartoon images from different internet sources and newspaper clippings from well-known cartoonists. This dataset consists of cartoon images containing many celebrity cartoon faces. Examples of the collection are shown in Fig. 3.

Fig. 3. Examples of celebrity cartoon images containing many celebrities were collected for our dataset.

Celebrity Cartoon Face Detector (CCFD). Onwards, we considered a subset of the collection and labelled those images using an annotating tool (LabelImg). Using a well-known Yolo-NAS deep architecture [9] with labelled images, we developed a cartoon face detector to detect and extract celebrities' faces named Celebrity Cartoon Face Detector (CCFD), specially designed for detecting celebrity cartoon faces. Because no unique face detector detects the cartoon faces. Yolo-NAS is a highly efficient, lightweight, deep architecture than the existing Yolo models. The process of celebrity cartoon face detection is demonstrated in Fig. 4. Following the manual grouping of faces, directories are established. To Accommodate multiple classes, each with cartoon faces of the same celebrity.

Fig. 4. Cartoon face detection and extraction using cartoon face detector (Yolo-NAS) (a) Input celebrity cartoon image (b) Detected and extracted cartoon faces.

Feature Analysis. Aim to automate the database creation process; however, analysing the suitable features for creation and automation is essential. Subsequently, using the detected face, we extract an appropriate discriminative feature extractor for cartoon faces such that each class has cartoon faces of the same celebrity was employed for this study with eight popular different deep feature extractors viz., AlexNet, EfficientNet, FaceNet, InceptionV3, MobileNet, ResNet, VGG16, and VGG19. Empirically, an appropriate discriminative feature extractor for celebrity cartoon face recognition was employed by examining five notable conventional learning models viz., Support Vector Machine (SVM) [10], K-Nearest Neighbor (KNN) [11], Random Forest [12], Decision Tree [13], and Gaussian Naïve Bayes [14].

Matching. A matching process is necessary to create a database. Hence, to determine whether the test samples belong to existing classes, a matching threshold must be utilised to differentiate between known and new classes. If the test sample matching similarity with a class is more significant than the matching threshold, the test sample belongs to the matched class. It will be stored in the corresponding class directory. In other ways, it creates a new directory with a new class label and stores. The matching threshold will be updated iteratively when a new class is created. In our work, the matching threshold (Th) is computed as,

In general, we considered the k number of classes for training such as $C = \{c_1, c_2, \ldots, c_k\}$ the matching threshold is,

$$Th = \frac{1}{k}\sum_{i=1}^{k} f(c_i) \qquad (1)$$

where the system will study with three different matching threshold values viz., $f(c_i) = \mu(Sim_{Intra}(c_i))$, $f(c_i) = \mu(Sim_{Intra}(c_i)) + \sigma(Sim_{Intra}(c_i))$, and $f(c_i) = \mu(Sim_{Intra}(c_i)) + 2 \times \sigma$, here $Sim_{Intra}(c_i)$ are intra-class similarities of ith class, $\forall\ i = \{1, \ldots, k\}$ and μ and σ represent mean and standard deviation, respectively.

3.2 Database Creation Phase

The following are the steps involved in the database creation process.

Step 1: Utilising the developed CCFD detector to detect and extract the cartoon faces from celebrities' cartoon images.
Step 2: The discriminant facial features are extracted for each extracted cartoon face using a suitable feature extractor.
Step 3: Compute the similarity value between extracted and existing cartoon facial features stored in the knowledge base.
Step 4: The decision will be made using a pre-computed matching threshold. If the computed similarity value is lesser than or equal to the matching threshold, the extracted face image is stored in the existing corresponding class directory; otherwise, a new directory is created and stored as a new celebrity.

4 Experimental Analysis

Initially, we collected 2000 images of celebrity cartoon images from various internet sources and labelled them to create a cartoon face detector. We randomly selected 1500 images from these images to train the YOLO-NAS architecture in developing the Cartoon Face Detector. The performance of the celebrity cartoon face detector is evaluated using a well-known metric called Mean Average Precision (mAP), which is calculated by the mean of the average precision value obtained from the 11-point interpolation method [15]. The customised Cartoon Face Detector model was tested with the remaining 500 cartoon images, and an impressive result of 79.09% mAP was achieved. Also, the performance of our CCFD is pictorially represented in Fig. 5. The mAP computation describes finding the average precision (AP) for each class and the average over the number of classes:

Fig. 5. Cartoon face detection results (a) correctly detected results (b), (c), and (d) wrongly detected results.

$$\mathbf{mAP} = \frac{1}{N} \sum_{i=1}^{N} AP_i \qquad (2)$$

where $N = 1$, as in our case, cartoon face is a single class. Therefore, the map is computed as,

$$\mathbf{mAP} = \frac{1}{11} \sum_{r \in \{0, 0.1, 0.2, \ldots, 0.9, 1\}} P_{inter_p}(r) \qquad (3)$$

where $P_{inter_p}(r) = {}_{r\prime : r\prime \geq r}{}^{max} P(r\prime)$ and empirically we computed the $P_{inter_p}(r)$ values for 11 precision scale points as {0,1,0.5,0.5,0.7,1,1,1,1,1,1}. Hence, the map for our cartoon detector is,

$$\mathbf{mAP} = \frac{1}{11}(0 + 1 + 0.5 + 0.5 + 0.7 + 1 + 1 + 1 + 1 + 1 + 1) = 79.09\%$$

Subsequently, we can observe that Fig. 5 demonstrates the correctly detected and few false cases as a working demonstration for a celebrity cartoon face detector. In database creation, initially, we created 20 classes of celebrity face images manually, which were extracted through the recommended cartoon face detector. Using these 20 classes, we studied the suitable feature extractor concerning the accuracy of models by combining various feature extraction techniques with five conventional classifiers. The obtained accuracies are shown in Fig. 6.

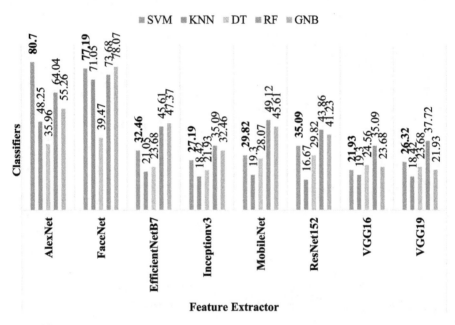

Fig. 6. Performance of combining five classifiers with various feature extractors.

From Fig. 6, it is evident that AlexNet and FaceNet features are performing better than others. Hence, we have chosen these two architectures for celebrity cartoon face analysis. However, for the database creation system, we utilised the FaceNet feature extractor because empirically, the FaceNet features are better performing than AlexNet features in terms of matching the test samples with existing classes and new classes and also having the capability to identify the new class sample. As explained in Sect. 3.1, we empirically computed the matching threshold (Th) and experimented with three matching threshold levels. A pool of new cartoon face images is fed into the model to classify them into one of the existing, if possible, based on the respective threshold, and if not, then a new directory gets created.

Table 1 tabulates the performance of our proposed system with the first threshold level (mean of mean values of all intra-class similarities). Similarly, one of the two remaining thresholds is computed by adding the standard deviation of all intra-class similarities to the first-level threshold. The other is calculated by adding a double standard deviation of all intra-class similarities to the first-level threshold. The performances are tabulated in Table 2 and Table 3, respectively.

Table 1. Statistics on outcomes of experimentation on database creation using a first-level threshold.

Class		No. of Test Samples	First Level Threshold			
			Correctly Classified	New Directory Created	Miss classification	
					Existing Classes Samples	Samples of Others
1_C		1	1	0	0	2
2_C		1	0	0	1	3
3_C		2	0	0	2	1
4_C		29	23	0	6	20
5_C		1	1	0	0	2
6_C		5	4	0	1	19
7_C		1	0	0	1	11
8_C		8	1	0	7	18
9_C		2	0	0	2	5
10_C		4	4	0	0	1
11_C		5	2	0	3	8
12_C		1	0	0	1	3
13_C		9	3	0	6	6
14_C		5	5	0	0	12
15_C		5	1	0	4	4
16_C		1	1	0	0	11
17_C		18	16	0	2	7
18_C		3	0	0	3	8
19_C		8	4	0	4	8
20_C		24	9	0	15	15
Total	Existing	133	75 (TP)	0	58 (FP)	-
	Others	175	11 (TN)	-	-	164 (FN)
Total		308	86	0	58	164
Accuracy (TP + TN) / (TP + FP + FN + TN)			(75 + 11)/(75 + 58 + 164 + 11) = 0.276			
Accuracy (%)			27.60			

Tables 1, 2, and 3 present the statistical results of our experimentation to create a database of cartoon faces of celebrities under different matching thresholds. We also presented the overall system accuracy for each threshold level when making the expected database with the required directories.

Table 2. Statistics on outcomes of experimentation on database creation using second-level threshold.

Class		No. of Test Samples	Second Level Threshold			
			Correctly Classified	New Directory Created	Miss classification	
					Existing Classes samples	Samples of Others
1_C		1	0	2 (1)	0	1
2_C		1	0	1 (1)	0	2
3_C		2	0	0	2	0
4_C		29	20	4 (2)	2	13
5_C		1	1	0	0	0
6_C		5	4	0	1	5
7_C		1	0	0	1	8
8_C		8	1	0	5	13
9_C		2	0	1 (1)	2	3
10_C		4	4	0	0	0
11_C		5	2	0	0	1
12_C		1	0	0	1	0
13_C		9	2	1 (1)	5	4
14_C		5	5	1 (1)	0	3
15_C		5	1	0	1	3
16_C		1	1	1 (1)	0	6
17_C		18	15	1 (1)	2	4
18_C		3	0	2 (1)	2	2
19_C		8	4	1 (1)	3	5
20_C		24	8	2 (1)	15	9
Total	Existing	133	68 (TP)	17 (12)	42	-
	Others	175	99 (TN)	-	-	82
Total		308	167	17	42	82
Accuracy (TP + TN) / (TP + FP + FN + TN)			(68 + 99)/(68 + 42 + 82 + 99) = 0.574			
Accuracy (%)			57.40			

Table 3. Statistics on outcomes of experimentation on database creation using a third-level threshold.

Class		No. of Test Samples	Third Level Threshold			
			Correctly Classified	New Directory Created	Miss classification	
					Existing Classes Samples	Samples of Others
1_C		1	0	4 (2)	0	0
2_C		1	0	1 (1)	0	0
3_C		2	0	1 (1)	0	0
4_C		29	12	31 (6)	0	3
5_C		1	1	0	0	0
6_C		5	4	0	1	1
7_C		1	0	1 (1)	0	1
8_C		8	1	0	1	1
9_C		2	0	1 (1)	1	0
10_C		4	3	1 (1)	0	0
11_C		5	2	0	0	0
12_C		1	0	0	0	0
13_C		9	2	2 (1)	2	2
14_C		5	3	6 (2)	0	0
15_C		5	1	0	0	1
16_C		1	0	2 (1)	0	0
17_C		18	12	7 (2)	1	3
18_C		3	0	1 (1)	0	0
19_C		8	4	1 (1)	0	0
20_C		24	7	5 (2)	4	2
Total	Existing	133	52 (TP)	64 (23)	10 (FP)	-
	Others	175	168 (TN)	-	-	14 (FN)
Total		308	220	64	10	14
Accuracy (TP + TN) / (TP + FP + FN + TN)			(52 + 168)/(52 + 10 + 14 + 168) = 0.90			
Accuracy (%)			90.00			

For better understanding, given the details of True Positive (TP), True Negative (TN), False Positive (FP), and False Negative (FN) statistics represent the number of face samples correctly matched with corresponding existing classes, correctly matched with corresponding new classes, miss matched between existing classes, and miss-matched new classes samples with existing classes respectively. For first-level threshold experimentation (See Table 1), five new directories of 11 samples were created, and no duplicates of existing classes were created. Subsequently, for the second-level threshold (See Table 2), 25 directories of 116 samples were created; 12 directories with 17 samples are duplication directories of existing classes. For the third-level threshold (See Table 3), 42 directories of 232 samples and 23 with 64 samples are duplication directories of existing classes. It is interesting to observe in Table 1, Table 2, and Table 3 that as the matching threshold level increases the model's accuracy in creating the database with an expected number of directories of different celebrity cartoon faces, the system becomes effective in identifying the new classes. Mathematically, the data spread is obtained by standard deviation. As it is small, it becomes narrower. If it is large, the data is dispersed more and broader.

5 Conclusion

Creating a suitable dataset would be immensely difficult and eventually require a lot of effort and time. Hence, this paper addresses an attempt to automate building the database of cartoon faces of celebrities extracted from general cartoon images through their detection. The results demonstrate that this attempt is the first of its kind. It is expected to open new dimensions and create a corpus in related domains in pattern recognition and machine learning applications. Extending this work to automate the creation of datasets of other domains shall be interesting for future work.

Acknowledgment. We thank Pavithra H N and Sharanya S for contributing to this research.

References

1. Arai, M.: Feature extraction methods for cartoon character recognition. In: 5th International Congress on Image and Signal Processing, pp. 445–448. IEEE (2012). https://doi.org/10.1109/CISP.2012.6469644
2. Gao, X, Liu, J., Lin, J., Liao, M., Xiang, L.: Contour-preserved retargeting of cartoon images. In: IEEE 17th International Conference on Computational Science and Engineering, pp. 1772–1778. IEEE (2014). https://doi.org/10.1109/CSE.2014.325
3. Takayama, K., Johan, H., Nishita, T.: Face detection and face recognition of cartoon characters using feature extraction. In: Image, Electronics and Visual Computing Workshop, vol. 48. (2012). http://www.iieej.org/trans/IEVC/IEVC2012/PDF/4B-1.pdf
4. Saito, M., Matsui, Y.: Illustration2vec: a semantic vector representation of illustrations. In: SIGGRAPH Asia 2015 Technical Briefs, pp. 1–4 (2015)
5. Zhou, Y., Jin, Y., Luo, A., Chan, S., Xiao, X., Yang, X.: ToonNet: a cartoon image dataset and a DNN-based semantic classification system. In: Proceedings of the 16th ACM SIGGRAPH International Conference on Virtual-Reality Continuum and its Applications in Industry, pp. 1–8 (2018)
6. Zheng, W., Yan, L., Wang, F.-Y., Gou, C.: Learning from the past: meta-continual learning with knowledge embedding for jointly sketch, cartoon, and caricature face recognition. In: Proceedings of the 28th ACM International Conference on Multimedia, pp. 736–743 (2020)

7. Jha, S., Agarwal, N., Agarwal, S.: Bringing cartoons to life: towards improved cartoon face detection and recognition systems. In: Computer Vision and Pattern Recognition (2018). arXiv preprint arXiv:1804.01753
8. Mishra, A., Rai, S.N., Mishra, A., Jawahar, C.V.: IIIT-CFW: a benchmark database of cartoon faces in the wild. In: Computer Vision–ECCV 2016 Workshops: Amsterdam, The Netherlands, 8–10 and 15–16 October 2016, Proceedings, Part I 14, pp. 35–47. Springer, Cham (2016). https://doi.org/10.1007/978-3-319-46604-0_3
9. Yao, L., Xu, H., Zhang, W., Liang, X., Li, Z.: SM-NAS: structural-to-modular neural architecture search for object detection. In: Proceedings of the AAAI Conference on Artificial Intelligence, vol. 34, no. 07, pp. 12661–12668 (2020)
10. Cortes, C.: Support-vector networks. Mach. Learn. (1995). https://doi.org/10.1007/BF00994018
11. Keller, J.M., Gray, M.R., Givens, J.A.: A fuzzy k-nearest neighbor algorithm. IEEE Trans. Syst. Man Cybern. **4**, 580–585. IEEE (1985)
12. Kremic, E., Subasi, A.: Performance of random forest and SVM in face recognition. Int. Arab J. Inf. Technol. **13**(2), 287–293 (2016)
13. Maturana, D., Mery, D., Soto, Á.: Face recognition with decision tree-based local binary patterns. In: Computer Vision–ACCV 2010: 10th Asian Conference on Computer Vision, Queenstown, New Zealand, 8–12 November 2010, Revised Selected Papers, Part IV 10, pp. 618–629. Springer, Heidelberg (2011). https://doi.org/10.1007/978-3-642-19282-1_49
14. Rish, I.: An empirical study of the naive Bayes classifier. In: IJCAI 2001 Workshop on Empirical Methods in Artificial Intelligence, vol. 3, no. 22, pp. 41–46 (2001). https://doi.org/10.1007/978-3-642-19282-1_49
15. Gao, X., Liu, J., Lin, J., Liao, M., Xiang, L.: Contour-preserved retargeting of cartoon images. In: IEEE 17th International Conference on Computational Science and Engineering, pp. 1772–1778. IEEE (2014). https://doi.org/10.1016/S0031-3203(99)00200-9

Deployable Solution for Real-Time Children Face Emotion Prediction System

D. L. Shivaprasad[1](✉)[⃝], D. S. Guru[1] [⃝], and R. Kavitha[2] [⃝]

[1] Department of Studies in Computer Science, University of Mysore, Manasagangotri, Mysuru, India
[2] Department of Data Science, CHRIST (Deemed to be University), Bangalore, India

Abstract. Nowadays, many parents struggle to comprehend their children's emotions, which can hinder the creation of a nurturing environment. While numerous models focus on predicting adult emotions, there is a lack of standardised datasets for studying children's emotions. To address this gap, our work attempts to establish a comprehensive children's emotion dataset that can facilitate the study of emotions across various pose orientations. Furthermore, we propose an efficient and deployable system for real-time children's emotion prediction. An effective face detector with deep architecture is designed to handle all pose orientations from key image frames. Optimal features are then selected by re-ranking the features using a hybrid feature selection mechanism. The emotion category is declared by carefully analysing sequences of emotion identification from these features. This system holds promise for educational institutions and healthcare facilities, offering insights into children's behaviour through emotional analysis. Through experimental comparisons with three state-of-the-art emotion prediction models, we observed that our proposed system consistently outperforms existing models. Hence, we strongly recommend the adoption of our proposed system. With its achievement of state-of-the-art results in children's facial emotion recognition, it offers a practical solution for real-time deployment across diverse settings.

Keywords: Key-frame Selection · Hybrid Feature Selection · Re-ranking · Emotion Prediction

1 Introduction

Emotion is one of the essential media for expressing non-verbal communication. Predicting children's emotions is a fascinating and challenging research area in artificial intelligence. Parents need to understand their children's emotions to nurture them better. Also, it helps teachers to enhance their teaching effectiveness by studying child behaviour. Similarly, doctors utilise emotion prediction to comprehend their patients' issues better. The emotion prediction brings out the true feelings of the children. In a real-life scenario, emotion prediction is handled by observing facial expressions and verbal communication. Recently, we noticed that computer vision is attempting to solve this problem by analysing facial expressions using facial images. Most of the researchers are directed toward adults, and no work was done on children's emotion prediction because of the unavailability of the children's emotion dataset. Hence, in this work, we created a sufficient and influential children's emotion dataset, including all facial poses, and proposed a new hybrid system for real-time facial expression recognition.

Here are the contributions of this work,

- Creation of a children's emotion dataset with different face orientations.
- Exploration of effective key-frame selection and proposing hybrid feature selection techniques to reduce dimensionality
- Develop a hybrid system for real-time children's emotion prediction by combining convolutional features with conventional classification techniques.

This paper is organised as follows: Sect. 2 provides the existing literature review of emotion prediction. Section 3 describes the proposed real-time children's emotion prediction system. Section 4 explores the created children's emotion dataset in detail. Experimental results and discussion are presented in Sect. 5. Finally, in Sect. 6, we conclude the paper.

2 Related Work

In real-time, emotion prediction is crucial in many scenarios. This problem can be addressed using machine learning models that analyse facial visual data, voice data, GSR (galvanic skin response) signals, and EEG (electroencephalogram) signals [1]. In the literature, numerous researchers focus on three critical areas of emotion prediction. Facial visual data, in particular, is a convenient and popular choice for real-time applications [2]. Utilising machine learning approaches, researchers have employed both traditional methods like Wavelet Gradient Transform [3], Landmark [4], and fully connected convolutional network models like fully Connected Convolutional Neural Network (CNN) [5], conditional Generative Adversarial Network (GCN) [6], ResNet50, VGG19, and InceptionV3 [7] for emotion classification. Additionally, hybrid models have been proposed [8-10]. Some researchers have combined conventional feature extraction techniques with convolutional classification [11-13], while others have used convolutional features with traditional classifiers [14-16] in a method known as transfer learning. Landmark or Keypoint based emotion prediction has also been explored [17-19]. Overall, a literature review reveals that, while numerous datasets are available for adult emotion studies, there is no standard dataset for studying children's emotions. Furthermore, no significant work has been directed toward predicting children's emotions. Table 1 details the existing standard datasets that include children's data, which, however, are insufficient for studying children's emotion models as they contain only frontal pose data. To fill this gap, we propose a children's emotion dataset that includes a comprehensive range of pose orientations for children aged 4–16. This dataset will support the development of a deployable system for a real-time emotion prediction system for children using convolutional features.

Table 1. Descriptions of Existing Datasets Containing Children's Data and Our Proposed Children's Emotion Dataset.

Dataset Name	Age Range (years)	Details	Facial pose angle	Subjects	Emotions
AffectNet [20]	1–77	8,62,620 face images	Frontal	330	Angry, Contempt, Disgust, Fear, Happy, Neutral, Sad and Surprise
CELEBI [21]	0–100	202,599 images	Frontal	10,177	(CelebFaces Attributes)
RAFD [22]	-	4,824 images	Frontal	67	Angry, Contempt, Disgust, Fear, Happy, Neutral, Sad and Surprise
LFW FACE [23]	0–100	13,233 frontal face images	Frontal	5,749	Angry, Disgust, Fear, Happy, Neutral, Sad and Surprise
Proposed Dataset	**4–16**	**360 videos, 8,324 images**	**0 – 90 Orientation**	**60 30 male & 30 female**	**Angry, Disgust, Happy, Neutral, Sad and Surprise**

3 Proposed System

We proposed a deployable system for real-time children's emotion prediction in this work. The system is divided into two phases: the training phase and the testing phase. The proposed system is illustrated in Fig. 1. The proposed system involves six significant stages: Data acquisition, Key-frame selection, Convolutional feature extraction, Hybrid feature selection, Expression identification, and Emotion prediction. Each stage is briefed in the following subsections.

3.1 Data Acquisition

Data acquisition involves collecting information from various sources. Our work used multiple cameras to capture real-time video data of children's emotions. During the training phase, we recorded videos over a set period, whereas in the testing phase, the video capture will be continuous and in real-time.

3.2 Key-Frame Selection

Key-frame selection involves selecting unique frames from a video collection. After acquiring the data, key-frames are collected using our proposed key-frame selection mechanism. The steps involved in the proposed key-frame selection are explained below:

Step 1: Collect all frames (F) from the input video data.

Step 2: Calculate the Histogram for all frames (HF) involving three channels (red, green, and blue).

Step 3: Compute a similarity matrix (SF) for all F using HF.

Step 4: Make unique groups using SF with a similarity threshold (th).

Step 5: Select a frame with the highest gradient value from each group. The gradient value represents the quality of the frame.

Step 6: Finally, we get high-quality, unique frames called key-frames, which will be utilised for further processing.

The above steps are the process for collecting key-frames in the training and testing phases. Due to we working on real-time scenario, the number of key-frame outcomes cannot be predetermined; they vary with video quality and duration. Especially in the testing phase, key-frames are collected within a specified time.

3.3 Face Detection

Subsequently, we focused on the regions of interest by extracting facial regions from key frames using our face detector. For this purpose, we adopted the well-known convolutional object detector 'YOLOv5', which we trained on our children's data and named the Face Detector. Existing face detectors are often inadequate for detecting faces in low-quality images and tend to remove essential regions of the face with different facial orientations.

3.4 Feature Extraction

Following the extraction of faces from critical frames, we proceeded to extract facial features. Our study employed three well-known convolutional models as feature extractors: FaceNet, MobileFaceNet, and MobileNet. Because these models are commonly used to build face recognition systems. FaceNet is suitable for recognising faces across all age categories, as noted in [24], while MobileFaceNet [25] is optimised for identifying children's faces. Similarly, MobileNet is often employed in developing mobile applications [26]. While all three feature extractors are adept at facial recognition, we focus on determining the most suitable for children's emotion prediction. It was also analysed with feature fusion. Indeed, two new conventional features are generated as horizontal and vertical facial pose coordinates computed using the nose point of the face detected by the media pipe [27] tool. These two features are also included in the convolutional features. This will provide 468 key point coordinates. The sample face angle estimation is represented in Fig. 2. Initially, the FaceNet and MobileFaceNet feature

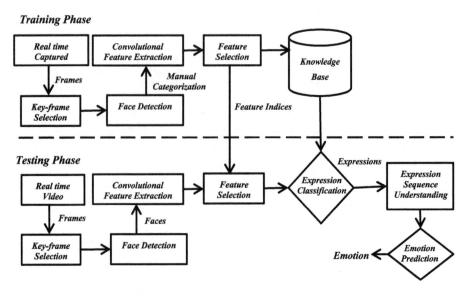

Fig. 1. Illustration of the proposed real-time children's emotion prediction system.

extractors produce highly discriminative 128-dimensional features. On the other hand, MobileNet, trained on the ImageNet dataset, generates 1000-dimensional features for each face image due to its 1000 classes. In this work, each feature extractor is augmented with two additional sets of features representing horizontal and vertical facial pose orientations and Normalised using the Min-Max normalisation technique.

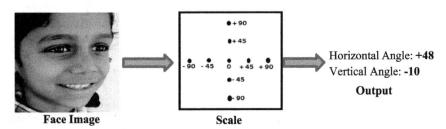

Fig. 2. Pictorial representation of computing facial pose orientation angles.

3.5 Feature Re-ranking Mechanism

Then, dimensionality reduction is applied to the feature space. To achieve this, we proposed a new hybrid feature selection mechanism that utilises five filter-based feature ranking techniques viz., Mutual-information (Msc), Chi-square (Csc), Fisher's score (Fsc), Mean Absolute Difference (MAD) and Inter-class variance (V_{Inter}). Using these techniques, the features are ranked. Generally, let D represent the features extracted by our feature extractor, resulting in d-dimensional features such that D = {f_1, f_2, ...,

f_d}. The features are then ranked using the five feature above ranking techniques, with the feature score lists denoted as S_1, S_2, S_3, S_4, and S_5. Subsequently, the features are ordered in descending ranking order for each of the five score lists, denoted as D_{S1}, D_{S2}, D_{S3}, D_{S4}, and D_{S5}. In our proposed method, the features are re-ranked using these five lists. Initially, we compile all lists into a 5xd dimension feature table. Next, we examine the feature subsets column-wise, removing repeated features and checking if they have already been considered. If a feature is new, it is added to the list; otherwise, it is skipped. The procedure of the proposed feature re-ranking mechanism is represented in Fig. 3.

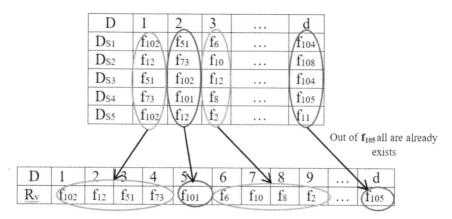

Fig. 3. Pictorial representation of our feature re-ranking mechanism.

From Fig. 3, we can observe that using the re-ranking mechanism, the f105 feature is the lowest-ranked feature. Finally, using this re-ranked feature sequence Rv, we iteratively analysed the learning models by adding features individually. The goal was to identify the most suitable learning model that delivers the best performance with the fewest features. In this work, we considered six different learning models: five conventional models—Support Vector Machine (SVM), K-Nearest Neighbor (KNN), Decision Tree (DT), Random Forest (RF), and Gaussian Naive Bayes (GNB)—and one convolutional model, Multilayer Perceptron (MLP).

3.6 Expression Identification

Expression identification is a crucial component of our proposed system, as the accuracy of expression identification directly impacts the accuracy of emotion prediction. Essentially, the success of the emotion prediction process hinges on precise expression identification. During the training phase, the video data undergoes key-frame selection, followed by face extraction from these key-frames using our Face Detector, as previously described. The cropped faces are manually categorised into six expressions: Angry, Disgust, Happy, Neutral, Sad, and Surprise. The samples for different expression classes are represented in Fig. 4.

After categorisation, convolutional features are extracted from all faces, and their dimensionality is reduced using our hybrid feature selection mechanism. The selected

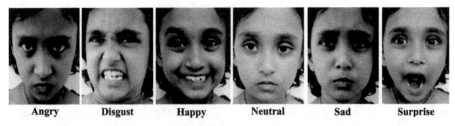

Fig. 4. Example samples of manually categorised expression classes.

feature indices and learning model are stored in a Knowledge Base. The same steps as the training phase are followed in the testing phase. Still, manual categorisation and feature selection are skipped instead of utilising the feature indices already stored in the Knowledge Base.

3.7 Emotion Prediction

In the testing phase, emotion prediction is managed using the learned model stored in the Knowledge Base. The process involves capturing frames in real time at specific intervals, reducing dimensionality both sample-wise and feature-wise, identifying expressions, and sequencing them. By analyzing these sequences, the most frequently occurring expressions are identified and declared. Analyzing the sequences allows for a deeper understanding of the emotions as they are not static but evolve over time. Also, it helps in predicting the emotional state more accurately than analyzing emotions in isolation. As mentioned, an effective emotion prediction system relies on an efficient expression identification model.

4 Dataset

The dataset comprises 360 videos of children aged 4–16 years, including 30 male and 30 female children. Each child has six videos depicting one of six expressions: Angry, Disgust, Happy, Neutral, Sad, and Surprise. These videos capture expressions from all facial pose orientations. By applying our key-frame selection technique, we obtained a total of 8,234 key-frames. Figure 5 provides a statistical breakdown of the dataset by gender, while Table 2 categorises the critical frames by pose angle. Further preprocessing was performed using our face detector. Sample preprocessed face images exhibiting different poses or orientations are shown in Fig. 6. These cropped faces were then resized to match the input size required by the feature extractor, preparing them for further processing.

5 Experimental Results and Analysis

This section explains the complete experimental setup and analyses the results. Our proposed system for evaluating the expression identification model utilised the created children's emotion dataset.

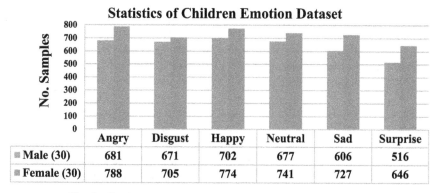

Fig. 5. Gender-wise statistics for our children's emotion dataset.

	Angry	Disgust	Happy	Neutral	Sad	Surprise
Male (30)	681	671	702	677	606	516
Female (30)	788	705	774	741	727	646

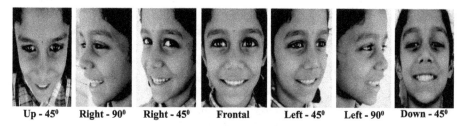

Up - 45⁰   Right - 90⁰   Right - 45⁰   Frontal   Left - 45⁰   Left - 90⁰   Down - 45⁰

Fig. 6. Sample face images of all pose orientations for the Happy expression class.

Table 2. Facial pose orientation-wise statistics for our dataset.

Expression	Number of Samples								
	0^0 to 5^0		0^0 to 10^0		0^0 to 45^0		0^0 to 90^0		Total
	Left	Right	Left	Right	Left	Right	Left	Right	
Angry	272	238	462	362	914	547	916	553	**1469**
Disgust	308	265	480	429	663	696	667	709	**1376**
Happy	312	349	409	555	497	961	504	972	**1476**
Neutral	299	308	389	500	473	927	479	939	**1418**
Sad	306	244	421	427	605	719	608	725	**1333**
Surprise	157	144	244	257	359	703	394	768	**1162**
Total	**1654**	**1548**	**2405**	**2530**	**3511**	**4553**	**3568**	**4666**	**8234**

5.1 Experimental Setup

The dataset comprises 8,234 images and key-frames, capturing a variety of pose orientations. First, we designed a Face Detector by randomly selecting 2,000 images from our collection, ensuring they covered all pose orientations. We manually labelled the face regions in these images. 1,500 labelled images were used to train the YOLOv5 model, resulting in an effective face detector. The remaining 500 images were used to validate our face detector, achieving an impressive 85% mean Average Precision (mAP) in detection. This validation was necessary because existing face detectors struggle to accurately detect faces with 90-degree pose orientations and often identify unwanted regions. Figure 7 compares our face detector with existing face detectors such as Img2Pose – C [19], FER [27], and MTCNN [2]. While MTCNN performs better than existing detectors, it still fails to detect upward-facing and 90-degree-oriented faces. In contrast, our face detector consistently provides accurate detection for all types of faces. Further, faces were extracted from all images using our Face Detector (FD). These faces were represented using convolutional features extracted by three different convolutional feature extractors. Additionally, two conventional features, horizontal and vertical facial pose coordinates, were computed using the nose point detected by the MediaPipe tool, as explained in Sect. 2.4. This process resulted in matrices with dimensions of 8,234 × 130 from FaceNet, 8,234 × 130 from MobileFaceNet, and 8,234 × 1002 from MobileNet. Finally, each matrix was normalised using the Min-Max normalisation technique. After normalisation, each feature matrix was analysed using train-test splits: 60–40, 70–30, and 80–20, ensuring all pose orientations were covered. Each split was evaluated in five trials, both with feature selection (WFS) and without feature selection (WoFS) was studied in each trial. Subsequently, the feature subsets' union set (WFS-U) from the five trials were analysed for their performance. For a contemporary analysis, we also evaluated the performance of three existing state-of-the-art expression identification models—FEAT [19], Deep Face [28, 29], and FER [27, 30] on Our children's face dataset.

The minimum, average, and maximum results for all splits of the existing expression identification models, as well as our proposed model with and without feature selection, are tabulated according to four different pose orientation ranges ($0-5^0$, $0-10^0$, $0-45^0$, and $0-90^0$). The consolidated results in terms of accuracy for our proposed expression model using FaceNet features, MobileFaceNet features, and MobileNet features are presented in Table 3. That table also includes the performance results of the existing models.

Table 3 demonstrates that the proposed model outperforms existing models by utilising three feature extractors: FaceNet, MobileFaceNet, and MobileNet. Notably, our proposed model with MobileFaceNet features performs best among the three. Additionally, our feature re-ranking mechanism reduces the feature dimension, with the union of selected sets performing on par with the original feature sets. Further extending the study, we analysed our proposed model using a fusion of these three convolutional features through concatenation. Including additional features, the fusion feature matrix has a dimension of 8,234 × 1,258 (128 + 128 + 1000 + 2). The results of this feature fusion are presented in the same table, showing the minimum, average, and maximum performances across the three splits and four different pose orientations ($0-5^0$, $0-10^0$, $0-45^0$, and $0-90^0$). Table 3 clearly shows that feature fusion outperforms the existing models. Additionally, our feature re-ranking mechanism effectively reduces the feature dimensions. The best average values of all feature extractors and the number of selected features are consolidated and presented in the same table.

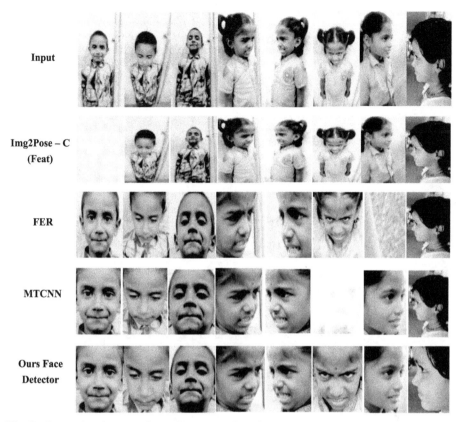

Fig. 7. Comparison between the performances of our face detector and the existing face detector.

5.2 Discussion

The overall study and results provide the following insights: the additional features representing horizontal and vertical facial pose coordinates significantly improve the model's performance, and the feature re-ranking mechanism effectively reduces feature dimensions. Table 3 demonstrates that feature fusion performs well for all facial pose orientations, though it involves higher feature dimensions. When we reduce the Feature space using our feature re-ranking mechanism, performance declines in each case. Notably, the MobileFaceNet feature extractor performs comparably to the fusion features while maintaining a lower dimension and supporting feature dimensionality reduction. Therefore, we recommend the MobileFaceNet feature extractor for extracting discriminant features of emotions in children's faces. Our analysis of suitable learning models for expression classification experimentally shows that the Support Vector Machine (SVM) with a Radial Basis Function (RBF) kernel outperforms other models. Thus, we recommend the combination of MobileFaceNet and SVM (RBF) for classifying expressions in children's face images.

Table 3. Consolidation of performance comparison of the proposed model with existing models.

Consolidation and Comparative Analysis Report

Parameters/Methods				Proposed Framework Performance						Existing Models Performance		
Pose	Splits	Method	Results	FaceNet	Number of Features	Mobile FaceNet	Number of Features	MobileNet	Number of Features	Fusion	Number of Features	FEAT	Deep Face	FER
Frontal (0^0 to 5^0)	60–40	WoF	Min	66.59	130	85.32	130	84.31	1002	88.47	1258	62.28	44.82	52.10
			Avg	68.73		86.32		85.52		89.02		62.55	46.14	53.28
			Max	70.38		87.96		86.36		89.63		63.00	47.07	54.25
		WFS	Min	65.19	49	82.44	66	69.70	78	72.74	86	62.28	44.82	52.10
			Avg	68.03	57	86.12	62	75.19	99	76.90	109	62.55	46.14	53.28
			Max	70.72	61	88.27	63	77.63	114	81.00	130	63.00	47.07	54.25
		WFS-U	Min	65.89	108	84.07	107	80.83	328	82.64	371	62.28	44.82	52.10
			Avg	68.12		85.92		82.19		84.65		62.55	46.14	53.28
			Max	69.78		88.04		83.03		85.81		63.00	47.07	54.25
	70–30	WoFS	Min	69.67	130	87.18	130	85.82	1002	89.86	1258	61.28	45.64	51.35
			Avg	71.79		88.82		87.14		90.35		62.50	47.25	53.33
			Max	73.65		90.46		88.69		91.29		63.69	49.07	55.07
		WFS	Min	67.53	46	86.93	52	73.86	80	65.73	48	61.28	45.64	51.35
			Avg	68.97	53	88.09	55	76.86	93	74.81	89	62.50	47.25	53.33
			Max	70.75	63	90.58	56	79.36	101	77.46	95	63.69	49.07	55.07
		WFS-U	Min	68.74	100	86.76	97	82.30	297	77.74	291	61.28	45.64	51.35

(continued)

Deployable Solution for Real-Time Children Face   215

Table 3. (continued)

Consolidation and Comparative Analysis Report

Parameters/Methods				Proposed Framework Performance						Existing Models Performance		
Pose	Splits	Method	Results	FaceNet	Number of Features	Mobile FaceNet	Number of Features	MobileNet	Number of Features	Fusion	Number of Features	FEAT	Deep Face	FER
Frontal (0⁰ to 10⁰)	80–20		Avg	70.81		**88.60**		83.55		83.12		62.50	47.25	53.33
			Max	72.61		**90.27**		84.23		85.20		63.69	49.07	55.07
		WoFS	Min	71.16	130	89.13	130	86.65	1002	**89.60**	1258	61.40	43.17	51.16
			Avg	73.20		89.99		87.57		**90.71**		62.89	46.01	53.25
			Max	75.27		91.45		88.18		**92.40**		65.63	48.05	54.76
		WFS	Min	67.29	45	**88.04**	51	61.86	57	68.53	62	61.40	43.17	51.16
			Avg	72.12	50	**89.34**	50	71.63	72	72.43	67	62.89	46.01	53.25
			Max	74.34	55	**90.20**	56	77.80	78	77.80	77	65.63	48.05	54.76
		WFS-U	Min	71.76	114	89.44	96	76.59	263	78.07	231	61.40	43.17	51.16
			Avg	72.96		**90.15**		81.45		81.38		62.89	46.01	53.25
			Max	75.58		**90.80**		84.09		83.70		65.63	48.05	54.76
	60–40	WoFS	Min	70.35	130	88.48	130	84.98	1002	**90.15**	1258	60.71	44.74	50.38
			Avg	71.59		89.27		87.56		**91.02**		61.72	45.27	51.31
			Max	72.56		90.20		88.99		**92.17**		62.94	45.76	52.12

(continued)

Table 3. (continued)

Consolidation and Comparative Analysis Report

Parameters/Methods				Proposed Framework Performance							Existing Models Performance		
Pose	Splits	Method	Results	FaceNet	Number of Features	Mobile FaceNet	Number of Features	MobileNet	Number of Features	Fusion	Number of Features	FEAT	Deep Face	FER
70–30		WFS	Min	67.93	57	**88.48**	**69**	71.33	115	64.14	56	60.71	44.74	50.38
			Avg	70.06	60	**89.36**	**71**	77.53	132	75.94	121	61.72	45.27	51.31
			Max	72.36	60	**90.75**	**75**	81.44	161	82.46	161	62.94	45.76	52.12
		WFS-U	Min	69.90	104	**88.78**	**113**	80.54	402	83.31	367	60.71	44.74	50.38
			Avg	71.06		89.31		84.36		85.42		61.72	45.27	51.31
			Max	72.36		90.30		86.10		87.17		62.94	45.76	52.12
		WoFS	Min	72.90	130	90.06	130	87.02	1002	**91.19**	1258	61.13	43.71	50.44
			Avg	73.96		91.42		89.13		**92.20**		62.30	45.58	51.56
			Max	75.52		92.48		90.01		**93.15**		63.26	47.38	52.68
		WFS	Min	70.05	53	**90.06**	**71**	76.53	127	78.08	135	61.13	43.71	50.44
			Avg	72.24	60	**91.04**	**65**	78.62	122	81.41	132	62.30	45.58	51.56
			Max	74.25	68	**91.62**	**66**	80.12	126	84.49	145	63.26	47.38	52.68
		WFS-U	Min	72.20	108	**89.99**	**104**	81.65	395	85.00	418	61.13	43.71	50.44
			Avg	73.50		91.65		86.70		88.19		62.30	45.58	51.56
			Max	74.71		92.68		88.87		90.47		63.26	47.38	52.68

(continued)

Table 3. (continued)

Consolidation and Comparative Analysis Report

Parameters/Methods				Proposed Framework Performance							Existing Models Performance		
Pose	Splits	Method	Results	FaceNet	Number of Features	Mobile FaceNet	Number of Features	MobileNet	Number of Features	Fusion	Number of Features	FEAT	Deep Face	FER
0^0 to 45^0	80–20	WoFS	Min	74.12	130	90.93	130	89.01	1002	90.02	1258	60.12	44.15	50.40
			Avg	75.46		91.99		90.30		**92.39**		61.94	45.21	51.65
			Max	77.16		92.45		91.06		**94.06**		64.16	46.73	52.21
		WFS	Min	69.39	45	**89.92**	56	72.58	80	66.16	67	60.12	44.15	50.40
			Avg	73.09	57	**91.16**	59	77.67	102	74.19	97	61.94	45.21	51.65
			Max	74.70	60	**92.45**	65	80.28	113	79.48	115	64.16	46.73	52.21
		WFS-U	Min	73.51	101	**91.13**	97	85.38	352	82.06	349	60.12	44.15	50.40
			Avg	74.58		**91.89**		86.19		85.95		61.94	45.21	51.65
			Max	75.96		**92.45**		87.73		90.54		64.16	46.73	52.21
	60–40	WoFS	Min	73.59	130	90.67	130	88.11	1002	**91.45**	1258	58.82	43.43	49.72
			Avg	74.65		91.25		88.98		**91.94**		59.66	44.08	50.23
			Max	75.77		91.50		89.52		**92.55**		60.37	44.84	50.53

(continued)

Table 3. (continued)

Consolidation and Comparative Analysis Report

Parameters/Methods				Proposed Framework Performance							Existing Models Performance		
Pose	Splits	Method	Results	FaceNet	Number of Features	Mobile FaceNet	Number of Features	MobileNet	Number of Features	Fusion	Number of Features	FEAT	Deep Face	FER
		WFS	Min	72.61	69	90.80	80	77.46	151	79.47	145	58.82	43.43	49.72
			Avg	73.51	78	91.22	81	79.70	162	81.72	175	59.66	44.08	50.23
			Max	74.56	79	91.81	78	82.39	182	83.62	197	60.37	44.84	50.53
		WFS-U	Min	73.16	119	90.73	124	85.55	467	86.94	469	58.82	43.43	49.72
			Avg	74.32		91.31		86.85		88.41		59.66	44.08	50.23
			Max	75.33		91.62		87.86		89.58		60.37	44.84	50.53
70–30		WoFS	Min	74.27	130	90.72	130	89.12	1002	92.28	1258	58.35	44.17	49.08
			Avg	75.89		92.03		90.20		92.74		59.56	44.92	50.03
			Max	77.21		92.65		91.23		93.51		60.52	45.60	51.44
		WFS	Min	73.62	67	91.18	75	76.53	138	80.39	145	58.35	44.17	49.08
			Avg	74.73	75	91.82	75	78.76	146	81.89	158	59.56	44.92	50.03
			Max	75.68	80	92.56	74	80.25	168	82.96	179	60.52	45.60	51.44
		WFS-U	Min	74.60	118	91.30	110	85.06	424	88.72	469	58.35	44.17	49.08
			Avg	75.90		92.22		87.08		89.44		59.56	44.92	50.03
			Max	76.96		93.02		88.91		90.26		60.52	45.60	51.44

(continued)

Table 3. (continued)

Consolidation and Comparative Analysis Report

Parameters/Methods					Proposed Framework Performance							Existing Models Performance		
Pose	Splits	Method	Results	FaceNet	Number of Features	Mobile FaceNet	Number of Features	MobileNet	Number of Features	Fusion	Number of Features	FEAT	Deep Face	FER
0^0 to 90^0	80–20	WoFS	Min	75.92	130	93.17	130	90.47	1002	92.87	1258	58.57	43.11	48.21
			Avg	77.77		93.64		90.93		93.48		59.57	43.50	49.42
			Max	79.40		94.15		91.27		93.97		59.96	44.12	50.18
		WFS	Min	72.11	47	92.44	61	73.00	83	75.83	87	58.57	43.11	48.21
			Avg	75.74	61	93.11	71	77.85	124	79.75	123	59.57	43.50	49.42
			Max	77.74	59	94.33	75	80.68	151	84.98	168	59.96	44.12	50.18
		WFS-U	Min	76.42	110	92.99	117	85.68	371	88.87	384	58.57	43.11	48.21
			Avg	77.77		93.54		86.74		89.63		59.57	43.50	49.42
			Max	79.77		94.03		87.70		90.40		59.96	44.12	50.18
	60–40	WoFS	Min	73.35	130	89.93	130	88.17	1002	**89.72**	1258	58.66	42.29	49.09
			Avg	73.99		90.41		88.59		**90.79**		59.20	43.23	49.30
			Max	74.63		90.96		89.11		**91.53**		59.69	44.01	49.71
		WFS	Min	71.52	63	**88.93**	69	77.68	139	78.28	187	58.66	42.29	49.09
			Avg	72.96	72	**89.68**	75	79.98	170	80.40	190	59.20	43.23	49.30
			Max	74.42	68	**90.96**	80	81.25	176	84.15	204	59.69	44.01	49.71
		WFS-U	Min	73.11	118	**89.93**	117	86.15	458	84.79	532	58.66	42.29	49.09

(continued)

Table 3. (continued)

Consolidation and Comparative Analysis Report

Parameters/Methods				Proposed Framework Performance							Existing Models Performance		
Pose	Splits	Method	Results	FaceNet	Number of Features	Mobile FaceNet	Number of Features	MobileNet	Number of Features	Fusion	Number of Features	FEAT	Deep Face	FER
	70–30		Avg	73.91		90.46		86.45		87.00		59.20	43.23	49.30
			Max	74.96		91.11		86.97		89.99		59.69	44.01	49.71
		WoFS	Min	75.08	130	92.34	130	88.91	1002	92.26	1258	59.02	42.92	48.17
			Avg	76.16		92.47		90.30		92.98		59.30	43.62	49.24
			Max	77.17		92.74		91.32		93.30		59.81	44.20	50.14
		WFS	Min	73.24	70	91.84	73	78.31	145	80.18	137	59.02	42.92	48.17
			Avg	73.98	67	92.28	79	79.61	149	81.77	158	59.30	43.62	49.24
			Max	75.33	74	92.90	83	81.26	152	84.08	186	59.81	44.20	50.14
		WFS-U	Min	75.28	121	92.22	121	86.52	427	89.13	451	59.02	42.92	48.17
			Avg	75.94		92.55		87.28		89.80		59.30	43.62	49.24
			Max	76.81		92.55		89.56		90.35		59.81	44.20	50.14
	80–20	WoFS	Min	76.73	130	93.45	130	90.02	1002	92.78	1258	57.84	41.60	47.75
			Avg	77.61		93.92		90.74		93.45		58.76	42.77	48.34

(continued)

Table 3. (continued)

Consolidation and Comparative Analysis Report

Parameters/Methods				Proposed Framework Performance								Existing Models Performance		
Pose	Splits	Method	Results	FaceNet	Number of Features	Mobile FaceNet	Number of Features	MobileNet	Number of Features	Fusion	Number of Features	FEAT	Deep Face	FER
			Max	78.32		94.11		91.66		94.05		59.41	43.72	49.43
		WFS	Min	74.91	51	92.36	64	76.47	106	80.30	140	57.84	41.60	47.75
			Avg	76.53	67	92.99	67	78.59	128	81.91	144	58.76	42.77	48.34
			Max	77.18	69	93.99	70	80.00	138	84.27	166	59.41	43.72	49.43
		WFS-U	Min	76.70	113	93.33	108	86.49	389	89.54	446	57.84	41.60	47.75
			Avg	77.39		93.64		87.28		90.39		58.76	42.77	48.34
			Max	78.14		94.18		88.53		91.05		59.41	43.72	49.43

6 Conclusion

This work presents a novel system for a real-time emotion prediction model for children. This system introduces a new mechanism for selecting key-frames and incorporates a deep architecture to design an effective face detector capable of handling all pose orientations. We evaluated three existing face recognition feature extractors to determine the most suitable features for emotion prediction and found that MobileFaceNet is particularly effective for extracting emotion features in children. We also developed a new hybrid feature selection method using a re-ranking mechanism, successfully reducing feature dimensions in all cases. Through hyperparameter tuning, we identified the Support Vector Machine (SVM) with an RBF kernel as the optimal learning model for expression classification. Additionally, we created a comprehensive children's emotion dataset comprising both images and videos. Our proposed model outperforms existing emotion prediction models, achieving state-of-the-art results. This study also demonstrates that emotion prediction models designed for adults are unsuitable for children. In the future, we aim to develop a generalised system capable of handling adult and children data.

Acknowledgment. The first author of this work would like to thank the Government of Karnataka for sponsoring the fellowship DST-KSTePs. Also, we gratefully acknowledge Miss. Nithyashree D R and Miss. Kavya N, for their support in creating the dataset.

Data Availability and Competing Interests. The dataset is available on request from the corresponding author. The authors declare no conflicts of interest / competing interests towards this article.

References

1. Khare, S.K., Blanes-Vidal, V., Nadimi, E.S., Rajendra Acharya, U.: Emotion recognition and artificial intelligence: a systematic review (2014–2023) and research recommendations. Inf. Fusion **102**, 102019 (2024)
2. Sajjad, M., Min Ullah, F.U., Ullah, M., Christodoulou, G., Cheikh, F.A., Hijji, M., Muhammad, K., Rodrigues, J.J.P.C.: a comprehensive survey on deep facial expression recognition: challenges, applications, and future guidelines. Alexandria Eng. J. **68**, 817–840 (2023)
3. Kumar, R.J.R., Sundaram, M., Arumugam, N.: Facial emotion recognition using subband selective multilevel stationary wavelet gradient transform and fuzzy support vector machine. The Visual Comput. **37**(8), 2315–2329 (2021)
4. Happy, S.L., Routray, A.: Automatic facial expression recognition using features of salient facial patches. IEEE Trans. Affective Comput. **6**(1), 1–12 (2014)
5. Sajjad, M., Zahir, S., Ullah, A., Akhtar, Z., Muhammad, K.: Human behavior understanding in big multimedia data using CNN based facial expression recognition. Mobile Networks Appl. **25**, 1611–1621 (2020)
6. Deng, J., Pang, G., Zhang, Z., Pang, Z., Yang, H., Yang, G.: cGAN based facial expression recognition for human-robot interaction. IEEE Access **7**, 9848–9859 (2019). https://doi.org/10.1109/ACCESS.2019.2891668

7. Giannopoulos, P., Perikos, I., Hatzilygeroudis, I.: Deep learning approaches for facial emotion recognition: a case study on FER-2013. Advances in hybridization of intelligent methods: Models, systems and applications, 1–16 (2018)
8. Sajjanhar, A., Wu, Z., Wen, Q.: Deep learning models for facial expression recognition. In: digital image computing: Techniques and applications, pp.1–6. IEEE (2018)
9. Li, C., Pourtaherian, A., van Onzenoort, L., Tjon a Ten, W.E., De With, P.H.N.: Infant facial expression analysis: towards a real-time video monitoring system using r-cnn and hmm. IEEE J. Biomed. Health Inf. **25**(5), 1429–1440 (2020)
10. Attention mechanism-based CNN for facial expression recognition: Li, Jing, Kan Jin, Dalin Zhou, Naoyuki Kubota, and Zhaojie Ju. Neurocomputing **411**, 340–350 (2020)
11. Liang, L., Lang, C., Li, Y., Feng, S., Zhao, J.: Fine-grained facial expression recognition in the wild. IEEE Trans. Inf. Forens. Secur. **16**, 482–494 (2020)
12. Minaee, S., Minaei, M., Abdolrashidi, A.: Deep-emotion: Facial expression recognition using attentional convolutional network. Sensors **21**(9), 3046 (2021)
13. Ruiz-Garcia, A., Elshaw, M., Altahhan, A., Palade, V.: A hybrid deep learning neural approach for emotion recognition from facial expressions for socially assistive robots. Neural Comput. Appl. **29**, 359–373 (2018)
14. Rodriguez, P., et al.: Deep pain: exploiting long short-term memory networks for facial expression classification. IEEE Trans. Cybern. **52**(5), 3314–3324 (2017)
15. Wang, F., Lv, J., Ying, G., Chen, S., Zhang, C.: Facial expression recognition from image based on hybrid features understanding. J. Visual Commun. Image Representation **59**, 84–88 (2019)
16. Durmuşoğlu, A., Kahraman, Y.: Facial expression recognition using geometric features. In: International Conference on Systems, Signals and Image Processing (IWSSIP), pp. 1–5. IEEE (2016)
17. Álvarez, V.M., Sánchez, C.N., Gutiérrez, S., Domínguez-Soberanes, J., Velázquez, R.: Facial emotion recognition: a comparison of different landmark-based classifiers. In: International Conference on Research in Intelligent and Computing in Engineering (RICE), pp. 1–4. IEEE (2018)
18. Farkhod, A., Bobomirzaevich Abdusalomov, A., Mukhiddinov, M., Cho, Y.-I.: Development of real-time landmark-based emotion recognition CNN for masked faces. Sensors **22**(22), 8704 (2022)
19. Cheong, J.H., Jolly, E., Xie, T., Byrne, S., Kenney, M., Chang, L.J.: Py-feat: Python facial expression analysis toolbox. Affective Science 4(4), 781–796 (2023)
20. Xiaohua, Wang, Peng Muzi, Pan Lijuan, Hu Min, Jin Chunhua, and Ren Fuji.: Two-level attention with two-stage multi-task learning for facial emotion recognition. J. Visual Commun. Image Representation **62**, 217–225 (2019)
21. Xu, T., White, J., Kalkan, S., Gunes, H.: Investigating bias and fairness in facial expression recognition. In: Computer Vision–ECCV 2020 Workshops: Glasgow, UK, August 23–28, 2020, Proceedings, Part VI 16, pp. 506–523. Springer International Publishing (2020)
22. Sun, N., Li, Q., Huan, R., Liu, J., Han, G.: Deep spatial-temporal feature fusion for facial expression recognition in static images. Pattern Recogn. Lett. **119**, 49–61 (2019)
23. Huang, G.B., Mattar, M., Berg, T., Learned-Miller, E.: Labeled faces in the wild: a database for studying face recognition in unconstrained environments. In: Workshop on faces in 'Real-Life' Images: detection, alignment, and recognition (2008)
24. Deb, D., Nain, N., Jain, A.K.: Longitudinal study of child face recognition. In: 2018 International Conference on Biometrics (ICB), pp. 225–232. IEEE (2018)
25. Oo, S.L.M., Nway Oo, A.: Child Face Recognition System Using Mobilefacenet. PhD diss., MERAL Portal (2019)
26. Sadik, R., Anwar, S., Reza, M.L.: Autismnet: recognition of autism spectrum disorder from facial expressions using mobilenet architecture. Int. J. **10**(1), 327–334 (2021)

27. Zhang, S., Zhang, Y., Zhang, Y., Wang, Y., Song, Z.: A dual-direction attention mixed feature network for facial expression recognition. Electronics **12**(17), 3595 (2023)
28. Serengil, S.I., Alper Ozpinar.: Lightface: a hybrid deep face recognition framework. In: Innovations in Intelligent Systems and Applications Conference (ASYU), pp. 1–5. IEEE (2020)
29. Serengil, S., Özpınar, A.: A benchmark of facial recognition pipelines and co-usability performances of modules. Bilişim Teknolojileri Dergisi **17**(2), 95–107 (2024)
30. Mellouk, W., Handouzi, W.: Facial emotion recognition using deep learning: review and insights. Procedia Comput. Sci. **175**, 689–694 (2020)

Vision Transformers in Evaluating Bread Edibility

D. S. Guru and D. Nandini(✉)

Department of Studies in Computer Science, Manasagangotri, University of Mysore, Mysore, Karnataka 570006, India
dsg@compsci.uni-mysore.ac.in, nandiniloku@gmail.com

Abstract. In this study, we introduce a novel approach for classifying bread edibility using Vision Transformer-based deep learning model, representing the first application of this technology in this domain. Our method segments bread images into patches, which are linearly projected and transformed into sequence of embeddings. To maintain positional context, we append a positional encoding to the embedding sequence. This sequence is processed through multiple multi-head self-attention (MSA) layers and these MSA mechanism adeptly captures complex spatial relationships, enabling the model to understand interactions between various bread image patches. This advanced spatial feature interpretation significantly enhances the model's edibility classification performance. This study was conducted on a novel dataset comprising 2,520 bread images classified into two categories: Edible and Inedible. To improve classification performance, five data augmentation techniques were employed to synthetically expand the training dataset. The proposed model was tested on various datasets, including our own, existing, and merged datasets. We evaluated multiple Vision Transformer (ViT) models, both with and without pre-trained weights, focusing on ViT_Base_16, ViT_Large_16, and ViT_Huge_14. Experimental results demonstrated that the ViT_Huge_14 model, leveraging pretrained weights and augmented data, achieved an average accuracy of 92%, outperforming current state-of-the-art approaches.

Keywords: Bread Edibility · Vision Transformers · Pre-trained weights

1 Introduction

Bread is a staple food worldwide, and its quality and edibility are vital for consumer satisfaction, food safety, and reducing waste. Traditional methods for assessing edibility, such as sensory evaluations or chemical analyses, are effective but often subjective, time-consuming, and impractical for large-scale operations. Environmental factors like humidity, temperature, and microbial growth further complicate spoilage detection, emphasizing the need for automated, reliable solutions for predicting bread edibility.

This study aims to classify bread images into edible and inedible categories using image analysis and deep learning. Bread quality and shelf life, typically 3–7 days, depend on factors like ingredient quality, baking time, and the use of preservatives or bread improvers. These factors, along with the baking process and resting time, play a crucial role in determining bread's edibility and freshness.

Computer vision and machine learning offer robust solutions for predicting bread edibility by analyzing visual cues like mold, texture, and deformation. Artificial intelligence has further advanced this process, automating classification with greater accuracy. Significant research efforts in this field are detailed below.

Quality assessment of wheat bread, especially under standard conditions, has traditionally relied on sensory evaluations and instrumental analyses like rheological measurements. Advanced techniques such as the Fuzzy Weighted Relevance Vector Machine and Local Binary Pattern Operators have been used for real-time evaluations. Studies like Gambo and Abubakar (2014) explored composite flours (wheat and maize) for improved bread quality, while Curica et al., (2008) developed an objective quality index for bake-off wheat breads. These efforts emphasize the importance of standardized, reliable evaluation methods to ensure consistent bread quality in the food industry.

Adebayo-Oyetoro et al., (2016) evaluated bread made with wheat and fermented banana flour, highlighting its potential to diversify raw materials and improve nutritional value. Similarly, Ibidapo et al., (2020) explored functional bread blends using wheat, malted millet, and 'Okara' flour, finding significant improvements in fiber content, protein quality, and overall acceptability. Kavitha et al., (2022) demonstrated the effectiveness of texture features in predicting bread edibility, emphasizing their role in advancing automated food quality assessment. Abinaya et al. (2024) emphasize AI's transformative role in enhancing food processing by optimizing supply chains, reducing waste, ensuring quality and safety, and exploring diverse technologies like machine learning and machine vision.

Advanced deep learning models enhance bread edibility assessment by detecting subtle changes, improving classification accuracy and reliability. Integrating AI elevates food safety, reduces waste, and optimizes supply chains. While CNNs have long dominated image classification due to their ability to capture spatial hierarchies, Vision Transformers (ViTs) represent a transformative innovation. Originating from NLP advancements like the transformer model by Vaswani et al., (2017), ViTs process entire images holistically using self-attention, capturing global relationships. Introduced by Dosovitskiy et al., (2019), ViTs leverage these principles to advance image-based tasks, surpassing traditional approaches in efficiency and performance.

Vision Transformers (ViTs) differ from CNNs in their approach to image processing. While CNNs use sliding filters to extract localized features hierarchically, they struggle to capture relationships between distant image regions. ViTs, in contrast, process entire images holistically using self-attention mechanisms, enabling them to identify global relationships and long-range dependencies, offering a broader understanding of complex spatial patterns.

Recent studies highlight ViTs versatility: Parez et al., (2023) optimized ViTs for plant disease detection, and Knott et al. (2023) achieved 90% accuracy in assessing banana ripeness and apple defects. Applications extend to remote sensing (Bazi et al., 2021), tomato grading (Khan et al., 2023), and leaf disease detection (Thai et al., 2022). ViTs have also been paired with GANs and attention modules for enhanced agricultural tasks like plant health monitoring and yield estimation (Dhanya et al., 2022; Wang et al.,

2022). This growing body of work underscores ViTs impact on precision agriculture and food quality assessment.

The survey reveals that most studies focus on assessing bread quality by evaluating raw ingredients or monitoring baking parameters, often requiring extensive lab procedures and manual input. Post-baking, bread edibility is typically judged by mold formation or sensory attributes like crust, texture, aroma, and taste subjective assessments relying on human intervention.

Empowering consumers with automated methods for evaluating bread edibility could improve food safety and quality assurance. Image based techniques hold promise, as visual cues like mold growth and texture changes effectively indicate spoilage. Despite this potential, studies leveraging deep learning models, particularly Vision Transformers, for image based bread edibility prediction remain scarce. Addressing this gap, our study explores the application of Vision Transformers to predict bread edibility through imaging, offering an innovative approach to food quality assessment.

To effectively tackle the aforementioned challenges, we propose a novel model for classifying Bread images into two categories: Edible and Inedible based on vision transformers.

The key contributions of this study include:

- Creating a novel bread dataset of 2,520 images from various bakeries, annotated with bounding boxes using LabelImg and processed with YOLOv5 for bread region detection.
- Enhanced the dataset using five augmentation techniques: rotation, flips, brightness adjustment, and distortion.
- Utilized pre-trained Vision Transformer models (ViT_Base_16, ViT_Large_16, ViT_Huge_14) to address dataset limitations and optimize resources.
- Demonstrated the significant impact of augmentations like rotation and flips on Vision Transformer performance.
- Integrated additional data from Kavitha et al., (2022) for experimentation and compared model performance with and without augmentation.
- Benchmarked the proposed model against CNNs and pre-trained networks like VGG16, InceptionV3, EfficientNetB0, and ResNet50.

2 Materials and Methods

2.1 Dataset Collection and Preparation

The proposed investigation offers significant strengths in light of the current literature, particularly in terms of dataset contributions that address multiple areas of improvement over existing models. Since no benchmark datasets are available for this type of study, a new dataset has been created to fill this gap.

Images were captured using a Moto G60 smartphone equipped with a 108MP + 2MP + 8MP rear camera. We collected bread samples by visiting 20 bakeries in and around Mysore and selecting white bread for our study. From each bakery, three slices of bread were sampled and photographed in six different orientations, as shown in Fig. 1. The detailed descriptions of images captured on each day are provided in Table 1.

Table 1. Description of our novel dataset.

Day	Day 1	Day 2	Day 3	Day 4	Day 5	Day 6	Day 7
Number of images	360	360	360	360	380	373	332
Class	Total No. of Edible Breads = 1440				Total No. of Non-Edible Breads = 1080		

The bread was stored at room temperature to monitor shelf life and gather supervised data. Each sample was observed continuously from day 1 to day 7 to note quality changes and other variations. Images were taken daily, and the samples were ultimately categorized into two classes: "Edible" (from day 1 to day 4) and "Inedible" (from day 5 to day 7). The progression of bread edibility is illustrated in Fig. 2, and Table 2 provides details of dataset 2.

Table 2. Description of dataset of Kavitha et al., (2022).

Day	Day 1	Day 2	Day 3	Day 4	Day 5	Day 6	Day 7
Number of images	24	51	147	147	102	78	38
Class	Total No. of Edible Breads = 369				Total No. of Non-Edible Breads = 218		

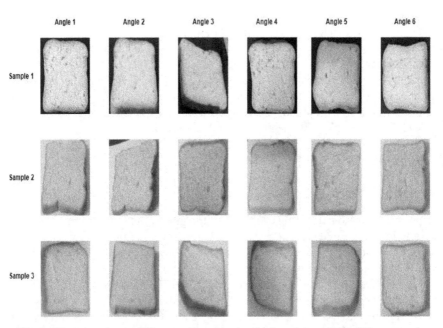

Fig. 1. Illustrates the six different orientations in which each bread sample is captured.

Fig. 2. Bread edibility progression of a single sample over different days (shelf life).

The raw bread images were manually annotated with bounding boxes using the LabelImg tool. Subsequently, a YOLOv5 model was trained on our custom dataset to detect the bread regions. Once the optimal model weights were obtained, all input images were detected, cropped, and stored separately for further analysis. This process is illustrated in Fig. 3.

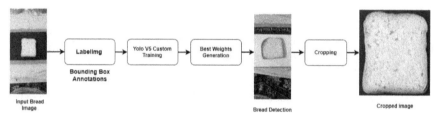

Fig. 3. Illustrates the process of raw bread image to its cropped image via the process for yolov5 segmentation

2.2 Experimentation Setup

The experimental setup for this study was conducted on Google Colab with NVIDI-ASMI 525.105.17, driver version 525.105.17, CUDA version 12.0, and GPU Tesla T4. The environment was configured with Python version 3.10.12, Torch version 2.0.1, and TensorFlow GPU 2.0.0.

2.3 Data Augmentation

Data augmentation (DA) involves expanding the original training set by applying label-preserving transformations, which can be represented as the mapping:

$$\phi : S \to A$$

Here, S denotes the original training set, and A represents the augmented set derived from S. The augmented training set is then defined as:

$$S^1 = S \cup A$$

where S^1 comprises, the original training set along with the corresponding transformations defined by ϕ. Our goal is to ensure that the augmented images maintain sufficient distinction from the originals while faithfully representing the same visual concept.

For each input image x in the original training set S, the five different images generated through transformations can be mathematically represented as:

$A(x) = \{\text{rotate}(x)_{(5,10)}, \text{flip}(x)_{(LR)}, \text{flip}(x)_{(TB)}, \text{distort}(x)_{(4,4,8)}, \text{brightness}(x)_{(0.3-1.2)}\}$

where:

- rotate(x) $_{(5,10)}$ denote images rotated by max left rotation of 5 and max right rotation of 10 degrees.
- flip(x)$_{(LR)}$ and flip(x)$_{(TB)}$ represent images flipped horizontally and vertically.
- distort(x) $_{(4,4,8)}$ denotes an image distorted with grid width 4, grid height 4, and magnitude 8,
- brightness(x) $_{(0.3-1.2)}$ denotes images with varying brightness factors ranging from 0.3 to 1.2.

Thus, the augmented set A for each image x in S is A(x), resulting in an augmented training set $S^1 = S \cup A$.

2.4 Proposed Methodology

The proposed model classifies bread images into two categories: Edible and Inedible, as shown in Fig 4. Various ViT configurations, both with and without pre-trained weights, are explored. When pre-trained weights are used, model weights are initialized accordingly. Additionally, the study addresses challenges of small datasets and limited computational resources by using self-supervised training with ViTs.

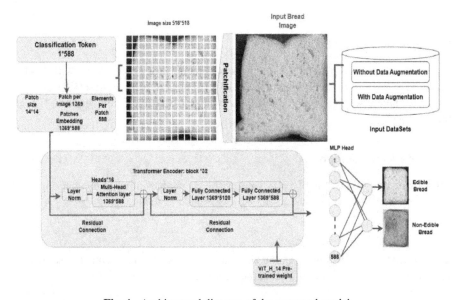

Fig. 4. Architectural diagram of the proposed model.

The proposed model divides the bread image into square patches. For example, an image of size 518 × 518 with patch size of 14 × 14 is split into 1369 patches, as outlined in Eq. (1).

$$\text{Number of patches (N)} = (H * W) \div (ph * pw) \tag{1}$$

Here, H and W represent the image height and width, while ph and pw denote the patch height and width. The stride, or the number of pixels the sliding window moves, is set to 16.

The patches are flattened into 1D vectors of size 588 and transformed into patch embeddings. Position embeddings are added to retain spatial sequence information, and a learnable class embedding is prepended for image classification.

To address overfitting challenges in Transformer based models, particularly with limited data, we integrate Conv2D layers into the Vision Transformer architecture. Conv2D layers assist in patch identification, leveraging CNN's strength in spatial feature extraction to improve model performance. This hybrid approach combines the global feature extraction of Transformers with the local spatial handling of CNNs, enhancing the model's ability to capture spatial relationships and improving classification accuracy.

Patches function similarly to filters (kernels) in our model, with a specified feature map size of 14. To flatten these patches, we use a flatten layer, implemented in PyTorch, as part of our architecture.

The linearly projected and flattened patches, position embeddings, and class tokens are input into the Transformer Encoder Block. The first layer, LayerNorm (LN), normalizes the input across its last dimension, improving training efficiency and model generalization by stabilizing the process. Next, the multi head self-attention (MSA) layer is configured with an embedding dimension of 1280, 16 attention heads, and a dropout rate of 0.

The multi head self-attention (MSA) mechanism allows each patch to attend to and gather information from other patches, capturing interdependencies and considering the overall image context. MSA assigns each patch three roles: Query (Q), Key (K), and Value (V). The Query (Q) seeks other patches, the Key (K) represents the patch being examined, and the Value (V) holds the patch's information. MSA computes attention by measuring the similarity between each patch's Query and the Key vectors of other patches. Attention weights are calculated using a softmax operation (Equation 2), determining how much attention each patch should allocate to others. Higher similarity indicates stronger relationships, helping the model capture critical information for improved predictions.

$$\text{Attention}(Q, K, V) = \text{Softmax}\left(\frac{QK^T}{\sqrt{d_k}}\right)V \tag{2}$$

where, d_k is the dimension of the key vector. After the multi head self-attention (MSA) layer, an "Add" operation (residual connection) is used to combine the output of the previous layer with that of the attention/feed-forward sub-layers. This operation preserves the original information while incorporating new insights from the sublayers. It creates shortcut paths for efficient gradient propagation, mitigating the vanishing gradient problem and enhancing the model's learning capabilities. When combined with LayerNorm, the "Add" operation improves information flow, stability, and overall training efficiency.

The model includes a multilayer perceptron (MLP) with an embedding dimension of 1280, an MLP size of 5120, and a 0.1 dropout after each dense layer. Each patch's output passes through a feed-forward network (FFN) to capture complex nonlinear relationships. Finally, a classification head maps the transformer's output to the desired output format.

3 Results and Discussion

The proposed model was optimized through extensive experimentation, with the dataset split into training and testing subsets in a 60:40 ratio. Table 4 presents the average accuracies for all three ViT models, each with four variants, across 20 trials, with each model trained for 30 epochs. Results for Dataset 2 (Kavitha et al., 2022) and the merged Dataset 3 are shown in Tables 5 and 6.

To assess model performance consistency across datasets, we applied five data augmentation strategies, resulting in a dataset of 4,320 Edible and 3,240 Inedible bread images. Without augmentation, the dataset contained 2,520 images. Experiments were conducted on both the original and augmented datasets, and comparisons were made using a merged dataset. Three ViT models were used, with their parameters outlined in Table 3.

Table 3 Shows parameters specification of all three ViT models.

ViT Models	Layers	Hidden Size D	MLP Size	Heads	Params
ViT_Base_16	12	768	3072	12	86M
ViT_Large_16	24	1024	4096	16	307M
ViT_Huge_14	32	1280	5120	16	632M

The experimentation showed that increasing the dataset from 2,520 to 4,320 images did not significantly improve accuracy. For instance, ViT_L_16 achieved 48.50% accuracy without data augmentation, and 48.89% with augmentation. Unlike CNNs, which benefit from techniques like cropping and flipping, Vision Transformers are more sensitive to patch order and position, limiting the impact of data augmentation.

The position encoding schema of proposed model plays a crucial role in its effectiveness for bread edibility prediction by facilitating accurate and context-aware feature extraction from images. Position embeddings play a crucial role in bread edibility classification by preserving spatial information critical for identifying mold growth, color changes, and texture variations. They enhance the Vision Transformer's attention mechanism by guiding focus to spatially relevant areas, such as crust edges or mold-affected regions, and improve generalization across diverse bread types with varying textures and shapes. These embeddings mitigate spatial ambiguities caused by lighting, occlusions, or background variations, enabling robust context-aware analysis. Additionally, they support multi-scale analysis by maintaining spatial coherence across features of varying sizes and adapt to real-world scenarios by encoding consistent spatial information, ensuring reliability in diverse conditions.

Table 4 Accuracy obtained by all three models considering data augmentation and pre trained weights for our Dataset.

Vision Transformer Models	Without pre-trained weights		With pre-trained weights	
	Without Data augmentation	With Data augmentation	Without Data augmentation	With Data augmentation
	Accuracy	Accuracy	Accuracy	Accuracy
ViT_B_16	54.21%	54.98%	74%	75%
ViT_L_16	55.50%	55.89%	84%	85.21%
ViT_H_14	56.72%	56.99%	91.21%	**92%**

Table 5 Accuracy obtained by all three models considering data augmentation and pre trained weights for Dataset 2 (Kavitha et al., (2022)).

Vision Transformer Models	Without pre-trained weights		With pre-trained weights	
	Without Data augmentation	With Data augmentation	Without Data augmentation	With Data augmentation
	Accuracy	Accuracy	Accuracy	Accuracy
ViT_B_16	44.22%	44.88%	80.01%	80.43%
ViT_L_16	45.40%	45.69%	82.21%	82.43%
ViT_H_14	46.22%	46.89%	87.01%	**87.52%**

Table 6 Accuracy obtained by all three models considering data augmentation and pre trained weights for Dataset 3 (merge of dataset1 and dataset 2).

Vision Transformer Models	Without pre-trained weights		With pre-trained weights	
	Without Data augmentation	With Data augmentation	Without Data augmentation	With Data augmentation
	Accuracy	Accuracy	Accuracy	Accuracy
ViT_B_16	55.01%	55.78%	73.89%	74.07%
ViT_L_16	56.00%	56.69%	83.01%	83.21%
ViT_H_14	57.12%	57.34%	91.02%	**92.32%**

Training Vision Transformers requires large datasets for good performance. To address this, pre-trained models on large datasets like ImageNet can be fine-tuned for the target task, reducing training time and improving accuracy. Initially, all ViT models in this study were trained from scratch, achieving around 55-56% accuracy. However, using pre-trained weights from ImageNet significantly improved the performance of each ViT model. For instance, the ViT_H_14 model trained from scratch achieves

56.72% accuracy, while using pre-trained ViT_H_14 weights boosts the accuracy to 92%, a 36.72% improvement. The use of pre-trained weights significantly enhances model performance and efficiency for bread edibility classification, benefiting from transfer learning and improved generalization. This approach combines the strengths of large-scale pre-training with task-specific fine-tuning, making the model both efficient and effective for diverse challenges in the application domain.

Table 7. Performance Comparison of the Proposed Model with Other Deep Learning Models.

Models	Proposed	CNN with 3 layers	Inception-V3		VGG-16		EffientNetB0		ResNet 50	
			WFT	FT	WFT	FT	WFT	FT	WFT	FT
Accuracy	92	86.01	83.4	85.4	81.0	82.2	86.2	90.4	80.3	81.6

Table 8. Performance Comparison of the Proposed Model with Existing Models

Models	Classification Method adopted	Number of classes	Accuracy
Kavitha et al., (2022) (Existing)	Conventional Machine Learning (LBP)	2	90.68%
Proposed	**Vision Transformers with pretrained weights**	2	**92.0%**

Table 4 presents the accuracies of each ViT model, with ViT_H_14 using pre-trained weights achieving the highest accuracy. Table 7 compares the proposed model with other deep learning models, showing accuracy with fine-tuning (FT) and without finetuning (WFT) for each model. The proposed model's success in bread edibility prediction is attributed to its attention mechanisms, effective representation learning, and adaptability through fine-tuning. These factors enable superior performance compared to CNN-based models. Figure 5 shows the accuracy and loss curves, indicating effective learning and generalization. Table 8 compares the proposed model with existing models, quoting their respective accuracies.

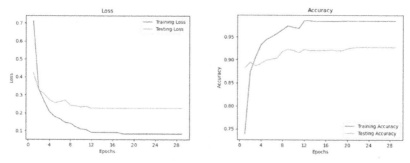

Fig. 5. Loss and Accuracy curve of the ViT_H_14 with pre-trained weights.

4 Conclusion

This study explores the applicability of Vision Transformers (ViTs) for bread edibility prediction, emphasizing their superior ability to utilize self-attention mechanisms and position embeddings for nuanced classification. Unlike CNNs, which rely on localized feature extraction and benefit significantly from traditional data augmentation methods like flipping and rotating, ViTs are sensitive to patch order and spatial arrangement. This sensitivity, enabled by position embeddings, allows ViTs to preserve spatial information and effectively identify critical visual cues such as mold patterns, texture variations, and discoloration factors essential for distinguishing between edible and inedible bread. Leveraging pre-trained weights overcame data limitations, with ViT_H_14 achieving the highest accuracy of 92%, surpassing state-of-the-art methods. Future work will focus on addressing the remaining 7% error by refining the model through reduced patch sizes, additional transformer layers, and exploring the role of position embeddings further. Real-time deployment solutions are also planned.

Acknowledgments. The authors would like to thank Ministry of Social Justice and Empowerment, Government of India for the financial support.

Data Availability Competing Interests. The dataset is available upon reasonable request from the corresponding author. The authors confirm the absence of any conflicts of interest concerning this article.

References

Ali, Z.N., Askerzade, I., Abdulwahab, S.: Estimation model for bread quality proficiency using fuzzy weighted relevance vector machine classifier. Applied Bionics and Biomechanics, Volume 2021 (2021)

Adebayo-Oyetoro, A.O., Ogundipe, O.O., Adeeko, K.N.: Quality assessment and consumer acceptability of bread from wheat and fermented banana flour. Food Sci. Nutrition **4**(3), 364–369 (2016)

Abinaya, S., Panghal, A., Kumar, S., Kumari, A., Kumar, N., Chhikara, N.: Artificial Intelligence (AI) in Food Processing. Nonthermal Food Engineering Operations, 154 (2024)

Bazi, Y., Bashmal, L., Rahhal, M.M.A., Dayil, R.A., Ajlan, N.A.: Vision transformers for remote sensing image classification. Remote Sens. **13**(3), 516 (2021)

Chen, Z., Xie, L., Niu, J., Liu, X., Wei, L., Tian, Q.: Visformer: the visionfriendly transformer. In: Proceedings of the IEEE/CVF International Conference on Computer Vision, pp. 589–598 (2021)

Curic, D., et al.: Design of a quality index for the objective evaluation of bread quality: application to wheat breads using selected bake off technology for bread making. Food Res. Int. **41**(7), 714–719 (2008)

Dosovitskiy, A., et al.: An image is worth 16x16 words: Transformers for image recognition at scale. arXiv preprint arXiv:2010.11929 (2020)

Devlin, J., Chang, M. W., Lee, K., Toutanova, K.: Bert: Pre-training of deep bidirectional transformers for language understanding. arXiv preprint arXiv:1810.04805 (2018)

Dhanya, V. G., et al.: Deep learning based computer vision approaches for smart agricultural applications. Artificial Intelligence in Agriculture (2022)

Gambo, A., Abubakar, S.J.: Production and Quality Evaluation of bread from composite flour of wheat and maize. Techno Sci. Africana J. **9** (2014)

Ibidapo, O.P., Henshaw, F.O., Shittu, T.A., Afolabi, W.A.: Quality evaluation of functional bread developed from wheat, malted millet (Pennisetum Glaucum) and 'Okara'flour blends. Sci. African **10**, e00622 (2020)

Khan, A., et al.: Convolutional Transformer for Autonomous Recognition and Grading of Tomatoes Under Various Lighting, Occlusion, and Ripeness Conditions. arXiv preprint arXiv:2307.01530 (2023)

Kavitha, R., Nandini, D., Guru, D.S., Parvathi, G.: Texture Features in Prediction of Bread Edibility. In: 2022 International Conference on Engineering and Emerging Technologies (ICEET), pp. 1–6. IEEE, October 2022

Khoje, S., Bodhe, S.K.: Comparative performance evaluation of fast discrete curvelet transform and color texture moments as texture features for fruit skin damage detection. Springer J. Food Sci. Technol. **52**, 6914–6926 (2015)

Nandi, C.S., Tudu, B., Koley, C.: Machine vision based techniques for automatic mango fruit sorting and grading based on maturity level and size. Sensing Technol. Current Status Future Trends **II**, 27–46 (2014)

Parez, S., Dilshad, N., Alghamdi, N.S., Alanazi, T.M., Lee, J.W.: Visual intelligence in precision agriculture: exploring plant disease detection via efficient vision transformers. Sensors **23**(15), 6949 (2023)

Shahi, T.B., Sitaula, C., Neupane, A., Guo, W.: Fruit classification using attention-based MobileNetV2 for industrial applications. Plos one **17**(2), e0264586 (2022)

Thai, H.T., Le, K.H., Nguyen, N.L.T.: FormerLeaf: an efficient vision transformer for cassava leaf disease detection. Comput. Electron. Agricult. **204**, 107518 (2023)

Vaswani, A., et al.: Attention Is All You Need. Advances in neural information system. 30 (2017)

Wang, Y., Chen, Y., Wang, D.: Convolution network enlightened transformer for regional crop disease classification. Electronics **11**(19), 3174 (2022)

Xiao, B., Nguyen, M., Yan, W.Q.: Fruit ripeness identification using transformers. Applied Intelligence, 1–12 (2023)

Yu, S., Xie, L., Huang, Q.: Inception convolutional vision transformers for plant disease identification. Internet Things **21**, 100650 (2023)

MobileNet Based Fruit Classification Using UNet Generated Segmented Images: GRAD-CAM Visualization

Sahitya Mondal[1], Tapashri Sur[1], Diganta Sengupta[2(✉)], and Chitrita Chaudhuri[3]

[1] Future Institute of Engineering and Management, Narendrapur, India
tapashri.sur@teamfuture.in
[2] Heritage Institute of Technology, Chowbaga Rd, Anandapur, Kolkata, India
sg.diganta@ieee.org
[3] Jadavpur University, Raja Subodh Chandra Mallick Rd, Jadavpur, Kolkata, India

Abstract. Accurate fruit segmentation from complex backgrounds, shadows, and overlapping objects, mainly leaves, can degrade the effectiveness of overall classification. Overcoming those obstacles can aid in automated fruit detection, efficient fruit disease identification, and decreased fruit rotten issues. To solve these fundamental issues, this study presents a hybrid framework over a comprehensive set of 30 fruits assessed using a publicly available dataset. This framework uses UNet as an image segmentation model to determine the region of interest (ROI) by generating masks of input images from a complicated background. This assists in the modified MobileNet-v2 to improve fruit categorization. Additionally, YOLO v8 is used to detect fruits from a group of fruits. Further understanding of prototypical behavior is achieved through the use of Gradient-weighted Class Activation Mapping (GRAD-CAM), which graphically identifies the crucial areas of the input images that influence the model's judgments. The mobileNet-v2 yields a classification accuracy of 96. 45%, followed by a precision, recall, and F1 score of 0.97, 0.96, and 0.96, respectively. The segmentation IoU and dice scores are 95.69% and 97.89%, respectively. In object detection, YOLO v8 gave an average mAp score of 0.95. This hybrid approach can automate procedures such as fruit quality assessment and categorising fruits for fast transportation, and its transparency in classification could be useful in AI-powered agricultural applications.

Keywords: Fruit Segmentation · MobileNet-v2 · YOLO v8 · UNet · GRAD-CAM · Agricultural AI

1 Introduction

The present agriculture and food sectors show a high demand for reliable and effective fruit classification methodologies. Modern supply chains demand consistent fruit quality, less waste and increased productivity, leading to reconsidering familiar fruit selection methods that rely heavily on manual labour. Recent advancements in computer vision [1,2] have demonstrated significant improvements in fruit detection, segmentation, and classification within the agricultural domain. These advances improve efficiency by reducing time and labor requirements and minimizing human errors arising from fatigue and exhaustion. Existing classification models may not yield promising results due to poorly structured datasets or images with complex backgrounds. As a result, the accuracy of those models can be sub-par. It's beneficial to detect the ROI in the images to improve classification. This approach can enhance both the results and the overall acceptability of the model.

This research utilizes the UNet model to segment fruits from images and a modified version of MobileNet-v2 to classify the fruits from 30 different classes. Although the YOLO v8 model can segment the images, due to the limited access for modification, only UNet is used here for the segmentation task. The dataset used in this study was not originally suitable for object detection, therefore the authors developed a module to convert it to comply with YOLO v8. This adaptation allows for an expansion of the object detection capabilities in the current study. To validate the classification task, the authors use GRAD-CAM to improve understanding of the model's outputs. The explainable model focuses on specific instances within certain areas by highlighting them in the image. This approach improves the model's acceptance among stakeholders through its results and explainability, particularly in agriculture, where poor outcomes can impact farmers' economies and may disrupt fruit supply chains.

The rest of the paper is organized as follows: Sect. 1.1: reviews related work, Sect. 2: provides an in-depth description of the proposed methodology, Sect. 3: analyzes the exploratory results, and Sect. 4: summarizes the key findings and further enhancements of this study.

1.1 Related Work

Recent studies show significant advancements in fruit classification, segmentation, and yield prediction [3] using computer vision techniques. The authors [4] introduced a novel methodology employing YOLOv7 for object identification and ArUco markers for size estimation in Banganapalle mangoes. YOLOv7 employs semantic segmentation to differentiate mango fruits from the background, while ArUco markers function as artificial references for size estimation among numerous objects within an image. This article [5] used AlexNet-SPP network combined with Mask R-CNN for enhancing mango classification. This approach utilizes Mask R-CNN for accurate segmentation and AlexNet-SPP for effective classification, surpassing conventional fruit classification models. This study, [6] contrasted Mask R-CNN with ViT models for on-tree fruit image segmentation and size estimation, specifically targeting pomegranate fruits using Mask R-CNN. It exhibited superior segmentation accuracy compared to ViT-based models such as grounding DINO and Segment Anything Model (SAM) and attained a median relative error of just 1.39%. The authors [7] presented a hybrid ensemble framework for plant disease detection with metaheuristic optimization techniques, such as Binary Dragonfly, Ant Colony Optimization, and Moth Flame Optimization, and has exhibited 99.8% accuracy in classifying diseases in apple and maize plants. The developed methodology [8] CottonSense, a high-throughput classification system, can segment and enumerate cotton fruit utilizing edge devices. It uses RGB-D cameras and a TensorRT-optimized Mask R-CNN model to acquire 2D and 3D data to identify and segment cotton fruits at different growth phases and got a segmentation precision of 79%. The authors [9] used the Mask Positioner technique, which employs a layer-by-layer filtering method to enhance feature maps for improved fruit segmentation. The method surpassed previous models in tests conducted on a green persimmon dataset, with a segmentation accuracy of 67.4% and a detection accuracy of 69.1%. This research [10] established a unique methodology for fruit segmentation, proposing two architectures, EFFS-Net and MDFS-Net, aimed at the robust segmentation of plant diseases and fruits. A significant problem in agricultural automation is the accessibility of high-quality datasets for model training. Here, the authors [11] filled this gap by presenting the 'FruitSeg30_Segmentation' dataset and mask annotations, including 1969 photos across 30 unique fruit classes. This study [12] presented an advanced CNN model that integrates spatial pyramid pooling and adaptive momentum backpropagation to increase feature extraction for illness diagnosis with an accuracy of 97.25% and an F1-score of 98.81% which helps for post-harvest Fruit Disease identification, classification and grading. The FCOS-EAM approach, as introduced in [13], handles the difficulties of segmenting overlapping green fruits, including apples and persimmons, in intricate orchard settings. It attained an accuracy of 81.2% on apple datasets and 77.9% on persimmons, surpassing several previous models.

Effective fruit classification is hampered by natural variations, shadows, overlapping, and uneven lighting in orchards. Current models like Mask R-CNN and Vision Transformers (ViTs) face challenges in these conditions. Integrating UNet, MobileNet-v2, and YOLO v8 with GRAD-CAM can improve detection and segmentation, making the approach suitable for edge devices.

2 Proposed Methodology

2.1 Architecture Overview

The proposed architecture in Fig. 1 details a three-step approach for image segmentation, classification and object detection. The methodology starts with Data incorporation from publicly available sources [11], which subsequently proceeds to the preprocessing module, where images are resized for standardization and undergo data augmentation to enhance the dataset. The ROI is extracted using UNet and MobileNetV2 handles the classification task on the basis of extracted ROI by UNet. The GRAD-CAM rendering module highlights critical areas of the fruit images. Additionally, the boundary box creation module takes the raw input data to create boundary boxes and prepare the YOLO-v8 object detection dataset.

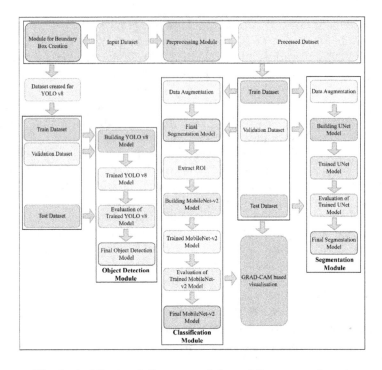

Fig. 1. Architectural diagram and flow of the proposed work

2.2 Data Augmentation and Preprocessing

The dataset consists of fruits, and their corresponding masks are denoted in Eq. 1 where $I_i, M_i \in \mathbb{R}^{h \times w \times c}$ represents the i-th image and mask of height h, width w, and c-channels (c = 3 for image and c = 1 for masks).

$$I = \{I_1, I_2, \ldots, I_n\}, \quad M = \{M_1, M_2, \ldots, M_n\} \qquad (1)$$

To ensure consistency in input dimensions required by the neural network architectures, the resize operation (128 × 128) is considered in both images and their masks by changing the h and w in I and M. Transformations such as 'flipping', 'rotation', 'scaling', and 'colour adjustments' are applied to generate augmented versions of I_i as I'_i, which enhances the model's ability to generalize, avoids class imbalance, and helps manage issues related to overfitting.

2.3 UNet Segmentation Model

Here, UNet architecture in Fig. 2(a) [15] is designed for 128 × 128 image segmentation. It features a contracting path with convolutional layers (3 × 3, ReLU), max pooling (2 × 2), and an expansive path with up-convolutions (2 × 2). The skip connections concatenate feature maps, ending with a 1 × 1 convolution layer and softmax for segmentation described in Fig. 2(a).

2.4 MobileNet-v2 Classification Model

This modified MobileNet-v2 architecture in Fig. 2(b) [16] processes a 128 × 128 RGB input image for classification into 30 Fruit classes. The Global Average Pooling Layer (GAP) reduces spatial dimensions into output shape (1280), Dense Layer with activation function Rectified Linear Unit (ReLU) transforms from 1280-dimensional space to 512-dimensional space. The softmax activation function in the final Dense layer gives probabilities among 30 classes as M in Eq. 2, where weights of dense layers are W_1 and W_2 and b_1 and b_2 are the bias.

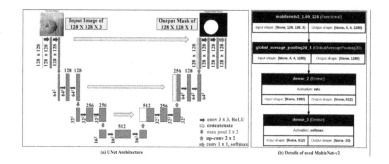

Fig. 2. Architecture of the UNet and MobileNet-v2

$$M = \text{softmax}(W_2 \cdot \text{ReLU}(W_1 \cdot \text{GAP}(\text{MobileNetV2}(\text{Input})) + b_1) + b_2) \quad (2)$$

2.5 Dataset Preparation for YOLO v8

The YOLO v8 model requires boundary box coordinates (x, y, w, h), where (x, y) is the top-left corner and w and h are the width and height of the box. The black and white pixels in the masked dataset [11] are not enough to train the model because it requires a boundary box around the object. Therefore, the threshold T is computed in Eq. 3 to isolate the object region. Additionally, the contours are computed using T, and each contour c obtained the boundary box coordinates (x, y, w, h) using the Python $OPENCV$ library [14]. Sometimes, the output comes with many boundary boxes but will only retain the boundary box with the largest area covered.

$$T(x, y) = \begin{cases} 255, & \text{if } mask(x, y) \geq 240 \\ 0, & \text{otherwise} \end{cases} \quad (3)$$

The normalized values $(x_{\text{norm}}, y_{\text{norm}}, w_{\text{norm}}, h_{\text{norm}})$ of (x, y, w, h) are computed in Eq. 4 with respect to the width W and height H of the image. Finally, $[C, x_{\text{norm}}, y_{\text{norm}}, w_{\text{norm}}, h_{\text{norm}}]$, $C \in 30\ Classes$, this information for each image will be stored in a text file for use in YOLO v8.

$$x_{\text{norm}} = \frac{x + \frac{w}{2}}{W}, \quad y_{\text{norm}} = \frac{y + \frac{h}{2}}{H}, \quad w_{\text{norm}} = \frac{w}{W}, \quad h_{\text{norm}} = \frac{h}{H} \quad (4)$$

2.6 YOLO v8 Object Detection

The input of the YOLO v8 model ($\mathcal{M}_{\text{YOLO v8}}$) is preprocessed image I'_i and output is bounding boxes $\mathcal{B}$ and corresponding class predictions $\mathcal{P}$ in Eq. 5, where $\mathcal{B} = \{B_1, B_2, \ldots, B_k\}$ represents the set of bounding boxes for k detected objects, and $\mathcal{P} = \{P_1, P_2, \ldots, P_k\}$ represents the class probabilities associated with each bounding box.

$$(\mathcal{B}, \mathcal{P}) = \mathcal{M}_{\text{YOLO v8}}(I'_i) \quad (5)$$

2.7 GRAD-CAM Visualization

GRAD-CAM (Gradient-weighted Class Activation Mapping) is applied to understand the model's decision-making process. The GRAD-CAM heatmap (L_{CAM}) highlights the regions of the input image that strongly influence the model's prediction. L_{CAM} is calculated from the Eq. 6. Where A^k is the activations of the k-th feature map in the last convolutional layer and $\frac{\partial y_{\text{class}}}{\partial A^k}$ is the gradient of the class score (y_{class}).

$$L_{\text{CAM}} = \text{ReLU}\left(\sum_k \frac{\partial y_{\text{class}}}{\partial A^k} A^k\right) \quad (6)$$

2.8 Dataset Description

The dataset 'FruitSeg30_Segmentation Dataset & Mask Annotations', collected from publicly available corpus [11], used in this study, contains 1969 high-resolution images of fruits and their corresponding masks over 30 different classes. The collection consists of 1,969 images and masks, each measuring 512 × 512 pixels. The distribution of images among the classes is shown in Fig 3. Figure 3 shows class imbalance, which is addressed using the data augmentation technique in Sect. 2.2.

2.9 Software and Hardware Used

The study utilized an 11th-gen Core i3 PC with 8 GB RAM and 256 GB SSD, running Windows 11. CNN models were developed on Google Colab with 32 GB RAM and L4/T4 GPUs.

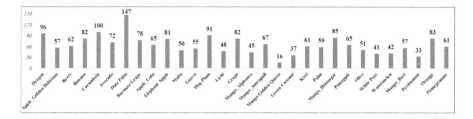

Fig. 3. Distribution of different classes in dataset

3 Results and Discussion

3.1 Results - UNet Segmentation

In Table 1, the model using Binary Crossentropy Loss achieved an Intersection over Union (IoU) of 88.05%, accompanied by a relatively low loss of 0.0874. The dice score is 96.93%; however, the IoU was moderate at 0.8805, indicating there is room for improvement in the overlap between predicted outcomes and actual targets. In contrast, the model configuration that employed Dice Loss produced superior results. It achieved an IoU of 95.69% and a shallow loss of 0.022. The dice score increased slightly to 97.89%, showcasing excellent identification of positive samples. Here, the improved IoU (95.69%) reflects more accurate overlapping predictions than the previous configuration.

Table 1. Performance comparison of UNet model with different loss functions

Model	Loss	Loss	DSC (%)	IoU (%)
UNet	Binary Crossentropy	0.0874	96.93	88.05
UNet	Dice Loss	**0.022**	**97.89**	**95.69**

In Fig. 4(a), during the initial training phase, the IoU improves rapidly in the early epochs, while the loss (Fig. 4(b)) decreases significantly. This trend suggests that the model may be generalizing well. However, after fine-tuning (as shown in Fig. 4(c, d)), the red dashed line indicates a slight increase in IoU. This suggests that the model is more stable and can perform well in various situations. The graph of the UNet model using Dice Loss is presented in Fig. 4(f, g). All metrics remain stable after fine-tuning begins, indicated by the red line (Fig. 4(h, i)) around epoch 40. This shows that the model generalizes well and is not prone to overfitting. Figure 4(e, j) illustrates the changes in Dice Loss and Binary Crossentropy Loss during training and validation. During the training phase, Dice Loss and Binary Crossentropy Loss decrease rapidly in the early epochs, indicating effective learning. While Dice Loss values drop to nearly zero faster, suggesting it may capture more accurate segmentations. Both variations

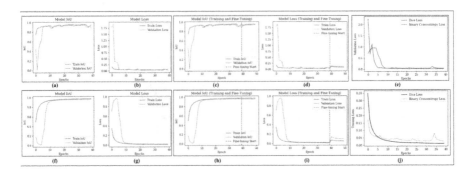

Fig. 4. IoU- Loss Curve of UNet model using different loss functions

of the UNet model perform well in segmentation, but the Dice Loss-oriented model offers better segmentation accuracy.

The test samples for the UNet model using Binary Cross Entropy Loss and Dice Loss are illustrated in Fig. 5 and Fig. 6, respectively. As discussed earlier, both variations of the UNet model can segment the test images correctly; however, the Dice Loss-oriented model performs better in complex environments, as shown in Fig. 6(a). In contrast, the model using Binary Cross Entropy Loss, depicted in Fig. 5(a), struggles with apple fruit images that have a complicated background. The Dice Loss model places greater emphasis on the fruits, effectively distinguishing them from the leaves in the background.

(a) Apple Fruit Outside dataset

Fig. 5. Test samples of UNet segmentation model using Binary Crossentropy Loss

3.2 Results MobileNet-v2 Classification

In this study, the authors utilize a modified MobileNet-v2 model that incorporates ROI identified by a prior segmentation model, UNet. This approach enhances focus on relevant areas of the images, thereby improving feature extraction for fruit classification. The Fig. 7(a) illustrates the model's accuracy and loss curves over 40 epochs. In the accuracy plot, both training and validation accuracy show significant improvement in the initial epochs and converge gradually, indicating model high accuracy. In the loss curve, both training and validation loss decrease sharply in the early epochs and then learn effectively and converge

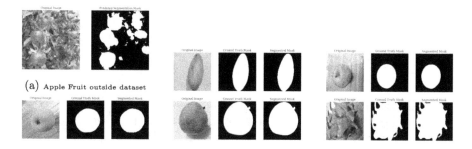

Fig. 6. Test samples of UNet segmentation model using Dice Loss

well. Overall, these curves indicate that the model has been effectively trained. The classification performance and confusion matrix for 30 classes are presented in Fig. 7(b) and Fig. 7(c), respectively. The results indicate a high overall accuracy of 96.45%. The macro averages for precision, recall and F1-Score were 0.97, 0.96, and 0.96, respectively, demonstrating a balanced performance across different classes. Particularly, fruits such as 'Dragon', 'Berry', 'Banana', and 'Burmese Grape' achieved perfect classification scores. For 'Golden Delicious apples', the model recorded a precision of 1.0 and a recall of 0.9, resulting in an F1-score of 0.947. In contrast, the classes with lower recall rates included 'Kiwi' (0.6) and 'Mango Amrapali' (0.67), indicating areas where the model could be improved further.

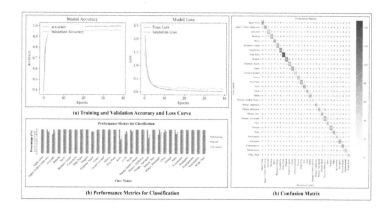

Fig. 7. Classification Outcome

3.3 Results - YOLO v8 Object Detection

The performance of the YOLO v8 model, trained over the prepared dataset described in Sect. 2.5, was evaluated after 50 epochs of initial training, followed

Table 2. Performance metrics of YOLO v8 model

Metric	Precision	Recall	mAP50	mAP50-95	Box Loss
Value	0.9803	0.9941	0.995	0.9501	0.2751

by 10 additional epochs of fine-tuning. Table 2 presents the key evaluation metrics, including Precision, Recall, mean Average Precision at 50% Intersection over Union (mAP50), mean Average Precision across IoU thresholds from 50% to 95% (mAP50-95), and Box Loss. The model achieved a high Precision of 0.9803 and a Recall of 0.9941, indicating correct identification of target objects by minimizing false positives. Furthermore, mAP50 reached 0.995, and mAP50-95 was 0.95017, underscoring the model's performance in terms of identifying and locating objects while considering different levels of overlap. The box loss value of 0.27512 suggests the model effectively minimizes errors in bounding box predictions. Figure 8 illustrates the performance metrics and object detection capabilities of YOLO v8. Figure 8(a) illustrates various loss functions that converge effectively, indicating successful model training without overfitting.

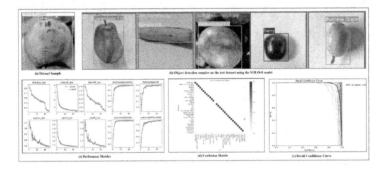

Fig. 8. Model Performance and output of YOLO v8

3.4 Results GRAD-CAM Visualizations

Grad-CAM visualizations highlight the regions that the MobileNet-v2 model focuses on the most when making the classification. The red and yellow areas represent the key features of the fruits, indicating where the model concentrates its attention to understand their shapes and characteristics. Figure 9 illustrates which parts of the input image significantly influence the final classification output.

3.5 Comparison with Related Works

Table 3 provides a comparative evaluation of the proposed model against the most recent existing AI models documented in this literature from 2023 to 2024.

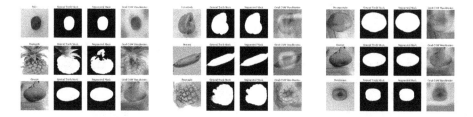

Fig. 9. GRAD-Cam based visualization of classification task by MobileNet-v2

This analysis includes GRAD-CAM and other metrics such as IoU, Dice Score, precision, accuracy, recall, and F1 score. The proposed model decisively outperforms all the metrics evaluated in this study.

Table 3. Comparative analysis of the proposed model with existing models

Ref	Year	GRAD-CAM	IoU	DSC (%)	Acc (%)	Precision	Recall	F1-Score
[4]	2023	×	-	-	84	0.84	0.89	-
[5]	2023	×	-	-	80.75	0.78	0.74	0.76
[6]	2024	×	81	-	92	0.957	0.96	0.923
[10]	2024	✓	-	95.1	90.7	-	-	-
[11]	2024	×	86	94.72	92.57	0.94	0.91	0.925
Proposed Work		✓	**95.69**	**97.89**	**96.45**	**0.97**	**0.96**	**0.96**

4 Conclusions and Future Work

This study developed a AI-based approach for the segmentation, classification and object detection of 30 different types of fruits. The proposed approach uses the UNet model to yield accurate segmentation masks for each fruit type. After segmentation with UNet, the targeted regions are inputted into the MobileNet-v2 model for fruit classification. The dice loss-oriented proposed UNet model achieved high performance in segmentation with an IoU of 0.9569, a loss of 0.022, and dice score of 97.89%. MobileNet-v2 demonstrated excellent classification with an accuracy of 96.45%, precision of 0.97, recall of 0.96, and an F1-score of 0.96, showing the model's effectiveness in classifying different types of fruits.

For object detection model, YOLO v8 was applied to identify and localize the fruit objects. YOLO v8 achieved a high mAP50 of 0.995, mAP(50-95) of 0.95, and a box loss of 0.275, demonstrating its efficiency and accuracy in detecting a variety of fruits across different classes. The results show that the proposed hybrid model is highly effective for segmenting, classifying, and detecting multiple types of fruit. This effectiveness could also lead to the development of an automated mechanical system using drones to capture images, which could benefit agriculture, fruit packaging delivery, and fruit logistics-related challenges.

In future work, several enhancements might be explored to improve the accuracy and practicality of this proposed approach. Firstly, advanced augmentation techniques could be utilized to create images from different angles and in varying lighting conditions, helping the model learn in a more realistic way. Secondly, classification techniques other than MobileNet-v2 can be applied, and there is scope for model optimization using methods like particle swarm optimization (PSO) and artificial bee colony (ABC) algorithms, which can be investigated in future studies. The object detection model's performance in challenging situations can be improved by enriching the training data with greater diversity and complexity, which may also add to the scalability of the work. Additionally, other models could be incorporated to extract various skin features of fruits, such as surface texture, color, and size. This information could aid in predicting fruit grading, which would help categorize fruits for business purposes.

References

1. Sun, M., Xu, L., Chen, X., Ji, Z., Zheng, Y., Jia, W.: BFP net: balanced feature pyramid network for small apple detection in complex orchard environment. Plant Phenomics (2022). Published by AAAS
2. Tang, Y., Zhou, H., Wang, H., Zhang, Y.: Fruit detection and positioning technology for a *Camellia oleifera* C. Abel Orchard based on improved YOLOv4-tiny model and binocular stereo vision. Expert Syst. Appl. **211**, 118573 (2023). Published by Elsevier
3. Mondal, S., Biswas, C., Chaudhuri, C.: Improved prediction of agronomic models with outlier detection and region-based clustering. In: Proceedings of the 2021 IEEE 18th India Council International Conference (INDICON), pp. 1–6 (2021). Organized by IEEE
4. Nenavath, D., Perumal, B.: Artificial Marker to Predict (Banganapalle) mango fruit size at multi-targets of an image using semantic segmentation. IEEE Access. https://doi.org/10.1109/ACCESS.2024.3351210. Accessed 01 2024
5. Yeh, J.F., Lin, K.M., Lin, C.Y., Kang, J.C.: Intelligent mango fruit grade classification using AlexNet-SPP with mask R-CNN-based segmentation algorithm. IEEE Trans. AgriFood Electron. https://doi.org/10.1109/TAFE.2023.3267617. Accessed 06 2023
6. Giménez-Gallego, J., Martinez-del-Rincon, J., González-Teruel, J.D., Navarro-Hellín, H., Navarro Lorente, P., Torres, R.: On-tree fruit image segmentation comparing Mask R-CNN and Vision Transformer models. Application in a novel algorithm for pixel-based fruit size estimation. Comput. Electron. Agricult. https://doi.org/10.1016/j.compag.2024.109077. Accessed 06 2024
7. Khaoula, T., Sohail, A., Shahzad, T., Khan, B., Khan, M., Ouahada, K.: An Ensemble hybrid framework: a comparative analysis of metaheuristic algorithms for ensemble hybrid CNN features for plants disease classification. IEEE Access. https://doi.org/10.1109/ACCESS.2024.3389648. Accessed 04 2024
8. Bolouri, F., Kocoglu, Y., Pabuayon, I.L., Ritchie, G., Sari-Sarraf, H.: CottonSense: A high-throughput field phenotyping system for cotton fruit segmentation and enumeration on edge devices. Comput. Electron. Agriculture. https://doi.org/10.1016/j.compag.2023.108531. Accessed 01 2024

9. Lu, Y., Ji, Z., Yang, L., Jia, W.: Mask Positioner: An effective segmentation algorithm for green fruit in complex environment. J. King Saud Univ. - Comput. Inf. Sci. https://doi.org/10.1016/j.jksuci.2023.101598. Accessed 06 2023
10. Haider, A.: Multi-scale and multi-receptive field-based feature fusion for robust segmentation of plant disease and fruit using agricultural images. Appl. Soft Comput.. https://doi.org/10.1016/j.asoc.2024.112300. Accessed 01 2024
11. Shamrat, F.M., Shakil, R., Idris, M., Akter, B., Zhou, X.: FruitSeg30_segmentation dataset & mask annotations: a novel dataset for diverse fruit segmentation and classification. Data Brief. https://doi.org/10.1016/j.dib.2024.110821. Accessed 08 2024
12. Patel, H., Patil, N.: Enhanced CNN for fruit disease detection and grading classification using SSDAE-SVM for postharvest fruits. IEEE Sensors J. https://doi.org/10.1109/JSEN.2023.3342833. Accessed 01 2023
13. Jia, W.: FCOS-EAM: an accurate segmentation method for overlapping green fruits. Computers and Electronics in Agriculture. https://doi.org/10.1016/j.compag.2024.109392. Accessed 01 2024
14. OpenCV-Python. OpenCV library for Python. https://pypi.org/project/opencv-python/
15. Ronneberger, O., Fischer, P., Brox, T.: U-Net: convolutional networks for biomedical image segmentation. In: Medical Image Computing and Computer-Assisted Intervention–MICCAI 2015: 18th International Conference, Munich, Germany, October 5–9, 2015, Proceedings, Part III**18**, 234–241. Springer (2015). https://doi.org/10.1007/978-3-319-24574-4_28
16. Sandler, M., Howard, A., Zhu, M., Zhmoginov, A., Chen, L.-C.: Mobilenetv2: inverted residuals and linear bottlenecks. In: Proceedings of the IEEE Conference on Computer Vision and Pattern Recognition, pp. 4510–4520 (2018). https://doi.org/10.1109/CVPR.2018.00474

RExAS: Relation Extraction Using Adaptive Self-attention

Madhusudan Ghosh[1(✉)], Partha Basuchowdhuri[1], and Sudip Kumar Naskar[2]

[1] Indian Association for the Cultivation of Science, Kolkata, India
madhusuda.iacs@gmail.com, partha.basuchowdhuri@iacs.res.in
[2] Jadavpur University, Jadavpur, India

Abstract. Relation extraction from unstructured text is essential for building knowledge bases or knowledge graphs, crucial in NLP tasks like question answering, information extraction, and intelligent applications (e.g., expert systems, search engines, chatbots). This paper introduces **RExAS**, a novel architecture leveraging adaptive self-attention for relation extraction. Our adaptive self-attention module learns a weighted adjacency representation from raw text, inputted into a Graph Convolution Network, bypassing dependency-parsed text and improving performance. Extensive experiments on **NYT**, **Wikidata**, **GIDS**, and **SemEval** datasets show **RExAS** outperforms or matches state-of-the-art methods across various evaluation setups.

Keywords: Sentential RE · GCN · LSTM · Self-Attention · BERT · Knowledge Graph

1 Introduction

Relation extraction (RE) from unstructured text focuses on identifying structured information by extracting semantic relationships between entity pairs within sentences. This process is often associated with knowledge discovery [15]. It generates knowledge in the Resource Description Framework (RDF) format, represented as SOP (<Subject, Object, Predicate>) triplets. The task of knowledge extraction is fundamental to numerous NLP applications, including knowledge base (KB) creation, KB population, question answering, and other knowledge-driven tasks. Over the years, it has gained significant traction within the NLP research community.

Initially, researchers employed OpenIE [4] to derive relational triplets, identifying verbs as relations due to the lack of robust supervised datasets. The advent of distant supervision [11] revolutionized relation extraction (RE), enabling distantly supervised RE (DSRE) for KB completion tasks [24] by leveraging background KBs [28]. Since then, supervised neural methods have advanced RE, broadly categorized into multi-instance and sentential RE. Multi-instance RE predicts relations for entity pairs across sentence bags, though contextual noise often hampers performance [21], prompting studies [24] to address noise issues. Sentential RE, in contrast, extracts relations directly from individual sentences without relying on entity-pair contexts [19]. Supplementary information, like entity types and KB-derived aliases, has also been explored to boost model performance.

Recently, a novel methodology was introduced to incorporate KB context information (i.e., entity attributes information, entity neighborhood triples from the underlying KBs) into sentential RE based neural models [1]. Subsequently, novel attention based methodology was proposed to integrate important part of KB context information in sentential RE settings [13]. In relation extraction literature, many of the Recurrent Neural Network (RNN) based sequential models cannot properly capture non-local syntactic information and also take exceedingly high amount of time to process the data. Although Convolutional Neural Network (CNN) based sequential models are faster, they cannot capture the semantic relationship between the entities, which are located far from each other in a sentence. Dependency based neural models take dependency trees, as opposed to sequences, as input into the models [2]. Generally, most of the dependency based models take into account pruned dependency trees[1] as input to the model. The author of the work [12] used the subtree rooted at the lowest common ancestor (LCA) of the entity pair as input. Later pruned trees were utilized, which contain tokens that are K distance away from the LCA in the dependency path. Sometimes these pruning strategies may exclude many relevant information from the subtree. To overcome this problem, attention guided Graph Convolution Network (GCN) [10] based approach was proposed to transform the dependency tree of the sentence into a weighted fully connected dependency graph by self-attention mechanism [5]. Similarly, in multi-instance RE settings, GCN was employed to encode sentence representation by taking dependency tree as input [21]. Instead of processing the adjacency representation of the dependency tree, our novel architecture **RExAS** internally learns the weighted adjacency representation for distantly supervised sentential RE settings. Then we provide this learned weighted adjacency representation as input to the graph convolution module to perform the relation classification task. Our adaptive self-attention module produces weighted adjacency representation of the sentences using BERT (Bidirectional Encoder Representations from Transformers) [3] pre-trained model. Pre-trained contextual language model (termed as PLM i.e., BERT) also helps to improve overall model performance for sentential RE paradigm without incorporating external information (i.e., entity label, entity alias, entity description, entity neighborhood triples generally taken from the existing KBs).

2 Related Work

Early research [16] used syntactic features for relation extraction with traditional machine learning. With the rise of distantly supervised data, recent works have leveraged neural networks. CNNs [23] and CNN-RNN hybrids [14,18] have been applied to classify relations. Attention-based models also improved feature representation from multiple sentences [9,20,27]. Dependency-based models, including LSTM for shortest dependency paths [26] and TreeLSTM for dependency subtrees [12], have shown strong performance. Recently, GCNs [10] using dependency trees were explored, with models like [5] focusing on attention-guided GCNs. Unlike these, our model learns weighted

---

[1] https://spacy.io/api/dependencyparser.

adjacency directly from sequence input. We compare against [14] on sentence-level relation extraction.

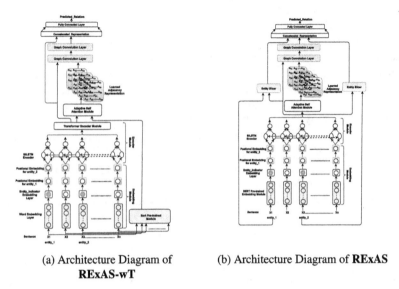

(a) Architecture Diagram of **RExAS-wT**

(b) Architecture Diagram of **RExAS**

Fig. 1. Architectures of the proposed models.

3 Model Description

Relation extraction classifies the semantic relation between an entity pair in a sentence into a predefined set of relations ($\mathcal{R}$). We introduce two novel architectures: **RExAS-wT**, combining GCN, Bi-LSTM, and a transformer encoder, and **RExAS**, which excludes the transformer encoder[2]. **RExAS** relies solely on pre-trained BERT [3] embeddings. Unlike traditional graph-based approaches that use external adjacency representations from dependency parse trees, our models learn the adjacency representation internally for GCN input. Architectures are shown in Fig. 1a and 1b.

3.1 Proposed Model: RExAS-wT

Embedding Module: In this module, we leverage BERT pre-trained word embeddings $w_b \in R^{d_b}$ alongside three additional types of embeddings: (i) word embeddings $w \in R^{d_w}$, (ii) entity indicator embeddings (EIE) $e \in R^{d_e}$, and (iii) positional embeddings (PE) for entity pairs $e^1 \in R^{d_z}$ and $e^2 \in R^{d_z}$. Here, d_b, d_w, and d_z denote the dimensions of BERT, entity indicator, and positional embeddings, respectively. To initialize the word embedding layer, we adopt embeddings trained with the Word2Vec algorithm from [14], which are further fine-tuned during the model's end-to-end training. The entity indicator embedding layer is initialized by assigning a label to each

---

[2] Code available at https://github.com/Madhu000/RExAS.git.

token in the sentence, where tokens belonging to the first entity e^1 are marked as *1*, those belonging to the second entity e^2 as *2*, and all other tokens as *3*. For the positional embedding layer, linear distances of words relative to the start of an entity are used as initialization.

Encoder Module: The four embeddings generated in the embedding module are concatenated to encode both semantic and relational information for the words and entity pairs. To process this representation, we employ a Bi-directional LSTM [7] combined with a transformer encoder module [22]. Given the computational overhead of LSTM for sequential data, a single-layer Bi-LSTM is utilized to capture local dependencies within a sentence $s = [w_1, w_2, \ldots, w_n]$ of length n. The concatenated input $x \in R^{(d_w + d_e + d_z + d_z)}$ is passed through the Bi-LSTM layer, producing output representations $h_t \in R^{2d_l}$, where d_l indicates the number of units per LSTM cell:

$$\begin{aligned}
x_t &= (w_t \cdot e_t \cdot e_t^1 \cdot e_t^2) \\
\overrightarrow{h_t} &= \overrightarrow{LSTM}(x_t, h_{(t-1)}) \\
\overleftarrow{h_t} &= \overleftarrow{LSTM}(x_t, h_{(t-1)}) \\
h_t &= (\overrightarrow{h_t} \cdot \overleftarrow{h_t})
\end{aligned} \quad (1)$$

To extract a global sentence representation, the Bi-LSTM output $h_t \in R^{2d_l}$ is fed into a transformer encoder. The core component of the transformer is the multi-head self-attention mechanism, paired with a position-wise feed-forward layer. As described in [22], the Bi-LSTM output is linearly transformed into Query ($Q = h_t W^q$), Key ($K = h_t W^k$), and Value ($V = h_t W^v$), using projection matrices $W^q \in R^{(d_{model} \times d'_l)}$, $W^k \in R^{(d_{model} \times d'_l)}$, and $W^v \in R^{(d_{model} \times d'_l)}$, where $d'_l = 2d_l$. Self-attention is then computed as follows:

$$Attn(Q, K, V) = \text{softmax}\left(\frac{QK^T}{\sqrt{d'_l}}\right) V \quad (2)$$

To apply the multi-head attention mechanism, self-attention is computed m times, concatenated, and linearly transformed to produce the final output representation $q_t \in R^{d_{model}}$ for the adaptive self-attention module:

$$\begin{aligned}
MultiH(Q, K, V) &= (head_1 \cdot head_2 \cdot \ldots \cdot head_m) W^o \\
head_i &= Attn(Q^i, K^i, V^i)
\end{aligned} \quad (3)$$

Here, the final projection matrix $W^o \in R^{(md'_l \times d_{model})}$ is trained during the end-to-end optimization of the model. All weights in this module are updated during training to ensure optimal performance.

Adaptive Self-Attention Module (ASM): This module automatically captures the adjacency representation from the sentence following the computations as shown in Eq. (2) and (3). Here, we process the pre-trained BERT embedding (w_b) and the transformer

Table 1. Dataset Statistics

		NYT_1	NYT_2	SemEval	Wikidata	GIDS
	# of relations	53	25	10	353	5
Training	# of sentences		455,412	335,843	7,200	372,059	11,297
	# of sentences with Valid relation tuples		124,636	100,671	5,913	548,587	8,526
	# of sentences with None/Other Relation tuples	330,776	235,172	1,287	228,894	2,771
Validation	# of sentences		113,853	37,010	800	123,824	1,864
	# of sentences with Valid relation tuples		31,401	10,939	677	178,0531	1,417
	# sentences with None/Other Relation tuples	82,452	26,071	123	73,746	447
Test	# of sentences		172,415	1,450	2,717	360,354	5,663
	# of sentences with Valid relation tuples		6,441	520	2,263	573,881	1,356
	# of sentences with None/Other Relation tuples	165,974	930	454	167,082	4,307

output (q_t) as input to this model. To apply the concept of self-attention mechanism, we need the query and key pair information. In the transformer module (cf. Sect. 3.1), to create query and key pair representation, linear transformation operation is applied on each of them by initializing random weight matrices. Here, BERT embedding is used as external knowledge to create a new query representation $Q' = q_t \sigma(W + w'_b)$, where $w'_b = w_b W^b$ and $W \in R^{d_{model}}$, $W^b \in R^{(d_{model} \times d_b)}$ are randomly initialized trainable weights. Here, $w'_b \in R^{d_{model}}$ is knowledge from an external source from the BERT embedding. Now, we compute the self-attention operation as in Eq. 4, taking q_t as the key term to get the adjacency representation.

$$A = softmax\left(\frac{Q' q_t^T}{\sqrt{d_{model}}}\right) \quad (4)$$

We perform the above computation m times followed by the concatenation operation to get the adjacency tensor representation ($Adj \in R^{m \times n \times n}$) as output.

Table 2. Model performance on **NYT** and **SemEval** datasets

Model	NYT_1			NYT_2			SemEval		
	P	R	F1	P	R	F1	P	R	F1
CNN [30]	0.413	0.591	0.486	0.444	0.625	0.519	-	-	-
PCNN [29]	0.380	0.642	0.477	0.446	0.679	0.538	-	-	-
EA [17]	0.443	0.638	0.523	0.419	0.677	0.517	-	-	0.843[a]
BGWA [9]	0.364	0.632	0.462	0.417	0.692	0.521	-	-	-
MFA [14]	**0.541**	0.595	0.566	0.507	0.652	0.571	-	-	-
RExAS-wT	0.514	0.669	0.584	0.426	0.736	0.540	0.802	0.789	0.796
RExAS	0.520	**0.695**	**0.595**	0.471	**0.750**	**0.577**	0.842	0.853	**0.847**

[a] [17] reported F1 score of 85.9 by adding two types of lexical features, WordNet hypernyms and words around nominals.

Graph Convolution Module: To capture relationships between entity pairs, context from nearby tokens is critical, often extracted via a sentence's dependency tree. Our model bypasses traditional parsing, learning this context with a weighted adjacency tensor $Adj \in \mathbb{R}^{m \times n \times n}$ in an adaptive self-attention framework (cf. Sect. 3.1). Leveraging GCNs, we use dual graph convolution layers to encapsulate entity relations, applying propagation rules as in [10] with Adj and a global feature vector $q_t \in \mathbb{R}^{d_{model}}$. To normalize adjacency, we define $Adj_{norm} = D^{-1/2} Adj D^{-1/2}$, computed with a degree tensor $D \in \mathbb{R}^{m \times n \times n}$ to represent node degrees.

This enables the GCN module to function effectively, where $W \in \mathbb{R}^{d_{model} \times d^{gcn}}$ is a trainable weight matrix, $v_e^0 = q_t$ is the initial output representation, and f is a non-linear activation function. Thus, the ith GCN layer yields a global entity contextual representation $v_e^i \in \mathbb{R}^{d^{gcn}}$ as $v_e^i = f(Adj_{norm} v_e^{(i-1)} W^{(i-1)})$.

Relation Extraction Module (REM): We concatenate the global feature representation of a sentence from the transformer encoder module and the global entity contextual representation from the GCN module. We apply a pooling operation on the concatenated representation. Then we pass the pooled output ($v_e^i \cdot q_t \in R^{d^{gcn}+d_{model}}$) to a fully connected layer with non-linear activation function softmax to map its corresponding relation vector with the highest probability. Thus, we get our final output relation vector (O_r) by computing Eq. 5, where $W \in R^{(d^{gcn}+d_{model}) \times n_r}$ is the learnable matrix, $b \in R^{n_r}$ is the bias vector and n_r is the number of relations present in the relation set $\mathcal{R}$.

$$P(O_r|(v_e^i \cdot q_t)) = \frac{\exp(W(v_e^i \cdot q_t) + b)}{\sum_{i=1}^{n_r} \exp(W(v_e^i \cdot q_t) + b)} \tag{5}$$

3.2 Proposed Model : RExAS

We present this model as a modification of the **RExAS-wT** model. Therefore, we only describe the incremental changes that we made on top of **RExAS-wT**.

Incremental Changes to RExAS-wT: The changes made to the **RExAS-wT** model are as follows.

1) Here, we replaced the word embedding module from **RExAS-wT** with the pre-trained BERT embedding module. This choice was made due to BERT's ability of efficiently representing word embeddings. In **RExAS**, unlike **RExAS-wT**, we do not feed pre-trained BERT embedding to the ASM.

2) The embedding module, to represent the semantic information of the words and the entity pairs, consists of BERT embedding, entity indicator embedding and positional embeddings. Therefore, the concatenated input representation $x \in R^{(d_b+d_e+d_z+d_z)}$ to the Bi-LSTM module is generated as follows,

$$x_t = (w_b \cdot e_t \cdot e_t^1 \cdot e_t^2) \tag{6}$$

The remaining equations in Eq. (1) stay same as mentioned in the encoder module (cf. Sect. 3.1) of **RExAS-wT**. Similarly, this module generates the required output representation $h_t \in R^{2d_l}$.

3) As in **RExAS-wT**, we pass the output representation h_t to our adaptive self-attention

Table 3. RExAS performance on NYT_1 dataset

Model	HRERE	Wu-2019	RESIDE	Ye-Ling-2019	Sorokin-LSTM	GP-GNN	RECON	KGPool	RExAS
P@10	0.861	0.817	0.736	0.789	0.754	0.813	0.875	0.901	**0.935**
P@30	0.766	0.618	0.595	0.624	0.587	0.631	0.741	0.867	**0.945**

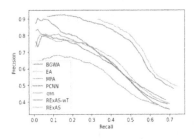

(a) Precision Recall Curve on NYT_1 dataset

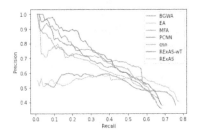

(b) Precision Recall Curve on NYT_2 dataset

Fig. 2. Precision Recall Curve

module to generate a weighted adjacency representation. This module computes self-attention as in Eq. (4) using the query $Q' = Wh_t$, where $W \in \mathbb{R}^{d_{model} \times d_{model}}$ ($d_{model} = 2d_l$) is a randomly initialized trainable weight matrix, and the key $q_t = h_t$. Like **RExAS-wT**'s ASM, this module generates the weighted adjacency tensor $Adj \in \mathbb{R}^{m \times n \times n}$.

4) We then pass the Adj representation and the hidden vector $q_t = h_t$ from the Bi-LSTM layer to the GCN module (cf. Sect. 3.1). to generate the contextual representation $v_e^i \in \mathbb{R}^{d_{gcn}}$.

5) In addition, we introduce the Entity Slicer module, which takes the masked entity representation and encoder output as input. Tokens belonging to the entity are marked as 1; otherwise, they are marked as 0, producing two masked representations $e_l \in v_b^n$ and $e_r \in v_b^n$ where $v_b \in \{0, 1\}$. We then apply a multiplication operation, yielding $e_l' = q_t * e_l$ and $e_r' = q_t * e_r$, which captures individual entity information ($e_l' \in \mathbb{R}^{d_{model}}, e_r' \in \mathbb{R}^{d_{model}}$). Next, we concatenate the GCN and Entity Slicer outputs, apply pooling, and feed the pooled output $v_e^i \cdot e_l' \cdot e_r' \in \mathbb{R}^{d_{gcn} + d_{model} + d_{model}}$ to a fully connected layer with softmax to map to the relation vector with the highest probability from the set $\mathcal{R}$. The final relation vector O_r is obtained as:

$$P(O_r | (v_e^i \cdot e_l' \cdot e_r')) = \frac{\exp(W(v_e^i \cdot e_l' \cdot e_r') + b)}{\sum_{i=1}^{n_r} \exp(W(v_e^i \cdot e_l' \cdot e_r') + b)}$$

where $W \in \mathbb{R}^{(d_{gcn} + d_{model} + d_{model}) \times n_r}$ are learnable parameters, and $b \in \mathbb{R}^{n_r}$ is the bias vector.

Baseline Models: We use the following baselines for the **NYT** dataset: CNN [30], PCNN [29], EA [17], BGWA [9], and MFA [14]. For **NYT**$_1$ with P@N metric, we include: Sorokin-LSTM [19], GP-GNN [31], HRERE [25], Wu-2019 [24], Ye-Ling-2019 [28], RESIDE [21], RECON [1], and KGPool [13]. For the **Wikidata** dataset,

Table 4. RExAS performance on **Wikidata** dataset

Model	Micro			Macro		
	P	R	F1	P	R	F1
Context-Aware [19]	0.721	0.720	0.721	0.692	0.137	0.172
GP-GNN [31]	0.823	0.823	0.823	0.422	0.246	0.311
RECON [1]	0.872	0.872	0.872	0.636	0.339	0.442
KGPool [13]	**0.886**	**0.886**	**0.886**	-	-	-
RExAS	0.861	0.813	0.836	**0.721**	**0.485**	**0.580**

we compare **RExAS** with Context-Aware LSTM [19], GP-GNN [31], RECON [1], and KGPool [13].

4 Experiments and Results

Dataset: We used four publicly available datasets: **NYT**, **Wikidata**, **GIDS**, and **SemEval**. The **NYT** corpus has two versions: NYT_1 by [16] and NYT_2 by [8], both using Freebase for distant supervision, with NYT_2 containing a manually created test set. The **SemEval** dataset, widely used for relation classification [6], contains 8,000 training and 2,717 test sentences across 10 relations, with 800 samples used for validation. We also use the distant supervision-based **Wikidata** [19] and **GIDS** [9] datasets. Dataset statistics are shown in Table 1[3].

Parameter Settings: In all experiments, sentence lengths (n) are fixed to 100 for **NYT** datasets, and to 98, 36, and 60 for **SemEval**, **Wikidata**, and **GIDS**, respectively. In **RExAS-wT**, word embedding dimension (d_w) is 50. For both **RExAS-wT** and **RExAS**, positional embedding (d_z) is 5, entity indicator embedding (d_e) is 10, and BERT embedding (d_b) is 768, with all embeddings except BERT trained end-to-end. Bi-LSTM hidden dimension (d'_l) is 128, $2d_l = d_{model} = 128$, and transformer encoder dimension (d_{model}) in **RExAS-wT** is also 128. Both models use 4 heads (m) for self-attention, and GCN hidden dimension (d^{gcn}) is 512. Dropout (p) is 0.5 for all modules except the transformer encoder in **RExAS-wT**, which uses residual dropout [22] with $p = 0.1$. We optimize with Adam and use categorical cross-entropy for multi-class classification. Batch sizes are 512 for **NYT** and **Wikidata**, 128 for **SemEval**, and 32 for **GIDS**. Experiments are conducted on Google Colab Pro's TPU free tier.

Results: The baseline models exclude test instances with *None* labels, and we follow the same approach. We adapt evaluation metrics for fair comparison with previous baselines. For NYT_1 and NYT_2, we use (micro) precision (P), recall (R), and F1 scores as in [14]. If a model predicts *None* for a **NYT** instance, it is kept unchanged. If a valid relation is predicted, we check if the confidence score is above a threshold; otherwise, it is marked as *None* to reduce false positives. Thresholds are set to maximize F1 on

---
[3] NYT datasets: https://github.com/nusnlp/MFA4RE, Wikidata: https://github.com/ansonb/RECON, GIDS: https://github.com/malllabiisc/RESIDE.

Table 5. RExAS performance comparison against previous basline models for individual relation prediction on **Wikidata** dataset

Relation type	Context-Aware		GP-GNN		RECON		RExAS	
	P	R	P	R	P	R	P	R
Country	0.449	0.435	0.873	0.931	**0.955**	**0.949**	0.893	0.892
Located in	**0.476**	0.130	0.463	0.074	0.398	**0.481**	0.430	0.420
Shares border	0.724	0.725	0.732	0.817	**0.862**	**0.829**	0.777	0.631
Instance of	0.748	0.745	0.780	0.748	**0.896**	**0.916**	0.886	0.884
Sport	0.966	0.968	0.962	0.975	**0.987**	**0.991**	0.986	0.978
Citizenship	0.853	0.895	0.848	0.913	**0.962**	**0.966**	0.916	0.952
Part of	0.462	0.427	0.443	0.441	**0.628**	0.565	0.623	**0.601**
Subclass of	0.469	0.375	0.435	0.498	0.588	**0.772**	0.622	0.626

Table 6. RExAS performance comparison using F1 score against previous SOTA models for individual relation prediction on **Wikidata** dataset

Relation Type	RExAS	KGPool	RECON	GP-GNN
Of works	0.00	**1.00**	0.00	0.00
Track gauge	0.83	**1.00**	0.92	0.00
Position played	0.83	**0.99**	**0.99**	0.92
Sport	0.98	**0.99**	**0.99**	0.97
Record label	0.85	**0.95**	0.90	0.64
List of episodes	0.85	**0.95**	0.00	0.49
Wing configuration	0.86	**0.94**	0.57	0.00
Numeric value	0.87	**0.93**	0.27	0.46
Vessel class	0.85	**0.87**	0.00	0.00

validation data. We use a similar approach for **SemEval** and **GIDS** datasets. Results on **NYT** and **SemEval** datasets are in Table 2. **RExAS-wT** outperforms baselines on NYT_1, while **RExAS** achieves state-of-the-art F1 on both NYT_1 and NYT_2. For precision-recall curves of **NYT**, we reproduce results as per [14], shown in Fig. 2[4]. **RExAS** consistently maintains higher precision across the recall range on NYT_1. On **GIDS**, **RExAS** achieves an F1 of 0.790, P of 0.747, and R of 0.839, demonstrating strong performance on smaller datasets. Additionally, we use micro P@N (P@10 and P@30) for NYT_1 following [25], averaging scores over four runs. Results, including *None* relation, are shown in Table 3, with **RExAS** achieving P@10 of 0.998 and P@30 of 0.984 when *None* is ignored, outperforming all baselines on P@N and setting new state-of-the-art results.

---

[4] Due to computational constraints, we report curves for **NYT** datasets only.

Table 7. Performance comparison of **RExAS+ExtAdj** vs **RExAS**

Model	NYT_1			NYT_2		
	P	R	F1	P	R	F1
RExAS + ExtAdj	0.397	0.687	0.503	0.398	0.769	0.524
RExAS	0.520	0.695	**0.595**	0.471	0.750	**0.577**

For the **Wikidata** dataset we consider the (micro and macro) precision (P), recall (R), and F-score (F1) evaluation metrics as mentioned in the work [19]. Table 4 summarizes the performance of **RExAS**. It can be observed that **RExAS** produces comparable results for micro P, R and F1, while it outperforms all the baseline models in terms of macro P, R and F1 score. All the performance metric scores of the baseline models as (reported in Table 3 and Table 4) have been taken from previous literature [1,13]. Additionally, to show the effectiveness of **RExAS**, we conduct smaller case studies by taking few top relation instances of **Wikidata** as reported in the previous work [1,13]. Table 5 presents the P and R scores[5] while Table 6 presents the F1 scores[6] for these relations. From these tables, it can be observed that for some relations **RExAS** performs better than RECON [1], while for some relations **RExAS** performs equivalent to RECON. It can also be observed from Table 6 that KGPool [13] performs better than **RExAS**. If we can incorporate finetuned PLM knowledge[7] properly for the downstream task, i.e., Sentential RE in distant supervision paradigm, model performance may improve.

5 Analysis and Discussions

We conducted an ablation study on $\mathbf{NYT_1}$ for the **RExAS** model. To validate our approach, we performed an additional experiment using adjacency representations from dependency parsing. In this setup, the GCN module takes the Bi-LSTM output and an external adjacency (ExtAdj) representation generated from a dependency parser as input. All other modules remain unchanged. Results in Table 7 demonstrate that the weighted adjacency from ASM in **RExAS** outperforms the ExtAdj representation.

To demonstrate the impact of various components in our **RExAS** model, we performed ablation studies by progressively incorporating individual model components. The findings from these experiments, as presented in Table 8, clearly highlight the significance of each component within the model architecture. The results in Table 8 indicate that the combination of Bi-LSTM, ASM, and GCN plays a pivotal role in enhancing the overall performance of the model. We also carried out experiments varying the number attention heads (m) and the number of layers in GCN. The results of these experiments are presented in Table 9. We obtained best results using GCN of 2 layers with number of attention heads 4 for the $\mathbf{NYT_1}$ dataset. Therefore, we carried out all the experiments with this setup.

---

[5] P and R values in Table 5 are taken from [1].
[6] F1 scores in Table 6 are taken from [13].
[7] We stick to use pre-trained BERT model and did not finetune it due to computational constraints.

Table 8. Effectiveness of different components of **RExAS**

Model Components	NYT_1			NYT_2		
	P	R	F1	P	R	F1
BERT →Entity Slicer	0.334	0.675	0.446	0.410	0.746	0.529
BERT→BiLSTM→Entity Slicer	0.450	0.669	0.538	0.433	0.734	0.545
BERT+EIE+PE→BiLSTM→Entity Slicer	0.462	0.698	0.556	0.436	0.761	0.554
RExAS	0.520	0.695	**0.595**	0.471	0.750	**0.577**

Table 9. **RExAS** performance analysis varying m and GCN layers

m		NYT_1		
	# of layers	P	R	F1
8	1	0.458	0.690	0.551
8	2	0.496	0.682	0.574
6	1	0.465	0.710	0.560
6	2	0.462	0.699	0.557
4	1	0.466	0.683	0.554
4	2	0.520	0.695	**0.595**

6 Conclusions

We present **RExAS**, a novel architecture for relation extraction from unstructured text. Our adaptive self-attention module learns weighted adjacency from sentence-level information, with the encoder capturing global features, the attention module capturing syntactic dependencies, and the GCN module identifying relevant neighboring tokens. Extensive experiments on NYT_1, NYT_2, **Wikidata**, and **GIDS** show **RExAS** achieves state-of-the-art results on the **NYT** corpus and competitive performance on other datasets, proving its robustness for both distantly supervised and manually curated RE datasets.

References

1. Bastos, A., et al.: Recon: relation extraction using knowledge graph context in a graph neural network. In: Proceedings of WWW 2021, pp. 1673–1685 (2021)
2. Bunescu, R., Mooney, R.: A shortest path dependency kernel for relation extraction. In: Proceedings of EMNLP, pp. 724–731 (2005)
3. Devlin, J., Chang, M.-W., Lee, K., Toutanova, K.: BERT: pre-training of deep bidirectional transformers for language understanding. In: Proceedings of the 2019 Conference of NAACL, pp. 4171–4186, Minneapolis, Minnesota, June 2019. ACL
4. Etzioni, O., Banko, M., Soderland, S., Weld, D.S.: Open information extraction from the web. Commun. ACM **51**(12), 68–74 (2008)
5. Guo, Z., Zhang, Y., Lu, W.: Attention guided graph convolutional networks for relation extraction. In: Proceedings of the 57th ACL, pp. 241–251. ACL, Florence, Italy, July 2019

6. Hendrickx, I., et al.: Semeval-2010 task 8: Multi-way classification of semantic relations between pairs of nominals. arXiv preprint arXiv:1911.10422 (2019)
7. Hochreiter, S., Schmidhuber, J.: Long short-term memory. Neural Comput. **9**(8), 1735–1780 (1997)
8. Hoffmann, R., Zhang, C., Ling, X., Zettlemoyer, L., Weld, D.S.: Knowledge-based weak supervision for information extraction of overlapping relations. In: Proceedings of the 49th ACL, pp. 541–550 (2011)
9. Jat, S., Khandelwal, S., Talukdar, P.: Improving distantly supervised relation extraction using word and entity based attention. arXiv preprint arXiv:1804.06987 (2018)
10. Kipf, T.N., Welling, M.: Semi-supervised classification with graph convolutional networks. In: ICLR 2017, Toulon, France, April 24–26, 2017, Conference Track Proceedings. OpenReview.net (2017)
11. Mintz, M., Bills, S., Snow, R., Jurafsky, D.: Distant supervision for relation extraction without labeled data. In: Proceedings of the Joint Conference of the 47th ACL and the 4th IJCNLP, pp. 1003–1011 (2009)
12. Miwa, M., Bansal, M.: End-to-end relation extraction using LSTMs on sequences and tree structures. In: Proceedings of the 54th ACL, pp. 1105–1116, Berlin, Germany, August 2016. ACL
13. Nadgeri, A., et al.: KGPool: dynamic knowledge graph context selection for relation extraction. In: Findings of the Association for Computational Linguistics: ACL-IJCNLP 2021, pp. 535–548, Online, August 2021. ACL (2021)
14. Nayak, T., Ng, H.T.: Effective attention modeling for neural relation extraction. In: Proceedings of the 23rd Conference on CoNLL, pp. 603–612. ACL, Hong Kong, China, November 2019
15. Quirk, C., Poon, H.: Distant supervision for relation extraction beyond the sentence boundary. In: Proceedings of the 15th Conference EACL: Volume 1, Long Papers, pp. 1171–1182. ACL, Valencia, Spain, April 2017
16. Riedel, S., Yao, L., McCallum, A.: Modeling relations and their mentions without labeled text. In: ECML-PKDD, pp. 148–163. Springer (2010)
17. Shen, Y., Huang, X.-J.: Attention-based convolutional neural network for semantic relation extraction. In: Proceedings of COLING 2016, pp. 2526–2536 (2016)
18. Shi, Z., Luo, H.: Cre-llm: a domain-specific Chinese relation extraction framework with fine-tuned large language model. arXiv preprint arXiv:2404.18085 (2024)
19. Sorokin, D., Gurevych, I.: Context-aware representations for knowledge base relation extraction. In: Proceedings of the 2017 Conference on EMNLP, pp. 1784–1789 (2017)
20. Tao, Y., Wang, Y., Bai, L.: Graphical reasoning: Llm-based semi-open relation extraction. arXiv preprint arXiv:2405.00216 (2024)
21. Vashishth, S., Joshi, R., Prayaga, S.S., Bhattacharyya, C., Talukdar, P.: RESIDE: improving distantly-supervised neural relation extraction using side information. In: Proceedings of the 2018 Conference on EMNLP, pp. 1257–1266. ACL, Brussels, Belgium, October-November 2018
22. Vaswani, A., et al.: Attention is all you need. In: Neurips, pp. 5998–6008 (2017)
23. Wang, L., Cao, Z., De Melo, G., Liu, Z.: Relation classification via multi-level attention cnns. In: Proceedings of the 54th ACL, pp. 1298–1307 (2016)
24. Shanchan, W., Fan, K., Zhang, Q.: Improving distantly supervised relation extraction with neural noise converter and conditional optimal selector. In: Proceedings of the AAAI, vol. 33, pp. 7273–7280 (2019)
25. Xu, P., Barbosa, D.: Connecting language and knowledge with heterogeneous representations for neural relation extraction. In: Proceedings of the 2019 Conference of NAACL, pp. 3201–3206. ACL, Minneapolis, Minnesota, June 2019

26. Xu, Y., Mou, L., Li, G., Chen, Y., Peng, H., Jin, Z.: Classifying relations via long short term memory networks along shortest dependency paths. In: Proceedings of the 2015 Conference on EMNLP, pp. 1785–1794 (2015)
27. Yang, X., Yu, Z., Guo, Y., Bian, J., Wu, Y.: Clinical relation extraction using transformer-based models. arXiv preprint arXiv:2107.08957 (2021)
28. Ye, Z.-X., Ling, Z.-H.: Distant supervision relation extraction with intra-bag and inter-bag attentions. In: Proceedings of the 2019 Conference of NAACL, pp. 2810–2819, Minneapolis, Minnesota. ACL, June 2019
29. Zeng, D., Liu, K., Chen, Y., Zhao, J.: Distant supervision for relation extraction via piecewise convolutional neural networks. In: Proceedings of the 2015 Conference on EMNLP, pp. 1753–1762 (2015)
30. Zeng, D., Liu, K., Lai, S., Zhou, G., Zhao, J.: Relation classification via convolutional deep neural network. In: Proceedings of COLING 2014, pp. 2335–2344 (2014)
31. Zhu, H., Lin, Y., Liu, Z., Fu, J., Chua, T.-S., Sun, M.: Graph neural networks with generated parameters for relation extraction. In: Proceedings of the 57th Annual Meeting of ACL, pp. 1331–1339. ACL, Florence, Italy, July 2019

Track C

Kontho: An AI-Driven Smart Glove for Enhanced Sign Language Communication

Dyuti Dasgupta[1], Soumyajit Datta[1], Sagnik Pramanik[2], Rohit Kumar Dey[2(✉)], Jeet Nandigrami[1], and Debaditya Ghosh[1]

[1] Department of Artificial Intelligence and Machine Learning, Heritage Institute of Technology, Kolkata, India
[2] Department of Computer Science and Engineering, Heritage Institute of Technology, Kolkata, India
rohit.kumardey.cse26@heritageit.edu.in

Abstract. In India, over 63 million individuals are affected by hearing loss, yet less than 350 certified sign language interpreters are available, thus leading to communication barriers and significant social and economic exclusion. This paper introduces Kontho, an ergonomic, AI-driven, multi-sensor glove integrated with a mobile app for real-time sign language communication via American Sign Language (ASL). Utilizing flex sensors, accelerometers, gyroscopes and EMG sensors, Kontho captures gestures and muscle activity which is processed through a combination of ensemble models and Large Language Models (LLMs) to enhance communication by predicting and completing incomplete gestures. Evaluated on a dataset of 23 ASL gestures at over 3867 data points with an accuracy of 99.61%, Kontho offers a scalable solution to foster social inclusion and address the economic isolation of hearing and speech-impaired individuals, enabling their active participation in the society.

Keywords: Ensemble Model · LLM · EMG · Bi-directional Communication

1 Introduction

Communication is a fundamental human need, yet for the deaf-mute population, engaging with the predominantly verbal world often presents significant challenges. According to a census by the World Federation of the Deaf, the deaf-mute make up about 72 million of the world's population [4]. In a world primarily designed for verbal communication, exchange of ideas by means of gestures or visual input still hinders many [5].

Traditional tools like sign language interpreters and text-based solutions have significant limitations. Interpreters are often scarce and expensive, with costs ranging from $50 to $185 per hour in developed countries [3]. Text-based approaches often fail to support real-time conversations, crucial for social integration and employment. The employment rate for deaf individuals is only 53.3% compared to 75.8% for hearing individuals [2], highlighting the impact of these barriers.

Recent advancements in technology have employed data gloves and deep learning algorithms to process information obtained from sensors, or computer vision systems to efficiently track, map, and decode sign language gestures into different linguistic vocabularies.

This study introduces Kontho, an innovative information technology-based solution designed as a prototype of a two-way multi sensored communication glove. Equipped with flex sensors, accelerometers, gyroscopes and a custom built EMG sensor, this prototype records nuanced data values corresponding to various Sign Language gestures which are then used to train a machine learning model. A mobile application enables the articulation of the text(as translated from ASL) to speech and vice versa thus enabling seamless bi-directional communication between the deaf and mute community and the general population. Open source large language models integrated within the system predict and construct coherent sentences from incomplete, imperfect, or erroneous sign language input.

2 Related Work

Assistive technologies for the deaf and mute have gained significant traction over recent years. Several approaches have been developed from wearable sensor-based systems to AI-driven solutions. Most studies have adopted the traditional approach using Arduino Mega, flex sensors, contact sensors, accelerometer, SD card Module and speaker [11]. More recent iterations employed the usage of ESP-32 to connect to an android application using the micro-controller's bluetooth support [5]. Also, utilization of MPU-6050 over ADXL has been preferred. While these may be considered to be the earliest iterations in this field, relying on sensor data and direct processing for ASL translation often produces inaccurate results.

Computer vision based techniques aiming to recognize hand gestures using deep learning show better results. A model is established by segmenting skin color, enabling hand gesture recognition through the difference between the skin tone of gestures and the surrounding environment. A LeNet-5 Convolutional Neural Network is employed to classify 10 common hand gestures. While this does give an accuracy rate of 98.3% [15], the LeNet-5 model struggles with 3D hand rotation and dynamic gesture recognition. Interpreting sign language through dynamic hand gesture recognition employs 3D Convolutional Neural Networks (3DCNN) to process and efficiently learn the local and global features of hand gestures. A key feature is the usage of MLP (Multilayer Perceptron) and Autoencoder for feature fusion [1]. The system limits its dataset to RGB frames and does not incorporate depth or skeletal data. With an accuracy of 87.69% [1], the system struggles due to variations in signer's height, clothing, and gesture speed.

Gesture or Sign Language detection by integrating the technology of sensors with Machine Learning techniques often prove to be efficient. Flex sensors, motion sensors and touch or pressure sensors positioned at strategic points of the fingers, wrist and forearm record the values for a certain gesture. The obtained data values for a set of predetermined gestures are used to train deep learning or classifier models. Multilayer Neural Network, with an accuracy of over 97% [6], clearly outperforms the other algorithms. K-Nearest Neighbour(KNN) remains the second alternative showing a slightly less accuracy. Random Forests tend to show an accuracy of 99.7% for ASL and 99.8% [6] for ArSL. When Multilayer Perceptron Feed-Forward Neural Network (MLPFFNN) was selected as a specific ANN algorithm suited for this purpose, the performance metric resulted in 99.6% [14]. While these algorithms do perform better, their use cases are limited to certain predefined Sign Language alphabets and numbers. Electromyographic techniques utilize decision trees and multistream Hidden Markov Models (HMMs) to classify hand gestures [16]. The system achieves user-specific classification accuracies of over 97% and user-independent accuracies of 90% [16].

SignAloud, developed by Thomas William Pryor, utilizes multiple sensors to capture gesture movements. The system outputs text or speech by comparing gestures with a predefined sign dictionary , thereby limiting it's flexibility and adaptability to unique communication needs [12]. Moreover, Signaloud remains out of reach for the general populace due to its high cost. Its inability to facilitate bidirectional communication also presents a significant drawback.

SignSpeak, on the other hand, incorporates 21 sensors and leverages Principal Component Analysis (PCA) for feature extraction and dimensionality reduction, enabling classification of ASL gestures. Initially achieving an accuracy of 85%, its performance improved to 92% [4] after addressing a faulty sensor and expanding its training dataset.

BrightSign Glove, developed by Hadeel Ayoub, offers a solution for two-way communication, with an accuracy rate of 97% [8]. It allows users to record and label their own gestures, thus reducing the limitations caused by the absence of social cues and body motions in the dataset. However, BrightSign's prohibitive cost, exceeding ₹2 lakh, renders it inaccessible to the average middle-class demographic. Additionally, while it enables gesture customization, it does not address the challenge of inconsistent or incoherent translations from specific sign languages.

3 Glove Design and Application Interface

3.1 Hardware Design

An array of sensors, including five flex sensors, MPU-6050 (3-axis accelerometer and gyroscope), and EMG sensors, is carefully embedded into a cotton ergonomic glove as shown in Fig. 2. This arrangement facilitates comprehensive data collection during each gesture. The collected data is then transmitted to an ESP-32 microcontroller to be relayed via bluetooth for further processing. The architecture of the entire system has been depicted in Fig. 1.

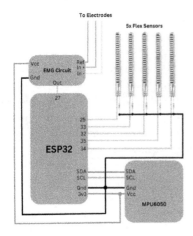
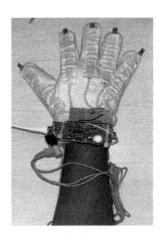

Fig. 1. Kontho Hardware Architecture   **Fig. 2.** Kontho Glove Prototype

Flex sensors (4.5") are attached to each of the five fingers to measure the degree of bending at the Metacarpophalangeal (MCP), Proximal Interphalangeal (PIP), and Distal Interphalangeal (DIP) joints [7]. As the finger bends, the sensor, which runs along the finger's length, bends as well, producing resistance values proportional to the degree of flexion. These resistance values, ranging from 7K to 15K ohms [13], are processed through a voltage divider circuit using a 4.7K ohm resistor and a 3.3V Vcc from the ESP-32.

The **MPU-6050** is a versatile motion-tracking device that integrates a 3-axis accelerometer and 3-axis gyroscope. When attached to the back of the hand, it effectively captures the hand's orientation and acceleration during movement. The accelerometer measures linear acceleration along three axes, while the gyroscope tracks angular velocity for pitch, roll, and yaw motions.

The device connects to an ESP-32 module using four pins. The data pins facilitate communication between the MPU-6050 and ESP-32 using the I2C protocol. This setup allows for comprehensive motion tracking of the hand, including forward-backward, side-to-side, and up-down movements, as well as rotations around different axes.

The design for the **custom-made EMG sensor** has been adapted from the Muscle BioAmp BisCute [9]. This sensor features a fixed gain of x2420 and a BandPass filter ranging from 72 Hz to 720 Hz, making it highly effective in capturing muscle signals while minimising noise. At the core of the sensor module is the LM324 quad operational amplifier (op-amp) integrated circuit (IC), which consists of four independent, high-gain, internally frequency-compensated op-amps. These op-amps are critical for signal amplification, filtering, and conditioning. In addition to the op-amp, the sensor circuit comprises specific resistors and capacitors that further aid in signal conditioning. The circuit diagram for the EMG Sensor has been given in Fig. 3.

The EMG sensor uses three electrodes to detect muscle activity in the forearm. A reference electrode on the back of the hand provides a baseline, while positive and negative electrodes on the inner forearm capture electrical signals from flexor muscles. These muscles are crucial for hand and finger movements. By recording the electrical activity during muscle contractions, the EMG sensor provides data on muscle performance and movement patterns, offering insights into the physiological aspects of sign language production.

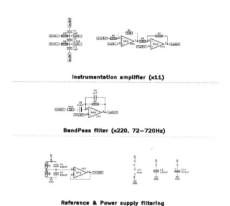 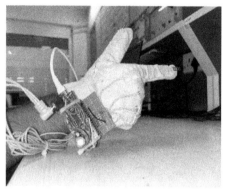

Fig. 3. Components of the custom made EMG module

Fig. 4. Sign Language gesturing "You"

3.2 Application Interface

The application, as shown in Fig. 6 is designed using MIT App Inventor and serves as a communication bridge between speech and hearing impaired individuals and the general population. It operates by receiving sensor data from an ESP-32 microcontroller via Bluetooth, which arrives as a comma-separated string. This data is then sent to a Flask server hosted on AWS(An EC2 instance with 2 vCPUs and 8 GB of memory running on Ubuntu OS) through an HTTP POST request. On the server, a machine learning model processes the received data to predict the corresponding English word that matches the input sign language gesture. The predicted word is transmitted back to the mobile application, where it's converted into speech using Google's text-to-speech engine and played through the mobile device's speakers. For reverse communication, the app uses speech-to-text conversion using Google's speech-to-text engine to help the impaired person understand spoken words.

270 D. Dasgupta et al.

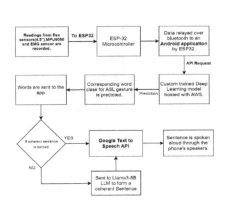 

Fig. 5. Workflow Diagram **Fig. 6.** Kontho Mobile App

3.3 Role of LLM

Sign languages primarily use a shorthand approach, focusing on key ideas rather than syntactic accuracy or linguistic intricacies. As a result, translations often produce incoherent or incomplete sentences. Additionally, the diversity of sign languages creates communication barriers between users of different dialects due to the lack of a universal medium.

To address these challenges, the application integrates an open-source Large Language Model (LLM), Llama3-8B-8192, hosted on Groq. Using Groq's Language Processing Unit (LPU) for ultra-fast, low-latency processing, the system employs few-shot prompting techniques to refine incoherent translations into coherent and meaningful text.

This refined text is then converted into speech using Google's Text-to-Speech engine. The LLM, thus, breaks down barriers that arise due to miscommunication of ideas and helps achieve an universal medium of exchange between individuals of varied dialects.

4 Proposed Algorithm

4.1 Dataset Collection and Labelling

The dataset for the algorithm was created by collecting data from five flex sensors(one for each finger), an MPU-6050 (3-axis accelerometer and gyroscope), and an EMG sensor. On average, each gesture occupies approximately 150 data points, containing real-time data captured from the sensors for each specific gesture. Each flex sensor recorded an analog value corresponding to finger flexion, while the MPU-6050 provided three analog values from its accelerometer (one for each axis: x, y, z) and three from its gyroscope (representing roll, yaw, and pitch angles). Additionally, the EMG sensor contributed a single analog value reflecting the contraction of the flexor muscles of the volar forearm. The data were compiled into 3,868 data points and distributed across 23 labels, each corresponding to gestures like hello, sorry, one, two, and you(as shown in Fig. 4). Each gesture is characterized by 12 key features, including the resistance achieved on finger flexion(One from each of 5 fingers), gyroscopic angles(pitch, roll and yaw respectively), linear accelerations(x,y and z axes), and EMG sensor readings. The data points representing some of the classes have been shown in Table 1.

Table 1. A sample dataset

F1	F2	F3	F4	F5	AX	AY	AZ	GX	GY	GZ	EMG	Label
971	573	264	204	437	−3.77	−1.79	9.08	−0.08	−0.02	0.01	1685	0
838	489	306	477	437	−3.49	8.69	3.04	−0.05	−0.02	0.02	2222	1
831	307	82	707	248	−8.51	1.45	4.83	−0.08	−0.04	0.04	1407	2
950	419	194	651	178	−8.78	4.06	1.95	−0.06	−0.01	0.03	1355	3
852	538	306	428	451	−9.22	1.70	−2.55	−0.04	−0.01	0.01	2221	4
943	293	54	693	220	−7.35	−5.88	−2.15	−0.04	−0.02	0.01	1666	5
901	384	173	679	269	−2.63	−0.21	−0.18	−0.05	0.50	−1.61	2266	6
999	594	201	337	395	−2.59	−6.50	−10.65	−0.02	3.01	−2.09	2224	7
950	657	362	358	563	−5.41	1.29	1.73	−0.90	−1.96	1.48	2193	8

4.2 Data Preprocessing

The preprocessing of sensor data for gesture recognition occurs in two key stages. These steps are outlined below:

Sensor Value Transformation. The sensor values from the flex sensors often show minimal differences between flexed and extended positions. To amplify these differences, a certain transformation formula is used to spread out the sensor values and enhance the distinction between gestures. The formula is mentioned in Eq. 1, where F_i represents the value from the i-th flex sensor.

$$F_i = (F_i \times 7) \% 1000 \qquad (1)$$

Standardization. After amplifying the sensor values, the data is standardized to ensure consistency across the diverse sensor types, including flex sensors, gyroscopes, accelerometers, and EMG sensors, which operate at different ranges and units. Z-score standardization, implemented via Scikit-Learn's 'StandardScaler', is used in this process. The 'scaler.fit_transform(X)' function computes the mean and standard deviation of each feature, and the data is standardized by subtracting the mean and dividing by the standard deviation for each feature as shown in Eq. 2

$$Z = \frac{X_1 - \mu_{X_1}}{\sigma_{X_1}} \qquad (2)$$

where Z represents the standardized value of feature X_1, μ_{X_1} is the mean of feature X_1, and σ_{X_1} is the standard deviation of feature X_1. This ensures that all sensor inputs, regardless of their original scale, contribute uniformly to the model, which is crucial for small-value features like EMG signals. Unlike normalization, which scales data to a fixed range (e.g., 0 to 1) but is sensitive to outliers, standardization maintains the distribution of features and works well with algorithms that assume normally distributed inputs. This helps preserve subtle differences in the data, improving gesture recognition accuracy. After preprocessing, the dataset is split into training and testing sets with an 80:20 ratio.

4.3 Model Selection and Training

Efficient interpretation of ASL involves predicting gestures based on data from 12 different sensor inputs, making it a multiclass classification problem. This approach is essential because each gesture corresponds to distinct patterns in the sensor data, thus requiring a model proficient at differentiating between multiple unique classes.

For this task, we have adopted a Stacked Generalization (stacking) ensemble model, with CatBoost Classifier serving as the final estimator. Stacking is a powerful ensemble learning technique that combines multiple base classifiers to enhance predictive performance. The base models in this ensemble are RandomForest Classifier, XGBClassifier, and SVC.

RandomForest Classifier builds multiple decision trees and aggregates their outputs for improved robustness and reduced overfitting. It excels in high dimensional datasets and provides feature importance insights from sensor readings. XGB Classifier utilizes gradient boosting for efficient error correction, optimizing speed and accuracy making it suitable for structured data and complex feature interactions like sensor-based datasets. Support Vector Classifier(SVC) handles high-dimensional spaces and models complex decision boundaries and is effective for datasets with many features and clear class margins.

CatBoost is highly accurate and provides fast training [10]. It's ideal for multiclass classification problems. CatBoost tends to be more robust to noisy data and less prone to overfitting, especially when combining predictions from different base models. As the final estimator in a stacking model, it is important to generalize well, even when the base models make conflicting predictions.

The stacking approach is crucial because it combines the features and benefits of multiple models–Random Forest, XGBoost, and SVM, allowing for a more robust prediction of sign language gestures from complex sensor data. The base models (Random Forest, XGBoost, and SVM) are trained on the dataset to learn patterns and relationships in the data. The predictions from the base models are then passed to the meta-classifier (CatBoost). The meta-classifier learns from these predictions, correcting the mistakes and making the final decision.

The Stacking Classifier training process begins with the initialization of three base models: Random Forest Classifier (C1), XGB Classifier (C2), and Support Vector Classifier (C3), each configured with specific parameters such as random state for reproducibility and appropriate settings for their respective algorithms. The meta-classifier, CatBoost Classifier (M_meta), is then initialized with its own parameters, including 1000 epochs and a learning rate of 0.083. The training vs validation loss graph is shown in Fig.7. Following this, the Stacking Classifier (M_stack) is created by combining the three base classifiers (C1, C2, and C3) and setting CatBoost Classifier (M_meta) as the final estimator. The base classifiers are first trained on the input dataset (X_train, Y_train), and their predictions are used as input for the meta-classifier. The meta-classifier is then trained on these predictions to optimize the final decision-making process. Once the stacking model has been trained, the complete model (M_stack) is fitted on the training data, resulting in a fully trained Stacking Classifier model, which is ready for predictions.

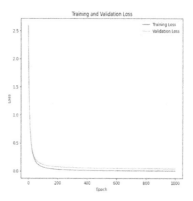

Fig. 7. Training vs Validation Loss Plot

5 Results and Discussion

Four different machine learning classifier configurations were tested, with the Stacking Classifier emerging as the top performer. This classifier used CatBoost as the final estimator and Random Forest, XGBClassifier, and Support Vector Classifier (SVC) as base models. Alternative configurations were also experimented with, including a Stacking Classifier with Logistic Regression as the final estimator and Random Forest and XGBClassifier as base models, as well as individual Support Vector Machine (SVM) and Random Forest models. The comparative analysis of these models, based on accuracy, precision, recall, and F1 score, is presented in a Sect. 5.1. Additionally, a feature importance analysis was conducted to understand the contribution of individual features to the classifiers' performance.

Table 2. Comparative analysis of all the ML classifiers with which we experimented

Model	Accuracy	Precision	Recall	F1 Score
Stacking Classifier: CatBoost final estimator, with Random Forest, XGB, SVC as base models	0.9961	0.9965	0.9975	0.9970
Stacking Classifier: Logistic Regression (final) with Random Forest & XGBoost (base).	0.9922	0.9933	0.9949	0.9940
Support Vector Machine	0.9871	0.9891	0.9863	0.9873
Random Forest	0.9406	0.9497	0.9256	0.9308

5.1 Comparative Analysis of Models

Table 2 presents the performance metrics of various machine learning classifiers evaluated in this study. The Stacking Classifier with CatBoost as the final estimator and Random Forest, XGB Classifier, and Support Vector Classifier as base models demonstrated superior performance, achieving an accuracy of 99.61%, precision of 99.65%, recall of 99.75%, and F1 score of 99.70%. The Stacking Classifier with Logistic Regression as the final estimator (using Random Forest and XGB Classifier as base models) showed comparable but slightly lower performance. Support Vector Machine and Random Forest models exhibited lower accuracy, with Random Forest yielding the lowest at 94.06%. To further assess the prediction capabilities of the best-performing model, a confusion matrix analysis was conducted, as illustrated in Fig. 8, demonstrating the model's ability to distinguish between different classes.

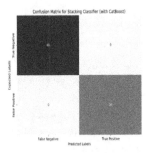

Fig. 8. Confusion matrix of the Stacking Classifier with CatBoost model.

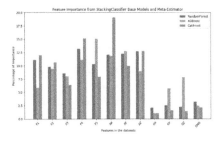

Fig. 9. Importance of Features in ASL dataset.

5.2 Feature Importance

Figure 9 illustrates the relative importance of features in the ML classifier predictions. Accelerometer features contributed most significantly to the model's predictive capabilities, followed by flex sensor features, which were crucial for distinguishing between gestures. Gyroscope and EMG sensors showed lower importance, possibly due to noisy and inconsistent readings in the dataset. Despite their lower significance, these sensors may still provide valuable auxiliary information when integrated with other features.

5.3 Real Time Testing

The model was found to deliver a theoretical accuracy of 99.61%, while in real-time testing with the app, it achieved an accuracy of only 76.22%. This clearly indicates that errors are natural during practical implementation compared to theoretical model predictions, primarily due to improper readings, calibration issues, and noise during the operation phase.

During real-world testing, the flex sensor values exhibited random variations or shifts in range for a given gesture upon restarting the device. In contrast, the accelerometer values for the same gesture remained consistent over time. To address these inconsistencies, we standardized the flex sensor readings to ensure that deviations did not disrupt the final predictions. Additionally, upon initializing the device, the hand and gloves had to remain in a neutral position for 5 s to allow the gyroscope to calibrate itself and accurately determine the x, y, and z axes.

6 Conclusion

The primary aim of Kontho is to bridge the communication gap for individuals who are deaf and mute by leveraging the potential of various machine learning models and techniques. The true novelty of Kontho lies in integrating LLMs into a cost-effective, customizable smart glove system that grows familiar with its user over time, making communication both intuitive and personal for a broader demographic.

However, the system deals with challenges like sensor noise, calibration inconsistencies, and an inability to process two-hand gestures effectively. Furthermore, reliance on MIT App Inventor for initial prototyping restricts scalability, limiting the system's readiness for real-world application.

To overcome these constraints, the next iteration will incorporate dual-hand gesture recognition and additional accelerometers for refined data precision. Shifting to frameworks like React Native or Flutter will enable an user-friendly application. The glove will feature lightweight, adaptive materials, breathable linings, and waterproof coatings, alongside adjustable straps for a tailored fit. Extended usability will be ensured through long-lasting batteries or portable power banks. By training diverse datasets and incorporating multilingual capabilities, the system will transcend linguistic barriers. Muscle bio-amp bands will replace electrolytic pads, enhancing signal accuracy and responsiveness. Partnerships with healthcare providers and disability organizations will amplify its reach, while intuitive tutorials and a focused marketing strategy will simplify user adoption, transforming the system into an indispensable bridge for seamless communication.

References

1. Al-Hammadi, M., et al.: Deep learning-based approach for sign language gesture recognition with efficient hand gesture representation. IEEE Access **8**, 192527–192542 (2020). https://doi.org/10.1109/ACCESS.2020.3032140
2. Anonymous: National deaf center on postsecondary outcomes (2019). https://nationaldeafcenter.org/
3. Anonymous: Registry of interpreters for the deaf (2019). https://rid.org/
4. Bukhari, J., Rehman, M., Malik, S.I., Kamboh, A.M., Salman, A.: American sign language translation through sensory glove; signspeak. Inter. J. u-and e-Ser. Sci. Technol. **8**(1), 131–142 (2015)
5. Burhani, Z., Prasetyo, J.: The sign language interpreting gloves. J. Appli. Sci. Adv. Eng. **1**(1), 18–27 (2023)
6. Elwahsh, H., Elkhouly, A., Nasr, E.A., Kamrani, A.K., El-Shafeiy, E.: A new intelligent approach for deaf/dumb people based on deep learning. Comput. Mater. Contin **72**, 6045–6060 (2022)
7. Jirapure, A.B., Thool, T., Kohale, U., Sonone, A., Raut, T.: Hand gesture recognization gloves with voice conversion for normal person (2024)
8. Kirkpatrick, K.: Technology for the deaf. Commun. ACM **61**(12), 16–18 (2018)
9. Labs, U.: Muscle bioamp biscute: A low-cost emg sensor (2024). https://github.com/upsidedownlabs/Muscle-BioAmp-BisCute
10. LLC, Y., Contributors, C.: Catboost: A fast, scalable, high performance gradient boosting on decision trees library. https://github.com/catboost/catboost (2023), used for ranking, classification, regression, and other machine learning tasks in Python, R, Java, C++. Supports computation on CPU and GPU. Accessed 12 Sep 2024
11. Pal, K., Padmukh, P., Patel, N.: Sign to speech smart glove (2020)
12. Pryor, T.W.: Hand motion interpretation and communication apparatus, 15 Oct (2019), uS Patent 10,446,059
13. Shahrukh, J., Ghousia, B., Aarthy, J., Ateequeur, R.: Wireless glove for hand gesture acknowledgment: sign language to discourse change framework in territorial dialect. Robot. Autom. Eng. J. **3**(2), 555609 (2018)
14. Sümbül, H.: A novel mems and flex sensor-based hand gesture recognition and regenerating system using deep learning model. IEEE Access (2024)
15. Sun, J.H., Ji, T.T., Zhang, S.B., Yang, J.K., Ji, G.R.: Research on the hand gesture recognition based on deep learning. In: 2018 12th International symposium on antennas, propagation and EM theory (ISAPE), pp. 1–4. IEEE (2018)
16. Zhang, X., Chen, X., Li, Y., Lantz, V., Wang, K., Yang, J.: A framework for hand gesture recognition based on accelerometer and emg sensors. IEEE Trans. Syst. Man. Cybernet.-Part A: Syst. Hum. **41**(6), 1064–1076 (2011)

Leveraging EfficientNetB4 Model with Multi-head Attentions for Maize Leaf Disease Detection

Nallamilli Eswar Venkata Reddiar, Pilla Veera Satya Sai Vikranth,
Teerdhala Kumar, Thota Siddartha, N. Rayvanth,
and Rimjhim Padam Singh[✉]

Department of Computer Science and Engineering, Amrita School of Computing,
Bengaluru, Amrita Vishwa Vidyapeetham, India
{BL.EN.U4AIE21087,BL.EN.U4AIE21100,BL.EN.U4AIE21131,
BL.EN.U4AIE21132}@bl.students.amrita.edu, ps_rimjhim@blr.amrita.edu

Abstract. Smart agriculture mainly stresses the improvements in early plant disease diagnostics, crop classification and management, and effective pest control. Maize being an important staple crop necessitates early and accurate disease detection on its leaves. Hence, this paper proposes a novel Convolutional neural network model based on EfficientNet-B4 model and multi-head attention for the effective classification of maize leaf diseases. The proposed model focuses on early-stage disease patterns with the help of a large amount of data. Compared to other architectures, it attains an outstanding F1-score of 96.75%. The proposed system not only helps farmers to get timely diagnosis but also offers them useful information to mitigate risks and improve production. This study benefits agricultural resilience, food security and farmer's welfare.

Keywords: Maize leaf · disease · attention · smart agriculture

1 Introduction

Maize crop is an important staple meal for millions of people in the world, and it is an important ingredient crop for several food industries like meat and milk production, energy production, chemicals and products produced from animal and plant waste, and medicine. Hence, maize crop diseases, pest infestation of the maize, and nutrient deficiencies also need to be managed in an efficient manner to ensure that the maize crop remains healthy and productive. Diseases caused to the leaves of maize cause a serious threat to the quality and production of maize and cause huge financial losses to farmers. Therefore, to implement control measures for maize disease control, it is crucial to be able to quickly identify the particular type of disease so that precision medication can be provided.

Today's disease identification is a slow, time-consuming, and highly subjective process that involves farmers' observations. The objectives of this study are to design an efficient deep learning model to diagnose diseases in maize leaves.

The proposed model specifically targets at identifying diseases like grey leaf spot, maize rust and northern blight through more complex convolutional neural networks since the task is primarily an image analysis task. The objective is to design a basic gadget that can be used by farmers and agronomists to diagnose diseases in the leaves of the maize crop early and in the process, be able to come up with sustainable measures to control the diseases.

It contributes to the field of smart and precision agriculture and its key contributions include:

- A novel approach fine-tuning EfficientNetB4 convolutional neural network by integrating multi-head attention mechanism optimally into the architecture.
- Analysis on the impact of multi-head attention mechanism added at different positions in the model architecture to find the most optimal architecture for disease classification.
- Analysis and implementation of five recent state-of-art convolutional neural networks for model selection and comparative performance analysis against the proposed model.

2 Literature Survey

Nowadays, there has been a lot of focus on smart agriculture, thereby, making several researchers focus on the development of automated systems for crop monitoring, disease detection, classification etc. This section discusses some of the notable works proposed to date for the detection and classification of different crop leaf diseases. Sun et al. [1] proposed a system for crop disease identification utilizing convolutional neural networks with multiplexed feature aggregation technique, Retinex enhancement, and huge RPN having a transmission module for enhanced localization accuracy. Their method shows a significant improvement in the degree of precision and perceptible FPS rates compared to earlier strategies.

Haque et al. [2] used deep learning for diagnosing diseases from field images in Ludhiana India by using synthetic photos with turning and light enhancement. To build a model for detecting watermelon diseases, they trained Inception-v3, and the results were good regardless of background settings. In the current study, Masood et al. [3] introduced MaizeNet, a deep learning model that integrates spatial channel attention and an improved Faster R-CNN for the identification of maize leaf diseases. This model showed that the system was stable in different climatic conditions and provided an answer to the problem of ecosystem productivity. Qian et al. [4] proposed a transformer-based model for the detection of Maize leaf diseases, reducing background distortion through self-attention and multi-source image datasets.

Rai et al. [5] reviewed NLB, a fungal disease that hazards maize. Several state-of-art models were trained from scratch with data augmentation techniques and Adam optimizers up to 50 epochs and the results were excellent. The attention U-Net proved to be better than other segmentation approaches, thus allowing accurate NLB disease segmentation using local features. Yin et al. [6] proposed DISE-Net for identifying the maize leaf spot disease that improves the feature transmission, cross-channel coupling, and multi-scale feature learning as a deeper network with better accuracy than InceptionV3, ResNet50, and VGG16. Grad-Cam visualization affirms its main area of interest, which is a handy tool for field classification. Waheed et al. [7], classified corn leaf disease using the DenseNet model, beating highly parameterized models such as EfficiencyNet and VGG19Net models while having a slight difference in classification accuracy, meaning that it consumes less computation resources.

Craze et al. [8] applied deep learning to maize leaf diseases' classification and specifically on GLD. Classifiers were trained on combined cornfield photos with diseases and it was noted that models from actual images are more generalized than simulated ones. In another research by Yu et al. [9], they integrated K-means clustering with highly advanced deep learning models to improve a precise maize disease diagnosis particularly the leaf spot, grey spot, and rust diseases with the help of models such as Inception v3, ResNet18, VGG-16, and VGG-19. Sibiya et al. [10] developed a CNN network for the estimation of maize common rust disease severity. The authors apply threshold segmentation with respect to the damaged leaf area and apply fuzzy decision rules to classify it with four severity classes. This AI-based operation introduces new interesting means for plant pathology assessment.

Deep Forest was used by Arora et al. [11] for classification of corn leaf diseases and the results demonstrated a higher accuracy and less time consumption than the traditional machine learning and artificial neural networks. The Deep Forest model almost achieved near to perfect accuracy with very little changes in hyperparameters which makes it suitable for maize leaf classification. To overcome the issue of delayed disease identification, Pan et al. [12] developed a deep learning method for white corn health diagnosis with more images for better decision and disease diagnosis. Pushpa et al. [13] worked on disease identification for early intervention for sustainable crop production with 92% accuracy after using train and test split.

Veni et al. [14] put forward a deep learning approach to mitigate the crop yield reduction by plant diseases. They employed the deep learning models in the classification of plant leaf diseases employing the support vector machines and k-nearest neighbour. Satvika et al. [15] used RGB to HSI conversion, k-means clustering, GLCM and SVM classifiers for crop disease recognition and the accuracy achieved was 93.5%. Indeed, Vijayakumar et al. [16] were engaged in the rice plant disease identification by using image processing techniques such as CNN, CNN with the data augmentation, and GAN to enhance the crop productivity through the early sign identification of a disease for appropriate fertilization.

Several other image classification techniques have been proposed to date in various computer vision applications like remote sensing, medical imaging, crop classification, disease predictions, etc. These techniques can be studied by referring to [17–21].

Haq et al. [23] developed an automated weed detection system based on a CNN LVQ model on 4400 UAV images with 100% accuracy of soil, 99.79% of soybean, and overall accuracy of 99.44%. The weed detection performance of the model was higher than previous studies after hyperparameter optimization. Haq et al. [24] proposed a five-layered CNN model for plant image identification with 300 images of nine plants. The model yielded a 96% accuracy on the NU108 and 97.8% on UAV images of the NU101 dataset, which proves the efficiency of the model in plant classification.

Haq et al. [25] employed high-resolution PlanetScope (PS) nanosatellite data to analyze temporal and spatial dynamics of agricultural land in the Al-Qassim region of Saudi Arabia. Compared with NDVI and Multinomial Logistic Regression (MLR), the Random Forest (RF) model yielded 98% accuracy in vegetation classes, which proved the model's ability to model complex variables and filter noise.

3 Dataset Details and Processing

For the purpose of this work, A standard Maize leaf dataset has been used. The dataset contains 4000 images of maize leaf diseases belonging to four different categories namely, Bercak Daun, Daun Sehat, Hawar Sehat and Karat Sehat. All the images in the dataset have been resized to a consistent image size of 200×200 pixels. Several image augmentation techniques have also been applied to increase the diversity of the dataset images. The applied transformations are the zoom_range with a value of 0.15, width_shift_range with a value of 0.2 and shear_range with a value of 0.15. This augmented dataset is used for the model training and testing purposes. For comprehensive model training, stability and testing, the dataset has been divided into three different sets namely, the train set, validation set and test set in the standard ratio of 60:20:20 with 600 images for each class in training and 200 images for each class in validation and test dataset.

4 Proposed Methodology

The methodology proposed in this paper exploits the efficiency of the recent EfficientNetB4 model and multi-head attention mechanism for automatically detecting and classifying diseases in the Maize crop leaf. Instead of blindly selecting the EfficientNetB4 model as the baseline model for the proposed approach, the work experiments with fine-tuning of five recent state-of-art and efficient convolutional neural networks for Maize leaf disease detection namely, DenseNet201, InceptionNetV3, MobileNetV3, XceptionNet and EfficientNetB4. All the models pre-trained on ImageNet dataset are selected and their weights are extracted as it is. The top layer of the models is removed and an additional Global average pooling layer is added followed by three additional dense layers having 1024, 1024 and 512 neurons with ReLU activation function. Finally, the last layer is added with 4 neurons and Softmax activation function. Here, the performance of EfficientNetB4 model surpasses all the models.

EfficientNetB4 convolutional neural network is a deep, wide, and high-resolution in architecture. This model uses compound scaling that balances depth, width and resolution rather than just depth scaling. It is designed to ensure better performance and efficiency by optimising layer width, depth and resolution. It contains the blocks which perform the implementation of the depth-wise separable convolutions with squeeze and excitation blocks, including the usage of batch normalisation and Swish activation functions.

Here, depthwise separable convolutions are substantially instrumental in reducing the number of parameters and computation for efficiency while Squeeze-and-excitation blocks further refine feature representations by explicitly modeling channel-wise dependencies. It also uses Global average pooling layers that reduce spatial dimensions, enabling generalization without over-fitting. It should be noted that the Swish function is recently favoured frequently due to its great performance. The model is advanced and performs better due to the increased scaling factors in higher ratings. Such meticulous design achieves state-of-the-art results for every image classification task, clearly demonstrating the fact that EfficientNetB4's architectural principles are functional in attaining high performance but with improved efficiency.

The rationale for selecting EfficientNetB4 over higher counterparts including EfficientNetB5, EfficientNetB6, or EfficientNetB7 was as follows. Although the higher variants provide higher scaling factors and potentially higher performance, they need much more GPU memory, higher computational capability and longer training time. Training or inferring with models like B5, B6, or B7 would have imposed actual limitations for computational hardware and exorbitant computational cost would ensue.

Based on these factors, the EfficientNetB4 model is a perfect middle ground between high performant model and a model with reasonable computational requirements. It provides very good performance for the maize leaf disease detection task and has reasonable resource consumption which is quite appropriate given the hardware and time limitations.

Multi-head attention, on the other hand, includes an inventory mechanism of different heads which, in transformer-based architectures, serve the purpose of capturing all the disparities that can exist in sequence inputs. Every day new attention head finds its own multi-level attention signatures by independently making attention scores for projected query, key, and value vectors. These scores are for the sake of computing weighted sums of values vector from multi-head attention output vector for the specific position in the sequence. Through simultaneously taking into account different representations of information from multiple subspaces, this kind of attention enables the model to efficiently learn how to understand and process the complex sequences which, in turn, results in improved accuracy of tasks.

The design of the multi-head attention is controlled by two key components (a) num_heads and (b) key_dim. *num_heads* in the multi-head attention mechanism specifies the number of parallel attention heads to be employed. Multiple attention heads enable the model in capturing and analyzing a variety of patterns and relationships in different regions of the input data images parallelly at the same time. Adjusting this parameter impacts model's process of learning and analyzing information from several different perspectives. The higher the value of num_heads, the more aspects of the input the model can attend to at the same time, possibly improving the performance, at the cost of higher computational complexity. The proposed model employs a total of eight attention heads. While the *key_dim* represents the projected key's dimensionality and value vectors' dimensions in each attention head. With the help of this parameter, it is able to decide the granularity of captured information in each attention head which increases the model's ability to understand relationships between tokens. The key_dim parameter should be large enough to capture meaningful information but small enough to make the computation efficient. Typical values for key_dim are between 64 and 512, but the best choice depends on the complexity of the task and the resources available. The proposed model employs a key_dim of value 64 only.

4.1 Integration of EfficientNetB4 Model and Multi-head Attention

Before the proposed solution – combination of the EfficientNetB4 CNN model with the Multi-head Attention (MHA) mechanism – the EfficientNetB4 model, pretrained on the ImageNet database, is further trained on the Maize leaf database. This is done by stacking a global pooling layer and a few dense layers way at the end of the model. The EfficientNetB4 model is loaded and the final classification layer is stripped off from the model. A GAP layer is then included to down sample spatial dimensions and three dense layers with 1024, 1024, and 512 neurons respectively. These layers employ rectifying linear unit nonlinearity function to make the computations faster. The final output dense layer comprised of 4 neurons to make multi-class predictions with the Softmax activation across the four diseases. The final layer employs categorical cross entropy for measuring the error for back propagation while the performance measure here is accuracy. EfficientNetB4 model is utilised with pre-trained weights at the base instance.

Once the architecture is optimized and the disease classification results are reasonable, the proposed methodology adds multi-head attention (MHA) layers at different positions between the dense layers. The different configurations tested are: We also compare the following architectures: (a) one MHA layer after the first dense layer (DL-1), (b) one MHA layer after the second dense layer (DL-2), and (c) two MHA layers after both DL-1 and DL-2. These multiple layers in the MHA means that the model can attend to a different part of the input sequence, the relationships within the data can be captured with more efficacy. These configurations were tested to determine an architecture that enhances the model's performance without adding more parameters or computational complexity.

The first two architectures enhanced the fine-tuned EfficientNetB4 model by a slightly better accuracy of classification of maize leaf diseases, while the three dense layers and two attention layers provided the best results. This combination enables the model to capture more complex features and relations in the data and thus perform better in the multi-class classification problem. The complete architecture can be seen in Fig. 1 below. EfficientNetB4 with multi-head attention layers is used to capture long-range dependencies in image data to capture dependencies that are important in complex pattern recognition tasks.

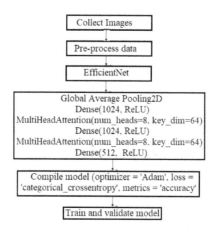

Fig. 1. Proposed system architecture for fine-tuned EfficientNetB4 model integrated with multi-head attention mechanism

5 Experiments

A common set of hyper-parameters is adopted for learning of all the deep learning models like DenseNet201, InceptionV3, etc., implemented for this work. Images are resized to 224 × 224 pixels and processed in batches of 32 for faster model training and error back-propagation. All the hidden layers employed ReLU activation function for faster computations while facilitating the multi-class classification, final output layer Softmax activation function. The Adam optimizer adjusts model parameters for optimal model learning by minimizing the categorical cross-entropy loss function over 30 epochs with a learning rate of 0.0001 (Table 1).

All the models have been comprehensively evaluated using Recall, Precision, Accuracy and F-score metrics (Fig. 2). Among the evaluated combinations of dense layers and multi-head attention layers, the proposed fine-tuned EfficientNetB4 model with three dense layers and two multi-head attention layers after DL-1 and DL-2 demonstrates the highest performance with an accuracy of 96.63% and the best F-score of 96.75% on the test set, indicating its effectiveness in making correct predictions. Following closely, EfficientNet (Layer 1) achieves an accuracy of 95.63%, while EfficientNet performs at 95.63%, EfficientNet (Layer 2) at 95.12%. Accuracy and F-score are the key metrics for

Table 1. Experiments of Fine-tuned EfficientNetB4 model with different combinations dense layers (DLs) and Multi-head attention (MHA) layers

Models	Precision	Recall	F1	Accuracy
3 DLs only	0.9575	0.9550	0.9575	0.9562
3 DLs + 1 MHA layer after DL-1	0.9575	0.9575	0.955 0	0.9563
3 DLs + 1 MHA layer after DL-2	0.9550	0.9500	0.9500	0.9513
3 DLs + 2 MHA layers after DL-1 DL-2	**0.9650**	**0.9625**	**0.9675**	**0.9663**

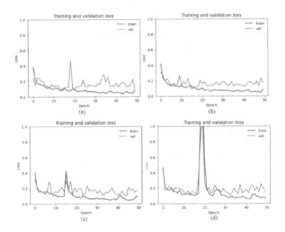

Fig. 2. Learning plots obtained for different combinations of Dense layers and multi-head attention layers applied for fine-tuning of EfficientNet-B4 model (a) without MHA layer, (b) with MHA layer after DL-1, (c) with MHA layer after DL-2 and (d) with MHA layers after DL-1 and DL-2

classification tasks, representing the percentage of correct predictions. However, the selection of the best model may also hinge on other considerations such as computational efficiency, interpretability, and alignment with specific task requirements. In this context, if the model is required to be kept lighter and to be installed on edge devices, one can opt for the EfficientNetB4 model fine-tuned with dense layers only.

The stability in the learning of different architecture of fine-tuned EfficientNetB4 model can be studied by referring to Fig. 1. The loss plots for all these different combinations over 50 epochs show a clear model convergence without over-fitting or under-fitting on the Maize leaf dataset images. It can be observed that during initial epochs, the models had huge fluctuations for both training and validation loss values but slowly towards the 50th epoch, the models converged properly with a stable learning process.

Amongst the different combinations of fine-tuned EfficientNetB4 model trained on the test set, fine-tuned EfficientNetB4 model with 3 dense layers only has the lowest test loss of 0.1404. While other combinations EfficientNetB4 with 3 dense layers and 2 multi-head attention layers had a loss of 0.1404, EfficientNetB4 with 3 dense layers and 1 multi-head attention layer after the first dense layer had a loss of 0.146 and EfficientNetB4 model with 3 dense layers and 1 multi-head attention layer after the second dense layer had a loss of 0.1794 which are relatively higher test losses. Lower loss values indicate that the model is better at minimizing the difference between its predictions and the actual target values. While loss is a crucial metric, the choice of the best model strongly depends on other metrics as well like F-score and accuracy which were the highest for the proposed model.

Table 2. Performance comparisons of proposed model against state-of-art models.

Models	Precision	Recall	F-score	Accuracy
MobileNetV2	0.84	0.8225	0.83	0.8312
DenseNet201	0.935	0.925	0.9275	0.9262
XceptionNet	0.87	0.87	0.8725	0.87
InceptionNetV3	0.86	0.8525	0.8575	0.8537
EfficientNetB4	0.9575	0.955	0.9575	0.9562
Proposed model	**0.9650**	**0.9625**	**0.9675**	**0.9663**

Table 2 compares several state-of-art deep learning models for Maize leaf disease classification tasks, with EfficientNetB4 model emerging as the best baseline performer model. DenseNet201 model also performed decently in identifying the leaf disease while MobileNetv2, XceptionNet, and InceptionNetV3 model had very low F-score and accuracy values in detecting the leaf disease. The efficientNetB4 model achieves the highest scores in Precision (0.9575), Recall (0.955), F1 Score (0.9575), and Accuracy (0.9562). This indicates that EfficientNetB4 excels in accurately identifying true positives while minimizing false positives to its maximum, making it the most effective model overall with a minimum of 3% improvement in all the metrics over all other state-of-art baseline methods. This made the EfficientNetB4 model our natural choice to further leverage the classification accuracies for the underlying Maize leaf disease detection task.

Finally, as discussed above, further leveraging the fine-tune EfficientNetB4 model with two additional multi-head attention layers increased the efficiency of the model in correctly detecting and classifying the disease type of Maize crop leaf with the highest F-score of 97% approximately. The multi-head attention layers proved to improve the alignment of the model on the parts of data which aided in focussing on the relatively important image regions to extract more informative features, thereby, increasing the model's efficiency.

Next, Fig. 3 presents the loss plots for the baseline models implemented. It can be seen that all the models learnt well and showed learning saturation within 50 epochs. The major difference to be noted here is that for MobileNetV2 model's validation loss kept fluctuating between a fixed range of 0.4 to 0.7 which

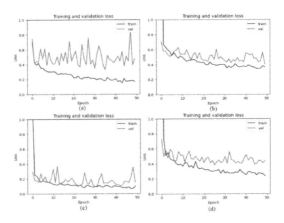

Fig. 3. Loss plots obtained for baseline models (a) MobileNetv2, (b) InceptionV3 (c) DenseNet201 and (d) XceptionNet on Maize leaf disease dataset

never got reduced and for InceptionV3 and XceptionNet models, the training and validation showed better convergence but the over-all validation loss never got lesser than 0.35 and 0.3. While for the DenseNet201 and EfficientNetB4 models also the model showed good convergence but EfficientNetB4 model had fewer fluctuations between a restricted loss range, allowing for better model learning.

Over all the proposed model achieved the minimum number of misclassification i.e. 27 for the dataset, thereby supporting the reliability of the model as presented in Fig. 4.

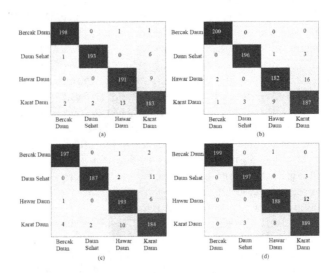

Fig. 4. Confusion matrices obtained for different combinations of Dense layers and multi-head attention layers applied for fine-tuning of EfficientNet-B4 model (a) without MHA layer,(b) with MHA layer after DL-1, (c) with MHA layer after DL-2 and (d) with MHA layers after DL-1 and DL-2

6 Conclusion

The paper proposed the novel classification model that integrated three dense layers and two multi-head attention layers for fine-tuning the architecture of EfficientNetB4 model for maize leaf disease detection. Multiple architectures comprising different combinations of dense and multi-head attention layers were tried and an alleviating change in accuracy and robustness of the model capabilities after a host of experiments was observed. Increased architectural depth through dense layers and feature weighting based on their relative importance allowed the distinction between healthy and diseased maize leaves effectively. The attention mechanisms particularly enabled the model to effectively focus on different regions in an input image adaptively, where it improves interpretability and decision-making of the proposed model against several other state-of-art networks. However, further work can be done to develop a unified system capable of classifying diseases in a variety of plants and crops at early stages for smart agricultural practices and effective management of crops.

References

1. Sun, J., Yang, Y., He, X., Wu, X.: Northern maize leaf blight detection under complex field environment based on deep learning. IEEE Access **8**, 33679–33688 (2020)
2. Haque, M.A., et al.: Deep learning-based approach for identification of diseases of maize crop. Sci. Rep. **12**(1), 6334 (2022)
3. Masood, M., et al.: MaizeNet: A deep learning approach for effective recognition of maize plant leaf diseases. IEEE Access (2023)
4. Qian, X., Zhang, C., Chen, L., Li, K.: Deep learning-based identification of maize leaf diseases is improved by an attention mechanism: self-Attention. Front. Plant Sci. **13**, 864486 (2022)
5. Rai, C.K. and Pahuja, R.: Northern maize leaf blight disease detection and segmentation using deep convolution neural networks. Multimedia Tools Appli., 1-18 (2023)
6. Yin, C., Zeng, T., Zhang, H., Fu, W., Wang, L., Yao, S.: Maize small leaf spot classification based on improved deep convolutional neural networks with a multi-scale attention mechanism. Agronomy **12**(4), 906 (2022)
7. Waheed, A., Goyal, M., Gupta, D., Khanna, A., Hassanien, A.E. and Pandey, H.M., 2020. An optimized dense convolutional neural network model for disease recognition and classification in corn leaf. Computers and Electronics in Agriculture, 175
8. Craze, H.A., Pillay, N., Joubert, F., Berger, D.K.: Deep learning diagnostics of gray leaf spot in maize under mixed disease field conditions. Plants **11**(15) (2022)
9. Yu, H., et al.: Corn leaf diseases diagnosis based on K-means clustering and deep learning. IEEE Access **9**, 143824–143835 (2021)
10. Sibiya, M., Sumbwanyambe, M.: Automatic fuzzy logic-based maize common rust disease severity predictions with thresholding and deep learning. Pathogens **10**(2), 131 (2021)
11. Arora, J., Agrawal, U.: Classification of Maize leaf diseases from healthy leaves using Deep Forest. J. Artifi. Intell. Syst. **2**(1), 14 (2020)

12. Pan, S.Q., Qiao, J.F., Wang, R., Yu, H.L., Cheng, W.A.: Of northern corn leaf blight with deep learning model. J. Integrative Agricult. **21**(4), 1094-1105
13. Pushpa, B.R., Av, S.H., Ashok, A.: Diseased leaf segmentation from complex background using indices based histogram. In: 2021 6th International Conference on Communication and Electronics Systems (ICCES), pp. 1502-1507 (July 2021)
14. Veni, S., Anand, R., Mohan, D., Sreevidya, P.: Leaf recognition and disease detection using content based image retrieval. In 2021 7th international conference on advanced computing and communication systems (ICACCS), vol. 1, pp. 243-247. IEEE (March 2021)
15. Satvika, A.S., Savitri Sreshta, G., Prathima, R.M., Bhavana, V.: Leaf disease detection using image processing techniques and offspring generation using genetic algorithm. In: Reddy, V.S., Prasad, V.K., Wang, J., Reddy, K. (eds.) Soft Computing and Signal Processing. AISC, vol. 1340, pp. 639–648. Springer, Singapore (2022). https://doi.org/10.1007/978-981-16-1249-7_60
16. Vijayakumar, A. and Ganga, P.L.: Rice plant leaf disease detection—a comparison of various methodologies. In: International Conference on Signal & Data Processing, pp. 325-336. Springer Nature Singapore, Singapore (June 2022). https://doi.org/10.1007/978-981-99-1410-4_27
17. Dong, P., Li, K., Wang, M., Li, F., Guo, W., Si, H.: Maize leaf compound disease recognition based on attention mechanism. Agriculture **14**(1), 74 (2023)
18. Anjali, K.S., Singh, R.P., Panda, M.K., Palaniappan, K.: An ensemble approach using self-attention based MobileNetV2 for SAR classification. Proc. Comput. Sci. **235**, 3207–3216 (2024)
19. Shalini, G., Singh, R.P., Khanna, M. and Kumar, P.: A Fine-Tuned MobileNetv2 based Approach for Weed Classification. In 2023 9th International Conference on Signal Processing and Communication (ICSC), pp. 504-509. IEEE (December 2023)
20. Sugunadevi, C., Singh, R.P., Maheswari, B.U., Kumar, P.: DiaMOS plant leaves disease classification using vision transformer. In 2023 9th International Conference on Signal Processing and Communication (ICSC), pp. 551-556). IEEE (December 2023)
21. Bajaj, A., Vishwakarma, D.K.: A state-of-the-art review on adversarial machine learning in image classification. Multimedia Tools Appli. **83**(3), 9351–9416 (2024)
22. Zhang, Z., et al.: NTIRE 2024 challenge on bracketing image restoration and enhancement: datasets methods and results. In: Proceedings of the IEEE/CVF Conference on Computer Vision and Pattern Recognition, pp. 6153-6166 (2024)
23. Haq, M.A.: CNN based automated weed detection system using UAV imagery. Comput. Syst. Sci. Eng. **42**(2) (2022)
24. Haq, M.A., Ahsan, A., Gyani, J.: Implementation of CNN for plant identification using UAV imagery. Inter. J. Adv. Comput. Sci. Appli. **14**(4) (2023)
25. Haq, M.A.: Planetscope nanosatellites image classification using machine learning. Comput. Syst. Sci. Eng. **42**(3) (2022)

Automated Module for Image Quality Assessment from Narrow-Banding Imaging Endoscopy Cameras

Van Hieu Bui[(✉)], Khac Long Pham, Thuan Thanh Nguyen, and The Anh Nguyen

Education Zone, FPT University, Hoa Lac Hi-Tech Park, Ha Noi, Vietnam
hieubv10@fe.edu.vn,
{longpkhe150157,thanhnthe150634,anhnthe151353}@fpt.edu.vn

Abstract. Gastrointestinal diseases pose a significant threat to human health, with gastrointestinal tumors ranking among the most common and fatal conditions. Narrow Band Imaging (NBI), an advanced endoscopic method, plays a crucial role in diagnosing these diseases by producing detailed imaging data. However, the large volume of generated data often includes low-quality images, making it challenging to identify frames with diagnostic value. This underscores the importance of an efficient image quality control mechanism for data optimization. In this study, we introduce a non-reference image quality assessment (IQA) framework specifically designed for NBI endoscopy. The proposed two-stage approach employs deep learning for accurate evaluation. In the first stage, a patch-based classification model assesses image regions by leveraging local features extracted through a convolutional neural network. In the second stage, a breadth-first search algorithm combines these patch-level outcomes to generate an overall image quality score. The framework achieves outstanding performance, with precision and recall rates of 96% and 97%, respectively. Additionally, it reduces storage requirements by approximately 90% and adapts effectively to various application needs.

Keywords: Image quality assessment · narrow-banding-imaging · endoscopy

1 Introduction

Gastrointestinal diseases are often marked by a variety of debilitating symptoms, including diarrhea, abdominal pain, bloating, gastrointestinal bleeding, bowel obstruction, malabsorption, and malnutrition. Functional Gastrointestinal Disorders (FGID), a subset of these diseases, are commonly associated with chronic pain syndromes such as fibromyalgia and functional conditions like chronic fatigue syndrome. Moreover, individuals with FGID frequently contend with mental health issues, including anxiety and depression [18]. These conditions substantially diminish the quality of life for affected individuals, often surpassing the burden experienced by those with other chronic illnesses, such as advanced congestive heart failure or rheumatoid arthritis [21].

Globally, gastrointestinal diseases impact approximately 40% of the population, with a higher prevalence among women and a decline in occurrence with age [20]. These disorders are responsible for 12% of primary care visits and 30% of gastroenterology consultations [11]. Notably, over two-thirds of FGID patients seek medical attention annually, with 40% requiring regular medication [3]. The economic burden is substantial; for example, during 2014-2015, the NHS spent at least £72.3 million on treatment, with the majority allocated to prescriptions, community care, and hospital services [17]. Without timely diagnosis and intervention, these conditions can escalate into gastrointestinal cancers, significantly increasing their physical, emotional, and financial toll. Early detection of abnormalities is critical for effective treatment, including targeted surgical interventions and complementary therapies.

Endoscopic imaging plays a pivotal role in diagnosing and managing gastrointestinal diseases. White Light Endoscopy (WLE) is widely used but has limitations, such as poor histopathological correlation and dependence on the endoscopist's expertise, making early lesion detection difficult [6]. Advanced imaging techniques, such as Narrow Band Imaging (NBI), address these challenges by enhancing visualization of vascular structures through specific light wavelengths, such as 415 nm (blue) and 540 nm (green). This improved visualization aids in detecting lesions and performing targeted biopsies [10]. Compared to WLE, NBI provides superior imaging of capillaries and mucosal structures, improving detection rates for conditions like gastric intestinal metaplasia.

Despite its advantages, endoscopic imaging faces significant challenges related to image quality. Factors such as occlusions caused by blood or medical instruments and technical issues like blurriness, noise, or low contrast can compromise image clarity [12]. High-quality images are essential for accurate diagnosis and monitoring. Endoscopic procedures, which last between 15 to 45 min, generate high-resolution videos stored in Picture Archiving and Communication Systems (PACS). However, only a fraction of the frames are diagnostically valuable, with many being affected by blurring due to manual handling or noise from fluid flushing or tissue manipulation. Storing entire videos is inefficient and complicates the extraction of diagnostically relevant frames.

Image quality assessment (IQA) is crucial for ensuring reliable diagnostic data. Automated IQA systems can assist in identifying and addressing quality issues, enhancing dataset curation and real-time image acquisition. These advancements are instrumental in improving early disease detection and patient care outcomes.

In this paper, we propose a two-stage framework to assess the quality of images obtained from NBI endoscopy. The first stage involves dividing the image into non-overlapping patches and categorizing them into four quality-impacting groups: Brightness, Darkness, Motion-blur, and High quality. The second stage aggregates these patch-level results using statistical methods to assign an overall quality rating to the image, categorizing it as Bad, Poor, Fair, Good, or Excellent.

Our approach not only achieves robust statistical performance but also aligns closely with medical professionals' perception of endoscopic image quality.

2 Related Works

2.1 Full-Reference Image Quality Assessment (FR-IQA)

FR-IQA approaches require both distorted and reference images as inputs to evaluate perceptual similarity. These methods can be broadly classified into two types: traditional evaluation metrics and learning-based models. Traditional metrics depend on predefined characteristics of the human visual system. However, due to the inherent complexity of visual perception, these methods often fall short of accurately replicating human vision. On the other hand, learning-based FR-IQA models utilize deep neural networks to extract features from training data. For instance, DeepQA [1] and DISTS [5] employ CNN-based architectures for tasks like score regression and similarity measurement. Similarly, Siamese-Difference neural networks enhanced with spatial and channel-wise attention mechanisms have been developed to predict image quality scores [2]. Despite their effectiveness, CNN-based models are limited in their ability to capture global features and are prone to locality bias [9].

To address this limitation, Vision Transformers (ViT) [7] were introduced, leveraging the capabilities of Transformers to capture global dependencies in visual data. These have achieved significant advancements across various computer vision tasks. Specifically for IQA, Shi et al. [19] utilized Transformers to encode features from distorted images at three different scales, addressing the challenge of variable image sizes. However, in practical applications such as medical imaging, obtaining reference images is often difficult, underscoring the importance of Non-Reference IQA (NR-IQA), also referred to as Blind Image Quality Assessment (BIQA).

2.2 Non-reference Image Quality Assessment (NR-IQA)

NR-IQA focuses on evaluating image quality without relying on a reference image, which presents unique challenges. To overcome these, researchers have explored diverse strategies. For instance, Ma et al. [16] developed a multi-stage network for classifying distortions and predicting quality scores. Hallucinated-IQA [14] proposed an innovative approach using generative adversarial networks to generate hallucinated reference information paired with distorted images. Zhu et al. [22] utilized meta-learning to capture shared prior knowledge across various distortion types, while Su et al. [22] employed deep models to extract content features at multiple scales for quality prediction.

Hyper-IQA [22] introduced a dual-feature strategy by dividing image features into low-level and high-level categories, transforming the latter to guide the former. Li et al. [15] proposed an unsupervised deep clustering technique for NR-IQA, while Kong et al. [13] developed metrics tailored for assessing image and video denoising algorithms. To address the challenge of small IQA datasets,

Liu et al. [15] used a Siamese Network to rank images by quality, training the network with synthetically generated distortions.

The key difficulty in NR-IQA lies in defining appropriate metrics to evaluate image quality in specific contexts and conditions, which requires identifying the most salient quality-related features. For gastroscopy applications, image quality varies considerably across regions due to factors like lighting and camera motion. As a result, applying a uniform IQA model to an entire image may not yield optimal results, necessitating tailored approaches that account for these variations.

3 Methods

Our implementation approach revolves around assessing the quality of each frame as a classification problem. However, it's important to note that within each frame, the quality of specific image areas can vary significantly, making it challenging to evaluate the overall quality of the entire frame. To address this issue, rather than subjecting the entire image to the model, we adopt a strategy of breaking down the image into smaller patches, each with a size of 128×128 pixels. Subsequently, we perform classification on each of these patches, and the results are then aggregated to form a final quality assessment for the entire image frame. Each image frame is divided into 20 consecutive image patches. Every image patch is classified into one of four groups based on their characteristics, as mentioned above. These individual patch-based assessments are then aggregated to determine the overall quality of the frame, categorized into one of five classes: Bad, Poor, Fair, Good, and Excellent.

3.1 Patch-base Classification Models

Patch-based classification model: Several factors can significantly impact or degrade image quality, often contingent upon the surrounding environment. In the realm of gastroscopy, as per the insights provided by medical professionals, the quality of each frame is predominantly influenced by four key factors: Brightness, Darkness, Motion blur, and High quality. Consequently, patches are categorized into four primary groups: Brightness (Fig. 1(a)): This is attributed to the reflection of gastric juice and the camera's light intensity. Darkness (Fig. 1(b)): Occurs when lighting cannot be uniformly distributed throughout the entire scene. Motion blur (Fig. 1(c)): Primarily caused by the relative motion of the camera and the stomach wall surface, making it a substantial contributor to endoscopic image quality issues. High quality (Fig. 1(d)): This category represents sharp areas, typically only observable when there is minimal relative camera motion and stomach surface movement.

To evaluate the quality of individual image patches, we propose a Convolutional Neural Network (CNN)-based model (Fig. 2). CNNs are well-suited for capturing the local structural information of images by applying convolutions with small filters. As a result, different layers of the network extract features

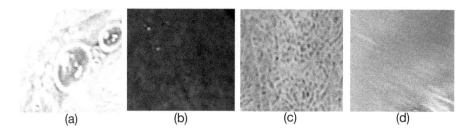

Fig. 1. The key feature classes affecting NBI endoscopic image quality: (a) Brightness; (b) Darkness; (c) Motion blur; (d) High quality.

with varying levels of semantic abstraction, with deeper layers focusing on more complex and intricate details. However, as CNNs become deeper, they may suffer from vanishing gradient issues, which can lead to a significant drop in performance during training [8]. To address this challenge, Kaiming He et al. introduced Residual Networks (ResNet), a robust architecture widely used in computer vision tasks. ResNet enables the efficient training of very deep networks, comprising hundreds or even thousands of layers, by incorporating shortcuts or skip connections that bypass one or more layers [23]. These connections help maintain gradient flow and prevent degradation in performance. The classification of image quality depends on the extraction of both low-level and high-level features, as highlighted in [7]. This means that different types of distortions may be represented in varying ways across the layers of a deep learning network (Fig. 2).

During the model development process, a significant challenge arose due to the high visual similarity between two categories of image patches: darkness and high-quality patches. This similarity made it difficult for the model to accurately distinguish between the two. To address this issue, we drew inspiration from the work in [8], which proposed a feature magnitude loss function to enhance the separability of normal and abnormal video snippets. In addition to the standard loss function used for classification, we incorporated a loss function specifically designed for the deep features of the aforementioned patch types. These deep features were extracted from the fully connected layer of the network, with the feature magnitudes being utilized to enhance discrimination. This feature magnitude loss function was designed to maximize the separability between the darkness and high-quality patches, effectively improving the model's ability to differentiate these visually similar categories.

3.2 Quality Assessment

Building upon the approaches outlined in prior works [4,8,23], this study performs an in-depth analysis of patch quality at a localized level. After evaluating the quality of individual patches within a frame, a comprehensive global assessment is conducted by aggregating the patch-level quality scores. This process enables the classification of frame quality into five categories: "Bad," "Poor,"

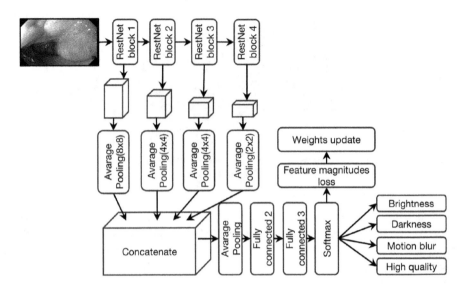

Fig. 2. The proposed model architecture for endoscope image patch quality classification.

"Fair," "Good," and "Excellent." Analysis of frames deemed "Good" or "Excellent" by medical experts revealed a tendency for high-quality patches to cluster together in horizontal or vertical alignments, forming regions dense in diagnostic information. To capture this phenomenon, a Breadth-first search algorithm was employed to calculate frame quality based on the percentage of adjacent high-quality patches. Simultaneously, the proportion of other patch types was calculated by dividing the count of each type by the total number of patches in the frame. Frames categorized as "Bad" or "Poor" often had a high proportion of motion blur patches, typically caused by rapid camera movement, which obscured essential diagnostic details.

Frames classified as "Fair" generally exhibited minimal motion and fewer blurred patches. However, uneven lighting in these frames often resulted in dominance by brightness and darkness patches, leaving only small regions of high-quality patches. The quality assessment criteria are defined as follows: frames with more than 45% blurred patches are labeled "Bad," while those with a blur rate between 35% and 45% are categorized as "Poor." "Fair" frames, which are considered to have acceptable quality, have fewer than 35% blurred patches and a low proportion of high-quality patches (less than 35%). This condition typically occurs in frames with limited camera movement and a small number of high-quality regions suitable for medical observation. Frames with 35% to 55% high-quality patches are labeled "Good," while those exceeding 55% are classified as "Excellent."

Figure 3 provides an overview of the distribution of patch types, shown in blue bars. The training dataset, consisting of 1,657 images, displayed a notable imbalance, with high-quality patches outnumbering darkness patches by a factor of six and brightness patches by a factor of twelve. To address this imbalance, data augmentation techniques were applied, including geometric transformations (e.g., rotation, flipping, cropping, stretching) and intensity adjustments (e.g., gamma correction, contrast modifications). After applying these methods, the input data was normalized to the range (0,1) and subsequently transformed back to a standard scale with mean values of [0.485, 0.456, 0.406] and standard deviations of [0.229, 0.224, 0.225]. These augmentation strategies effectively balanced the patch-type distribution, as demonstrated by the orange bars in Fig. 3.

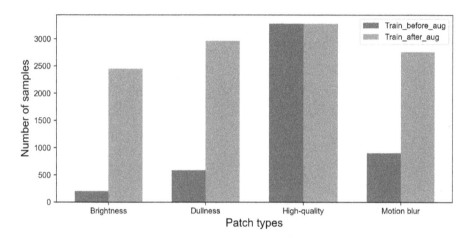

Fig. 3. The distribution of each patch type before and after augmentation Techniques.

4 Results

During the training phase, the Adam optimizer was employed with a learning rate of 1e-4 and a weight decay of 5e-3. A batch size of 32 was utilized to balance computational efficiency and model performance. To improve the model's ability to escape local optima, the Cosine Annealing Restart strategy was applied for learning rate scheduling. For the patch classifier, the Cross-Entropy loss function was adopted, with hyperparameters $\alpha = 0.2$ and a margin value of $m = 15$, aligning with the feature magnitude learning framework. Standard metrics such as accuracy, precision, recall, and F1-score were used to evaluate model performance.

Figure 4 compares the extracted features from the proposed model, which integrates multiple feature layers and feature magnitude loss, with those from a baseline model that utilizes a basic CNN. The results illustrate that the proposed approach achieves better class separation, particularly in distinguishing high-quality patches from darkness patches. This demonstrates the effectiveness of the proposed pipeline in enhancing feature discrimination. Figure 5 shows two test results from a real-world environment. For images labeled as 'Fair,' the majority are composed of brightness and darkness patches, with only a small

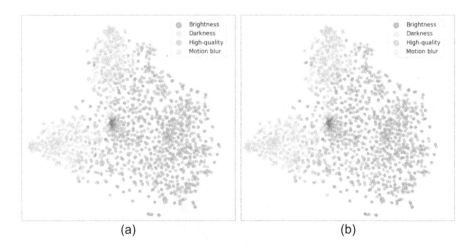

Fig. 4. t-SNE plots of patch-based classification: (a) Baseline model; (b) Proposed model.

number of high-quality patches present. As seen in Fig. 5(a), 25% of the patches are part of adjacent high-quality regions, while brightness and darkness patches account for 15% and 55%, respectively. In contrast, images categorized as 'Good' quality exhibit very few motion-blur patches, with high-quality patches being the dominant feature. Notably, in Fig. 5(b), representing 'Excellent' quality images, more than 60% of the patches consist of adjacent high-quality regions. These observations suggest that the model demonstrates strong performance in distinguishing between high and low-quality images. Figure 6 illustrates the prediction outcomes of the proposed model. The model performed optimally when predicting a single brightness patch as high quality and classifying three motion-

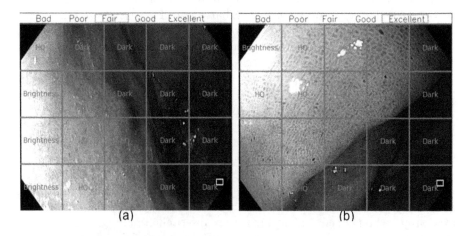

Fig. 5. Image quality assessment results: (a) Fair; (b) Excellent

blur patches as brightness. Nevertheless, the model continues to face challenges in accurately classifying darkness and high-quality patches. Despite these difficulties, incorporating feature magnitude significantly improved performance by reducing the number of misclassified patches from 23 to 13.

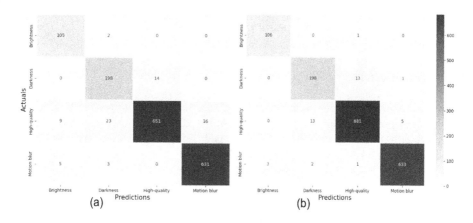

Fig. 6. Confusion matrixes of model

Table 1 summarizes the performance metrics, including Precision, Recall, and F1 score for each patch type. Data imbalance was partially addressed through the application of various data augmentation techniques, leading to notable improvements in the precision of both brightness and darkness patches, with values reaching 97.25% and 92.96%, respectively. This improvement also resulted in corresponding enhancements to the F1-score, achieving 98.15% for brightness patches and 93.18% for darkness patches, highlighting the importance of numerical balance among patch categories.

Moreover, the introduction of the feature magnitude loss function reduced the misclassification between high-quality and darkness patches, improving the recall of high-quality patches to 97.42%. The proposed model also achieved an overall accuracy of 97.70%, representing a 2.00% increase over the baseline model. These results collectively demonstrate that the integration of these strategies significantly enhanced the performance of the patch-based classification model across multiple evaluation metrics.

We evaluated storage savings using two videos captured by Endoscopy Cameras through the image quality assessment (IQA) module. The results demonstrated storage savings between 57.66% and 79.90% for the first video and between 81.64% and 89.90% for the second video, depending on the chosen quality threshold. These findings highlight the IQA module's effectiveness in optimizing storage by significantly reducing the amount of required space. Additionally, the results emphasize the module's flexibility, allowing users to adjust storage settings based on specific needs or different use-case scenarios.

Table 1. Performance of model

Classes	Precision	Recall	F1-score
Brightness patches	97.25	99.07	98.15
Darkness patches	92.96	93.40	93.18
Motion blur patches	99.06	99.06	99.06
High-quality patches	97.84	97.42	97.63

5 Conclusion

Robust endoscopic image quality control in gastroscopy optimizes medical imaging data management and contributes to improved patient outcomes. By excluding suboptimal images, the proposed approach minimizes storage requirements, enhances the identification of diagnostically critical frames, and streamlines the review process. This, in turn, supports better treatment decisions. Furthermore, the proposed framework offers valuable assistance in the training and evaluation of novice surgeons and technicians.

This study introduced a two-stage image quality assessment (IQA) framework based on deep learning. The first stage involves segmenting images into non-overlapping patches and classifying them into distinct quality categories using a multi-layer convolutional neural network (CNN). The second stage determines the overall image quality by aggregating statistical data from these classified patches. To optimize performance, we incorporated feature magnitude to enhance the discrimination of patch types and applied an efficient inference method to expedite processing. The proposed approach achieved a patch classification accuracy of nearly 98%, with favorable feedback from medical professionals.

Nevertheless, the framework does have some limitations. The use of fixed patch sizes and non-overlapping divisions can lead to ambiguities, particularly when patches exhibit mixed quality traits, such as being simultaneously high-quality and dark. Additionally, the framework's validation has relied on feedback from a limited number of medical professionals, which may affect its generalizability in broader clinical settings. Future research will aim to involve a larger and more diverse group of medical experts to address these limitations, validate the framework further, and enhance its practical application.

References

1. Ahn, S., Choi, Y., Yoon, K.: Deep learning-based distortion sensitivity prediction for full reference image quality assessment. In: IEEE Conference on Computer Vision and Pattern Recognition Workshops, pp. 344–353 (2021)
2. Ayyoubzadeh, S., Royat, A.: (asna) an attention based siamese-difference neural network with surrogate ranking loss function for perceptual image quality assessment. In: IEEE Conference on Computer Vision and Pattern Recognition Workshops, pp. 388–397 (2021)

3. Aziz, I., Palsson, O., Tornblom, H., et al.: The prevalence and impact of overlapping rome iv-diagnosed functional gastrointestinal disorders on somatization, quality of life, and healthcare utilization: a cross-sectional general population study in three countries. Am. J. Gastroenterol. **113**, 86–96 (2018)
4. Bosse, S., Maniry, D., Müller, K.R., Wiegand, T., Samek, W.: Deep neural networks for no-reference and full-reference image quality assessment. IEEE Trans. Image Process. **27**(1), 206–219 (2017)
5. Ding, K., Ma, K., Wang, S., Simoncelli, E.: Image quality assessment: unifying structure and texture similarity. IEEE Trans. Pattern Anal. Mach. Intell. (2020)
6. Dinis-Ribeiro, M., da Costa-Pereira, A., Lopes, C., et al.: Magnification chromoendoscopy for the diagnosis of gastric intestinal metaplasia and dysplasia. Gastrointest Endosc (2003)
7. Dosovitskiy, A., Beyer, L., Kolesnikov, A., et al.: An image is worth 16x16 words: Transformers for image recognition at scale. arXiv preprint arXiv:2010.11929 (2020)
8. Gao, F., Wang, Y., Li, P., et al.: Deepsim: deep similarity for image quality assessment. Neurocomputing **257**, 104–114 (2017)
9. Golestaneh, S.A., Dadsetan, S., Kitani, K.M.: No-reference image quality assessment via transformers, relative ranking, and self-consistency. In: Proceedings of the IEEE/CVF Winter Conference on Applications of Computer Vision (2022)
10. Gono, K., Obi, T., Yamaguchi, M., et al.: Appearance of enhanced tissue features in narrow-band endoscopic imaging. J. Biomed. Opt. **9**(3), 568–577 (2004)
11. Jones, M., Crowell, M., Olden, K., Creed, F.: Functional gastrointestinal disorders: an update for the psychiatrist. Psychosomatics **48**, 93–102 (2007)
12. Kim, G.H., et al.: Effort to increase image quality during endoscopy: the role of pronase. National Library of Medicine (2016)
13. Kong, X., Yang, Q.: No-reference image quality assessment for image autodenoising. Int. J. Comput. Vis. **126**, 537–549 (2018)
14. Lin, K.Y., Wang, G.: Hallucinated-iqa: no-reference image quality assessment via adversarial learning. In: Proceedings of the IEEE Conference on Computer Vision and Pattern Recognition, pp. 732–741 (2018)
15. Liu, X., van de Weijer, J., Bagdanov, A.D.: Rankiqa: learning from rankings for no-reference image quality assessment. In: Proceedings of the IEEE International Conference on Computer Vision (ICCV), pp. 1040–1049 (2017)
16. Ma, K., Liu, W., Zhang, K., et al.: End-to-end blind image quality assessment using deep neural networks. IEEE Trans. Image Process. **27**(3), 1202–1213 (2017)
17. Mahon, J., Lifschitz, C., Ludwig, T., et al.: The costs of functional gastrointestinal disorders and related signs and symptoms in infants: a systematic literature review and cost calculation for england. BMJ Open **7**, e015594 (2017)
18. Petersen, M., Schroder, A., Jorgensen, T., et al.: Irritable bowel, chronic widespread pain, chronic fatigue and related syndromes are prevalent and highly overlapping in the general population: Danfund. Sci. Rep. **10**, 3273 (2020)
19. Shi, J., Gao, P., Qin, J.: Transformer-based no-reference image quality assessment via supervised contrastive learning. In: Proceedings of the AAAI Conference on Artificial Intelligence, vol. 38, pp. 4829–4837 (2024)
20. Sperber, A., Bangdiwala, S., Drossman, D., et al.: Worldwide prevalence and burden of functional gastrointestinal disorders, results of rome foundation global study. Gastroenterology (2020)
21. Spiegel, B., Harris, L., Lucak, S., et al.: Developing valid and reliable health utilities in irritable bowel syndrome: results from the ibs proof cohort. Am. J. Gastroenterol. **104**, 1984–1991 (2009)

22. Su, S., Yan, Q., Zhu, Y., et al.: Blindly assess image quality in the wild guided by a self-adaptive hyper network. In: Proceedings of the IEEE Conference on Computer Vision and Pattern Recognition, pp. 3667–3676 (2020)
23. Zhang, R., Isola, P., Efros, A.A., Shechtman, E., Wang, O.: The unreasonable effectiveness of deep features as a perceptual metric. In: Proceedings of the IEEE Conference on Computer Vision and Pattern Recognition, pp. 586–595 (2018)

Does Varied Developer Interactions Cause Bugs to Be Resolved Faster? A Study of Open Source Software Ecosystems

Reshma Roychoudhuri[✉], Subhajit Datta, and Subhashis Majumder

Heritage Institute of Technology, Kolkata, India
reshma.roychoudhuri@gmail.com, subhajit.datta@acm.org,
subhashis.majumder@heritageit.edu
https://www.heritageit.edu/

Abstract. Open-source software systems have proliferated over the past few decades, with increasing penetration across domains. The wide availability of development data from such systems has led to studies on various aspects of the software development life cycle. A large majority of these studies conduct correlational analysis of historical data to identify associations between variables of interest. Due to their correlational nature, such studies cannot isolate causal effects on key software engineering outcomes. In this paper, we investigate how the uniformity of developer interaction affects bug resolution time. In large and complex ecosystems, developer interaction is influenced by the experience levels of participating developers. Accordingly, we classify developers on their co-commenting experience levels and identify different types of interactions across levels. Using the causal inference technique, inverse probability of treatment weighting (IPTW), and real-world data from two large-scale software development ecosystems, we establish a causal relationship between the distribution of developer co-commenting activities across multiple categories and bug resolution times. We find consistent evidence across both datasets that increasing uniformity of interaction distribution leads to increasing bug resolution time up to a limit, beyond which the effect is reversed. Our results can inform team assembly and governance, and guide individual developers in their choice of interactions with peers.

Keywords: Software development · Bugs resolution · Causal inference · IPTW

1 Introduction and Motivation

Almost every aspect of life and society, from healthcare to transportation, finance, education, entertainment, is now impacted by software [22]. Large software development ecosystems have processes to deal with bugs and their resolution so that cost, time, and quality are not adversely impacted. In large and complex software systems, reducing the number of bugs, as well their resolution times is an area of active research. This paper aims to study a key aspect of software development - interaction among developers - and its impact on bug resolution time.

Engineering disciplines such as mechanical, electrical, chemical etc. are underpinned by laws of physics and chemistry. However, laws governing software development are yet to be established. A key component in the formulation of laws is the identification of causal relations. Most existing studies in software development are correlational in nature. In many such cases, correlation may not necessarily imply causation. A previous study pointed to an interesting dynamic between the interaction among developers and bug resolution time, indicating that *more diverse* types of interactions among developers associated with *increased* bug resolution time [23].

The counter-intuitive nature of the outcome and the dearth of causal studies in software development motivated us to explore the causal relationship between our variables of interest.

One of the most effective methods to establish causation is a randomized control trial (RCT). RCT works on the principle of the formation of two groups: one that receives an intervention – *treatment* group – and another that does not – *control* group. To eliminate selection bias, study subjects are randomly placed in treatment and control groups. In a real-world software development scenario, it is not feasible to execute a study design based on RCT, as intervention in the form of resolution effort by developers can not be randomly withheld from some bugs (who happen to be in the control group), while made available to while made available to other bugs (who happen to be in the treatment group). Thus, in this work we use an established statistical technique that examines historical data to infer causal effects between variables of interest.

Our paper studies the bug resolution data from two large open-source software development ecosystems - Eclipse[1], which is a popular integrated development platform, and OpenStack[2], a popular cloud-computing platform. We delve deep into communication among the developers in the bug resolution system via co-commenting activities and conclude that these communications are not all alike and could be divided into multiple categories. We then investigate our research question -

Is there any causal relationship between the distribution of developer co-commenting activities across multiple categories and bug resolution time?

2 Methodology

In this section, we elaborate on the steps that were followed in implementing this study. The first step is to identify the different levels in which the developers would be classified according to the number of comments they posted in the bug resolution system. Then we describe the dynamic process of identification of the

---

[1] https://www.eclipse.org/.
[2] https://www.openstack.org/.

level of the developer and identification of the interaction category. Once the different interaction categories are in place, we compute the uniformity of distribution of developer interactions across multiple categories. We then describe our datasets and end this section by elucidating our hypotheses.

2.1 Developer Categorisation

The number of comments posted by a developer is often an indicator of the time the developer has engaged with the bug resolution system, with more comments possibly indicating more time and engagement. More comments posted imply greater time expended in the bug resolution system and thus lead to a better understanding and more experience of how the system works. The number of comments made is a metric that has been used to quantify developer contribution and experience in prior studies as well [4,8]. For our study, we have segregated developers based on their *co-commenting engagement* (CCE), into four *levels - 1, 2, 3, 4*. To ascertain the comment count that marks the threshold of each CCE level, we first listed the developers in each dataset in descending order of the number of comments they made. It was found that almost 80% of the comments, in each dataset, were contributed by developers who belonged in the top 10%. Thus, the comment count by the uppermost 10% was considered and was divided into four quartiles. The boundary of each quartile marked the threshold of a developer CCE level. For example, for the Eclipse dataset, developers with the number of comments between one and 33 belong to CCE *level 1*, between 34 and 61 belong to CCE *level 2*, between 62 and 184 belong to CCE *level 3*, and 185 and more belong to CCE *level 4*. The corresponding numbers for OpenStack datasets are:- one to 139 comments for CCE *level 1*, 140 to 230 comments for CCE *level 2*, 231 to 475 comments for CCE *level 3*, 476 and above comments for CCE *level 4*.

All developers start at CCE level one, then with time as they log more comments, they gradually move to other CCE levels. The process in which this dynamic change of developer CCE level is recorded and used to categorize different types of interactions is described in the next section.

2.2 Developer Co-commenting Interaction Identification

Developer co-commenting interactions (DCI) are categorized in our study based on two factors:- (i) the CCE level of the participating developers and, (ii) the prior co-commenting experience of the participating developers. When two developers co-comment for the first time on a bug they get to know the work methods of each other. When they co-comment with each other on other bugs, the interaction dynamics for such subsequent times usually differ from that of the first time since the participating developers are now familiar with each other's working methods. In the algorithm given below, we describe the strategy used to process the data extracted from the bug resolution to ascertain the various interaction categories for every bug. We take as input a pre-processed list that contains the bug ID, the ID of the developer who has commented on the bug, and the comment posting time. Each row of this preprocessed list is processed to generate the output, a network of developers, connected on the basis of their co-commenting activity. The construction of the co-commenting network is explained with the help of example data and diagram in Fig. 1.

With four levels of developer co-commenting experience and two identifiers (*first* and *repeat*) to track prior co-commenting interactions among developers, our study generates 20 $(2(C(4,2) + C(4,1)) = 2(6+4) = 20)$ different DCI categories for each dataset. For example, a first co-commenting experience between two developers one with CCE level 1 and another CCE level 2 will be labeled as *L1L2F*; a repeat co-commenting experience between two developers one with CCE level 3 and another CCE level 4 will be labeled as *L3L4R*.

Algorithm to identify developer co-commenting interaction categories

---

1: **INPUT:** Pre-processed list containing the bug ID, the ID of the developer who has commented on the bug, and the comment posting time.
2: **OUTPUT:** Developer co-commenting categories.
3: **for** Every row of the pre-processed list **do**
4:     Extract *developer_id* and *bug_id*
5:     **if** *developer_id* commenting for the first time **then**
6:         set *developer_comment_count* to 1
7:         set *experience_level* of *developer_id* to *level_1*
8:         add *developer_id* to the *network*
9:         **if** this *bug_id* has been commented on before **then**
10:             find out *prev_developer(s)* who has commented on this bug
11:             draw an edge between current *developer_id* and each *prev_developer(s)*
12:             mark interaction as *first* and record the CCE level of the edge
13:         **end if**
14:     **else**
15:         increase *developer_comment_count* by 1
16:         record *experience_level* of *developer_id* to appropriate level
17:         **if** this *bug_id* has been commented on before **then**
18:             find out *prev_developer(s)* who has commented on this bug
19:             **if** $\nexists$ edge between *developer_id* and *prev_developer(s)* **then**
20:                 draw edge between *developer_id* and each *prev_developer(s)*
21:                 mark interaction as *first* and record the CCE level of edge
22:             **else**
23:                 increase *edge_weight* by 1
24:                 mark interaction as *repeat* and record the CCE level of edge
25:             **end if**
26:         **end if**
27:     **end if**
28: **end for**

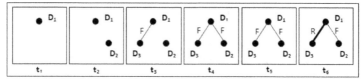

Part A: Sample bug resolution system

Part B: Snapshot at every time-step of the co-commenting network generated by the algorithm while processing each row of the sample bug resolution system given in part A. In time step t_1 and t_2 developers D_1 and D_2 are added to the network. In time-step t_3, D_3 is added to the network and an edge (undirected link) is drawn between D_1 and D_3 as they have co-commented on the same bug B_1. Since this is the first interaction between D_1 and D_3 this edge is labelled as F, signifying first interaction between them. Similarly at time-step t_4 an edge is drawn between D_1 and D_2 and labelled as F. As D_3 is already a part of the network, no new node is added in t_5. At t_6 a new edge is added to the network between D_1 and D_3. Since they already had an edge between them, this edge is marked as R, signifying repeat co-commenting interaction.

Fig. 1. Visualization of the construction of the co-commenting network

2.3 Calculating Uniformity of Developer Interaction Distribution

With 20 different DCI categories in place for each bug, we next seek to investigate how uniformly developer co-commenting interactions are distributed across these categories. For this purpose, we use an established distribution metric, the Gini coefficient [5,20,25]. The Gini coefficient is a measure of inequality and is given as a number that ranges from 0 to 1 with higher numbers denoting a more unequal distribution of an element of interest. Though the Gini coefficient was originally introduced for measures of economic disparity, it has since been used in a variety of fields, including software engineering [5,20,25]. That Gini coefficient takes into account the entire set of values and arrives at a single number as the outcome gives a couple of advantages that make the Gini coefficient well-suited for our purpose. We define the Gini coefficient for each bug $Gini(Bug_i)$ to denotes how disparately the developer co-commenting interactions are distributed across the 20 DCI categories for Bug_i. From this measure of inequality, we determine the uniformity of interaction distribution as:

$$InteractionUniformity = 1 - Gini(Bug_i)$$

2.4 Datasets and Hypotheses

We have used the bug resolution data of two large-scale diverse open-source development datasets for our study - Eclipse and OpenStack [15]. While Eclipse is a well-known integrated development environment, OpenStack is a popular infrastructure for cloud computing. Each dataset has multiple attributes to capture the characteristics of a bug, such as - bug ID, description, status, owner, date on which a comment was posted. With 20 different possible DCI categories for every bug, our study aims to investigate the causal relations between the time taken to resolve a bug and the extent to which the developer interactions are uniformly distributed across the DCI categories. With this perspective, we derived the following null hypothesis (H_0) and alternate hypothesis (H_a) from our research question:-

H_0: *Uniformity of distribution of developer co-commenting interactions and bug resolution time are not causally related.*

H_a: *Uniformity of distribution of developer co-commenting interactions and bug resolution time are causally related.*

3 Model Development

In this section, we will describe our model variables and explain the process of causal estimation conducted in our study.

3.1 Model Parameters

We have estimated the causal impact our treatment variable has on our outcome variable in the presence of the control variables (covariates). These covariates have been identified as variables that have the potential to influence the outcome and need to be controlled for to isolate the impact of the treatment on the outcome.

- **Outcome Variable:**
    - *BugResolutionTime*: This is our outcome variable that denotes the time between the first and last comment on a bug. Time taken to resolve a bug is a critical factor that is directly related to the overall project health and outcome [10, 26, 27].

- **Exposure:**
    - *InteractionUniformity*: This variable denotes how uniformly developer interactions are distributed across the various categories of interaction, for every bug. The calculation of this variable is described in Sect. 2.3.

- **Covariates:**
    - *Commenters*: This variable captures the total number of distinct developers who have commented on the bug [9].

- *CommentByOwnerOtherBugs*: This variable aims to capture the overall engagement of the owner of the current bug and denotes the number of comments made on bugs in the bug resolution ecosystem that are not owned by him/her [11,13].
- *CommentByOwnerOwnBugs*: This variable aims to capture the engagement of the owner of the current bug and denotes the number of comments made across all the bugs owned by him/her [11].
- Interaction categories: This denotes a group of variables and represents the 20 categories of interaction identified by our algorithm, for example, L1L2F, L2L3F, L1L3R etc., as introduced in Sect. 2.2.

Construction of DAG: To analyze the correlation among our model variables we have first constructed a directed acyclic graph (DAG), given in Fig. 2. The DAG portrays the relationship between our model variables. The covariates *Commenters*, *CommentsByOwnerOtherBugs*, and *CommentsByOwnerOwnBugs* depicted in the DAG capture the co-commenting activity of the developers and thus influence our interaction category variables. The interaction category variables directly impact both the treatment variable *InteractionUniformity* and the outcome variable *BugResolutionTime*. The directed arrow between the treatment variable and the outcome variable depicts the causal relationship that our study investigates.

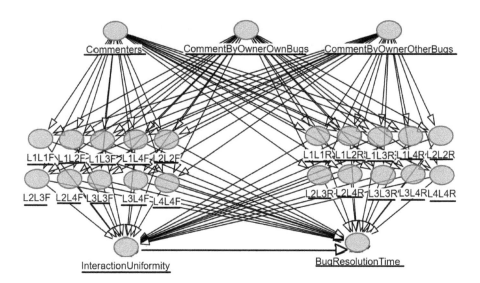

Fig. 2. DAG representing the relationship between our model variables

The DAG constructed is used as an input for the calculation of the Pearson correlation coefficient and the p-value of our model variables for each of the conditional independence relationships that are implied by our model structure. From the Pearson correlation coefficient and *p*-values, we note that the dependencies of our model parameters are not highly correlated and that conditional independence is true for our data to a reasonable extent. The correlation coefficients and *p*-values for both our datasets, are provided in the supplementary materials[3].

3.2 IPTW Estimation

Causal models have a treatment variable and an outcome, where treatment is the variable whose effect is measured on the outcome variable. In our model, the treatment variable is *InteractionUniformity* and the outcome variable is *BugResolutionTime*. To estimate the causal impact of our treatment on the outcome we have used the standard statistical method of *inverse probability of treatment weighting* (IPTW) estimation, which has been found to be more effective than other causal study methods in multiple studies [1,2,6]. IPTW controls for the effect of parameters that have the potential to influence both the treatment and the outcome. Such parameters, known as *confounders*, need to be controlled for to ensure that the true causal effect of the treatment on the outcome can be estimated. IPTW method starts by calculating the probability - or *propensity score* - of a subject being treated given its characteristics. The subjects are then assigned weights based on the inverse of their propensity score. Thus, subjects with a higher probability of receiving treatment are assigned a lower weight, and vice versa. This assignment of weights results in a *pseudo population* where the confounders are evenly distributed into two groups - the exposed group and the unexposed group. With the confounders distributed in these two groups, their impact on the treatment and the outcome are controlled for.

4 Results and Discussion

4.1 Applying IPTW for Causal Inference

IPTW works in two steps. In the first step, IPTW models the treatment to assign weights. In the second step, it uses the weights to model the outcome. Our treatment variable *InteractionUniformity* being continuous in nature, IPTW uses a regression-based approach. Having observed a non-linear relationship between our treatment and outcome variable in the scatterplots[4], we expressed their relationship in the quadratic form $outcome = a(treatment)^2 + b(treatment) + c$, where a, b, and c are constants.

For the models pertaining to each of the two datasets Eclipse and OpenStack, the coefficients, significance levels, and standard errors of the model parameters are given in Table 1, along with the overall model parameters such as number

---

[3] https://bit.ly/3YD8t0A.
[4] https://bit.ly/3YD8t0A.

of data points (N), goodness of fit (R^2), degrees of freedom (Df), Fischer's F-statistics (F), and significance level. We observe that both the models are statistically significant and a majority of the model parameters have a statistically significant relationship with our outcome variable, bug resolution time.

Table 1. Model Details of Eclipse and OpenStack. p-values ≤ 0.001, ≤ 0.01, ≤ 0.05, ≤ 0.1, and ≥ 0.1 are denoted by "****", "***", "**", "*", "+" respectively

Model Parameter	Eclipse Estimate and Significance	Eclipse Standard Error	OpenStack Estimate and Significance	OpenStack Standard Error
Intercept	9.530×10^{-02} ***	6.725×10^{-04}	0.090 ***	6.155×10^{-04}
Commenters	-5.953×10^{-03} ***	8.885×10^{-05}	-0.009 ***	1.59×10^{-04}
CommentByOwnerOtherBugs	-7.125×10^{-06}	1.412×10^{-05}	0.001 ***	3.336×10^{-04}
CommentByOwnerOwnBugs	5.703×10^{-06}	1.407×10^{-05}	-0.003 ***	0.0003305
$L1L1F$	1.298×10^{-02} ***	8.772×10^{-04}	0.017 ***	5.410×10^{-04}
$L1L2F$	3.045×10^{-02} ***	1.049×10^{-03}	0.026 ***	6.313×10^{-04}
$L1L3F$	3.263×10^{-02} ***	9.091×10^{-04}	0.031 ***	6.235×10^{-04}
$L1L4F$	2.904×10^{-02} ***	7.413×10^{-04}	0.031 ***	3.979×10^{-04}
$L2L2F$	9.864×10^{-03} ***	2.762×10^{-03}	0.002	0.002
$L2L3F$	1.902×10^{-02} ***	1.518×10^{-03}	0.019 ***	0.001
$L2L4F$	1.614×10^{-02} ***	1.133×10^{-03}	0.009 ***	0.001
$L3L3F$	1.179×10^{-02} ***	1.693×10^{-03}	0.010	0.001
$L3L4F$	1.549×10^{-02} ***	9.857×10^{-04}	0.008 ***	0.001
$L4L4F$	1.249×10^{-02} ***	1.317×10^{-03}	-0.004 **	0.001
$L1L1R$	1.092×10^{-02} ***	8.498×10^{-04}	0.018 ***	4.685×10^{-04}
$L1L2R$	1.671×10^{-02} ***	7.678×10^{-04}	0.024 ***	4.722×10^{-04}
$L1L3R$	1.767×10^{-02} ***	6.303×10^{-04}	0.033	4.635×10^{-04}
$L1L4R$	1.312×10^{-02} ***	5.287×10^{-04}	0.008	2.865×10^{-04}
$L2L2R$	1.061×10^{-02} ***	1.200×10^{-03}	0.022 ***	0.001
$L2L3R$	2.312×10^{-02} ***	8.091×10^{-04}	0.028 ***	7.365×10^{-04}
$L2L4R$	9.549×10^{-03} ***	3.643×10^{-04}	0.021 ***	3.334×10^{-04}
$L3L3R$	4.694×10^{-03} ***	5.054×10^{-04}	0.021 ***	8.090×10^{-04}
$L3L4R$	7.525×10^{-03} ***	2.764×10^{-04}	0.017	3.190×10^{-04}
$L4L4R$	-3.563×10^{-03} ***	2.117×10^{-04}	0.008	2.935×10^{-04}
Overall Model Parameters	Eclipse		OpenStack	
N	13248		25531	
R^2	0.836		0.828	
Df	13222		25505	
F	2720		4932	
Significance level	$p \leq 2.210^{-16}$		$p \leq 2.210^{-16}$	

For each dataset, the coefficients, significance levels, and standard errors of the quadratic term, linear term, and intercept are given in Table 2. We see that for both Eclipse and OpenStack, the coefficient of the linear term (2498151 and 89273.7 respectively) and the coefficient of the quadratic term (−4030439 and −208086.9 respectively), have a statistically significant relationship with the outcome variable. We can thus reject our null hypothesis in favor of our alternate hypothesis. The plots representing the relationship between our treatment and outcome variable are available in the supplementary materials[5]. We observe a

---

[5] https://bit.ly/3YD8t0A.

Table 2. Treatment and outcome of Eclipse, and OpenStack. p-values ≤ 0.001, ≤ 0.01, ≤ 0.05, ≤ 0.1, and ≥ 0.1 are denoted by "****", "***", "**", "*", "+" respectively

	Eclipse Estimate and Significance level	Eclipse Standard Error	OpenStack Estimate and Significance level	OpenStack Standard Error
Intercept	−305421 **	115940	−6696.4 ***	284.8
Coefficient of x	2498151 ***	719855	89273.7 ***	2322.6
Coefficient of x^2	−4030439 ***	1028125	−208086.9 ***	4443.4

generally concave nature of the relationship for both datasets. This implies that as uniformity of distribution of co-communication interaction across various categories increases, the time taken to resolve a bug too increases, but only up to a certain point. Beyond that, more uniformity reduces the bug resolution time. The degree of concavity is more pronounced for Eclipse than OpenStack. The OpenStack dataset has more data points than Eclipse, and that can be a reason for lesser pronounced nature of the curve.

4.2 Importance of Our Study

In the context of the research question introduced in Sect. 1, our results indicate that there is a causal relationship between the distribution of developer co-commenting activities across multiple categories, and bug resolution time. This provides critical insight that developer co-commenting interaction has the potential to affect a key software outcome. Optimizing bug resolution time has been looked into by researchers and software stakeholders since it has an impact on overall project cost and quality. Hence our results are useful to industry and academic stakeholders. In particular, they provide insights to organizations and managers on team composition. Our result also encourage diverse team composition that would lead to communication among developers with varied experience levels. For individual developers, our results encourage seeking out collaborators beyond a known circle of peers.

5 Threats to Validity and Future Work

In this section we aim to address the threats arising from *construct validity*, *internal validity*, *external validity*, and *reliability*.

Construct validity addresses threats arising from the measurement of the variables. Some of our model variables (*Commenters*, *CommentByOwnerOtherBugs*, and *CommentByOwnerOwnBugs*) are extracted directly from the dataset. The model variables pertaining to the developer co-commenting interaction categories are measured by the systematic processing of the datasets using the steps mentioned in Sect. 2.2. The steps ensure that the variables are measured consistently across the two datasets. The choice of Gini coefficient as a measure of uniformity was motivated by its wide acceptance in various disciplines, along with its closer relevance to our study than other measures such as Hoover index[6] or Palma ratio[7]. Thus threats to **construct validity** are not present to a notable extent in this study.

We have used historical data from two large open-source software development ecosystems that are available in the public domain. These datasets were collected, curated, and shared for research [15,24]. The historical nature of the data ensures there are no threats to maturity or mortality and does not introduce any systemic error or bias that could pose a threat to **internal validity**.

Threats to **external validity** arise from the generalizability of a study's results. To mitigate such threats we have conducted our study on two datasets. Both our datasets are from open-source systems, as proprietary datasets are not available in the public domain. Even as our results are not fully generalizable yet, we believe they present helpful insights for researchers and practitioners.

Reliability is concerned with the replicability of a study's results. Towards that end, we have shared the replication package of our work[8].

In our **future work** we seek to replicate the results of this study on additional datasets. We also plan to investigate how other causal inference techniques can be used to examine factors affecting software engineering outcomes.

6   Related Work

Developers form a critical component of large-scale software development ecosystems [12]. Various factors related to developers have the potential to impact the schedule, cost, and quality of software systems in multiple ways [14,16]. Developer inter-communication plays a critical role in influencing outcomes of software projects [8].

While developers communicate throughout the software development life cycle, bug resolution is a phase when such interaction is most intense [19,29]. This is evident from the co-commenting activities between developers during bug resolution. Time to resolve bugs is an important software development outcome. Significant research has been dedicated to investigating factors that affect bug resolution time [18,28]. Most studies in this area are correlational in nature.

A survey on causal studies in software engineering yielded papers mostly on testing and fault localization [3,7,17,21]. Our work aims to complement such existing studies by looking into the causal impact of a critical dynamic of developer communications on bug resolution times.

7   Summary and Conclusions

Developer interaction plays an important role in influencing the outcomes of large-scale software development. In this study, we categorize developer interaction based on their co-commenting in the bug resolution process. Using the

---

[6] https://en.wikipedia.org/wiki/Hoover_index.
[7] https://views-voices.oxfam.org.uk/2023/07/what-is-palma-ratio-inequality/.
[8] https://bit.ly/4Oo6zT3.

inverse probability of treatment weighting (IPTW) technique and data from two large-scale software development ecosystems – Eclipse and OpenStack, we investigate the causal relationship between the distribution of developer co- commenting activities across multiple categories and bug resolution time. Our results can inform decisions at the individual, team, and organizational levels towards more effective development outcomes. To the best of our knowledge, this is one of the pioneering studies identifying causal effects on bug resolution times.

References

1. Austin, P.C.: The performance of different propensity-score methods for estimating differences in proportions (risk differences or absolute risk reductions) in observational studies. Stat. Med. **29**(20), 2137–2148 (2010)
2. Austin, P.C., Stuart, E.A.: Moving towards best practice when using inverse probability of treatment weighting (iptw) using the propensity score to estimate causal treatment effects in observational studies. Stat. Med. **34**(28), 3661–3679 (2015)
3. Baah, G.K., Podgurski, A., Harrold, M.J.: Mitigating the confounding effects of program dependences for effective fault localization. In: Proceedings of the 19th ACM SIGSOFT Symposium and the 13th European Conference on Foundations of Software Engineering, pp. 146–156 (2011)
4. Brasil-Silva, R., Siqueira, F.L.: Metrics to quantify software developer experience: a systematic mapping. In: Proceedings of the 37th ACM/SIGAPP Symposium on Applied Computing, pp. 1562–1569 (2022)
5. Chełkowski, T., Gloor, P., Jemielniak, D.: Inequalities in open source software development: analysis of contributor's commits in apache software foundation projects. PLoS ONE **11**(4), e0152976 (2016)
6. Chesnaye, N.C., et al.: An introduction to inverse probability of treatment weighting in observational research. Clin. Kidney J. **15**(1), 14–20 (2022)
7. Clark, A.G., et al.: Testing causality in scientific modelling software. arXiv preprint arXiv:2209.00357 (2022)
8. Datta, S., Roychoudhuri, R., Majumder, S.: Understanding the relation between repeat developer interactions and bug resolution times in large open source ecosystems: a multisystem study. J. Softw. Evolut. Process **33**(4) (Apr 2021). https://doi.org/10.1002/smr.2317, https://onlinelibrary.wiley.com/doi/10.1002/smr.2317
9. Datta, S., Sarkar, P., Das, S., Sreshtha, S., Lade, P., Majumder, S.: *How many eyeballs does a bug need?* an empirical validation of linus' law. In: Cantone, G., Marchesi, M. (eds.) XP 2014. LNBIP, vol. 179, pp. 242–250. Springer, Cham (2014). https://doi.org/10.1007/978-3-319-06862-6_17
10. Eiroa-Lledo, E., Ali, R.H., Pinto, G., Anderson, J., Linstead, E.: Large-scale identification and analysis of factors impacting simple bug resolution times in open source software repositories. Appli. Sci. **13**(5), 3150 (Feb 2023). https://doi.org/10.3390/app13053150, https://www.mdpi.com/2076-3417/13/5/3150
11. Espinosa, J.A., Slaughter, S.A., Kraut, R.E., Herbsleb, J.D.: Familiarity, complexity, and team performance in geographically distributed software development. Organizat. Sci. **18**(4), 613–630 (Jul 2007). https://doi.org/10.1287/orsc.1070.0297, http://orgsci.journal.informs.org/content/18/4/613
12. Fahmy, S., Deraman, A., Yahaya, J.H., Ngah, A., Salman, F.A.: A model for people-centric software configuration management. J. Telecommun. Electr. Comput. Eng. (JTEC) **9**(3-5), 7–13 (2017)

13. Fong Boh, W., Slaughter, S.A., Espinosa, J.A.: Learning from experience in software development: a multilevel analysis. Manage. Sci. **53**(8), 1315–1331 (Aug 2007). https://doi.org/10.1287/mnsc.1060.0687
14. Girardi, D., Lanubile, F., Novielli, N., Serebrenik, A.: Emotions and perceived productivity of software developers at the workplace. IEEE Trans. Software Eng. **48**(9), 3326–3341 (2021)
15. Gonzalez-Barahona, J.M., Robles, G., Izquierdo-Cortazar, D.: The MetricsGrimoire database collection. In: 2015 IEEE/ACM 12th Working Conference on Mining Software Repositories, pp. 478–481. IEEE, Florence, Italy (May 2015).https://doi.org/10.1109/MSR.2015.68, http://ieeexplore.ieee.org/document/7180122/
16. Hirao, T., Kula, R.G., Ihara, A., Matsumoto, K.: Understanding developer commenting in code reviews. IEICE Trans. Inf. Syst. **102**(12), 2423–2432 (2019)
17. Küçük, Y., Henderson, T.A., Podgurski, A.: Improving fault localization by integrating value and predicate based causal inference techniques. In: 2021 IEEE/ACM 43rd International Conference on Software Engineering (ICSE), pp. 649–660. IEEE (2021)
18. Lee, Y., Lee, S., Lee, C.G., Yeom, I., Woo, H.: Continual prediction of bug-fix time using deep learning-based activity stream embedding. IEEE Access **8**, 10503–10515 (2020)
19. Mani, S., Nagar, S., Mukherjee, D., Narayanam, R., Sinha, V.S., Nanavati, A.A.: Bug resolution catalysts: identifying essential non-committers from bug repositories. In: 2013 10th Working Conference on Mining Software Repositories (MSR), pp. 193–202. IEEE (2013)
20. Masuda, A., Matsuodani, T., Tsuda, K.: Team activities measurement method for open source software development using the gini coefficient. In: 2019 IEEE International Conference on Software Testing, Verification and Validation Workshops (ICSTW), pp. 140–147. IEEE (2019)
21. Oh, S., Lee, S., Yoo, S.: Effectively sampling higher order mutants using causal effect. In: 2021 IEEE International Conference on Software Testing, Verification and Validation Workshops (ICSTW), pp. 19–24. IEEE (2021)
22. Pontin, J.: The problem with programming. https://www.technologyreview.com/2006/11/28/227399/the-problem-with-programming/ Accessed 11 July 2023 (2023)
23. Roychoudhuri, R., Datta, S., Majumder, S.: More equal than others? parity in developer interaction and its relation to bug resolution time. Innovations Syst. Softw. Eng., 1–13 (2024)
24. Shihab, E., Kamei, Y., Bhattacharya, P.: Mining challenge 2012: the Android platform. In: 2012 9th IEEE Working Conference on Mining Software Repositories (MSR), pp. 112–115 (2012). https://doi.org/10.1109/MSR.2012.6224307, iSSN: 2160-1860
25. Vasa, R., Lumpe, M., Branch, P., Nierstrasz, O.: Comparative analysis of evolving software systems using the gini coefficient. In: 2009 IEEE International Conference on Software Maintenance, pp. 179–188. IEEE (2009)
26. Weiss, C., Premraj, R., Zimmermann, T., Zeller, A.: How long will it take to fix this bug? In: Fourth International Workshop on Mining Software Repositories (MSR 2007: ICSE Workshops 2007), Minneapolis, MN.IEEE (May 2007). https://doi.org/10.1109/MSR.2007.13, https://ieeexplore.ieee.org/document/4228638/
27. Zhang, F., Khomh, F., Zou, Y., Hassan, A.E.: An empirical study on factors impacting bug fixing time. In: 2012 19th Working Conference on Reverse Engineering, pp. 225–234. IEEE, Kingston, ON, Canada (Oct 2012). https://doi.org/10.1109/WCRE.2012.32, http://ieeexplore.ieee.org/document/6385118/

28. Zhang, T., Jiang, H., Luo, X., Chan, A.T.: A literature review of research in bug resolution: tasks, challenges and future directions. Comput. J. **59**(5), 741–773 (May 2016). https://doi.org/10.1093/comjnl/bxv114, https://academic.oup.com/comjnl/article-lookup/doi/10.1093/comjnl/bxv114
29. Zhang, W., Wang, S., Yang, Y., Wang, Q.: Heterogeneous network analysis of developer contribution in bug repositories. In: 2013 International Conference on Cloud and Service Computing, pp. 98–105. IEEE (2013)

Movie Recommendation Using Web Crawling

Pronit Raj, Chandrashekhar Kumar, Harshit Shekhar, Amit Kumar, Kritibas Paul, and Debasish Jana[✉]

Department of Computer Science and Engineering, Heritage Institute of Technology, Kolkata, India
{pronit.raj.cse25,chandrashekhar.kumar.cse25,harshit.shekhar.cse25, amit.kumar.cse25,kritibas.paul.cse25}@heritageit.edu.in, debasish.jana@heritageit.edu

Abstract. In today's digital world, streaming platforms offer a vast array of movies, making it hard for users to find content matching their preferences. This paper explores integrating real-time data from popular movie websites using advanced HTML scraping techniques and APIs. It also incorporates a recommendation system trained on a static Kaggle dataset, enhancing the relevance and freshness of suggestions. By combining content-based filtering, collaborative filtering, and a hybrid model, we create a system that utilizes both historical and real-time data for more personalized suggestions. Our methodology shows that incorporating dynamic data not only boosts user satisfaction but also aligns recommendations with current viewing trends.

Keywords: Movie Recommendation · Web Crawling · Content-Based and Collaborative Filtering · Machine Learning · Hybrid Model · Data Analysis

1 Introduction

The rise of digital streaming platforms has revolutionized how people access movies and shows, with services from platforms like Netflix, Amazon Prime, Hulu, and others offering extensive catalogs of content [20]. Users increasingly face the challenge of finding the right content among thousands of options, leading to a growing demand for sophisticated recommendation systems [23].

Many streaming services are leveraging big data and analytics to shape their strategic decisions. By utilizing vast amounts of user data and advanced algorithms, these platforms can better understand viewer preferences, guiding decisions on content acquisition, investment, and marketing. This approach enables them to provide personalized recommendations that keep existing subscribers engaged while attracting new users in diverse global markets [19]. However, balancing subscriber satisfaction with growth is an ongoing challenge. As users' tastes evolve and new competitors emerge, recommendation systems must adapt to accurately reflect the preferences of a global, ever-expanding customer base.

The goal is not only to prevent users from leaving but also to keep them engaged and satisfied in an increasingly competitive streaming landscape.

Recommendation engines [2] are crucial, leveraging data-driven insights and machine learning to curate content that aligns with individual tastes while addressing the diverse demands of global markets. Traditional recommendation systems fall into three main categories [7]: (a) **Content-based systems** [10] recommend items similar to those a user has liked in the past. (b) **Collaborative systems** [3] leverage the preferences of other users to make recommendations. (c) **Hybrid systems** [24] combine both approaches for improved accuracy. However, these systems typically rely on static datasets that fail to capture real-time trends. Our research explores integrating web crawling techniques to collect up-to-date data on movie releases and user preferences, addressing this gap.

Objective. The primary objectives of this paper are:

1. To design a movie recommendation system that combines static and real-time data sources.
2. To build and evaluate various recommendation techniques, including content-based, collaborative, and hybrid models.
3. To demonstrate the effectiveness of web crawling in updating movie recommendations to match users' current interests.

Scope and Contributions. This research contributes to the field of movie recommendation systems by integrating static datasets with real-time web-scraped data, offering a more dynamic and responsive solution to user preferences. The paper demonstrates the effectiveness of combining context-based, collaborative, and hybrid models to enhance recommendation accuracy. Additionally, it highlights the importance of web crawling techniques in continuously updating the dataset, ensuring that recommendations reflect the latest trends and user interests. The methodology presented serves as a framework for future research in real-time recommendation systems across various domains.

Organization of the Paper. The organization of this paper is as follows. Section 1 discusses the significance of recommendation systems in the context of digital streaming platforms, highlighting existing challenges and the necessity for real-time data integration to enhance user satisfaction. Section 2 the background and development of recommendation systems, covering foundational approaches like content-based and collaborative filtering, along with the emergence of hybrid models to enhance personalization and accuracy. Additionally, it discusses the role of web crawling for integrating real-time data into recommendation systems, comparing existing systems with the proposed approach, which combines both static and dynamic data sources to deliver relevant, up-to-date recommendations. Section 3 provides an in-depth analysis of the challenges associated with traditional movie recommendation systems and the proposed solution for integrating web-scraped data with a static dataset to address these limitations.

It outlines the problem statement, the methodologies used for data collection and processing, and the development of a recommendation model that leverages content-based, collaborative, and hybrid filtering approaches. Additionally, Sect. 3 delves into the technical processes, including data sourcing, scraping techniques, and the structuring of recommendation algorithms, designed to enhance the relevance of movie recommendations. Section 4 concludes the paper by discussing the effectiveness of integrating real-time web-crawled data with static datasets for a more dynamic recommendation system. It also outlines future work, including expanding data sources, incorporating advanced modeling techniques, and integrating real-time feedback loops to enhance personalization and adaptability in recommendation systems.

2 Related Work

2.1 Recommendation Systems

The evolution of recommendation systems is vast, with early systems primarily using content-based approaches, recommending items with similar attributes like genre or keywords [15]. Hooda et al. [5] discussed the adoption of recommender systems in social networks, covering key concepts like collaborative recommendation, content-based recommendation, and hybrid recommendation. Collaborative filtering, however, gained popularity by leveraging user-item interactions to suggest items based on what similar users enjoyed [22]. More recently, hybrid models have been developed to combine the strengths of both methods, improving accuracy and personalization. For instance, in movie recommendation, content-based filtering might recommend movies by genre or cast, while collaborative filtering suggests movies based on the viewing patterns of similar users [1].

2.2 Web Crawling for Real-Time Data

Web crawling [12] has emerged as a crucial method for extracting real-time data from the internet. With improved techniques in data scraping, real-time data can be collected efficiently and used in recommendation systems to capture trends, popularity metrics, and new releases. Khder [8] emphasized that code reuse and maintenance are essential in web scraping, as reusable code allows efficient handling of common tasks like site access, while maintenance ensures scrapers remain functional despite changes in site structure or behavior. Recent studies on e-commerce recommendation systems show how web scraping enhances user experiences by integrating frequently updated data on products, which provides relevance and keeps recommendations fresh. Onyenwe et al. [13] applied web crawling and scraping techniques to an e-commerce site to extract HTML data for identifying real-time product updates. Rathod et al. [16] built one system with Python on PyCharm, featureed web scraping and data mining modules to search for user-desired products within specified discounts and budgets, storing preferences for future recommendations and ranking products through a Product Rank Algorithm. Kumar et al. [9] applied Web scraping useing open-source tools to automate data extraction from the internet, and Python's extensive libraries [6] to make it a popular choice for web crawling process. Tools like BeautifulSoup [14] and Scrapy are commonly used for web crawling [4], allowing seamless extraction and processing of structured information.

2.3 Comparison with Existing Work

Most current movie recommendation systems rely on static datasets, which limits their ability to provide timely recommendations [11]. Some hybrid models do exist, but they lack real-time updates [21], which can be a drawback for users seeking newly released movies or trending films. This research introduces a novel approach by integrating static and dynamic data, leveraging web-crawled real-time information along with a dataset of movie metadata from Kaggle, to create a more comprehensive and up-to-date recommendation system.

3 Problem Statement and Proposed Methodology

Problem Statement. Existing movie recommendation systems often lack real-time data, leading to a gap in capturing new releases or trending movies, which are crucial for accurate user recommendations. This paper aims to solve the problem by integrating static datasets and web-scraped data to deliver a dynamic recommendation system. By utilizing both historical and fresh data, the aim is to create a system that better reflects current user interests and preferences. In this paper, we outline a structured approach for building a movie recommendation system through web crawling techniques. It comprises the following stages: dataset creation, data processing, recommendation modeling (encompassing context-based, collaborative, and hybrid approaches).

3.1 Web Scrapping

3.1.1 Data Source

To create a reliable and informative dataset, we collected data from Rotten Tomatoes (https://www.rottentomatoes.com/) and IMDb (https://www.imdb.com/). These platforms were chosen because of their large repository of movie-related information, including user ratings, reviews, genre classifications, cast, and release dates, which are essential for recommendation modeling. We used web scraping to extract this data programmatically, using Python's BeautifulSoup [18] and `requests` [17] libraries.

Rotten Tomatoes, like many other websites, actively blocks scraping attempts through JavaScript or other mechanisms designed to prevent automated access. As such, prior permission is required to engage in such activities. In the following sections, we provide examples for clarity. The best practice is to use the API access offered by many review and ratings aggregators today to fetch data legally. We present code examples based on a hypothetical or similar site-scraping approach to gather reviews and explain the general steps, keeping ethics in mind.

3.1.2 Data Collection Process

We scrape the Rotten Tomatoes website to gather key information for each movie, including the title of the movie, the release date, the genre, the ratings of the critics, the ratings of the audience and the top reviews. Additional data, such as cast and crew information, was also collected from IMDb to expand the contextual information on each movie, thus enriching the dataset for more accurate recommendations.

For example, consider the recent release of the movie Oppenheimer. By scraping real-time data from Rotten Tomatoes and IMDb, the system dynamically identified Oppenheimer as trending and updated its recommendations to include this movie for users interested in biographical dramas.

Rotten Tomatoes. Rotten Tomatoes is a widely used website for movie ratings and reviews, providing extensive information on films, TV shows, and audience opinions. It serves as a valuable resource for movie enthusiasts, analysts, and developers interested in trends and viewer preferences. Users can access professional critic reviews and audience scores that reflect public sentiment about films. The available key information includes movie titles, genres, release dates, synopses, and lists of cast and crew. By tracking ratings over time, users can observe trends in genre, director, or actor popularity. The *Tomatometer* displays critic consensus, while audience scores provide information on general public preferences. Data from Rotten Tomatoes can be utilized to build personal databases, compare films across different years, and analyze changes in ratings and genres.

The Rotten Tomatoes API provides JSON feeds for data extraction. We employ the **requests** and **simplejson** libraries (packages) to fetch and process data, creating a script to retrieve information on movies that are currently playing. The purpose of this web scraping from the Rotten Tomatoes site is to extract valuable data on movies, such as titles, ratings, and audience opinions, which can help analyze trends and preferences in the film industry. Using the Rotten Tomatoes API, we gather up-to-date information on movies currently playing for further downstream analysis. To scrape information from Rotten Tomatoes, first, we obtain an API key and construct the appropriate API URL to request data on movies in theaters. Next, we use the **requests** library to make a GET request to the API and retrieve the response content. Then, we parse the JSON response using a library like **simplejson** to access the relevant movie data, such as titles, and finally loop through the list of movies to print or further process the desired information. A code snippet is given below to show use of APIs to extract needed information.

```
api_key = "ACTUAL_API_KEY_FROM_ROTTEN_TOMATOES"
api_url = "http://api.rottentomatoes.com/api/public/v1.0/lists/"+
          "movies/in_theaters.json?apikey=%s"
# Make a GET request to the Rotten Tomatoes API
response = requests.get(api_url % api_key)
# Parse the response content to JSON
response_content = response.content
parsed_data = simplejson.loads(response_content)
movies_list = parsed_data["movies"]
```

```python
# Loop through each movie and print its title
for movie in movies_list:
    print(movie["title"])
```

We have all the movie information now and thus, we can use the following Python function `get_movie_details()` to extract additional movie details and pass the key and the movie title: The purpose of this code is to retrieve detailed information about a specific movie from the Rotten Tomatoes API using its title and an API key. To perform web scraping, the code first checks for spaces in the movie title and replaces them with plus signs for URL formatting, constructs a request URL with the API key and movie title, sends a GET request to the API, parses the JSON response, and then extracts and displays various details such as the movie's rating, synopsis, cast, runtime, and scores.

```python
def get_movie_details(api_key, movie_title):
    if " " in movie_title:
        title_parts = movie_title.split(" ")
        movie_title = "+".join(title_parts)

    base_url = "http://api.rottentomatoes.com/api/public/v1.0/movies.json"
    request_url = "%s?apikey=%s&q=%s&page_limit=1"
    request_url = request_url % (base_url, api_key, movie_title)

    response = requests.get(request_url)
    json_data = simplejson.loads(response.content)

    for film in json_data["movies"]:
        print("Rated: %s" % film["mpaa_rating"])
        print("Movie Synopsis: " + film["synopsis"])
        print("Critics Consensus: " + film["critics_consensus"])
        print("Major Cast:")

        for actor in film["abridged_cast"]:
            print("%s as %s" % (actor["name"], actor["characters"][0]))

        film_ratings = film["ratings"]
        print("Runtime: %s" % film["runtime"])
        print("Critics Score: %s" % film_ratings["critics_score"])
        print("Audience Score: %s" % film_ratings["audience_score"])
        print("For more information: %s" % film["links"]["alternate"])
```

To extract data from Rotten Tomatoes with Python, we use requests to send HTTP requests and use BeautifulSoup to parse the HTML content. At the 96th Academy Awards (2024), Christopher Nolan's epic biopic Oppenheimer, about the father of the atomic bomb, dominated by winning seven Oscars, including Best Picture, Best Director, and Best Actor for Cillian Murphy. The URL for the Rotten Tomatoes page of "Oppenheimer" is: https://www.rottentomatoes.com/m/oppenheimer_2023 (Fig. 1). We can send a GET request to the webpage, as below:

```python
response = requests.get(url)
soup = BeautifulSoup(response.text, "html.parser")
```

Fig. 1. Snapshot from Rotten Tomatoes site for biopic Oppenheimer(2023) (a) web page (b) Cast & Crew

We use the movie's Rotten Tomatoes URL to access the webpage, then parse it to find the element containing the director's name. Note that if Rotten Tomatoes updates its page structure, we might need to adjust the HTML tags and attributes used. We can find the director's name by locating the appropriate HTML element as:

```
director = soup.find("a", {"data-qa": "movie-info-director"})
```

Then we can extract and get the director's name as

```
director.get_text()
```

IMDb. IMDb, or the Internet Movie Database, is a wholly owned subsidiary of Amazon.com that serves as a comprehensive resource for information about movies, TV shows, video games, and other forms of entertainment. The site features details such as cast and crew lists, release dates, plot summaries, trailers, trivia, and reviews. The IMDb API allows users to access data related to movies, TV shows, video games, and celebrities. It also provides information on box office performance, cast and crew details, and IMDb ratings.

Fig. 2. Snapshot from IMDb site for biopic Oppenheimer(2023) (a) web page (b) Full Cast & Crew

```
# AWS Data Exchange IMDb endpoint
url = "https://api.imdbws.com/graphql"
# API key (obtained from AWS credentials after subscribing)
```

```
headers = {
    "x-api-key": "AWS_API_KEY",
    "Content-Type": "application/json"
}
# GraphQL query to retrieve movie titles
query = """
{
    movies {
        edges {
            node {
                title
                releaseDate
            }
        }
    }
}
"""
# Send the request
response = requests.post(url, json={'query': query}, headers=headers)
# Check if the request was successful
if response.status_code == 200:
    data = response.json()
    # Process the data to extract movie titles
    for movie in data['data']['movies']['edges']:
        print(f"Title: {movie['node']['title']}" +
              ", Release Date: {movie['node']" +
              "['releaseDate']}")
else:
    print(f"Failed to fetch data: {response.status_code}")
    print(response.text)
```

This code snippet uses **requests** package and retrieves movie titles and release dates from the IMDb database using AWS Data Exchange's GraphQL API. It sends a query to the IMDb API endpoint to access specific movie information, displaying the results if successful.

The code starts by setting the IMDb GraphQL API endpoint and preparing authentication headers that include the AWS API key. It then defines a GraphQL query to fetch movie titles and release dates. Using requests.post, it sends an HTTP POST request with the query and headers to the API endpoint. If the request succeeds, the response data is processed and each movie's title and release date are printed; otherwise, an error message is displayed.

Scrapping. IMDb's structure typically doesn't allow direct scrapping as it's protected by rules and terms of service. Additionally, IMDb prefers that its data be accessed through its official APIs (available via AWS Data Exchange), which provide a stable and authorized way to access movie data. However, since we wanted to proceed with scraping for research purposes, here is an example code snippet that demonstrates how we extract the director's name from the IMDb page for "Oppenheimer" (2023) using BeautifulSoup. Figure 2 shows snapshot from IMDb site for biopic Oppenheimer(2023)

(a) web page (b) Full Cast & Crew. To run this code, we save the HTML page locally because IMDb blocks bots and scraping scripts. In the HTML of our file, the director's name for Oppenheimer (2023) can be found in a JSON-LD section, specifically in:

```
<script type="application/ld+json">
{
  "@context": "https://schema.org",
  "@type": "Movie",
  "url": "https://www.imdb.com/title/tt15398776/",
  "name": "Oppenheimer",
  ...
  "director": [
    {
      "@type": "Person",
      "url": "https://www.imdb.com/name/nm0634240/",
      "name": "Christopher Nolan"
    }
  ],
  ...
}
</script>
```

This <script> tag with type="application/ld+json" contains structured data for the page in JSON format. We find the "director" Field: Inside this JSON data, then look for the "director" field, which lists directors as an array of objects. We extract the Name: The director's name, "Christopher Nolan", is found under the "name" key within the "director" object. Using BeautifulSoup and Python, we parse this JSON content to extract the director's name. Here's a Python code snippet that uses json and BeautifulSoup packages to extract the director's name from the JSON-LD data in our HTML file:

```python
# Load the offline saved IMDb HTML page
with open("oppenheimer.html", "r", encoding="utf-8") as file:
    page_content = file.read()
# Parse the HTML content
soup = BeautifulSoup(page_content, "html.parser")
# Find the JSON-LD script tag containing movie information
json_ld_script = soup.find("script", type="application/ld+json")
if json_ld_script:
    # Load JSON data from the script tag
    movie_data = json.loads(json_ld_script.string)
    # Extract the director's name
    director_info = movie_data.get("director", [])
    if director_info:
        director_name = director_info[0].get("name", "Director not found")
        print(f"Director: {director_name}")
    else:
        print("Director information not found")
else:
    print("JSON-LD script with movie data not found")
```

3.2 Data Processing Through Kaggle

For developing a movie recommendation system in this paper, we utilize the TMDB Movies Dataset 2023 (tmdb-movies-dataset-2023-930k-movies) from Kaggle, which includes over 930,000 records. This dataset is rich in information, containing attributes like movie titles, genres, release dates, ratings, and cast information, providing a comprehensive base for personalized recommendations. Each record represents a unique movie entry, allowing us to design recommendation algorithms that explore relationships based on both user preferences and the inherent characteristics of movies. Our approach leverages both content-based filtering and collaborative filtering techniques, along with a potential hybrid model to achieve balanced recommendations. Figure 3 shows Top-5 recommendations as obtained from processing the TMDB Movies Dataset 2023.

index	id	title	vote_average	vote_count	status	release_date	revenue
0	0	27205	Inception	8.364	34495	Released	2010-07-15	825532764
1	1	157336	Interstellar	8.417	32571	Released	2014-11-05	701729206
2	2	155	The Dark Knight	8.512	30619	Released	2008-07-16	1004558444
3	3	19995	Avatar	7.573	29815	Released	2009-12-15	2923706026
4	4	24428	The Avengers	7.710	29166	Released	2012-04-25	1518815515

Fig. 3. Top-5 movie recommendations derived from processing the TMDB Movies Dataset 2023

We further evaluated our approach on the MovieLens 25M dataset, which comprises an extensive collection of 25,000,095 ratings and 1,093,360 tag applications across 62,423 movies. As with Fig. 3, which presents our movie recommendation results on TMDB, we generated similar movie recommendations by processing the MovieLens 25M dataset. By evaluating our approach across multiple benchmarks, we demonstrate robustness across various movie pools and feature sets.

3.3 Recommendation Model

Content-Based Filtering. In content-based filtering, key features from movie attributes (e.g., genres, keywords, descriptions) are extracted to measure similarity among movies using cosine similarity. This approach recommends movies with characteristics similar to those a user has previously enjoyed. Specifically, context-based recommendations suggest movies based on attributes like genre, director, or primary cast members. For example, if a user shows interest in action movies featuring certain actors, the system will recommend other action movies with similar features. Our content-based model utilizes cosine similarity on feature vectors representing genres, directors, and cast members to generate relevant suggestions.

Example: If a user has expressed interest in films directed by Christopher Nolan, the model prioritizes other movies by Nolan or those with similar stylistic elements. When a user searches for science-fiction movies, real-time scraping identifies popular trending movies like Dune: Part Two. By integrating this real-time data with the user's historical preferences, the system provides timely, accurate recommendations.

Collaborative Filtering. Collaborative filtering leverages user interaction data, such as ratings, to recommend based on the assumption that users with similar tastes will enjoy similar content. This technique uses matrix factorization, specifically Singular Value Decomposition (SVD), to break down the user-item interaction matrix and discover latent factors that represent user preferences and movie characteristics. By employing collaborative filtering methods, such as matrix factorization or nearest neighbors, the system recommends movies that align with the viewing behavior of similar users.

Example: If Users A and B both rate several action-thrillers highly, the system may recommend a top-rated movie from B's list that A hasn't seen yet.

Hybrid Model. The hybrid model combines content-based and collaborative filtering to provide comprehensive recommendations. Collaborative filtering first generates a recommendation list based on user preferences, which is then refined using specific context-based criteria. This approach combines individual preferences with dataset trends, enhancing recommendations from large datasets like the Kaggle TMDB dataset. By combining content features (such as genres and keywords) and collaborative insights from user interactions, the model effectively adapts to new and recurring user interests.

Example: For a user who favors high-rated science fiction movies, the hybrid model first identifies top-rated options through collaborative filtering, then refines results with context-based filtering to include positively reviewed films or those by specific directors, creating a more personalized recommendation.

4 Conclusion and Future Work

This research proposes integrating real-time web-crawled data with static datasets to build a dynamic movie recommendation system. By combining content-based, collaborative, and hybrid filtering models, the system provides personalized suggestions based on historical and current trends. Real-time data from sources like Rotten Tomatoes and IMDb ensures the model stays relevant, addressing the limitations of traditional systems. The system could be integrated into platforms like Netflix and Amazon Prime to offer personalized recommendations based on seasonal and holiday-specific trends. Future work could expand data sources, incorporate more streaming platforms, and include user feedback from social media. Additionally, integrating multiple datasets like MovieLens and TMDB with real-time data could further improve recommendation accuracy. Advanced techniques such as neural collaborative filtering and deep learning models, along with real-time feedback loops, would enhance adaptability and enable more sophisticated recommendation systems.

References

1. Amangeldieva, A., Kharmyssov, C.: A hybrid approach for a movie recommender system using content-based, collaborative and knowledge-based filtering methods. In: 2024 IEEE 4th International Conference on Smart Information Systems and Technologies (SIST), pp. 93–99. IEEE (2024)
2. Barwal, D., Joshi, S., Obaid, A.J., et al.: The impact of netflix recommendation engine on customer experience. In: AIP Conference on Proceedings. AIP Publishing (2023)
3. Degemmis, M., Lops, P., Semeraro, G.: A content-collaborative recommender that exploits wordnet-based user profiles for neighborhood formation. User Model. User-Adap. Inter. **17**, 217–255 (2007)
4. Dikilitaş, Y., Çakal, Ç., et al.: Performance analysis for web scraping tools: case studies on beautifulsoup, scrapy, htmlunit and jsoup. In: International Conference on Emerging Trends and Applications in Artificial Intelligence, pp. 471–480. Springer, Heidelberg (2023). https://doi.org/10.1007/978-3-031-56728-5_39
5. Hooda, R., Singh, K., Dhawan, S.: A study of recommender systems on social networks and content-based web systems. IJCA **97**(4), 23–28 (2014)
6. Jarmul, K., Lawson, R.: Python Web Scraping. Packt Publishing Ltd. (2017)
7. Javed, U., Shaukat, K., Hameed, I.A., Iqbal, F., et al.: A review of content-based and context-based recommendation system. Int. J. Emerg. Technol. Learn. (iJET) **16**(3), 274–306 (2021)
8. Khder, M.A.: Web scraping or web crawling: state of art, techniques, approaches and application. Int. J. Adv. Soft Comput. Appl. **13**(3) (2021)
9. Kumar, S., Roy, U.B.: A technique of data collection: web scraping with python. In: Statistical Modeling in Machine Learning, pp. 23–36. Elsevier (2023)
10. Maidel, V., Shoval, P., et al.: Ontological content-based filtering for personalised newspapers: a method and its evaluation. Online Inf. Rev. **34**(5), 729–756 (2010)
11. Marcuzzo, M., Zangari, A., Albarelli, A., Gasparetto, A.: Recommendation systems: an insight into current development and future research challenges. IEEE Access **10**, 86578–86623 (2022)
12. Olston, C., Najork, M., et al.: Web crawling. Found. Trends® Inf. Retr. **4**(3), 175–246 (2010)
13. Onyenwe, I., Onyedinma, E., Nwafor, C., Agbata, O.: Developing products update-alert system for e-commerce websites users using html data and web scraping technique. arXiv preprint arXiv:2109.00656 (2021)
14. Pant, S., Yadav, E.N., Sharma, M., Bedi, Y., Raturi, A., et al.: Web scraping using beautiful soup. In: 2024 International Conference on Knowledge Engineering and Communication Systems (ICKECS), vol. 1, pp. 1–6. IEEE (2024)
15. Permana, A.H.J.P.J., Wibowo, A.T.: Movie recommendation system based on synopsis using content-based filtering with TF-IDF and cosine similarity. Int. J. Inf. Commun. Tech. (IJoICT) **9**(2), 1–14 (2023)
16. Rathod, U., Pavate, A., Patil, V.: Recommendation system using product rank algorithm for E-commerce. IOSR J. Eng. (IOSRJEN) **5**, 56–61 (2018). http://www.iosrjen.org
17. Reitz, K.: Requests: HTTP for Humans (2024). https://pypi.org/project/requests/
18. Richardson, L.: Beautiful Soup (2007). https://pypi.org/project/beautifulsoup4/
19. Shattuc, J.: Netflix, inc. and online television. In: A Companion to Television, pp. 145–164. Wiley Online Library (2020)

20. Singh, K.K., Makhania, J., et al.: Impact of ratings of content on OTT platforms and prediction of its success rate. Multimedia Tools Appl. **83**(2) (2024)
21. Sunny, B.K., Janardhanan, P., Francis, A.B., Murali, R.: Implementation of a self-adaptive real time recommendation system using spark machine learning libraries. In: 2017 IEEE International Conference on Signal Processing, Informatics, Communication and Energy Systems (SPICES), pp. 1–7. IEEE (2017)
22. Wang, Z.: Intelligent recommendation model of tourist places based on collaborative filtering and user preferences. Appl. Artif. Intell. **37**(1), 2203574 (2023)
23. Zangerle, E., Bauer, C.: Evaluating recommender systems: survey and framework. ACM Comput. Surv. **55**(8), 1–38 (2022)
24. Zhuhadar, L., Nasraoui, O.: A hybrid recommender system guided by semantic user profiles for search in the e-learning domain. J. Emerg. Technol. Web Intell. **2**(4) (2010)

A Quadrant Partitioned-RRT* (QP-RRT*) Autonomous Agent

Aritra Saha[✉] and Saikat Roy

Heritage Institute of Technology, Kolkata 700107, West Bengal, India
aritra.saha@heritageit.edu, saikat.roy.cse23@heritageit.edu.in

Abstract. Path planning is crucial in robotics and autonomous systems, but traditional algorithms like Rapidly Exploring Random Tree Star (RRT*) face limitations in exploration efficiency and adaptability.

We propose Quadrant Partitioned-RRT* (QP-RRT*), which addresses these challenges by dividing the map into quadrants and focusing exploration efforts dynamically based on a density threshold. If the threshold is exceeded, the start point shifts to a new quadrant, enabling efficient and adaptive exploration.

Experimental results demonstrate that QP-RRT* outperforms RRT* in path quality, exploration efficiency, and adaptability. Future research will focus on integrating obstacle avoidance and dynamic environments. QP-RRT* provides a promising solution for complex path-planning challenges.

Keywords: RRT* · QP-RRT* · Path Planning · Path Optimization · Robotics · Obstacle Avoidance · Quadrant-Based Search · Dynamic Density Threshold · Disaster Management

1 Introduction

Path planning underpins efficient navigation in robotics and autonomous systems. Algorithms such as RRT* are renowned for their ability to explore high-dimensional spaces and generate near-optimal paths. However, RRT* often suffers from inefficiencies in exploration and adaptability, particularly in complex environments with varying point densities or narrow passages.

This paper introduces Quadrant Partitioned-RRT* (QP-RRT*), an algorithm designed to enhance RRT*'s capabilities. By dividing the environment into quadrants and focusing on relevant regions, QP-RRT* reduces the search space and improves computational efficiency. A dynamic density threshold mechanism further enhances adaptability by shifting the start point to unexplored quadrants when point density exceeds a threshold, facilitating new region exploration and avoiding local minima.

The paper evaluates QP-RRT*'s performance against RRT* using metrics like path quality, computational efficiency, and adaptability in complex environments. The experimental results highlight its significant improvements in path quality and exploration efficiency.

2 Literature Review

Path planning algorithms are essential for enabling autonomous systems to navigate complex environments. This section reviews related algorithms, focusing on the strengths and weaknesses of the traditional RRT* algorithm.

Numerous studies have explored and enhanced robotic path planning algorithms, particularly RRT and RRT* variants, to address challenges like computational efficiency, optimality, robustness, and adaptability in dynamic environments. Below are key contributions:

Foundational Algorithms: LaValle, S. M. (1998). Rapidly – exploring random trees: A new tool for path planning [1]. This seminal paper introduces the Rapidly – exploring Random Trees (RRT) algorithm, which has been widely adopted in robotics for efficient path planning in complex environments. Karaman, S., Frazzoli, E. (2011). Sampling–based algorithms for optimal motion planning [2]. This paper presents the RRT* algorithm, an extension of RRT that aims to find optimal paths by incorporating cost functions and re–wiring techniques. J. J. Kuffner Jr., S. M. LaValle (2000). RRT – Connect: An efficient approach to single – query path planning [3]. This paper introduces the RRT–connect algorithm, which addresses motion planning for systems with differential constraints and has been widely applied to robotic motion planning problems.

Specific Constraints and Dynamic Environments: Phillips, M., Mian, O., Likhachev, M., (2011). SIPP: Safe interval path planning for dynamic environments [4]. This paper presents the Safe Interval Path Planning (SIPP) algorithm, which addresses path planning in dynamic environments by considering time-varying obstacles and generating collision-free paths with respect to time intervals. Huang, H., Zhou, Y., Sun, Y. (2015). Dynamic PRM: A path planning algorithm with adjustable exploration-exploitation balance [5]. This paper presents the Dynamic PRM algorithm, which dynamically adjusts the balance between exploration and exploitation to efficiently find paths in changing environments. Liu, Y., Hu, H., Zhang, M., Yang, F. (2018) [6]. Fast searching in cluttered environments with hybrid RRT*. This paper introduces a hybrid variant of RRT* that combines deterministic and random sampling strategies to efficiently search for paths in cluttered environments.

Multi-objective and Advanced Approaches: Song, Y., Yang, J. (2017) [7]. Multi–objective RRT* algorithm for path planning of mobile robot. This paper presents a multi–objective variant of RRT* that considers multiple criteria, such as path length, smoothness, and obstacle avoidance, to generate high quality paths for mobile robots. Tang, J., Song, X., (2018). An improved RRT* - based algorithm for path planning of mobile robot [8]. This paper presents an improved version of RRT* that integrates a local searching strategy to enhance the efficiency and effectiveness of path planning for mobile robots. Zhang, J., Yang, C. (2019). Improved RRT* algorithm for unmanned aerial vehicle path planning in dynamic environments [9]. This paper introduces an improved RRT* algorithm specifically designed for path planning of unmanned aerial vehicles (UAVs) in dynamic environments, considering factors such as obstacle avoidance and dynamic trajectory tracking.

Emerging Techniques: Zhou, Y., Hu, S., Tang, J. (2022). Self–Supervised Learning for Path Planning: A Comparative Study [10]. This paper investigates the application of self–supervised learning approaches for path planning, comparing their performance with traditional sampling-based algorithms and highlighting their potential advantages. Zhang, Y., Liu, W., Wu, C. (2023). Ensemble Path Planning: A Multi-Model Approach for Autonomous Navigation [11]. This paper proposes an ensemble path-planning approach that combines multiple path-planning models to improve the robustness and adaptability of autonomous navigation systems.

The initial studies lay the foundation for RRT and RRT*. The next works provide valuable insights into state-of-the-art path planning techniques. Combined, they serve as the cornerstone for developing and evaluating novel algorithms like QP-RRT*.

Introduction to QP-RRT*. To address the limitations of traditional RRT*, we propose *Quadrant Partitioned-RRT (QP-RRT)**, a strategy leveraging quadrant-based exploration and dynamic density thresholds.

QP-RRT* divides the environment into quadrants, performing independent RRT* expansions to reduce search space and improve computational efficiency. A dynamic density threshold mechanism shifts the start point diagonally when point density exceeds a predefined limit, enhancing adaptability, exploring new spaces, and avoiding local minima and narrow passages.

This approach improves exploration efficiency, adaptability to diverse environments, and path quality. The following sections detail the QP-RRT* methodology, experimental setup, evaluation metrics, results, discussion, and applications.

3 Methodology

This section presents the methodology of the QP-RRT* algorithm, through quadrant-based exploration and a dynamic density threshold mechanism.

By dividing the problem space, monitoring density, and adjusting the start point, QP-RRT* balances exploration and optimization, dynamically adapting the search space for improved path-finding in complex environments.

Quadrant Division. QP-RRT* divides the map into four quadrants, centered at the origin (0, 0): Q1 (top right), Q2 (top left), Q3 (bottom left), and Q4 (bottom right). This division minimizes search space and boosts computational efficiency.

Endpoint Position. Identify the quadrant containing the endpoint to help QP-RRT* focus on the relevant region for expansion.

Expansion within Quadrants. After the partitioning of the quadrants, QP-RRT * performs independent expansions of RRT * within each quadrant by sampling random points and connecting them to the nearest node in the tree, progressively growing the tree toward the endpoint.

Dynamic Density Threshold Refinement. QP-RRT* adapts to varying point densities using a dynamic density threshold mechanism. It calculates density by dividing the number of points by the area enclosed between the minimum and maximum X and Y coordinates. If density exceeds a predefined threshold *Density_Threshold*, a density check counter increases, and once a set threshold is reached *Density_Threshold_Points*, the start point shifts to balance exploration.

Relocation of the Start Point. When the density check counter reaches the threshold, the start point is shifted diagonally opposite the endpoint quadrant (e.g. from Q3 to Q1). This shift allows exploration in new regions and helps escape local minima and narrow passages. The algorithm resumes the RRT* expansion in the new quadrant until a path is found, or another shift is triggered.

Incremental Search Space. With the adjusted starting point, continue the expansion process of RRT* in the expanded search space. The algorithm aims to find a route by exploring the newly added regions while avoiding high-density areas.

3.1 Pseudo-Code

```
1   QP-RRT* (start, end, max_iter, density_thresh, density_thresh_pts)
2   Initialize an empty tree T; add start node to T
3   while (iterations < max_iter) do
4       if (points < density_thresh_pts) then
5           check density in the current region
6           area = (X_max - X_min) * (Y_max - Y_min)
7           density = points/area
8       if (density > density_thresh) then
9           shift start to opposite quadrant of endpoint
10          recreate search region based on new start
11          clear T; add new start node to T
12      q_rand = generate random config
13      q_near = nearest node in T to q_rand
14      extend q_near towards q_rand with step size delta
15      if obstacle encountered, continue
16      cost = cost from start to q_near + cost (q_near, q_new)
17      set q_new as child of q_near
18      for each q_near_neighbor in neighborhood of q_new do
19          if (cost(q_new) + cost(q_new, q_near_neighbor)
                              < cost(q_near_neighbor)) then
20              rewire q_near_neighbor to have q_new as parent
21      iterations = iterations + 1
22  Return path P from start to node closest to end in T
```

3.2 Mathematical Representation

We have explained the QP-RRT* algorithm's working principle and its algorithmic steps. Below is the mathematical representation of QP-RRT*.

Initialization: Let X be the state space representing all possible configurations or states of the system. Define the initial state x_{init}. Create an empty tree T with x_{init} as the root node.

Quadrant Division: Divide the state space X into four quadrants based on the start point x_{start}:

Quadrant 1 (Q1): $\theta \in [0, \pi/2]$
Quadrant 2 (Q2): $\theta \in [\pi/2, \pi]$
Quadrant 3 (Q3): $\theta \in [-\pi, -\pi/2]$
Quadrant 4 (Q4): $\theta \in [-\pi/2, 0]$

Iterative Expansion. Repeat until termination:

1. Sample a random state x_{rand} from X.
2. Determine the quadrant Q_n of x_{rand}.
3. Find the nearest node x_{near} in T within Q_n.
4. Steer from x_{near} towards x_{rand}, generating x_{new} at δ distance:
   $x_{\text{new}} = \text{steer}(x_{\text{near}}, x_{\text{rand}})$.
5. Perform collision checking.
6. If x_{new} is valid:
   - Find neighboring nodes n_{near} within radius r.
   - Evaluate cost-to-come:
     $g(x_{\text{new}}) = g(x_{\text{near}}) + c(x_{\text{near}}, x_{\text{new}})$.
7. Update the parent of x_{new} to minimize cost-to-come.
8. Add x_{new} to T; rewire the tree if necessary.

Density Threshold and Start Point Adjustment. Adjust and Set

- Define density threshold density_threshold_points.
- Monitor point density during RRT* expansion.
- If point density exceeds density_threshold_points:
  - Determine the quadrant Q of x_{goal}.
  - Shift x_{start} opposite to x_{goal} by distance α.
  - Recompute quadrants and reset density count.

Path Selection. Find the goal node x_{goal} in T closest to the desired goal state. Trace back from x_{goal} to the root to obtain the optimal path.

4 Experimental Setup

In this section, we describe the experimental setup used to evaluate the effectiveness of the Quadrant Partitioned-RRT* (QP-RRT*) algorithm, including the evaluation metrics, test environments, and implementation details. To assess the performance of QP-RRT*, we utilize the following evaluation metrics:

Path Length: Measures the length of the generated path from start to endpoint. Shorter paths indicate better efficiency and optimality.

Exploration Efficiency: Counts the total number of nodes expanded during execution. Fewer nodes indicate more efficient exploration.

Path Complexity: Counts the number of turns in the path. Fewer turns indicate simpler paths.

Computation Time: Measures the time taken to generate a path. Shorter times indicate faster execution.

Test Environments. Experiments were conducted in 2D problem spaces with multiple obstacles, designed to mimic real-world scenarios including narrow passages, open areas, and obstacle-rich regions. Different start and endpoint configurations were tested to observe the algorithm's adaptability.

Implementation Details. The QP-RRT* algorithm was implemented in Python, utilizing the following libraries:

> **cv2:** For visualizing and plotting results.
> **NumPy:** For efficient array manipulation and mathematical operations.
> **math:** For mathematical functions.
> **random:** For generating random points during RRT* expansion.
> **argparse:** For handling command-line arguments, allowing specification of input parameters.

Experiments were performed on a computer with an Intel Core i5 8th generation processor (1.6 GHz), 4 GB DDR4 RAM, and a 2 GB NVIDIA GeForce MX150 GPU, providing sufficient computational power and visualization capabilities.

5 Results and Analysis

In this section, we present the results and analysis of the Quadrant Partitioned-RRT* (QP-RRT*) algorithm, comparing its performance to the traditional RRT* algorithm on four key aspects: the number of turns taken, the path length, the time taken, and the number of nodes generated.

These comparisons are made across different problem maps labeled *World 1* to *World 6* with varying start and endpoints.

Path Complexity. The number of turns required to reach the endpoint is a critical measure of path efficiency. QP-RRT* aims to minimize unnecessary turns, producing smoother trajectories. Comparisons showed that QP-RRT* consistently required lesser or equal turns than RRT*.

Path Length. The path length is a key metric for evaluating path planning performance. Shorter paths indicate more direct and optimal routes. Our experiments showed that QP-RRT* consistently produced paths of similar or shorter lengths than RRT*, demonstrating its efficiency in finding more efficient paths.

Computation Time. Computation time is crucial, especially for real-time applications. QP-RRT* generally exhibited faster path generation due to its quadrant-based division, which reduces the search space and focuses exploration in relevant regions.

Table 1. Selected summary comparing RRT* and QP-RRT* on the above metrics.

Method	RRT*				QP-RRT*			
Map	Turns	Length	Time	Nodes	Turns	Length	Time	Nodes
World 1	3.63	308.78	5.31	250.13	3.75	288.98	1.34	58.50
World 2	4.00	293.37	14.93	391.88	3	318.14	3.59	90.50
World 3	3.25	204.41	1.79	86.50	2.75	165.01	0.68	26.25
World 4	3.38	220.50	1.18	66.50	3.38	142.71	0.61	17.00
World 5	4.00	458.28	8.47	314.38	4.00	313.10	1.38	71.13
World 6	4.50	489.61	14.24	415.75	4.38	454.96	2.87	120.00
Average	**3.79**	**329.158**	**7.65**	**254.19**	**3.54**	**280.48**	**1.74**	**63.90**
World 7	*4.13*	*335.72*	*7.86*	*256.25*	*4.63*	*331.93*	*9.14*	*239.80*
World 8	*5.50*	*609.03*	*9.32*	*291.63*	*5.63*	*575.17*	*10.93*	*262.88*
Average	***4.81***	***472.37***	***8.59***	***273.94***	***5.13***	***453.55***	***10.03***	***251.31***

All experiments with Shift Threshold = 0.1, Density Threshold = 0.005, and Density Check Threshold = 20.

Exploration Efficiency. The number of nodes generated during expansion reflects exploration efficiency. Fewer nodes indicate reduced computational overhead and more effective search space exploration. Experiments confirmed that QP-RRT* consistently generated fewer nodes than RRT*, resulting in faster convergence (Table 1).

5.1 Summary of the Results

We selectively compare QP-RRT* with RRT* in the various world maps. Each map was tested for at least 10 iterations, keeping the constants the same. The average values over the test runs have been reported in the table. Lower values indicate better performance for each metric.

For the first six instances, labelled as *World 1* to *World 6*, QP-RRT* shows far better performance. The next two results, *World 7* and *World 8*, show instances where QP-RRT* might be behind in some metric or the other.

5.2 Analysis

The results highlight the superior performance of QP-RRT* compared to the traditional RRT* across multiple metrics. QP-RRT* consistently demonstrated advantages in terms of computation time and the number of nodes generated.

The faster computation time of QP-RRT* suggests its suitability for applications requiring immediate response. The quadrant-based division significantly reduces the search space, focusing exploration in relevant regions and leading to faster convergence and path generation.

The reduced number of nodes generated by QP-RRT* signifies its exploration efficiency and computational effectiveness. With fewer nodes expanded, QP-RRT* achieves more efficient exploration, reducing computational overhead and improving scalability.

QP-RRT* offers several implications for practical path-planning applications. By incorporating a quadrant-based approach, it adapts the exploration strategy to the spatial distribution of the start and end points, enabling it to handle complex environments more efficiently and find shorter, smoother paths.

The improved performance of QP-RRT* in computation time and the number of nodes generated makes it suitable for various real-world scenarios. Applications such as autonomous navigation and robot motion planning can benefit from QP-RRT*'s efficiency and optimality.

Furthermore, the flexibility of QP-RRT* in accommodating different start and end point configurations enhances its versatility. It can adapt to varying initial conditions and generate paths tailored to specific requirements, expanding its applicability in diverse environments.

Some pictorial comparisons between RRT* and QP-RRT* algorithms are given here (Figs. 1, 2, 3 and 4):

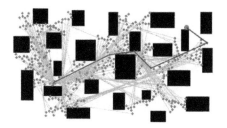

Fig. 1. RRT* Path for World 5.

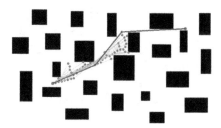

Fig. 2. QP-RRT* Path for World 5.

Fig. 3. RRT* Path for World 6.

Fig. 4. QP-RRT* Path for World 6.

These pictorial comparisons illustrate how QP-RRT* performs more efficiently than the traditional RRT* algorithm.

5.3 Limitations

While QP-RRT* demonstrates promising performance in most scenarios, it has limitations. A key limitation arises when an obstacle blocks access to the entire quadrant where the end point lies. In such cases, QP-RRT* may not provide the best outcome compared to traditional RRT*.

When an obstacle obstructs the entire quadrant containing the end point, QP-RRT* may need to navigate around the obstacle, leading to suboptimal results. The quadrant-based division and exploration strategy of QP-RRT* may not effectively navigate complex obstacles in such situations. In contrast, RRT* can explore the entire search space without quadrant restrictions, potentially finding better paths.

QP-RRT* excels in scenarios with distributed start and end points and moderate obstacles. However, its performance can be compromised in highly obstructed environments or when obstacles entirely block access to a quadrant. Alternative algorithms or modifications to QP-RRT* may be needed in such challenging scenarios.

Fig. 5. RRT* path for World 7.   **Fig. 6.** QP-RRT* path for World 7.

Despite this limitation, QP-RRT* offers significant advantages in computation time and exploration overhead reduction in many scenarios. It remains a valuable tool for path planning in various applications, provided that its limitations and specific constraints are carefully considered and mitigated as necessary. It is evident from Figs. 5 and 6, how QP-RRT* performs better by gradually increasing its search region based on point density and finding the path. We can fine-tune this result by modifying the density_threshold, density_threshold_points, and delta variables.

6 Applications and Future Work

In this section, we discuss the application scenarios of the Quadrant-based RRT* (QP-RRT*) algorithm and potential modifications to improve its performance.

6.1 Applications

The QP-RRT* algorithm has broad applications across various domains requiring efficient path planning. Some potential applications include:

Autonomous Navigation. QP-RRT* can be utilized in autonomous vehicles, drones, and mobile robots to plan optimal paths, avoiding obstacles and minimizing travel time. Its ability to generate smoother paths quickly makes it suitable for real-time navigation in dynamic environments.

Robotics. QP-RRT* can be employed in industrial robotics, collaborative robots (cobots), and manipulators to optimize motion planning, enabling robots to perform tasks efficiently and avoid collisions.

Computer Graphics and Animation. QP-RRT* can be used in computer graphics and animation to generate natural and realistic paths for virtual characters and objects. Its efficiency in finding smooth and optimal trajectories enhances the visual quality and realism of animated scenes.

Manufacturing and Warehouse Robotics. QP-RRT* aids in planning motions for robots operating in manufacturing facilities or warehouses. It helps optimize robot movements, considering obstacles, workspace constraints, and operational objectives, such as minimizing cycle time or energy consumption.

Motion Planning for Manipulators. QP-RRT* can plan paths for robotic arms or manipulators in various industrial or research settings. It enables robots to move efficiently and avoid obstacles while performing tasks such as grasping, assembly, or inspection.

Disaster Management and Response Services. QP-RRT* can play a crucial role in search and rescue operations during natural disasters or emergencies. It helps plan optimal paths for search teams or robotic systems, such as drones or robots, to explore disaster-stricken areas and locate survivors. By considering the dynamics of the disaster environment, including collapsed structures, debris, and other hazards, QP-RRT* generates paths that avoid obstacles and ensure the safety of search and rescue teams.

6.2 Future Work

While the QP-RRT* algorithm demonstrates promising performance, several avenues for practical implementation and development exist:

Handling Dynamic Obstacles. Enhancing QP-RRT* to handle dynamic obstacles would make it more robust in dynamic environments. Incorporating mechanisms to detect and react to moving obstacles in real time can further improve the algorithm's adaptability.

Multi-agent Planning. Extending QP-RRT* to handle multi-agent planning scenarios can enable coordinated path planning for multiple agents. Developing efficient strategies for collision avoidance and cooperative exploration among agents is a potential area of research.

Hybrid Approaches. Investigating hybrid approaches that combine QP-RRT* with other planning algorithms or techniques can leverage the strengths of different algorithms, leading to even more efficient and effective path-planning solutions.

The QP-RRT* algorithm holds promise in a wide range of applications, including autonomous navigation, robotics, and computer graphics. The research directions highlighted above can further advance the field of path planning and contribute to the development of intelligent and efficient systems.

7 Conclusion

The Quadrant-based RRT* (QP-RRT*) algorithm offers a novel approach to path planning, leveraging the spatial distribution of start and endpoints. Extensive experiments show QP-RRT*'s superior performance over traditional RRT* in terms of path efficiency, computation time, number of turns, and nodes generated.

QP-RRT*'s quadrant-based division and dynamic density threshold adjustment enable efficient exploration of complex environments, resulting in smoother and more direct paths. This adaptability enhances its versatility in various scenarios.

The algorithm's faster computation times and reduced node generation contribute to its scalability and real-time applicability, improving efficiency and safety in autonomous systems.

However, QP-RRT* has limitations, especially when obstacles obstruct the entire quadrant containing the endpoint. In such cases, alternative algorithms or modifications may be necessary.

Overall, QP-RRT* significantly advances path-planning techniques with its quadrant-based approach and dynamic density adjustments. The research highlights its benefits in path efficiency, computation time, and exploration overhead reduction.

The contributions of this paper include the proposal, implementation, experimental evaluation, and comparative analysis of QP-RRT* with RRT*. By integrating innovative algorithms and computational techniques, QP-RRT* enhances path-planning methodologies.

The algorithm holds promise for various applications, including autonomous navigation, robotics, UAV path planning, and computer graphics. Future research can explore dynamic obstacle handling, machine learning integration, multi-agent planning, real-world validations, and hybrid approaches.

In conclusion, QP-RRT* is a valuable tool for optimizing path generation, enabling autonomous systems to navigate complex environments efficiently and safely.

References

1. LaValle, S.M.: Rapidly – exploring random trees: a new tool for path planning. Technical Report No. TR-CIM-98-22, Computer Science Department, Iowa State University (1998)
2. Karaman, S., Frazzoli, E.: Sampling-based algorithms for optimal motion planning. Int. J. Rob. Res. **30**(7), 846–894 (2011)
3. Kuffner Jr., J.J., LaValle, S.M.: RRT – connect: an efficient approach to single–query path planning. In: Proceedings of the IEEE International Conference on Robotics and Automation (ICRA), vol. 2, pp. 995–1001 (2000)
4. Philips, M., Mian, O., Likhachev , M.: SIPP: safe interval path planning for dynamic environments. In: Proceedings of the IEEE International Conference on Robotics and Automation (ICRA), pp. 5628–5633 (2011)
5. Huang, H., Zhou, Y., Sun, Y.: Dynamic PRM: a path planning algorithm with adjustable exploration-exploitation balance. IEEE Trans. Autom. Sci. Eng. **12**(2), 456–467 (2015)
6. Liu, Y., Hu, H., Zhang, M., Yang, Y.F.: Fast searching in cluttered environments with hybrid RRT*. In: Proceedings of the IEEE International Conference on Robotics and Automation (ICRA), pp. 4186–4192 (2018)
7. Song, Y., Yang, J.: Multi–objective RRT* algorithm for path planning of mobile robot. In: Proceedings of the 12th World Congress on Intelligent Control and Automation (WCICA), pp. 1412–1417 (2017)
8. Tang, J., Song, X.: An improved RRT*—based algorithm for path planning of mobile robot. In: Proceedings of the 10th International Conference on Modelling, Identification and Control (ICMIC), pp. 77–82 (2018)
9. Zhang, J., Yang, C.: Improved RRT* algorithm for unmanned aerial vehicle path planning in dynamic environments. In: Proceedings of the 5th International Conference on Mechanical, Control and Computer Engineering (ICMCCE), pp. 428–432 (2019)
10. Zhou, Y., Hu, S., Tang, J.: Self – supervised learning for path planning: a comparative study (2022). arXiv preprint arXiv: 2207.01234
11. Zhang, Y., Liu, W., Wu, C.: Ensemble path planning: a multi-model approach for autonomous navigation (2023). arXiv preprint arXiv: 2301.12345
12. Sertac, K., Frazzoli, E.: Kinodynamic RRT*: asymptotically optimal motion planning for robots with linear dynamics. In: Proceedings of the IEEE International Conference on Robotics and Automation (ICRA), vol. 2, pp. 2005–2011 (2004)
13. Karaman, S., Frazzoli, E.: Incremental sampling-based algorithms for optimal motion planning. Rob. Sci. Syst. **6**, 7 (2010)
14. Smith, A., Johnson, B., Anderson, C.: A comparative study of path planning algorithms for unmanned aerial vehicles. J. Intell. Rob. Syst. **77**(1), 59–76 (2015)
15. Liu, Y., Zhang, J., Zhu, X.: Enhanced RRT*-connect algorithm for UAV path planning. In: Proceedings of the IEEE International Conference on Robotics and Biomimetics (ROBIO), pp. 34–39 (2017)

Framework of a Smart Contract System for Improved Supply Chain Management

Aniket Pal[✉], Aniket Chatterjee, and Rituparna Chaki[ID]

A K Choudhury School of IT, University of Calcutta, Kolkata, India
aniketpal621@gmail.com

Abstract. In this work, we focus on integrating supply chain management with blockchain technology, emphasizing the use smart contracts on EVM based Polygon network using solidity. A framework for implementing smart contract in supply chain management is presented. The proposed system aims to improve the reliability, manageability, and traceability of supply chains while addressing vulnerabilities and data alteration. The successful implementation of this framework demonstrates the significant potential of smart contract to improve supply chain management practices, paving the way for a more secure and efficient supply chain ecosystem.

Keywords: Supply Chain Management · Blockchain · Smart Contract · Solidity · Polygon

1 Introduction

Of late, supply chain management is gaining significant attention of researchers due to growing demand and advancements in digital technologies. For effective management of supply chain, it is important to have streamlined processes with secure transaction and automated enforcement of agreements in a transparent manner. It is [7] noted that digital supply chain transformation towards blockchain integration is a significant trend, indicating the potential for blockchain to disrupt traditional industries. This necessitates the development smart contracts. Blockchain technology, a decentralized and secure public ledger, offers significant potential to enhance transparency, security, and efficiency in managing logistics and ensuring timely deliveries. Smart contracts, a feature of blockchain platforms, automate agreements by executing predefined clauses when conditions are met. These contracts are coded and stored as immutable transactions, ensuring a tamper-proof record of the contract lifecycle from deployment to completion. These technologies improve sourcing, procurement, and logistics while providing transparency, reducing reliance on intermediaries, and creating an immutable, trustworthy system for managing operations. Our aim is to establish a foundation for employing similar technologies in the supply chain management process, demonstrating their potential to streamline operations and improve efficiency.

This paper aims to solve the problems faced in the mentioned research by integrating blockchain and smart contract technology in a single system to enhance supply chain management. Specifically, it explores the implementation of supply chain management using smart contracts on the Polygon network.

2 Literature Review

Researchers [6] proposed that blockchain technology can realize traceability and ensure food safety in the entire agri-food supply chain by gathering, transferring, and sharing authentic data. This finding is supported by [9], which emphasized that blockchain can streamline and benefit modern supply chains, particularly enhancing value chain networks and improving food traceability, information transparency, and recall efficiency. [13] showcased the application of blockchain in ensuring the authenticity of organic products, further underlining its potential in enhancing transparency and trust in agri-food supply chains. [10] reinforced this view, stating that blockchain technology has the potential to improve supply chain transparency but is still in its infancy. Recent research [14] explored the impact of blockchain on supply chain resilience, highlighting its role in mitigating disruptions and enhancing adaptability in dynamic environments. [8, 12] focused on the relationship between blockchain technology and sustainable supply chain management, emphasizing the need to explore adoption barriers. These studies highlight the theoretical aspects of adopting blockchain in sustainable supply chains, pointing towards the need for further empirical research to address these barriers. Recent research [14] investigated the environmental impact of blockchain adoption in supply chains, shedding light on its potential to promote sustainability initiatives.

From the above study, it is observed that traceability, transparency and cost efficiency in blockchain models need to be addressed for effective utilization of its' potentials. These observations lead to the proposed novel approach towards smart contract development based on polygon blockchain.

3 Description of Proposed Logic

3.1 Assumptions

Our proposed system has the following assumptions:

1. Only owner can register and deregister a supplier and update the shipment status of an order.
2. Only verified suppliers can add, and update products.
3. Suppliers can update the products only which they added.
4. Buyer can only order a product at a time.
5. Until the payment for an order is done, the shipment status of that specific order cannot be updated.
6. The payment is directly going to the supplier from the buyer.

The proposed system for supply-chain management in Fig. 1, takes advantage of Polygon blockchain. It outlines a comprehensive strategy, detailing involved stakeholders, process, regulations and constraints to bolster system reliability.

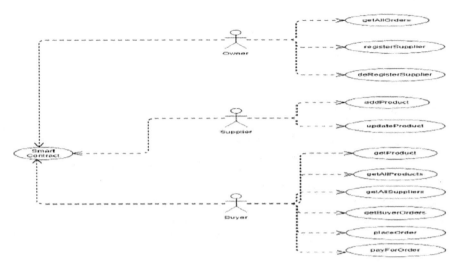

Fig. 1. Component of the proposed System

3.2 Data Dictionary

(See Table 1).

Table 1. Data Structures with Definition

Data Structures	Definition
Product[id, name, Description, price, quantity, supplier]	Stores product details
Order[ID, product ID, quantity, total price, fulfillment status, shipment status, buyer]	Records order's details
Supplier[registration status, address]	Supplier's verified status & address
BuyerOrders[]	all orders by a buyer
ShipmentStatus[Pending, InTransition, Shipped, Delivered]	Status of a shipment

3.3 Functions

Smart contracts are developed using Solidity, the programming language native to the Ethereum Virtual Machine (EVM). The Remix Integrated Development Environment (IDE) facilitates the creation, testing, debugging, and deployment of these contracts, while the Polygon Amoy test net offers a budget-friendly testing platform. Following are the functions functions within the contract and their respective roles.

Modifier Functions:

1. *onlyOwner()*: Gives modification rights only permitted to the owner.
2. *onlySupplier()*: Modification rights only permitted to the supplier.

Constructor Function:

1. *constructor()*: Sets the deployer of the contract as the owner of the contract.

Public Functions:

1. *addProduct()*: Addition of a new product by accepting input data within the product struct as its argument.
2. *updateProduct():*. By leveraging this functionality, suppliers can update the product catalog in real-time, ensuring that buyers have access to the latest information on available products and their attributes.
3. *placeOrder()*: This function enables buyers to order a product from a registered and verified supplier and generates an order id for the order.
4. *payForOrder()*: This function enables buyers to pay for a specific order linked with the order id.
5. *registerSupplier()*: The owner can register a user who want to be a supplier.
6. *deregisterSupplier()*: Through this function, the owner can remove a supplier form the list of registered suppliers.
7. *updateShipmentStatus()*: Through this function, the owner can update the shipment status of a specific order.

Public View Functions: They utilize a view modifier, signifying that they are restricted to read-only operations.

1. *getProduct()*: Through this, buyer can see the details of a specific product.
2. *getProducts()*: Through this, buyer can see the details of all the products available in the chain.
3. *getAllSuppliers()*: Through this, buyer can see list of all registered suppliers.
4. *getAllOrders()*: Through this function, owner can see all the orders.
5. *getBuyerOrders()*: This function returns all the orders of a specific buyer.

Internal View Functions: The *hasOrder()* function checks that the buyer has any order or not; also incorporates a view modifier, denoting its restriction to read-only access.

3.4 Workflow

The workflow of the proposed system revolves around the journey of the products from supplier to their ultimate destination. This process is segmented into three modules: the first module manages the owner's workflow, the second module handles the buyer's workflow, and the third module oversees the workflow of the supplier (Figs. 2, 3 and 4).

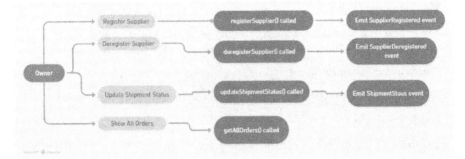

Fig. 2. Workflow of the owner

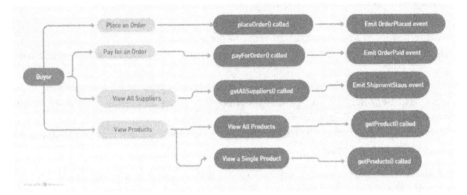

Fig. 3. Workflow of the buyer

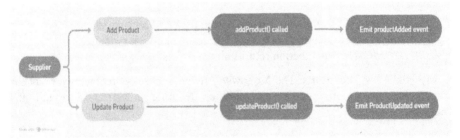

Fig. 4. Workflow of the supplier

4 Conclusion

Research has opened the transformative potential of integrating smart contracts and harnessing blockchain technology to improve business transactions, ensuring heightened security, transparency, efficiency, and traceability. In this work, we have used the Solidity smart contract for supply chain optimization on the Polygon blockchain. For automating and enhancing critical supply chain processes. This hierarchical access control mechanism safeguards sensitive operations and also fosters trust and accountability within the supply chain ecosystem. By capturing transactional data in a transparent and auditable manner, the contract fosters trust among participants and facilitates effective decision-making. The proposal enables the owner to seamlessly onboard new suppliers or remove existing ones, thereby maintaining control over the network's composition. This flexibility ensures that the supply chain remains adaptable to changing business requirements and market dynamics. As the contract allows suppliers to update the product catalog in real-time, the timely dissemination of information enhances supply chain efficiency and enables buyers to make informed purchasing decisions.

References

1. Yigit, E., Dag, T.: Improving supply chain management processes using smart contracts in the ethereum network written in solidity (2024). https://doi.org/10.3390/app14114738
2. Agrawal, T.K., Angelis, J., Khilji, W.A., Kalaiarasan, R., Wiktorsson, M.: Demonstration of a blockchain-based framework using smart contracts for supply chain collaboration. Int. J. Prod. Res. **61**(5), 1497–1516 (2023)
3. Monrat, A.A., Schelén, O., Andersson, K.: A survey of blockchain from the perspectives of applications, challenges, and opportunities. IEEE Access **7**, 117134–117151 (2019)
4. Prause, G.: Smart contracts for smart supply chains. IFAC-Papers OnLine **52**(13), 2501–2506 (2019)
5. Zheng, Z., et al.: An overview on smart contracts: challenges, advances and platforms. Future Gener. Comput. Syst. **105**, 475–491 (2020)
6. Tian, F.: An agri-food supply chain traceability system for China based on RFID & blockchain technology. In: 2016 13th International Conference on Service Systems and Service Management, pp. 1–6 (2013)
7. Korpela, K., Hallikas, J., Dahlberg, T.: Digital Supply Chain Transformation toward Blockchain Integration (2017)
8. Saberi, S., Kouhizadeh, M., Sarkis, J., Shen, L.: Blockchain technology and its relationships to sustainable supply chain management. Int. J. Prod. Res. **57**, 2117–2135 (2018)
9. Cole, R., Stevenson, M., Aitken, J.: Blockchain technology: implications for operations and supply chain management (2019)
10. Dutta, P., Choi, T., Somani, S., Butala, R.: Blockchain technology in supply chain operations: applications, challenges and research opportunities. Transport. Res. Part E Logist. Transport. Rev. **142**, 102067 (2020)
11. Kouhizadeh, M., Saberi, S., Sarkis, J.: Blockchain technology and the sustainable supply chain: theoretically exploring adoption barriers. Int. J. Prod. Econ. **231**, 107831 (2021)
12. Wang, X., Liu, Y., Wang, J., Chai, J.: Environmental impact assessment of blockchain-based sustainable supply chains. J. Clean. Prod. **341**, 130846 (2022)
13. Huckle, S., White, M.: Enhancing trust and transparency in organic food supply chains through blockchain technology. J. Clean. Prod. **323** (2023)
14. Zhang, L., Xu, L., Liao, Z., Wang, Y.: Blockchain-enabled supply chain resilience: conceptualization and empirical examination. Int. J. Prod. Econ. **241**, 108390 (2023)

Integrating AI, IoT, and Drones for Sustainable Apple Orchard Monitoring in Society 5.0

Ankana Datta[1], Sukalpa Paul[2], Anidipta Pal[1], Sounav Biswas[2], Anil Kumar Bag[2(✉)], and Diganta Sengupta[3]

[1] Department of Computer Science and Engineering - AIML, Heritage Institute of Technology, Chowbaga Road, Kolkata 700107, India
[2] Department of Applied Electronics and Instrumentation Engineering, Heritage Institute of Technology, Chowbaga Road, Kolkata 700107, India
anilkumar.bag@heritageit.edu
[3] Department of Computer Science and Engineering, Heritage Institute of Technology, Chowbaga Road, Kolkata 700107, India

Abstract. Sustainable smart agriculture forms one of the focal points in Society 5.0. We propose an AI-IOT enabled framework capable of processing multi-modal data for apple orchard monitoring. Real-time data acquisition is done from ground sensors as well as drone fitted cameras. The ground sensors monitor soil moisture, pH levels, nutrient composition (nitrogen, phosphorous, and potassium), ambient temperature, and humidity, while ESP32-CAMs fitted on drones capture images of apples, leaves, and trees. IOT enabled Unmanned Aerial Vehicle (UAV) as well as the ground sensor framework feed the data to the cloud. YOLOv8 and ResNet152 have been used to process the images for classifying the health of the apple plants. Machine learning models predict the farm yield using the ground sensor data reflecting the soil conditions. Our framework fares better than prior art in terms of accuracy. Although existing literature exhibits processing of soil data for prediction of health and yield, our study takes into consideration three further nutrient components - nitrogen, phosphorous, and potassium. Our study shows accuracy of 98.19% (apple counting) 53.66% (apple classification) 96.00% (leaf classification). To the entirety of our understanding, this study is the first to use multi-modal data inclusive of extended soil nutrients.

Keywords: Smart Apple Orchard Monitoring System (SAOMS) · IOT sensors · Computer vision · YOLOv8 and ResNet152 · UAV · agricultural yield · Sustainable Development Goals (SDG) · AutoRegressive Integrated Moving Average with Exogenous Variables (ARIMAX)

1 Introduction

Society 5.0 calls for the development of Smart Apple Orchard Monitoring System (SAOMS) which marks a recognizable step towards precision agriculture, integrating cutting-edge technologies like IoT, AI, sensors, and drone/UAV imagery

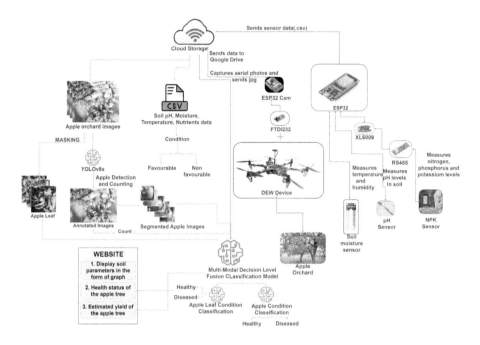

Fig. 1. High level diagram for the proposed framework

[1]. Automatic orchard management optimization frameworks [2] project potentials for SDG by enabling orchardists to make data-driven informed decisions, thereby improving productivity. Decision making [3] in precision agriculture requires a comprehensive service platform [4]. Figure 1 presents the High level diagram for the proposed framework. The proposed SAOMS collects data on soil conditions and plant health in real time coupled with the UAV captured images. We deploy deep learning models to analyze the images, and machine learning models to extract information from the soil data. The collected data is fed to the cloud which is processed further.

This study introduces an innovative approach to Smart Apple Orchard Monitoring. By integrating AI, IoT, UAVs, and sensors, the proposed framework classifies apples and leaves, counts them, and predicts yields based on soil parameters.

The rest of the paper is organized as follows. Section 2 presents the related work. Section 3 presents the proposed work. We present the results and discussions in Sect. 4 followed by Conclusion.

2 Related Work

Elumalai et al. [5] focus on developing an IoT-powered smart farm that leverages drone technology to boost crop yields and monitor plant health. Hu et al. [6] introduced a novel model that combines Vision Transform and the YOLOv7 object detection system, utilizing attention mechanisms like the Convolutional Block Attention Module (CBAM) and channel attention. This model showed significant improvements in accuracy and multi-object tracking. Jemaa et al. [7] proposed a two-stage UAV-based framework which uses RGB UAV images for tree detection and multi-band imagery-derived vegetation indices for health classification, achieving an F1-score of 86.24% and an overall accuracy of 97.52%. Kiktev et al. [8] developed a monitoring system which uses a neural network to identify apple fruits on tree crowns, count them, determine diseases, ripening rates, and crop volume per hectare. Experiments demonstrated high accuracy in estimating fruit numbers (94.72%) and counting infected fruits (90.44%).

3 Materials and Methods

Data for monitoring the apple orchard is obtained from two sources - the UAV mounted ESP32-CAM and the sensors placed on the ground throughout the apple orchard. All these sensor data are uploaded to cloud via ESP32. The image capture rate is one image per 2 s. The drone has a 4GB memory card that stores the photos taken throughout that period in case it loses its network connection. The images are moved to Google Drive as soon as the network is restored. A soil pH sensor board is used to monitor the pH of the soil. $SoilpH \propto 1/(VoltageDifference)$. The electrical resistivity of the soil, which is influenced by the moisture content, is measured by this sensor. $SoilMoisture \propto 1/(ElectricalResistiity)$. The most important nutrients for determining the level of nutrients in soil are calcium (Ca), phosphorus (P), potassium (K), and nitrogen (N), though in smaller amounts. The Soil NPK Sensor is used to measure the aforementioned parameters. Temperature is measured between 0 °C and 50 °C with a maximum variance of 2 °C, while humidity is measured between 20% and 80% with 95% accuracy.

The annotated apple images are segmented and stacked together, creating an array of annotated apple images. We have used YOLOv8 as it uses C2F modules for feature extraction with multiple layers stacked. A publicly available dataset comprising of 600 images of an apple orchard is used [9], having a combination of various view angles, lighting conditions, and angle deviation. The images are resized at 640 × 640 pixels. The data is fed into the YOLOv8x model and trained with 100 epochs. Model summary: 365 layers, 68,153,571 parameters, 68,153,555 gradients, 258.1 GFLOPs. The optimizer used is AdamW ($momentum = 0.9, lr = 0.002$) with parameter groups 97 weight (decay = 0.0), 103 bias ($decay = 0.0$) 104 weight ($decay = 0.0005$). After detection of the apples, each apple in an image is given a unique ID, which is essential for tracking individual apples across multiple frames in a video. To maintain consistency in identification across frames, the Euclidean distance is computed between the bounding boxes of apples in successive frames. This distance helps to track and match apples by their proximity in successive frames. If the distance is small enough, the apples are considered the same across frames, and the unique ID is retained, minimizing multi-counting of the same apple

Table 1. Soil parameters from IoT sensors

Sensor name	Parameters	Unit
Soil Moisture Sensor (Resistive Type)	Moisture	%
Soil pH Sensor	pH	-
NPK Sensor	Nitrogen, Phosphorus, Potassium	mg/kg
DHT 11	Temperature, Humidity	°C,%

Table 2. Observed soil parameters from IoT sensors

Sensor name	Normal range of parameters	Observed values
Soil Moisture Sensor	20–40 %	28% (average)
Soil pH Sensor	5.5–6.5	5.1 (average)
NPK Sensor	N: 30–40 mg/kg, P: 10–20 mg/kg, K: 100–150 mg/kg	43.5 mg/kg, 15 mg/kg, 120 mg/kg
DHT 11	Temp: 7–30, Humidity: 35–65 °C	Within range, 40%

overtime. The ResNet152 classifier model was trained on a dataset comprising 3961 apple images, categorized into four classes: Normal_Apple, Rot_Apple, Blotch_Apple, and Scab_Apple. The images were uniformly resized to 128×128 pixels. The model achieved a test accuracy of 53.66%. The ResNet152 model was trained on a dataset of 996 apple leaf images, categorized into four classes: Healthy, Black Rot, Scab, and Cedar Rust, which are common diseases in apple leaves. The images were resized to 128 × 128 pixels. RMSProp was used as the optimizer, with Cross-Entropy Loss. The model achieved a test accuracy of 98.56% and a validation accuracy of 96.54%. Yield prediction involves forecasting the potential yield of crops based on various factors such as soil quality, weather conditions, and crop management practices. The predictions and counts are combined to predict the yield of the orchard. These predicted counts are integrated with the data from IoT sensors. Data from sensors monitoring soil parameters along with their units for measurement are shown in Table 1. The pre-trained ARIMAX model is used to train the dataset with the following characteristics: AR coefficient (ar.L1) = 0.2675 significant (p-value = 0.000), MA coefficient (ma.L1) = −0.9453 significant (p-value = 0.000), Variance of error term (sigma2) = 28.3473 highly significant, Ljung-Box test (Q) = 0.02 p-value = 0.89 (no significant autocorrelation), and arque-Bera test = 6158.00 p-value = 0.00 (non-normal residuals).

4 Result and Discussions

We recorded the normal data ranges for the environmental parameters and fed this data into our classification model. The normal and observed values are presented in Table 2. The YOLOv8 model fetched an F1-Score of 0.612, precision of 0.585, recall of 0.558, mAP50 value of 0.515, and mAP50-90 value of 0.29. Figure 2 illustrates the model's training over 100 epochs. The mAP values are calculated as follows: $mAP = \frac{1}{n}\sum_{i=1}^{n} AP_i$. We utilized ResNet152 with 5-fold cross-validation, the final model having K-fold value = 2. We calculated

Table 3. Performance metrics reported in notable existing proposals for other datasets.

#Ref	Efficiency	Accuracy	Precision	Recall	F1(%)
[7]	-	98.06% (classification)	-	-	-
[8]	-	94.72% (detection) 90.44% (counting)	-	-	-
[10]	-	89% (detection) 88.67% (overlapping fruit) 93.64% (obscured fruit)	-	-	-
This study	88.65%	98.19% (apple counting) 53.66% (apple classification) 96.00% (leaf classification)	96.57% (leaf) 68.70% (apple)	96.00%	96.14

a composite performance score, combining the F1-Score and loss, to determine the final model. The composite score is calculated as $CompositeScore = \frac{F_1}{L}$. We selected ResNet152 following a comparative analysis of the Soft Voting Classifier. The Voting Classifier used are Random Forest, Logistic Regression, Support Vector Classifier, Decision Tree, Categorical Boosting and LGBM. The performance value sets in terms of {Accuracy (%), Precision, Recall, F1-Score} for the Voting Classifier and ResNet152 are {36.00, 0.4, 0.5, 0.45} and {96.0, 0.9657, 0.96, 0.9617} respectively. We observed that ResNet152 fares better. The ARIMAX model predicts apple yield having values for MAE = 3.62, MSE = 57.19, RMSE = 7.56, MBD = 1.8, R2 = 0.075, and a variance score of 0.867. The total expected harvest at the end of the season is calculated using $TotalPredictedYield = \sum_{t=1}^{n} \hat{Y}_t$, where $\hat{Y}_t$ is the predicted yield at each time step. Peer Comparison with literary proposals in terms of accuracy and is presented in Table 3.

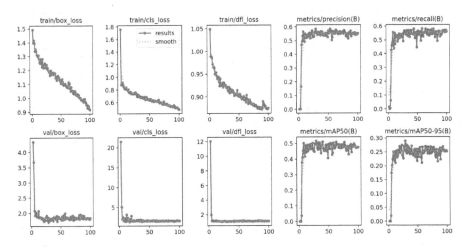

Fig. 2. Performance results of the YOLO model

5 Conclusion and Future Scope

This study presents a transformative approach for Smart Apple Orchard Monitoring. The proposed framework classifies apples and leaves, counts, and also predicts the yields based on soil parameters. Additionally, we can implement a more effective filtering mechanism for sorting good and bad apples. By deploying a model for bad apple detection and placing a camera on the conveyor belt in the apple segregation area, the system can automatically detect bad apples.

References

1. Ahamed, T.: IoT and AI in Agriculture. Springer, Singapore (2023)
2. Nakaguchi, V.M., Ahamed, T.: Artificial intelligence in agriculture: commitment to establish society 5.0: an analytical concepts mapping for deep learning application. In: IoT and AI in Agriculture: Self-sufficiency in Food Production to Achieve Society 5.0 and SDG's Globally, pp. 133–152. Springer, Singapore (2023)
3. Araújo, S.O., et al.: Intelligent data-driven decision support for agricultural systems-ID3SAS. IEEE Access **11**, 115798–115815 (2023). https://doi.org/10.1109/ACCESS.2023.3324813
4. Xie, L., Luan, D., Liu, H., Wei, W.: Design and implementation of a smart orchard comprehensive service platform. In: 2023 IEEE International Conference on Electrical, Automation and Computer Engineering (ICEACE), pp. 64–69 (2023). https://doi.org/10.1109/ICEACE60673.2023.10442478.
5. Elumalai, M., Fernandez, T.F., Ragab, M.: Machine learning (ML) algorithms on IoT and drone data for smart farming. In: Balasubramanian, S., Natarajan, G., Chelliah, P.R. (eds.) Intelligent Robots and Drones for Precision Agriculture, pp. 179–206. Springer, Cham (2024). https://doi.org/10.1007/978-3-031-51195-0_10
6. Hu, J., Fan, C., Wang, Z., Ruan, J., Wu, S.: Fruit detection and counting in apple orchards based on improved Yolov7 and multi-object tracking methods. Sensors **23**(13), Art. no. 5903 (2023). https://doi.org/10.3390/s23135903
7. Jemaa, H., Bouachir, W., Leblon, B., LaRocque, A., Haddadi, A., Bouguila, N.: UAV-based computer vision system for orchard apple tree detection and health assessment. Remote Sens. **15**(14), Art. no. 3558 (2023). https://doi.org/10.3390/rs15143558
8. Kiktev, N., Kutyrev, A., Mazurchuk, P.: International scientific symposium 'intelligent solutions' IntSol-2023. In: CEUR Workshop Proceedings, Kyiv-Uzhhorod, Ukraine, 27–28 September 2023. Available under Creative Commons License Attribution 4.0 International (CC BY 4.0)
9. https://www.kaggle.com/datasets/royvoetman/generated-apple-tree-dataset-prompt-engineering
10. Behera, S.K., Sethy, P.K., Sahoo, S.K., Panigrahi, S., Rajpoot, S.C.: On-tree fruit monitoring system using IoT and image analysis. Concurr. Eng. **29**(1), 6–15 (2021). https://doi.org/10.1177/1063293X20988395

SHIKSHA: Smart Hybrid Intelligent Knowledge System for Helping Academia

Aishik Paul[1(✉)], Abhisri Shaha[2], Arijit Mukherjee[1], Debajit Guha[2], Priyam Das[1], Ankan Das[3], Anurina Tarafdar[2], and Anindya Sen[1]

[1] Department of Electronics and Communication Engineering, Heritage Institute of Technology, Kolkata 700107, West Bengal, India
{aishik.paul.ece26,arijit.mukherjee.ece26, priyam.das.ece26}@heritageit.edu.in, anindya.sen@heritageit.edu

[2] Department of Computer Science and Engineering, Heritage Institute of Technology, Kolkata 700107, West Bengal, India
{abhisri.shaha.cse26,debajit.guha.cse27}@heritageit.edu.in, anurina.tarafdar@heritageit.edu

[3] Department of Computer Science and Engineering (AIML), Heritage Institute of Technology, Kolkata 700107, West Bengal, India
ankan.das.aiml26@heritageit.edu.in

Abstract. Our Smart Hybrid Intelligent Knowledge System for Helping Academia (SHIKSHA) addresses critical challenges in classroom and examination management by offering a fully automated solution. Key features consist automated attendance tracking with integrated intruder detection which eliminates manual errors and enhances security. The system also improves examination management using the Coordinate and Area-based Row Column Mapping (CAB-RCM) algorithm ensuring accurate seat-matrix mapping via face recognition. SHIKSHA automates student performance monitoring by analyzing behavior with face tracking and seating patterns to help educators make data-driven decisions. It supports resource management by sending maintenance alerts based on projector usage with a brightness-based algorithm. It monitors classroom audio to assess attentiveness and track syllabus progress. Utilizing existing CCTV cameras and microphones, SHIKSHA operates with minimal hardware requirements and offers an eco-friendly, cost-effective and scalable solution that enhances academic efficiency across a wide range of educational institutions.

Keywords: Fully Automated Attendance · Behavior Detection · Seat Matrix Based Row Column Mapping · Computer Vision · Signal Processing · Noise Voice Segmentation

1 Introduction

Smart education uses advanced technologies to improve learning and classroom management. The proposed Smart Hybrid Intelligent Knowledge System for

Helping Academia (SHIKSHA) is a comprehensive solution that addresses key problems in classroom and examination environments using various algorithms. It includes an *automated attendance system* that eliminates long queues at biometric kiosks, reduces human error, and prevents unauthorized entry. The system uses *Coordinate and Area-based Row Column Mapping (CAB-RCM)* to map and cross-check students' registered seat matrix during examinations. SHIKSHA also provides *student behavior monitoring* through seating pattern analysis, a brightness-based *projector management* method, and a *real-time fire alert system* based on fire intensity. These features make SHIKSHA a scalable, cost-effective solution for academic institutions of all sizes, with minimal hardware requirements. The system helps students, teachers and administrators with data-driven insights, making it a cost-effective solution for all educational institutions. The rest of the paper is structured as follows: Sect. 2: Related Work; Sect. 3: Methodology; Sect. 4: Experimental Results. Section 5: Conclusion.

2 Related Work

Recent studies have explored various methods for classroom automation. Ambre et al. [1] and Kumar et al. [2] have proposed few methods to monitor attendance using HAAR cascades and a CNN model. In [2] the authors have trained ResNet-18 and ResNet-50 models on the FER2013 dataset to monitor attendance. Contrarily, we have used a combination of YOLOv8 and DeepFace to detect and recognize students' faces, which outperform HAAR cascades and CNN as it handles multiple faces simultaneously, making it ideal for crowded classrooms. Moreover, DeepFace requires only a few images for accurate recognition. Surantha et al. [3] used SRGAN to enhance the quality of captured images and FaceNet architecture to recognize faces. Our model works better, being adaptable to resolutions and is faster by avoiding image enhancement. Llurba et al. [4] and Rawat et al. [5] detected behavior using an emotion recognition model that detects students' faces and tracks Action Units (facial muscle movements) to classify their emotions based on their facial movements. Contrarily, our approach uses a custom trained YOLOv8 model to detect faces and classify the behaviors with face tracking, thus not relying totally on the facial expressions of the students. Alqahtani et al. [6] measured classroom noise levels, compared them with international standards and used ANOVA to analyze their impact on student behavior. We have monitored student attention using classroom audio data by detecting voice and noise through signal processing methods. This approach reduces computation time and allows the audio data to be used for various purposes.

3 Methodology

This section presents the proposed Smart Hybrid Intelligent Knowledge System for Helping Academia (SHIKSHA) technique, outlining its key features and presenting a workflow schematic diagram in Fig. 1.

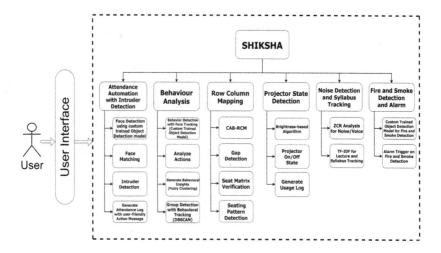

Fig. 1. Schematic diagram of SHIKSHA.

3.1 Attendance Automation with Intruder Detection

The automated attendance system uses CCTV footage to detect student faces, analyzing input video frames at specific intervals ensuring detection of every face. A combination of object detection model and DeepFace is used in order to reduce the requirement of a huge database of students. Classrooms have databases and faces are matched using DeepFace library and mapped with roll numbers, identifying intruders with cosine distance value. The cosine distance between two face embeddings **A** and **B** is calculated as Cosine Distance = (1 - Cosine Similarity), where, Cosine Similarity = $\frac{\mathbf{A} \cdot \mathbf{B}}{\|\mathbf{A}\| \|\mathbf{B}\|}$.

3.2 Behavior Analysis

Our system automates classroom behavior tracking using behavior detection with **face tracking** ensuring student individual behavior detection continuity even when a face is temporarily undetected. To associate behaviors with students, the system uses maximum Intersection over Union (IoU) between face bounding box (A) and the behavior bounding box (B) as, IoU = $\frac{\text{Area of Intersection}}{\text{Area of Union}} = \frac{(x_B - x_A) \cdot (y_B - y_A)}{\text{Area}(A) + \text{Area}(B) - \text{Area of Intersection}}$. Fuzzy clustering categorizes behaviors dynamically and assign marks based on students' behavior data. The system is used in exam halls for automated cheating detection. **Group Detection** of students is performed using DBSCAN which detects student clusters based on seating arrangements using center points from face detection defining neighborhood of point p as the set of points in the dataset D that are within a radius ϵ: $N_\epsilon(p) = \{q \in D \mid \text{dist}(p, q) \leq \epsilon\}$. Group frequency and behavior data help identify disruptive groups for management or seating changes to promote productive clusters for collaboration.

3.3 Row Column Mapping (CAB-RCM Algorithm)

The Coordinate and Area-Based Row Column Mapping (CAB-RCM) algorithm (Algorithm 1) combines Coordinate-Based (CB-RCM) and Area-Based (AB-RCM) methods to map students' seating to a predefined matrix. We consider that there are m rows and n columns in the classroom. CB-RCM clusters students by detecting face center points and grouping by similar vertical (y_i) and horizontal (x_i) coordinates. AB-RCM calculates the average bounding box area in each row for spatial consistency. A gap detection mechanism identifies missing students by analyzing gaps (G_n) with tolerance (ΔG) ensuring correct mapping if any student is absent in a row. While CB-RCM struggles with irregular camera angles and AB-RCM requires spatial uniformity, the combined CAB-RCM ensures accurate student-to-seat mapping through a robust grid system.

Algorithm 1 CAB-RCM Algorithm

Input: CCTV footage data; m=number of rows; n=number of columns; Face Bounding Box Center Points
Output: Grid of student positions mapped to their assigned seating arrangement
1: Define allowable threshold x_i for column similarity, tolerance ΔG for gap detection;
2: Initialize empty matrices for rows and columns;
3: **for** each frame in the footage **do**
4:     **for** each detected face bounding box **do**
5:         Compute enter coordinates (x_i, y_i) and area A_i of the bounding box;
6:     **end for**
7:     Group students by similar y-coordinates ($y_1 \approx y_2 \approx \cdots \approx y_n$); // (**Row Detection**)
8:     Group students by similar x-coordinates ($x_1 \approx x_2 \approx \cdots \approx x_m$); // (**Column Detection (CB-RCM)**)
9:     Compute average area for each row, $A_{i_{avg}} = \frac{A_{i1}+A_{i2}+\cdots+A_{in}}{n}$, as ($A_1 \approx A_2 \approx \cdots \approx A_n$);
10:     Traverse along x-axis, matching each bounding box with the average area for that row; // (**Column Detection (AB-RCM)**)
11:     For each row, calculate average gap G_{avg} between adjacent x-coordinates, $G_{avg} = \frac{|x_2-x_1|+|x_3-x_2|+\cdots+|x_n-x_{n-1}|}{n}$; // (**Gap Detection**)
12:     **if** $G_n > G_{avg} + \Delta G$ **then**
13:         Mark as a missing student;
14:     **end if**
15: **end for**

3.4 Projector State Detection

Projector state detection monitors the usage and prevents malfunctions. Using a custom object detection model projector's Region of Interest (ROI) is restricted in CCTV footage. A mathematical computer vision algorithm determines its ON/OFF state based on the brightness of the brightest point in the ROI, with positive or negative spikes indicating state changes from OFF to ON and ON to OFF respectively with a defined threshold (Figs. 2, 3, and 4).

3.5 Noise Detection and Syllabus Tracking

Classroom attentiveness is monitored using Noise-Voice Segmentation fetched with Zero Crossing Rate (ZCR) analysis (Fig. 5) with a threshold (red dotted

Fig. 2. Brightest point (green circle) at projector lens and high brightness value(ON state) (Color figure online)

Fig. 3. Brightest point (green circle) at projector body and low brightness value (OFF state) (Color figure online)

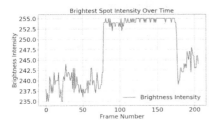
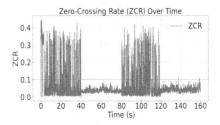

Fig. 4. Graph Showing brightness change spikes used to detect changes in projector state

Fig. 5. Zero Crossing Rate Plot

line). Noise and silent segments are trimmed, leaving only lectures and teacher-student conversations, which are transcribed into daily text files. TF-IDF vectorization helps in tracking syllabus progress by assigning weight to words based on frequency across files, with Inverse Document Frequency highlighting term importance across documents compared with registered syllabus keyword files with cosine similarity.

We used the formulae, $\text{TF}(t,d) = \frac{\text{Number of times term } t \text{ appears in document } d}{\text{Total number of terms in document } d}$; and $\text{IDF}(t) = \log\left(\frac{N \text{ (Total number of documents to be compared)}}{1+\text{DF}(t) \text{ (Number of documents containing term "t")}}\right)$. $\text{TF-IDF}(t,d) = \text{TF}(t,d) \times \text{IDF}(t)$. Cosine Similarity $= \frac{\mathbf{A} \cdot \mathbf{B}}{\|\mathbf{A}\|\|\mathbf{B}\|}$, where $A \cdot B = \sum_{i=1}^{n} A_i \times B_i$, $\|B\| = \sqrt{\sum_{i=1}^{n} B_i^2}$ and $\|A\| = \sqrt{\sum_{i=1}^{n} A_i^2}$ (X_i=i-th term).

3.6 Fire and Smoke Detection and Alarm

To address risks from fire hazards, an automated algorithm detects fire or smoke in classrooms using a custom-trained object detection model, raising alarms based on severity (determined by the area of fire) and triggering an automated emergency call when it exceeds a threshold.

4 Experimental Results

The study evaluates the proposed SHIKSHA approach, using a student database (created by registering our face images in the system), Face Detection Dataset[1], Fire & Smoke Dataset[2]. The model achieved a 92% mAP for face detection, 96% mAP for behavior detection, 98% mAP for projector detection, and 97% mAP for fire detection. The system was tested for six different behaviors of students ("looking forward", "raising hand", "reading", "writing", "sleeping", "using phone", and "turning around"), including face detection, projector detection, and fire detection, with various datasets and videos. A computer with 8 GB RAM, 512 GB SSD, 12th Generation Intel® Core™ i5 processor was used for experimental setup, and the classroom data was collected using a phone camera of 13MP. The proposed system has been implemented in a three-layer web-interface where the Students can access dashboard; the Teachers can view students with details; and the Administrators can access all details.

Fig. 6. Classroom Attendance

Fig. 7. Intruder Detection

Fig. 8. Detected Behavior in a Classroom

Fig. 9. Detected Groups in a Classroom

Fig. 10. RCM Algorithm Applied on a Classroom Image

Fig. 11. Student Faces Mapped with Seat Matrix

The **Attendance Automation with Intruder Detection** system generates a video with student names and detected intruders (Figs. 6 and 7), attendance CSV file, and teacher-friendly action messages. The **Behaviour Analysis**

---

[1] https://www.kaggle.com/datasets/fareselmenshawii/face-detection-dataset.
[2] https://www.kaggle.com/datasets/gautamrmenon/fire-and-smoke-roboflow.

system generates student behavior-tracking videos with names (Fig. 8), CSV file with behavior timings, insights, and recommendations, while group detection (Fig. 9) outputs a CSV of student groupings and behavioral analysis. The **Row Column Mapping** system uses CAB-RCM algorithm to map student faces to seating arrangements for exams (Figs. 10 and 11). The **Projector State Detection** system detects projector on/off states using brightness, generating videos, CSV files, and maintenance reports. The **Noise Detection and Syllabus Tracking** system outputs a CSV with voice/noise durations and tracks syllabus progress by topic. The **Fire and Smoke Detection and Alarm** system sends real-time alerts with dynamic intensity based alarming system.

5 Conclusion and Future Scope

The Smart Hybrid Intelligent Knowledge System for Helping Academia (SHIKSHA) streamlines classroom and examination settings with various automated methods with reduced computation time and GPU requirement. Future improvements could focus on enhancing detection in low-resolution video inputs and expanding datasets while integrating advanced lightweight deep learning models for better student performance analysis. Moreover, we would also explore SHIKSHA's deployment in diverse educational environments, ensuring its adaptability and effectiveness across different academic contexts.

References

1. Ambre, N., Pitale, R., Rao, P., Mote, H., Chavan, S.: A-eye: attendance monitoring using face detection and recognition from CCTV footage. In: 2024 4th International Conference on Emerging Smart Technologies and Applications (eSmarTA), pp. 1–6. IEEE (2024)
2. Kumar, M.V., Ramesh, G.P., Pareek, P.K., Deepak, H.A., Babu, J.A.: Robotic attendance scheme in the classroom using artificial intelligence and internet of things. In: 2023 International Conference on Applied Intelligence and Sustainable Computing (ICAISC), pp. 1–6. IEEE (2023)
3. Surantha, N., Yose, E., Isa, S.M.: Low-resolution face recognition for CCTV and edge-powered smart attendance systems. In: 2024 IEEE 48th Annual Computers, Software, and Applications Conference (COMPSAC), pp. 676–681. IEEE (2024)
4. Llurba, C., Fretes, G., Palau, R.: Classroom emotion monitoring based on image processing. Sustainability **16**(2), 916 (2024)
5. Rawat, S., Rodrigues, M., Sheregar, P., Wagaskar, K.A., Tripathy, A.K.: Computer vision based hybrid classroom attention monitoring. In: 2024 IEEE International Conference on Information Technology, Electronics and Intelligent Communication Systems (ICITEICS), pp. 1–6. IEEE (2024)
6. Alqahtani, A.Y., Makki, A.A., Alidrisi, H.M.: Revealing factors influencing classroom noise in the universities teaching and learning environment: a design of experiments approach. J. Eng. Res. **11**(1), 100009 (2023)

Analyzing Social Networks of Actors in Movies and TV Shows

Sarthak Giri[1(✉)], Sneha Chaudhary[1], and Bikalpa Gautam[2]

[1] ION Group, Noida, Uttar Pradesh, India
sarthak.giri@iongroup.com
[2] KC Construction, Pokhara, Gandaki Province, Nepal

Abstract. The paper offers a comprehensive analysis of social networks among movie actors and directors in the film industry. Utilizing data from IMDb and Netflix, we leverage Python and NetworkX to uncover valuable insights into the movie industry's intricate web of collaborations. Key findings include identifying the top actors and directors in the OTT sector, tracking the rise of movies on OTT platforms, and analyzing centrality measures for actors. We also explore the hidden patterns within the movie data, unveiling the shortest paths between actors and predicting future collaborations. Cluster analysis categorizes movies based on various criteria, revealing the most insular and liberal clusters and identifying crossover actors bridging different segments of the industry. The study highlights that actors predominantly collaborate within language groups, transcending national boundaries. We investigate the degree of isolation of Bollywood from global cinema and identify actors working across world clusters. The project provides valuable insights into the evolving dynamics of the film industry and the impact of OTT platforms, benefiting industry professionals, scholars, and enthusiasts.

Keywords: Social Network Analysis · Clustering · Sentiment Analysis · Link Prediction · OTT Platforms

The following abbreviations are used in this manuscript:

OTT	Over-The-Top
SNA	Social Network Analysis
IMDb	Internet Movie Database
EDA	Exploratory Data Analysis
NLP	Natural Language Processing
QoE	Quality of Experience
PCA	Principal Component Analysis
ANN	Artificial Neural Network

1 Introduction

The rapid rise of Over-the-top (OTT) streaming services alongside the long-established film industry is driving a major and transformative shift in the entertainment landscape [1–4]. A lot of research has been done already that studied the performance of OTT platforms and their impact on the market [5–7]. For performers and artists, this is a critical time that offers them a unique chance to engage with audiences around the world [8,9]. In this digitally infused era, a strong online presence has become essential to success, and the OTT sector has become a vital platform for actors and filmmakers to flourish on. But in the fiercely competitive OTT space, the complex web of interactions and relationships between market players becomes a critical determinant of success [10,11]. A thorough understanding of the interactions between actors, directors, producers, and the industry at large is imperative in this digital age. The implications of the entertainment industry's ongoing digital age adaptation are wide-ranging, encompassing aspects such as cross-industry dynamics, collaboration patterns, and the changing nature of actor relationships.

SNA, a data science discipline, provides a powerful framework for investigating these interactions by leveraging the power of networks and graph theory [12–15]. SNA has a long history of revealing hidden patterns in a variety of fields, from determining how illnesses spread to tracking the dissemination of ideas. In order to investigate the intricate connections within the traditional film industry and the OTT industry, we are utilizing SNA for movie network analysis. Our data collection includes publicly available sources, with platforms like IMDb and Netflix functioning as crucial repositories. Using the NetworkX package and the Python programming language, the analysis allows us to carefully examine this data and reveal important insights.

Additionally, our study explores the centrality metrics of different players, illuminating their roles within the networks and exposing the dominant figures that influence the sector. We investigate the idea of the shortest path between players, revealing hidden relationships that specify the paths leading to cooperation. Furthermore, in order to predict future partnerships, we utilize advanced link prediction approaches like resource allocation, Jaccard cosine similarity, common neighbour analysis, and Adamic Adar index. The study explores the fascinating world of clusters within the network, exposing subclusters within clusters, raising important questions about Bollywood's level of exclusion from the international film industry, and identifying performers who work across different countries. This research project is motivated by the investigation of these interrelated networks and the complex relationships that characterize the cinema and over-the-top (OTT) industries. The following sections of the paper include a literature survey, methodology, results, and conclusion, as well as future work.

2 Related Works

The related literature provides valuable insights into sentiment and social network analysis in movie data. However, our research builds on these studies by expanding the scope, applying deeper network analysis, and using more extensive datasets, as summarized in Table 1.

Table 1. Comparison of related works with our research.

Author(s)	Contributions	Limitations/How Our Research Addresses Them
Dangi et al. [16]	Framework for sentiment and pattern analysis in movie data	Lacked community detection, centrality, and database expansion beyond movies. We include OTT content and broader network metrics
Hodeghatta [17]	Twitter sentiment analysis of Hollywood movies	Focused on Hollywood only. Our research covers a wider database, including OTT platforms
Weng et al. [18]	Semantic movie analysis using role-based social networks	Applied to only three types of storylines. We extend the analysis to more complex movie narratives and databases
Ha et al. [19]	CosMovis for sentiment relationships in movie reviews	Inefficient for large networks. Our system handles large datasets more effectively
Weng and Chu [20]	RoleNet: character exploration in stories	Limited databases affect accuracy. We use larger, more diverse datasets for improved results
Rathor and Prakash [21]	Sentiment analysis using IMDB reviews	Limited to IMDB. Our research includes both movie and OTT databases, covering actor-movie/series networks
Li and Lin [22]	Key player identification in social networks	Focused on egocentric networks. Our work applies these methods to actor networks with broader metrics
Lee et al. [23]	ActRec: Actor recommendation using word embeddings	Focused on actor-role recommendations. Our research delves into actor networks using advanced analysis
Hu et al. [24]	Movie and actor recommendations based on YAGO and IMDB	Limited to movie recommendations. Our analysis applies to actor networks, using comprehensive datasets
Liu et al. [25]	SMAS: Social media analysis for box office prediction	Focused on revenue prediction. Our study extends to actor network analysis across movies and OTT platforms
Landherr et al. [26]	Reviewed centrality measures in social networks	Centrality measures are not applied to actor networks. Our research implements these metrics for actor network analysis
Wang et al. [27]	Heterogeneous graph attention network with sentiment markers	Focused on graph representation. Our research performs extensive network analysis beyond representation
Yuliana et al. [28]	SNA applied to an online fan group	Limited to online fan analysis. Our research covers larger real-world datasets in movies and OTT content
Lewis et al. [29]	Social networks and cultural tastes on Facebook	Focused on changing traits like hobbies. We use a constant movie dataset for more stable insights
Tang et al. [30]	TAP model for social influences in large networks	Focused on connections and relationships. Our research extends to centrality measures and community detection

3 Keyword Network Analysis of Actor Collaborations in Movies and OTT Platforms

We conducted a keyword co-occurrence analysis to investigate the evolving dynamics of social networks within the movie and television industries, particularly focusing on the role of actors and directors. This analysis aimed to uncover research trends and highlight domains shaping the industry in the era of digital disruption. A keyword co-occurrence network represents relationships between frequently appearing keywords in a collection of documents. In such a network, vertices represent keywords, and edges connect two keywords that co-occur within the same document.

The co-occurrence network in this study was constructed using VOSviewer, a bibliometric tool that extracts and visualizes keyword relationships from bibliographic data. Keywords were derived from the titles and abstracts of research papers using VOSviewer's text-mining functionality. For instance, if a paper listed five keywords, each keyword would connect to the others, forming a fully connected subnetwork for that paper. Similarly, if a keyword appeared in multiple papers, it would link to all keywords from those papers, creating a web of associations that reflects the shared thematic focus of the literature. The dataset comprised research papers sourced from the Web of Science (WoS) database. To ensure relevance, we conducted an advanced search using terms such as "Social Network Analysis in Movies," "Actor Collaboration," "OTT Platforms," and "Digital Media." The search was further refined to include papers published between 2014 and 2022, focusing on the intersection of social networks and digital transformations within the movie industry. Initially, 2146 research papers were identified. These papers were filtered based on criteria such as the presence of relevant keywords in their titles, abstracts, and research areas. After rigorous screening for thematic alignment and removing duplicates, a final set of 617 papers was retained for analysis.

The resulting co-occurrence network (see Fig. 1) provides a comprehensive visualization of research trends in the field. Dominant clusters of keywords such as "character," "story," and "experience" underscore traditional areas of focus, highlighting the social and creative dimensions of actor collaborations. Emerging keywords like "smartphone use" and "OTT streaming services" reflect the growing influence of digital platforms such as Netflix and Amazon Prime, which are reshaping audience interactions and narrative structures. These trends point to a paradigm shift from traditional cinematic practices to new forms of digital storytelling and engagement.

The temporal analysis of keywords, spanning from 2014 to 2022, reveals a progressive emphasis on "multimedium" and "smartphone use," indicating pivotal research directions. Keywords like "quality" and "experience" emphasize the role of audience perception and technical critique in the success of films, particularly in the context of OTT platforms. These observations suggest that the increasing integration of digital technologies is transforming collaboration networks within the film industry, warranting further exploration of this intersection. This keyword co-occurrence network serves as a framework for

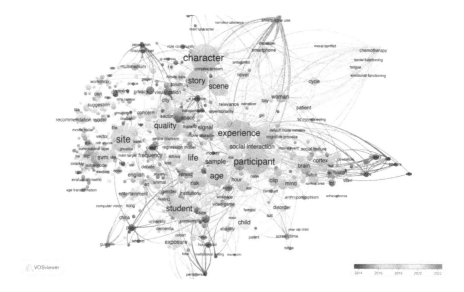

Fig. 1. Keyword co-occurrence network illustrating key themes in social network analysis of actors and directors, and the role of digital platforms and character centrality in shaping film and OTT collaborations between 2014–2022

understanding the evolving research landscape in the movie and OTT platform industries.

4 Proposed Architecture

This proposed architecture given in Fig. 2 outlines a comprehensive approach to conducting social network analysis within the OTT and movie industries. It encompasses data collection from diverse sources, like Kaggle[1] and IMDb[2]. By leveraging the NetworkX library in Python, the architecture facilitates network construction to visualize relationships between various actors. Centrality measures, such as degree, betweenness, and eigenvector centrality, are applied to identify influential actors who play pivotal roles in connecting disparate groups and influencing information flow. Additionally, link prediction algorithms like the Jaccard coefficient calculate the likelihood of potential collaborations, with the caveat that some probabilities may exceed 1 due to high connectivity within the network. Visualization tools further enhance the understanding of actor relationships, while community detection methods, such as the Louvain method, reveal clusters of collaboration and shared interests among actors. Ultimately, this analysis aims to provide valuable insights into viewer preferences and emerging trends, identifying potential future leaders and collaborations in the movie industry landscape.

---

[1] https://www.kaggle.com/datasets/shivamb/netflix-shows.
[2] https://developer.imdb.com/non-commercial-datasets/.

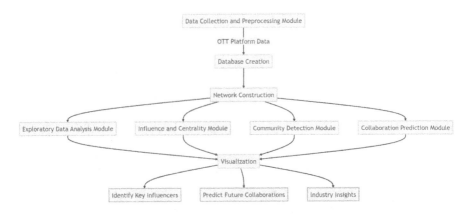

Fig. 2. Proposed architecture outlining the workflow for social network analysis within OTT platforms, incorporating data collection, network construction, and centrality analysis to identify key influencers.

5 Methodology

This paper's methodology involves the following sequential steps: Firstly, we will carefully choose a suitable database to establish the network. Subsequently, we will conduct preprocessing and culling of the database to eliminate undesirable data and entries that are not useful for our analysis. Next, we will construct a social network from this refined database, with a preference for representing it as an adjacency matrix. This matrix will serve as a foundational tool for our analysis. We will then engage in a series of operations on the matrix to draw meaningful conclusions, such as determining centralities and exploring various factors like identifying actors with the highest number of film credits, pinpointing actors with extensive co-star collaborations, and uncovering co-stars who have participated in the most acting partnerships.

5.1 Dataset

The study conducts a social network analysis of movie actors using data from Netflix, a leading global OTT platform, and IMDb, an open-source database rich in information on movies, series, and entertainment figures. The dataset includes actor names, titles, release dates, and co-appearance details, which are crucial for building the social network. The OTT data is sourced from Kaggle and contains over 8,807 unique streaming titles, while the movie data is taken from IMDb. The IMDb dataset provides rich metadata crucial for network construction containing unique identifiers like titles and individuals, their roles (category), specific jobs, character names and language. This enables precise mapping of collaborative relationships between actors. The Kaggle dataset complements this with additional contextual information such as release years, countries of production, and cast details. Together, these datasets offer a multi-dimensional view of cinematic collaborations to construct and analyze intricate social networks of actors across different genres, periods, nationalities and production contexts.

5.2 Modules

In this research, we developed multiple interconnected modules to systematically analyze the collaboration patterns in the film and OTT industries (Fig. 3). First, the Data Collection and Preprocessing module handled the input data, performing essential pre-processing and cleaning steps to create a structured dataset and a network graph for further analysis in Python. Then we had the Exploratory Data Analysis (EDA) module, which provided a basic overview of the dataset by revealing key patterns and trends within the OTT and movie industries. Through graphical visualizations, this module showcased critical metrics such as the number of movies released per year, average cast size, content type distribution, rating categories, and viewer preferences.

Following this, the Actor Collaboration Network module used the network graph to evaluate metrics such as the shortest path between any two actors and the likelihood of their collaboration based on the path length. By analyzing these connections, we gained insights into actor partnerships and identified actors with significant collaboration histories.

To further analyze influence within the network, the Influence and Centrality Analysis module applied several centrality measures. Degree Centrality measured the number of connections [31] each actor had, quantifying their collaborative activity, as captured by the equation:

$$C_D(n_i) = \frac{x_{i+}}{g-1}$$

where x_{i+} denotes the number of connections or edges linked to node n_i. This metric highlighted actors with a high number of collaborations. Betweenness Centrality [31] evaluated actors who bridged different clusters, such as actors working across Hollywood and British cinema. It is represented by the equation:

$$C_B(v) = \sum_{s,t \in V} \frac{\sigma(s,t \mid v)}{\sigma(s,t)}$$

where $\sigma(s,t)$ is the total number of shortest paths between nodes s and t, and $\sigma(s,t \mid v)$ is the number of those shortest paths that pass through node v. Closeness Centrality [31] measured how close an actor was to others in the network, providing a metric for accessibility and potential collaboration opportunities. It is represented by the equation:

$$C_C(n_i) = \frac{g-1}{\sum_{j=1}^{g} d(n_i, n_j)}$$

where $d(n_i, n_j)$ denotes the length of the shortest path between node n_i and node n_j. Eigen Centrality [31] went beyond simple connections, evaluating actors based on their ties to other well-connected figures, highlighting influential actors and directors within the network. It is represented by the equation:

$$x_v = \frac{1}{\lambda} \sum_{t \in M(v)} x_t = \frac{1}{\lambda} \sum_{t \in G} a_{v,t} x_t$$

where λ represents the eigenvalue, M(v) is the set of neighbors of vertex v and $a_{v,t}$ is the adjacency matrix entry (1 if connected, 0 if not). In order to anticipate future collaborations, the Collaboration Prediction module applied algorithms such as Common Neighbour [32], Jaccard Coefficient [33,34], Resource Allocation [35], Adamic-Adar Index [36], and Preferential Attachment [37]. For example, the Jaccard Coefficient measured the similarity of actors' collaborative networks through the formula:

$$\sigma_{\text{Jaccard}}(v_i, v_j) = \frac{|N(v_i) \cap N(v_j)|}{|N(v_i) \cup N(v_j)|}$$

where the numerator represents the size of the intersection of the neighbor sets of node v_i and node v_j while the denominator represents the size of their union. These algorithms enabled the prediction of potential future collaborations by examining the shared connections between actors and directors, offering a probabilistic outlook on future industry partnerships.

Next we had Community Detection Module, where we employed Louvain Clustering to group actors into distinct communities based on their collaborative patterns. Interaction frequency in this study refers to the threshold of collaborative engagements required for different clusters, such as movie industries or genres, to be considered interconnected. A higher interaction frequency, like 5%, highlights strong, frequent collaborations, while a lower frequency, such as 0.25%, reveals broader, less frequent connections. By adjusting this frequency, the analysis uncovers how clusters evolve and expand, with new collaborations emerging across global film industries as the threshold decreases. This approach helps in understanding the dynamic nature of inter-cluster interactions and industry growth. The clustering technique identified clusters of actors who frequently work together, forming subcommunities within the broader industry network. By analyzing these subclusters, we discovered smaller, tightly knit groups of actors with recurring collaborations. Furthermore, by extending this analysis to examine cross-cluster connections, we identified key actors who serve as bridges between different sections of the industry. These bridging actors facilitate the flow of talent and ideas across both regional and international film markets, highlighting influential individuals who contribute to cross-market collaborations .

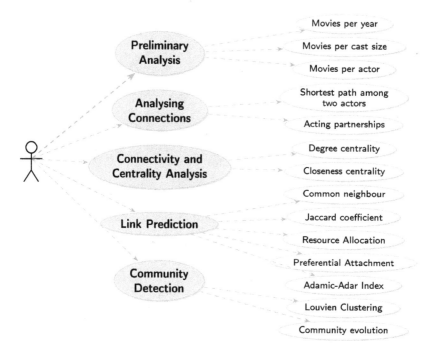

Fig. 3. Network Analysis Workflow

6 Results and Analysis

Our research on actor collaboration networks in the traditional film industry and OTT platforms introduces several insights that challenge existing conclusions in the field. While Rathor and Prakash [21] examined movie sentiment analysis from user reviews, our network-based approach reveals the structural dynamics driving those sentiments. Using network analysis and centrality measures, we focused on top actors, including Anupam Kher, Takahiro Sakurai, and others, to identify their influence in bridging different groups. As shown by Table 2 and Table 3, degree centrality identified Kher and Sakurai as the most connected actors, highlighting their role in fostering cross-industry collaborations, while Fred Tatasciore and Fred Armisen showed the highest closeness centrality, underscoring their importance as connectors between diverse clusters. Further, the analysis of the shortest path between actors exposed fascinating details of acting relationships, such as Robin Williams' connection to Angelina Jolie through movies like "Dead Poets Society" and "Taking Lives".

Our analysis further explored the formation and evolution of clusters, representing different movie industries, such as Hollywood, British, Spanish, Brazilian, and more (Fig. 4). We observed how these clusters gradually evolved, with the degree of constraints influencing the degree of intercluster interactions. At a 5% interaction frequency, we witnessed clusters like Hollywood pairing with

Table 2. Actors with highest betweenness centrality

Anupam Kher	Takahiro Sakurai	Yuichi Nakamura	Fred Tatasciore
0.00750	0.00677	0.006192	0.006134

Table 3. Actors with highest closeness centrality

Fred Tatasciore	Fred Armisen	Anupam Kher	Yuichi Nakamura
0.255	0.2518	0.2415	0.2080

Table 4. Link prediction probabilities between actors in the OTT and movie industry, representing the likelihood of future collaborations based on existing connections and collaborative history, as calculated using the Jaccard Coefficient.

Probability of Connections	Actors
0.84	(Joseph Gordon, Gary Oldman), (Gary Oldman, Marion Cotillard)
0.63	(Liam Neeson, Gary Oldman), (Tom Hardy, Tom Wilkinson), (Marion Cotillard, Rutger)
0.54	(Liam Neeson, Aaron Eckhart), (Maggle G, Rutger Hauser)

Hollywood Horror, TV, and British, indicating their propensity to collaborate only within their niche. As constraints were reduced, Hollywood expanded its reach, forging connections with German, French, Czech, Yugoslavian, and Italian actors, forming a substantial connected cluster. This evolution showcased the adaptability of the industry in transcending traditional boundaries and affiliations. Intriguingly, we found that actors primarily collaborate based on language rather than country, reflecting the significance of linguistic bonds within the industry. Temporal analysis revealed that older American actors clustered separately from contemporary Hollywood figures, with genre-specific clusters such as Hollywood TV and Hollywood Horror remaining isolated.

However, as the interaction frequency reduced to 2%, collaboration patterns expanded further, revealing significant partnerships. At 2% interaction frequency shown by Fig. 5, the Hollywood cluster starts interacting with Old American, Italian, and Yugolovakian clusters, while the French cluster starts interacting with the Italian cluster.

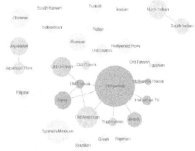

Fig. 4. Initial raw clusters before applying interconnection frequency filters

Fig. 5. Visualization of cluster interconnection at 2% frequency rate

The dataset also highlighted co-acting relationships, with actors like Adoor Bhasi and Bahadur collaborating in over 187 films and Japanese actors Kijaku Otani and Matsunosuke Onoe co-acting in 146 films. The Louvain clustering technique resulted in a high modularity score of 90.8%, indicating a strong, diverse network structure. The diversity of collaborations was further illustrated through high fit scores (94.9%) and a notable variety of industry interactions. The analysis also identified Jackie Chan as the most versatile actor, adept at co-acting across different clusters, showcasing his unique role in bridging various industry segments. Link prediction estimated a high probability of future collaborations, with an 84% likelihood of partnerships, between Joseph Gordon and Gary Oldman, as well as Gary Oldman and Marion Cotillard, as shown by Table 4. Furthermore, our general analysis of the industry's growth trends indicated an increase in TV shows while a slight decrease of movies on OTT platforms from 2011 to 2020 (see Fig. 6). Figure 8 and 9 show that Rajiv Chilaka and Jan Suter are the top directors who have directed the highest number of movies, while Anupam Kher and Om Puri are the actors who have acted in the highest number of movies. We also observed that traditional Bollywood actors appeared to be relatively isolated from the global cinema landscape, although exceptions existed.

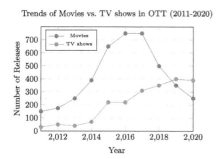
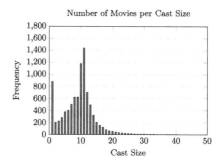

Fig. 6. Comparative trends between TV shows and movies on OTT platforms from 2011–2020

Fig. 7. Distribution of movies categorized by cast size, i.e., the frequency of movies featuring varying numbers of actors in the OTT industry.

Bollywood actors such as Om Puri and Gulshan Grover were identified as the top Indian actors collaborating with Hollywood, reflecting the inter-industry connections forged. The analysis of movies and cast size as shown in Fig. 7 indicates that the majority of movies have a cast size of less than 10, with very few featuring a cast size above 20. The high value for a cast size of 1 is primarily attributable to autobiographical and documentary films, which typically feature a single actor.

The study uncovered vibrant cross-language connections, with Chinese and South Korean actors leading a dynamic transnational cluster. Hollywood, ever adaptive, expanded its reach to embrace collaborations with Scandinavian, Spanish, Polish, Brazilian, and Nigerian films, showcasing its global flexibility.

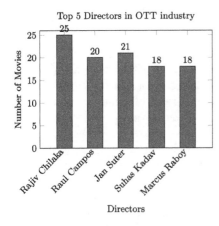 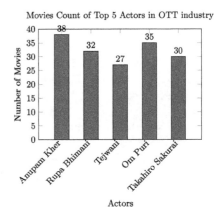

Fig. 8. The top 5 directors in the OTT industry by the number of movies directed

Fig. 9. Total number of movies produced by the top 5 actors in the OTT industry

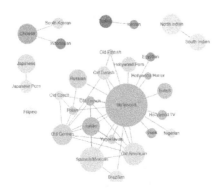 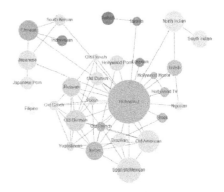

Fig. 10. Visualization of cluster interconnection at 0.5% frequency rate

Fig. 11. Visualization of cluster interconnection at 0.25% frequency rate

However, industries like Russian, Greek, Egyptian, and even Hollywood Porn remained more secluded, limited by fewer interactions.

As shown by Fig. 10, at the 0.5% interaction frequency, our analysis revealed that actors started collaborating with groups beyond their own. Examples of such collaborations include Turkish and Iranian actors, Indonesian and South Korean actors interacting with Chinese actors, and Hollywood actors expanding to collaborate with Russian, Greek, and Egyptian actors. At the 0.25% interaction frequency, shown in Fig. 11, our analysis revealed a more interconnected collaboration pattern, where almost all actor groups engaged with one another. Notably, major collaborations emerged between Japanese, Chinese, Iranian, and North Indian cinema with Hollywood, as well as between North Indian and British films. Hollywood also expanded its network to include South Korean cinema. Chinese and Japanese cinemas began collaborating with each other. It is worth noting that at 2%, North and South Indian cinemas began interacting, forming new edges, but it was at the 0.25% frequency that the Indian film industry began reaching beyond their own and engaging with Hollywood and other international actors. This shift provides important insights into how Bollywood is becoming more connected with global cinema.

In summary, the network analysis, centrality measures, and cluster exploration allowed us to gain a comprehensive understanding of the film and OTT industry's intricate social networks. These findings offer valuable insights that can inform industry professionals, content creators, and streaming platforms, enabling them to make informed decisions about collaborations, partnerships, and content creation strategies in the ever-evolving entertainment landscape.

7 Conclusion and Future Scope

In conclusion, our comprehensive analysis of social networks among movie actors and directors has provided valuable insights into the intricate web of collaborations in the modern film industry. By leveraging data from IMDb and Netflix, we identified key players, top actors, and directors who play central roles in the industry's network. We explored the increasing trend of TV shows on OTT platforms and unveiled patterns in centrality measures like degree, betweenness, and closeness centrality, highlighting influential actors who act as bridges between different clusters. Our cluster analysis revealed categorizations based on various criteria, emphasizing that actors predominantly collaborate within language groups, transcending national boundaries. Link prediction techniques offered valuable insights into potential future collaborations. The study also addressed key questions regarding the industry's isolation, indicating that it operates more on linguistic, temporal, and genre-based divisions than national boundaries. This research has significant implications for industry professionals, scholars, and enthusiasts, guiding decision-making processes in the dynamic world of film and entertainment. While our study provides valuable insights into the collaborative patterns within the film and OTT industries, several limitations must be acknowledged. First, the use of a heuristic, non-ML-based approach for link prediction, while computationally efficient, might oversimplify the complexities of real-world collaborations and fail to capture nuanced factors that machine learning models could address. Second, the clustering methodology, though methodologically sound, assumes static interactions over time, potentially overlooking dynamic shifts in industry trends. Additionally, the criteria for defining clusters may be subjective, influencing the interpretation of intercluster interactions. These limitations highlight areas for further research and refinement to enhance the robustness and generalizability of our findings.

Looking ahead, many exciting opportunities for exploration await. Temporal analysis could shed light on how collaboration patterns change over time. The influence of genre on actor collaborations and content analysis can provide deeper insights into storytelling and network dynamics. Machine learning models like SVM, deep learning models like ANN, and NLP techniques, also suggested by key word network analysis, can further increase knowledge and uncover insights of actor collaboration and also provide advanced link prediction and network analysis possibilities. The impact of globalization on the film industry's cross-country, cross-language collaborations remains largely unexplored. Investigating the economic implications and social media's role in shaping actor collaborations are promising research areas. These future directions will enrich our understanding of the film industry's social networks and evolving dynamics, offering valuable insights to entertainment stakeholders.

References

1. Kim, M.S., Kim, S.: Policy responses to the rise of global OTT platforms in Korea. Sci. Public Policy (2024). Early Access
2. Patnaik, R., Patra, S.K., Mahapatra, D.M., Baral, S.K.: Adoption and challenges underlying OTT platform in India during pandemic: a critical study of socio-economic and technological issues. FIIB Bus. Rev. **13**(3), 356–363 (2024). https://doi.org/10.1177/23197145221101676
3. Khanna, P., Sehgal, R., Gupta, A., Dubey, A.M., Srivastava, R.: Over-the-top (OTT) platforms: a review, synthesis and research directions. Mark. Intell. Plan. (2024). Early Access. https://doi.org/10.1108/MIP-03-2023-0122
4. Sharma, R.R., Mishra, P.: Investigating OTT subscription intention antecedents: a review of online entertainment motivations. In: Kaiser, M.S., Xie, J., Rathore, V.S. (eds.) Information and Communication Technology for Competitive Strategies (ICTCS 2022). LNNS, vol. 615, pp. 373–380. Springer, Singapore (2023). https://doi.org/10.1007/978-981-19-9304-6_35
5. Kim, M.S., Kim, E., Hwang, S., Kim, J., Kim, S.: Willingness to pay for over-the top-services in China and Korea. Telecommun. Policy **41**(3), 197–207 (2017). https://doi.org/10.1016/j.telpol.2016.12.011
6. Sanson, K., Steirer, G.: Hulu, streaming, and the contemporary television ecosystem. Media Cult. Soc. **41**(8), 1210–1227 (2019). https://doi.org/10.1177/0163443718823144
7. Wayne, M.: Netflix, Amazon, and branded television content in subscription video on-demand portals. Media Cult. Soc. **40** (2017). https://doi.org/10.1177/0163443717736118
8. Kim, J., Kim, E., Hong, A.: OTT streaming distribution strategies for dance performances in the post-COVID-19 age: a modified importance-performance analysis. Int. J. Environ. Res. Public Health **19**(1), 327 (2022). https://doi.org/10.3390/ijerph19010327
9. Dear, C., Muller, E.: On the table: an open invitation. Choreogr. Pract. **13**(2), 180–192 (2022). https://doi.org/10.1386/chor_00050_3
10. Gao, K.: Will OTT service providers and telecom operators end the competition? A case study based on dispute between Tencent and China Mobile about micro-letter charges. Adv. Inf. Sci. Serv. Sci. **5**(13), 120–125 (2013)
11. Oh, S.-J., Lee, Y.-S.: Movie watching through cinemas or OTT services: focused on the 2021 national survey of cultural participation. J. Media Econ. Cult. **22**(2), 7–36 (2024)
12. Rani, P., Tayal, D., Bhatia, M.: Sociocentric SNA on fuzzy graph social network model. Res. Square (2021). https://doi.org/10.21203/rs.3.rs-991418/v1

13. Zaefarian, G., Misra, S., Koval, M., et al.: Social network analysis in marketing: a step-by-step guide for researchers. Ind. Mark. Manage. **107**, A11–A24 (2022). https://doi.org/10.1016/j.indmarman.2022.01.011
14. Zhou, X., Yang, J., Lin, Z., Zhang, G., Liu, Y.: Research on identifying the BBS active users with SNA. In: 2015 International Conference on Intelligent Human-Machine Systems and Cybernetics (IHMSC), pp. 70–73. IEEE (2015). https://doi.org/10.1109/IHMSC.2015.32
15. Mandic, M., Škobić, D., Martinović, G.: Clique comparison and homophily detection in telecom social networks. Int. J. Electr. Comput. Eng. **9**(2), 81–87 (2018). https://doi.org/10.32985/ijeces.9.2.5
16. Dangi, D., Bhagat, A., Bakariya, B.: Efficient framework for sentiment and pattern analysis on movie data. In: 2021 IEEE International Conference on Technology, Research, and Innovation for Betterment of Society (TRIBES), pp. 1–5. IEEE (2021)
17. Hodeghatta, U.R.: Sentiment analysis of Hollywood movies on Twitter. In: Proceedings of the 2013 IEEE/ACM International Conference on Advances in Social Networks Analysis and Mining, pp. 1401–1404 (2013)
18. Weng, C.Y., Chu, W.T., Wu, J.L.: Movie analysis based on roles' social network. In: 2007 IEEE International Conference on Multimedia and Expo, pp. 1403–1406. IEEE (2007)
19. Ha, H., Kim, G.N., Hwang, W., Choi, H., Lee, K.: CosMovis: analyzing semantic network of sentiment words in movie reviews. In: 2014 IEEE 4th Symposium on Large Data Analysis and Visualization (LDAV), pp. 113–114. IEEE (2014). https://doi.org/10.1109/LDAV.2014.7013215
20. Weng, C.Y., Chu, W.T., Wu, J.L.: Rolenet: movie analysis from the perspective of social networks. IEEE Trans. Multimedia **11**(2), 256–271 (2009). https://doi.org/10.1109/TMM.2008.2009684
21. Rathor, S., Prakash, Y.: Application of machine learning for sentiment analysis of movies using IMDB rating. In: 2022 IEEE 11th International Conference on Communication Systems and Network Technologies (CSNT), pp. 196–199 (2022). https://doi.org/10.1109/CSNT54456.2022.9787663
22. Li, C.T., Lin, S.D.: Egocentric information abstraction for heterogeneous social networks. In: 2009 International Conference on Advances in Social Network Analysis and Mining, pp. 255–260. IEEE (2009). https://doi.org/10.1109/ASONAM.2009.38
23. Lee, A.N., Chen, K.Y., Li, C.T.: ActRec: a word embedding-based approach to recommend movie actors to match role descriptions. In: 2020 IEEE/ACM International Conference on Advances in Social Networks Analysis and Mining (ASONAM), pp. 389–392. IEEE (2020). https://doi.org/10.1109/ASONAM49781.2020.9381452
24. Hu, Y., Wang, Z., Wu, W., Guo, J., Zhang, M.: Recommendation for movies and stars using YAGO and IMDB. In: 2010 12th International Asia-Pacific Web Conference, pp. 123–129. IEEE (2010). https://doi.org/10.1109/APWeb.2010.51
25. Liu, Z., Chen, K., Qu, Y., Guo, S., Liu, C., Jia, C.: SMAS: an investor-oriented social media analysis system for movies. In: 2018 IEEE International Conference on Big Data (Big Data), pp. 3691–3694. IEEE (2018). https://doi.org/10.1109/BigData.2018.8622414
26. Landherr, A., Friedl, B., Heidemann, J.: A critical review of centrality measures in social networks. Bus. Inf. Syst. Eng. **2**(6), 371–385 (2010)
27. Wang, X., et al.: Heterogeneous graph attention network. In: The World Wide Web Conference, pp. 2022–2032 (2019). https://doi.org/10.1145/3308558.3313562

28. Yuliana, I., Santosa, P.I., Setiawan, N.A.: Finding the most important actor in online crowd by social network analysis. J. Phys. Conf. Ser. **812**(1) (2017)
29. Lewis, K., Gonzalez, M., Kaufman, J.: Social selection and peer influence in an online social network. Proc. Natl. Acad. Sci. **109**(1), 68–72 (2012). https://doi.org/10.1073/pnas.1109739109
30. Tang, J., Sun, J., Wang, C., Yang, Z.: Social influence analysis in large-scale networks. In: Proceedings of the 15th ACM SIGKDD International Conference on Knowledge Discovery and Data Mining, pp. 807–816 (2009). https://doi.org/10.1145/1557019.1557108
31. Golbeck, J.: Analyzing networks. In: Golbeck, J. (ed.) Introduction to Social Media Investigation, pp. 221–235 (2015). https://doi.org/10.1016/B978-0-12-801656-5.00021-4
32. Daminelli, S., Thomas, J., Durán, C., Cannistraci, C.: Common neighbours and the local-community-paradigm for topological link prediction in bipartite networks. New J. Phys. **17** (2015). https://doi.org/10.1088/1367-2630/17/11/113037
33. Niwattanakul, S., Singthongchai, J., Naenudorn, E., Wanapu, S.: Using of Jaccard coefficient for keywords similarity. In: The 2013 IAENG International Conference on Internet Computing and Web Services (ICICWS 2013) (2013)
34. Survarachakan, S., et al.: Deep learning for image-based liver analysis – a comprehensive review focusing on malignant lesions. Artif. Intell. Med. **130** (2022). https://doi.org/10.1016/j.artmed.2022.102331
35. Chen, J., Du, T., Xiao, G.: A multi-objective optimization for resource allocation of emergent demands in cloud computing. J. Cloud Comput. **10**(20) (2021). https://doi.org/10.1186/s13677-021-00237-7
36. Hesamipour, S., Balafar, M.A.: A new method for detecting communities and their centers using the Adamic/Adar Index and game theory. Phys. A **535** (2019). https://doi.org/10.1016/j.physa.2019.122354
37. Karyotis, V., Khouzani, M.H.R.: Malware-propagative Markov random fields. In: Karyotis, V., Khouzani, M.H.R. (eds.) Malware Diffusion Models for Wireless Complex Networks, pp. 107–138 (2016). https://doi.org/10.1016/B978-0-12-802714-1.00015-3

Author Index

A
Akram, Waseem 15
Amruth, S. Jaya 117
Azgor, Sk Ruhul 3

B
Bag, Anil Kumar 346
Basappa, Manjanna 39
Basuchowdhuri, Partha 250
Bera, Nilina 65
Bhattacharya, Bhargab B. 65
Bhowmick, Partha 51
Biswas, Sounav 346
Bui, Van Hieu 157, 180, 289

C
Cao, Minh Son 157
Chaki, Rituparna 340
Chatterjee, Aniket 340
Chaudhary, Sneha 359
Chaudhuri, Chitrita 237

D
Das, Ankan 352
Das, Priyam 352
Dasgupta, Ananyo 143
Dasgupta, Dyuti 265
Dasgupta, Shibaranjani 92
Datta, Ankana 143, 346
Datta, Soumyajit 265
Datta, Subhajit 301
Dey, Rohit Kumar 265
Dinh, Quoc Lap 180
Dutta, Diptendu 92

G
G. Basu, Nilanjana 51
Gautam, Bikalpa 359
Ghosh, Debaditya 265
Ghosh, Madhusudan 250

Giri, Sarthak 359
Guha, Debajit 352
Gunjal, Sachin 27
Guru, D. S. 192, 204, 225

H
Harshitha, Talluri 130
Hossain, Md. Iqbal 105

J
Jagadale, Uday 27
Jana, Debasish 92, 315
Jaswanthi, Thadakuluru 130

K
Kar, Mohuya B. 143
Kavitha, R. 204
Khan, Arifa 79
Kumar, Amit 315
Kumar, Chandrashekhar 315
Kumar, Teerdhala 277

M
Maity, Chandan 92
Majumder, Subhashis 51, 65, 301
Malavadkar, Prashant 27
Moitra, Agnij 168
Mondal, Sahitya 237
Mukherjee, Arijit 352
Mukherjee, Somdip 92
Muttakin, Md. Nurul 105

N
Nandigrami, Jeet 265
Nandini, D. 225
Naskar, Sudip Kumar 250
Nguyen, Ba Hoang Nam 180
Nguyen, Quang Dung 180
Nguyen, The Anh 289
Nguyen, Thuan Thanh 289

P

Pal, Anidipta 143, 346
Pal, Aniket 340
Paul, Aishik 352
Paul, Kritibas 315
Paul, Sukalpa 346
Pham, Khac Long 289
Prajna, S. 192
Pramanik, Sagnik 265

R

Rahman, Md. Saidur 3, 105
Raj, Pronit 315
Rayvanth, N. 117, 130, 277
Reddiar, Nallamilli Eswar Venkata 277
Resmi, S. 117
Roy, Saikat 328
Roychoudhuri, Reshma 301

S

Saha, Aritra 328
Saravanan, P. 79
Saxena, Sanjeev 15
Sen, Anindya 352
Sengupta, Diganta 237, 346
Shaha, Abhisri 352
Shekhar, Harshit 315
Shikare, M. M. 27
Shivaprasad, D. L. 192, 204
Siddartha, Thota 277
Simhadri, Tanya 130
Singh, Rimjhim Padam 117, 130, 277
Singh, Rohan 92
Singireddy, Vishwanath R. 39
Sur, Tapashri 237
Suryaa, E. 117

T

Tarafdar, Anurina 352
Tran, Khanh Nam 157
Tran, Trung Dinh 157

V

Venkatesan, S. K. 79
Vikranth, Pilla Veera Satya Sai 277

W

Waphare, B. N. 27

GPSR Compliance
The European Union's (EU) General Product Safety Regulation (GPSR) is a set of rules that requires consumer products to be safe and our obligations to ensure this.

If you have any concerns about our products, you can contact us on

ProductSafety@springernature.com

In case Publisher is established outside the EU, the EU authorized representative is:

Springer Nature Customer Service Center GmbH
Europaplatz 3
69115 Heidelberg, Germany

www.ingramcontent.com/pod-product-compliance
Lightning Source LLC
Chambersburg PA
CBHW071551270425
25794CB00006BA/45